Dear Launey:

Congratulations and celebrations on your retirement from Texas Southern University. Your distinguished career in educational leadership and your commitment to intellectual excellence has been matched only by your faith in the betterment of human kind.

Very sincerely yours,

Jim and Sandy Anderson

9/29/14

BARTLETT'S
FAMILIAR
BLACK
QUOTATIONS

BARTLETT'S FAMILIAR BLACK QUOTATIONS

RETHA POWERS, GENERAL EDITOR

FOREWORD BY HENRY LOUIS GATES, JR.

Little, Brown and Company

BOSTON · NEW YORK · LONDON

Little, Brown and Company
Hachette Book Group
237 Park Avenue, New York, NY 10017
littlebrown.com

First Edition: November 2013

Little, Brown and Company is a division of Hachette Book Group, Inc.
The Little, Brown name and logo are trademarks of Hachette Book Group, Inc.

The publisher is not responsible for websites (or their content)
that are not owned by the publisher.

The Hachette Speakers Bureau provides a wide range of authors for speaking events.
To find out more, go to hachettespeakersbureau.com or call (866) 376-6591.

ISBN 978-0-316-01017-7
LCCN 2013950703

10 9 8 7 6 5 4 3 2

RRD-C

Printed in the United States of America

Contents

Foreword

I've listened to and delivered enough speeches in my life to know how handy *Bartlett's Familiar Quotations* can be to anyone hoping to inspire others with the collective wisdom of those who've gone before: their insights, humor, irony, and wit; their doubts, fears, and frustrations; their observations about the nobility and frailties of the human condition; and their beliefs about the purpose of the life well-lived and even the possibilities and prospects of a life beyond this one. Sometimes *Bartlett's* introduces us to nuggets of thoughts of writers we've never heard of, or it reminds us of the brilliance of those we've read long ago, whose canonical status we take for granted but whose thinking about a particular subject we either missed or have forgotten.

The most compelling quotations from the works of our most original thinkers can, in just a few words or lines, move us in profound ways, and (in quite a mysterious and uncanny process) *name* feelings and thoughts that are, paradoxically, deeply familiar to us yet still inchoate, lacking in form — ideas, we realize as soon as we read them clothed in expressive language, that we have *felt*, even though we hadn't found a way to give voice to them. Encountering these ideas, digested for us in reference works like *Bartlett's,* yields the sheer pleasure of recognition of a shared humanity, through the realization that we are not alone in either how we view the world or our existence in that world. Ideas such as these, rendered so easily accessible by a careful and thoughtful editor, can explain and even reshape our understanding of the world in a single moment of clarity, beauty, epiphany. And when we repeat them, when we make them part of ourselves and our work, we give them life in multiple dimensions: then and now, here and there, point and counterpoint, first- and second-hand. A precious few quotations, the ones we know by heart, alter the landscape so fundamentally that attribution, though richly deserved (and required), no longer even seems necessary. A few of these come readily to mind:

> "The problem of the twentieth century is the problem of the color line."
> "What happens to a dream deferred? / Does it dry up / like a raisin in the sun?"
> "They seemed to be staring at the dark, but their eyes were watching God."
> "I may not get there with you, but I want you to know tonight, that we as a people will get to the promised land!"
> "Yes, we can!"

Many of us will recognize these words as first written, respectively, by the philosopher and historian W. E. B. Du Bois, the poet Langston Hughes, the novelist Zora Neale Hurston, the Reverend Dr. Martin Luther King, Jr., and President Barack Obama. And through the familiarity bred of repetition, these words are part of our common culture. Reference works like *Bartlett's* are tools that shape our common culture, the sum total of thoughtful reflection that, collectively, we all share and to which we are all heir, regardless of the nationality, gender, or ethnicity of the authors, the time or place when their words were first uttered or written, or the conditions (sometimes dire) that spawned them. The wisdom of the human community is the common property of us all.

As a literary critic and a historian of the African and African American intellectual traditions, I can be a fanatic about recording lost and familiar quotations. As a person who loves archival research and preserving the achievements of people of color by editing encyclopedias, anthologies, and biographical dictionaries, I am particularly grateful to and admiring of Retha Powers for her magnificent achievement in compiling and editing this impressively researched and documented collection of the finest thought produced by writers throughout the African diaspora (as well as citations from key ancient, classical African texts and the King James Bible, which has long been the "silent second text" of so very much of black literature and oratory).

Bartlett's Familiar Black Quotations is the first of its kind in the *Bartlett's* family, and its enormous historical significance derives from what it signifies about the longer journey in thought and feeling that its pages so invitingly contain. When my fellow Cantabridgian John Bartlett printed the first private edition of his *Collection of Familiar Quotations* in 1855, race-based slavery in America was still legal in 15 states and the District of Columbia, and many slaveholders, mindful of laws forbidding their "property" from learning to read and write, would have punished them (or worse) for even looking at a book like *Bartlett's,* out of fear that it would talk back to them (a recurring trope in the first half-dozen slave narratives) — and thus incite them to think for themselves, to recognize their common humanity with their putative owners, and then to run away or revolt.

The leading black abolitionist of his day, Frederick Douglass, himself an ex-slave, wrote in his second slave narrative, *My Bondage and My Freedom,* in the very same year Bartlett published his book of quotations, that his former master had warned his wife not to teach the young Douglass or any other slave to read the Bible: "'learning would do him no good,'" his master warned, and even worse "'probably, a great deal of harm — making him disconsolate and unhappy.'" He was right, Douglass later explained in his own book; for once he had learned to read, in secret, he "had penetrated the secret of all slavery and oppression, and had ascertained their true foundation to be in the pride, the power and the avarice of man." In other words, learning to read freed the slave-child long before he managed to escape to the North and become "free," and the one book that had inspired him more than any other was *The Columbian Orator,* a book of political essays, dialogues, and quotations.

For Frederick Douglass and countless slaves and ex-slaves, language was power, *literal* power that they used to comprehend, critique, and ultimately dismantle the system that for centuries had chained them and their families, the system that was constructed in every meaningful way to convince human beings that they were, *by nature,* meant to be chattel slaves. Not even in the free states of the North would it have been easy for a black person to gain access to a book of such canonical importance as *Bartlett's*; indeed, in John Bartlett's own home state of Massachusetts, several decades before, the first African American to publish a book of poetry, Phillis

Wheatley, had had to submit to examination by the leading lights of Boston to ascertain that the poems she had written were not mere quotations of others' work but her own original creations, the creations of a rational fellow human being.

"I sit with Shakespeare, and he winces not," W. E. B. Du Bois, the first African American to receive a Ph.D. at Harvard, wrote in *The Souls of Black Folk* (1903) during the height of the Jim Crow era, when African Americans, even when they could attend school, found it extremely difficult to gain access to textbooks or canonical literature in separate, poorly funded, and extremely unequal institutions. "Across the color line I move arm and arm with Balzac and Dumas, where smiling men and welcoming women glide in gilded halls," Du Bois continued. "From out of the caves of evening that swing between the strong-limbed Earth and the tracery of stars, I summon Aristotle and Aurelius and what soul I will, and they come all graciously with no scorn nor condescension. So, wed with Truth, I dwell above the Veil."

The marriage of the most cosmopolitan sense of *truth* with intellectual freedom has been the hallmark of Bartlett's expertly edited reference work since Emily Morrison Beck "boldly revamped the book," Powers reminds us, "adding many more black and female speakers, thus deepening the international scope." Retha Powers's edition contributes dramatically to the growing tendency of subsequent *Bartlett's* editors to mine increasingly various intellectual traditions for the best that has been thought and said by an ever-widening array of thinkers.

The denial of access to literacy throughout early American history increased the magical powers of language in African American culture, particularly in song and speech. We see these magical powers at work in Douglass's mastery of the dialogues in *The Columbian Orator*. We see them in Du Bois's appropriation of Shakespeare and much of the canon of Western culture. We see them in Thurgood Marshall's nimble citation of precedents in arguments for school desegregation in *Brown v. Board of Education*. We see them in the Reverend Dr. Martin Luther King, Jr.'s resonant interweaving of verses from the King James Bible throughout his mellifluous speeches and writings, summoning them so effortlessly, seemingly at will. And we see these magical powers at work throughout *Bartlett's Familiar Black Quotations*, the publication of which would have been a cause for great celebration by the authors quoted here, another example of Dr. King's certainty that the "arc of the moral universe...bends toward justice."

But quotations "bend," too, not in the proper order of their words, but in their various (and often unforeseen) contacts across time and space. This practice of "bending" or peppering black discourse with familiar quotations is also another hallmark of African and African American culture and doubtlessly one of the potential uses of this new edition; for in publishing a collection of familiar quotations by black people, *Bartlett's* has not only produced a handy reference guide for the stumped writer; it has provided a counter-narrative in a land where so much for so long was repressed for so many. To "sit with Shakespeare" and for him to "wince not," the disinherited have to have access. And while no anthology can possibly be a substitute for the fullest and deepest encounter with the corpus and fabric of a writer's body of work, anthologies do provide an introduction to that work, and they do, in the case of the original *Bartlett's*, open up the canon of Western thought even to those who, historically, have had the least direct access to it. And now Retha Powers's *Bartlett's* will serve to open up the canon of African American, African, and Caribbean thought to those with the least historical access to it, including younger generations of black people not versed in the best that has been thought and said in their own tradition.

To be sure, this is not the first book to undertake this awesome task. Indeed, the first book of black quotations that I have been able to identify is Victoria Earle Matthews's *Black-Belt Diamonds: Gems from the Speeches, Addresses, and Talks to Students of Booker T. Washington*, published as early as 1898. In 1910, Izett Anderson and Frank Cundall edited *Jamaica Negro Proverbs and Sayings*, while seven years later, Mitchell Davis published *One Hundred Choice Quotations by Prominent Men and Women of the Negro Race: A Valuable Little Gift Book*. In somewhat the same vein, Alice Moore Dunbar (the widow of the poet Paul Laurence Dunbar) in 1914 published the very valuable compendium of *Masterpieces of Negro Eloquence: The Best Speeches Delivered by the Negro from the Days of Slavery to the Present Time*, just as Carter G. Woodson, the renowned historian would also do in 1925 with his *Negro Orators and Their Orations*.

In 1981, Anita King pioneered the contemporary field with her first edition of *Quotations in Black*, a book that filled readers emerging from the

Black Arts Movement with enormous pride. In 1993, three important books of quotations appeared, including Dorothy Winbush Riley's *My Soul Looks Back, 'Less I Forget: A Collection of Quotations by People of Color*; Eric Copage's *Black Pearls: Daily Meditations, Affirmations, and Inspirations for African-Americans*; and Terri L. Jewell's delightful collection, *The Black Woman's Gumbo Ya-Ya: Quotations by Black Women*. Anita Doreen Diggs's *Talking Drums: An African-American Quote Collection* and Venice Johnson's *Heart Full of Grace: A Thousand Years of Black Wisdom* appeared two years later, the same year Janet Cheatham Bell published *Famous Black Quotations*, the first of eleven well-edited volumes of quotations by African Americans that this pioneering editor would go on to publish. Since then, the field has proliferated with a marvelous array of titles. Among many others out there, I am particularly fond of the 1998 collection edited by Richard Newman, my late friend and colleague at Harvard's Du Bois Institute, titled *African American Quotations*, and most recently, the collected quotations of Frederick Douglass, edited by John R. McKivigan and Heather L. Kaufman and published in 2012 as *In the Words of Frederick Douglass: Quotations from Liberty's Champion*. But none of these reference works compares with the scope of Retha Powers' collection, which (unlike almost all of the other books of black quotations cited above), thankfully, includes the original source and the date of each quotation's publication, a considerable boon to further research and a guarantee of accuracy.

In following them, Retha Powers both honors their work and reaffirms something essential about black culture: quoting or "sampling," both versions of the larger African American language practice of signifying. As I have written elsewhere, quoting the past is more than mere repetition; it is an act both of homage and revision; building incrementally on what "was" within the context of what is now and what might be still. It is about finding the perfect break in a passage or song and riffing on it, so that the underlying quotation, its adaptation, and everything in between exist simultaneously in multiple dimensions — the original and the invoked. As in jazz, "the dozens," and hip-hop, quoting, signifying, sampling, you name it, are at once acts of respect, critique, and improvisation; and in many cases, the results stand among the highest art Americans have given the world.

So whenever one might sample or signify using this new addition to the *Bartlett's Familiar Quotations* family, I hope you will invoke the quotations that Retha Powers has gathered and documented inside to inspire and be inspired, to improvise, and at all times to be reminded of the preciousness and power of accessing language in a land where for centuries its value was so great it had to be forbidden by law and guarded with chains. "I had a great curiosity to talk to the books," Olaudah Equiano writes in his 1789 slave narrative, "and so to learn how all things had a beginning: for that purpose I have often taken up a book, and have talked to it, and then put my ears to it, when alone, in hopes it would answer me; and I have been very much concerned when I found it remained silent." May this first edition of *Bartlett's Familiar Black Quotations* always "answer" you and, in answering, help you to unlock the deep, long-silenced truths of the black intellectual tradition.

Writing in his fourth edition, John Bartlett ruminates on his use of the word *familiar* in the title of his pioneering and quite popular collection: "What is familiar to one class of readers," he writes, "may be quite new to another." I think that Bartlett's hope in undertaking his project was *to make* these quotations *familiar,* the stuff of a collective commonplace book — the commonplace book of canonical Anglo-American culture — and to do so by gathering them together into a readily accessible reference work to be held and cherished "in common" by the educated general public, which, in turn, would *preserve and perpetuate* what Bartlett saw as the best of Anglo-English literature and philosophy for future generations. And that is what he — and they — did. Now, Retha Powers has done the same for what is "familiar" to African Americans about their own intellectual history, and what should be equally "familiar" to all Americans about African American history and culture. I cannot stress how important publications such as this are to reflecting, and creating, a deeper, shared understanding of the richness, complexity, and variety of a truly multicultural American culture. Every family that owns *Bartlett's Familiar Quotations* should own *Bartlett's Familiar Black Quotations* as well, since the two volumes talk to one another and, in that never-ending conversation, talk to us.

Henry Louis Gates, Jr.
Harvard University

Preface

[Learning to read] was a new and special revelation, explaining dark and mysterious things, with which my youthful understanding had struggled, but struggled in vain. I now understood what had been to me a most perplexing difficulty — to wit, the white man's power to enslave the black man. It was a grand achievement, and I prized it highly. From that moment, I understood the pathway from slavery to freedom.

Narrative of the Life of Frederick Douglass [1845]

We have to do with the past only as we can make it useful to the present and to the future.

The Meaning of the Fourth of July to the Negro.
Speech, Rochester, New York [July 5, 1852]

In 1855 Frederick Douglass published his second enduring autobiography, *My Bondage and My Freedom.* That same year John Bartlett, a bookstore owner in Cambridge, Massachusetts, published a 258-page volume titled *A Collection of Familiar Quotations.* Douglass, who had long been known as a stirring orator in the cause of abolition and for his nationally best-selling *Narrative of the Life of Frederick Douglass, An American Slave* (which also received international attention), did not make it into Bartlett's collection; nor did any women, save Mrs. Barbauld. But, then again, neither did George Washington or Thomas Jefferson. In fact, Benjamin Franklin was the most prominent founding father to gain inclusion, alongside such notables as Shakespeare and Lord Byron. Both Douglass and Bartlett published their books just before the Civil War, amid a bitter battle over the enslavement of people of African descent that would continue to challenge notions of who was and what it meant to be American, making Douglass's absence from Bartlett's anthology even more glaring.

Up until the fourteenth edition, in 1968, only a few black voices could be found in what came to be known as *Bartlett's Familiar Quotations*. Editor Emily Morrison Beck boldly revamped the book, adding many more black and female speakers, and deepened the international scope. She added Frederick Douglass, Harriet Tubman, Sojourner Truth, Barbara Jordan, and writers such as Nikki Giovanni, Derek Walcott, and Ralph Ellison. Morrison Beck was criticized for expanding the international definition in *Bartlett's* beyond Europe and redefining ancient and contemporary speakers, but by doing so she set the tone for broader inclusion in future editions.

John Bartlett wrote that the purpose of his book was "to show, to some extent, the obligations our language owes to various authors for numerous phrases and familiar quotations which have become household words." This first edition of *Bartlett's Familiar Black Quotations* does the same specifically for black cultures while also restoring words lost, omitted, or forgotten during slavery and the struggles for freedom and equality.

Sources range from African proverbs to the rhyming verse of Muhammad Ali; from the separatist philosophy of Marcus Garvey to the humanistic, visionary grace of Nelson Mandela; from the musings of Benjamin Banneker to the Nobel Prize–winning words of Toni Morrison. *Bartlett's Familiar Black Quotations* also records the "folks" from various eras, through popular sayings and anonymous speakers. It was, after all, a church elder known as Mother Pollard who said during the Montgomery bus boycott, "My feets is tired, but my soul is rested." Quotations have been selected for popularity and familiarity, originality, historical significance, and sometimes simply for eloquence and beauty.

Quotations have been culled from novels, poems, speeches, essays, memoirs, slave narratives, films, television shows and appearances, radio interviews, song lyrics, letters, biographies, and black and mainstream periodicals. Speakers in *Bartlett's Familiar Black Quotations* include writers, artists, musicians, poets, philosophers, politicians, athletes, activists, playwrights, singers, actors, religious leaders, and others whose words were significant in their time and have endured beyond it. Many of these speakers have never been represented in such a collection before.

Building *Bartlett's Familiar Black Quotations* has been a process of reaching back and reaching forward. Various schools of thought are represented: Huey P. Newton's black power stance is given a place at the table, along with the nationalist philosophy of Malcolm X and the civil disobedience of Bayard Rustin. The result is a range of speakers and well-known quotes: "I have a dream" (Martin Luther King, Jr.); "What happens to a dream deferred?" (Langston Hughes); "Look up, you mighty race!" (Marcus Garvey). And lesser-known but equally powerful quotations are included, such as "When and where I enter, in the quiet, undisputed dignity of my womanhood, without violence and without suing or special patronage, then and there the whole *Negro race enters with me*" (Ana Julia Cooper).

In *Notes of a Native Son*, James Baldwin writes, "They face each other, the Negro and the African, over a gulf of three hundred years — an alienation too vast to be conquered in an evening's good-will, too heavy and too double-edged ever to be trapped in speech.... [The Negro] cannot deny them, nor can they ever be divorced." Although a majority of the quotations in this collection come from African Americans, Africa and the African diaspora are also represented.

Challenges linked to racism and oppression have been continuous in black lives, and so the recurrence of themes leads sometimes to a similarity of sentiment and conversations within and across eras. Opposition to slavery and oppression is as old as the "peculiar institution" itself, as evidenced by King Afonso's sixteenth-century letter to the king of Portugal: "We cannot reckon how great the damage is, since the...merchants daily seize our subjects, sons of the land and sons of our noblemen, and vassals and our relatives.... They grab them and cause them to be sold; and so great, Sir, is their corruption and licentiousness that our country is being utterly depopulated." And as the enslaved African playwright and poet Terence writes, "In fact, nothing is said that has not been said before."

Although black speakers have had much to say about the struggle against oppression, *Bartlett's Familiar Black Quotations* does not limit itself to protest alone. Once again in the words of Terence, "While there's life, there's hope." Nikki Giovanni writes about love as often as she does about race, and comedians such as Bert Williams, Richard Pryor, and Chris Rock have blended highly quotable humor with social insight.

In his introduction to the Fourth Edition of *Bartlett's Familiar Quotations*, John Bartlett writes, "It has been thought better to incur the risk of erring on the side of fullness." In that tradition, the reader of *Bartlett's Familiar Black Quotations* will find quotes that are urgent ("If a race has no history, if it has no worthwhile tradition, it becomes a negligible factor in the thought of the world, and it stands in danger of being exterminated" — Carter G. Woodson); exuberant ("*Imagination!* who can sing thy force? / Or who describe the swiftness of thy course?" — Phillis Wheatley); saucily defiant ("Sometimes, I feel discriminated against, but it does not make me angry. It merely astonishes me. How can any deny themselves the pleasure of my company?" — Zora Neale Hurston); and lyrical ("This is the urgency: Live! / and have your blooming in the noise of the whirlwind" — Gwendolyn Brooks). As a whole, the quotations included capture humor, strivings, insights, history, and moments of controversy as observed by black people.

As in *Bartlett's Familiar Quotations*, the Bible is a major source in *Bartlett's Familiar Black Quotations*. In defiance of the use of "the good book" by some to justify slavery, enslaved black people embraced the Bible as an important tool of activism and an inspiration for black oratory. Other holy texts are quoted as well, including the Koran and the Kebra Nagast.

Literary sources in *Bartlett's Familiar Black Quotations* range from Phillis Wheatley to Jupiter Hammon, Chinua Achebe to Wole Soyinka, Alice Walker to Jamaica Kincaid. Early writers such as Harriet E. Wilson and Frances Ellen Watkins Harper captured the harsh realities and emotional toll of slavery. More than half a century later, Countee Cullen asked, "What is Africa to me?" Still later, Amiri Baraka and Sonia Sanchez used words as protest. Writers such as Rita Dove, Aimé Césaire, and August Wilson documented the intimate moments of their times. "I am invisible, understand, simply because people refuse to see me," writes Ralph Ellison in *Invisible Man*. The art of the written word makes black lives visible despite such refusals.

The impact of music on black culture and of black music on world culture is undeniable; thus a wealth of words from songwriters and performers is quoted here. Black American musicians and songwriters in all genres have had a particularly strong impact on the national lexicon. The reader will find James Brown exclaiming, "Say it loud, I'm black and I'm proud!" The volume includes lyrics by songwriters such as Holland-Dozier-Holland and Otis Blackwell and by writer/performers such as Nick Ashford and Valerie Simpson, Chuck Berry, Chuck D, Prince, and Muddy Waters.

Notable political figures include Nelson Mandela of South Africa and Ellen Johnson Sirleaf of Liberia. During the course of this book's development, President Barack Obama transformed from being the keynote speaker at the 2004 Democratic National Convention to becoming a senator to being the first black person elected to the highest office of the United States. Frederick Douglass wrote in 1857, "Power concedes nothing without a demand. It never did and it never will." Douglass agitated on behalf of oppressed African Americans and continues to challenge generations of Americans, and his legacy echoes in the eloquent words of President Obama: "Nothing can stand in the way of the power of millions of voices calling for change."

Many of the quotes illuminate and debate what blackness is and what it means to be human. As Henry Louis Gates, Jr., writes, "I want to be black, to know black, to luxuriate in whatever I might be calling blackness at any particular time — but to do so in order to come out the other side, to experience a humanity that is neither colorless nor reducible to color. Bach *and* James Brown. Sushi *and* fried catfish." This collection underscores the complexity of the black experience the world over.

Many thanks to researchers Ashley Williams and Marc Powers and to the following for kindly serving as advisors offering comments and suggestions: Valerie Boyd, Catherine Clinton, Veronica Chambers, Lisa Dent, Steven G. Fullwood, Michael A. Gomez, E. Ethelbert Miller, Ishmael Reed, Franklin Sirmans, and Ben Zimmer. I am eternally grateful to Henry Louis Gates, Jr., for generously writing the foreword.

I am indebted to Neeti Madan for sharing her wisdom, to Tracy Behar for her patience and guidance with this project, and to Michael Pietsch and Mary Tondorf-Dick for the opportunity to work on this volume. Many thanks to Little, Brown and Company's Christina Rodriguez, Jenny Tai, and Peggy Freudenthal and to copyeditors Liz Duvall, Laura Lawrie, Katherine Kiger, Cynthia Lindlof, Michael Neibergall, and Kathryn Rogers.

Thanks also to James Powers, Christopher Nickelson, Martin Jamison, Kakuna Kerina, Carolyn Ferrell, Robyn Crawford, John Howard, David Unger, Robert L. Harris, Jr., Walter Fluker, Ruth Shoge, Carla Whyte, Efua Morgan, and Deborah Baker.

This book would not have been possible without the generosity of David Silverman, who lent his technical skills and eagle eye to troubleshooting style and formatting issues. Nor could I have completed this undertaking in the absence of the encouragement, support, handholding, and cheerleading of Jen Silverman. Isa, you were but a hope when this work began, but you've been my North Star, and this book is for you. Finally, I am grateful to the librarians and pages of the Schomburg Center for Research in Black Culture, who cheerfully pulled many hundreds, if not thousands, of books from its estimable stacks. As Toni Morrison observes, "Access to knowledge is the superb, the supreme act of truly great civilizations." The Schomburg makes this quite evident.

Retha Powers

New York, 2013

Guide to the Use of *Bartlett's Familiar Black Quotations*

BASIC INFORMATION

Like its predecessor, *Bartlett's Familiar Black Quotations* arranges speakers chronologically by year of birth. Every attempt has been made to include the most important, memorable quotations of each. Authors born in the same year are arranged alphabetically, and under each speaker, quotations appear with the name of the source, arranged by publication date.

Anonymous quotations appear at the back of the book and under the subgroups African, American, Caribbean, and Spirituals. Most blues lyrics are attributed to specific songwriters, but when the writer is unknown, they appear under Anonymous: American. Sources without a specific author, such as the March on Washington for Jobs and Marcher's Pledge, are listed chronologically by name.

Ellipses are employed when text has been abridged, but longer versions of quotations often have been chosen from controversial speakers. Too often the words and language of black speakers are misunderstood, misapplied by some, and even misquoted by others. The intention has been to include the words in as close to their original form and context as possible.

To find a specific author, refer to the Index of Authors, and when in search of a specific quotation, see the index in the back of the book.

SPEAKERS AND LANGUAGE

Many speakers, male and female, especially those from earlier eras, use the default "man" to refer to men, women, and children. The editor assumes that when Frances Ellen Watkins Harper penned the words "Men grow strong in action, but in solitude their thoughts are ripened," she was referring to women and men alike.

In some early entries, English has been standardized for clarity, but when an author intentionally uses vernacular language and spelling, the entries reflect the original source. For example, see Paul Laurence Dunbar's *When Malindy Sings:*

> When it comes to real right singin',
> 'T ain't no easy thing to do.

"Black" in reference to black people is capitalized or lowercased depending on the author's preference, as indicated in the source.

All speakers, whether in song, speech, movie line, or another source, are black, so some of the words most closely associated with speakers have not been included. For example, Billie Holiday's signature song, the lynching protest anthem "Strange Fruit" — "Southern trees bear a strange fruit, / Blood on the leaves and blood at the root, / Black bodies swinging in the Southern breeze, / Strange fruit hanging from the poplar trees" — was written in the 1930s by Abel Meerpool, a Jewish schoolteacher. Holiday did coauthor "God Bless the Child" with Irving Mills, and this and other wonderful lyrics are in *Bartlett's Familiar Black Quotations.* Similarly, Paul Robeson made famous the lyrics "Ol' man river, 'at ol' man river, / He mus' know sumpin', / But don't say nuthin', / He jes' keeps rollin', / He keeps on rollin' along," but they were written by Oscar Hammerstein II for *Showboat* and are thus not included here. Cuba Gooding, Jr.'s line "Show me the money!" helped him win an Oscar, but credit for the sentence goes to the filmmaker Cameron Crowe, so it's not considered a black quotation. Some singers may seem to be missing, but while many vocalists, such as Roberta Flack, are known for emblematic lyrics, they didn't always write them.

QUOTATION SOURCES

Each quotation is accompanied by its title or source, publication date if known, and other information that may be helpful to the reader. If no precise date is known, then the quote appears in order according to the approximate date. If there is no approximate date, then it is placed before or after all dated quotations. Every effort has been made to verify the speaker as the originator of attributed quotes. If the speaker cannot be verified as the originator but the quote is closely associated with the speaker, then "attributed" appears with the quote.

Character names are usually indicated in brackets when dialogue is quoted from works of fiction. For example, in *A Raisin in the Sun*, Lorraine Hansberry's character Mama says, "When you starts measuring somebody — measure him right, child. Measure him right. Make sure you done taken into account what hills and valleys he come through before he got wherever he is." In her own voice, Hansberry proclaims, "Though it be a thrilling and marvelous thing to be merely young and gifted in such times, it is doubly so, doubly dynamic — to be young, gifted and black."

FOOTNOTES

The vast majority of quotations are taken from original sources; when those are unavailable, works of scholarship such as history texts and biographies are credited. Footnotes are employed where necessary to explain context, note a translator, or cite a secondary source. As in *Bartlett's Familiar Quotations*, footnotes are also used to note relationships to other quotations where appropriate.

INDEX OF AUTHORS

The Index of Authors for *Bartlett's Familiar Black Quotations* comprises birth and death dates and page numbers for each author, as well as the page numbers for any additional quotations that appear in footnotes.

In cases in which a speaker has both a given and a chosen name, if a speaker was first known by his or her given name, the given name is noted first and both names are cross-referenced in the index — for example, Stokely Carmichael [Kwame Toure]. However, if the chosen name is better or solely known, the speaker's given name is bracketed — for example, Muhammad Ali [Cassius Marcellus Clay, Jr.]. Female speakers who are known by both their married and their maiden name are listed with both when the married name is used publicly.

To find a particular book in the Bible, see the Bible section; books are listed alphabetically.

INDEX

The index is arranged by keywords, not topics. The spelling and capitalization in the index entry match those of the quotation. Some older or variant spellings are indexed, as are "made" words, such as *jazzers*, and dialectal words, such as *chitlins* and *gri-gri*. Compound names, such as *United States*, are indexed as one word. Elided letters found in many quotations, such as *'d* for *ed*, are supplied in the index entries.

Alphabetization of keywords is word-by-word, not letter-by-letter. Thus, *New York* precedes *Newspaper*. The order of plural and possessive keywords is from singular possessive to plural to plural possessive: for example, *Lover's, Lovers, Lovers'*. The number at the end of each index entry shows the page on which the quotation starts and the number of the quotation on the page — 139:7, for example, is the seventh quotation on page 139. Entries for footnote quotations are cited by page and note number, such as 139:*n*2 for the second footnote on page 139.

The index entry line is usually a short form of the indexed phrase, and the words generally appear in the same order, with the keyword abbreviated unless it starts the entry. Index entry lines are alphabetized, with articles, prepositions, and conjunctions included.

> Heart, a lot of h., and soul, 384:2
>> as big as a whale, 226:5
>> black labs of the h., 354:4
>> full of grace, 320:10
>> heat wave burnin' in my h., 408:5
>> of a woman, 169:3

    of Muhammad, 56:13
    sorrow in my h., 72:3
    vista of your h., 415:6

Occasionally, words not in the actual quotations are supplied in the index entries to make the entries clear.

    Readers who cannot find a particular quotation under one keyword are advised to scan that keyword entry in its entirety (since there are many ways of indexing one phrase) or to try other keywords.

Kathryn Rogers

Index of Authors

BARTLETT'S
FAMILIAR
BLACK
QUOTATIONS

Familiar Black Quotations

The Song of the Harper[1,2]   c. 2650–2600 B.C.

1   There is no one who can return from there,
     To describe their nature, to describe their dissolution,
     That he may still our desires,
     Until we reach the place where they have gone.   *St. 5*

2   Remember: it is not given to man to take his goods with him.
     No one goes away and then comes back.   *St. 10*

Ptahhotep   Twenty-fourth century B.C.

3   Teach him what has been said in the past; then he will set a good
     example to the children of the magistrates, and judgment and all exactitude
     shall enter into him. Speak to him, for there is none born wise.
          The Maxims of Ptahhotep [c. 2350 B.C.],[3]
          introduction

4   Do not be arrogant because of your knowledge, but confer with the
     ignorant man as with the learned. . . . Good speech is more hidden than mala-
     chite, yet it is found in the possession of women slaves at the millstones.
                              The Maxims of Ptahhotep, 1

5   Truth is great and its effectiveness endures.
                              The Maxims of Ptahhotep, 5

6   Follow your desire as long as you live and do not perform more than
     is ordered; do not lessen the time of following desire, for the wasting of time

---

[1]Ancient Egyptian quotations from *The Song of the Harper,* Ptahhotep, *The Teaching for Merikare,* and *Love Songs of the New Kingdom* are from *The Literature of Ancient Egypt* [1973], edited by WILLIAM KELLY SIMPSON.

[2]From the tomb of King Inyotef. Translated by WILLIAM KELLY SIMPSON.

[3]Translated from the earliest manuscript of the *Maxims* (the Prisse Papyrus in Paris) by R. O. FAULKNER.

is an abomination to the spirit.... When riches are gained, follow desire, for riches will not profit if one is sluggish.

The Maxims of Ptahhotep, 11

1 One who is serious all day will never have a good time, while one who is frivolous all day will never establish a household.

The Maxims of Ptahhotep, 25

2 Be cheerful while you are alive.

The Maxims of Ptahhotep, 34

The Teaching for Merikare[1]   c. 2135–2040 B.C.

3 Be skillful in speech, that you may be strong; [...] it is the strength of [...] the tongue, and words are braver than all fighting; a wise man is a school for the magnates, and those who are aware of his knowledge do not attack him.   *Parable 4*

4 Do justice, that you may live long upon earth. Calm the weeper, do not oppress the widow, do not oust a man from his father's property, do not degrade magnates from their seats. Beware of punishing wrongfully; do not kill, for it will not profit you.   *Parable 8*

5 Instill the love of you into all the world, for a good character is what is remembered.   *Parable 24*

The Book of the Dead   c. 1700–1000 B.C.

6 Hail to you gods
On that day of the great reckoning.
Behold me, I have come to you,
Without sin, without guilt, without evil,
Without a witness against me,
Without one whom I have wronged...
Rescue me, protect me,
Do not accuse me before the great god!

I am one pure of mouth, pure of hands.   *The Address to the Gods*[2]

7 As for him who knows this book on earth, he shall come out into the day, he shall walk on earth among the living, and his name shall not perish forever.   *Theban Recension, ch. 70*[3]

---

[1]A treatise on kinship addressed by a king of Heracleopolis, whose name is lost, to his son and successor, Merikare. Translated by R. O. FAULKNER.

[2]*Ancient Egyptian Literature* [1976], *vol. II, The New Kingdom*, translated by MIRIAM LICHTHEIM.

[3]Translated from the earliest manuscript of the *Maxims* (the Prisse Papyrus in Paris) by R. O. FAULKNER.

1   The bright Eye of Horus comes, the glorious Eye of Horus comes; welcome, O you who shine like Re in the horizon. It drives off the powers of Seth from upon the feet of Him who brings it. It is Seth who would take possession of it, but its heat is against him; the torch comes. When will it arrive? It comes now, traversing the sky behind Re on the hands of your two sisters, O Re. Live, live, O Eye of Horus within the Great Hall! Live, live, O Eye of Horus, for he is the Pillar-of-his-Mother priest.

Chapter for kindling a torch for N[1]

Love Songs of the New Kingdom[2]

c. 1550–1080 B.C.

2   My love for you is mixed throughout
my body
So hurry to see your lady,
like a stallion on the track,
or like a falcon swooping down to its
papyrus marsh.
Heaven sends down the love of her
as a flame falls in the hay.
                                                            Song no. 2

3   The voice of the wild goose,
caught by the bait, cries out.
Love of you holds me back,
and I can't loosen it at all . . .
I did not set my traps today;
love of you has thus entrapped me.
                                                            Song no. 10

4   Sweet pomegranate wine in my mouth
is bitter as the gall of birds.
But your embraces
alone give life to my heart;
may Amun give me what I have found
for all eternity.
                                                            Song no. 12

5   The voice of the turtledove speaks out. It says:
Day breaks, which way are you going?
Lay off, little bird,
must you so scold me?
I found my lover on his bed,
and my heart was sweet to excess.
                                                            Song no. 14

---

[1]Translated from the earliest manuscript of the *Maxims* (the Prisse Papyrus in Paris) by R. O. FAULKNER.
[2]Translated by WILLIAM KELLY SIMPSON.

Hatshepsut

Fifteenth century B.C.
d. 1468 B.C.

1   I have made bright the truth....I eat of its brightness....My fame makes the great ones of the countries to bow down.   *Obelisk engraving*[1]

2   My command stands firm like the mountains, and the sun's disk shines and spreads rays over the titulary of my august person, and my falcon rises high above the kingly banners unto all eternity.   *Obelisk engraving*[2]

3   Now my heart turns this way and that, as I think what the people will say. Those who shall see my monuments in years to come, and who shall speak of what I have done.   *Obelisk engraving*[3]

Suti and Hor[4]

Fifteenth–fourteenth centuries B.C.

4   Creator uncreated.
Sole one, unique one, who traverses eternity,
Remote one, with millions under his care;
Your splendor is like heaven's splendor.   *First Hymn to the Sun God*

5   Beneficent mother of gods and men
Valiant shepherd who drives his flock,
Their refuge, made to sustain them...
He makes the seasons with the months,
Heat as he wishes, cold as he wishes...
Every land rejoices at his rising,
Every day gives praise to him.

Second Hymn to the Sun God

The Great Hymn to the Aten[5]

c. 1350 B.C.

6   Splendid you rise in heaven's lightland,
O living Aten, creator of life!   *St. 1*

7   When you set in western lightland,
Earth is in darkness as if in death.   *St. 2*

---

[1]From EVELYN WELLS, *Hatshepsut* [1969].

[2]From JOYCE ANN TYLDESLEY, *Hatchepsut: The Female Pharaoh* [1996].

[3]Translated by S. R. SNAPE.

[4]Architects to Amenhotep III (reigned c. 1411–1375 B.C.). Translated by MIRIAM LICHTHEIM.

[5]From the reign [1365–1349 B.C.] of Amenhotep IV, Akhenaten. Translated by MIRIAM LICHTHEIM.
   Amenhotep IV...converted the supreme god [Aten, the sun disk] into the sole god by denying the reality of all the other gods. — MIRIAM LICHTHEIM, *Ancient Egyptian Literature* [1976], *vol. II, The New Kingdom, pt. II*

1   Every lion comes from its den,
All the serpents bite;
Darkness hovers, earth is silent,
As their maker rests in lightland.
Earth brightens when you dawn in lightland,
When you shine as Aten of daytime;
As you dispel the dark,
As you cast your rays,
The Two Lands are in festivity.
Awake they stand on their feet,
You have roused them.   *St. 2, 3*

2   The entire land sets out to work,
All beasts browse on their herbs;
Trees, herbs are sprouting,
Birds fly from their nests
Ships fare north, fare south as well,
Roads lie open when you rise;
The fish in the river dart before you,
Your rays are in the midst of the sea.   *St. 3*

3   How many are your deeds,
Though hidden from sight,
O Sole God beside whom there is none!
You made the earth as you wished, you alone.   *St. 5*

The Holy Bible[1]
The Old Testament[2]

4   In the beginning God created the heaven and the earth.
And the earth was without form, and void; and darkness was upon the face
    of the deep.
And the Spirit of God moved upon the face of the waters.
And God said, Let there be light:[3] and there was light.
                      The First Book of Moses, Called Genesis, ch. 1, verses 1–3

---

[1]Bible quotations are from the Authorized (King James) Version [1611]. Numbers in Bible citations represent chapter and verse. The oldest part of the Bible, Song of the Sea (*Exodus 15:1–18;* see 9:17–10:2), dates from the tenth century B.C., the era of Solomon, but the material used by the author (called J, or the Yahwist) was much older. Next oldest is the Song of Deborah (*Judges 5:1–12*, 12:13–14).

[2]The Hebrew Scriptures. The first five books (the Pentateuch, or the five books of Moses) are the Jewish Torah. The Pentateuch is considered by Jews and many Christians to embody the law revealed to Moses on Mount Sinai.

[3]Fiat lux. — *The Vulgate*

1   And the evening and the morning were the first day.   *1:5*

2   And God saw that it was good.   *1:10*

3   And God said, Let us make man in our image, after our likeness.   *1:26*

4   Male and female created he them.   *1:27*

5   Be fruitful, and multiply, and replenish the earth, and subdue it: and have dominion over the fish of the sea, and over the fowl of the air, and over every living thing that moveth upon the earth.   *1:28*

6   And on the seventh day God ended his work which he had made.   *2:2*

7   And the Lord God formed man of the dust of the ground, and breathed into his nostrils the breath of life; and man became a living soul.   *2:7*

8   And the Lord God planted a garden eastward in Eden.   *2:8*

9   But of the tree of the knowledge of good and evil, thou shalt not eat of it: for in the day that thou eatest thereof thou shalt surely die.   *2:17*

10   It is not good that the man should be alone; I will make him an help meet for him.   *2:18*

11   And the Lord God caused a deep sleep to fall upon Adam, and he slept: and he took one of his ribs, and closed up the flesh instead thereof.
And the rib, which the Lord God had taken from man, made he a woman.   *2:21–22*

12   Bone of my bones, and flesh of my flesh.   *2:23*

13   Therefore shall a man leave his father and his mother, and shall cleave unto his wife: and they shall be one flesh.
And they were both naked, the man and his wife, and were not ashamed.   *2:24–25*

14   Your eyes shall be opened, and ye shall be as gods, knowing good and evil.   *3:5*

15   And they heard the voice of the Lord God walking in the garden in the cool of the day.   *3:7–8*

16   The woman whom thou gavest to be with me, she gave me of the tree, and I did eat.   *3:12*

17   What is this that thou hast done? And the woman said, The serpent beguiled me, and I did eat.
And the Lord God said unto the serpent, Because thou hast done this, thou art cursed above all cattle, and above every beast of the field; upon thy belly shalt thou go, and dust shalt thou eat all the days of thy life.   *3:13–14*

1   In the sweat of thy face shalt thou eat bread, till thou return unto the ground; for out of it wast thou taken: for dust thou art, and unto dust shalt thou return.

And Adam called his wife's name Eve; because she was the mother of all living.   *3:19–20*

2   So he drove out the man: and he placed at the east of the garden of Eden cherubims, and a flaming sword which turned every way, to keep the way of the tree of life.   *3:24*

3   And Abel was a keeper of sheep, but Cain was a tiller of the ground.

4:2

4   Am I my brother's keeper?   *4:9*

5   The voice of thy brother's blood crieth unto me from the ground.

4:10

6   My punishment is greater than I can bear.   *4:13*

7   And the Lord said unto him, Therefore whoever slayeth Cain, vengeance shall be taken on him sevenfold. And the Lord set a mark upon Cain, lest anyone finding him should kill him.   *4:15*

8   And all the days of Methuselah were nine hundred sixty and nine years.   *5:27*

9   There were giants in the earth in those days, mighty men which were of old, men of renown.   *6:4*

10   And of every living thing of all flesh, two of every sort shalt thou bring into the ark.   *6:19*

11   And the rain was upon the earth forty days and forty nights.

7:12

12   And, lo, in her mouth was an olive leaf pluckt off.   *8:11*

13   Whoso sheddeth man's blood, by man shall his blood be shed: for in the image of God made he man.   *9:6*

14   And Noah awoke from his wine, and knew what his younger son had done unto him.   *9:24*

15   And he said, Cursed be Canaan; a servant of servants shall he be unto his brethren.   *9:25*

16   And he said, Blessed be the Lord God of Shem; and Canaan shall be his servant.   *9:26*

17   God shall enlarge Japheth, and he shall dwell in the tents of Shem; and Canaan shall be his servant.   *9:27*

1   Therefore is the name of it called Babel; because the Lord did there confound the language of all the earth.   *11:9*

2   Abram dwelled in the land of Canaan, and Lot dwelled in the cities of the plain, and pitched his tent toward Sodom.   *13:12*

3   In a good old age.   *15:15*

4   Thy name shall be Abraham; for a father of many nations have I made thee.   *17:5*

5   My Lord, if now I have found favor in thy sight, pass not away, I pray thee, from thy servant.   *18:3*

6   But his [Lot's] wife looked back from behind him, and she became a pillar of salt.   *19:26*

7   My son, God will provide himself a lamb for a burnt offering.   *22:8*

8   He [Jacob] dreamed, and behold a ladder set up on the earth, and the top of it reached to heaven: and behold the angels of God ascending and descending on it.   *28:12*

9   Surely the Lord is in this place; and I knew it not.   *28:16*

10   This is none other but the house of God, and this is the gate of heaven.   *28:17*

11   And Jacob was left alone; and there wrestled a man with him until the breaking of the day.   *32:24*

12   I will not let thee go, except thou bless me.   *32:26*

13   Behold, this dreamer cometh.   *37:19*

14   They stript Joseph out of his coat, his coat of many colors.   *37:23*

15   The Lord made all that he did to prosper in his hand.   *39:3*

16   God forbid.   *44:7*

17   And ye shall eat the fat of the land.   *45:18*

18   I have waited for thy salvation, O Lord.   *49:18*

19   Unto the utmost bound of the everlasting hills.   *49:26*

20   Now there arose up a new king over Egypt, which knew not Joseph.
The Second Book of Moses, Called Exodus 1:8

21   I have been a stranger in a strange land.   *2:22*

22   Behold, the bush burned with fire, and the bush was not consumed.   *3:2*

23   Put off thy shoes from off thy feet, for the place whereon thou standest is holy ground.   *3:5*

1   And Moses hid his face; for he was afraid to look upon God.   *3:6*

2   A land flowing with milk and honey.   *3:8*

3   And God said unto Moses, I AM THAT I AM.   *3:14*

4   Let my people go.   *5:1*

5   Thou shalt say unto Aaron, Take thy rod, and cast it before Pharaoh, and it shall become a serpent.   *7:9*

6   They [Pharaoh's wise men] cast down every man his rod, and they became serpents: but Aaron's rod swallowed up their rods.
And he hardened Pharaoh's heart.   *7:12–13*

7   This is the finger of God.   *8:19*

8   Yet will I bring one plague more upon Pharaoh, and upon Egypt.   *11:1*

9   And they shall eat the flesh in that night, roast with fire, and unleavened bread; and with bitter herbs they shall eat it.   *12:8*

10   And thus shall ye eat it; with your loins girded, your shoes on your feet, and your staff in your hand; and ye shall eat it in haste: it is the Lord's passover.
For I will pass through the land of Egypt this night, and will smite all the firstborn in the land of Egypt, both man and beast; and against all the gods of Egypt I will execute judgment: I am the Lord.   *12:11–12*

11   This day [Passover] shall be unto you for a memorial; and ye shall keep it a feast to the Lord throughout your generations.   *12:14*

12   Seven days shall ye eat unleavened bread.   *12:15*

13   There was a great cry in Egypt; for there was not a house where there was not one dead.   *12:30*

14   Remember this day, in which ye came out from Egypt, out of the house of bondage.   *13:3*

15   And the Lord went before them by day in a pillar of a cloud, to lead them the way; and by night in a pillar of fire, to give them light.   *13:21*

16   And the children of Israel went into the midst of the sea upon the dry ground: and the waters were a wall unto them on their right hand, and on their left.   *14:22*

17   I will sing unto the Lord, for he hath triumphed gloriously: the horse and his rider hath he thrown into the sea.
The Lord is my strength and song, and he is become my salvation.   *15:1–2*

1   The Lord is a man of war.   *15:3*

2   Thy right hand, O Lord, is become glorious in power: thy right hand, O Lord, hath dashed in pieces the enemy.   *15:6*

3   It is manna.   *16:15*

4   I am the Lord thy God.   *20:2*[1]

5   Thou shalt have no other gods before me.
      Thou shalt not make unto thee any graven image.   *20:3–4*

6   For I the Lord thy God am a jealous God, visiting the iniquity of the fathers upon the children unto the third and fourth generation of them that hate me;
      And showing mercy unto thousands of them that love me, and keep my commandments.
      Thou shalt not take the name of the Lord thy God in vain.   *20:5–7*

7   Remember the sabbath day, to keep it holy.
      Six days shalt thou labor, and do all thy work:
      But the seventh day…thou shalt not do any work.   *20:8–10*

8   Honor thy father and thy mother: that thy days may be long upon the land which the Lord thy God giveth thee.
      Thou shalt not kill.
      Thou shalt not commit adultery.
      Thou shalt not steal.
      Thou shalt not bear false witness against thy neighbor.
      Thou shalt not covet thy neighbor's house, thou shalt not covet thy neighbor's wife, nor his manservant, nor his maidservant, nor his ox, nor his ass, nor any thing that is thy neighbor's.   *20:12–17*

9   Eye for eye, tooth for tooth, hand for hand, foot for foot.   *21:24*

10   Behold, I send an Angel before thee, to keep thee in the way.   *23:20*

11   Thou canst not see my face: for there shall no man see me, and live.
                                                                                     33:20

12   And he [Moses] was there with the Lord forty days and forty nights; he did neither eat bread, nor drink water. And he wrote upon the tables the words of the covenant, the Ten Commandments.   *34:28*

13   Whatsoever parteth the hoof, and is cloven-footed, and cheweth the cud, among the beasts, that shall ye eat.
                                                            The Third Book of Moses, Called Leviticus 11:3

---

[1]*Exodus 20:2–17* contain the Ten Commandments (the Decalogue). Tradition holds that God handed down the commandments to Moses on Mount Sinai.

1   And the swine is unclean to you.
     Of their flesh shall ye not eat.   *11:7–8*

2   Let him go for a scapegoat into the wilderness.   *16:10*

3   And when ye reap the harvest of your land, thou shalt not wholly reap the corners of thy field, neither shalt thou gather the gleanings of thy harvest.

     And thou shalt not glean thy vineyard, neither shalt thou gather every grape of thy vineyard; thou shalt leave them for the poor and stranger.

                                                                        19:9–10

4   Thou shalt love thy neighbor as thyself.[1]   *19:18*

5   The Lord bless thee, and keep thee:
     The Lord make his face shine upon thee, and be gracious unto thee:
     The Lord lift up his countenance upon thee, and give thee peace.
          The Fourth Book of Moses,
          Called Numbers 6:24–26

6   Moses lifted up his hand, and with his rod he smote the rock twice: and the water came out abundantly.   *20:11*

7   He whom thou blessest is blessed.   *22:6*

8   What hath God wrought!   *23:23*

9   How goodly are thy tents, O Jacob, and thy tabernacles, O Israel!

                                                                        24:5

10   Be sure your sin will find you out.   *32:23*

11   I call heaven and earth to witness.
                    The Fifth Book of Moses, Called Deuteronomy 4:26

12   Hear, O Israel: The Lord our God is one Lord.   *6:4*

13   The Lord thy God hath chosen thee to be a special people unto himself.   *7:6*

14   Man doth not live by bread only,[2] but by every word that proceedeth out of the mouth of the Lord doth man live.   *8:3*

15   A land of wheat, and barley, and vines, and fig trees, and pomegranates; a land of oil olive, and honey;

     A land wherein thou shalt eat bread without scarceness, thou shalt not lack any thing in it; a land whose stones are iron, and out of whose hills thou mayest dig brass.   *8:8–9*

---

[1]Also in *Matthew 19:19* and *22:39* (30:1), *Mark 12:31* and *33, Romans 13:9, Galatians 5:14, James 2:8.*
[2]Man shall not live by bread alone. — *Matthew 4:4*

1   A dreamer of dreams. *13:1*

2   The poor shall never cease out of the land. *15:11*

3   And thou shalt become an astonishment, a proverb, and a byword, among all nations. *28:37*

4   He is the Rock, his work is perfect: for all his ways are judgment: a God of truth. *32:4*

5   As thy days, so shall thy strength be. *33:25*

6   The eternal God is thy refuge, and underneath are the everlasting arms. *33:27*

7   And the priests that bare the ark of the covenant of the Lord stood firm on dry ground in the midst of Jordan, and all the Israelites passed over on dry ground, until all the people were passed clean over Jordan. *The Book of Joshua 3:17*

8   Mighty men of valor. *6:2*

9   And it came to pass, when the people heard the sound of the trumpet, and the people shouted with a great shout, that the wall fell down flat, so that the people went up into the city [Jericho]. *6:20*

10   Hewers of wood and drawers of water. *9:21*

11   I am going the way of all the earth. *23:14*

12   They shall be as thorns in your sides. *The Book of Judges 2:3*

13   I Deborah arose ... I arose a mother in Israel. *5:7*

14   Awake, awake, Deborah: awake, awake, utter a song: arise, Barak, and lead thy captivity captive. *5:12*

15   The Philistines be upon thee, Samson. *16:9*

16   The Philistines took him [Samson], and put out his eyes, and brought him down to Gaza, and bound him with fetters of brass; and he did grind in the prison house. *16:21*

17   So the dead which he slew at his death were more than they which he slew in his life. *16:30*

18   All the people arose as one man. *20:8*

19   In those days there was no king in Israel: every man did that which was right in his own eyes. *21:25*

20   Whither thou goest, I will go; and where thou lodgest, I will lodge: thy people shall be my people, and thy God my God. *The Book of Ruth 1:16*

21   Let me glean and gather after the reapers among the sheaves. *2:7*

1   In the flower of their age.   *The First Book of Samuel 2:33*

2   The Lord called Samuel: and he answered, Here am I.   *3:4*

3   Speak, Lord; for thy servant heareth.   *3:9*

4   God save the king.   *10:24*

5   A man after his own heart.   *13:14*

6   Every man's sword was against his fellow.   *14:20*

7   For the Lord seeth not as man seeth; for man looketh on the outward appearance, but the Lord looketh on the heart.   *16:7*

8   Go, and the Lord be with thee.   *17:37*

9   And he [David] chose him five smooth stones out of the brook.   *17:40*

10   So David prevailed over the Philistine with a sling and with a stone.   *17:50*

11   Saul hath slain his thousands, and David his ten thousands.   *18:7*

12   And Jonathan loved him [David] as he loved his own soul.   *20:17*

13   Wickedness proceedeth from the wicked.   *24:13*

14   I have played the fool.   *26:21*

15   Saul and Jonathan were lovely and pleasant in their lives, and in their death they were not divided: they were swifter than eagles, they were stronger than lions.   *The Second Book of Samuel 1:23*

16   How are the mighty fallen in the midst of the battle!   *1:25*

17   Thy love to me was wonderful, passing the love of women.
      How are the mighty fallen, and the weapons of war perished!   *1:26–27*

18   Abner ... smote him under the fifth rib.   *2:23*

19   And David and all the house of Israel played before the Lord on all manner of instruments made of fir wood, even on harps, and on psalteries, and on timbrels, and on cornets, and on cymbals.   *6:5*

20   David danced before the Lord.   *6:14*

21   Thou art the man.   *12:7*

22   Would God I had died for thee, O Absalom, my son, my son!   *18:33*

23   The Lord is my rock, and my fortress, and my deliverer.   *22:2*

24   A wise and an understanding heart.   *The First Book of the Kings 3:12*

1 He [Solomon] spake three thousand proverbs: and his songs were a thousand and five. *4:32*

2 The wisdom of Solomon. *4:34*

3 When the queen of Sheba heard of the fame of Solomon she came to prove him with hard questions. *10:1*

4 There appeared a chariot of fire, and horses of fire, and parted them both asunder; and Elijah went up by a whirlwind into heaven.
The Second Book of the Kings 2:11

5 The chariot of Israel, and the horsemen thereof. And he saw him no more. *2:12*

6 He [Elisha] took up also the mantle of Elijah. *2:13*

7 What hast thou to do with peace? Turn thee behind me. *9:18*

8 Jezebel heard of it; and she painted her face, and tired her head, and looked out at a window. *9:30*

9 Set thine house in order. *20:1*

10 His mercy endureth for ever.
The First Book of the Chronicles 16:41

11 Our days on the earth are as a shadow. *29:15*

12 He [David] died in a good old age, full of days, riches, and honor.
29:28

13 Thou art a God ready to pardon, gracious and merciful, slow to anger, and of great kindness.
The Book of Nehemiah 9:17

14 The man whom the king delighteth to honor.
The Book of Esther 6:7

15 One that feared God, and eschewed evil.
The Book of Job 1:1

16 Satan came also. *1:6*

17 And the Lord said unto Satan, Whence comest thou? Then Satan answered the Lord, and said, From going to and fro in the earth, and from walking up and down in it. *1:7*

18 And I only am escaped alone to tell thee. *1:15*

19 Naked came I out of my mother's womb, and naked shall I return thither: the Lord gave, and the Lord hath taken away; blessed be the name of the Lord. *1:21*

14 20 Skin for skin, yea, all that a man hath will he give for his life. *2:4*

1   Curse God, and die.

             2:9

2   Who ever perished, being innocent? or where were the righteous cut off?

             4:7

3   Fear came upon me, and trembling.

             4:14

4   Then a spirit passed before my face; the hair of my flesh stood up.

             4:15

5   Shall mortal man be more just than God? shall a man be more pure than his maker?

             4:17

6   Man is born unto trouble, as the sparks fly upward.

             5:7

7   How forcible are right words!

             6:25

8   But ask now the beasts, and they shall teach thee; and the fowls of the air, and they shall tell thee:

      Or speak to the earth, and it shall teach thee; and the fishes of the sea shall declare unto thee.

             12:7–8

9   But man dieth, and wasteth away: yea, man giveth up the ghost, and where is he?

             14:10

10   If a man die, shall he live again?

             14:14

11   My days are past.

             17:11

12   I am escaped with the skin of my teeth.

             19:20

13   Oh that my words were now written! oh that they were printed in a book!

             19:23

14   Seeing the root of the matter is found in me.

             19:28

15   The womb shall forget him; the worm shall feed sweetly on him; he shall be no more remembered.

             24:20

16   But where shall wisdom be found? and where is the place of understanding?

             28:12

17   The land of the living.

             28:13

18   The price of wisdom is above rubies.

             28:18

19   I was eyes to the blind, and feet was I to the lame.

             29:15

20   Great men are not always wise.

             32:9

21   One among a thousand.

             33:23

22   Out of the mouth of babes and sucklings hast thou ordained strength, because of thine enemies; that thou mightest still the enemy and the avenger.

      When I consider thy heavens, the work of thy fingers, the moon and the stars, which thou hast ordained;

What is man, that thou art mindful of him? and the son of man, that thou visitest him?

For thou hast made him a little lower than the angels.

The Book of Psalms 8:2–5

1   How long wilt thou forget me, O Lord? *13:1*

2   The fool hath said in his heart, There is no God. *14:1 and 53:1*

3   The lines are fallen unto me in pleasant places; yea, I have a goodly heritage. *16:6*

4   Keep me as the apple of the eye, hide me under the shadow of thy wings. *17:8*

5   He rode upon a cherub, and did fly: yea, he did fly upon the wings of the wind. *18:10*

6   The judgments of the Lord are true and righteous altogether.

More to be desired are they than gold, yea, than much fine gold: sweeter also than honey and the honeycomb. *19:9–10*

7   Cleanse thou me from secret faults. *19:12*

8   Thou hast given him his heart's desire. *21:2*

9   My God, my God, why hast thou forsaken me? Why art thou so far from helping me, and from the words of my roaring? *22:1*

10   The Lord is my shepherd; I shall not want.

He maketh me to lie down in green pastures: he leadeth me beside the still waters.

He restoreth my soul: he leadeth me in the paths of righteousness for his name's sake.

Yea, though I walk through the valley of the shadow of death, I will fear no evil: for thou art with me; thy rod and thy staff they comfort me.

Thou preparest a table before me in the presence of mine enemies: thou anointest my head with oil; my cup runneth over.

Surely goodness and mercy shall follow me all the days of my life: and I will dwell in the house of the Lord for ever. *23*

11   The Lord is my light and my salvation; whom shall I fear? the Lord is the strength of my life; of whom shall I be afraid? *27:1*

12   The Lord is my strength and my shield. *28:7*

13   Weeping may endure for a night, but joy cometh in the morning. *30:5*

14   I am forgotten as a dead man out of mind: I am like a broken vessel. *31:12*

1   The meek shall inherit the earth.   *37:11*

2   Be still, and know that I am God.   *46:10*

3   Every beast of the forest is mine, and the cattle upon a thousand hills.   *50:10*

4   I was shapen in iniquity; and in sin did my mother conceive me.   *51:5*

5   Oh that I had wings like a dove! for then would I fly away, and be at rest.   *55:6*

6   Thou crownest the year with thy goodness.   *65:11*

7   Make a joyful noise unto God, all ye lands.   *66:1*

8   We went through fire and through water.   *66:12*

9   Princes shall come out of Egypt; Ethiopia shall soon stretch out her hands unto God.   *68:31*

10   His enemies shall lick the dust.   *72:9*

11   His name shall endure for ever.   *72:17*

12   A stubborn and rebellious generation.   *78:8*

13   But ye shall die like men, and fall like one of the princes.   *82:7*

14   How amiable are thy tabernacles, O Lord of hosts!   *84:1*

15   They go from strength to strength.   *84:7*

16   Lord, why castest thou off my soul? why hidest thou thy face from me?   *88:14*

17   Lord, thou hast been our dwelling place in all generations.

Before the mountains were brought forth, or ever thou hadst formed the earth and the world, even from everlasting to everlasting, thou art God.

Thou turnest man to destruction; and sayest, Return, ye children of men.

For a thousand years in thy sight are but as yesterday when it is past, and as a watch in the night.

Thou carriest them away as with a flood; they are as a sleep: in the morning they are like grass which groweth up.

In the morning it flourisheth, and groweth up; in the evening it is cut down, and withereth.   *90:1–6*

18   We spend our years as a tale that is told.   *90:9*

19   So teach us to number our days, that we may apply our hearts unto wisdom.   *90:12*

20   Establish thou the work of our hands upon us; yea, the work of our hands establish thou it.   *90:17*

1	O sing unto the Lord a new song.	*96:1*
2	My days are consumed like smoke.	*102:3*
3	The fear of the Lord is the beginning of wisdom.	*111:10*
4	From the rising of the sun unto the going down of the same the Lord's name is to be praised.	*113:3*
5	They have mouths, but they speak not: eyes have they, but they see not.	
	They have ears, but they hear not.	*115:5–6*
6	The darkness and the light are both alike to thee.	*139:12*
7	I am fearfully and wonderfully made.	*139:14*
8	Thou openest thine hand, and satisfiest the desire of every living thing.	*145:16*
9	Put not your trust in princes.	*146:3*
10	He telleth the number of the stars; he calleth them all by their names.	*147:4*
11	To give subtilty to the simple, to the young man knowledge and discretion.	*The Proverbs 1:4*
12	Be not afraid of sudden fear.	*3:25*
13	Wisdom is the principal thing; therefore get wisdom: and with all thy getting get understanding.	*4:7*
14	He that trusteth in his riches shall fall.	*11:28*
15	He that troubleth his own house shall inherit the wind.	*11:29*
16	A righteous man regardeth the life of his beast: but the tender mercies of the wicked are cruel.	*12:10*
17	He that spareth his rod hateth his son: but he that loveth him chasteneth him betimes.	*13:24*
18	Before honor is humility.	*15:33 and 18:12*
19	Pride goeth before destruction, and an haughty spirit before a fall.	*16:18*
20	A fool's mouth is his destruction.	*18:7*
21	Wealth maketh many friends.	*19:4*
22	Wine is a mocker, strong drink is raging.	*20:1*
23	The borrower is servant to the lender.	*22:7*
24	Rob not the poor, because he is poor: neither oppress the afflicted in the gate.	*22:22*

1 Riches certainly make themselves wings; they fly away as an eagle toward heaven.   *23:5*

2 As he thinketh in his heart, so is he.   *23:7*

3 If thou faint in the day of adversity, thy strength is small.   *24:10*

4 Answer a fool according to his folly.   *26:5*

5 Boast not thyself of tomorrow; for thou knowest not what a day may bring forth.   *27:1*

6 Better is a neighbor that is near than a brother far off.   *27:10*

7 He that giveth unto the poor shall not lack.   *28:27*

8 Where there is no vision, the people perish.   *29:18*

9 Give me neither poverty nor riches.   *30:8*

10 Strength and honor are her clothing.   *31:25*

11 All the rivers run into the sea; yet the sea is not full.
Ecclesiastes; or The Preacher 1:7

12 The thing that hath been, it is that which shall be; and that which is done is that which shall be done: and there is no new thing under the sun.
1:9

13 There is no remembrance of former things; neither shall there be any remembrance of things that are to come with those that shall come after.
1:11

14 In much wisdom is much grief: and he that increaseth knowledge increaseth sorrow.   *1:18*

15 One event happeneth to them all.   *2:14*

16 How dieth the wise man? as the fool.   *2:16*

17 To every thing there is a season, and a time to every purpose under the heaven.

A time to be born, and a time to die; a time to plant, and a time to pluck up that which is planted;

A time to kill, and a time to heal; a time to break down, and a time to build up;

A time to weep, and a time to laugh; a time to mourn, and a time to dance;

A time to cast away stones, and a time to gather stones together; a time to embrace, and a time to refrain from embracing;

A time to get, and a time to lose; a time to keep, and a time to cast away;

A time to rend, and a time to sew; a time to keep silence, and a time to speak;

A time to love, and a time to hate; a time of war, and a time of peace. *3:1–8*

1   As he came forth of his mother's womb, naked shall he return to go as he came, and shall take nothing of his labor, which he may carry away in his hand. *5:15*

2   A good name is better than precious ointment; and the day of death than the day of one's birth. *7:1*

3   The heart of the wise is in the house of mourning; but the heart of fools is in the house of mirth. *7:4*

4   Be not righteous over much. *7:16*

5   There is not a just man upon earth, that doeth good, and sinneth not. *7:20*

6   One man among a thousand have I found; but a woman among all those have I not found. *7:28*

7   There is no discharge in that war. *8:8*

8   A man hath no better thing under the sun, than to eat, and to drink, and to be merry. *8:15*

9   I returned, and saw under the sun, that the race is not to the swift, nor the battle to the strong, neither yet bread to the wise, nor yet riches to men of understanding, nor yet favor to men of skill; but time and chance happeneth to them all.

For man also knoweth not his time: as the fishes that are taken in an evil net, and as the birds that are caught in the snare; so are the sons of men snared in an evil time, when it falleth suddenly upon them. *9:11–12*

10   Cast thy bread upon the waters: for thou shalt find it after many days. *11:1*

11   Remember now thy Creator in the days of thy youth, while the evil days come not, nor the years draw nigh, when thou shalt say, I have no pleasure in them;

While the sun, or the light, or the moon, or the stars, be not darkened, nor the clouds return after the rain:

In the day when the keepers of the house shall tremble, and the strong men shall bow themselves, and the grinders cease because they are few, and those that look out of the windows be darkened,

And the doors shall be shut in the streets, when the sound of the grinding is low, and he shall rise up at the voice of the bird, and all the daughters of music shall be brought low. *12:1–4*

1   Of making many books there is no end; and much study is a weariness of the flesh.

    Let us hear the conclusion of the whole matter: Fear God, and keep his commandments: for this is the whole duty of man.

    For God shall bring every work into judgment, with every secret thing, whether it be good, or whether it be evil.   *12:12–14*

2   The song of songs, which is Solomon's.

The Song of Solomon 1:1

3   I am black, but comely, O ye daughters of Jerusalem, as the tents of Kedar, as the curtains of Solomon.   *1:5*

4   O thou fairest among women.   *1:8*

5   I am the rose of Sharon, and the lily of the valleys.   *2:1*

6   His banner over me was love.

    Stay me with flagons, comfort me with apples: for I am sick of love.

2:4–5

7   Take us the foxes, the little foxes, that spoil the vines: for our vines have tender grapes.   *2:15*

8   How much better is thy love than wine!   *4:10*

9   Awake, O north wind; and come, thou south; blow upon my garden, that the spices thereof may flow out. Let my beloved come into his garden, and eat his pleasant fruits.   *4:16*

10   His mouth is most sweet: yea, he is altogether lovely. This is my beloved, and this is my friend, O daughters of Jerusalem.   *5:16*

11   Who is she that looketh forth as the morning, fair as the moon, clear as the sun, and terrible as an army with banners?   *6:10*

12   Thy neck is as a tower of ivory.   *7:4*

13   I am my beloved's, and his desire is toward me.   *7:10*

14   Set me as a seal upon thine heart, as a seal upon thine arm: for love is strong as death; jealousy is cruel as the grave.   *8:6*

15   Many waters cannot quench love, neither can the floods drown it.

8:7

16   The whole head is sick, and the whole heart faint.

The Book of the Prophet Isaiah 1:5

17   Learn to do well; seek judgment, relieve the oppressed, judge the fatherless, plead for the widow.

    Come now, and let us reason together…though your sins be as scarlet, they shall be as white as snow.   *1:17–18*

1   They shall beat their swords into plowshares, and their spears into pruning hooks: nation shall not lift up sword against nation, neither shall they learn war any more.[1]   *2:4*

2   Then said I, Lord, how long?   *6:11*

3   For unto us a child is born, unto us a son is given: and the government shall be upon his shoulder: and his name shall be called Wonderful, Counselor, The mighty God, The everlasting Father, The Prince of Peace.
Of the increase of his government and peace there shall be no end.   *9:6–7*

4   The nations shall rush like the rushing of many waters.   *17:13*

5   The burden of the desert of the sea. As whirlwinds in the south pass through; so it cometh from the desert, from a terrible land.   *21:1*

6   Babylon is fallen, is fallen; and all the graven images of her gods he hath broken unto the ground.   *21:9*

7   Let us eat and drink; for tomorrow we shall die.   *22:13*

8   I will fasten him as a nail in a sure place.   *22:23*

9   As with the maid, so with her mistress.   *24:2*

10 He will swallow up death in victory; and the Lord God will wipe away tears from off all faces.   *25:8*

11 Awake and sing, ye that dwell in dust.   *26:19*

12 Hide thyself as it were for a little moment, until the indignation be overpast.   *26:20*

13 The voice of him that crieth in the wilderness, Prepare ye the way of the Lord, make straight in the desert a highway for our God.   *40:2–3*

14 Every valley shall be exalted, and every mountain and hill shall be made low: and the crooked shall be made straight, and the rough places plain.   *40:4*

15 He shall feed his flock like a shepherd: he shall gather the lambs with his arm, and carry them in his bosom, and shall gently lead those that are with young.   *40:11*

16 The nations are as a drop of a bucket, and are counted as the small dust of the balance.   *40:15*

17 There is no peace, saith the Lord, unto the wicked.   *48:22*

18 They shall see eye to eye.   *52:8*

---

[1]Also in *Joel 3:10* and *Micah 4:3*.

1   All we like sheep have gone astray. *53:6*

2   He is brought as a lamb to the slaughter. *53:7*

3   Behold, I have given him for a witness to the people, a leader and commander to the people. *55:4*

4   Peace to him that is far off, and to him that is near. *57:19*

5   Arise, shine; for thy light is come, and the glory of the Lord is risen upon thee. *60:1*

6   A little one shall become a thousand, and a small one a strong nation. *60:22*

7   I am holier than thou. *65:5*

8   Hear now this, O foolish people, and without understanding; which have eyes, and see not; which have ears, and hear not.

The Book of the Prophet Jeremiah 5:21

9   Saying, Peace, peace; when there is no peace. *6:14 and 8:11*

10   Amend your ways and your doings. *7:3 and 26:13*

11   The harvest is past, the summer is ended, and we are not saved. *8:20*

12   Is there no balm in Gilead? *8:22*

13   Can the Ethiopian change his skin, or the leopard his spots? *13:23*

14   The heart is deceitful above all things, and desperately wicked: who can know it? *17:9*

15   With my whole heart and with my whole soul. *32:41*

16   How doth the city sit solitary, that was full of people! how is she become as a widow! *The Lamentations of Jeremiah 1:1*

17   As is the mother, so is her daughter.

The Book of the Prophet Ezekiel 16:44

18   The king of Babylon stood at the parting of the way. *21:21*

19   The valley was full of bones
and lo, they were very dry. *37:1–2*

20   Can these bones live? *37:3*

21   O ye dry bones, hear the word of the Lord. *37:4*

22   Every man's sword shall be against his brother. *38:21*

23   His legs of iron, his feet part of iron and part of clay.

The Book of Daniel 2:33

24   Shadrach, Meshach, and Abednego, fell down bound into the midst of the burning fiery furnace. *3:23*

1   Ye are the sons of the living God.   *Hosea 1:10*

2   Like people, like priest.   *4:9*

3   After two days will he revive us: in the third day he will raise us up, and we shall live in his sight.   *6:2*

4   He shall come unto us as the rain, as the latter and former rain unto the earth.   *6:3*

5   For I desired mercy, and not sacrifice; and the knowledge of God more than burnt offerings.   *6:6*

6   They have sown the wind, and they shall reap the whirlwind.   *8:7*

7   Your old men shall dream dreams, your young men shall see visions.
                                                                      Joel 2:28

8   They sold the righteous for silver, and the poor for a pair of shoes.
                                                                      Amos 2:6

9   Can two walk together, except they be agreed?   *3:3*

10   And Jonah was in the belly of the fish three days and three nights.
                                                                      Jonah 1:17

11   What doth the Lord require of thee, but to do justly, and to love mercy, and to walk humbly with thy God?   *Micah 6:8*

12   I have spread you abroad as the four winds of the heaven.
                                                                      Zechariah 2:6

13   Prisoners of hope.   *9:12*

14   So they weighed for my price thirty pieces of silver.   *11:12*

15   What are these wounds in thine hands? Those with which I was wounded in the house of my friends.   *13:6*

16   Have we not all one father? hath not one God created us?
                                                                      Malachi 2:10

17   Behold, I will send my messenger, and he shall prepare the way before me.   *3:1*

18   Behold, I will send you Elijah the prophet before the coming of the great and dreadful day of the Lord.   *4:5*

The Apocrypha[1]

19   Great is Truth, and mighty above all things.   *I Esdras 24:41*

---

[1]"The Apocrypha" (The Hidden Books) is a term used to describe the books found in the Alexandrine Greek Scripture (the Septuagint) but absent from the Orthodox Hebrew Scripture (the Masoretic Text). These books are regarded as canonical only by Roman Catholics.

1   I shall light a candle of understanding in thine heart, which shall not be put out.   *14:25*

2   Put on her garments of gladness.   *Judith 10:3*

3   The ear of jealousy heareth all things.

The Wisdom of Solomon 1:10

4   Our time is a very shadow that passeth away.   *2:5*

5   For God created man to be immortal, and made him to be an image of his own eternity.

Nevertheless through envy of the devil came death into the world.

2:23–24

6   Even so we in like manner, as soon as we were born, began to draw to our end.   *5:13*

7   Profess not the knowledge that thou hast not.
A stubborn heart shall fare evil at the last.   *3:25–26*

8   Wisdom exalteth her children, and layeth hold of them that seek her.
He that loveth her loveth life.   *Ecclesiasticus 4:11–12*

9   Observe the opportunity.   *4:20*

10   A faithful friend is the medicine of life.   *6:16*

11   Miss not the discourse of the elders.   *8:9*

12   So is a word better than a gift.   *18:16*

13   Many have fallen by the edge of the sword: but not so many as have fallen by the tongue.   *28:18*

14   Let the counsel of thine own heart stand.   *37:13*

15   Let us now praise famous men, and our fathers that begat us.   *44:1*

16   When he was at the last gasp.   *The Second Book of the Maccabees 7:9*

The New Testament[1]

17   Behold, a virgin shall be with child, and shall bring forth a son, and they shall call his name Emmanuel, which being interpreted is, God with us.
The Gospel According to Saint Matthew 1:23

18   Now when Jesus was born in Bethlehem of Judaea in the days of Herod the king, behold, there came wise men from the east to Jerusalem,
Saying, Where is he that is born King of the Jews? For we have seen his star in the east, and are come to worship him.   *2:1–2*

---

[1]The earliest Christian writings [A.D. c. 50–c. 64] are the Letters (Epistles) of Paul the Apostle. The Gospels were written later, between the years 70 and 100.

1   They saw the young child with Mary his mother, and fell down, and worshipped him: and they…presented unto him gifts; gold, and frankincense, and myrrh.

And being warned of God in a dream that they should not return to Herod, they departed into their own country another way.   *2:11–12*

2   Out of Egypt have I called my son.   *2:15*

3   Rachel weeping for her children, and would not be comforted, because they are not.   *2:18*

4   He shall be called a Nazarene.   *2:23*

5   Repent ye: for the kingdom of heaven is at hand.   *3:2*

6   The voice of one crying in the wilderness, Prepare ye the way of the Lord, make his paths straight.   *3:3*

7   And his meat was locusts and wild honey.   *3:4*

8   The Spirit of God descending like a dove.   *3:16*

9   This is my beloved Son, in whom I am well pleased.   *3:17*

10   And when he had fasted forty days and forty nights, he was afterward an hungred.   *4:2*

11   Follow me, and I will make you fishers of men.   *4:19*

12   Blessed are the poor in spirit: for theirs is the kingdom of heaven.
Blessed are they that mourn: for they shall be comforted.
Blessed are the meek: for they shall inherit the earth.
Blessed are they which do hunger and thirst after righteousness: for they shall be filled.
Blessed are the merciful: for they shall obtain mercy.
Blessed are the pure in heart: for they shall see God.
Blessed are the peacemakers: for they shall be called the children of God.
Blessed are they which are persecuted for righteousness's sake: for theirs is the kingdom of heaven.
Blessed are ye, when men shall revile you, and persecute you, and shall say all manner of evil against you falsely, for my sake.   *5:3–11*

13   Ye are the salt of the earth: but if the salt have lost his savor, wherewith shall it be salted?   *5:13*

14   Whosoever looketh on a woman to lust after her hath committed adultery with her already in his heart.

And if thy right eye offend thee, pluck it out, and cast it from thee: for it is profitable for thee that one of thy members should perish, and not that thy whole body should be cast into hell.

And if thy right hand offend thee, cut it off.   *5:28–30*

1 Love your enemies, bless them that curse you, do good to them that hate you, and pray for them which despitefully use you, and persecute you.

5:44

2 After this manner therefore pray ye: Our Father which art in heaven, Hallowed be thy name.

Thy kingdom come. Thy will be done in earth, as it is in heaven.

Give us this day our daily bread.

And forgive us our debts, as we forgive our debtors.[1]

And lead us not into temptation, but deliver us from evil: For thine is the kingdom, and the power, and the glory, for ever. Amen.   *6:9–13*

3 No man can serve two masters: for either he will hate the one, and love the other; or else he will hold to the one, and despise the other. Ye cannot serve God and mammon.

6:24

4 Consider the lilies of the field, how they grow; they toil not, neither do they spin.

6:28

5 Judge not, that ye be not judged.   *7:1*

6 Neither cast ye your pearls before swine.   *7:6*

7 Ask, and it shall be given you; seek, and ye shall find; knock, and it shall be opened unto you.

7:7

8 Therefore all things whatsoever ye would that men should do to you, do ye even so to them: for this is the law and the prophets.[2]   *7:12*

9 Or what man is there of you, whom if his son ask bread, will he give him a stone?

7:9

10 Wide is the gate, and broad is the way, that leadeth to destruction, and many there be which go in thereat:

Because strait is the gate, and narrow is the way, which leadeth unto life, and few there be that find it.   *7:13–14*

11 Beware of false prophets, which come to you in sheep's clothing, but inwardly they are ravening wolves.   *7:15*

12 [The house] fell not: for it was founded upon a rock.   *7:25*

13 A foolish man, which built his house upon the sand.   *7:26*

14 Follow me; and let the dead bury their dead.   *8:22*

15 Why are ye fearful, O ye of little faith?   *8:26*

---

[1]And forgive us our trespasses, / As we forgive those who trespass against us. — *Book of Common Prayer, Morning Prayer*

[2]The Golden Rule. Common form: Do unto others as you would have others do unto you.

1   They that be whole need not a physician, but they that are sick.

9:12

2   Freely ye have received, freely give.   *10:8*

3   Whosoever shall not receive you, nor hear your words, when ye depart out of that house or city, shake off the dust of your feet.   *10:14*

4   Ye shall be hated of all men for my name's sake.   *10:22*

5   The disciple is not above his master, nor the servant above his lord.

10:24

6   He that hath ears to hear, let him hear.   *11:15*

7   The Son of man came eating and drinking, and they say, Behold a man gluttonous, and a winebibber, a friend of publicans and sinners. But wisdom is justified of her children.   *11:19*

8   Come unto me, all ye that labor and are heavy laden, and I will give you rest.
    Take my yoke upon you, and learn of me; for I am meek and lowly in heart: and ye shall find rest unto your souls.
    For my yoke is easy, and my burden is light.   *11:28–30*

9   He that is not with me is against me.   *12:30*

10   The tree is known by his fruit.   *12:33*

11   Out of the abundance of the heart the mouth speaketh.   *12:34*

12   Some seeds fell by the way side.   *13:4*

13   Because they had no root, they withered away.   *13:6*

14   The care of this world, and the deceitfulness of riches.   *13:22*

15   The kingdom of heaven is like to a grain of mustard seed.   *13:31*

16   The kingdom of heaven is like unto a net, that was cast into the sea, and gathered of every kind.   *13:47*

17   Is not this the carpenter's son?   *13:55*

18   A prophet is not without honor, save in his own country.   *13:57*

19   Give me here John Baptist's head in a charger.   *14:8*

20   We have here but five loaves, and two fishes.   *14:17*

21   And they did all eat, and were filled: and they took up of the fragments that remained twelve baskets full.   *14:20*

22   And in the fourth watch of the night Jesus went unto them, walking on the sea.   *14:25*

    23   Be of good cheer; it is I; be not afraid.   *14:27*

1   O thou of little faith, wherefore didst thou doubt?   *14:31*

2   Of a truth thou art the Son of God.   *14:33*

3   They be blind leaders of the blind. And if the blind lead the blind, both shall fall into the ditch.   *15:14*

4   The dogs eat of the crumbs which fall from their masters' table.
    15:27

5   When it is evening, ye say, It will be fair weather: for the sky is red.
    16:2

6   The signs of the times.   *16:3*

7   Thou art the Christ, the Son of the living God.   *16:16*

8   Thou art Peter, and upon this rock I will build my church; and the gates of hell shall not prevail against it.
    And I will give unto thee the keys of the kingdom of heaven.
    16:18–19

9   Get thee behind me, Satan.   *16:23*

10   Whosoever will save his life shall lose it: and whosoever will lose his life for my sake shall find it.
    For what is a man profited, if he shall gain the whole world, and lose his own soul?   *16:25–26*

11   Where two or three are gathered together in my name, there am I in the midst of them.   *18:20*

12   Until seventy times seven.   *18:22*

13   What therefore God hath joined together, let not man put asunder.
    19:6

14   It is easier for a camel to go through the eye of a needle, than for a rich man to enter into the kingdom of God.   *19:24*

15   Many that are first shall be last; and the last shall be first.   *19:30*

16   Borne the burden and heat of the day.   *20:12*

17   Is it not lawful for me to do what I will with mine own?   *20:15*

18   Overthrew the tables of the moneychangers.   *21:12*

19   My house shall be called the house of prayer; but ye have made it a den of thieves.   *21:13*

20   They made light of it.   *22:5*

21   Many are called, but few are chosen.   *22:14*

29

1   Thou shalt love the Lord thy God with all thy heart, and with all thy soul, and with all thy mind.

This is the first and great commandment.

And the second is like unto it, Thou shalt love thy neighbor as thyself.[1]

On these two commandments hang all the law and the prophets.

22:37–40

2   Whosoever shall exalt himself shall be abased; and he that shall humble himself shall be exalted.   *23:12*

3   Ye shall hear of wars and rumors of wars: see that ye be not troubled: for all these things must come to pass, but the end is not yet.

For nation shall rise against nation.   *24:6–7*

4   And he shall send his angels with a great sound of a trumpet.

24:31

5   Heaven and earth shall pass away, but my words shall not pass away.

24:35

6   The one shall be taken, and the other left.   *24:40*

7   Then shall the kingdom of heaven be likened unto ten virgins, which took their lamps, and went forth to meet the bridegroom.

And five of them were wise, and five were foolish.   *25:1–2*

8   Well done, thou good and faithful servant . . . enter thou into the joy of thy lord.   *25:21*

9   Unto every one that hath shall be given, and he shall have abundance: but from him that hath not shall be taken away even that which he hath.

25:29

10   And before him shall be gathered all nations: and he shall separate them one from another, as a shepherd divideth his sheep from the goats.

25:32

11   For I was hungred, and ye gave me meat: I was thirsty, and ye gave me drink: I was a stranger, and ye took me in:

Naked, and ye clothed me: I was sick, and ye visited me: I was in prison, and ye came unto me.   *25:35–36*

12   Inasmuch as ye have done it unto one of the least of these my brethren, ye have done it unto me.   *25:40*

13   For ye have the poor always with you; but me ye have not always.

26:11

---

[1]See also *Leviticus 19:18* (11:4).

1   What will ye give me, and I will deliver him unto you? And they covenanted with him for thirty pieces of silver.   *26:15*

2   My time is at hand.   *26:18*

3   Verily I say unto you, that one of you shall betray me.   *26:21*

4   And they were exceeding sorrowful, and began every one of them to say unto him, Lord, is it I?   *26:22*

5   It had been good for that man [Judas] if he had not been born.   *26:24*

6   Jesus took bread, and blessed it, and brake it, and gave it to the disciples, and said, Take, eat; this is my body.

    And he took the cup, and gave thanks, and gave it to them, saying, Drink ye all of it;

    For this is my blood of the new testament, which is shed for many for the remission of sins.

    But I say unto you, I will not drink henceforth of this fruit of the vine, until that day when I drink it new with you in my Father's kingdom.   *26:26–29*

7   This night, before the cock crow, thou shalt deny me [Jesus] thrice.   *26:34*

8   O my Father, if it be possible, let this cup pass from me: nevertheless, not as I will, but as thou wilt.   *26:39*

9   Could ye not watch with me one hour?

    Watch and pray, that ye enter not into temptation: the spirit indeed is willing, but the flesh is weak.   *26:40–41*

10   Behold, the hour is at hand, and the Son of man is betrayed into the hands of sinners.   *26:45*

11   He came to Jesus, and said, Hail, Master; and kissed him.   *26:49*

12   All they that take the sword shall perish with the sword.   *26:52*

13   The potter's field, to bury strangers in.   *27:7*

14   Have thou nothing to do with that just man.   *27:19*

15   Let him be crucified.   *27:22*

16   [Pilate] took water, and washed his hands before the multitude, saying, I am innocent of the blood of this just person: see ye to it.   *27:24*

17   His blood be on us, and on our children.   *27:25*

18   This is Jesus the King of the Jews.   *27:37*

31

1   He saved others; himself he cannot save.   *27:42*

2   Eli, Eli, lama sabachthani? that is to say, My God, my God, why hast thou forsaken me?[1]   *27:46*

3   His countenance was like lightning, and his raiment white as snow.   *28:3*

4   Go ye therefore, and teach all nations, baptizing them in the name of the Father, and of the Son, and of the Holy Ghost.   *28:19*

5   Lo, I am with you always, even unto the end of the world.   *28:20*

6   There cometh one mightier than I[2] after me, the latchet of whose shoes I am not worthy to stoop down and unloose.
The Gospel According to Saint Mark 1:7

7   Arise, and take up thy bed, and walk.   *2:9*

8   The sabbath was made for man, and not man for the sabbath.   *2:27*

9   If a house be divided against itself, that house cannot stand.   *3:25*

10   What manner of man is this?   *4:41*

11   My name is Legion: for we are many.   *5:9*

12   Clothed, and in his right mind.   *5:15*

13   I see men as trees, walking.   *8:24*

14   Suffer the little children to come unto me, and forbid them not; for of such is the kingdom of God.   *10:14*

15   He is risen.   *16:6*

16   Go ye into all the world, and preach the gospel to every creature.   *16:15*

17   Hail, thou that art highly favored, the Lord is with thee: blessed art thou among women.   *The Gospel According to Saint Luke 1:28*

18   For with God nothing shall be impossible.   *1:37*

19   Blessed is the fruit of thy womb.   *1:42*

20   My soul doth magnify the Lord.   *1:46*

21   He hath scattered the proud in the imagination of their hearts.
He hath put down the mighty from their seats, and exalted them of low degree.   *1:51–52*

22   He hath filled the hungry with good things; and the rich he hath sent empty away.   *1:53*

---

[1]See *Psalm 22:1* (16:9).

[2]John the Baptist.

1   Blessed be the Lord God of Israel; for he hath visited and redeemed his people.   *1:68*

2   As he spake by the mouth of his holy prophets, which have been since the world began:

That we should be saved from our enemies, and from the hand of all that hate us.   *1:70–71*

3   Through the tender mercy of our God; whereby the dayspring from on high hath visited us,

And she brought forth her firstborn son, and wrapped him in swaddling clothes, and laid him in a manger; because there was no room for them in the inn.   *2:7*

4   There were in the same country shepherds abiding in the field, keeping watch over their flock by night.

And, lo, the angel of the Lord came upon them, and the glory of the Lord shone round about them: and they were sore afraid.

And the angel said unto them, Fear not: for, behold, I bring you good tidings of great joy, which shall be to all people.

For unto you is born this day in the city of David a Savior, which is Christ the Lord.   *2:8–11*

5   Glory to God in the highest, and on earth peace, good will toward men.   *2:14*

6   Lord, now lettest thou thy servant depart in peace.   *2:29*

7   Jesus increased in wisdom and stature, and in favor with God and man.   *2:52*

8   [The devil] showed unto him all the kingdoms of the world in a moment of time.   *4:5*

9   For it is written, He shall give his angels charge over thee, to keep thee:

And in their hands they shall bear thee up, lest at any time thou dash thy foot against a stone.   *4:10–11*

10   Physician, heal thyself.   *4:23*

11   Woe unto you, when all men shall speak well of you!   *6:26*

12   Nothing is secret, that shall not be made manifest.   *8:17*

13   Peace be to this house.   *10:5*

14   I beheld Satan as lightning fall from heaven.   *10:18*

15   Many prophets and kings have desired to see those things which ye see, and have not seen them; and to hear those things which ye hear, and have not heard them.   *10:24*

33

1	A certain man went down from Jerusalem to Jericho, and fell among thieves.	*10:30*
2	A certain Samaritan had compassion on him.	*10:33*
3	Go, and do thou likewise.	*10:37*
4	But Martha was cumbered about much serving.	*10:40*
5	But one thing is needful: and Mary hath chosen that good part, which shall not be taken away from her.	*10:42*
6	Let your loins be girded about, and your lights burning.	*12:35*
7	For unto whomsoever much is given, of him shall be much required: and to whom men have committed much, of him they will ask the more.	*12:48*
8	Rejoice with me; for I have found my sheep which was lost.	*15:6*
9	[The prodigal son] wasted his substance with riotous living.	*15:13*
10	Bring hither the fatted calf, and kill it.	*15:23*
11	For this my son was dead, and is alive again; he was lost, and is found.	*15:24*
12	Son, thou art ever with me, and all that I have is thine.	*15:31*
13	He that is faithful in that which is least is faithful also in much: and he that is unjust in the least is unjust also in much.	*16:10*
14	Between us and you there is a great gulf fixed.	*16:26*
15	The kingdom of God is within you.	*17:21*
16	Remember Lot's wife.	*17:32*
17	If these should hold their peace, the stones would immediately cry out.	*19:40*
18	He is not a God of the dead, but of the living.	*20:38*
19	This do in remembrance of me.	*22:19*
20	Not my will, but thine, be done.	*22:42*
21	The place, which is called Calvary.	*23:33*
22	Father, forgive them; for they know not what they do.	*23:34*
23	Lord, remember me when thou comest into thy kingdom.	*23:42*
24	Today shalt thou be with me in paradise.	*23:43*
25	Father, into thy hands I commend my spirit.	*23:46*
26	He gave up the ghost.	*23:46*
27	He was a good man, and a just.	*23:50*

1   Why seek ye the living among the dead?   *24:5*

2   Their words seemed to them as idle tales.   *24:11*

3   Did not our heart burn within us, while he talked with us?   *24:32*

4   The Lord is risen indeed.   *24:34*

5   In the beginning was the Word, and the Word was with God, and the Word was God.   *The Gospel According to Saint John 1:1*

6   There was a man sent from God, whose name was John.   *1:6*

7   The true Light, which lighteth every man that cometh into the world.   *1:9*

8   The Word was made flesh, and dwelt among us full of grace and truth.   *1:14*

9   No man hath seen God at any time.   *1:18*

10   Behold the Lamb of God, which taketh away the sin of the world.   *1:29*

11   Can there any good thing come out of Nazareth?   *1:46*

12   Hereafter ye shall see heaven open, and the angels of God ascending and descending upon the Son of man.   *1:51*

13   Woman, what have I to do with thee? mine hour is not yet come.   *2:4*

14   The water that was made wine.   *2:9*

15   Except a man be born again, he cannot see the kingdom of God.   *3:3*

16   The wind bloweth where it listeth, and thou hearest the sound thereof, but canst not tell whence it cometh, and whither it goeth: so is every one that is born of the Spirit.   *3:8*

17   How can these things be?   *3:9*

18   God so loved the world, that he gave his only begotten Son, that whosoever believeth in him should not perish, but have everlasting life.   *3:16*

19   He was a burning and a shining light.   *5:35*

20   Search the scriptures.   *5:39*

21   What are they among so many?   *6:9*

22   Gather up the fragments that remain, that nothing be lost.   *6:12*

23   I am the bread of life: he that cometh to me shall never hunger; and he that believeth on me shall never thirst.   *6:35*

24   It is the spirit that quickeneth; the flesh profiteth nothing.   *6:63*

1   Judge not according to the appearance.   *7:24*

2   Never man spake like this man.   *7:46*

3   He that is without sin among you, let him first cast a stone at her.

8:7

4   Neither do I condemn thee: go, and sin no more.   *8:11*

5   The truth shall make you free.   *8:32*

6   Whether he be a sinner or no, I know not: one thing I know, that, whereas I was blind, now I see.   *9:25*

7   I am the door.   *10:9*

8   I am the good shepherd: the good shepherd giveth his life for the sheep.   *10:11*

9   Other sheep I have, which are not of this fold.   *10:16*

10   I am the resurrection, and the life: he that believeth in me, though he were dead, yet shall he live:
And whosoever liveth and believeth in me shall never die.

11:25–26

11   Jesus wept.   *11:35*

12   A new commandment I give unto you, That ye love one another.

13:34

13   Let not your heart be troubled: ye believe in God, believe also in me.
In my Father's house are many mansions: if it were not so, I would have told you. I go to prepare a place for you.   *14:1–2*

14   I will come again, and receive you unto myself; that where I am, there ye may be also.   *14:3*

15   I am the way, the truth, and the life.   *14:6*

16   I will not leave you comfortless.   *14:18*

17   Peace I leave with you, my peace I give unto you: not as the world giveth, give I unto you. Let not your heart be troubled, neither let it be afraid.   *14:27*

18   Greater love hath no man than this, that a man lay down his life for his friends.   *15:13*

19   Ye have not chosen me, but I have chosen you.   *15:16*

20   Ask, and ye shall receive, that your joy may be full.   *16:24*

21   Be of good cheer; I have overcome the world.   *16:33*

22   Pilate saith unto him, What is truth?   *18:38*

1. Behold the man![1]   *19:5*

2. Woman, behold thy son!   *19:26*

3. It is finished.   *19:30*

4. Touch me not.[2]   *20:17*

5. Blessed are they that have not seen, and yet have believed.
                                                                          20:29

6. Suddenly there came a sound from heaven as of a rushing mighty wind.   *The Acts of the Apostles 2:2*

7. There appeared unto them cloven tongues like as of fire, and it sat upon each of them. And they were all filled with the Holy Ghost, and began to speak with other tongues.   *2:3–4*

8. Silver and gold have I none; but such as I have give I thee.
                                                                          3:6

9. And distribution was made unto every man according as he had need.
                                                                          4:35

10. Thy money perish with thee.   *8:20*

11. He is a chosen vessel unto me.   *9:15*

12. God is no respecter of persons.   *10:34*

13. God that made the world, and all things therein, seeing that he is Lord of heaven and earth, dwelleth not in temples made with hands;
    Neither is worshipped with men's hands, as though he needed any thing, seeing he giveth to all life, and breath, and all things;
    And hath made of one blood all nations of men for to dwell on all the face of the earth.   *17:24–26*

14. It is more blessed to give than to receive.   *20:35*

15. And the chief captain answered, With a great sum obtained I this freedom. And Paul said, But I was free born.   *22:28*

16. God shall smite thee, thou whited wall.   *23:3*

17. Revilest thou God's high priest?   *23:4*

18. I [Paul] am a Pharisee, the son of a Pharisee.   *23:6*

19. A conscience void of offense toward God, and toward men.
                                                                          24:16

20. When I have a convenient season, I will call for thee.   *24:25*

---

[1]Ecce homo. — *The Vulgate*
[2]Noli me tangere. — *The Vulgate*

1   Paul, thou art beside thyself; much learning doth make thee mad.

26:24

2   I am not mad but speak forth the words of truth and soberness.

26:25

3   For this thing was not done in a corner.   *26:26*

4   Wherein thou judgest another, thou condemnest thyself.

The Epistle of Paul the Apostle to the Romans 2:1

5   These, having not the law, are a law unto themselves.   *2:14*

6   The things that are more excellent.   *2:18*

7   Who against hope believed in hope.   *4:18*

8   Death hath no more dominion over him.   *6:9*

9   I speak after the manner of men.   *6:19*

10   The wages of sin is death; but the gift of God is eternal life.   *6:23*

11   The good that I would I do not: but the evil which I would not, that
I do.   *7:19*

12   Who shall deliver me from the body of this death?   *7:24*

13   Heirs of God, and joint-heirs with Christ.   *8:17*

14   If God be for us, who can be against us?   *8:31*

15   Who shall separate us from the love of Christ?   *8:35*

16   Neither death, nor life, nor angels, nor principalities, nor powers, nor
things present, nor things to come,
Nor height, nor depth, nor any other creature, shall be able to separate
us from the love of God, which is in Christ Jesus our Lord.   *8:38–39*

17   Be kindly affectioned one to another with brotherly love.   *12:10*

18   Given to hospitality.   *12:13*

19   Be not wise in your own conceits.
Recompense to no man evil for evil.   *12:16–17*

20   If it be possible, as much as lieth in you, live peaceably with all men.

12:18

21   Vengeance is mine; I will repay, saith the Lord.   *12:19*

22   Be not overcome of evil, but overcome evil with good.   *12:21*

23   Render therefore to all their dues: tribute to whom tribute is due;
custom to whom custom; fear to whom fear; honor to whom honor.
Owe no man anything, but to love one another.   *13:7–8*

24   Let every man be fully persuaded in his own mind.   *14:5*

1 Let us therefore follow after the things which make for peace.

14:19

2 We then that are strong ought to bear the infirmities of the weak, and not to please ourselves. *15:1*

3 God hath chosen the foolish things of the world to confound the wise; and God hath chosen the weak things of the world to confound the things which are mighty.

The First Epistle of Paul the Apostle to the Corinthians 1:27

4 Every man's work shall be made manifest: for the day shall declare it, because it shall be revealed by fire; and the fire shall try every man's work of what sort it is. *3:13*

5 For the temple of God is holy, which temple ye are. *3:17*

6 We are made a spectacle unto the world, and to angels, and to men.

4:9

7 Absent in body, but present in spirit. *5:3*

8 For even Christ our Passover is sacrificed for us. *5:7*

9 The fashion of this world passeth away. *7:31*

10 Knowledge puffeth up, but charity edifieth. *8:1*

11 I am made all things to all men. *9:22*

12 Know ye not that they which run in a race run all, but one receiveth the prize? *9:24*

13 All things are lawful for me, but all things are not expedient. *10:23*

14 Take, eat: this is my body, which is broken for you: this do in remembrance of me. *11:24*

15 This cup is the new testament in my blood: this do ye, as oft as ye drink it, in remembrance of me. *11:25*

16 Charity suffereth long, and is kind; charity envieth not; charity vaunteth not itself, is not puffed up,

Doth not behave itself unseemly, seeketh not her own, is not easily provoked, thinketh no evil;

Rejoiceth not in iniquity, but rejoiceth in the truth;

Beareth all things, believeth all things, hopeth all things, endureth all things. *13:4–8*

17 When I was a child, I spake as a child, I understood as a child, I thought as a child: but when I became a man, I put away childish things.

For now we see through a glass, darkly; but then face to face: now I know in part; but then shall I know even as also I am known.

And now abideth faith, hope, charity, these three; but the greatest of these is charity. *13:9–13*

1   If the trumpet give an uncertain sound, who shall prepare himself to the battle? *14:8*

2   Let all things be done decently and in order. *14:40*

3   And last of all he was seen of me also, as of one born out of due time.

For I am the least of the apostles, that am not meet to be called an apostle, because I persecuted the church of God.

But by the grace of God I am what I am. *15:8–10*

4   But now is Christ risen from the dead, and become the first fruits of them that slept.

For since by man came death, by man came also the resurrection of the dead.

For as in Adam all die, even so in Christ shall all be made alive. *15:20–22*

5   The last enemy that shall be destroyed is death. *15:26*

6   Evil communications corrupt good manners. *15:33*

7   Behold, I show you a mystery; We shall not all sleep, but we shall all be changed,

In a moment, in the twinkling of an eye, at the last trump: for the trumpet shall sound, and the dead shall be raised incorruptible, and we shall be changed.

For this corruptible must put on incorruption, and this mortal must put on immortality. *15:51–53*

8   Death is swallowed up in victory.

O death, where is thy sting? O grave, where is thy victory? *15:54–55*

9   Not of the letter, but of the spirit: for the letter killeth, but the spirit giveth life. *The Second Epistle of Paul the Apostle to the Corinthians 3:6*

10   We are troubled on every side, yet not distressed; we are perplexed, but not in despair; Persecuted, but not forsaken; cast down, but not destroyed. *4:8–9*

11   We walk by faith, not by sight. *5:7*

12   Now is the accepted time. *6:2*

13   As having nothing, and yet possessing all things. *6:10*

14   Though I be rude in speech. *11:6*

15   For ye suffer fools gladly, seeing ye yourselves are wise. *11:19*

1   A thorn in the flesh.   *12:7*

2   My strength is made perfect in weakness.   *12:9*

3   The right hands of fellowship.
                          The Epistle of Paul the Apostle to the Galatians 2:9

4   Weak and beggarly elements.   *4:9*

5   It is good to be zealously affected always in a good thing.   *4:18*

6   Ye are fallen from grace.   *5:4*

7   Every man shall bear his own burden.   *6:5*

8   Be not deceived; God is not mocked: for whatsoever a man soweth,
that shall he also reap.   *6:7*

9   To be strengthened with might by his Spirit in the inner man.
                          The Epistle of Paul the Apostle to the Ephesians 3:16

10   Carried about with every wind of doctrine.   *4:14*

11   Put on the whole armor of God.   *6:11*

12   To live is Christ, and to die is gain.
                          The Epistle of Paul the Apostle to the Philippians 1:21

13   Whatsoever things are true, whatsoever things are honest, whatsoever
things are just, whatsoever things are pure, whatsoever things are lovely,
whatsoever things are of good report; if there be any virtue, and if there
be any praise, think on these things.   *4:8*

14   By him were all things created, that are in heaven, and that are in
earth, visible and invisible all things were created by him, and for him:
        And he is before all things, and by him all things consist.
                          The Epistle of Paul the Apostle to the Colossians 1:16–17

15   Set your affection on things above, not on things on the earth.   *3:2*

16   Where there is neither Greek nor Jew, circumcision nor uncircumci-
sion, Barbarian, Scythian, bond nor free: but Christ is all, and in all.   *3:11*

17   Fathers, provoke not your children to anger, lest they be discouraged.
                                                                                    3:21

18   Luke, the beloved physician.   *4:14*

19   Labor of love.
                          The First Epistle of Paul the Apostle to the Thessalonians 1:3

20   The day of the Lord so cometh as a thief in the night.   *5:2*

21   Ye are all the children of light, and the children of the day: we are not
of the night, nor of darkness.   *5:5*

1   Putting on the breastplate of faith and love; and for an helmet, the hope of salvation.   *5:8*

2   Pray without ceasing.   *5:17*

3   Prove all things; hold fast that which is good.   *5:21*

4   The law is good, if a man use it lawfully.
The First Epistle of Paul the Apostle to Timothy 1:8

5   Speaking lies in hypocrisy; having their conscience seared with a hot iron.   *4:2*

6   Every creature of God is good, and nothing to be refused, if it be received with thanksgiving.   *4:4*

7   Let them learn first to show piety at home.   *5:4*

8   We brought nothing into this world, and it is certain we can carry nothing out.   *6:7*

9   The love of money is the root of all evil.   *6:10*

10   Fight the good fight of faith, lay hold on eternal life.   *6:12*

11   Rich in good works.   *6:18*

12   A workman that needeth not to be ashamed.
The Second Epistle of Paul the Apostle to Timothy 2:15

13   I have fought a good fight, I have finished my course, I have kept the faith.   *4:7*

14   The Lord reward him according to his works.   *4:14*

15   Unto the pure all things are pure.   *The Epistle of Paul to Titus 1:15*

16   Who maketh his angels spirits, and his ministers a flame of fire.
The Epistle of Paul the Apostle to the Hebrews 1:7

17   The word of God is quick, and powerful, and sharper than any two-edged sword, piercing even to the dividing asunder of soul and spirit, and of the joints and marrow, and is a discerner of the thoughts and intents of the heart.   *4:12*

18   Faith is the substance of things hoped for, the evidence of things not seen.   *11:1*

19   Let brotherly love continue.
Be not forgetful to entertain strangers: for thereby some have entertained angels unawares.   *13:1–2*

20   Jesus Christ the same yesterday, and to day, and for ever.   *13:8*

21   For here have we no continuing city, but we seek one to come.   *13:14*

1. Blessed is the man that endureth temptation: for when he is tried, he shall receive the crown of life.   *The General Epistle of James 1:12*

2. Be ye doers of the word, and not hearers only.   *1:22*

3. As the body without the spirit is dead, so faith without works is dead also.   *2:26*

4. Resist the devil, and he will flee from you.   *4:7*

5. Ye have heard of the patience of Job.   *5:11*

6. Hope to the end.   *The First Epistle General of Peter 1:13*

7. Honor all men. Love the brotherhood. Fear God. Honor the king.   *2:17*

8. Charity shall cover the multitude of sins.   *4:8*

9. A crown of glory that fadeth not away.   *5:4*

10. Be sober, be vigilant; because your adversary the devil, as a roaring lion, walketh about, seeking whom he may devour.   *5:8*

11. And the day star arise in your hearts.
     The Second Epistle General of Peter 1:19

12. God is light, and in him is no darkness at all.
     The First Epistle General of John 1:5

13. If any man sin, we have an advocate with the Father, Jesus Christ the righteous:
And he is the propitiation for our sins: and not for ours only, but also for the sins of the whole world.   *2:1–2*

14. He that loveth not, knoweth not God; for God is love.   *4:8*

15. There is no fear in love; but perfect love casteth out fear.   *4:18*

16. I John, who also am your brother, and companion in tribulation, and in the kingdom and patience of Jesus Christ, was in the isle that is called Patmos, for the word of God, and for the testimony of Jesus Christ.
     The Revelation of Saint John the Divine 1:9

17. And being turned, I saw seven golden candlesticks.   *1:12*

18. His feet like unto fine brass, as if they burned in a furnace; and his voice as the sound of many waters.   *1:15*

19. When I saw him, I fell at his feet as dead.   *1:17*

20. To him that overcometh will I give to eat of the tree of life.   *2:7*

21. Be thou faithful unto death, and I will give thee a crown of life.   *2:10*

22. I will give him the morning star.   *2:28*

1   I will not blot out his name out of the book of life.   *3:5*

2   Behold, I stand at the door, and knock.   *3:20*

3   The first beast was like a lion, and the second beast like a calf, and the third beast had a face as a man, and the fourth beast was like a flying eagle.
And the four beasts had each of them six wings about him; and they were full of eyes within: and they rest not day and night, saying, Holy, holy, holy, Lord God Almighty, which was, and is, and is to come.   *4:7–8*

4   Thou hast created all things, and for thy pleasure they are and were created.   *4:11*

5   A book sealed with seven seals.   *5:1*

6   He went forth conquering, and to conquer.   *6:2*

7   Behold a pale horse: and his name that sat on him was Death, and Hell followed with him.   *6:8*

8   Four angels standing on the four corners of the earth, holding the four winds of the earth.   *7:1*

9   Hurt not the earth, neither the sea, nor the trees.   *7:3*

10   All nations, and kindreds, and people, and tongues.   *7:9*

11   These are they which came out of great tribulation, and have washed their robes, and made them white in the blood of the lamb.   *7:14*

12   They shall hunger no more, neither thirst any more; neither shall the sun light on them, nor any heat.   *7:16*

13   The kingdoms of this world are become the kingdoms of our Lord and of his Christ.   *11:15*

14   There was war in heaven: Michael and his angels fought against the dragon; and the dragon fought and his angels,
And prevailed not.   *12:7–8*

15   The great dragon was cast out, that old serpent, called the Devil, and Satan, which deceiveth the whole world.   *12:9*

16   No man might buy or sell, save he that had the mark, or the name of the beast.   *13:17*

17   The voice of many waters.   *14:2*

18   Babylon is fallen, is fallen, that great city.   *14:8*

19   Blessed are the dead which die in the Lord that they may rest from their labours.   *14:13*

20   And he gathered them together into a place called in the Hebrew tongue Armageddon.   *16:16*

1   He is Lord of lords, and King of kings.   *17:14*

2   Another book was opened, which is the book of life.   *20:12*

3   I saw a new heaven and a new earth: for the first heaven and the first earth were passed away; and there was no more sea.

And I John saw the holy city, new Jerusalem, coming down from God out of heaven, prepared as a bride adorned for her husband.   *21:1–2*

4   God shall wipe away all tears from their eyes; and there shall be no more death, neither sorrow, nor crying, neither shall there be any more pain: for the former things are passed away.   *21:4*

5   There shall be no night there.   *22:5*

6   He that is unjust, let him be unjust still: and he which is filthy, let him be filthy still: and he that is righteous, let him be righteous still: and he that is holy, let him be holy still. And, behold, I come quickly.   *22:11–12*

7   I am Alpha and Omega, the beginning and the end, the first and the last.   *22:13*

Aesop[1]

fl. c. 550 B.C.

8   The lamb...began to follow the wolf in sheep's clothing.

The Wolf in Sheep's Clothing

9   Appearances often are deceiving.   *The Wolf in Sheep's Clothing*

10   Do not count your chickens before they are hatched.[2]

The Milkmaid and Her Pail

11   I am sure the grapes are sour.[3]   *The Fox and the Grapes*

12   No act of kindness, no matter how small, is ever wasted.

The Lion and the Mouse

13   Slow and steady wins the race.   *The Hare and the Tortoise*

14   Familiarity breeds contempt.   *The Fox and the Lion*

15   The boy cried "Wolf, wolf!" and the villagers came out to help him.

The Shepherd Boy and the Wolf

---

[1]Animal fables from before Aesop's time and after were attributed to him. The first collection was made two hundred years after his death.

[2]To swallow gudgeons ere they're catched / And count their chickens ere they're hatched. — SAMUEL BUTLER, *Hudibras* [1664], *pt. 2, canto III, 1. 923*

[3]The fox, when he cannot reach the grapes, says they are not ripe. — GEORGE HERBERT, *Jacula Prudentum* [1651]

"They are too green," he said, "and only good for fools." — JEAN DE LA FONTAINE, *Fables* [1668], *bk. III, fable 11, The Fox and the Grapes*

AESOP

1   A crust eaten in peace is better than a banquet partaken in anxiety.
The Town Mouse and the Country Mouse

2   Borrowed plumes.   *The Jay and the Peacock*

3   It is not only fine feathers that make fine birds.
The Jay and the Peacock

4   Self-conceit may lead to self-destruction.   *The Frog and the Ox*

5   People often grudge others what they cannot enjoy themselves.
The Dog in the Manger

6   It is thrifty to prepare today for the wants of tomorrow.
The Ant and the Grasshopper

7   Be content with your lot; one cannot be first in everything.
Juno and the Peacock

8   A huge gap appeared in the side of the mountain. At last a tiny mouse
came forth.[1]   *The Mountain in Labor*

9   Any excuse will serve a tyrant.   *The Wolf and the Lamb*

10 Beware lest you lose the substance by grasping at the shadow.
The Dog and the Shadow

11 Who shall bell the cat?   *The Rats and the Cat*

12 I will have nought to do with a man who can blow hot and cold with
the same breath.   *The Man and the Satyr*

13 Thinking to get at once all the gold the goose could give, he killed it
and opened it only to find — nothing.
The Goose with the Golden Eggs

14 Put your shoulder to the wheel.   *Hercules and the Wagoner*

15 The gods help them that help themselves.[2] *Hercules and the Wagoner*

16 We would often be sorry if our wishes were gratified.
The Old Man and Death

17 Union gives strength.   *The Bundle of Sticks*

18 While I see many hoof marks going in, I see none coming out. It is
easier to get into the enemy's toils than out again.
The Lion, the Fox, and the Beasts

---

[1]A mountain was in labor, sending forth dreadful groans, and there was in the region the highest
expectation. After all, it brought forth a mouse. — PHAEDRUS, *Fables, IV, 22:1*

[2]God loves to help him who strives to help himself. — AESCHYLUS, *Fragment 223*
Heaven helps not the men who will not act. — SOPHOCLES, *Fragment 288*
Try first thyself, and after call in God; / For to the worker God himself lends aid. — EURIPIDES,
Hippolytus, Fragment 435

46

1   The haft of the arrow had been feathered with one of the eagle's own plumes. We often give our enemies the means of our own destruction.[1]

The Eagle and the Arrow

Terence[2] *[Publius Terentius Afer]*   c. 190–159 B.C.

2   Moderation in all things.

Andria (The Lady of Andros), l. 61

3   Hence these tears.[3]   *Andria, l. 126*

4   Lovers' quarrels are the renewal of love.[4]

Andria, l. 555

5   Charity begins at home.[5]   *Andria, l. 635*

6   I am a man: nothing human is alien to me.[6]

Heauton Timoroumenos (The Self-Tormentor), l. 77

7   Draw from others the lesson that may profit yourself.[7]

Heauton Timoroumenos, l. 221

8   Time removes distress.   *Heauton Timoroumenos, l. 421*

9   Nothing is so difficult but that it may be found out by seeking.[8]

Heauton Timoroumenos, l. 675

10   Some people ask, "What if the sky were to fall?"[9]

Heauton Timoroumenos, l. 719

---

[1]So in the Libyan fable it is told / That once an eagle, stricken with a dart, / Said, when he saw the fashion of the shaft, / "With our own feathers, not by others' hands, /Are we now smitten." — AESCHYLUS, *Fragment 135*; translated [1868] by EDWARD HAYES PLUMPTRE

[2]Translated by JOHN SARGEAUNT (Loeb Classical Library), with occasional adaptations.

[3]Hinc illae lacrimae.

The phrase is proverbial for "That's the cause of it" and was often quoted by Horace in *Epistles, I, xix*, and by others.

Hence rage and tears [Inde irae et lacrimae]. — JUVENAL, *Satires, bk. I, l. 168*

[4]Amantium irae amoris integratio est.

The anger of lovers renews the strength of love. — PUBLILIUS SYRUS, *Maxim 24*

The falling out of faithful friends renewing is of love. — RICHARD EDWARDS, *The Paradise of Dainty Devices* [1576]

Let the falling out of friends be a renewing of affection. — JOHN LYLY, *Euphues* [1579]

The falling out of lovers is the renewing of love. — ROBERT BURTON, *Anatomy of Melancholy* [1621–1651], *pt. 3, sec. 2*

[5]Proximus sum egomet mihi.

[6]Homo sum: humani nil a me alienum puto. Quoted by CICERO in *De Officiis, bk. I, 30.*

[7]Periculum ex aliis facito tibi quod ex usu siet. (A saying.)

[8]Nil tam difficile est quin quaerendo investigari possiet.

[9]Quid si nunc caelum ruat?

Some ambassadors from the Celtae, being asked by Alexander what in the world they dreaded most, answered, that they feared lest the sky should fall upon them. — LUCIUS FLAVIUS ARRIANUS, *bk. I, 4*

1   Extreme law is often extreme injustice.[1]

Heauton Timoroumenos, l. 796

2   There is nothing so easy but that it becomes difficult when you do it reluctantly.   *Heauton Timoroumenos, l. 805*

3   While there's life, there's hope.   *Heauton Timoroumenos, l. 981*

4   In fact, nothing is said that has not been said before.

Eunuchus (The Eunuch), l. 41, prologue

5   I have everything, yet have nothing; and although I possess nothing, still of nothing am I in want.   *Eunuchus, l. 243*

6   There are vicissitudes in all things.   *Eunuchus, l. 276*

7   I don't care one straw.[2]   *Eunuchus, l. 411*

8   Take care and say this with presence of mind.[3]   *Eunuchus, l. 769*

9   He is wise who tries everything before arms.   *Eunuchus, l. 789*

10   I know the disposition of women: when you will, they won't; when you won't, they set their hearts upon you of their own inclination.

Eunuchus, l. 812

11   I took to my heels as fast as I could.   *Eunuchus, l. 844*

12   Fortune helps the brave.[4]   *Phormio, l. 203*

13   So many men, so many opinions; every one his own way.[5]

Phormio, l. 454

14   I bid him look into the lives of men as though into a mirror, and from others to take an example for himself.   *Adelphoe (The Brothers), l. 415*

Nag Hammadi[6]   Fourth century

15   I was sent forth from [the] power,

---

[1]Ius summum saepe summa est malitia.
Extreme law, extreme injustice, is now become a stale proverb in discourse. — CICERO, *De Officiis, bk. 1, 33*
Extreme justice is often injustice. — JEAN RACINE, *La Thébaïde* [1664], *act IV, sc. iii*
Mais l'extrême justice est une extrême injure. — VOLTAIRE, *Oedipe* [1718], *act III, sc. iii*

[2]Ego non flocci pendere.
Nor do they care a straw. — CERVANTES, *Don Quixote* [1605] *pt. 1, bk. III, ch. 9*

[3]Fac animo haec praesenti dicas. Literally, "with a present mind" — equivalent to Caesar's "praesentia animi" *(De Bello Gallico, bk. V, 43, 4)*

[4]Pliny the Younger says *(bk. VI, letter 16)* that Pliny the Elder said this during the eruption of Vesuvius: "Fortune favors the brave."

[5]Quot homines tot sententiae: suo quoque mos.

[6]Translated by GEORGE W. McRAE. From *The Nag Hammadi Library, rev. ed.* [1990], edited by JAMES M. ROBINSON. The Nag Hammadi Library is a collection of fourth-century Gnostic manuscripts found in Egypt in 1945.

and I have come to those who reflect upon me,
and I have been found among those who seek after me.
The Thunder: Perfect Mind, Gnostic manuscripts, codex VI, 2

1   Do not be ignorant of me.
For I am the first and the last.
I am the honored one and the scorned one.
I am the whore and the holy one.
I am the wife and the virgin.
I am <the mother>[1] and the daughter.
I am the members of my mother.
I am the barren one
    and many are her sons.
I am she whose wedding is great,
  and I have not taken a husband.
I am the midwife and she who does not bear.
I am the solace of my labor pains.
I am the bride and the bridegroom,
    and it is my husband who begot me.
I am the mother of my father
    and the sister of my husband
    and he is my offspring.
I am the slave of him who prepared me.
I am the ruler of my offspring.   *The Thunder: Perfect Mind, VI, 2*

2   I am the silence that is incomprehensible
    and the idea whose remembrance is frequent.
I am the voice whose sound is manifold
    and the word whose appearance is multiple.
I am the utterance of my name.   *The Thunder: Perfect Mind, VI, 2*

3   Why, you who hate me, do you love me,
    and hate those who love me?
You who deny me, confess me,
    and you who confess me, deny me.
You who tell the truth about me, lie about me,
    and you who have lied about me, tell the truth about me.
You who know me, be ignorant of me,
    and those who have not known me, let them know me.
For I am knowledge and ignorance.

---

[1]Correction made by translator.

I am shame and boldness.

I am shameless; I am ashamed.

I am strength and I am fear.

I am war and peace.   *The Thunder: Perfect Mind, VI, 2*

1   And do not cast me out among those who are slain in violence.

But I, I am compassionate and I am cruel.

The Thunder: Perfect Mind, VI, 2

2   Be on your guard!

Do not hate my obedience

and do not love my self-control.

In my weakness, do not forsake me,

and do not be afraid of my power.

For why do you despise my fear

and curse my pride?

But I am she who exists in all fears

and strength in trembling.

I am she who is weak,

and I am well in a pleasant place.

I am senseless and I am wise.   *The Thunder: Perfect Mind, VI, 2*

3   Why have you hated me in your counsels?

For I shall be silent among those who are silent,

and I shall appear and speak,

Why then have you hated me, you Greeks?

Because I am a barbarian among [the] barbarians?

For I am the wisdom [of the] Greeks

and the knowledge of the barbarians.

I am the judgment of [the] Greeks and of the barbarians.

[I] am the one whose image is great in Egypt

and the one who has no image among the barbarians.

I am the one who has been hated everywhere

and who has been loved everywhere.

I am the one whom they call Life,

and you have called Death.

I am the one whom they call Law,

and you have called Lawlessness.

I am the one whom you have pursued,

and I am the one whom you have seized.

I am the one whom you have scattered,

and you have gathered me together.

I am the one before whom you have been ashamed,
    and you have been shameless to me.   *The Thunder: Perfect Mind, VI, 2*

1   I am the one whom you have reflected upon,
    and you have scorned me.
I am unlearned,
    and they learn from me.
I am the one whom you have despised,
    and you reflect upon me.
I am the one whom you have hidden from,
    and you appear to me.
But whenever you hide yourselves,
    I myself will appear.
For [whenever] you [appear],
I myself [will hide] from you.   *The Thunder: Perfect Mind, VI, 2*

2   Why do you curse me and honor me?
You have wounded and you have had mercy.
Do not separate me from the first ones whom you have [known].
[And] do not cast anyone [out nor] turn anyone away.
    The Thunder: Perfect Mind, VI, 2

3   And I am an alien and a citizen.   *The Thunder: Perfect Mind, VI, 2*

4   Hear me in gentleness, and learn of me in roughness.
I am she who cries out,
    and I am cast forth upon the face of the earth.
I prepare the bread and my mind within.
I am the knowledge of my name,
I am the one who cries out,
    and I listen.   *The Thunder: Perfect Mind, VI, 2*

5   Hear me, you hearers
    and learn of my words, you who know me.
I am the hearing that is attainable to everything;
    I am the speech that cannot be grasped.
I am the name of the sound
    and the sound of the name.
I am the sign of the letter
    and the designation of the division.   *The Thunder: Perfect Mind, VI, 2*

6   For I am the one who alone exists,
    and I have no one who will judge me.
    The Thunder: Perfect Mind, VI, 2   *51*

1   For many are the pleasant forms which exist in
       numerous sins,
       and incontinencies,
       and disgraceful passions,
       and fleeting pleasures,
          which (men) embrace until they become sober
       and go up to their resting-place.
    And they will find me there,
       and they will live,
       and they will not die again.   *The Thunder: Perfect Mind, VI, 2*

Saint Augustine

354–430

2   The weakness of little children's limbs is innocent, not their souls.
       Confessions [397–401], bk. I, ch. 7

3   To Carthage I came, where all about me resounded a caldron of dissolute loves.   *Confessions, III, 1*

4   I was in love with loving.   *Confessions, III, 1*

5   In the usual course of study I had come to a book of a certain Cicero.   *Confessions, III, 4*

6   Give me chastity and continence, but not just now.
       Confessions, VIII, 7

7   Take up, read! Take up, read![1]   *Confessions, VIII, 12*

8   Too late I loved you, O Beauty ever ancient and ever new! Too late I loved you! And, behold, you were within me, and I out of myself, and there I searched for you.   *Confessions, X, 27*

9   Give what you command, and command what you will.
       Confessions, X, 29

10   Hear the other side.[2]   *De Duabus Animabus, bk. XIV, ch. 2*

11   I would not have believed the gospel had not the authority of the Church moved me.   *Contra Epistulam Fundamenti [c. 410], ch. 5*

12   Necessity has no law.   *Soliloquiorum. Animae ad Deum [c. 410], 2*

13   We make a ladder of our vices, if we trample those same vices underfoot.   *Sermones, no. 3*

---

[1]Tolle lege, tolle lege.
   What the bell seemed to say to Augustine at the moment of his conversion. He opened the Bible and read *Romans 13:12–14.*

[2]Audi partem alteram.

1   Anger is a weed; hate is the tree.   *Sermones, 58*

2   The dove loves when it quarrels; the wolf hates when it flatters.
                                                          Sermones, 64

3   Rome has spoken; the case is closed.[1]   *Sermones, 131*

4   He who created you without you will not justify you without you.
                                                         Sermones, 169

5   The most glorious city of God.
                                              De Civitate Dei [415], vol. I, preface

6   Two cities have been formed by two loves: the earthly by the love of
self, even to the contempt of God; the heavenly by the love of God, even
to the contempt of self.   *De Civitate Dei, XIV, ch. 28*

The Koran[2]

7   In the name of the most merciful God: Praise be to God, the Lord of
all Being; the most merciful, the Master of the day of judgment. Thee do we
worship, and of Thee do we beg assistance. Direct us in the right path, in the
path of those to whom Thou hast been gracious; not of those against whom
Thou art incensed, nor of those who go astray.   *Ch. 1, verses 1–3*

8   Do not veil the truth with falsehood, nor conceal the truth knowingly.   *2:42*

9   We believe in God, and in that which has been sent down on us and
sent down on Abraham, Ishmael, Isaac and Jacob, and the Tribes, and that
which was given to Moses and Jesus and the Prophets, of their Lord; we
make no division between any of them, and to Him we surrender.[3]

                                                             2:135–136

10 A believing slave is better than an idolater, even though ye admire
him.   *2:221*

11 God will not take you to task for vain words in your oaths, but He will
take you to task for what your hearts have amassed.   *2:225*

---

[1]Roma locuta est; causa finita est.

[2]Also spelled Qur'an; Quran. Muslim tradition holds that the Koran is of divine origin, revealed by God
to the prophet Muhammad [c. 570–632].

The word Koran, derived from the verb *karaa, to read,* signifies properly in Arabic "the reading," or
rather, "that which ought to be read.". . . The Koran is divided into 114 larger portions of very unequal
length, which we call chapters, but the Arabians *sowar,* in the singular *sura,* a word rarely used on any
other occasion. — GEORGE SALE, *The Koran* [1734], *The Preliminary Discourse, sec. 2*

Translations by GEORGE SALE [1734], E. H. PALMER [1900], J. M. RODWELL [1909], RICHARD BELL [1927],
M. M. PICKTHALL [1953], and A. J. ARBERRY [1955], edited and adapted by SARI NUSEIBAH.

[3]"Surrender" is the literal translation of the word "Islam."

1   I [Muhammad] have no power over benefit or hurt to myself except as God willeth.... I am only a warner, and a bringer of good tidings to a people who believe.   *7:188*

2   God sufficeth me: there is no God but He. In Him I put my trust.
                                                                     9:129

3   In the alternation of night and day, and what God has created in the heavens and the earth — surely there are signs for a god-fearing people.   *10:6*

4   Surely God wrongs not men, but themselves men wrong.   *10:44*

5   Not so much as the weight of an ant in earth or heaven escapes from the Lord, neither is aught smaller than that, or greater, but is clearly written in God's book.   *10:61*

6   God changes not what is in a people, until they change what is in themselves.   *13:11*

7   We [God] never sent a messenger save with the language of his folk, that he might make (the message)[1] clear for them.   *14:4*

8   Seest thou not how God hath coined a parable? A good word is like a good tree whose root is firmly fixed, and whose top is in the sky. And it produces its edible fruit every season, by the permission of its Lord.... And a corrupt word is like a corrupt tree which has been torn off the ground, and has no fixity. God makes those who believe stand firm in this life and the next by His firm Word.   *14:24–27*

9   Our [God's] word to a thing when We will it, is but to say, "Be," and it is.   *16:40*

10   Glory be to Him who carried His servant by night from the sacred temple of Mecca to the temple of Jerusalem that is more remote, whose precinct We have blessed, that We might show him of Our tokens.   *17:1*

11   Thy Lord hath decreed that ye worship none save Him, and (that ye show) kindness to parents.... Lower unto them the wing of submission through mercy, and say, "My Lord, have mercy on them both as they took care of me when I was little."   *17:23–24*

12   Walk not on the earth exultantly, for thou canst not cleave the earth, neither shalt thou reach to the mountains in height.   *17:37*

13   They will question thee concerning the soul. Say: "The soul is the concern of my Lord, and you have been given of knowledge but a little." *17:85*

14   They say: "We will not believe thee till thou makest a spring to gush forth from the earth for us, or ... bringest God and the angels as a

---

[1]Throughout these quotations from the Koran, parentheses indicate additions to the Arabic.

surety.". . . And naught prevented men from believing when the guidance came to them, but that they said, "Has God sent forth a mortal as messenger?" Say: "Had there been in the earth angels walking at peace, We would have sent down upon them out of heaven an angel as messenger."

17:90–95

1   And do not say, regarding anything, "I am going to do that tomorrow," but only, "if God will."   *18:23–24*

2   Wealth and children are the adornment of this present life: but good works, which are lasting, are better in the sight of thy Lord as to recompense, and better as to hope.   *18:46*

3   Man says: "How is it possible, when I am dead, that I shall then be brought forth alive?"

Does he not remember that We have created him once, and that he was nothing then?   *19:66–67*

4   Do not the unbelievers see that the skies and the earth were both a solid mass, and that We clave them asunder, and that by means of water We give life to everything? Will they not then believe?   *21:30*

5   O men, if you are in doubt as to the Resurrection, surely We created you of dust, then of a sperm drop, then of a blood clot, then of a lump of flesh. . . . And thou beholdest the earth blackened; then, when We send down water upon it, it quivers, and swells, and puts forth herbs of every joyous kind.   *22:5*

6   We [God] charge not any soul save to its ability.   *23:62*

7   God is the light of the heavens and of the earth. His light is like a niche in which is a lamp — the lamp encased in glass — the glass, as it were, a glistening star. From a blessed tree it is lighted, the olive neither from the East nor of the West, whose oil would well nigh shine out, even though fire touched it not. It is light upon light. God guideth whom He will to His light, and God setteth forth parables to men.   *24:35*

8   As for the unbelievers, their works are as a mirage in a spacious plain which the man athirst supposes to be water, till, when he comes to it, he finds it is nothing; there indeed he finds God, and He pays him his account in full; and God is swift at the reckoning. Or they are as shadows upon a sea obscure, covered by a billow above which is a billow, above which are clouds, shadows piled upon one another; when he puts forth his hand, wellnigh he cannot see it. And to whomsoever God assigns no light, no light has he.   *24:39–40*

9   Thou seest the mountains and thou deemest them affixed, (verily) they are as fleeting as the clouds.   *27:88*

1   Thou truly canst not guide whom thou lovest; but God guideth whom He will; and He best knoweth those who yield to guidance.   *28:55*

2   The present life is naught but a diversion and a sport; surely the Last Abode is Life, did they but know.   *29:64*

3   And of His [God's] signs is the creation of the heavens and earth and the variety of your tongues and hues. Surely in that are signs for all living beings.   *30:22*

4   Whosoever surrenders his face to God and performs good deeds, he verily has grasped the surest handle, and unto God is the sequel of all things.   *31:22*

5   If whatever trees are in the earth were pens, and He should after that swell the seas into seven seas of ink, the Words of God would not be exhausted.   *31:27*

6   We offered this trust[1] to the heavens and the earth and the mountains, but they were humbled by it, and shrank from bearing it. Yet, man bore it. Truly he is ever in the darkness of injustice, and of ignorance.

    33:72

7   He makes the night seep into the day, and makes the day seep into the night; He has subordinated the sun and the moon, making each of them journey towards a preordained time.   *35:13*

8   And on that day no soul shall be wronged at all, nor shall ye be rewarded for aught but that which ye have done.   *36:54*

9   They say: "We only have the life of this world. We die and we live, and nothing destroys us but time." Yet, not true knowledge have they of this; only belief.   *45:24*

10   O true believers, let not men laugh other men to scorn, who peradventure may be better than themselves. . . . Neither let the one of you speak ill of another in his absence.   *49:10–13*

11   The Arabs of the desert say, We believe. Answer, Ye do by no means believe; but say, We have embraced Islam: for the faith hath not yet entered into your hearts.   *49:14*

12   We [God] created Man, and We know what his soul whispereth within him; and We are nearer unto him than his jugular vein.   *50:16*

13   The heart of Muhammad did not falsely represent that which he saw. Will you therefore dispute with him concerning that which he saw?

    53:11–12

---

[1]The message conveyed in the Koran.

1   O tribe of spirits and of men, if you are able to slip through the parameters of the skies and the earth, then do so. You shall not pass through them save with My [the Lord's] authority.   *55:33*

2   He is the first and the last, the manifest and the hidden: and He knoweth all things.   *57:3*

3   Let every soul look upon the morrow for the deed it has performed.   *59:18*

4   Is he, therefore, who goeth groveling upon his face, better directed than he who walketh upright in a straight way?   *67:22*

5   Man is a witness unto his deeds.   *75:14*

6   Recite: In the name of thy Lord who created,
Created Man of a blood clot.
Recite: And thy Lord is the most
Generous, who taught by the Pen,
Taught Man that he knew not.   *96:1–5*

7   Whoso has done an atom's weight of good shall see it; and whoso has done an atom's weight of evil shall see it.   *99:7–8*

8   Say: "He is God, One God, the Everlasting Refuge, who has not begotten, and has not been begotten, and equal to Him is not anyone."   *112*

Sunjata[1]   Thirteenth century

9   If you call a great man, no great man answers your call;
You must lay your hand upon the earth;
Many a great man is under the ground, a youthful king.
Had the ground a mouth, it would say, "Many great men are under me."

Afonso I [Nzinga Mebeba]   c. 1461–1543

10   We cannot reckon how great the damage is, since the … merchants daily seize our subjects, sons of the land and sons of our noblemen, and vassals, and our relatives. … They grab them and cause them to be sold: and so great, Sir, is their corruption and licentiousness that our country is being utterly depopulated.

Letter to the king of Portugal [1526][2]

---

[1]BAMBA SUSO, *Sunjata: Gambian Versions of the Mande Epic* [1974]. Translated by GORDON INNES.
[2]From BASIL DAVIDSON, *The African Slave Trade* [1980].

Leo Africanus   Sixteenth century

1   No one makes war on anyone, and no one steps outside his own territory. Some worship the sun, and prostrate when they see it rising above the horizon. Others worship fire.... Yet others are Christians in the style of the Egyptians.

Description of Africa [1526][1]

2   There are numerous regions there, but most are unknown to us, either because of the length and difficulty of the journey, or because of the diversity of the languages and beliefs, which hinders them from having relations with the countries that are known to us, just as they hinder ours from having relations with theirs.

Description of Africa

The Kebra Nagast   Sixteenth century

3   And the Queen [Makeda] said unto her subjects: "Ye who are my people, listen to my words for I desire wisdom and my heart seeketh to find understanding."

I am smitten with the love of wisdom, for wisdom is far better than treasures of gold and silver, and wisdom is the best of everything that hath been created on the earth. Unto what under the heavens shall wisdom be compared? It is sweeter than honey and it makes one to rejoice more than wine; it shines more than the sun and it is beloved more than precious stones. It fattens more than oil, and it satisfies more than dainty meats, and it gives more fame than thousands of gold and silver. It is a source of joy for the heart, a bright and shining light for the eyes and a giver of speed to the feet; a shield for the breast and a helmet for the head.

*Pt. 2, sec. 22. The Queen of Ethiopia Prepares for
Her Journey to Jerusalem*[2]

4   He who heaps up gold and silver does so to no profit without wisdom, but he who heaps up wisdom no man can snatch it from his heart.

*Pt. 2, sec. 22. The Queen of Ethiopia Prepares for
Her Journey to Jerusalem*[2]

5   And [Solomon] spoke further to the Queen, saying: What is the use of us, the children of men, if we do not exercise kindness and love upon earth?

Pt. 2, sec. 25. Solomon and the Workman[2]

---

[1]From *Timbuktu and the Songhay Empire* [1999], translated and edited by JOHN O. HUNWICK.
[2]Translated by MIGUEL F. BROOKS [1955].

1   The word of the Lord cutteth like a straight, sharp sword, and in like manner the Scriptures cut from men's hearts the danger caused by deceitful fables and imaginings.   *Pt. 4, sec. 60. Concerning the Prophecy of Christ*[1]

2   The people of Ethiopia were chosen from among idols and graven images, and the people of Israel were rejected. The daughters of Zion were rejected, and the daughters of Ethiopia were honoured...for God accepted the peoples who had been cast away, and rejected Israel, *for Zion was taken away from them and she came into the country of Ethiopia...for wherever God is pleased for her to dwell, there is her habitation.*

        Pt. 4, sec. 78. How Queen Makeda Made
        Her Son King of Ethiopia[1]

3   Then all the saints who were gathered together said:
    "In all truth the King of Ethiopia is more exalted and more honorable than any other king upon the earth, because of the glory and the greatness of the heavenly Zion."

        Pt. 4, sec. 83. How the Authority of Bayna-Lehkem
        Was Universally Accepted[1]

Ahmad Baba   c. 1556–1627

4   O traveler to Gao, turn off to my city. Murmur my name there and greet all my dear ones,

    With scented salams from an exile who longs for his homeland and neighbors, companions and friends.   *Written in exile from Timbuktu*[2]

5   Adam was created from a handful taken from the whole earth. Thus, his sons carried exactly the nature of the colors of the earth. Some were red, others white and some were black. Some were good-natured, others ill-natured while some were vicious and some were virtuous.

        Quoting another scholar, al-Ash 'ari[3]

Njinga [Donna Anna de Sousa][4]   1582–1663

6   I was born Queen and must at all times live like a Queen. Thus the natural order has it and no one debates this. But the governors of Angola, officials of Portugal who are born vassals in Europe, through great pride and

---

[1] Translated by MIGUEL F. BROOKS [1955].

[2] From *Timbuktu and the Songhay Empire* [1999], translated and edited by JOHN O. HUNWICK.

[3] From *The Mi' raj: A Legal Treatise on Slavery by Ahmad Baba*, translated by BERNARD BARBOUR and MICHELLE JACOBS. From *Slaves and Slavery in Muslim Africa* [1985], *vol. I*, edited by JOHN RALPH WILLIS.

[4] Also spelled *Nzinga*. Donna Anna de Sousa was the name Njinga took upon Christian baptism.

ambitions which fills their head, want here in Africa to live like Kings to the detriment and at the expense of these countries and therefore, they can no longer henceforth be endured, and they are hateful to all; and if God does not help here they will reduce us to ultimate despair.

Letter, La Marvigliosa Conversione all Santa Fede di Cristo della Regina Signa e del svo Regno di Matamba nell'Africa Meridonale [1668][1]

1   Sometimes force is able to exterminate the wicked customs of those that do not use reason and do not understand any argument without punishment.

Descrição histórica dos três reinos do Congo, Matamba e Angola by Cavazzi de Montecòccolo, Giovanni Antonio [1965][1]

'Abd al-Rahman Al-Sa 'di

Seventeenth century

2   To proceed: we understand that our forefathers used mainly to divert one another in their assemblies by talking of the Companions and the pious folk — may God be pleased with them, and have mercy upon them. Then they would speak of the chiefs and kings of their lands, their lives and deaths, their conduct, their heroic exploits, and other historical information and tales relating to them. This was what they most delighted in telling, and what they most desired to speak of among themselves.

Then that generation passed away — may the mercy of God Most High be upon them. In the following generation there was none who had any interest in that, nor was there anyone who followed the path of their deceased ancestors, nor anyone greatly concerned about respect for elders. If there were indeed any such, then they were few, and finally the only folk remaining were those whose motivations were base, and who concerned themselves with hatred, jealousy, back-biting tittle-tattle, scandal-mongering, and concocting lies about people. God preserve us from such things, for they lead to evil consequences.

Ta 'rikh al-Sudan,[2] *introduction*

3   [On Timbuktu] It is a city unsullied by the worship of idols, where none has prostrated save to God the Compassionate, a refuge of scholarly and righteous folk, a haunt of saints and ascetics and a meeting place of caravans and boats.   *Ta 'rikh al-Sudan, ch. 7*

---

[1]From CATHY JEAN SKIDMORE-HESS, *Queen Njinga: 1582–1663: Ritual, Power and Identity in the Life of a Pre-colonial African Ruler* [1995].

[2]The History of the Sudan.

Gassire's Lute[1]   Seventeenth century

1   Four times
        Wagadu rose.[2]
        A great city, gleaming in the light of day.
    Four times
        Wagadu fell.
        And disappeared from human sight.
        Once through vanity.
        Once through dishonesty.
        Once through greed.
        Once through discord.

    The guinea hen sang:
    "All creatures must die, be buried, and vanish.
    Kings and heroes die, are buried and vanish.
    I, too, shall die, shall be buried, and vanish."

    The smith spoke:
    "The lute is but a piece of wood.
    Without a heart it cannot sing."

    And while we should not like to live fameless,
        we have no wish to die for fame alone.

Felix   Eighteenth century

2   We have no Property! We have no Wives! No Children! We have no
    City! No Country!   *Petition for Freedom, Boston [January 6, 1773]*[3]

Briton Hammon   Eighteenth century

3   Having been informed by some of the ship's crew that she was to sail
    in a few days, I had nothing now to do, but seek an opportunity how I
    should make my escape.
                    *A Narrative of the Uncommon Sufferings, and Surprizing
                    Deliverance of Briton Hammon, a Negro Man [1760]*

4   I think I have not deviated from Truth, in any particular of this my
    Narrative, and tho' I have omitted a great many things, yet what is wrote
    may suffice to convince the Reader, that I have been most grievously

---

[1]Translated and adapted by Alta Jablow [1971].
[2]Wagadu was a Soninke city-state that ruled in four areas, including Ghana.
[3]From George Washington Williams, *History of the Negro Race in America, 1619–1880* [1883], *vol. I.*

afflicted, and yet thro' the Divine Goodness, as miraculously preserved, and delivered out of many Dangers.

A Narrative of the Uncommon Sufferings, and Surprizing
Deliverance of Briton Hammon, a Negro Man

Othello

Eighteenth century

1   To whom are the wretched sons of Africa to apply for redress, if their cruel master treats them with unkindness? To whom will they resort for protection if he is base enough to refuse it to them? The law is not their friend; — alas! too many statutes are enacted against them. The world is not their friend — the iniquity is too general and extensive. No one who hath slaves of his own, will protect those of another, less the practice should be retorted. Thus when their masters abandon them, their situation is destitute and forlorn and God is their only friend![1]   *[1788]*

Job Ben Solomon [Ayuba Suleiman Diallo]   c. 1702–c. 1773

2   One of my wives had got another husband in my room and the other gave me over, my father died soon after my misfortune of being seized and sold for a slave, but my children are all well, my redemption was so remarkable and surprising that my messengers and letters sent on my arrival here were not credited, but how elated and amazed they were at my arrival, I must leave you to guess at, as being inexpressible as is likewise the raptures and pleasure I enjoy'd, floods of tears burst their way and some little time afterwards we recover'd so as to have some discourse and in time I acquainted them and all the country how I had been redeem'd . . . from such distant parts as are beyond their capacity to conceive.

Letter from son of Fulani high priest on returning home many
years after being sold into slavery in the United States [1735/6][2]

James Albert Ukawsaw Gronniosaw   c. 1710–1775

3   I was frequently lost in wonder at the works of the Creation: was afraid, uneasy and restless, but could not tell for what. I wanted to be informed of things that no person could tell me: and was always dissatisfied. . . . I should have perceived that I had much more to suffer than I had before experienced, and that my troubles had as yet barely commenced.

Narrative of the Most Remarkable Particulars in the Life of James
Albert Ukawsaw Gronniosaw, an African Prince [1772]

---

[1]From *The Journal of Negro History* [1916], *vol. I*, edited by CARTER G. WOODSON.

[2]From *Documents Illustrative of the History of the Slave Trade to America* [1931], *vol. II*, edited by ELIZABETH DONNAN.

1   I who, at home, was surrounded and guarded by slaves, so that no indifferent person might approach me, and clothed with gold, have been inhumanly threatened with death; and have frequently wanted clothing to defend me from the inclemency of the weather....I am willing, and even desirous to be counted as nothing, a stranger in the world, and a pilgrim here.

A Narrative of the Most Remarkable Particulars in the Life of
James Albert Ukawsaw Gronniosaw, an African Prince

Jupiter Hammon [1]   c. 1711–1806

2   Come Blessed Jesus, Heavenly Dove,
        Accept Repentance here;
    Salvation give, with tender Love;
        Let us with Angels share.   *An Evening Thought [December 25, 1760]*

3   While thousands tossed by the sea,
        And others settled down,
    God's tender mercy set thee free,
        From dangers that come down.
                    An Address to Miss Phillis Wheatly [sic] [August 4, 1778]

4   Thus, the Dialogue shall end,
        Strive to obey the word;
    When ev'ry Nation acts like friends,
        Shall be the sons of God.   *A Dialogue [1782]*

5   Let us remember the uncertainty of human life, and that we are many of us within a step of the grave, hanging only by the single thread of life, and we know not how soon God may send the cold hand of death to cut the thread of life.   *A Winter Piece [1782]*

6   Now whether it is right, and lawful, in the sight of God, for them to make slaves of us or not, I am certain that while we are slaves, it is our duty to obey our masters, in all their lawful commands and mind them unless we are bid to do that which we know to be sin, or forbidden in God's word.... It may seem hard for us, if we think our masters wrong in holding us slaves, to obey in all things, but who of us dare dispute with God! He has commanded us to obey, and we ought to do it cheerfully, and freely.

Address to the Negroes of the State of New York [1787] [2]

---

[1]From *America's First Negro Poet: The Complete Works of Jupiter Hammon of Long Island* [1970], edited by STANLEY AUSTIN.

[2]Hammon's views mirrored those of slaveholders who used Christianity to justify slavery.

1   I acknowledge that liberty is a great thing, and worth seeking for, if we can get it honestly; and by our good conduct prevail on our masters to set us free: though for my own part I do not wish to be free, yet I should be glad if others especially the young Negroes, were to be free; for many of us who are grown up slaves and have always had masters to take care of us, should hardly know how to take care of ourselves; and it may be more for our own comfort to remain as we are. . . . I must say that I have hoped that God would open their eyes, when they were so much engaged for liberty, to think of the state of the poor blacks, and to pity us. He has done it in some measure, and has raised us up many friends; for which we have reason to be thankful, and to hope in his mercy.   *An Address to the Negroes of the State of New York*[1]

2   There are but two places where all go after death, white and black, rich and poor; those places are Heaven and Hell.

An Address to the Negroes of the State of New York

Belinda   c. 1713–c. 1787

3   Nations must be agitated, and the world convulsed for the preservation of the freedom which the Almighty Father intended for all the human Race. . . . The face of your Petitioner, is now marked with the furrows of time, and her frame bending under the oppression of years, while she, by the Laws of the Land, is denied the employment of one morsel of that immense wealth, apart whereof hath been accumulated by her own industry, and the whole augmented by her servitude.

*From petition for pension submitted in Massachusetts
by former slave [February 1783]*[2]

Crispus Attucks   c. 1723–1770

4   Be not afraid, they dare not fire.

Said during Boston Massacre [March 5, 1770][3]

Ignatius Sancho[4]   c. 1729–1780

5   Lord! What is man? — and what business have such lazy, lousy, paltry beings of a day to form friendships, or to make connections? Man is an absurd

---

[1]Hammon also believed that if the enslaved were devout enough, God would eventually free them without struggle.

[2]From *Unchained Voices* [1996], edited by VINCENT CARRETTA. Belinda's petition was successful, but the $15 pension was paid only once, and she repetitioned in 1787.

[3]From MARTIN ROBISON DELANY, *The Condition, Elevation, Emigration and Destiny of the Colored People of the United States, Politically Considered* [1852].

[4]From *Letters of the Late Ignatius Sancho, an African: In Two Volumes. To Which Are Prefaced the Memoirs of His Life* [1782].

animal — yea, I will ever maintain it — in his vices, dreadful — in his few virtues, silly — he has religion without devotion — philosophy without wisdom — the divine passion (as it is called) love too oft without affection — and anger without cause — friendship without reason — hate without reflection — knowledge . . . without judgment — and wit without discretion.   *Letter 2 [August 7, 1768]*

1   Happy, happy lad! What a fortune is thine! — Look round upon the miserable fate of almost all of our unfortunate color — superadded to ignorance — see slavery, and the contempt of those very wretches who roll in affluence from our labors.   *Letter 14 [October 11, 1772]*

2   Alas! Time leaves the marks of his rough fingers upon all things.
                                    Letter 18 [November 26, 1774]

3   Philosophy is best practiced, I believe, by the easy and affluent.
                                    Letter 30 [October 16, 1775]

4   Zounds! If alive — what ails you?   *Letter 42 [February 9, 1777]*

5   Make human nature thy study — wherever though residest — whatever the religion — or the complexion — study their hearts.   *Letter 2 [1778]*

Venture Smith   1729–1805

6   I crossed the waters to come here, and I am willing to cross them to return.   *A Narrative of the Life and Adventures of Venture [1798]*

7   My freedom is a privilege which nothing else can equal.
                            A Narrative of the Life and Adventures of Venture

8   A father's lips are closed in silence and in grief!
                            A Narrative of the Life and Adventures of Venture

Lucy Terry Prince   c. 1730–1821

9   August 'twas the twenty-fifth,
       Seventeen hundred and forty-six;
       The Indians did in ambush lay,
       Some very valiant men to slay,
       The names of whom I'll not leave out.
       Samuel Allen like a hero fout
       And though he was so brave and bold,
       His face no more shall we behold.
                    Bars Fight [c. 1746] in History of Western Massachusetts [1855][1]

---

[1] By Josiah Gilbert Holland.

Benjamin Banneker

1731–1806

1   Sir, I have long been convinced, that if your love for yourselves, and for those inestimable laws, which preserved to you the rights of human nature, was founded on sincerity, you could not but be solicitous, that every individual, of whatever rank or distinction, might with you equally enjoy the blessings thereof; neither could you rest satisfied short of the most active effusion of your exertions, in order to their promotion from any state of degradation, to which the unjustifiable cruelty and barbarism of men may have reduced them.

Letter to Thomas Jefferson [August 19, 1791][1]

2   Sir, how pitiable is it to reflect, that although you were so fully convinced of the benevolence of the Father of Mankind, and of his equal and impartial distribution of these rights and privileges, which he hath conferred upon them, that you should at the same time counteract his mercies, in detaining by fraud and violence so numerous a part of my brethren, under groaning captivity and cruel oppression, that you should at the same time be found guilty of that most criminal act, which you professedly detested in others, with respect to yourselves.

Letter to Thomas Jefferson

Prince Hall

1735–1807

3   [A Mason] should lend his helping hand to a brother in distress, and relieve him. This we may do in various ways; for we may sometimes help him to a cup of cold water, and it may be better to him than a cup of wine. Good advice may be sometimes better than feeding his body, helping him to some lawful employment, better than giving him money; so defending his case and standing by him when wrongfully accused, may be better than clothing him; better to save a brother's house when on fire, than to give him one.

A Charge Delivered to the Brethren of the African Lodge
[June 25, 1792]

4   So in states and kingdoms; sometimes in tranquility, then wars and tumults; rich today and poor tomorrow; which shows that there is not an independent mortal on earth: but dependent one upon the other from the king to the beggar.

A Charge Delivered to the African Lodge [June 24, 1797]

---

[1]Banneker responded to *Notes on the State of Virginia*, in which Jefferson wrote: "Misery is often the parent of the most affecting touches in poetry. Among the blacks is misery enough, God knows, but not poetry. Love is the peculiar oestrum of the poet. Their love is ardent, but it kindles the senses only, not the imagination. Religion, indeed, has produced a Phyllis Whatley (*sic*); but it could not produce a poet. The compositions published under her name are below the dignity of criticism."

1   The passion of fear, like pride and envy, hath slain its thousands.

A Charge Delivered to the African Lodge

2   Be always ready to give an answer to those that ask you a question; give the right hand of affection and fellowship to whom it justly belongs, let their color and complexion be what it will; let their nation be what it may, for they are your brethren and it is your indispensable duty to do so.

A Charge Delivered to the African Lodge

Joseph Boulogne [Le Chevalier de Saint-George][1]   1739–1799

3   I can no longer remain in this cruel uncertainty; I have nothing in the world with which to reproach myself; everywhere I have given proofs of my good citizenship and my republican sentiments, which are innate in me.

Letter requesting reinstatement to commanding post in French military [September 29, 1793]

4   Oh the joy of being loved tenderly,
And yet what disappointment follows in its wake!
    Why do you approach so slowly
    And then so quickly turn away?

The Other Day Beneath the Trees[1]

5   Sighing for what one adores is the hardest thing to bear.

Romances (Songs)[1]

Elizabeth Freeman [Mum Bett]   c. 1742–1829

6   By keepin' still and mindin' things.

Response when asked how she learned about the Bill of Rights, which she used as the basis to sue successfully for her freedom [1781][2]

Toussaint L'Ouverture   1743–1803

7   I was born in slavery, but I received from nature the soul of a freeman.

Letter [August 26, 1797][3]

8   There cannot exist slaves on this territory, servitude is therein forever abolished. All men are born, live and die free and French.
    All men, regardless of color, are eligible to all employment.

---

[1]From ALAIN GUÉDÉ, *Monsieur de Saint-George* [2003], translated by GILDA M. ROBERTS.
[2]From HARRIET MARTINEAU, *Retrospect of Western Travel* [1838].
[3]From RALPH KORNGOLD, *Citizen Toussaint* [1944].

There shall exist no distinction other than those based on virtue and talent, and other superiority afforded by law in the exercise of a public function. The law is the same for all whether in punishment or in protection.

Title II, Haitian Constitution [1801], articles 3–5

1   It is my duty to render to the French Government an exact account of my conduct. I shall relate the facts with all the simplicity and frankness of an old soldier, adding to them the reflections that naturally suggest themselves. In short, I shall tell the truth, though it be against myself.

Memoir of General Toussaint L'Ouverture Written by Himself [1802],[1] opening lines

2   Means have been employed against me which are only used against the greatest criminals. Doubtless, I owe this treatment to my color; but my color, — my color, — has it hindered me from serving my country with zeal and fidelity? Does the color of my skin impair my honor and my bravery?

Memoir of General Toussaint L'Ouverture

3   They have sent me to France destitute of everything; they have seized my property and my papers, and have spread atrocious calumnies concerning me. Is it not like cutting off a man's legs and telling him to walk? Is it not like cutting out a man's tongue and telling him to talk? Is it not burying a man alive?

Memoir of General Toussaint L'Ouverture

4   I have been a slave; I am willing to own it; but I have never received reproaches from my masters.

Memoir of General Toussaint L'Ouverture

5   There are men who appear outwardly to love liberty for all, but who are inwardly its sworn enemies.

Letter[2]

6   Men in general are so inclined to envy the glory of others, are so jealous of good which they have not themselves accomplished, that a man often makes himself enemies by the simple fact that he has rendered great service.

Letter

Olaudah Equiano [Gustavus Vassa]   1745–1797

7   It is difficult for those who publish their own memoirs to escape the imputation of vanity; nor is this the only disadvantage under which they labor: it is also their misfortune, that what is uncommon is rarely, if ever believed, and what is obvious we are apt to turn from with disgust. . . .

---

[1]From JOHN R. BEARD, *Toussaint L'Ouverture: A Biography and Autobiography* [1863].

[2]From C. L. R. JAMES, *The Black Jacobins* [1963].

People generally think those memoirs only worthy to be read or remembered which abound in great or striking events, those in short which in a high degree excite either admiration or pity: all others they consign to contempt and oblivion.

The Interesting Narrative of the Life of Olaudah Equiano, or Gustavus Vassa, the African [1789], ch. 1

1   Did I consider myself an European, I might say my sufferings were great: but when I compare my lot with that of most of my countrymen, I regard myself as a particular favorite of heaven.

The Interesting Narrative of the Life of Olaudah Equiano, or Gustavus Vassa, the African, 1

2   The first object which saluted my eyes when I arrived on the coast was the sea, and a slave ship, which was then riding at anchor, and waiting for its cargo. These filled me with astonishment, which was soon converted into terror, when I was carried on board. I was immediately handled, and tossed up to see if I were sound, by some of the crew; and I was now persuaded that I had gotten into a world of bad spirits, and that they were going to kill me. . . . I would have freely parted with them all to have exchanged my condition with that of the meanest slave in my own country. When I looked round the ship too and saw a large furnace or copper boiling, and a multitude of black people of every description chained together, every one of their countenances expressing dejection and sorrow, I no longer doubted of my fate.

The Interesting Narrative of the Life of Olaudah Equiano, or Gustavus Vassa, the African, 2

3   *[On the Middle Passage:]* The closeness of the place, and the heat of the climate, added to the number in the ship, which was so crowded that each had scarcely room to turn himself, almost suffocated us. This produced copious perspirations, so that the air soon became unfit for respiration, from a variety of loathsome smells, and brought on a sickness among the slaves, of which many died, thus falling victims to the improvident avarice, as I may call it, of their purchasers. This wretched situation was again aggravated by the galling of the chains, now become insupportable; and the filth of the necessary tubs, into which the children often fell, and were almost suffocated. The shrieks of the women, and the groans of the dying, rendered the whole a scene of horror almost inconceivable.

The Interesting Narrative of the Life of Olaudah Equiano, or Gustavus Vassa, the African, 2

4   Is not the slave trade entirely at war with the heart of man? And surely that which is begun by breaking down the barriers of virtue, involves

in its continuance destruction to every principle, and buries all sentiments in ruin!

> *The Interesting Narrative of the Life of Olaudah Equiano,*
> *or Gustavus Vassa, the African, 5*

1   When you make men slaves you deprive them of half their virtue, you set them, in your own conduct, an example of fraud, rapine, and cruelty, and compel them to live with you in a state of war.

> *The Interesting Narrative of the Life of Olaudah Equiano,*
> *or Gustavus Vassa, the African, 5*

Absalom Jones   1746–1818

2   We implore thy blessing, O God, upon the President, and all who are in authority in the United States. Direct them by thy wisdom, in all their deliberations, and O save thy people from the calamities of war. Give peace in our day, we beseech thee, O thou God of peace! and grant, that this highly favoured country may continue to afford a safe and peaceful retreat from the calamities of war and slavery, for ages yet to come.

> *On Account of the Abolition of the Slave Trade.*
> *A Thanksgiving Sermon [January 1, 1808]*

George Liele   c. 1750–c. 1828

3   I agree to election, redemption, the fall of Adam, regeneration and perseverance, knowing the promise is to all who endure, in grace, faith and good works to the end, shall be saved.

> *Letter, Kingston, Jamaica [December 18, 1791]*[1]

Lemuel Haynes[2]   1753–1833

4   Liberty and freedom is an innate principle, which is unmoveably placed in the human species; and to see a man aspire after it, is not enigmatical, seeing he acts no ways incompatible with his own nature.... Liberty is a Jewel which was handed down to man from the cabinet of heaven.

> *Liberty Further Extended [1776]*

5   An African, or in other terms,... a Negro may justly challenge and has an undeniable right to his liberty: Consequently, the practice of slave-keeping, which so much abounds in this Land is illicit.... Liberty is equally as precious to a Black man as it is to a white one, and bondage equally as intolerable to the one as it is to the other.   *Liberty Further Extended*

---

[1]From *Journal of Negro History* [January 1916], *vol. I, no. 1*, edited by CARTER G. WOODSON.
[2]From *Black Preacher to White America: The Collected Writings of Lemuel Haynes 1774–1833* [1990], edited by RICHARD NEWMAN.

1   *[On the devil:]* He is an old preacher. He lived above one thousand seven hundred years before Abraham; above two thousand four hundred and thirty years before Moses; four thousand and four years before Christ. By this time he must have acquired great skill in the art.

Universal Salvation [June 1805]

2   The reality of a future punishment is at times so clearly impressed on the human mind, that even Satan is constrained to own that there is a hell.

Universal Salvation

Phillis Wheatley[1]   c. 1753–1784

3   Wisdom is higher than a fool can reach.   *On Virtue*

4   Twas mercy brought me from my *Pagan* land,
    Taught my benighted soul to understand
    That there's a God, that there's a *Saviour* too:
    Once I redemption neither sought nor knew,
    Some view our sable race with scornful eye,
    "Their colour is a diabolic die."
    Remember, *Christians*, *Negroes*, black as *Cain*,
    May be refin'd, and join th' angelic train.

On Being Brought from Africa to America

5   Hail, happy saint, on thine immortal throne,
    Possest of glory, life, and bliss unknown:
    We hear no more the music of thy tongue,
    Thy wonted auditories cease to throng.

On the Death of the Reverend Mr. George Whitfield. 1770

6   *Aurora* hail, and all the thousand dies,
    Which deck thy progress through the vaulted skies:
    The morn awakes, and wide extends her rays,
    On ev'ry leaf the gentle zephyr plays;
    Harmonious lays the feather'd race resume,
    Dart the bright eye, and shake the painted plume.

A Hymn to the Morning

7   Let placid slumbers sooth each weary mind,
    At morn to wake more heav'nly, more refin'd.   *A Hymn to the Evening*

8   *Imagination!* who can sing thy force?
    Or who describe the swiftness of thy course?   *On Imagination*

---

[1]From *Poems on Various Subjects, Religious and Moral* [1773].

1 Descend to earth, there place thy throne;
    To succour man's afflicted son
      Each human heart inspire:
    To act in bounties unconfin'd
    Enlarge the close contracted mind,
      And fill it with thy fire.   *A Hymn to Humanity*

John Marrant   1755–1791

2   I now and then found, that my affections to my family and country were not dead; they were sometimes very sensibly felt, and at last strengthened into an invincible desire of returning home.

On his decision to return home after years of living among the Cherokee. A Narrative of the Lord's Wonderful Dealings with John Marrant [1785]

3   I saw my call to the ministry fuller and clearer; had a feeling concern for the salvation of my countrymen: I carried them constantly in the arms of prayer and faith to the throne of grace, and had continual sorrow in my heart for my brethren, for my kinsmen, according to the flesh.

A Narrative of the Lord's Wonderful Dealings with John Marrant

4   Man is a wonderful creature, and not undeservedly said to be a little world, a world within himself, and containing whatever is found in the Creator.   *Sermon preached at the African Lodge, Boston [June 24, 1789]*

5   Slavery... is not a just cause of our being despised; for if we search history, we shall not find a nation on earth [that] has at some period or other of their existence been in slavery, from the Jews down to the English nation under many Emperors, Kings and Princes.

Sermon preached at the African Lodge, Boston

[Quobna] Ottobah Cugoano   c. 1757–c. 1791

6   No necessity, or any situation of men, however poor pitiful and wretched they may be, can warrant them to rob others, or oblige them to become thieves because they are poor, miserable and wretched: But the robbers of men, the kidnappers, ensnarers and slave holders, who take away the common rights and privileges of others to support and enrich themselves, are universally those pitiful and detestable wretches; for the ensnarings of others, and taking away their liberty by slavery and oppression is the worst kind of robbery.

Thoughts and Sentiments on the Evil and Wicked Traffic of the Slavery and Commerce of the Human Species [1787]

1   When a vessel arrived to conduct us away to the ship, it was a most horrible scene; there was nothing to be heard but rattling of chains, smacking of whips, and the groans and cries of our fellow men.... All my help was cries and tears and these could not avail.

> *On being brought onto a slave ship. Thoughts and Sentiments on the Evil and Wicked Traffic of the Slavery and Commerce of the Human Species*

2   I must own, to the shame of my own countrymen, that I was first kidnapped and betrayed by some of my own complexion, who were the first cause of my exile and slavery; but if there were no buyers, there would be no sellers.

> *Thoughts and Sentiments on the Evil and Wicked Traffic of the Slavery and Commerce of the Human Species*

Jean-Jacques Dessalines   1758–1806

3   We have dared to be free — let us continue free by ourselves, and for ourselves; let us imitate the growing child; his own strength breaks his leading-strings, which become useless and troublesome to him in his walk. What are the people who have fought us? What people would reap the fruits of our labors? And what a dishonorable absurdity, to conquer to be slaves!

> *Proclamation of Haiti's Independence [January 1, 1804]*[1]

4   Remember that I have sacrificed everything to fly to your defense — parents, children, fortune, and am now only rich in your liberty — that my name has become a horror to all friends of slavery, or despots; and tyrants only pronounce it cursing the day that gave me birth. If ever you refuse or receive with murmuring the laws, which the protecting angel that watches over your destinies, shall dictate to me for your happiness, you will merit the fate of an ungrateful people. But away from me this frightful idea: You will be the guardians of the liberty you cherish.

> *Proclamation of Haiti's Independence*

Paul Cuffe[2]   1759–1817

5   My soul feels free to travel for the welfare of my fellow creatures both here and hereafter.

> *Letter, Westport [February 22, 1813]*

---

[1]From MARCUS RAINSFORD, *An Historical Account of the Black Empire of Hayti* [1805].
[2]From *Captain Paul Cuffe's Logs and Letters 1808–1817* [1996], edited by ROSALIND COBB WIGGINS.

Agrippa Hull

1759–1848

1   It is not the cover of the book, but what the book contains is the question. Many a good book has dark covers. Which is the worst, the white black man or the black white man? To be black outside, or to be black inside?

> *From Electa F. Jones, Stockbridge,*
> *Past and Present* [1854]

2   Sir, he was half black and half white; I liked my half, how did you like yours?

> *Response when asked by white master how he enjoyed*
> *"nigger preaching" after the two heard the sermon of*
> *a "distinguished mulatto preacher."* [1]
> *From Stockbridge, Past and Present*

Richard Allen

1760–1831

3   Men must be willfully blind and extremely partial, that cannot see the contrary effects of liberty and slavery upon the mind of man. I truly confess the vile habits often acquired in a state of servitude are not easily thrown off; the example of the Israelites shows, who with all that Moses could do to reclaim them from it, still continued in their habits more or less; and why will you look for better from us? ... It is in our posterity enjoying the same privileges with your own that you ought to look for better things.

> *The Life, Experience and Gospel Labors of the Rt. Rev.*
> *Richard Allen* [1833]. *An Address to Those Who Keep*
> *Slaves and Oppose the Practice*

4   The bands of bondage were so strong that no way appeared for my release: yet at times a hope arose in my heart that a way would open for it.

> *The Life, Experience and Gospel Labors of the Rt. Rev.*
> *Richard Allen. To the People of Colour*

5   Much depends upon us for the help of our color — more than many are aware. If we are lazy and idle, the enemies of freedom plead it as a cause why we ought not to be free, and say we are better in a state of servitude, and that giving us our liberty would be an injury to us, and by such conduct we strengthen the bands of oppression and keep many in bondage who are more worthy than ourselves.

> *The Life, Experience and Gospel Labors of the Rt. Rev.*
> *Richard Allen. To the People of Colour*

---

[1] The "distinguished mulatto preacher" may have been Lemuel Haynes, per Sidney Kaplan and Emma Nogrady Kaplan. *The Black Presence in the Era of the American Revolution*, rev. ed. [1989].

1   The tear of sensibility trickles from your eye, to see the sufferings that keep us from increasing....You see our race more effectually destroyed, than was in Pharaoh's power to effect upon Israel's sons; you blow the trumpet against the mighty evil; you make the tyrants tremble; you strive to raise the slave to the dignity of a man; you take our children by the hand, to lead them in the path of virtue.

> *The Life, Experience and Gospel Labors of the Rt. Rev.*
> *Richard Allen. A Short Address to the Friends*
> *of Him Who Hath No Helper*

Boston King   c. 1760–1802

2   To escape this cruelty, I determined to go to Charles Town, and throw myself into the hands of the English. They received me readily, and I began to feel the happiness of liberty, of which I knew nothing before, although I was most grieved at first to be obliged to leave many friends, and remain among strangers.

> *On joining the British during the American Revolution.*
> *Memoirs of the Life of Boston King, a Black Preacher,*
> *Written by Himself [1796]*

3   We saw our old masters coming from Virginia, North Carolina and other parts, and seizing upon their slaves in the streets of New York, or even dragging them out of their beds. Many of the slaves had very cruel masters, so that the thoughts of returning home with them embittered life to us. For some days we lost our appetite for food and sleep departed from our eyes.

> *On the end of the American Revolution. Memoirs of the Life*
> *of Boston King, a Black Preacher, Written by Himself*

Henri Christophe[1]   1767–1820

4   My subjects inherit the ignorance and prejudice that belong to slavery. At this moment they have made but very little progress in knowledge. Where could they acquire it, for, in gaining their liberty, they have seen nothing but camps and war?

> *Undated letter to Thomas Clarkson*

5   Nothing short of absolute independence in both government and commerce will satisfy us. This we shall have or cease to live.

> *Letter to Thomas Clarkson, Sans Souci*
> *[February 5, 1816]*

---

[1]From *Henri Christophe and Thomas Clarkson: A Correspondence* [1952], edited by EARL LESLIE GRIGGS and CLIFFORD H. PRATOR.

Denmark Vesey
1767–1822

1   The work of insurrection will go on.

Remark after being sentenced to death for planning slave rebellion[1]

Pierre Toussaint
1778–1853

2   I go to a great many places; I go into one house and they cry, cry, cry, — somebody dead. I go into another, and it is all laugh, laugh — they are happy and glad. I go to another, it is all shut up dark, they move very softly, they speak in a whisper, — somebody very sick. I come here it is all, dance and sing, and flowers and wedding dresses. I say nothing; but it makes me think a great deal.   *Memoir of Pierre Toussaint [1853]*

3   I have enough for myself, but if I stop work, I have not enough for others.

*Response when the wealthy philanthropist was asked
why he didn't retire. Memoir of Pierre Toussaint*

Peter Williams, Jr.
1780–1840

4   The festivities of this day serve but to impress upon the minds of reflecting men of color a deeper sense of the cruelty, the injustice, and oppression, of which they have been the victims. While others rejoice in their deliverance from a foreign yoke, they mourn that a yoke a thousand-fold more grievous is fastened upon them. Alas, they are slaves in the midst of freedom; they are slaves to those who boast that freedom is the unalienable right of all; and the clanking of their fetters, and the voice of their wrongs, make a horrid discord in the songs of freedom which resound through the land.   *Speech [July 4, 1830]*[2]

5   We are NATIVES of this country, we ask only to be treated as well as FOREIGNERS. Not a few of our fathers suffered and bled to purchase its independence; we ask only to be treated as well as those who fought against it. We have toiled to cultivate it, and to raise it to its present prosperous condition; we ask only to share equal privileges with those who come from distant lands, to enjoy the fruits of our labor.   *Speech*

Jarena Lee
1783–c. 1855

6   If the man may preach, because the Saviour died for him, why not the woman? Seeing he died for her also. Is he not a whole Saviour, instead of a

---

[1]From THOMAS WENTWORTH HIGGINSON, *Black Rebellion* [1998]. Reprint of an earlier edition that quotes a witness who said that Vesey, before his death, insisted "the work of insurrection would go on."

[2]From *The Black Abolitionist Papers* [1991], *vol. III*, edited by C. PETER RIPLEY ET AL.

half one? As those who hold it wrong for a woman to preach, would seem to make it appear.

Religious Experience and Journal of
Mrs. Jarena Lee [1849]

1   I felt as if aided from above. My tongue was cut loose, the stammerer spoke freely; the love of God, and of his service, burned with a vehement flame within me — his name was glorified among the people.

Religious Experience and Journal of Mrs. Jarena Lee

2   It is known that the blind have the sense of hearing in a manner much more acute than those who can see: also their sense of feeling is exceedingly fine, and is found to detect any roughness on the smoothest surface, where those who can see find none. So it may be with such as I am, who has never had more than three months schooling; and wishing to know much of the way and law of God, have therefore watched the more closely, the operations of the Spirit, and have in consequence been led thereby.

Religious Experience and Journal of Mrs. Jarena Lee

William Grimes   1784–1865

3   If it were not for the stripes on my back which were made while I was a slave, I would in my will leave my skin a legacy to the government, desiring that it might be taken off and made into parchment, and then bind the constitution of glorious happy and free America. Let the skin of an American slave bind the charter of American Liberty.

Life of William Grimes [1825]

David Walker   1785–1830

4   Having traveled over a considerable portion of these United States, and having, in the course of my travels, taken the most accurate observations of things as they exist — the result of my observations has warranted the full and unshaken conviction, that we, (coloured people of these United States,) are the most degraded, wretched, and abject set of beings that ever lived since the world began; and I pray God that none like us ever may live again until time shall be no more.

David Walker's Appeal [1829]

5   I declare, it does appear to me, as though some nations think God is asleep, or that he made the Africans for nothing else but to dig their mines and work their farms, or they cannot believe history, sacred or profane.

David Walker's Appeal

1   Are we MEN!! — I ask you, O my brethren! are we MEN? Did our creator make us to be slaves to dust and ashes like ourselves?

David Walker's Appeal

2   The whites have always been an unjust, jealous, unmerciful, avaricious and blood-thirsty set of beings, always seeking after power and authority.

David Walker's Appeal

3   Let no man of us budge one step and let slaveholders come to beat us from our country. America is more our country, than it is the whites — we have enriched it with our blood and tears.   *David Walker's Appeal*

4   Throw away your fears and prejudices then, and enlighten us and treat us like men, and we will like you more than we do now hate you. . . . Americans, I declare to you, while you keep us and our children in bondage, and treat us like brutes, to make us support you and your families, we cannot be your friends. You do not look for it, do you? Treat us then like men, and we will be your friends.   *David Walker's Appeal*

5   See your Declaration Americans!!! Do you understand your own language? Hear your language, proclaimed to the world, July 4th, 1776 — "We hold these truths to be self evident — that ALL MEN ARE CREATED EQUAL!! that they are endowed by their Creator with certain unalienable rights; that among these are life, liberty, and the pursuit of happiness!!" Compare your own language above, extracted from your Declaration of Independence, with your cruelties and murders inflicted by your cruel and unmerciful fathers and yourselves on our fathers and on us — men who have never given your fathers or you the least provocation!!!!!!

David Walker's Appeal

Mary Prince

1788–1833

6   I was soon surrounded by strange men, who examined and handled me in the same manner that a butcher would a calf or a lamb he was about to purchase, and who talked about my shape and size in like words — as if I could no more understand their meaning than the dumb beasts. . . . When the sale was over, my mother hugged and kissed us, and mourned over us, begging of us to keep up a good heart, and do our duty to our new masters. It was a sad parting; one went one way, one another, and our poor mammy went home with nothing.

On being sold away from her family. The History of Mary Prince, a West Indian Slave [1831]

7   I have been a slave myself — I know what slaves feel — I can tell by myself what other slaves feel, and by what they have told me. The man that

says slaves be quite happy in slavery — that they don't want to be free — that man is either ignorant or a lying person. I never heard a slave say so.

The History of Mary Prince

1   We don't mind hard work, if we had proper treatment, and proper wages like English servants, and proper time given in the week to keep us from breaking the Sabbath. But they won't give it: they will have work-work-work, night and day, sick or well, till we are quite done up; and we must not speak up nor look amiss, however much we be abused. And then when we are quite done up, who cares for us, more than for a lame horse? This is slavery.

The History of Mary Prince

Josiah Henson   1789–1883

2   [*On* Uncle Tom's Cabin, *by* HARRIET BEECHER STOWE:] The truth has never been half-told; the story would be too horrible to hear. I could fill this book with cases that have come under my own experience and observation, by which I could prove that the slaveholder could and did break every one of the ten commandments with impunity.

Uncle Tom's Story of His Life [1876], ch. 25

Samuel E[li] Cornish[1]   1795–1858

3   On our conduct, in great measure, their salvation depends. Let us show that we are worthy to be freemen; it will be the strongest appeal to the judgment and conscience of the slaveholder and his abettors, that can be furnished; and it will be a sure measure of our elevation in society, and to the possession of all of our rights, as men and citizens.

Responsibility of Colored Americans in Free States
[March 4, 1837]. Editorial published in Colored American

4   You are COLORED AMERICANS. The Indians are RED AMERI-CANS and the white people are WHITE AMERICANS and you are as good as they are, and they are no better than you — God made all of the same blood.

Colored American [March 15, 1838]. Editorial

5   The time has come when the question has got to be met. When our friends must face it, if they are our friends, or do as some will, take to their heels and run. Prejudice against color, after all is the test question — at least among us. . . . Here comes the tug; and here our friends have to grapple with slavery not at arm's length but with a backhold. Here the slimy serpent is among them coiled up in their own hearts and houses.

Colored American [June 9, 1838]. Editorial

---

[1]From *The Black Abolitionist Papers* [1991], *vol. III*, edited by C. PETER RIPLEY ET AL.

Samuel E[li] Cornish
1795–1858

and

John B[rown] Russwurm
1799–1851

1   We wish to plead our own cause. Too long have others spoken for us. Too long has the public been deceived by misrepresentations, in things which concern us dearly.

Editor's statement, first issue of Freedom's Journal
[March 16, 1827][1]

Samuel E[li] Cornish
1795–1858

and

Theodore S. Wright
1797–1847

2   The question whether or not the colored man can "rise" in this country is, as yet wholly undecided. We do not pronounce that he *could,* or that he could *not,* for the experiment that will satisfy a philosophical mind as to either remains to be made.... Release him from his chains! — strike off his fetters! — relieve him from the stifling pressure of your own weight! — try him! and if, after time allowed for restoring the circulation of his blood to its free and wonted course, and for supplying his muscles, numbed and deadened by the ligatures that bind him — if after this, he be unable to rise, your assertion may gain credit but not until then.

The Colonization Scheme Considered [April 1, 1840]

3   Slaves, of any color, becoming free in countries where their own race are in bondage, show as much if not more eagerness (when they possess the means) to become masters, than such as are born free. And their treatment of their slaves is generally more cruel.

The Colonization Scheme Considered

Rebecca Cox Jackson
1795–1871

4   One day I was sitting finishing a dress in haste and in prayer. This word was spoken in my mind, "Who learned the first man on earth?" "Why, God." "He is unchangeable, and if He learned the first man to read, He can learn you." I laid down my dress, picked up my Bible, ran upstairs, opened it, and kneeled down with it pressed to my breast, prayed earnestly to Almighty God if it was consisting to His holy will, to learn me to read His

[1]America's first black-owned and -operated newspaper.

holy word. And when I looked on the word, I began to read. And when I found I was reading, I was frightened — then I could not read one word. I closed my eyes again in prayer and then opened my eyes, began to read. So I done, until I read the chapter....Oh how thankful I feel for this unspeakable gift of Almighty God to me! Oh may I make a good use of it all the days of my life!

Gifts of Power[1]

George M[oses] Horton[2]

c. 1797–1883

1   Creation fires my tongue!
      Nature thy anthems raise;
  And spread the universal song
      Of thy Creator's praise!   *The Hope of Liberty [1829]. Praise of Creation*

2   Alas! Am I born for this,
      To wear this slavish chain?
  Deprived of all created bliss,
      Through hardship, toil and pain!

The Hope of Liberty. On Liberty and Slavery

3   Something still my heart surveys,
  Groping through this dreary maze;
  Is it Hope? — then burn and blaze
      Forever!   *The Hope of Liberty. The Slave's Complaint*

4   Alas! how quick it is the case,
      The scion of youth is grown —
  How soon it runs its morning race,
      And beauty's sun goes down.   *The Hope of Liberty. On Winter*

5   Love which can ransom every slave,
      And set the pris'ner free;
  Gild the dark horrors of the grave.
      And still the raging sea.   *The Hope of Liberty. Heavenly Love*

6   True nature first inspires the man.

Naked Genius [1865]. The Art of a Poet

Juan Francisco Manzano

1797–1854

7   Behold, his conscience! Oh what deep repose,

---

[1]From *Gifts of Power: The Writings of Rebecca Jackson* [1987], edited by JEAN MCMAHON HUMEZ.
[2]From GEORGE MOSES HORTON, *Poems by a Slave* [1837], and *The Black Bard of North Carolina: George Moses Horton and His Poetry* [1997], edited by JOAN R. SHERMAN.

It slumber in one long deadly doze:
Why do you wonder that it thus does sleep;
That crime should prosper, or that guilt so deep,
So long unfelt should seem unscathed, in fine,
Should know no shame, and fear no law divine.

The Slave Trade Merchant[1]

1   Oh, though great scourge and terror of our race,
While thy strong hand bows down the proudest head,
Filling the earth with cries in every place,
And grief and wailing o'er the silent dead.

To Death[1]

2   Yes, tho' in gloom and sadness I may rise,
One blessed strain can soothe my troubled soul,
No sooner wakened than with streaming eyes,
Upward I look, and there I seek my goal.

Religion, an Ode[1]

3   In vain I was forbidden to write, for when everybody went to bed,
I used to light a piece of candle, and when at my leisure I copied the best
verses thinking that I could imitate these, I would become a poet.

The Life of the Negro Poet Written by Himself
[1840]

4   I resolved to venture on my escape, and in case of detection, to suffer
for something.... I saddled the horse for the first time in my life, put on the
bridle, but with such trembling that I hardly knew what I was about....
When I was going away, I heard the sound of a voice saying "God bless you,
make haste."

On running away to freedom.
The Life of the Negro Poet Written by Himself

Sojourner Truth [Isabella Van Wagenen]   c. 1797–1883

5   Frederick, is God dead?

Question to speaker Frederick Douglass[2] *[c. 1850]*

6   That man...says that women need to be helped into carriages, and
lifted over ditches, and to have the best place everywhere. Nobody ever helps
me into carriages, or over mud puddles, or gives me any best place, and
aren't I a woman?...I have plowed, and planted, and gathered into barns,

[1]From *Poems by a Slave in the Island of Cuba* [1840], translated by R. R. MADDEN.
[2]As reported by HARRIETT BEECHER STOWE in *Sojourner Truth: The Libyan Sibyl* [1863].

and no man could head me—and aren't I a woman? I could work as much and eat as much as a man (when I could get it), and bear the lash as well—and aren't I a woman? I have borne thirteen children and seen them most all sold off into slavery, and when I cried out with a mother's grief, none but Jesus heard—and aren't I a woman?

Speech at Woman's Rights Convention,
Akron, Ohio [1851]

1   That...man...says women can't have as much rights as man, 'cause Christ wasn't a woman. Where did your Christ come from? From God and a woman. Man had nothing to do with him.

Speech at Woman's Rights Convention,
Akron, Ohio

2   If the first woman God ever made was strong enough to turn the world upside down all alone, these women together ought to be able to turn it back, and get it right side up again!

Speech at Woman's Rights Convention, Akron, Ohio

3   I sell the shadow to support the substance.

Caption under photographs of Truth [c. 1864]

4   It is hard for the old slaveholding spirit to die. But die it must.[1]

Letter [October 1, 1865]

5   There is a great stir about colored men getting their rights, but not a word about the colored women; and if colored men get their rights, and not colored women theirs, you see the colored men will be masters over the women, and it will be just as bad as it was before.

Speech at the American Equal Rights Association
[May 9, 1867]

6   *[Response upon hearing that Democrats would burn down an Angola, Indiana, building if she spoke, 1863:]* Then I will speak upon the ashes.

Narrative of Sojourner Truth [1875]. Book of Life

7   Our nerves and sinews, our tears and blood have been sacrificed on the altar of this nation's avarice. Our unpaid labor has been a stepping-stone to its financial success. Some of its dividends must surely be ours.

Narrative of Sojourner Truth. Book of Life

8   Religion without humanity is a poor human stuff.

Narrative of Sojourner Truth [1884].
A Memorial Chapter

[1]From *We Are Your Sisters* [1984], edited by DOROTHY STERLING.

1   I isn't goin' to die, honey, Ise goin' home like a shootin' star.
From HALLIE Q. BROWN, *Homespun Heroines and Other*
Women of Distinction [1926]

2   The rich rob the poor and the poor rob one another.   *Saying*

Theodore S. Wright   1797–1847

3   The prejudice which exists against the colored man, the free man is
like the atmosphere, everywhere felt by him. It is true that in these
United States and in this State, there are men, like myself, colored with
a skin like my own, who are not subjected to the lash; who are not liable
to have their wives and their infants torn from them; from whose hand
the Bible is not taken. It is true that we may walk abroad; we may enjoy
our domestic comforts, our families; retire to the closet; visit the sanctuary, and may be permitted to urge on our children and our neighbors
in well doing. But sir, still we are slaves — everywhere we feel the chain
galling us.   *Speech, New York State Anti-Slavery Society [1837]*

James P[ierson] Beckwourth   c. 1798–1866

4   Whatever is their fortune, good or bad, the leader is the person on
whom the praise or blame falls.
The Life and Adventures of James P. Beckwourth [1856]

5   If you will not kill me, I will live with you.
Said to Native Americans. The Life and Adventures of
James P. Beckwourth

6   The restless, youthful mind, that wearies with the monotony of
peaceful everyday existence, and aspires after a career of wild adventure and
thrilling romance, will find by my experience that such a life is by no means
one of comfort, and that the excitement which it affords is very dearly purchased by the opportunities lost of gaining far more profitable wisdom.
The Life and Adventures of James P. Beckwourth

7   You are all fools and old women; come with me, if any of you are
brave enough, and I will show you how to fight.
From FRANCIS PARKMAN, *The Oregon Trail [1872]*

Alexander Sergeyevich Pushkin   1799–1837

8   Reason's icy intimations,
and records of a heart in pain.   *Eugene Onegin [1823],*[1] *dedication*

---

[1]From *The Works of Alexander Pushkin* [1936], edited by AVRAHM YARMOLINSKY. Translated by CHARLES
JOHNSTON.

1   Unforced, as conversation passed,
     he had the talent of saluting
     felicitously every theme,
     of listening like a judge supreme
     while serious topics were disputing,
     or, with an epigram-surprise,
     of kindling smiles in ladies' eyes.   *Eugene Onegin, ch. 1, st. 5*

2   Always contented with his life,
     and with his dinner, and his wife.   *Eugene Onegin, 1, st. 12*

3   Why fight what's known to be decisive?
     Custom is despot of mankind.   *Eugene Onegin, 1, st. 25*

4   The illness with which he'd been smitten
     should have been analyzed when caught,
     something like *spleen,* that scourge of Britain,
     or Russia's *chondria,* for short.   *Eugene Onegin, 1, st. 38*

5   When, wrapped in storm, shall I be battling
     The billows, while the shrouds are rattling,
     And roam the sea's expanse unpent,
     Quit of the shore's dull element?
     'Tis time to seek the southern surges
     Beneath my Afric's sunny sky,
     And, there at home, for Russia sigh,
     Lamenting in new songs and dirges
     The land that knew my love, my pain,
     Where long my buried heart is lain.   *Eugene Onegin, 1, st. 50*[1]

6   Habit is Heaven's own redress:
     it takes the place of happiness.   *Eugene Onegin, 2, st. 31*

7   Love passed, the muse appeared, the weather
     of mind got clarity newfound;
     now free, I once more weave together
     emotion, thought, and magic sound.   *Eugene Onegin, 2, st. 59*

8   *Pimen [writing by lamplight]:* One more, the final record, and my annals
     Are ended, and fulfilled the duty laid
     By God on me, a sinner. Not in vain
     Hath God appointed me for many years

---

[1]Translated by ALFRED HAYES.

A witness, teaching me the art of letters;
A day will come when some laborious monk
Will bring to light my zealous, nameless toil,
Kindle, as I, his lamp, and from the parchment
Shaking the dust of ages, will transcribe
My chronicles. *Boris Godunov [written 1825]*[1]

1   Like to some magistrate grown gray in office
Calmly he contemplates alike the just
And unjust, with indifference he notes
Evil and good, and knows not wrath nor pity. *Boris Godunov*

2   *Mosalsky:* Good folk! Maria Godunov and her son Feodor have poisoned themselves. We have seen their dead bodies. [*The people are silent with horror.*] Why are you silent? Cry, Long live Czar Dimitri Ivanovich! [*The people are speechless.*]

Boris Godunov

3   Generally the young Negro was regarded in the light of a curiosity; people used to surround him and overwhelm him with compliments and questions—and this curiosity, concealed by a show of graciousness offended his vanity.... He felt that he was for them a kind of rare beast, a peculiar alien creature, accidentally brought into a world, with which he had nothing in common. He envied people who remained unnoticed, and considered them fortunate in their insignificance.

The Negro of Peter the Great [1827]

4   Nothing inflames love so much as the encouraging observation of a bystander: love is blind, and having no trust in itself, readily grasps hold of every support. *The Negro of Peter the Great*

5   Nothing is hidden from the eyes of the observing world.

The Negro of Peter the Great

6   To me; here, my Madonna, thou shalt throne:
Most pure exemplar of the purest grace. *Madonna [1830]*

7   And thus he[2] mused: "From here, indeed
Shall we strike terror in the Swede;
And here a city, by our labor
Founded, shall gall our haughty neighbor;
'Here cut'—so Nature gives command—

---

[1]Translated by ALFRED HAYES.
[2]Peter I (the Great) [1672–1725].

'Your window through on Europe: stand
Firm-footed by the sea, unchanging!'"

The Bronze Horseman [written 1833][1]

1   Disrespect for one's ancestors is the first sign of barbarity and immorality.   *Polnoe sobranie sochinenii [1937–1954], vol. VIII*[2]

John B[rown] Russwurm   1799–1851

2   Our time is short in this transitory world, and it therefore becomes us to labor with all our might, lest the darkness overtake us before we are aware of it.   *Letter [April 1830]*[3]

Nat Turner   1800–1831

3   You have asked me to give a history of the motives which induced me to undertake the late insurrection, as you call it. — To do so I must go back to the days of my infancy, and even before I was born.

The Confessions of Nat Turner [1831][4]

4   Having soon discovered to be great, I must appear so, and therefore studiously avoided mixing in society, and wrapped myself in mystery, devoting my time to fasting and prayer.

The Confessions of Nat Turner

5   I had a vision — and I saw white spirits and black spirits engaged in battle, and the sun was darkened — the thunder rolled in the Heavens, and blood flowed in streams — and I heard a voice saying, "Such is your luck, such you are called to see, and let it come rough or smooth you must surely bare [*sic*] it."   *The Confessions of Nat Turner*

6   I heard a loud noise in the heavens, and the Spirit instantly appeared to me and said the Serpent was loosened, and Christ had laid down the yoke he had borne for the sins of men, and that I should take it on and fight against the Serpent, for the time was fast approaching when the first should be last and the last should be first.[5]   *The Confessions of Nat Turner*

7   'Twas my object to carry terror and destruction wherever we went.

The Confessions of Nat Turner

---

[1]Translated by OLIVER ELTON.

[2]From *The Cambridge Companion to Pushkin* [2006], edited by ANDREW KAHN.

[3]From *The African Repository and Colonial Journal* [1831], *vol. VI.*

[4]Lawyer Thomas R. Gray, who was white, wrote the pamphlet *The Confessions of Nat Turner*, reportedly assembling the text from Turner's oral jailhouse account of the 1831 slave rebellion.

[5]Many that are first shall be last; and the last shall be first. — *Matthew 19:30*

Marie Laveau

1801–1881

1   Here is the day, we must welcome it with song.

New Orleans Times [June 28, 1872] [1]

Alexandre Dumas the Elder

1802–1870

2   All for one, one for all, that is our motto.

The Three Musketeers [1844], ch. 9

3   Never forget that until the day when God will deign to reveal the future to man, all human wisdom is contained in these two words — "*Wait and hope.*"

The Count of Monte Cristo [1845], vol. III,
ch. 42 [Edmond Dantés]

4   Nothing succeeds like success.   *Ange Pitou [1854], vol. I*

5   Let us look for the woman.

The Mohicans of Paris [1854–1855], vol. III, ch. 10, 11

Lunsford Lane

1803–c. 1863

6   Ever after I entertained the first idea of being free, I had endeavored so to conduct myself as not to become obnoxious to the white inhabitants, knowing as I did their power, and their hostility to the colored people. The two points necessary in such a case I had kept constantly in mind. First, I made no display of the little property or money I possessed, but in every way I wore as much as possible the aspect of poverty. Second, I had never appeared to be even so intelligent as I really was. This all colored people at the south, free and slaves, find it peculiarly necessary to their own comfort and safety to observe.   *The Narrative of Lunsford Lane [1842]*

Maria W. Stewart

1803–1879

7   O, ye daughters of Africa, awake! Awake! Arise! No longer sleep nor slumber, but distinguish yourselves. Show forth to the world that ye are endowed with noble and exalted faculties. O ye daughters of Africa! What have ye done to immortalize your names beyond the grave? What examples have ye set before the rising generation? What foundation have ye laid for generations yet unborn? Where are our union and love?

Religion and the Pure Principles of Morality
[October 1831] [2]

---

[1] From ROBERT TALLANT, *Voodoo in New Orleans* [1974].
[2] From *Meditations from the Pen of Mrs. Maria W. Stewart* [1879].

1   How long shall the daughters of Africa be compelled to bury their minds and talents beneath a load of iron pots and kettles? Until union, knowledge and love begin to flow among us. How long shall a mean set of men flatter us with their smiles, and enrich themselves with our hard earnings; their wives' fingers sparkling with rings, and they themselves laughing at our folly? Until we begin to promote and patronize each other. Shall we be a by-word among the nations any longer? Shall they laugh us to scorn forever? Do you ask, what we can do? Unite and build a store of your own.... We have spent more than enough for nonsense, to do what building we should want. We have never had an opportunity of displaying our talents; therefore the world thinks we know nothing.

Religion and the Pure Principles of Morality

2   Possess the spirit of independence. The Americans do, and why should not you? Possess the spirit of men, bold and enterprising, fearless and undaunted. Sue for your rights and privileges. Know the reason that you cannot attain them. Weary them with your importunities. You can but die if you make the attempt; and we shall certainly die if you do not.

Religion and the Pure Principles of Morality

3   Oh, America, America, foul and indelible is thy stain! Dark and dismal is the cloud that hangs over thee, for thy cruel wrongs and injuries to the fallen sons of Africa.

Religion and the Pure Principles of Morality

4   Why sit here and die? If we say we will go to a foreign land, the famine and the pestilence are there, and there we shall die. If we sit here, we shall die. Come let us plead our case before the whites: if they save us alive, we shall live — and if they kill us, we shall but die.

Speech to the New England Anti-Slavery Society,
Boston [September 21, 1832][1]

5   Ingratitude is one of the worst passions that reigns in the human breast; it is this that cuts the tender fibers of the soul.

Speech to the Afric-American Female Intelligence
Society of Boston [1832][1]

6   O woman, woman! Your example is powerful, your influence great; it extends over your husbands, and your children, and throughout the circle of your acquaintance.

Speech to the Afric-American Female Intelligence
Society of Boston

---

[1]From *Meditations from the Pen of Mrs. Maria W. Stewart* [1879].

1   What if I am a woman; is not the God of ancient times the God of these modern days? Did he not raise up Deborah, to be a mother, and a judge in Israel? Did not Queen Esther save the lives of the Jews? And Mary Magdalene first declare the resurrection of Christ from the dead?

Farewell address [September 21, 1833][1]

2   It is not the color of the skin that makes the man or the woman, but the principle formed in the soul. Brilliant wit will shine, come from whence it will; and genius and talent will not hide the brightness of its luster.

Farewell address

Mary Seacole   1805–1881

3   "Americans" (even from the Northern States) are always uncomfortable in the company of colored people, and very often show this feeling in stronger ways than by sour looks and rude words. . . . I have a few shades of deeper brown upon my skin which shows me related — and I am proud of that relation — to those poor mortals whom you once enslaved and whose bodies America still owns. And having this bond, and knowing what slavery is; having seen with my eyes and heard with my ears proof positive enough of its horrors — let others affect to doubt them if they will — is it surprising that I should be somewhat impatient of the airs of superiority which many Americans have endeavored to issue over me?

The Wonderful Adventures of Mrs. Seacole
in Many Lands [1857], ch. 2

4   I am not ashamed to confess that I love to be of service to those who need a woman's help. And wherever the need arises — on whatever distant shore — I ask no greater or higher privilege than to minister to it.

The Wonderful Adventures of Mrs. Seacole in
Many Lands, 4

5   Beside the nettle, ever grows the cure for its sting.

The Wonderful Adventures of Mrs. Seacole in
Many Lands, 7

6   All death is trying to witness — even that of the good man who lays down his life hopefully and peacefully; but on the battlefield, when the poor body is torn and rent in hideous ways, and the scared spirit struggles to loose itself from the still strong frame that holds it tightly, to the last, death is fearful indeed.

The Wonderful Adventures of Mrs. Seacole in
Many Lands, 16

---

[1]From *Meditations from the Pen of Mrs. Maria W. Stewart* [1879].

Ira [Frederick] Aldridge
c. 1807–1867

1   I risk my all upon thy power —
    Life — son — yea, country too;
To free my brethren, fetter'd slaves
From sinking in inglorious graves.

Farewell address [April 2, 1832][1]

2   A child of the sun, black my countenance, yet I stand before you in the light of my soul.

Epilogue, Berlin [January 13, 1853][2]

3   As usual the leading man is grumbling about the disadvantage he says he will be at not understanding English. He forgets that I am at a greater disadvantage, his language is understood by the entire audience while I am but partially so. However this is easily got over.

Letter to wife on playing Othello in Stockholm[3]

James W[illiam] C[harles] Pennington
1807–1870

4   There is one sin that slavery committed against me, which I never can forgive. It robbed me of my education; the injury is irreparable.... It cost me two years' hard labor, after I fled, to unshackle my mind; it was three years before I had purged my language of slavery's idioms; it was four years before I had thrown off the crouching aspect of slavery; and now the evil that besets me is a great lack of that general information.... I am grievously overwhelmed with a sense of my deficiency, and more especially as I can never hope to make it up.

The Fugitive Blacksmith [1849]

5   The colored population of the United States have no destiny separate from that of the nation of which they form an integral part. Our destiny is bound up with that of America. Her ship is ours; her pilot ours; her storms ours; her calms are ours. If she breaks upon any rock, we break with her.

Speech delivered in Glasgow and London [1850][4]

Plácido [Gabriel de la Concepción Valdés]
1809–1844

6   Let them who fear be dumb, for not of them am I!

The Living Age [1860]

---

[1]From *Notes and Queries* [July–December 1872].

[2]From HERBERT MARSHALL and MILDRED STOCK, *Ira Aldridge: The Negro Tragedian* [1958].

[3]From OWEN MORTIMER, *Speak of Me As I Am: The Story of Ira Aldridge* [1995].

[4]From WILLIAM COOPER NELL, *The Colored Patriots of the American Revolution* [1855].

1   If the unfortunate fate engulfing me,
The ending of my history of grief,
The closing of my span of years so brief,
Mother, should wake a single pang in thee,
Weep not.

Farewell to My Mother,[1] *written the night before execution*
[June 27, 1844]

2   But if 'tis fixed by the decree divine,
That I must bear the pain of guilt and shame,
And that my foes this cold and senseless frame
Shall rudely treat with scorn and shouts malign;
Give thou the word, and I my breath resign
Obedient to thy will; blest be thy holy name.

My Prayers to God[2]

Charles Lenox Redmond   1810–1873

3   Complexion can in no sense be construed into crime, much less be
rightfully made the criterion of rights.

Speech before the Legislative Committee, Massachusetts
House of Representatives [1842][3]

4   What a burning shame it is, that many of the pieces on the subject of
slavery and the slavetrade, contained in different school books have been
lost sight of, or been subject to the pruning knife of the slaveholding expur-
gatorial system! To make me believe that those men, or bodies of men, who
have regulated the educational institutions of our country, have humanity
in their hearts, is to make me believe a lie; and not less in making me believe
those Christian ministers who profess to love God in words, and hate their
brother in works.

Letter to William Lloyd Garrison [March 5, 1842][3]

5   I do not feel as many may feel today, to make an appeal over the prostrate form of some slave mother; nor do I care to repeat the sayings of some
noble slave father.... I have only to speak for myself; to speak for freedom
for myself; to determine for freedom for myself, and in doing so, I speak and
determine for the freedom of every slave on every plantation.

Speech. The Liberator [July 10, 1857]

---

[1]From *The Book of American Negro Poetry, second edition* [1931], translated by James Weldon Johnson.
[2]From Arthur A. Schomburg, *Plácido: A Cuban Martyr* [December 25, 1909].
[3]From Patricia W. Romero, *I Too Am America: Documents from 1619 to the Present* [1968].

David Ruggles   1810–1849

1   Every man that can read and has sense sufficient to put two ideas together without losing one, knows what the abolitionists mean when they speak of elevating us "according to our equal rights." But why is it that it seems to you so "repugnant" to marry your sons and daughters to colored persons?
The Extinguisher Extinguished [1834]

2   A man is sometimes lost in the dust of his own raising.
The Extinguisher Extinguished

3   Liberty is the word for me, above all, Liberty.
Mirror of Liberty [July 1838]

Martin R[obison] Delany   1812–1885

4   We have speculated and moralized much about equality — claiming to be as good as our neighbors, and everybody else — all of which may do very well in ethics — but not in politics.
The Condition, Elevation, Emigration and Destiny of the Colored People of the United States [1852]

5   White men are producers — we are consumers. They build houses, and we rent them. They raise produce, and we consume it. They manufacture cloths and wares, and we garnish ourselves with them. They build coaches, vessels, cars, hotels, saloons, and other vehicles and places of accommodation and we deliberately wait until they have got them in readiness, then walk in, and contend with as much assurance for a "right" as though the whole thing was bought by, paid for, and belonged to us.
The Condition, Elevation, Emigration and Destiny of the Colored People of the United States

6   Our elevation must be the result of self-efforts, and work of our own hands. No other human power can accomplish it.
The Condition, Elevation, Emigration and Destiny of the Colored People of the United States

7   We are slaves in the midst of freedom, waiting patiently, and unconcernedly — indifferently, and stupidly, for masters to come and lay claim to us, trusting to their generosity, whether or not they will own us and carry us into endless bondage. The slave is more secure than we; he knows who holds the heel upon his bosom — we know not the wretch who may grasp us by the throat.
The Condition, Elevation, Emigration and Destiny of the Colored People of the United States

1   A serpent is a serpent, and none the less a viper, because nestled in the bosom of an honest hearted man.

The Condition, Elevation, Emigration and Destiny of the Colored People of the United States

2   No people are ever elevated above the condition of their *females;* hence, the condition of the *mother* determines the condition of the child. To know the position of a people, it is only necessary to know the *condition* of their *females;* and despite themselves, they cannot rise above their level.

The Condition, Elevation, Emigration and Destiny of the Colored People of the United States

3   We love our country, dearly love her, but she don't love us — she despises us, and bids us begone, driving us from her embraces; but we shall not go where she desires us; but when we do go, whatever love we have for her, we shall love the country none the less that receives us as her adopted children.

The Condition, Elevation, Emigration and Destiny of the Colored People of the United States

John Jasper   1812–1901

4   There is a mighty difference between a dream and a vision. A dream am an empty thing, but a vision are a reality.

The Sun Do Move [1882]

5   If we only reads what is on one page, without looking underneath, on the other side, we can't understand its meaning.   *The Sun Do Move*

6   If every man had to say when he should die, he would live on to a hundred, a thousand years — he would never die. But you all has to go! And when Providence calls you! Death am universal!   *The Sun Do Move*

Harriet Ann Jacobs [Linda Brent]   1813–1897

7   [My parents] lived together in a comfortable home; and, though we were all slaves I was so fondly shielded that I never dreamed I was a piece of merchandise, trusted to them for safe keeping, and liable to be demanded of them at any moment.

Incidents in the Life of a Slave Girl [1861], ch. 1

8   Notwithstanding my grandmother's long and faithful service to her owners, not one of her children escaped the auction block. These God-breathing machines are no more, in the sight of their masters, than the cotton they plant, or the horses they tend.

Incidents in the Life of a Slave Girl, 1

1   No matter whether the slave girl be as black as ebony or as fair as her mistress. In either case there is no shadow of law to protect her from insult, from violence, or even from death; all these are inflicted by fiends who bear the shape of men.

Incidents in the Life of a Slave Girl, 5

2   Southern women often marry a man knowing that he is the father of many little slaves. They do not trouble themselves about it. They regard such children as property, as marketable as the pigs on the plantation.

Incidents in the Life of a Slave Girl, 6

3   Slavery is a curse to the whites as well as to the blacks. It makes the white fathers cruel and sensual; the sons violent and licentious; it contaminates the daughters, and makes the wives wretched.

Incidents in the Life of a Slave Girl, 9

4   To be an object of interest to a man who is not married, and who is not her master, is agreeable to the pride and feelings of a slave, if her miserable condition has left her any pride or sentiment. It seems less degrading to give one's self, than to submit to compulsion. There is something akin to freedom in having a lover who has no control over you, except that which he gains by kindness and attachment.   *Incidents in the Life of a Slave Girl, 10*

5   Reader, my story ends with freedom; not in the usual way, with marriage. I and my children are now free!

Incidents in the Life of a Slave Girl, 41

James McCune Smith[1]   1813–1865

6   Nations which are pleased to term themselves civilized, have one sort of faith which they hold to one another, and another sort which they entertain towards people less advanced in refinement. The faith which they entertain towards the latter, is very often treachery, in the vocabulary of the civilized.   *A Lecture on the Haytien Revolutions [1841]*

7   By remaining in this country, the scene of our enslavement, we shall overcome slavery and consequently confute, by the resistless evidence of facts, the doctrines upon which slavery rests. This will do more for human Liberty than could be accomplished by emigration. By the latter course we might escape from, but would leave untouched, an evil institution, which by our present course, we are destined to overthrow.

The Destiny of the People of Color [1843]

---

[1]From *The Works of James McCune Smith* [2006], edited by John Stauffer.

1   The great hindrance to the advancement of the free colored people is the want of unity in action. If we were to unite in the pursuit of any one object, I can imagine no possibility beyond our power to compass. But we are not united as a people; and the main reason why we are not united is that we are not equally oppressed. This is the grand secret of our lack of union.

Letter. Frederick Douglass' Papers [May 12, 1854]

2   When a man raises himself from the lowest condition of society to the highest, mankind pay him the tribute of their admiration; when he accomplishes this elevation by native energy guided by prudence and wisdom, their admiration is increased; but when his course, onward and upward, excellent in itself, furthermore proves a possible . . . reform, then he becomes a burning and a shining light, on which the aged may look with gladness, the young with hope, and the downtrodden, as a representative of what they may themselves become.

Introduction to FREDERICK DOUGLASS,
My Bondage and My Freedom [1855]

James McCune Smith   1813–1865

and

G. B. Wilson   Nineteenth century

and

William H. Topp   1812–1857

3   Among ourselves we need a press that shall keep us steadily alive to our responsibilities, which shall constantly point out the principles which should guide our conduct and our labors, which shall cheer us from one end of the land to the other, by recording our acts, our sufferings, our temporary defeats and our steadily approaching triumph — or rather the triumph of the glorious truth, "Human Equality," whose servants and soldiers are we.

*Report by the Committee on a National Press of the National
Convention of Colored People and Their Friends,
Troy, New York [October 6, 1847]*[1]

William Wells Brown   1814–1884

4   I had long since made up my mind that I would not trust myself in the hands of any man, white or colored. The slave is brought up to look upon

---

[1]From *Proceedings of the National Convention of Colored People and Their Friends* [October 6–9, 1847].

every white man as an enemy to him and his race; and twenty-one years in slavery had taught me that there were traitors, even among colored people.
Narrative of William W. Brown [1847], ch. 13

1   The appearance of Clotel on the auction block created a deep sensation amongst the crowd. There she stood, with a complexion as white as most of those who were waiting with a wish to become her purchasers.
Clotel; or, the President's Daughter [1853], ch. 1

2   Known to God only is the amount of human agony and suffering which sends its cry from the slave markets and Negro pens, unheard and unheeded by man up to his ear; mothers weeping for their children, breaking the night-silence with the shrieks of their breaking hearts.
Clotel; or, the President's Daughter, 5

3   Society did not take me up; I took myself up. I did not ask society to take me up. All I asked of the white people was to get out of the way.
Speech [May 6, 1862][1]

4   Why, every man must make equality for himself. No society, no government can make this equality. I do not expect the slave of the south to jump into equality; all I claim for him is, that he may be allowed to jump into liberty, and let him make equality for himself.
The Black Man: His Antecedents, His Genius,
and His Achievements [1863]

5   The last great struggle for our rights; the battle for our civilization, is entirely with ourselves.   *My Southern Home [1880]*

Joseph Cinqué [Sengbe Pieh]   c. 1814–1879

6   They say we are like dogs without any home. But if you send us home, you will see whether we be dogs or not. We want to see no more snow. We no say this place no good, but we afraid of cold. Cold catch us all the time. We have great many friends here and we love them just as we love our brethren.
Letter to President John Tyler [October 5, 1841][2]

Sarah L[ouisa] Forten   c. 1814–1883

7   It has often engendered feelings of discontent and mortification in my breast when I saw that many were preferred before me, who by education — birth — or worldly circumstances were no better than

---

[1]From PATRICIA W. ROMERO, *I Too Am America: Documents from 1619 to the Present* [1968].
[2]From *African Repository* [December 1841], *vol. XVII.*

myself — their sole claim to notice depending on the superior advantage of being white — but I am striving to live above such heart burnings… believing that a spirit of forbearance under such evils is all that we as a people can exert.   *Letter to Angelina E. Grimké [April 15, 1837]*[1]

Mary Ellen Pleasant[2]   c. 1814–1904

1   I'd rather be a corpse than a coward.   *Letter [1889]*

2   You tell those newspaper people that they may be smart, but I'm smarter. They deal with words. Some folks say that words were made to reveal thoughts. That ain't so. Words were made to conceal thought.
San Francisco Call [1901]

3   I am a whole theater unto myself.
Memoirs and Autobiography, Pandex of the Press
[January 1902]

Henry [Walton] Bibb   1815–1854

4   To be compelled to stand by and see you whip and slash my wife without mercy, when I could afford her no protection, not even by offering myself to suffer the lash in her place, was more than I felt it to be the duty of a slave husband to endure.
Letter to former master W. H. Gatewood [March 23, 1844]

5   Believe me when I say, that no tongue nor pen ever has or can express the horrors of American Slavery.
Narrative of the Life and Adventures of Henry Bibb,
an American Slave, Written by Himself [1849]

6   Slaves were not allowed books, pen, ink, nor paper to improve their minds. But it seems to me now, that I was particularly observing, and apt to retain what came under my observation. But more especially, all that I heard about liberty and freedom to the slaves, I never forgot. Among other good trades I learned the art of running away to perfection. I made a regular business of it, and never gave it up, until I had broken the bands of slavery.
Narrative of the Life and Adventures of Henry Bibb

7   That the slave is a human being, no one can deny. It is his lot to be exposed in common with other men, to the calamities of sickness, death, and the misfortunes incident to life. But unlike other men, he is denied the consolation of struggling against external difficulties, such as destroy the life,

---

[1]From *The Black Abolitionist Papers* [1991], *vol. III*, edited by C. PETER RIPLEY ET AL.
[2]From LYNN M. HUDSON, *The Making of Mammy Pleasant* [2002].

liberty, and happiness of himself and family. A slave may be bought and sold in the market like an ox. He is liable to be sold off to a distant land from his family. He is bound in chains hand and foot; and his sufferings are aggravated a hundred fold, by the terrible thought, that he is not allowed to struggle against misfortune, corporeal punishment, insults and outrages committed upon himself and family; and he is not allowed to help himself, to resist or escape the blow, which he sees impending over him.

Narrative of the Life and Adventures of Henry Bibb

1   My strong attachments to friends and relatives, with all the love of home and birth place which is so natural among the human family, twined about my heart and were hard to break away from. And withal, the fear of being pursued with guns and bloodhounds, and of being killed, or captured and taken to the extreme South, to linger out my days in hopeless bondage on some cotton or sugar plantation, all combined to deter me. But I had counted the cost, and was fully prepared to make the sacrifice. . . . I must forsake friends and neighbors, wife and child, or consent to live and die a slave.   *Narrative of the Life and Adventures of Henry Bibb*

2   My affinity with the Anglo-Saxon race, and even slaveholders, worked well for my escape. But no thanks to them for it. While in their midst they have not only robbed me of my labor and liberty, but they have almost entirely robbed me of my dark complexion.

Narrative of the Life and Adventures of Henry Bibb

3   Reverse the circumstances which lead to these results; cut off from a society its most highly cultivated minds, let education cease, enslave the mass, let toiling, eating and sleeping constitute their only employment; let their whole time be devoted to ministering the wants of the animal portion of their nature, while the moral and intellectual are lost sight of—what a marked change will be observable in a few generations!

To Our Old Masters [1851][1]

4   Colorphobia is a contagious disease. It is more destructive to the mind than to the body. . . . Its symptoms are various. It makes them sing out "darkey, darkey, nigger.". . . It frightens them up from the dining table at public houses, not because of a black man's cooking the dinner or waiting on the table, but because of his sitting down to eat. . . . When they have it bad they will turn up their noses when they get near a colored person, as if they smelt something disagreeable.

Editorial. Voice of the Fugitive [May 21, 1851]

---

[1]From *The Black Abolitionist Papers* [1991], *vol. III*, edited by C. Peter Ripley et al.

Henry Box Brown   1815–?

1   I prayed fervently that he who seeth in secret and knew the inmost desires of my heart, would lend me his aid in bursting my fetters asunder, and in restoring me to the possession of those rights, of which men had robbed me; when the idea suddenly flashed across my mind of shutting myself up in a box, and getting myself conveyed as dry goods to a free state. . . . I was willing to dare even death itself rather than endure any longer the clanking of those galling chains.

Narrative of the Life of Henry Box Brown,
Written by Himself [1851]

2   A number of persons soon collected round the box after it was taken in to the house, but as I did not know what was going on I kept myself quiet. I heard a man say, "Let us rap upon the box and see if he is alive"; and immediately a rap ensued and a voice said, tremblingly, "Is all right within?" to which I replied — "All right." . . . When they heard that I was alive they soon managed to break open the box, and then came my resurrection from the grave of slavery.

Narrative of the Life of Henry Box Brown

Henry Highland Garnet   1815–1882

3   Neither god, nor angels, nor just men, command you to suffer for a single moment. Therefore it is your solemn and imperative duty to use every means, both moral, intellectual, and physical that promise success. . . . All you desire is FREEDOM, and that nothing else will suffice.

Address to the Slaves of the United States of America. Speech
delivered before the National Convention of Colored Citizens,
Buffalo, New York [August 1843]

4   It is impossible, like the children of Israel to make a grand Exodus from the land of bondage. THE PHARAOHS ARE ON BOTH SIDES OF THE BLOOD-RED WATERS!

Address to the Slaves of the United States of America

5   You cannot be more oppressed than you have been — you cannot suffer greater cruelties than you have already. RATHER DIE FREEMEN, THAN LIVE TO BE SLAVES.

Address to the Slaves of the United States of America

6   You are a patient people. You act as though you were made for the special use of these devils. You act as though your daughters were born to pamper the lusts of your masters and overseers. And worse than all, you tamely submit while your lords tear your wives from your embraces, and

defile them before your eyes. In the name of God we ask are you men? Where is the blood of your fathers? Has it all run out of your veins? Awake, awake, millions of voices are calling you! Your dead fathers speak to you from their graves. Heaven, as with a voice of thunder, calls you to arise from this dust.

Address to the Slaves of the United States of America

1   Let your motto be RESISTANCE! RESISTANCE! RESISTANCE! No oppressed people have ever secured their Liberty without resistance. What kind of resistance you had better make, you must decide by the circumstances that surround you, and according to the suggestion of expediency.

Address to the Slaves of the United States of America

2   But slavery attempts to make a man a brute. It treats him as a beast. Its terrible work is not finished until the ruined victim of its lusts and pride and avarice and hatred is reduced so low that with tearful eyes and feeble voice he faintly cries, "I am happy and contented. I love this condition."

A Memorial Discourse [February 12, 1865] [1]

3   The caged lion may cease to roar, and try no longer the strength of the bars of his prison, and lie with his head between his mighty paws.... But is he contented? Does he not instinctively long for the freedom of the forest and the plain? Yes, he is still a lion.

A Memorial Discourse

4   If such are the deeds of mercy wrought by angels, then tell me what works of iniquity there remain for devils to do? This commerce in human beings has been carried on until three hundred thousand have been dragged from their native land in a single year. While this foreign trade has been pursued, who can calculate the enormities and extent of the domestic traffic which has flourished in every slave state, while the whole country has been open to the hunters of men.

A Memorial Discourse

5   Is it right to lay heavy burdens on other men's shoulders which you would not remove with one of your fingers?

A Memorial Discourse

6   We ask no special favors, but we plead for justice. While we scorn unmanly dependence; in the name of God, the universal Father, we demand the right to live and labor and enjoy the fruits of our toil.

A Memorial Discourse

---

[1]Delivered in the hall of the House of Representatives during the debate over the Thirteenth Amendment. From *Masterpieces of Negro Eloquence* [1914], edited by Alice Moore Dunbar.

Moses Roper

c. 1815–1891

1   My resembling my father so very much, and being whiter than the other slaves, caused me to be soon sold to what they call a Negro trader, who took me to the southern states of America, several hundred miles from my mother. As well as I can recollect, I was then about six years old.

A Narrative of the Adventures and Escape of
Moses Roper from American Slavery [1838]

2   When the slave runs away, the master always adopts a more rigorous system of flogging. Having determined from my youth to gain my freedom, I made several attempts, was caught and got a severe flogging of one hundred lashes each time.

A Narrative of the Adventures and Escape of
Moses Roper from American Slavery

3   Just before we started, my grandmother came to bid me farewell; I gave her my hand as well as I could, and she having given me two or three presents, we parted. I had felt enough, far too much for the weak state I was in; but how shall I describe my feelings upon parting with the last relative I ever saw? The reader must judge by what would be his own feelings under similar circumstances.

A Narrative of the Adventures and Escape of Moses
Roper from American Slavery

William Cooper Nell

1816–1874

4   Any person, of ordinary caliber, must know that to become elevated they must cultivate and practice the same traits which are elevating others around them; and if it is (as indeed we all feel it to be) harder for the colored man than others, why then let him work harder, and eventually the summit will be attained.

Report on the 1847 National Convention of
Colored Americans and Their Friends [October 25, 1847][1]

5   So sure as night precedes day, war ends in peace, and winter wakes spring, just so sure will the preserving efforts of Freedom's army be crowned with victory's perennial laurels!

Letter to William Lloyd Garrison
[January 23, 1848][1]

---

[1]From *William Cooper Nell: 19th-Century African American Abolitionist, Historian, Integrationist: Selected Writings: 1832–1874* [2002], edited by DOROTHY PORTER WESLEY and CONSTANCE PORTER UZELAC.

1   Be awake! No man, or body of men have a claim upon your liberty, but yourselves.

North Star [May 5, 1848]

2   Of the services and sufferings of the Colored Soldiers of the Revolution, no attempt has, to our knowledge, been made to preserve a record. They have no historian.

The Colored Patriots of the American Revolution [1855], introduction

Victor Séjour
1817–1874

3   How many times has experience taught him that his good deeds count for nothing, and that he should love neither his wife nor his son; for one day the former will be seduced by the master, and his own flesh and blood will be sold and transported away despite his despair? What then, can you expect him to become? Shall he smash his skull against the paving stones? Shall he kill his torturer? Or do you believe the human heart can find a way to bear such misfortune?

The Mulatto [1837] [Antoine][1]

Samuel Ringgold Ward
1817–1866

4   The real political issue is, not whether the black man's slavery shall be perpetuated, but whether the freedom of any Americans can be permanent.

Autobiography of a Fugitive Negro [1855]

5   Justice, even-handed justice, for the Negro — that which, according to American profession, is every man's birthright — that I claimed, nothing less.

Autobiography of a Fugitive Negro

6   Why should slaves be expected to be better than what they have been made, by the institution which has crushed them? Indeed, though I recollect nothing of slavery, I am every day showing something of my slave origin. It is among my thoughts, my superstitions, my narrow views, my awkwardness of manners. Ah, the infernal impress is upon me, and I fear I shall transmit it to my children, and they to theirs! How deeply seated, how far reaching, a curse it is!

Autobiography of a Fugitive Negro

7   The Negro, especially the American Negro, has no encouragement.... His sky is sunless, starless; deep, black clouds, admitting no ray of light, envelope his horizon. What is there for him in past history? Slavery. What is the condition of the majority of his class? Slavery. What are the signs of the times, so far as the disposition of their oppressors is concerned? Continual slavery. If educated, what position may he acquire? That of a menial.

---

[1]From *The Norton Anthology of African American Literature* [1997], edited by Henry Louis Gates and Nelly Y. McKay. Translated by Phillip Barnard.

What are the opportunities for education? Such only as may be inferred from the rejection of Negroes from most of the halls of learning in the land. What encouragements has he from friends, from the feelings of the mass of the people, from the institutions of his native country? None, absolutely none. *Autobiography of a Fugitive Negro*

Frederick Douglass

1818–1895

1   Every tone [of the songs of the enslaved] was a testimony against slavery, and a prayer to God for deliverance from chains. Slaves sing most when they are most unhappy. The songs of the slave represent the sorrows of his heart; and he is relieved by them, only as an aching heart is relieved by its tears.   *Narrative of the Life of Frederick Douglass [1845], ch. 2*

2   It [learning to read] was a new and special revelation, explaining dark and mysterious things, with which my youthful understanding had struggled, but struggled in vain. I now understood what had been to me a most perplexing difficulty — to wit, the white man's power to enslave the black man. It was a grand achievement, and I prized it highly. From that moment, I understood the pathway from slavery to freedom.
Narrative of the Life of Frederick Douglass, 6

3   You have seen how a man was made a slave; you shall see how a slave was made a man.   *Narrative of the Life of Frederick Douglass, 10*

4   I have found that, to make a contented slave, it is necessary to make a thoughtless one. It is necessary to darken his moral and mental vision, and, as far as possible, to annihilate the power of reason. He must be able to detect no inconsistencies in slavery; he must be made to feel that slavery is right; and he can be brought to that only when he ceases to be a man.
Narrative of the Life of Frederick Douglass, 10

5   Agitate! Agitate! Agitate!
Speech in Dundee, Scotland [March 10, 1846]
(frequent invocation)

6   Every blow of the sledge hammer, wielded by a sable arm, is a powerful blow in support of our cause. Every colored mechanic, is by virtue of circumstances, an elevator of his race. Every house built by black men, is a strong tower against the allied hosts of prejudice.
An Address to the Colored People of the United States
[September 6, 1848]

7   We have to do with the past only as we can make it useful to the present and to the future. To all inspiring motives, to noble deeds which can be gained from the past, we are welcome. But now is the time, the important

time. Your fathers have lived, died. . . . You live and must die, and you must do your work.

Speech at Rochester, New York [July 5, 1852].
The Meaning of the Fourth of July to the Negro

1   America is false to the past, false to the present and, solemnly binds herself to be false to the future.   *Speech at Rochester, New York*

2   O! had I the ability, and could I reach the nation's ear, I would, today, pour out a fiery stream of biting ridicule, blasting reproach, withering sarcasm, and stern rebuke. For it is not light that is needed, but fire; it is not the gentle shower, but thunder. We need the storm, the whirlwind, and the earthquake.   *Speech at Rochester, New York*

3   What, to the American slave, is your Fourth of July? I answer: A day that reveals to him, more than all other days in the year, the gross injustice and cruelty to which he is the constant victim. To him your celebration is a sham.   *Speech at Rochester New York*

4   You profess to believe that "of one blood God made all nations of men to dwell on the face of all the earth" and hath commanded all men, everywhere, to love one another—yet you notoriously hate (and glory in your hatred!) all men whose skins are not colored like your own!
        Speech at Rochester, New York

5   The ground which a colored man occupies in this country is, every inch of it, sternly disputed.

Speech at the American and Foreign Anti-Slavery Society
annual meeting, New York City [May 11, 1853]

6   I say nothing of *father,* for he is shrouded in a mystery I have never been able to penetrate. Slavery does away with fathers, as it does away with families.   *My Bondage and My Freedom [1855], ch. 3*

7   A man who will enslave his own blood, may not be safely relied on for magnanimity.   *My Bondage and My Freedom, 3*

8   Men do not love those who remind them of their sins.
        My Bondage and My Freedom, 3

9   The whole history of the progress of human liberty shows that all concessions yet made to her august claims have been born of earnest struggle. . . . If there is no struggle, there is no progress. Those who profess to favor freedom, and yet deprecate agitation, are men who want crops without plowing up the ground, they want rain without thunder and lightning. They want the ocean without the awful roar of its many waters.

Speech at Canandaigua, New York [August 3, 1857]

1   Power concedes nothing without a demand. It never did and it never will.

Speech at Canandaigua, New York

2   The destiny of the colored American ... is the destiny of America.

Speech at the Emancipation League, Boston [February 12, 1862]

3   The relation subsisting between the white and colored people, of this country, of all other questions is the great, paramount, imperative, and all-commanding question for this age and nation to solve.

Speech at the Church of the Puritans, New York [May 1863]

4   All I ask is give him [the black person] a chance to stand on his own legs! Let him alone! If you see him on his way to school, let him alone, — don't disturb him! If you see him going to the dinner table at a hotel, let him go! If you see him going to the ballot-box, let him alone, — don't disturb him! If you see him going into a workshop, just let him alone, — your interference is doing him a positive injury.

Speech at the American Anti-Slavery Society, Boston [April 1865]

5   Slavery has been fruitful in giving itself names. It has been called "the peculiar institution," "the social system," and the "impediment."... It has been called by a great many names, and it will call itself by yet another name; and you and I and all of us had better wait and see what new form this old monster will assume, in what new skin this old snake will come forth next.

Speech at the American Anti-Slavery Society, Boston [May 10, 1865]

6   Despite of it all, the Negro remains like iron or granite, cool, strong, imperturbable, and cheerful.

Speech on the twenty-first anniversary of emancipation in the District of Columbia, Washington, D.C. [April 1883]

7   Our destiny is largely in our own hands. If we find, we shall have to seek. If we succeed in the race of life, it must be by our own energies, and our own exertions. Others may clear the road, but we must go forward, or be left behind in the race of life.

Speech on the twenty-first anniversary of emancipation in the District of Columbia

8   In all the relations of life and death, we are met by the color line.

Speech at the Convention of Colored Men, Louisville, Kentucky [September 24, 1883]

9   No man can put a chain about the ankle of his fellow man without at last finding the other end fastened about his own neck.

Speech at civil rights mass meeting, Washington, D.C. [October 22, 1883]

1   The life of the nation is secure only while the nation is honest, truthful, and virtuous.

> *Speech on the twenty-third anniversary of emancipation*
> *in the District of Columbia, Washington, D.C.*
> *[April 1885]*

2   Where justice is denied, where poverty is enforced, where ignorance prevails, and where any one class is made to feel that society is in an organized conspiracy to oppress, rob, and degrade them, neither persons nor property will be safe.

> *Speech on the twenty-fourth anniversary of emancipation*
> *in the District of Columbia, Washington, D.C.*
> *[April 1886]*

3   We Negroes love our country. We fought for it. We ask only that we be treated as well as those who fought against it.

> *Speech at the World's Columbian Exposition*
> *[August 25, 1892]*

Ethiop [William J. Wilson]   1818–?

4   The country affords pleasure, the city if nothing else abundant information. If the country gives vigor to the spirits, the city induces many profitable reflections.

> *Letter to Frederick Douglass. Frederick Douglass' Papers*
> *[March 11, 1853]*

5   We despise, we almost hate ourselves and all that favors us. Well may we scoff at black skins and wooly heads, since every model set before us for admiration has pallid face and flaxen head.... A black girl would as soon fondle an imp as a black doll — such is the force of this species of education upon her.   *Letter to Frederick Douglass*

6   Indeed, the question may seem presumptuous, quizzical, ridiculous; but truth is, that these white people themselves, through their Press and Legislative Halls, in their pulpits, and on their Rostrums, so constantly talk of nothing but us black people, and have apparently got so far beyond every thing else, that it would seem that their very instincts regard us in a measure able to settle and make quiet their restlessness, and hence they have actually forced upon us the question.... It has indeed become a serious question with us: What shall we do with the white people?

> *What Shall We Do with the White People.*
> *Anglo-African Magazine [1860]*[1]

---

[1]From *Black on White: Black Writers on What It Means to Be White* [1998], edited by DAVID R. ROEDIGER.

Elizabeth [Hobbs] Keckley

1818–1907

1   A cruel custom deprived me of my liberty, and since I was robbed of my dearest right, I would not have been human had I not rebelled against the robbery.

Behind the Scenes, or Thirty Years a Slave and Four Years
in the White House [1868]

2   The past is a mirror that reflects the chief incidents of my life. To surrender it is to surrender the greatest part of my existence.

Behind the Scenes, or Thirty Years a Slave and Four Years
in the White House

3   Friends are a recompense for all the woes of the darkest pages of life.

Behind the Scenes, or Thirty Years a Slave and Four Years
in the White House

Alexander Crummell

1819–1898

4   Oppression not only makes a wise man mad, it robs him also of his self-respect. And this is our loss; but having emerged from slavery, it is our duty to cast off its grave-clothes and resist its deadly influences.

To Africa. A Letter [1861]

5   When colored men question the duty of interest in Africa because they are not Africans, I beg to remind them of the kindred duty of self-respect.... I remark that the abject state of Africa is a most real and touching appeal to any heart for sympathy and aid. It is an appeal, however, which comes with a double force to every civilized man who has Negro blood flowing in his veins.

To Africa. A Letter

6   Among the various evils to which society has been subjected, none have been more general or more deadly than slavery. No portion of the globe has been exempt from this curse.

The Future of Africa.
The Negro Race Is Not Under a Curse

Paul Bogle

c. 1820–1865

7   Skin for skin,[1] the iron bars is now broken in this parish, the white people send a proclamation to the Governor to make war against us,... we all must put our shoulder to the wheels and pull together.... Every one of you must leave your house, take your guns, who don't have guns, take your cutlasses down at once!...Blow your shells, roll your drums, house

---

[1]Skin for skin, yea, all that a man hath will he give for his life. — *The Book of Job 2:4*

to house take out every man; . . . War is at us, my black skins. War is at hand from today to tomorrow. Every black man must turn out at once, for the oppression is too great. The white people are now cleaning up they guns for us, which we must prepare to meet them to. Cheer men, cheer in the heart we looking for you a part of the night before day break.

Letter found in a house after the Morant Bay Rebellion
[October 1865][1]

Ann Plato

1820–?

1   Our whole life is often a life of suffering. We can not engage in business, or dissipate ourselves in pleasure and riot as irreligious men too often do: We must bear our sorrows in silence, unknown and unpitied. We must often put on a face of serenity and cheerfulness when our hearts are torn with anguish, or sinking in despair.

Essays. Including Biographies and Miscellaneous Pieces in
Prose and Poetry [c. 1841]. Religion

2   A society or people are always considered as advancing, when they are found paying proper respect to education. The observer will find them erecting buildings for the establishment of schools, in various sections of their country, on different systems, where their children many at an early age commence learning, and having their habits fixed for higher attainments.   *Essays. Education*

3   It is owing to the preservation of books, that we are led to embrace their contents. . . . They may sleep for a while and be neglected; but whenever the desire of information springs up in the human breast, there they are with mild wisdom ready to instruct and please us.

Essays. Education

4   In proportion to the education of a nation, it is rich and powerful.

Essays. Education

5   Education is a system which the bravest men have followed.

Essays. Education

6   Our whole life is but one great school; from the cradle to the grave we are all learners; nor will our education be finished until we die.

Essays. Education

7   Then when in silence thou doest walk,

Nor being round with whom to talk;

---

[1]From Don Robotham, *The "Notorious Riot": The Socio-Economic and Political Bases of Paul Bogle's Revolt* [1981].

When thou art on the mighty deep,
And do in quiet action sleep;
If we no more on earth do meet,
Forget me not.

Essays. Forget Me Not

1   I begged him, father do not go,
For when you left me last,
You said you would not go again:
My childish joys are past.

Essays. Daughter's Inquiry

William Still   1821–1902

2   I think abundant evidence may be found . . . to convince the most prejudiced against the colored man, that he is by no means so sadly degraded
and miserably poor as the public have generally been led to suppose from all
that has been said of him.
Letter to the editor, North American and United States Gazette
[August 30, 1859]

3   Nobody insults a colored man or woman in the Tax Receiver's Office,
however full it may be.
A Brief Narrative of the Struggle for the Rights of the Colored
People of Philadelphia in the City Railway Cars and a Defense
of William Still [April 8, 1867]

4   Those who come after us seeking for information in regard to the existence, atrocity, struggles and destruction of Slavery, will have no trouble in
finding this hydra-headed monster ruling and tyrannizing over Church and
State, North and South, white and black, without let or hindrance for at
least several generations. Nor will posterity have any difficulty in finding the
deeds of the brave and invincible opposers of Slavery, who in the language
of William Lloyd Garrison declared without concealment and without compromise: "I am earnest, I will not equivocate — I will not excuse — I will not
retreat a single inch and I will be heard."
The Underground Railroad: A Record of Facts, Authentic
Narratives, Letters, etc. [1871], preface

5   The slave and his particular friends could only meet in private to
transact the business of the Underground Railroad. All others were outsiders. The right hand was not to know what the left hand was doing. Stock-
holders did not expect any dividends nor did they require special reports to
be published. Indeed prudence often dictated that even the recipient of our

favor should not know the names of their helpers, and vice versa they did not desire to know them.   *The Underground Railroad, preface*

Harriet Tubman   c. 1822–1913

1   I grew up like a neglected weed — ignorant of liberty, having no experience of it.

From BENJAMIN DREW, *A North-side View of Slavery* [1856]

2   I had reasoned this out in my mind; there was one of two things I had a right to, liberty or death; if I could not have one, I would have the other; for no man should take me alive.

To her biographer Sarah H. Bradford [c. 1868]

3   I looked at my hands to see if I was the same person now I was free. There was such a glory over everything. . . . I had crossed the line of which I had so long been dreaming.[1]   *To her biographer Sarah H. Bradford*

4   I can say what most conductors can't say — I never run my train off the track and I never lost a passenger.

From SARAH H. BRADFORD, *Harriet, the Moses of Her People [1901]*

5   If you are tired, keep going; if you are scared, keep going; if you are hungry, keep going; if you want to taste freedom, keep going.   *Attributed*

Mary Ann Shadd Carey   1823–1893

6   We have been holding conventions for years — have been assembling together and whining over our difficulties and afflictions, passing resolutions on resolutions to any extent; but it does really seem that we have made but little progress, considering our resolves. We have put forth few practical efforts to an end. I, as one of the people, see no need for distinctive meetings, if we do not do something. We should do more, and talk less.

Letter to Frederick Douglass. North Star [January 25, 1849][2]

7   *[On teaching:]* The field is very important, but the work is incessant.

Letter [October 24, 1852]

8   Self-reliance Is the Fine Road to Independence.

Slogan for the Provincial Freeman

9   Were it not for the monster of slavery, we would have a common destiny here — in the land of our birth.   *Speech [April 6, 1858][3]*

---

[1] On her first escape from slavery [1845].

[2] From *The Black Abolitionist Papers* [1985], *vol. II: Canada 1830–1865*, edited by C. PETER RIPLEY ET AL.

[3] From JANE RHODES, *Mary Ann Shadd Cary* [1998].

William Craft

1824–1900

and

Ellen Craft

1826–1891

1   It is true, our condition as slaves was not by any means the worst;
but the mere idea that we were held as chattels, and deprived of all legal
rights—the thought that we had to give up our hard earnings to a tyrant
to enable him to live in idleness and luxury—the thought that we could not
call the bones and sinews that God gave us our own: but above all, the fact
that another man had the power to tear from our cradle the newborn babe
and sell it in the shambles like a brute, and then scourge us if we dared to lift
a finger to save it from such a fate, haunted us for years.

Running a Thousand Miles for Freedom [1860]

Alexandre Dumas the Younger

1824–1895

2   Business? It's quite simple. It's other people's money.
La Question d'Argent (The Question of Money) [1857], act II, sc. vii

3   All generalizations are dangerous, even this one.

Attributed

Frances Ellen Watkins Harper

1825–1911

4   Heard you that shriek? It rose
       So wildly on the air,
It seemed as if a burden'd heart
       Was breaking in despair.
Poems on Miscellaneous Subjects [1854].[1] *The Slave Mother*

5   Oh! how shall I speak of my proud country's shame
Of the stains on her glory, how give them their name?
How say that her banner in mockery waves—
Her star-spangled banner—o'er millions of slaves?
Poems on Miscellaneous Subjects. Eliza Harris

6   On my people's blighted bosom
       Mountain weights of sorrow lay,
Stop not now to ask the question
       Who shall roll the stone away?
Be Active. Frederick Douglass' Papers
[January 11, 1856][1]

---

[1]From *Complete Poems of Frances E. Harper* [1988], edited by MAYEMMA GRAHAM.

1   I have seen the ocean singing its wild chorus of sounding waves, and ecstasy has thrilled upon the living chords of my heart. I have since then seen the rainbow-crowned Niagara ... chanting the choral hymn of Omnipotence, girdled with grandeur, and robed with glory; but none of these things have melted me as the first sight of Free Land.

Letter [September 12, 1856][1]

2   Our heart may grow more hopeful for humanity when it sees the sublime sacrifice it is about to receive from his hands. Not in vain has your dear husband periled all, if the martyrdom of one hero is worth more than the life of a million cowards.

Letter to John Brown's widow [November 14, 1859][1]

3   Our fault in a land of Bibles and churches, of baptisms and prayers, is that in our veins flows the blood of an outcast race; a race oppressed by power and proscribed by prejudice, a race cradled in wrong and nurtured in oppression.

An Appeal to Christians Throughout the World
[January 1860][2]

4   Some of the exiles have left children, who were very dear but to stay with them was to involve ourselves in a lifetime of slavery. Some left dear companions; they were enslaved and we had no other alternative than slavery or exile. We were weak, our oppressors were strong. We were a feeble, scattered people; they, being powerful, placed before us slavery or banishment. We chose the latter. Poverty, trials, and all the cares incident to a life of freedom are better, far better than slavery.

An Appeal to Christians Throughout the World

5   What hath God wrought! ... In the crucible of disaster and defeat God has stirred the nation, and permitted no permanent victory to crown her banners while she kept her hand upon the trembling slave and held him back from freedom.

Speech in response to Emancipation Proclamation
[1863][1]

6   From the crimson sods of war springs the white flower of freedom, and songs of deliverance mingle with the crash and roar of war. The shadow of the American army becomes a covert for the slave, and beneath

---

[1]From *The Underground Rail Road: A Record of Facts, Authentic Narratives, Letters, &c: Narrating the Hardships, Hair-breadth Escapes, and Death Struggles of the Slaves in Their Efforts for Freedom* [1872], edited by WILLIAM STILL.

[2]From *The Black Abolitionist Papers* [1992], vol. V, edited by C. PETER RIPLEY ET AL.

the American Eagle he grasps the key of knowledge and is lifted to a higher destiny.

Letter [1865][1]

1   Sorrow treads on the footsteps of the nation's joy.... Let the whole nation resolve that the whole virus shall be eliminated from its body; that in the future slavery shall only be remembered as a thing of the past that shall never have the faintest hope of a resurrection.

Letter regarding the assassination of
Abraham Lincoln [1865][1]

2   We are all bound up together in one great bundle of humanity, and society cannot trample on the weakest and feeblest of its members without receiving the curse in its own soul.

We Are All Bound Up Together. Speech at the Woman's
Rights Convention, New York [May 1866][2]

3   You white women speak here of rights. I speak of wrongs. I as a colored woman have had in this country an education which has made me feel as if I were in the situation of Ishmael, my hands against every man, and every man's hand against me.

We Are All Bound Up Together

4   Men grow strong in action, but in solitude
Their thoughts are ripened.

Moses: A Story of the Nile [1869],[3] ch. 4

5   Now is the time for our women to begin to try to lift up their heads and plant roots of progress under the hearthstone.

Lecture to Freedwomen [March 29, 1870][3]

6   After all whether they encourage or discourage me, I belong to this race, and when it is down I belong to a down race; when it is up I belong to a risen race.

Letter [1870][1]

7   A landless people must be dependent upon the landed people.

Lecture [1871][1]

8   Make me a grave where'er you will,
In a lovely plain, or a lofty hill;

---

[1]From *The Underground Rail Road: A Record of Facts, Authentic Narratives, Letters, &c: Narrating the Hardships, Hair-breadth Escapes, and Death Struggles of the Slaves in Their Efforts for Freedom* [1872], edited by WILLIAM STILL.

[2]From *A Brighter Coming Day* [1990], edited by FRANCES SMITH FOSTER.

[3]From *Complete Poems of Frances E. Harper* [1988], edited by MAYEMMA GRAHAM.

Make it among earth's humblest graves,
But not in a land where men are slaves.

Bury Me in a Free Land [1871][1]

1   But we soon got used to freedom,
         Though the way at first was rough;
      But we weathered through the tempest,
         For slavery made us tough.

Sketches of a Southern Life [1872].[1] *Aunt Chloe.*
The Deliverance

2   The most important question before us colored people is not simply
what the Democratic party may do against us or the Republican party do for
us; but what are we going to do for ourselves?

The Great Problem to Be Solved. Lecture, Philadelphia
[April 14, 1875][2]

3   Apparent failure may hold in its rough shell the germs of a success that
will blossom in time, and bear fruit throughout eternity.

The Great Problem to Be Solved

4   What's the use of praying for a thing, if when it comes, you won't
take it?   *Iola Leroy [1893] [Robert]*

5   I am not despondent to the future of my people; there's too much
elasticity in their spirits, too much hope in their hearts, to be crushed out
by unreasoning malice.

Iola Leroy [Iola]

6   Slavery is dead, but the spirit which animated it still lives.

Iola Leroy [Iola]

7   It is easier to outgrow the dishonor of crime than the disabilities of
color.   *Iola Leroy [Iola]*

8   Let me make the songs for the people,
         Songs for the old and young;
      Songs to stir like a battle-cry
         Wherever they are sung.

Songs for the People [1896]

9   Have ye not, oh, my favored sisters,
         Just a plea, a prayer or a tear,

---

[1]From *Complete Poems of Frances E. Harper* [1988], edited by MAYEMMA GRAHAM.
[2]From *A Brighter Coming Day* [1990], edited by FRANCES SMITH FOSTER.

For mothers who dwell 'neath the shadows
Of agony, hatred and fear?

An Appeal to My Countrywomen [1896][1]

Harriet E. Wilson   1825–1900

1   Lonely Mag Smith! See her as she walks with downcast eyes and heavy heart. It was not always thus. She had a loving, trusting heart.

Our Nig [1859], opening lines

2   Expert with the needle, Frado soon equaled her instructress; and she sought also to teach her the value of useful books; and while one read aloud to the other of deeds historic and names renowned, Frado experienced a new impulse. She felt herself capable of elevation; she felt that this book information supplied an undefined dissatisfaction she had long felt, but could not express.

Our Nig, ch. 11

3   Enough has been unrolled to demand your sympathy and aid.

Our Nig, 12

Edward Mitchell Bannister   1826–1901

4   All that I would do I cannot, that is all I would say in Art, simply for the want of proper training. With God's help, however, I hope to be able to deliver the messages instructed to me.

Letter to George W. Whitaker [1887][2]

5   He becomes the interpreter of the infinite, subtle qualities of the spiritual idea centering in all created things, expounding for us the laws of beauty...revealing to us glimpses of the absolute idea of perfect harmony.

On the role of the artist [1886][3]

James Madison Bell   1826–1902

6   No longer 'neath the weight of years—
No longer merged in hopeless fears—
Is now that good time, long delayed,
When right, not might, shall all pervade.

---

[1]From *Complete Poems of Frances E. Harper* [1988], edited by MAYEMMA GRAHAM.

[2]From *Edward Mitchell Bannister, 1828–1901: Research Chronology and Exhibition Record* [1992], edited by JUANITA MARIE HOLLAND.

[3]From ROMARE BEARDEN and HARRY HENDERSON, *A History of African-American Artists* [1993].

Drive hence despair — no longer doubt,
Since friends within and foes without
Their might and main conjointly blend
To reach the same great, glorious end —
The sweeping from this favored land
The last foul chain and slavish brand.

The Day and the War [1864]

1   The wrong cannot forever last —
        The right is mightier than the chain.

The Progress of Liberty [1866]

2   There is no right a freeman has
        So purely sacred as his choice.

The Triumph of Liberty [1870]

3   Deep in the unrecorded past,
        There was an age of darkness vast,
    And boundless as the realms of space.
        An age that held, in its embrace
    And in an embryotic state,
    All worlds and systems, small and great.
            The Poetical Works of James Madison Bell [1901].
            Creation Light

4   Shall they, because their skins are dark,
        Forever wear the galling chain?
    Has hope for them no cheering spark
        That wrong will one day cease to reign?
            The Poetical Works of James Madison Bell.
            The Black Man's Wrongs

5   For O, there is in earth or Heaven
        No sweeter note or purer key
    To mortals known, or angels given,
        Than peerless, chainless LIBERTY!
            The Poetical Works of James Madison Bell.
            The Dawn of Freedom

Hiram [Rhoades] Revels   1827–1901

6   The responsibilities of being the exponent of such a constituency as I
    have the honor to represent are fully appreciated by me.... That feeling
    prompts me now to lift my voice for the first time in this council chamber

of the nation; and I stand today on this floor to appeal for protection from the strong arm of the government for her loyal children, irrespective of color and race.

First speech before United States Senate [March 16, 1870][1]

1   I am in favor of removing the disabilities of those upon whom they are imposed in the South just as fast as they give evidence of having become loyal men and of being loyal....I am in favor of removing his disabilities; and if you can find one hundred men that the same is true of I am in favor of removing their disabilities. If you can find a whole State that this is true of I am in favor of removing the disabilities of all its people.

Speech before United States Senate [May 17, 1870][1]

Kale

c. 1828–?

2   We want you to ask the court what we have done wrong. What for Americans keep us in prison. Some people say Mendi people crazy, Mendi people dolt because we no talk America language. Merica people no talk Mendi language; Merica people dolt?

Letter to John Quincy Adams, on being held in
Amistad *mutiny trial [January 4, 1841]*[2]

John Mercer Langston

1829–1897

3   The history of the emancipated classes of the world, whether they have been serfs or slaves, abundantly sustains the assertion that in most cases in which emancipation has occurred, and the emancipated class has been left under the control of the former master class, in the midst of the old associations of its slavery, upon the plantations or estates where it was wont to labor, such class thus situated and thus controlled does not and cannot rise until it has by some means freed itself from the dependence connected with such condition.

Freedom and Citizenship [1883]

Lucy A[nn] Delaney

c. 1830–c. 1890

4   Slavery! cursed slavery! what crimes has it invoked! and, oh! what retribution has a righteous God visited upon these traders in human flesh! The rivers of tears shed by us helpless ones, in captivity, were turned to lakes

---

[1]From Elizabeth Lawson, *The Gentleman from Mississippi* [1960].

[2]From *Slave Testimony* [1977], edited by W. John Blassingame. Originally appeared in *African Repository* [December 1841], *vol. XVII.*

of blood! How often have we cried in our anguish, "Oh! Lord, how long, how long?"

> *From the Darkness Cometh the Light, or,*
> *Struggles for Freedom [1890s]*

1   The uses of adversity is a worn theme, and in it there is much of weak cant, but when it is considered how much of sacrifice the poverty-stricken must bear in order to procure the slightest gratification, should it not impress the thinking mind with amazement, how much of fortitude and patience the honest poor display in the exercise of self-denial! Oh! ye prosperous! prate of the uses of adversity as poetically as you please, we who are obliged to learn of them by bitter experience would greatly prefer a change of surroundings.

> *From the Darkness Cometh the Light, or,*
> *Struggles for Freedom*

2   There are abounding in public and private libraries of all sorts, lives of people which fill our minds with amazement, admiration, sympathy, and indeed with as many feelings as there are people.

> *From the Darkness Cometh the Light, or,*
> *Struggles for Freedom*

E[dward] W[ilmont] Blyden   1832–1912

3   Let us teach our children from their infancy — for they need to be taught — that no curse except that which every day follows the impenitent, hangs upon us; that it is the force of circumstances, induced, as we have endeavored to show, by our iniquities, that keep us down; and that we have as much right as any other people to strive to rise to the very zenith of national glory.   *A Vindication of the African Race [1857]*[1]

4   The regeneration of Africa will doubtless be the final transforming power of her downtrodden descendants. And as they rise in the lands of their exile, by education and culture, to the threshold of a higher life — as their minds are strengthened and expanded by the wide and glorious prospects which literature and science open before them — they will become less pachydermatous than they now are; they will feel the pressure of influences which they now regard as natural and normal. The avenues they now traverse with ease will become too narrow for them. . . . Shaking themselves free from the traditions and associations of the past, they will find that it is one thing to enjoy the hospitalities of a mansion erected by and for others, and another to occupy a dwelling, be it ever so humble, constructed by

---

[1]From *Black Spokesman: Selected Published Writings of E. W. Blyden* [1971], edited by HOLLIS R. LYNCH.

oneself for one's own purposes, and adapted to one's tastes.... En Afrique, soyouz Africains!

Africa for the African. African Repository,
vol. XLVIII [January 1872]

1   The African spirit is a spirit of service. I do not mean in a degrading sense, but in the highest sense, in which the Son of man came not to be ministered unto but to minister — the sense He took upon Himself the form of a servant — slave in the original. The spirit of service in the black man is born of his spiritual genius.

Letter to Booker T. Washington. New York Age
[January 24, 1895][1]

John Sella Martin   1832–1876

2   I hold that that is a false logic which talks about good slaveholders.... It is folly for us to talk about the slaveholders being kind. Cruelty is part and parcel of the system. If slavery is right at all, then all its terrors and horrors, — the whip, the manacle, the thumbscrew, the paddle, the stake, the gibbet — are right also; if it is not right, then all these are wrong.

Speech on the death of John Brown. The Liberator
[December 9, 1859]

3   Certainly, great injustice is done to a people who are excluded on account of a complexion which they did not give themselves.

Letter to the Editors of the Saturday Evening Post.
The Liberator [May 5, 1865][2]

4   The simple fact is this: prejudice and proscription in free society during the time of slavery kept the white people away from the Negroes, so that they knew, and still know, but little of colored people; and the slaveholder, though knowing better, found it in his interest to keep his knowledge to himself.

Speech before the Paris Anti-Slavery Conference
[August, 1867][3]

Rebecca Crumpler   1833–1895

5   Selfish prudence is too often allowed to come between duty and human life.   *A Book of Medical Discourses in Two Parts [1883]*

---

[1] From *Black Spokesman: Selected Published Writings of E. W. Blyden* [1971], edited by HOLLIS R. LYNCH.
[2] The *Evening Post* refused to print the original letter, dated April 24, 1865. From *The Black Abolitionist Papers* [1991], *vol. VIII*, edited by C. PETER RIPLEY and MICHAEL F. HEMBREE.
[3] From PATRICIA W. ROMERO, *I Too Am America: Documents from 1619 to the Present* [1968].

1   Our women work hard, seemingly, and many of them against a heavy tide; nor does there ever seem to be an end to their toils. Especially do some of the laboring women of my race appear to work under heavy disadvantages; if the family is small, they are never through with their work; if it is large, there is a double excuse for having no time to rest; yet many real needful things are left undone.... The laboring men of my race, generally speaking, take much better care of the horses entrusted to their care than they do of their own health.   *A Book of Medical Discourses in Two Parts*

Anthony Burns   1834–1862

2   I began to hear about a North, and to feel the necessity for freedom of soul and body. I heard of a North where men of my color could live without any man daring to say to them, "You are my property"; and I determined by the blessing of God, one day to find my way there. My inclination grew on me, and I found my way to Boston.
Speech to black church who bought his freedom.
The Liberator [March 9, 1855]

3   [On being taken as a fugitive slave:] I was taken down, with the bracelets on my wrists — not such as you wear, ladies, of gold and silver — but iron and steel, that wore into the bone.
Speech to black church who bought his freedom. The Liberator

Henry McNeal Turner[1]   1834–1915

4   I hold that I am a member of this body. Therefore, sir, I shall neither fawn nor cringe before any party, nor stoop to beg them for my rights.
Speech to the Georgia Legislature after being denied a seat.
[September 3, 1868]

5   God has weaved and tissued variety and versatility throughout the boundless space of His creation. Because God saw fit to make some red, and some white, and some black, and some brown, are we to sit here in judgment upon what God has seen fit to do?
Speech to the Georgia Legislature

6   There is no instance mentioned in history where an enslaved people of an alien race rose to respectability upon the same territory of their enslavement and in the presence of their enslavers, without losing their identity or individuality by amalgamation.
African Repository, vols. 51–53 [July 1876]

---

[1]From *Respect Black: The Writings and Speeches of Henry McNeal Turner* [1971], edited by EDWIN S. REDKEY.

1   I know we are Americans to all intents and purposes. We are born here, raised here, fought, bled and died here, and have a thousand times more right here than hundreds of thousands of those who help to snub, proscribe and persecute us, and that is one of the reasons I almost despise the land of my birth. *Letter [February 22, 1883]*

2   Neither the Republican nor Democratic party can do for the colored race what they can do for themselves. Respect Black.

Remarks at symposium [1884]

3   Every race of people since time began who have attempted to describe their God by words, or by paintings, or by carvings, or by any other form or figure, have conveyed the idea that the God who made them and shaped their destinies was symbolized in themselves.... We do not believe that there is any hope for a race of people who do not believe that they look like God. *God Is a Negro. The Voice of Missions [February 1898]*

4   I used to love what I thought was the grand old flag, and sing with ecstasy about the Stars and Stripes, but to the Negro in this country the American flag is a dirty and contemptible rag.

The American Flag. The Atlanta Constitution
[February 16, 1906]

5   It was indeed a time of times, and a half time, nothing like it will ever be seen again in this life. Our entrance into Heaven itself will only form a counterpart.

Recalling Emancipation Day. The Negro in Slavery,
War and Peace [1913]

Hannah Crafts   c. 1837–?

6   In most cases there is something horrible in the idea of being bought and sold; it sent a thrill to my heart, a shiver through my brain. For a moment I felt dizzy, but a moment only. I had experienced too much trouble and anxiety to be overwhelmed by this. Then, too, I thought that though my perishable body was at their disposal, my soul was beyond their reach.

[c. 1850s]. From The Bondwoman's Narrative by Hannah
Crafts [2002], edited by HENRY LOUIS GATES, JR.

Charlotte Forten Grimké   1837–1914

7   I wonder that every colored person is not a misanthrope. Surely we have everything to make us hate mankind.

[September 12, 1855]. From Journals of Charlotte Forten
Grimké [1988], edited by BRENDA STEVENSON

1   But oh, how inexpressibly bitter and agonizing it is to feel oneself an outcast from the rest of mankind, as we are in this country! To me it is dreadful, dreadful.... Oh, that I could do much towards bettering our condition. I will do all, all the very little that lies in my power, while life and strength last!   *[January 17, 1857]. From Journals of Charlotte Forten Grimké*

2   Let me not forget again that I came not here for friendly sympathy or for anything else but to work, and to work hard. Let me do that faithfully and well.

St. Helena Island [December 14, 1862].
From Journals of Charlotte Forten Grimké

3   The long, dark night of the Past, with all its sorrows and its fears, was forgotten; and for the Future—the eyes of these freed children see no clouds in it. It is full of sunlight, they think, and they trust in it, perfectly.

Life on the Sea Islands. The Atlantic Monthly [June 1864]

4   *[On teaching ex-slaves:]* I shall dwell again among "mine own people." I shall gather my scholars about me, and see smiles of greeting break over their dusky faces. My heart sings a song of thanksgiving, at the thought that even I am permitted to do something for a long-abused race.

Life on the Sea Islands

P[inckney] B[enton] S[tewart] Pinchback[1]   1837–1921

5   The customs and habits contacted during 241 odd years of slavery and oppression cannot pass away in a day. Nor will it ever pass away unless we seek that information which will qualify us for a higher station. No nation ever born has, or ever can, obtain the respect and confidence of other nations of the earth until it has made some efforts on its own behalf.

Speech [c. 1866]

6   Wealth is the great lever that moves the earth.   *Speech [c. 1866]*

7   They say it is a pity that the harmonious relations heretofore existing between the slave and the master (some go so far to say the happy relations) should be disturbed. I need not dwell long upon that subject as all of us know how happy we have been. I dare not refer to the many causes that should have made us happy lest I slip up, indeed a feeling of hatred that would demand blood.   *Speech [c. 1866]*

8   Sir, we are told do not legislate on this subject; time will bring it about. Give the people time to get over their prejudices.... If left to time the time will never come. Unless this matter is regulated by law, we will not only fail

---

[1]From JAMES HASKINS, *Pinckney Benton Stewart Pinchback* [1973].

to have these privileges, but Sir, we may look to have all of our rights, one by one or in fell swoop, taken away from us.

Speech introducing civil rights bill to Louisiana Senate
[January 1869]

1 I am infamous because I cannot be frightened nor coaxed into supporting the Democracy, I am infamous because from the very day the constitutional convention met in this city, I have championed the cause of the down-trodden colored people. From that day to this I have not failed, whenever the opportunity presented itself, to cast my vote and raise my voice in behalf of the class I represent. I have stood firm at my post of duty. *Speech to United States Senate [1872]*

2 That this great act was a Godsend and an immeasurable blessing to the colored race, I admit, but I declare in the same breath that it was dictated and performed more in the interest of the white people of the North and to aid them in conquering the rebellion than from love or a disposition to help the Negro. *On the Emancipation Proclamation [1880]*[1]

3 A large number of white people feel just as sad as we do, but unfortunately for them, they dare not come out and express their opinion. They are ground down in a slavery worse than ours. They are slaves to a mistaken public opinion. *On the Colfax, Louisiana, Massacre [1873]*

Robert Smalls   1839–1915

4 Some morning you may wake up to find that the bone and sinew of your country is gone.... I tell you the Negro is the bone and sinew of your country and you cannot do without him.

Speech. South Carolina Constitutional Convention [October 27, 1895]

5 My race needs no special defense, for the past history of them in this country proves them to be the equal of any people anywhere. All they need is an equal chance in the battle of life. *Speech [November 1, 1895]*[2]

Cudjo Lewis[3]   c. 1840–1935

6 After dey free us, you understand me, we so glad, we make de drum and beat it lak in de Affica soil. *Interview with Zora Neale Hurston [1928]*[4]

---

[1]From Josh Gottheimer, *Ripples of Hope* [2003].

[2]From Okon Edet Uya, *From Slavery to Public Service: Robert Smalls 1839–1915* [1971].

[3]In 1860 Lewis was one of 110 enslaved Africans aboard the *Clotilda*, the last slave ship to the United States. At his death he was the longest-living survivor of that journey.

[4]Lewis's words were used as the theme of the United Nations International Day of Remembrance of the Victims of Slavery and the Transatlantic Slave Trade [March 25, 2009].

Blanche Kelso Bruce   1841–1898

1   We simply demand the practical recognition of the rights given us in the Constitution, and laws, and ask from our white fellow citizens only the consideration and fairness that we so willingly extend to them.

Speech to United States Senate [March 31, 1876]

2   I have confidence, not only in my country and her institutions, but in the capacity and destiny of my people.

Speech to United States Senate

3   We are determined that the great government that gave us liberty and rendered its gift valuable by giving us the ballot shall not find us wanting in a sufficient response to any demand that humanity or patriotism may make upon us; and we ask such action as will not only protect us in the enjoyment of our constitutional rights, but will preserve the integrity of our republican institutions.

Speech to United States Senate

Hallie Q[uinn] Brown   c. 1845–1949

4   It is the cultivation of our own natures that is aimed at and not the imitation of the nature of another. The powers of our own mind are to be drawn out.

Bits and Odds [1880]

5   It is our anxious desire to preserve for future reference an account of these women, their life and character and what they accomplished under the most trying and adverse circumstances, — some of whom passed scatheless through fires of tribulation, only to emerge the purer and stronger, — some who received their commission even at the furnace door, the one moment thinking their all was lost forever, the next in secure consciousness of the Everlasting Arms.

Homespun Heroines and Other Women of Distinction [1926], introduction

Edmonia Lewis   c. 1845–c. 1911

6   Some praise me because I am a colored girl, and I don't want that kind of praise. I had rather you would point out my defects, for that will teach me something.

Interview by Lydia Maria Child. The Liberator [February 19, 1864][1]

---

[1]From WILLIAM LOREN KATZ, *The Black West* [2005].

John R[oy] Lynch

1847–1939

1   Mr. Speaker, if this unjust discrimination is to be longer tolerated by the American people, which I do not, cannot, and will not believe until I am forced to do so, then I can only say with sorrow and regret that our boasted civilization is a fraud; our republican institutions a failure; our social system a disgrace; and our religion a complete hypocrisy. But I have an abiding confidence ... in the patriotism of this people, in their devotion to the cause of human rights, and in the stability of our republican institutions. I hope that I will not be deceived. I love the land that gave me birth; I love the Stars and Stripes. This country is where I intend to live, where I expect to die.

Speech to the United States House of Representatives [1867][1]

Louis H[oward] Latimer

1848–1928

2   *[On electric light:]* Like the light of the sun, it beautifies all things on which it shines, and is no less welcome in the palace than in the humblest home.   *Incandescent Electric Lighting [1890]*

Susie King Taylor

1848–1912

3   It seems strange how our aversion to seeing suffering is overcome in war, — how we are able to see the most sickening sights, such as men with their limbs blown off and mangled by the deadly shells, without a shudder; and instead of turning away, how we hurry to assist in alleviating their pain, bind up their wounds, and press the cool water to their parched lips, with feelings only of sympathy and pity.

Reminiscences of My Life in Camp [1902][2]

4   I wonder if our white fellow men realize the true sense or meaning of brotherhood? For two hundred years we had toiled for them; the war of 1861 came and was ended, and we thought our race was forever freed from bondage, and that the two races could live in unity with each other, but when we read almost every day of what is being done to my race by some whites in the South, I sometimes ask, "Was the war in vain? Has it brought freedom, in the full sense of the word, or has it not made our condition more hopeless?"

Reminiscences of My Life in Camp

---

[1]From PATRICIA W. ROMERO, *I Too Am America: Documents from 1619 to the Present* [1968].
[2]New York: The Digital Schomburg, The New York Public Library.

1   Justice we ask, — to be citizens of these United States, where so many of our people have shed their blood with their white comrades, that the stars and stripes should never be polluted.

Reminiscences of My Life in Camp

George Washington Williams   1849–1891

2   I have tracked my bleeding countrymen through the widely scattered documents of American history; I have listened to their groans, their clanking chains, and melting prayers, until the woes of a race and the agonies of centuries seem to crowd upon my soul as a bitter reality. Many pages of this history have been blistered with my tears; and, although having lived but a little more than a generation, my mind feels as it were cycles old.

A History of the Negro Race in America [1883], vol. II, introduction

Francis J[ames] Grimké   1850–1937

3   There are enemies ever about us and are ever plotting our ruin — enemies within the race and without it. If we assume that all is well, that there is nothing to fear, and so relax our vigilance, so cease to be watchful, we need not be surprised if our enemies get the better of us, if we are worsted in the conflict.

Equality of Rights for All Citizens Black and White Alike [March 7, 1889][1]

4   If we are ever to be free from invidious distinction in this country, based upon race, color, previous condition, we have got to be alive, wide-awake to our own interest. If we are not, we have no right to expect others to be; we have no right to expect anything but failure, but defeat. And we deserve defeat if ours is the spirit of indifference, of unconcern. We are not going to secure our rights in this land without a struggle.

Equality of Rights for All Citizens Black and White Alike

5   A program of silence on the part of the race is a fool's program. . . . A race that sits quietly down and rests in sweet content in the midst of the wrongs from which it is suffering, is not worth contending for, is not worth saving. . . . If justice sleeps in this land, let it not be because we have helped to lull it to sleep by our silence and our indifference; let it not be from lack of effort on our part to arouse it from its slumbers.

Equality of Rights for All Citizens Black and White Alike

---

[1]From *Masterpieces of Negro Eloquence* [1914], edited by ALICE MOORE DUNBAR.

1   The black race is not a race of criminals. . . . Whenever crimes are committed by Negroes, especially crimes of a glaring nature, a sense of shame, of regret is felt by the better elements of the race; not only because of the crime itself, but also because of its tendency to discredit the race, and to increase the already unfavorable impression which so many have of it.

Lynching: Its Causes: The Crimes of the Negro.
Sermon [June 18, 1899][1]

2   If the time ever comes when the Negro himself acquiesces in that condition of things then his fate is sealed, and ought to be sealed. Such a race is not fit to be free. . . . The Negro is an American citizen and he will never be eliminated as a political factor with his consent. He has been terrorized and kept from the polls by bloody ruffians; but he has never felt that it was right; has never acquiesced in it, and never will.

Discouragements. Sermon [November 20, 1900]

Charles Albert Tindley   1851–1933

3   This world is one great battlefield,
With forces all arrayed;
If in my heart I do not yield
I'll overcome someday.   *I'll Overcome Someday [1901]*

4   By and by, when the morning comes,
All the saints of God are gathered home,
We'll tell the story how we've overcome.
For we'll understand it better by and by.
We'll Understand It Better By and By [1905]

5   When the storms of life are raging, stand by me.
When the world is tossing me, like a ship upon the sea,
Thou who rulest wind and water, stand by me.   *Stand by Me [1905]*

6   Beams of heaven as I go
Through this wilderness below
Guide my feet in peaceful ways
Turn my midnights into days.   *Beams of Heaven (Some Day)*

A[lbery] A[llson] Whitman   1851–1901

7   Full blue-eyed Summer, stately coming on,
With shouting harvests stood the hills upon;

[1]From *The Works of Francis J. Grimké* [1942], edited by CARTER G. WOODSON.

The breath of wasting juices did inhale,
With bloomy cotton whitened in the vale,
Spread out the ripened cane along the steep
And waving rice fields in the swamp did reap.

Not a Man and yet a Man [1877]

1   Oh! sing it in the light of freedom's morn,
Tho' tyrant wars have made the earth a grave;
The good, the great, and true, are, if so born,
And so with slaves, chains do not make the slave!

The Rape of Florida [1884]

Lucy Parsons[1]   1853–1942

2   We now live under the pay system, in which, if you can't pay, you can't have.   *What Freedom Means. The Liberator [December 20, 1886]*

3   Governments never lead; they follow progress. When the prison, stake or scaffold can no longer silence the voice of the protesting minority progress moves on a step, but not until then.

The Principles of Anarchism [c. 1905]

4   We are the slaves of slaves. We are exploited more ruthlessly than men. Whenever wages are to be reduced the capitalist class use women to reduce them.

*Speech, founding convention of the Industrial Workers
of the World [1905]*

5   The "new woman" has made her bow upon the stage of life's activities as an independent human being, and she feels her importance; she feels very different from her man-tagged sisters of past generations, who imagined they couldn't move on without man's assistance.

The Liberator [October 3, 1905]

6   The sooner men learn to make companions and equals of their wives and not subordinates, the sooner the marriage relation will be one of harmony.   *The Liberator*

7   I am an anarchist: I have no apology to make to a single man, woman or child, because I am an anarchist, because anarchism carries the very germ of liberty in its womb.

*I'll Be Damned If I Go Back to Work Under Those Conditions
[May 1, 1930]*

---

[1]From *Lucy Parsons: Writings & Speeches 1878–1937* [2004], edited by GALE AHERNS.   *129*

James A[llen] Bland

1854–1911

1   Carry me back to old Virginny,
There's where the cotton and the corn and taters grow;
There's where the birds warble sweet in the springtime,
There's where this old darky's heart am longed to go.

Carry Me Back to Old Virginny [1875]

2   Oh, dem golden slippers!
Oh, dem golden slippers!
Golden slippers I'm gwinter to wear,
To walk the golden streets.   *Oh! Dem Golden Slippers [1879]*

Nat Love

1854–1921

3   Lariat near my hand, and my trusty guns in my belt and the broad plains stretching away for miles and miles. . . . I felt I could defy the world. What man with the fire of life and youth and health in his veins could not rejoice in such a life?   *The Life and Adventures of Nat Love [1907]*

4   It is a terrible thing to kill a man, no matter what the cause.

The Life and Adventures of Nat Love

5   Isn't it a wonder that some of us are alive to tell the tale? One moment we are rejoicing that we are alive; the next we are so near the jaws of death that it seems it would be almost a miracle that our lives be saved.

The Life and Adventures of Nat Love

Fannie Barrier Williams

1855–1944

6   Slavery in America was debasing, but the debasement of the Negro woman was deeper than that of the Negro man. Slavery made her the only woman in all America for whom virtue was not an ornament and a necessity.   *Club Movement Among Colored Women [1903]*[1]

7   Whether I live in the North or the South, I cannot be counted for my full value, be that much or little. I dare not cease to hope and aspire and believe in human love and justice, but progress is painful and my faith is often strained to the breaking point.   *A Northern Negro's Autobiography [1904]*[1]

Henry O[ssian] Flipper

1856–1940

8   *[On being the first black soldier at West Point:]* I simply do as the Romans do. If they are friendly, so am I; if they scorn me, I do not obtrude

---

[1] From *The New Woman of Color: The Collected Writings of Fannie Barrier Williams* [2002], edited by Mary Jo Deegan.

myself upon them. If they are indifferent, I am indifferent, too.... It is not my desire to go through life feared by anyone. I can derive no pleasure from anything which is accorded me through motives of fear. The grant must be spontaneous and voluntary to give me the most pleasure. I want nothing, not even recognition, unless it be freely given, hence have I not forced myself upon my comrades.

The Colored Cadet at West Point [1878]

T[imothy] Thomas Fortune   1856–1928

1   To tell a man he is free when he has neither money nor the opportunity to make it is simply to mock him. To tell him he has no master when he cannot live except by permission of the man who under favorable conditions, monopolizes all the land, is to deal in the most tantalizing contradiction of terms.

Black and White [1884]

2   Mob law is the most forcible expression of an abnormal public opinion; it shows that society is rotten to the core.

Black and White

3   The truth should be told, though it kill.

Black and White

4   There are so many privileges and immunities denied us as citizens, which we are entitled to enjoy equally with others, that we would be discouraged at the prospect of the long fight we have before us to secure them, if we did not stop to reflect that, by our history as well as the history of others, they only succeed who refuse to fail and who fight all the time for theirs whatever the obstacles. I feel that way about it now at the age of 75 as I did at the age of 21. I want all the young and the old people of the race to feel about it in the same way.

The Negro World [1928]. Editorial

Booker T[aliaferro] Washington   1856–1915

5   Cast down your bucket where you are — cast it down in making friends in every manly way of the people of all races by whom you are surrounded.

Speech at the Cotton States and International Exposition,
Atlanta [September 18, 1895]

6   No race can prosper till it learns that there is as much dignity in tilling a field as in writing a poem. It is at the bottom of life we must begin, and not the top. Nor should we permit our grievances to overshadow our opportunities.

Speech at the Cotton States and International Exposition

1   In all things that are purely social we [black and white] can be as separate as the fingers, yet one as the hand in all things essential to mutual progress.

Speech at the Cotton States and International Exposition

2   The unprecedented leap the Negro made when freed from the oppressing withes of bondage is more than deserving of a high place in history. It can never be chronicled. The world needs to know of what mettle these people are built. It needs to understand the vast possibility of a race, so much despised and so thoroughly able to prove without blare and flourish of trumpet its ability to hold its own and compete.

Progress of a Race [1897]

3   We are led into saying that there is no difference between us and other people. We must admit that there is a difference produced by the unequal opportunities. To argue otherwise is to discredit the effects of slavery.

From Stumbling Blocks, quoted in Black-Belt Diamonds [1898], edited by VICTORIA EARLE MATTHEWS

4   No race or people ever got upon its feet without severe and constant struggle, often in the face of the greatest discouragement.

The Case of the Negro. Atlantic Monthly [November 1899]

5   In the exercise of his political rights I should advise the Negro to be temperate and modest, and more and more to do his own thinking, rather than to be led or driven by a political "boss" or by political demagogues.

The Race Problem in the United States. Appleton's Popular Science Monthly [July 1899]

6   Ignorance is more costly to the State than education.

The Future of the American Negro [1899], ch. 6

7   It is not in the highest degree helpful to a race to be continually praised, and thus have its weaknesses overlooked; neither is it the most helpful thing to have its faults alone continually dwelt upon. What is needed is downright, straightforward honesty in both directions.

The Future of the American Negro, 7

8   Success is to be measured not so much by the position that one has reached in life as by the obstacles which he has overcome while trying to succeed.

Up from Slavery [1901], ch. 2

9   I would permit no man, no matter his color might be, to narrow and degrade my soul by making me hate him.

Up from Slavery, 11

1   Nothing ever comes to one, that is worth having, except as a result of hard work.

Up from Slavery, 12

2   We are to be tested in our patience, our forbearance, our perseverance, our power to endure wrong, to withstand temptations, to economize, to acquire and use skill; in our ability to compete, to succeed in commerce, to disregard the superficial for the real, the appearance for the substance, to be great and yet small, learned and yet simple, high and yet the servant of all.

Up from Slavery, 17

3   I would set no limits to the attainments of the Negro in arts, in letters or statesmanship, but I believe the surest way to reach those ends is by laying the foundation in the little things of life that lie immediately about one's door. I plead for industrial education and development for the Negro not because I want to cramp him, but because I want to free him.

Industrial Education for the Negro.
From The Negro Problem [1903]

4   Patiently, quietly, doggedly, persistently, through summer and winter, sunshine and shadow, by self-sacrifice, by foresight, by honesty and industry, we must reinforce argument with results.

Industrial Education for the Negro

5   There are two ways of exerting one's strength; one is pushing down, the other is pulling up.

The Value of Educating the Negro [1904]

6   I would find no interest in living in an age when there were no weak parts of the human family to be helped, no wrongs to be righted. Men grow strong in proportion as they reach down and help others up.

The American Negro of Today. Putnam's Monthly
[October 1907]

7   You can't hold a man down without staying down with him.

Attributed

Charles W[addell] Chesnutt   1858–1932

8   I will live down the prejudice, I will crush it out. I will show to the world that a man may spring from a race of slaves, and yet far excel many of the boasted ruling race. If I can exalt my race, if I can gain the applause of the good, and the approbation of God, the thoughts of the ignorant and prejudiced will not concern me. If a man be too proud, too selfconceited, or so blinded by prejudice as not to recognize and honor true merit wherever

discovered, I want not his good opinion. Let him reserve it for those whom it will please or displease!

Journal entry [1878][1]

1   It is evident that where the intermingling of the races has made such progress as it has in this country, the line which separates the races must in many instances have been practically obliterated.

What Is a White Man? [1889][2]

2   Mr. Ryder might aptly be called the dean of the Blue Veins. The original Blue Veins were a little society of colored persons organized in a certain Northern city shortly after the war. Its purpose was to establish and maintain correct social standards among a people whose social condition presented almost unlimited room for improvement. By accident, combined perhaps with some natural affinity, the society consisted of individuals who were, generally speaking, more white than black. Some envious outsider made the suggestion that no one was eligible for membership who was not white enough to show blue veins. The suggestion was readily adopted by those who were not of the favored few, and since that time the society though possessing a longer and more pretentious name, had been known far and wide as the "Blue Vein Society" and its members as the "Blue Veins."

The Wife of His Youth [1898]

3   Time touches all things with destroying hand: and if he seem now and then to bestow the bloom of youth, the sap of spring, it is but a brief mockery, to be surely and swiftly followed by the wrinkles of old age, the dry leaves and bare branches of winter. And yet there are places where Time seems to linger lovingly long after youth has departed, and to which he seems loath to bring the evil day. Who has not known some even-tempered old man or woman who seemed to have drunk of the fountain of youth? Who has not seen somewhere an old town that, having long since ceased to grow, yet held its own without perceptible decline?

The House Behind the Cedars [1900], opening lines

4   Truth, it has been said, is mighty and must prevail; but it sometimes leaves a bad taste in the mouth.   *The Marrow of Tradition [1901], ch. 7*

5   The workings of the human heart are the profoundest mystery of the universe. One moment they make us despair of our kind, and the next we see in them the reflection of the divine image.

The Marrow of Tradition, 27

---

[1]From *The Journals of Charles W. Chesnutt* [1993], edited by Richard H. Brodhead.
[2]From *Charles Chesnutt: Essays and Speeches* [1999], edited by Joseph R. McElrath, Jr., Robert C. Leitz III, and Jesse S. Crisler.

1   Nations do not first become rich and learned and then free, but the lesson of history has been that they first become free and then rich and learned, and oftentimes fall back into slavery again because of too great wealth, and the resulting luxury and carelessness of civic virtues.

From The Disenfranchisement of the Negro [1903].
From The Negro Problem [1903],
edited by BOOKER T. WASHINGTON

Ana Julia Cooper   1858–1964

2   One muffled strain in the Silent South, a jarring chord and a vague and uncomprehended cadenza, has been and still is the Negro. And of that muffled chord, the one mute and voiceless note has been the sadly expectant Black Woman.... Caucasian barristers are not to blame if they cannot *quite* put themselves in the dark man's place, neither should the dark man be wholly expected fully and adequately to reproduce the exact Voice of the Black Woman.
Voice from the South [1892]

3   True progress is never made by spasms. Real progress is growth. It must begin in the seed.
Voice from the South

4   We are the heirs of a past which was not our fathers' molding.
Voice from the South

5   Only the BLACK WOMAN can say "when and where I enter, in the quiet, undisputed dignity of my womanhood, without violence and without suing or special patronage, then and there the whole *Negro race enters with me.*"
Voice from the South

6   We need men who can let their interest and gallantry extend outside the circle of their aesthetic appreciation; men who can be a father, a brother, a friend to every weak, struggling unshielded girl.
Voice from the South

7   I constantly felt (as I suppose many an ambitious girl has felt) a thumping from within unanswered by any beckoning from without.
Voice from the South

8   Bullies are always cowards at heart and may be credited with a pretty safe instinct in scenting their prey.
Voice from the South

9   The cause of freedom is not the cause of a race or a sect, a party or a class — it is the cause of humankind, the very birthright of humanity.
Voice from the South

10   *[On the liberation of women:]* The world has had to limp along with the wobbling gait and one-sided hesitancy of a man with one eye. Suddenly the bandage is removed from the other eye and the whole body is filled with

light. It sees a circle where before it saw a segment. The darkened eye restored, every member rejoices with it.

Voice from the South

1   One needs occasionally to stand aside from the hum and rush of human interests and passions to hear the voices of God.

Voice from the South

Pauline E[lizabeth] Hopkins   1859–1930

2   Fiction is of great value to any people as a preserver of manners and customs — religious, political and social. It is a record of growth and development from generation to generation.

Contending Forces [1900], preface

3   Conservatism, lack of brotherly affiliation, lack of energy for the right and the power of the almighty dollar which deadens men's hearts to the sufferings of their brothers, and makes them feel that only if *they* can rise to the top of the ladder may God help the hindmost man, are the forces which are ruining the Negro in this country.... *These are the contending forces that are dooming this race to despair!*

Contending Forces, ch. 14 [Luke Sawyer]

4   The one drop of black blood neutralized all her virtues, and she became, from the moment of exposure, an unclean thing.

Hagar's Daughter. Colored American Magazine [1901]

5   No man can draw the dividing line between the two races, for they are both of one blood![1]   *Of One Blood [1903]*

Henry O[ssawa] Tanner   1859–1937

6   It has very often seemed to me that many painters of religious subjects seem to forget that their pictures should be as much works of art as are other paintings with less holy subjects. To suppose that the fact of the religious painter having a more elevated subject than his brother artist makes it unnecessary for him to consider his picture as an artistic production, or that he can be less thoughtful about a color harmony, for instance, than he who selects any other subject, simply proves that he is less of an artist than he who gives the subject his best attention.

[1902] From Dewey F. Mosby, Darrell Sewell, *and* Rae Alexander-Minter, Henry Ossawa Tanner *[1991]*

---

[1]And hath made of one blood all nations of men for to dwell on all the face of the earth. — *Acts 17:24–26*

1 My effort has been to not only put the biblical incident in the original setting, but at the same time, to give the human touch which makes the whole world kin, and which ever remains the same.

Artist's statement quoted in the New York Times
[January 27, 1924]

Esteban Montejo   1860–1973

2 Because of being a runaway I never knew my parents. I never even saw them. But this is not sad, because it is true.... I was a runaway from birth.

The Autobiography of a Runaway Slave [1968][1]

3 I think trees' shadows must be like men's spirits. The spirit is the reflection of the soul.   *The Autobiography of a Runaway Slave*

4 When slavery ended I stopped being a runaway.... I realized from the way people were cheering and shouting that slavery had ended, so I came out of the forest. They were shouting "We free now." But I didn't join in; I thought it might be a lie.   *The Autobiography of a Runaway Slave*

5 Murderers don't turn into patriots.

The Autobiography of a Runaway Slave

6 I say I don't want to die so I can fight in all the battles to come. And I'm not going into the trenches or using any of those modern weapons. A machete will do for me. *The Autobiography of a Runaway Slave, last lines*

Bill Pickett   c. 1860–1932

7 I'm promised for this world just so long, and when I go that will be the end of it.... Sometime, I suppose, I'll make a mistake, a fatal mistake... and it will be all over.

Reply when asked if he was afraid of getting killed.
Arizona Republican [1905][2]

Joseph S[eamon] Cotter, Sr.   1861–1949

8 Neber min' folks' good opinion
  So you habe a way to slay it.

A White Song and a Black One [1909]. The Don't-Care Negro

9 Go train your head and hands to do,
  Your head and heart to dare.

Collected Poems of Joseph S. Cotter, Sr. [1938]. The Negro Child

---

[1]Translated by JOCASTA INNES.
[2]From CECIL JOHNSON, *Guts* [1994].

Callie House[1]   c. 1861–1928

1   If the government had the right to free us she had a right to make some provision for us and since she did not make it soon after Emancipation she ought to make it now.   *Letter [1899]*

2   My face is black is true, but it's not my fault but I love my name and my honesty in dealing with my fellow man.   *Letter [1899]*

Victoria Earle Matthews   1861–1907

3   Though Race Literature be founded upon the traditionary history of a people, yet its fullest and largest development ought not to be circumscribed by the narrow limits of race or creed, for the simple reason that literature in its loftiest development reaches out to the utmost limits of soul enlargement and outstrips all earthly limitations.

The Value of Race Literature. Address [1895]

4   The awakening of the Afro-American woman is one of the most promising facts in our national life. That she deserves the active sympathy and co-operation of all the female forces of the Republic, I think I have sufficiently shown. We need them. We have always needed them. We need them in the work of religion, of education, of temperance, of morality, of industrialism; and above all we need their assistance in combating the public opinion and laws that degrade our womanhood because it is black and not white; for of a truth, and as a universal law, an injury to one woman is an injury to all women.   *The Awakening of the Afro-American Woman [1897]*

Ida B[ell] Wells-Barnett   1862–1931

5   There is little difference between the Antebellum South and the New South. Her white citizens are wedded to any method however revolting, any measure however extreme, for the subjugation of the young manhood of the race. They have cheated him out of his ballot, deprived him of civil rights or redress therefore in the civil courts, robbed him of the fruits of his labor, and are still murdering, burning and lynching him.

Southern Horrors: Lynch Law in All Its Phases [1892].
The South's Position

6   The strong arm of the law must be brought to bear upon lynchers in severe punishment, but this cannot and will not be done unless a healthy public sentiment demands and sustains such action.

Southern Horrors. The South's Position

---

[1]From MARY FRANCES BERRY, *My Face Is Black Is True* [2005].

1   Nothing is more definitively settled than he [the Black American] must act for himself. He may employ the boycott, emigration, and the press, and I feel that by a combination of all of these agencies can be effectually stamped out lynch law, that last relic of barbarism and slavery. "The gods help those who help themselves."[1]   *Southern Horrors. Self-Help*

2   The white man's dollar is his god.   *Southern Horrors. Self-Help*

3   Nobody in this section of the country believes in the old threadbare lie that Negro men rape white women. If southern white men are not careful, they will overreach themselves, and public sentiment will have a reaction; a conclusion will then be reached which will be very damaging to the moral reputation of their women.   *Free Speech. Editorial [May 21, 1892]*[2]

4   During the slave regime, the Southern white man owned the Negro body and soul. . . . While slaves were scourged mercilessly . . . the white owner rarely permitted his anger to go so far as to take a life, which would entail upon him a loss of several hundred dollars. . . . But Emancipation came and the vested interests of the white man in the Negro's body were lost.
       A Red Record [1895]. The Case Stated

5   The government which had made the Negro a citizen, found itself unable to protect him. It gave him the right to vote, but denied him the protection which should have maintained that right. Scourged from his home; hunted through the swamps; hung by midnight raiders, and openly murdered in the light of day, the Negro clung to his right of franchise with a heroism which would have wrung admiration from the hearts of savages. He believed that in that small white ballot there was a subtle something which stood for manhood as well as citizenship, and thousands of brave black men went to their graves exemplifying the one by dying for the other.   *A Red Record*

6   The Negro has suffered much and is willing to suffer more. He recognizes that the wrongs of two centuries cannot be righted in a day, and he tries to bear his burden with patience for today and be hopeful for tomorrow.   *A Red Record*

7   Virtue knows no color line, and the chivalry which depends upon complexion of skin and texture of hair can command no honest respect.
       A Red Record

8   The only excuse which capital punishment attempts to find is upon the theory that the criminal is past the power of reformation and his life is a constant menace to the community.   *A Red Record*

---

[1]See Aesop, 46:15.

[2]On eight men being lynched in one week, five of them charged with rape. The office of Wells-Barnett's Memphis newspaper was destroyed in response.

1   Our country's national crime is lynching. It is not the creature of an hour, the sudden outburst of uncontrolled fury, or the unspeakable brutality of an insane mob. It represents the cool, calculating deliberation of intelligent people who openly avow that there is an "unwritten law" that justifies them in putting human beings to death without complaint under oath, without trial by jury, without opportunity to make defense, and without right of appeal.   *Lynch Law in America. The Arena [January 1900]*

2   The Negro has been too long associated with the white man not to have copied his vices as well as his virtues.   *Lynch Law in America*

3   Our watchword has been "the land of the free and the home of the brave." Brave men do not gather by thousands to torture and murder a single individual, so gagged and bound he cannot make even feeble resistance or defense. Neither do brave men or women stand by and see such things done without compunction of conscience, nor read of them without protest.   *Lynch Law in America*

4   One had better die fighting against injustice than to die like a dog or a rat in a trap.

Crusade for Justice: The Autobiography of Ida B. Wells [1970]

Mary Church Terrell   1863–1954

5   Lifting as we climb, onward and upward we go, struggling and striving and hoping that the buds and blossoms of our desires will burst into glorious fruition ere long....Seeking no favors because of our color nor patronage because of our needs, we knock at the bar of justice and ask for an equal chance.

*What Role Is the Educated Negro Woman to Play
in the Uplifting of Her Race? [1902]*[1]

6   It is impossible for any white person in the United States, no matter how sympathetic and broad, to realize what life would mean to him if his incentive to effort were suddenly snatched away. To the lack of incentive to effort, which is the awful shadow under which we live, may be traced the wreck and ruin of scores of colored youth.

*What It Means to Be Colored in the Capital
of the United States [1907]*

7   Surely nowhere in the world do oppression and persecution based solely on the color of the skin appear more hateful and hideous than in the capital of the United States, because the chasm between the principles upon

---

[1]"Lifting As We Climb" was the motto of the National Association of Colored Women. From BEVERLY WASHINGTON JONES, *Quest for Equality: The Life and Writings of Mary Church Terrell* [1990].

which the Government was founded, in which it still professes to believe, and those which are daily practiced under the protection of the flag, yawns so wide and deep.

What It Means to Be Colored in the Capital of the United States

1   I will not shrink from undertaking what seems wise and good, because I labor under the double handicap of race and sex; but, striving to preserve a calm mind with a courageous, cheerful spirit, barring bitterness from my heart, I will struggle all the more earnestly to reach the goal.

Creed written for Delta Sigma Theta [1914]

2   A white woman has only one handicap to overcome—that of sex. I have two—both sex and race.... Colored men have only one—that of race.   *A Colored Woman in a White World [1940], introduction*

3   I cannot help wondering sometimes what I might have become and might have done if I had lived in a country which had not circumscribed and handicapped me on account of my race, but had allowed me to reach any height I was able to attain.   *A Colored Woman in a White World*

4   It is a great pity the word "Negro" was not outlawed in the Emancipation Proclamation as it certainly should have been. After people have been freed it is a cruel injustice to call them by the same name they bore as slaves.

Letter to the Editor. Washington Post [May 14, 1949][1]

George Washington Carver   1864–1943

5   No individual has any right to come into the world and go out of it without leaving behind him distinct and legitimate reasons for having passed through it.   *Letter to Booker T. Washington [May 25, 1915][2]*

6   Inspiration is never at variance with information; in fact the more information one has, the greater will be the inspiration.

Letter to the New York Times [November 24, 1924][3]

7   I never have to grope for methods: the method is revealed at the moment I am inspired to create something new.

Speech at the Marble Collegiate Church [November 1924][3]

8   We must disabuse our people of the idea that there is a shortcut to achievement. Life requires thorough preparation. Veneer isn't worth anything.   *Speech [October 11, 1927][4]*

---

[1]From *Daughters of Africa* [1992], edited by MARGARET BUSBY.

[2]From BASIL MATHEWS, *Booker T. Washington: Educator and Interracial Interpreter* [1948].

[3]From *George Washington Carver in His Own Words* [1987], edited by GARY R. KREMER.

[4]From RALEIGH H. MERRITT, *From Captivity to Fame, or The Life of George Washington Carver* [1929].

1   Creative genius is what makes people respect you. It's not a color question, it's a question of whether you have what the world wants.

Speech

2   The primary idea in all of my work was to help the farmer and fill the poor man's empty dinner pail.   *Letter [January 16, 1929]*[1]

3   More and more, as we come closer and closer in touch with nature and its teachings, are we able to see the Divine and are therefore fitted to interpret correctly the various languages spoken by all forms of nature about us.   *How to Search for Truth [1930]*

4   I love to think of nature as unlimited broadcasting stations, through which God speaks to us every day, every hour and every moment of our lives, if we will only tune in and remain so.   *How to Search for Truth*

5   It is not the style of clothes one wears, neither the kind of automobile one drives, nor the amount of money one has in the bank, that counts. These mean nothing. It is simply service that measures success.   *Attributed*

Charles Young   1864–1922

6   The American officers that I brought with me have been loyal and worked well. The troops are natives, not Liberians. They are not one whit inferior in the soldier spirit to our best black troops of our own Army, which as you know is saying much.

Letter sent from Monrovia, Liberia [July 26, 1915][2]

Madame C. J. Walker [Sarah Breedlove]   1867–1919

7   I am a woman that came from the cotton fields of the South. I was promoted from there to the washtub. Then I was promoted to the cook kitchen, and from there I promoted myself into the business of manufacturing hair goods and preparations....Everybody told me I was making a mistake by going into this business, but I know how to grow hair as well as I know how to grow cotton.

Speech to the National Negro Business League, Chicago [August 1912]

Robert S[engstacke] Abbott   1868–1940

8   IF YOU CAN FREEZE TO DEATH in the North and be free why FREEZE to death in the South and be a slave, where your mother, sister and

---

[1]From BASIL MATHEWS, *Booker T. Washington: Educator and Interracial Interpreter* [1948].
[2]From PATRICIA W. ROMERO, *I Too Am America: Documents from 1619 to the Present* [1968].

daughter are raped, and burned at the stake, where your father, brother and sons are treated with contempt and hung to a pole, riddled with bullets at the least mention that he does not like the way he has been treated? Come north then, all of you folks both good and bad. If you don't behave yourself up here, the jails will certainly make you wish you had. For the hard working man there is plenty of work — if you really want it. The *Defender* says come.

Chicago Defender [February 24, 1917]

W[illiam] E[dward] B[urghardt] Du Bois   1868–1963

1   The problem of the twentieth century is the problem of the color line.

To the Nations of the World. Address to Pan-African Conference, London [1900]

2   The Negro race, like all races, is going to be saved by its exceptional men. The problem of education, then, among Negroes must first of all deal with the Talented Tenth; it is the problem of developing the Best of this race that they may guide the Mass away from the contamination and death of the Worst, in their own and other races.

The Talented Tenth. From The Negro Problem [1903]

3   Education and work are the levers to uplift a people. Education must not simply teach work — it must teach Life.   *The Talented Tenth*

4   The Talented Tenth of the Negro race must be made leaders of thought and missionaries of culture among their people.

The Talented Tenth

5   Why did God make me an outcast and a stranger in mine own house?   *The Souls of Black Folk [1903], ch. 1*

6   It is a peculiar sensation, this double-consciousness, this sense of always looking at one's self through the eyes of others.... One ever feels his twoness — an American, a Negro; two souls, two thoughts, two unreconciled strivings; two warring ideals in one dark body, whose dogged strength alone keeps it from being torn asunder.   *The Souls of Black Folk, 1*

7   To be a poor man is hard, but to be a poor race in a land of dollars is the very bottom of hardships.   *The Souls of Black Folk, 1*

8   While it is a great truth to say that the Negro must strive and strive mightily to help himself, it is equally true that unless his striving be not simply seconded, but rather aroused and encouraged, by the initiative of the richer and wiser environing group, he cannot hope for great success.

The Souls of Black Folk, 3

---

[1]From *W. E. B. Du Bois: A Reader* [1995], edited by DAVID LEVERING LEWIS.

1   The worlds within and without the Veil of Color are changing and changing rapidly, but not at the same rate, not in the same way; and this must produce a peculiar wrenching of the soul, a peculiar sense of doubt and bewilderment. Such a double life, with double thought, double duties and double social classes, must give rise to double words and double ideals, and tempt the mind to pretence or to revolt, to hypocrisy or to radicalism.   *The Souls of Black Folk, 10*

2   Herein lies the tragedy of the age: not that men are poor—all men know something of poverty; not that men are wicked—who is good? Not that men are ignorant—what is truth? Nay, but that men know so little of men.   *The Souls of Black Folk, 12*

3   The Negro folk-song—the rhythmic cry of the slave—stands today not simply as the sole American music, but as the most beautiful expression of human experience born this side the seas. It has been neglected, it has been, and is, half despised, and above all it has been persistently mistaken and misunderstood; but notwithstanding, it still remains as the singular spiritual heritage of the nation and the greatest gift of the Negro people.
                                                    The Souls of Black Folk, 14

4   Your country? How came it yours?   *The Souls of Black Folk, 14*

5   Would America have been America without her Negro people?
                                                    The Souls of Black Folk, 14

6   I believe that all men, black and brown and white, are brothers, varying through Time and Opportunity, in form and gift and feature, but differing in no essential particular, and alike in soul and the possibility of infinite development.   *Credo. The Independent [October 6, 1904][1]*

7   I believe in pride of race and lineage and self; in pride of self so deep as to scorn injustice to other selves; in pride of lineage so great as to despise no man's father; in pride of race so chivalrous as neither to offer bastardy to the weak nor beg wedlock of the strong, knowing that men may be brothers in Christ, even though they be not brothers-in-law.   *Credo*

8   The cost of liberty is less than the price of repression.
                                                    John Brown [1909], ch. 13

9   Liberty trains for liberty. Responsibility is the first step in responsibility.   *John Brown, 13*

10   Save us World Spirit from our lesser selves!
     Grant us that war and hatred cease,
     Reveal our souls in every race and hue!

---

[1]From *W. E. B. Du Bois: A Reader* [1995], edited by DAVID LEVERING LEWIS.

Help us, O Human God, in this thy truce
To make Humanity divine.

A Hymn to the Peoples, read before the Races Congress [1911]

1   The cause of war is preparation for war.

Of the Children of Peace [1914]

2   We do not countenance violence. Our fight is against violence. We are fighting as we always have fought — for the reign of law over the reign of the mob.   *Essay. The Crisis [November 1919]*

3   The discovery of personal whiteness among the world's peoples is a very modern thing — a nineteenth and twentieth century matter, indeed. The ancient world would have laughed at such a distinction. The Middle Age regarded skin color with mild curiosity; and even up into the eighteenth century we were hammering our national manikins into one, great, Universal Man, with fine frenzy which ignored color and race even more than birth. Today we have changed all that, and the world in a sudden, emotional conversion has discovered that it is white and by that token, wonderful!

Darkwater [1920], ch. 2, The Souls of White Folk

4   The Dark World is going to submit to its present treatment just as long as it must and not one moment longer.   *Darkwater, 2*

5   There is a curious assumption in some quarters that intelligent and law-abiding Negroes like, encourage and sympathize with Negro crime and defend Negro criminals. They do not. They suffer more from the crime of their fellows than white folk suffer, not only vicariously, but directly. The black criminal knows that he can prey on his own people with the least danger of punishment because they control no police or courts.

Essay. The Crisis [February 1920]

6   We cannot refuse to cooperate with white Americans and simultaneously demand the right to cooperate!

*In response to criticism that the NAACP had white people
in its organization. The Crisis [May 1920]*

7   There are still a few of us who are running away to avoid each other with the vague feeling that we shall thus lose ourselves in the world and be free.   *Essay. The Crisis [November 1920]*

8   The attempt to make black men American citizens was in a certain sense all a failure, but a splendid failure.

Black Reconstruction in America [1935]

9   As I face Africa I ask myself: what is it between us that constitutes a tie which I can feel better than I can explain?   *Dusk of Dawn [1940], ch. 5*

10   The return from your work must be the satisfaction which that work brings you and the world's need of that work. With this, life is heaven, or as

near heaven as you can get. Without this — with work which you despise, which bores you, and which the world does not need — this life is hell.

To His Newborn Great-Grandson. Address on his ninetieth birthday [1958]

1   As you live, believe in life! Always human beings will live and progress to greater, broader, and fuller life.

Last message to the world [written 1957].
Read at his funeral [1963]

Scott Joplin

1868–1917

2   Let me see you do the ragtime dance.
Turn left and do the Cakewalk prance,
Turn the other way and do the Slow drag,
Now take your lady to the worlds fair
and do the ragtime dance.

The Ragtime Dance [1902]

3   Aunt Dinah has blowed de horn,
An' we'll go home to stay until dawn.
Get ready, put yo' sack on yo' back,
I'm so happy I don't know how to act.

Treemonisha [1911], no. 18. Aunt Dinah Has Blowed de Horn

4   Wrong is never right,
And it will never be.

Treemonisha, no. 22

5   We will trust you as our leader,
We will trust you as our leader,
No one else could lead like you,
For you know what is best to do.

Treemonisha, no. 26

Olivia Ward Bush-Banks

1869–1944

6   Yes, drifting, drifting; and I thought that life,
When nearing death is like the sunset sky
And death is but the slow, sure drifting in,
To rest far more securely, by and by.

Driftwood [1914].[1] Drifting [Newport, June 12, 1898]

7   Prejudice, the floating wreckage of chattel slavery, rises ever to the surface of the turbulent waters of a Nation's life, obstructing each best attempt toward a safe course to its highest citizenship.   *Driftwood. Hope*

---

[1]From *The Collected Works of Olivia Ward Bush-Banks* [1991], compiled and edited by BERNICE F. GUILLAUME.

Sissieretta Jones
1869–1933

1   The flowers absorb the sunshine because it is their nature. I give out
melody because God filled my soul with it.

From Black Women in America [1993],
edited by DARLENE CLARKE HINE

James Weldon Johnson
1871–1938

2   Lift ev'ry voice and sing,
Till earth and heaven ring,
Ring with the harmonies of Liberty.   *Lift Every Voice and Sing [1900]*

3   Sing a song full of the faith that the dark past has taught us,
Sing a song full of the hope that the present has brought us;
Facing the rising sun of our new day begun,
Let us march on till victory is won.   *Lift Every Voice and Sing*

4   The colored people of this country know and understand the white
people better than the white people know and understand them.

The Autobiography of an Ex-Colored Man [1912], ch. 2

5   Every race and every nation should be judged by the best it has been
able to produce, not by the worst.

The Autobiography of an Ex-Colored Man, 10

6   All the while I understood that it was not discouragement or fear or
search for a larger field of action and opportunity that was driving me out
of the Negro race. I knew that it was shame, unbearable shame. Shame at
being identified with a people that could with impunity be treated worse
than animals.   *The Autobiography of an Ex-Colored Man, 10*

7   I have sold my birthright for a mess of pottage.[1]

The Autobiography of an Ex-Colored Man, last line

8   O black and unknown bards of long ago,
How came your lips to touch the sacred fire?
How, in your darkness, did you come to know
The power and beauty of the minstrel's lyre?

O Black and Unknown Bards [1917], st. 1

9   A people may become great through many means, but there is only
one measure by which its greatness is recognized and acknowledged. The
final measure of the greatness of all peoples is the amount and standard of
the literature and art they have produced. The world does not know that a

---

[1]And he [Esau] sold his birthright unto Jacob.
Then Jacob gave Esau bread and pottage of lentils. —*Genesis 25:33–34*

people is great until that people produces great literature and art. No people that has produced great literature and art has ever been looked upon by the world as distinctly inferior.

The Book of American Negro Poetry [1922], preface

1   And God stepped out on space,
     And He looked around and said,
     "I'm lonely—
     I'll make me a world."   *God's Trombones [1927]. The Creation, st. 1*

2   And far as the eye of God could see
     Darkness covered everything,
     Blacker than a hundred midnights.   *God's Trombones. The Creation, st. 2*

3   With His head in His hands,
     God thought and thought,
     Till He thought: I'll make me a man!

God's Trombones. The Creation, st. 10

4   Your arm's too short to box with God.[1]

God's Trombones. Prodigal Son, st. 1

5   Weep not, weep not,
     She is not dead;
     She's resting in the bosom of Jesus.
     Heart-broken husband—weep no more;
     Grief-stricken son—weep no more;
     Left-lonesome daughter—weep no more;
     She's only just gone home.

God's Trombones. Go Down Death (A Funeral Sermon), st. 1

6   Find Sister Caroline.
     She's borne the burden and heat of the day,
     She's labored long in my vineyard,
     And she's tired—
     She's weary—
     Go down, Death, and bring her to me.

God's Trombones. Go Down Death, st. 5

7   It is from the blues that all that may be called *American music* derives
         its most distinctive characteristic.   *Black Manhattan [1930], ch. 11*

---

[1]First published as "Yo' arm's too short to box wid God," in *The Autobiography of an Ex-Colored Man* [1912], *ch. 10.*
    Vinette Carroll [1922–2002] popularized this phrase by using it as the title of her musical *Your Arms Too Short to Box with God* [1975].

Paul Laurence Dunbar[1]   1872–1906

1   Folks ain't got no right to censuah othah folks about dey habits.
                                                    Lyrics of a Lowly Life [1896]. Accountability

2   A crust of bread and a corner to sleep in,
    A minute to smile and an hour to weep in,
    A pint of joy to a peck of trouble,
    And never a laugh but the moans come double;
        And that is life!   *Lyrics of a Lowly Life. Life*

3   Oh, dere's lots o' keer an' trouble
        In dis world to swaller down;
    An' ol' Sorrer's purty lively
        In her way o' gittin' roun'.
    Yet der's times when I furgit 'em, —
        Aches an' pains an' troubles all, —
    An' it's when I tek at ebenin'
        My ol' banjo f'om de wall.   *Lyrics of a Lowly Life. A Banjo Song*

4   If the muse were mine to tempt it
        And my feeble voice were strong,
    If my tongue were trained to measures,
        I would sing a stirring song.
    I would sing a song heroic
        Of those noble sons of Ham,
    Of the gallant colored soldiers
        Who fought for Uncle Sam!   *Lyrics of a Lowly Life. The Colored Soldiers*

5   Wearily I sit and listen
        To the water's ceaseless drip.
        To my lip
    Fate turns up the bitter cup,
        Forcing me to sip;
    'Tis a bitter, bitter drink,
    Thus I sit and think.   *Lyrics of a Lowly Life. Melancholia*

6   Why, de 'lectric light o' Heaven
        Seems to settle on de spot,
    When yo' mammy says de blessin'
        An' de co'n pone's hot.

                    Lyrics of a Lowly Life. When de Co'n Pone's Hot

---

[1]From *The Complete Poems of Paul Laurence Dunbar* [1962].

1   An Angel, robed in spotless white,

      Bent down and kissed the sleeping Night.

      Night woke to blush; the sprite was gone.

      Men saw the blush and called it Dawn.   *Lyrics of a Lowly Life. Dawn*

2   We wear the mask that grins and lies,

      It hides our cheeks and shades our eyes, —

      This debt we pay to human guile;

      With torn and bleeding hearts we smile.

      And mouth with myriad subtleties.

                                    Lyrics of a Lowly Life. We Wear the Mask

3   When hit comes to real right singin',

        'T ain't no easy thing to do.   *Lyrics of a Lowly Life. When Malindy Sings*

4   I know why the caged bird sings, ah me,

      When his wing is bruised and his bosom sore, —

      When he beats his bars and he would be free;

      It is not a carol of joy or glee,

      But a prayer that he sends from his heart's deep core...

      I know why the caged bird sings!

                                Lyrics of the Hearthside [1899]. Sympathy, st. 3

5   There is a heaven, for ever, day by day,

      The upward longing of my soul doth tell me so.

      There is a hell, I'm quite as sure; for pray,

      If there were not, where would my neighbors go?

                                  Lyrics of the Hearthside. Theology

6   But it's easy 'nough to titter w'en de stew is smokin' hot,

        But hit's mighty ha'd to giggle w'en dey's nuffin' in de pot.

                    Lyrics of Love and Laughter [1903]. Philosophy

7   Slight was the thing I bought,

      Small was the debt I thought,

      Poor was the loan at best —

      God! but the interest!   *Lyrics of Love and Laughter. The Debt*

8   Since thou[1] and those who died with thee for right

        Have died, the Present teaches, but in vain!

               Lyrics of Love and Laughter. Robert Gould Shaw, st. 2

---

[1]Colonel Robert Gould Shaw, white commander of the 54th Massachusetts regiment (the first enlisted black regiment in the Civil War), died with many others of the regiment at Fort Wagner [July, 18, 1863].

1   This, this it is to be accursed indeed;
>   For if we mortals love, or if we sing,
We count our joys not by what we have,
>   But by what kept us from the perfect thing.

Lyrics of Love and Laughter. Life's Tragedy

2   I found you and I loved you,
>   And all the world was mine.

Lyrics of Sunshine and Shadow [1905]. A Golden Day

W[illiam] C[hristopher] Handy[1]   1873–1958

3   I hate to see de evenin' sun go down.   *St. Louis Blues [1914]*

4   Got de St. Louis Blues jes as blue as ah can be.
Dat man got a heart lak a rock cast in the sea,
Or else he wouldn't have gone so far from me.   *St. Louis Blues*

5   Susan Johnson lost her Jockey, Lee
There has been much excitement, more to be
You can hear her moaning night and morn.
Wonder where my Easy Rider's gone?   *Yellow Dog Blues [1914]*

6   Tell me how long will I have to wait?
Oh, won't you tell me now, why do you hesitate?

Hesitating Blues [1915]

7   You'll never miss the water till your well runs dry.   *Joe Turner Blues [1915]*

8   You'll see pretty Browns in beautiful gowns
You'll see tailor-mades and hand-me-downs
You'll meet honest men and pickpockets skilled,
You'll find that business never closes till somebody gets killed.
    . . . if Beale Street could talk.   *Beale Street Blues [1917]*

9   I'd rather be here than any place I know,
It's going to take the Sergeant for to make me go,
Goin' to the river, maybe by and by
Goin' to the river and there's a reason why
Because the river's wet, and Beale Street's done gone dry.   *Beale Street Blues*

10   Love, oh loveless love
You set our hearts on goalless goals
With dreamless dreams and

---

[1]From *Blues: An Anthology* [1926], edited by W. C. HANDY, revised by JERRY SILVERMAN [1972].

Schemeless schemes,
We wreck our boats on the shoals.

Loveless Love [1921]

1   In everything we find a flaw,
Even love, oh love, oh loveless love.

Loveless Love

Enoch Sontonga

1873–1905

2   Nkosi, sikelel' iAfrika[1]

Song title [1897][2]

[Arturo]Arthur A[lfonso] Schomburg

1874–1938

3   The American Negro must remake his past in order to make his
future. Though it is orthodox to think of America as the one country where
it is unnecessary to have a past, what is a luxury for the nation as a whole
becomes a prime social necessity for the Negro. For him, a group tradition
must supply compensation for persecution, and pride of race the antidote
for prejudice. History must restore what slavery took away, for it is the social
damage of slavery that the present generations must repair and offset.

The Negro Digs Up His Past. Survey Graphic [March 1925]

Mary McLeod Bethune

1875–1955

4   What does the Negro want? His answer is very simple. He wants only
what all other Americans want. He wants opportunity to make real what the
Declaration of Independence and the Constitution and the Bill of Rights say,
what the Four Freedoms establish. While he knows these ideals are open to
no man completely, he wants only his equal chance to obtain them.

*Certain Unalienable Rights. From What the Negro Wants
[1944], edited by* Rayford W. Logan

5   If we simply accept and acquiesce in the face of discrimination, we
accept the responsibility ourselves and allow those responsible to salve their
conscience by believing that they have our acceptance and concurrence. We
should, therefore, protest openly everything . . . that smacks of discrimination or slander.

Certain Unalienable Rights

---

[1]God, bless Africa.

[2]Sontonga's original hymn, composed in Xhosa, was best known as the anthem of the African National
Congress as well as an international symbol of the struggle against apartheid. After the country's first
democratic election in 1994, *Nkosi, sikelel' iAfrika* and *Die Stem van Suid Afrika* (The Call of South
Africa), the official song, were combined to create the South African National Anthem: Nkosi sikelel'
iAfrika / Maluphakanyisw' uphondo lwayo, / Yizwa imithandazo yethu, / Nkosi sikelela, thina lusapho
lwayo (Lord, bless Africa / May her spirit rise high up / Hear thou our prayers / Lord bless us).

From http://www.anc.org.za/misc/nkosi.html and http://www.southafrica.info/ess_info/sa_glance/
history/anthem.htm.

1   We must remake the world. The task is nothing less than that.
> *Address to a World Assembly for Moral Re-armament,*
> *Caux, Switzerland [July 27, 1954]*[1]

2   Knowledge is the prime need of the hour.
> *My Last Will & Testament. Ebony [August 1955]*

3   We live in a world which respects power above all things. Power, intelligently directed, can lead to more freedom. Unwisely directed, it can be a dreadful, destructive force.   *My Last Will & Testament*

4   Without faith, nothing is possible. With it, nothing is impossible.
> *My Last Will & Testament*

5   My color has never destroyed my self-respect nor has it ever caused me to conduct myself in such a manner as to merit the disrespect of any person. I have not let my color handicap me. Despite many crushing burdens and handicaps, I have risen from the cotton fields of South Carolina to found a college, administer it during its years of growth, become a public servant in the government of our country and a leader of women. I would not exchange my color for all the wealth in the world, for had I been born white I might not have been able to do all that I have done or yet hope to do.   *My Last Will & Testament*

Samuel Coleridge-Taylor   1875–1912

6   *[On music:]* Should it not rather come from the heart as well as the brain?
> *Essay [January 1911]. From W. C. BERWICK SAYERS, Samuel*
> *Coleridge-Taylor, Musician: His Life and Letters [1915]*

Alice Dunbar-Nelson[2]   1875–1935

7   To an independent spirit there is a certain sense of humiliation and wounded pride in asking for money, be it five cents or five hundred dollars.
> *Violets and Other Tales [1895]. The Woman*

8   Marriages might be made in Heaven, but too often they are consummated right here on earth.
> *Violets and Other Tales. The Woman*

9   It is dark, like the passionate women of Egypt; placid, like their broad brows; deep, silent like their souls. Within its bosom are hidden romances

---

[1]From *Mary McLeod Bethune: Building a Better World: Essays and Selected Documents* [1999], edited by AUDREY THOMAS MCCLUSKEY and ELAINE M. SMITH.

[2]From *The Works of Alice Dunbar-Nelson* [1988], edited by GLORIA T. HULL.

and stories, such as were sung by minstrels of old. From the source to the mouth is not far distant, visibly speaking, but in the life of the bayou a hundred heart-miles could scarce measure it.

The Goodness of St. Roque and Other Tales [1899].
By the Bayou St. John

1   And now — unwittingly you've made me dream
Of violets, and my soul's forgotten dream.

Violets. The Crisis [August 1919]

2   I sit and sew — a useless task it seems,
My hands grown tired, my head weighed down with dreams —
The panoply of war, the martial tred of men,
Grim-faced, stern-eyed, gazing beyond the ken
Of lesser souls, whose eyes have not seen Death,
Nor learned to hold their lives but as a breath —
But — I must sit and sew.

I Sit and Sew [1920]

3   There are a thousand subtleties of refined cruelty which every fair colored person must suffer at the hands of his or her own people. And every fair colored woman or man, girl or boy who reads this knows that I have not exaggerated.... It is not to be wondered at that lighter skinned Negroes cling together in their respective communities.... The "yaller niggers," the "Brass Ankles," must bear the hatred of their own and the prejudice of the white race.

Brass Ankles Speaks [1929]

Carter G[odwin] Woodson   1875–1950

4   The citizenship of the Negro in this country is a fiction.

The Journal of Negro History [January 1921], vol. VI

5   Real education means to inspire people to live more abundantly, to learn to begin with life as they find it and make it better.

The Mis-education of the Negro [1933], ch. 4

6   When you determine what a man shall think you do not have to concern yourself about what he will do. If you make a man feel that he is inferior, you do not have to compel him to accept an inferior status, for he will seek it himself. If you make a man think that he is justly an outcast, you do not have to order him to the back door. He will go without being told; and if there is no back door, his very nature will demand one.

The Mis-education of the Negro, 9

1   If the Negro could abandon the idea of leadership and instead stimulate a larger number of the race to take up definite tasks and sacrifice their time and energy in doing these things efficiently the race might accomplish something. The race needs workers, not leaders. Such workers will solve the problems which race leaders talk about and raise money to enable them to talk more and more about. When you hear a man talking, then, always inquire as to what he is doing or what he has done for humanity. Oratory and resolutions do not avail much. If they did, the Negro race would be in a paradise on earth.   *The Mis-education of the Negro, 11*

2   You cannot serve people by giving them orders as to what to do. The real servant of the people must live among them, think with them, feel for them, and die for them.

The Mis-education of the Negro, 12

3   The world does not want and will never have the heroes and heroines of the past. What this age needs is an enlightened youth not to undertake the tasks like theirs but to imbibe the spirit of these great men and answer the present call of duty with equal nobleness of soul.

The Mis-education of the Negro, 13

4   History shows that it does not matter who is in power or what revolutionary forces take over the government, those who have not learned to do for themselves and have to depend solely on others never obtain any more rights or privileges in the end than they had in the beginning.

The Mis-education of the Negro, 17

5   If a race has no history, if it has no worthwhile tradition, it becomes a negligible factor in the thought of the world, and it stands in danger of being exterminated.   *The Story of the Negro Retold [1935]*

6   Most historians know practically nothing about the Negroes in Africa prior to their enslavement and there has been little systematic effort to study them.... The fact is that we know less about Africa than about any other part of the world.

The Negro in Our History, 9th ed. [1947]

Alex Rogers   1876–1930

7   My hard luck started when I was born,
leas' so the old folks say.
Dat same hard luck been my bes' fren'
up to dis very day.   *I'm a Jonah Man [1900]*

8   I May Be Crazy, but I Ain't No Fool   *Song title [1904]*   155

1   Adam never had no Mammy, fur to take him on her knee
An' teach him right from wrong an' show him
Things he ought to see.
I knows down in my heart dat he'd a let dat apple be.

Why Adam Sinned [1904]

2   When life seems full of clouds and rain
And I am full of nothin' and pain
Who soothes my thumpin', bumpin' brain? . . .   *Nobody. Nobody [1905]*

3   I ain't never done nothin' to nobody
I ain't never got nothin' from nobody no time
And until I get somethin' from somebody sometime
I don't 'tend to do nothin' for nobody no time.   *Nobody*

Bert Williams
1876–1922

4   I have never been able to discover that there was anything disgraceful in being a colored man. But I have found it inconvenient — in America.

The Comic Side of Trouble. The American Magazine
[January 1918]

Bert Williams
1876–1922

and

George Walker
1873–1911

5   Money is de root of evil
No matter where you happen to go;
But nobody has any objections to de root; now ain't dat so?

When It's All Going Out and Nothing Coming In [1902]

Dantés Bellegarde[1]
1877–1966

6   Intelligence is a flame. The more vivacious it is, the better it shines.

Pour une Haiti heureuse [1927, 1929]

7   To await one's salvation from another but oneself, or to consume oneself in the apprehension of a catastrophe — which only our inaction can make inevitable — is the policy of a people that will die, more speedily perhaps because it will have pronounced its own death sentence.

Un Haitien parle [1934]

---

[1]From PATRICK BELLEGARDE-SMITH, *In the Shadow of Powers: Dantés Bellegarde in Haitian Social Thought* [1985].

1   The interplay of institutions is not...as perfect as one would have
desired. The machinery creaks, its springs screech and the principles emerge
badly cracked.   *Dessalines a parlé [1948]*

2   In a specific community, general progress will result from the progress
accomplished by individuals that form it. In the international society, progress will be the results accomplished by the ensemble of nations that constitute it. To develop maximally, all forces of one's nation — moral,
intellectual, economic forces — is to work for the progress and the welfare
of humanity in its entirety.

Éducation pour la paix et le bien-être social.
Journal of American Studies [January 1959]

[Charles] Buddy Bolden   1877–1931

3   I thought I heard Buddy Bolden say,
Funky butt, funky butt, take it away!

Funky Butt (Buddy Bolden's Blues)

Benjamin Oliver Davis, Sr.[1]   c. 1877–1970

4   I did my duty. That's what I set out to do — to show that I could make
my way if I knew my job.   *Interview [June 2, 1968]*

5   Segregation fosters intolerance, suspicion and friction.

Statement regarding need for integration of
United States military

Meta Vaux Warrick Fuller   1877–1968

6   Art must be the quintessence of meaning. Creative art means that you
create yourself.   *Speech at Livingstone College [1950]*[2]

William Stanley Braithwaite   1878–1962

7   Two women on the lone wet strand
(*The wind's out with a will to roam*)
The waves wage war on rocks and sand,
(*And a ship is long due home!*)   *The Watchers [1904]*

8   Heart free, hand free,
        Blue above, brown under,

---

[1]From MARVIN E. FLETCHER, *America's First Black General* [1989].
[2]From SHONETTE KOONTZ, *Profiles of Negro Womanhood* [2003], *vol. II, From a Collection of the Life and Work of Meta Vaux Warrick Fuller 1877–1968.*

All the world to me
    Is a place of wonder.   *Sic Vita [1908]*

1   I must go on with Time, and leave him there
In Autumn's house where dreams will soon grow thin.
When Time shall close the door unto the house
And opens that of Winter's soon to be,
And dreams go moving through the ruined boughs —
He who went in comes out a Memory.
From his deep sleep no sound may e'er arouse, —
The moaning rain, nor wind-embattled sea.
        To the House of Falling Leaves [1908], pt. 4

2   Poetry is one of the realities that persist. The façade and the dome of
the palace and temple, the monuments of heroes and saints, crumble before
the ruining breath of time, while the Psalms last.
      Anthology of Magazine Verse [1913],
      introduction

3   I kissed a kiss in youth
    Upon a dead man's brow;
And that was long ago —
    And I'm a grown man now.   *Scintilla [1915]*

4   Sandy Star and Willie Gee,
Count 'em two, you make 'em three:
Pluck the man and boy apart
And you'll see into my heart.
      Sandy Star and Willie Gee [1922], prologue

5   His thoughts were a loose skein of threads,
    And tangled emotions, vague and dim;
And sacrificing what he loved
    He lost the dearest part of him.
      Sandy Star and Willie Gee. Sandy Star, sec. 1

6   Let me dream my dream entire.
      Turn Me into Yellow Leaves [1922]

7   Quiet has a hidden sound
Best upon a hillside street,
When the sunlight on the ground
Is luminous with heat.

        Selected Poems [1948]. Quiet Has a Hidden Sound

Jack [John Arthur] Johnson   1878–1946

1   I have known the tremendous exaltation of victory in the ring, in love, in business and in controversies of all kinds, and I have been cast down into the despair that sometimes comes with failure. I have traveled in nearly every country of the world and wherever I have gone I have had adventures that men of my race and nation have never had.

Jack Johnson in the Ring and Out [1927]

2   [*On taking the heavyweight championship from Tommy Burns:*] I was supremely glad I had attained the championship, but I kept this feeling to myself. I did not gloat over the fact that a white man had fallen. My satisfaction was only in the fact that one man had conquered another, and that I had been the conqueror. To me it was not a racial triumph, but there were those who were to take this view of the situation, and almost immediately a great hue and cry went up because a colored man was holding the championship.

Jack Johnson in the Ring and Out

3   There have been countless women in my life. They have participated in my triumphs, and suffered with me in my moments of disappointment. They have inspired me to attainment and they have balked me; they have caused me joy and they have heaped misery upon me; they have been faithful to the utmost and they have been faithless; they have prized and loved me and they have hated and denounced me. Always a woman has swayed me.

Jack Johnson in the Ring and Out

4   The search for the "white hope" not having been successful, prejudices were being piled up against me, and certain unfair persons, piqued because I was champion, decided that if they could not get me one way, they would another.

Jack Johnson in the Ring and Out

5   The possession of muscular strength and the courage to use it in contests with other men for physical supremacy does not necessarily imply a lack of appreciation for the finer and better things of life. Brutish qualities and base inclinations are prevalent in all classes. A man's vocation is no measure of his inner feelings nor a guarantee of his earnest desire to live right and attain the highest standards.

Jack Johnson in the Ring and Out

6   I have found no better way of avoiding race prejudice than to act with people of other races as if prejudice did not exist.

Jack Johnson in the Ring and Out

Bill Bojangles [Luther] Robinson

1878–1949

1   Everything is copacetic.

Attributed

Major Taylor

1878–1932

2   I hold no animosity towards any man. This includes those who so bitterly opposed me and did everything possible to injure me and prevent my success.... When I am called home I shall rest easy, knowing that I always played the game fairly and tried my hardest, although I was not always given a square deal or anything like it. When I am finally run off my feet and flattened by that mighty champion Father Time, the last thought to remain in my mind will be that throughout life's great race I always gave the best that was in me. Life is too short for a man to hold bitterness in his heart, and that is why I have no feeling against anybody.

The Fastest Bicycle Rider in the World [1928]

Nannie Helen Burroughs

1879–1961

3   The Negro must stop charging his failures up to his "color" and to white people's attitudes.

12 Things the Negro Must Do for Himself and
12 Things White People Must Stop Doing to the Negro
[early 1900s]

4   We Specialize in the Wholly Impossible.

Motto of the National Training School for Women and Girls,
Washington, D.C. [1909]

5   At times we feel wounded, hurt, disappointed, disgusted, resentful, sick of it all. At other times we feel skeptical, outraged, robbed, beaten. We chafe, hate, overlook. Then again we feel like ignoring, defying and fighting for every right that belongs to us as human beings.

What Do You Think? [1950].
How Does It Feel to Be a Negro?

6   Education and justice are democracy's only life insurance....

Think on These Things [1982].
Education and Justice

Charlotta Spears Bass

c. 1880–1969

7   I make this pledge — to my people, the dead and the living — to all Americans black and white. I will not retire nor will I retreat, not one inch, so long as God gives me vision to see what is happening and strength to fight for the things I know are right. For I know that my kingdom, my people's

kingdom, and the kingdom of all the peoples of the world, is not beyond the skies, the moon, and the stars, but right here at our feet.

> *Acceptance speech on being nominated as Progressive*
> *Party vice presidential candidate [March 30, 1952].*
> *Forty Years [1960]*

1   The Americans who came across the plains in covered wagons and those who followed the trail later in trains drawn by the iron horse were interested in home ownership and a new life. Especially was this true of the Negro pioneers. They knew it was not a case of starting again. For them it was the dawn of a new life in an atmosphere of freedom.   *Forty Years*

Angelina Weld Grimké   1880–1958

2   He breathes your air so free,
You hang him to a tree,
You hound of deviltry.
You burn him if he speak,
Until your freelands reek
From gory peak to peak.

> *Beware Lest He Awakes, Pilot [1902]*[1]

3   And so this nation — this white Christian nation — has deliberately set its curse upon the most beautiful — the most holy thing in life — motherhood! Why it makes you doubt — God!

> *Rachel [1916], act I [Rachel]*

4   I am afraid to go to sleep, for every time I do my children come and beg me weeping not to bring them here to suffer. Tonight, they came when I was awake.   *Rachel, act III, final scene [Rachel]*

5   I have just seen a beautiful thing
        Slim and still,
Against a gold, gold sky,
        A straight black cypress,
        Sensitive
        Exquisite,
    A black finger
    Pointing upwards.
Why, beautiful still finger, are you black?
And why are you pointing upwards?   *The Black Finger [1925]*

---

[1]From MARK PERRY, *Lift Up Thy Voice: The Grimké Family's Journey from Slaveholders to Civil Rights Leaders* [2001].

1   Each one must make his way alone —
                    And this is Life!   *Life(1)*[1]

2   And to us here, ah! she remains
    A lovely memory,
    Until Eternity;
    She came, she loved and then she went away.
                    To Keep the Memory of Charlotte Forten
                    Grimké[1]

3   Lure of you, eye and lip;
    Yearning, yearning,
    Languor, surrender;
        Your mouth,
    And madness, madness,
    Tremulous, breathless, flaming.   *El Beso*[1]

J[oel] A[ugustus] Rogers   1880–1966

4   One of the world's greatest needs has ever been unboastful, unbiased
    history.   *World's Great Men of Color [1947]*

5   It does appear that a past is as necessary to man as roots to a tree.
                                      World's Great Men of Color

6   As with almost everything else, ancestry is what you make of it.
                                      World's Great Men of Color

William Pickens   1881–1954

7   If prejudice could only reason, it would dispel itself.
                                      The New Negro [1916]

8   The new Negro is a sober, sensible creature, conscious of his environ-
    ment, knowing that not all is right, but trying hard to become adjusted to
    this civilization in which he finds himself by no will or choice of his own.
    He is not the shallow, vain, shadowy creature which he is sometimes adver-
    tised to be. He still hopes that the unreasonable opposition to his forward
    and upward progress will relent. But, at any rate, he is resolved to fight and
    live or die on the side of God and the Eternal Verities.

                                      The New Negro

9   I believe in Africa for the African, white and black, and I believe in
    America for the Americans, native, naturalized and all colors — and I

---

[1]From *Selected Works of Angelina Weld Grimké* [1991], edited by Carolivia Herron.

believe that any of these Americans would be foolish to give up their citizenship for a thousand-year improbability in Africa or anywhere else.

Letter to Marcus Garvey [July 24, 1922][1]

Jimmie Cox

c. 1882–1925

1   It's mighty strange without a doubt,
nobody knows you when you're down and out.

Nobody Knows You When You're Down and Out [1922]

Father Divine [George Baker]

c. 1882–1965

2   Peace, it's wonderful.   *Motto of the Peace Mission Movement*

3   I am a free gift to mankind. Of the plenty and abundance which I have I give to you freely. I ask of you only faith. I take from you nothing. I take your sorrows and give you joy. I take your sickness and give you health. I take your poverty and give you peace and prosperity, for I am the spirit of success and health.   *Amsterdam News, New York [December 23, 1931]*

4   That which has been termed race, is not a race.... It is a curse, and a cursed, vulgar name that was given to low-rate you, in short, to DIS-GRACE you.   *Sermon. Spoken Word [November 1935]*[2]

5   Real education consists of more than merely teaching men the subjects taught in a school curriculum. It comes after the learning of these subjects and consists of putting into practice in daily life the actual virtues of right thinking, right speaking and right living.

If I Were a College Professor [July 25, 1939]

Jessie Redmon Fauset

1882–1961

6   It comes to every colored man and every colored woman, too, who has any ambition.... But every colored man feels it sooner or later. It gets in the way of his dreams, of his education, of his marriage, of the rearing of his children. The time comes when he thinks, "I might just as well fall back; there's no use pushing on. A colored man just can't make any headway in this awful country." Of course, it's a fallacy. And if a fellow sticks it out he finally gets past it, but not before it has worked considerable confusion in his life.   *There Is Confusion [1924]. [Brian]*

7   "All right," she [Angela] said to herself wearily, "I'll keep on living." She thought then of black people, of the race of her parents and of all the odds against living which a cruel, relentless fate had called on them to

---

[1]From Sheldon Avery, *Up from Washington* [1989].
[2]From Robert Weisbrot, *Father Divine and the Struggle for Racial Equality* [1983].

endure. And she saw them as a people powerfully, almost overwhelmingly endowed with the essence of life. They had to persist, had to survive because they did not know how to die.   *Plum Bun [1929]*

1   Rather like spent swimmers, who had given up the hope of rescue and then had suddenly met with it, they were sensing with all their being, the feel of the solid ground beneath their feet, the grateful monotony of the skies above their heads,...and everywhere about them the immanence of God....The Chinaberry Tree became a Temple.

The Chinaberry Tree [1931], last lines

2   To be a colored man in America and enjoy it, you must be greatly daring, greatly stolid, greatly humorous and greatly sensitive and at all times a philosopher.   *Comedy American Style [1933]. [Phebe]*

Sweet Daddy [Charles Emanuel] Grace   c. 1882–1960

3   I do not take any title, call me anything you wish.

Baltimore Afro-American [December 15, 1956]

4   A lot of people are dead, but they haven't been buried yet.

Baltimore Afro-American [February 20, 1960]

5   If you sin against God, Grace can save you, but if you sin against Grace, God cannot save you.

From ARTHUR HUFF FAUSET, *Black Gods of the Metropolis [1971]*

Anne Spencer[1]   1882–1975

6   I know you — a glance, and what you are
Sits-by-the-fire in my heart.
My Limousine-Lady knows you, or
Why does the slant-envy of her eye mark
Your straight air and radiant inclusive smile?
Guilt pins a fig-leaf; Innocence is its own adoring.   *At the Carnival [1922]*

7   We trekked into a far country,
My friend and I.
Our deeper content was never spoken,
But each knew all the other said.   *Translation [1922]*

8   Most things are colorful things — the sky, earth and sea.
        Black men are most men; but the white are free!
White things are rare things so rare, so rare
They stole from out a silvered world — somewhere.   *White Things [1923]*

---

[1]From J. LEE GREENE, *Time's Unfading Garden: Anne Spencer's Life and Poetry* [1977].

1 Lady, Lady, I saw your hands,
Twisted, awry, like crumpled roots,
Bleached poor white in a sudsy tub,
Wrinkled and drawn from your rub-a-dub.
Lady, Lady, I saw your heart,
And altered there in its darksome place,
Were the tongues of flames the ancients knew,
Where the good God sits to spangle through.   *Lady, Lady [1925]*

2 This you may do:
Lock your heart, then, quietly,
And lest they peer within,
Light no lamp when dark comes down
Raise no shade for sun;
Breathless must your breath come through
If you'd die and dare deny
The gods their god-like fun.   *Letter to My Sister [1927]*

3 Once the world was young
For I was twenty and very old
And you and I knew all the answers
What the day was, how the hours would turn
One dial was there to see
Now the world is old and I am still young
For the young know nothing, nothing.   *Epitome*

Jimmy Winkfield
1882–1974

4 To be a great jockey, you have to have a stopwatch in your head. You keep your horse in hand until you're ready to take him out front — but you don't move out there until you're sure you can stay out there.
Statement [1973]. From ED HOATLING, Wink [2005]

Eubie [James Herbert] Blake
1883–1983

5 *[On marking his 100th birthday:]* If I'd known I was going to live this long, I'd have taken better care of myself.   *Attributed [February 1983]*

Hubert Harrison[1]
1883–1927

6 We thank honest white people everywhere who take up our cause, but we wish them to know that we have already taken it up ourselves. While

---

[1]From *A Hubert Harrison Reader* [2001], edited by JEFFREY B. PERRY.

they were refusing to diagnose our case we diagnosed it ourselves, and, now that we have prescribed the remedy — Racial Solidarity — they came to us with their prescription — Class Solidarity. It is too late, gentlemen! ... We say Race First because you have all along insisted on Race First and class after when you didn't need our help.

Race First Versus Class First, Negro World [March 27, 1920]

1   The destiny of the American Negro lies in the future of America. ... While the racial heart of the American Negro will always beat in response to the call of the blood, he recognizes that he is part and parcel of the American civilization. It is here that he has been the burden-bearer; having borne the burden and heat of the day he intends to receive the wages due him here for that work.

The Negro and the Nation. Radio address, New York [June 21, 1923]

2   To attempt to unite the "intellectuals" at the top is not the same thing as uniting the Negro masses. For, very often the "intellectuals" assume the air of superior beings who are made of finer clay and expect that others will run to seek them out. ... The way to unity lies through the hearts of the multitude. First set those hearts on fire with a common zeal for a common object, equally desired and equally attained by all in common, and the fire of that common feeling will flame in every lodge, every church, every city and state in the nation. ... Unselfishness, humility, courage and helpfulness must be the fuel that will go to the kindling of such a flame. But light the fire at the bottom of the pile.

The Right Way to Unity. Boston Chronicle [May 10, 1924]

3   Out of the bosom of the Common People rise the sources of our literature and art, and the real, living virile society is the genuine life they live. Divorced from that, art is finical and literature flabby and what is called "society" becomes only the drumming of drones. It is better to have their good opinion when you are dead than the blessing of the Brahmins while you live.   *The Common People. Boston Chronicle [May 17, 1924]*

4   It is easy to win applause and approval among our people by charging every one of our shortcomings up to the white people. But, just the same, it isn't true. For instance: the white people, instead of being responsible for color prejudice among us, have done their best to discourage it by calling us all by the same contemptuous epithets and by lynching and jim crowing us impartially.   *The Roots of Power. Boston Chronicle [June 21, 1924]*

Ernest Everett Just   1883–1941

5   A group is often slower to see the flame of truth than a single open-minded individual. A group must be conservative and being so may run the

danger of attempting to hold with both the old and the new — an impossibility when one is incompatible with the other.

Letter to John D. Rockefeller, Jr. [June 22, 1936][1]

1   The world today needs a spiritual regeneration. If this can come from biology as biology it has a power in this age of science over those who see science as the end-all of life, and gives strength to others who know by faith alone. But spiritually poverty-stricken as the world is today, how few realize this plight! Where is there given adequate emphasis on things of the spirit? And yet, what is man and all his science but the reflected light of this inner flame?

Letter to John D. Rockefeller, Jr.

2   We feel the beauty of Nature because we are part of Nature and because we know that however much in our separate domains we abstract from the unity of Nature, this unity remains. Although we may deal with particulars, we return finally to the whole pattern woven out of these. So in our study of the animal egg: though we resolve it into constituent parts the better to understand it, we hold it as an integrated thing, as a unified system: in it life resides and in its moving surface life manifests itself.

The Biology of the Cell Surface [1939]

Oscar Micheaux   1884–1951

3   His heritage, then, had been his indefatigable will; his firm determination to make his way; his great desire to make good.

The Homesteader [1917], ch. 2

4   The completed picture is a miniature replica of life and all the varied forces which help to make life so complex.

Quoted in the Philadelphia Afro-American [January 25, 1925][2]

Alain Locke   1885–1954

5   Of all the voluminous literature on the Negro, so much is mere external view and commentary that we may warrantably say that nine-tenths of it is *about* the Negro rather than of him, so that it is the Negro problem rather than the Negro that is known.

The New Negro [1925], foreword

6   The Sociologist, The Philanthropist, the Race-leader are not unaware of the New Negro, but they are at a loss to account for him. He simply cannot be swathed in their formulae. For the younger generation is vibrant

[1]From Kenneth R. Manning, *Black Apollo of Science* [1983].
[2]From Carol Van Epps-Taylor, *Oscar Micheaux: A Biography* [1999].

with a new psychology; the new spirit is awake in the masses, and under the very eyes of the professional observers is transforming what has been a perennial problem into the progressive phases of contemporary Negro life.

The New Negro

1   Hitherto, it must be admitted that American Negroes have been a race more in name than in fact, or to be exact, more in sentiment than in experience. The chief bond between them has been that of a common condition rather than a common consciousness; a problem in common rather than a life in common.

The New Negro

2   The pioneer American Negro artists were, really, unbeknown to themselves, starting the Negros' second career in art and unconsciously trying to recapture a lost artistic heritage.... How was this heritage lost?... Slavery is the answer. Slavery not only physically transplanted the Negro, it cut him off sharply from his cultural roots, and by taking away his languages, abruptly changing his habits, putting him in the context of a strangely different civilization, reduced him, so to speak, to cultural zero.

Negro Art: Past and Present [1936]

Elise Johnson McDougald   1885–1971

3   Negro women are of a race which is free neither economically, socially nor spiritually. Like women in general, but more particularly like those of other oppressed minorities, the Negro woman has been forced to submit to over-powering conditions. Pressure has been exerted upon her, both from without and within her group.

The Double Task. Survey Graphic: Harlem
[March 1925]

Nate Shaw [Ned Cobb]   1885–1973

4   All God's dangers ain't a white man.

From All God's Dangers: The Life of Nate Shaw [1974],
compiled by THEODORE ROSENGARTEN

Lucy Diggs Slowe   1885–1937

5   Negro women, no less than white women, must be prepared for the responsibilities of citizenship if they are to discharge their duties to the government under which they live and if they are to be capable of watching intelligently their own interests, and of using their ballot in preserving and promoting these interests.

Higher Education of Negro Women.
The Journal of Negro Education [July 1933]

Matthew Henson   1886–1955

1   I think I'm the first man to sit on top of the world.
              Greeting to Robert E. Peary when he arrived at the
              North Pole [April 6, 1909][1]

Clementine Hunter   c. 1886–1988

2   Painting is a lot harder than pickin' cotton. Cotton's right there for
you to pull off the stalk, but to paint, you got to sweat your mind.
              Quoted in SHELBY R. GILLEY, *Painting by Heart:*
              The Life and Art of Clementine Hunter [2000]

Georgia Douglas Johnson   1886–1966

3   The heart of a woman falls back with the night,
And enters some alien cage in its plight,
And tries to forget it has dreamed of the stars
While it breaks, breaks, breaks on the sheltering bars.
                                     The Heart of a Woman [1918]

4   I want to die while you love me,
              Oh, who would care to live
Till love has nothing more to ask
              And nothing more to give!
              An Autumn Love Cycle [1928]. I Want to Die While You Love Me

5   Your world is as big as you make it.
I know, for I used to abide.
In the narrowest nest in a corner.
My wings pressing close to my side.   *Share My World [1962]. Your World*

[Gertrude] Ma Rainey   1886–1939

6   Oh, C. C. Rider, a see what you done done.   *See See Rider [1924]*[2]

7   Lord, I wonder what is worryin' me
If it ain't my regular, must be my used to be.   *Broken Hearted Blues [1926]*[3]

8   Now I'm gon' show you all my black bottom
They stay to see that dance

---

[1]From ROBERT H. FOWLER, The Negro Who Went to the Pole with Peary, *American History Illustrated* [May 1966]. In a 1953 interview with Fowler, Henson stated that he arrived at the North Pole before Peary.

[2]First recorded by Rainey. Also known as "C. C. Rider."

[3]From ANGELA DAVIS, *Blues Legacies and Black Feminism* [1998].

> Wait until you see me do my big black bottom
> It'll put you in a trance.   *Ma Rainey's Black Bottom [1927]*[1]

1   They say I do do it, ain't nobody caught me,
    Sure got to prove it on me.
    Went out last night with a crowd of my friends,
    They must've been women, 'cause I don't like no men.
                                               Prove It on Me Blues [1928]

James Van Der Zee   1886–1983

2   Happiness is a sort of perfume. You can't pour it on somebody else
    without getting a few drops on yourself.
                    Quoted in a print advertisement for Bell System
                    [1982]

Lovie Austin [Cora Calhoun]   1887–1972

3   My man ain't actin' right
    He stays out late at night
    And still he says he loves no one but me.
                                               Any Woman's Blues [1923]

4   Lord, I love my man better than I love myself
    And if he don't have me, he won't have nobody else.
                                               Any Woman's Blues

Marcus Garvey   1887–1940

5   One God! One Aim! One Destiny!
                    Motto of the United Negro Improvement Association
                    [founded 1914]

6   Everybody knows there is absolutely no difference between the native
    African and the American and West Indian Negro, in that we are descen-
    dant of one common family stock. It is only a matter of accident that we
    have been divided and kept apart...but it is felt that when the time has
    come for us to get back together, we shall do so in the spirit of brotherly
    love.   *Africa for the Africans [1919].*[2] *Oneness of Interests*

7   We are the descendants of a suffering people. We are the descendants
    of a people determined to suffer no longer.... We do not desire what has

---

[1]From ANGELA DAVIS, *Blues Legacies and Black Feminism* [1998].

[2]*Marcus Garvey: Life and Lessons. A Centennial Companion to The Marcus Garvey and Universal Negro Improvement Association Papers* [1987], *introduction*, edited by ROBERT A. HILL and BARBARA BAIR.

belonged to others, though others have always sought to deprive us of that which belonged to us.

> *Speech at the First International Convention of the*
> *Negro Peoples of the World [August 2, 1920]*

1   We shall ask, demand and expect of the world a free Africa.

> *Speech at the First International Convention of the*
> *Negro Peoples of the World*

2   We shall strive that by our labors, succeeding generations of our own shall call us blessed, even as we call the generation past blessed.... They were blest with a patience not yet known to man. A patience that enabled them to endure the tortures and the sufferings of slavery for two hundred and fifty years. Why? Was it because they loved slavery? No. It was because they loved this generation more. Isn't it wonderful? Transcendent? What then are you going to do to show your appreciation of this love, what gratitude are you going to manifest in return for what they have done for you?

> *Liberty Hall Emancipation Day Speech*
> *[January 1, 1922]*[1]

3   We are not engaged in domestic politics, in church building or in social uplift work, but we are engaged in nation building.

> *The Principles of the Universal Negro Improvement*
> *Association. Speech at Liberty Hall, New York City*
> *[November 25, 1922]*

4   We are organized not to hate other men, but to lift ourselves and to demand respect of all humanity.... We declare to the world that Africa must be free, that the entire Negro race must be emancipated from industrial bondage, peonage and serfdom; we make no compromise; we make no apology in this declaration. We do not desire to create offense on the part of other races, but we are determined that we shall be heard, that we shall be given the rights to which we are entitled.

> *The Philosophy and Opinions of Marcus Garvey,*
> *vol. I, The Future As I See It [1923],*
> *edited by* AMY JACQUES GARVEY

5   We must realize that upon ourselves depend our destiny, our future; we must carve out that future, that destiny.

> *The Philosophy and Opinions of Marcus Garvey, I*

6   It is history, and history will repeat itself. Beat the Negro, brutalize the Negro, kill the Negro, burn the Negro, imprison the Negro, scoff at the

---

[1]*Marcus Garvey: Life and Lessons. A Centennial Companion to The Marcus Garvey and Universal Negro Improvement Association Papers* [1987], *introduction,* edited by ROBERT A. HILL and BARBARA BAIR.

Negro, deride the Negro, it may come back to you one of these fine days because the supreme destiny of man is in the hands of God.
The Philosophy and Opinions of Marcus Garvey, I

1   Today the one race is up, tomorrow it has fallen; today the Negro seems to be the footstool of the other races and nations of the world; tomorrow the Negro may occupy the highest rung of the great human ladder. *The Philosophy and Opinions of Marcus Garvey, I*

2   Black men, you were once great; you shall be great again.... The thing to do is to get organized; keep separated and you will be exploited, you will be robbed, you will be killed. Get organized and you will compel the world to respect you. *The Philosophy and Opinions of Marcus Garvey, I*

3   The only protection against INJUSTICE in man is POWER.
The Philosophy and Opinions of Marcus Garvey, I

4   The masses make the nation and the race.
The Philosophy and Opinions of Marcus Garvey, I

5   EDUCATION is the medium by which a people are prepared for the creation of their own particular civilization, and the advancement and glory of their own race. *The Philosophy and Opinions of Marcus Garvey, I*

6   Africa for the Africans; those at home and those abroad![1]
Motto. The Philosophy and Opinions of Marcus Garvey, I

7   Look for me in the whirlwind or the storm, look for me all around you, for, with God's grace, I shall come and bring with me countless millions of black slaves who have died in America and the West Indies and the millions in Africa to aid you in the fight for Liberty, Freedom and Life.
Letter from Atlanta Prison [February 10, 1925]

8   If others laugh at you, return the laughter to them; if they mimic you, return the compliment with equal force.
African Fundamentalism. Editorial, Negro World [June 6, 1925]

9   Let no voice but your own speak to you from the depths. Let no influence but your own raise you in time of peace and time of war. Hear all, but attend only that which concerns you. *African Fundamentalism*

10   God and Nature first made us what we are, and then out of our own creative genius we make ourselves what we want to be.
African Fundamentalism

11   Let the sky and God be our limit and Eternity our measurement.
African Fundamentalism

---

[1]See William Pickens, 162:9.

1   There is no sense in hate; it comes back to you; therefore, make your history so laudable, magnificent and untarnished, that another generation will not seek to repay your seed for the sins inflicted upon their fathers. The bones of injustice have a peculiar way of rising from the tombs to plague and mock the iniquitous.

> *The Philosophy and Opinions of Marcus Garvey [1925], II.*
> *The Sins of the Fathers*

2   Look Up, You Mighty Race!   *[c. 1936]*[1]

Cyril Valentine Briggs   1888–1966

3   There can be neither geographical nor racial lines where Democracy is concerned. It is for all or for none.

> *The Crusader [September 18, 1918], vol. I, no. 1*

Fenton Johnson[2]   1888–1958

4   There is music in me, the music of a peasant people.

> *The Banjo Player*

5   We are children of the sun,
>   Rising sun!   *Children of the Sun, st. 1*

6   Once I was good like the Virgin Mary and the Minister's
>   wife.
> My father worked for Mr. Pullman and white people's
>   tips; but he died two days after his insurance expired.
> I had nothing, so I had to go to work.   *The Scarlet Woman, st. 1*

7   I am tired of work; I am tired of building up somebody
>   else's civilization.   *Tired, st. 1*

Horace Pippin   1888–1946

8   Pictures just come to my mind and I tell my heart to go ahead.

> *American Artist [1945]*

Sarah [Sadie] Delany   1889–1999

9   Life is short, and it's up to you to make it sweet.

> *Having Our Say [1993]*

---

[1]*Marcus Garvey: Life and Lessons. A Centennial Companion to The Marcus Garvey and Universal Negro Improvement Association Papers* [1987], *introduction,* edited by Robert A. Hill and Barbara Bair.
[2]From *The Book of American Negro Poetry, second edition* [1931], edited by James Weldon Johnson.

Lead Belly[1] *[Huddie Ledbetter]* 1889–1949

1   Go down, ol' Hannah,
     Don't you rise, no more,
     Well, if you rise in the mornin'
     Set this world on Fire.   *Go Down, Old Hannah [1936][2]*

2   Goodnight, Irene, goodnight, Irene,
     I'll kiss you in my dreams.   *Goodnight Irene [1936]*

3   Home of the brave, land of the free
     I don't wanna be mistreated by no bourgeoisie.   *Bourgeois Blues [1937]*

4   It may sound a little funny
     But you didn't make very much money
     In them old cotton fields at home.   *Cotton Fields [1940]*

5   Good mornin' blues, how do you do?   *Good Morning Blues [1940]*

6   On a Monday I was arrested,
     On a Tuesday I was locked up in jail,
     On a Wednesday my trial was attested,
     On a Thursday nobody wouldn't go my bail.
     Yes, I'm almost done,
     Yes, I'm almost done.   *On a Monday [1941]*

Claude McKay[3] 1889–1948

7   Dere is no land dat can compare
       Wid you where'er I roam;
     In all de wul' none like you fair,
       My native land, my home.

       My Native Land, My Home [1912]

8   Upon her swarthy neck black shiny curls
     Luxuriant fell; and tossing coins in praise,
     The wine-flushed, bold-eyed boys, and even girls,
     Devoured her shape with eager, passionate gaze;
     But looking at her falsely-smiling face,
     I knew her self was not in that strange place.

       The Harlem Dancer [1917]

---

[1] Also Leadbelly.
[2] Also recorded as "If you rise up in the mornin', / Bring Judgment Day," as in the traditional work song.
[3] From *Complete Poems of Claude McKay* [2004], edited by WILLIAM J. MAXWELL.

1 Ah, heart of me, the weary, weary feet
  In Harlem wandering from street to street.

Harlem Shadows [1918]

2 Be not deceived, for every deed ye do
    I could match — out match: am I not Afric's son,
    Black of that black land where black deeds are done?

To the White Friends [1918]

3 If we must die, let it not be like hogs
  Hunted and penned in an inglorious spot.

If We Must Die [1919]

4 Like men we'll face the murderous, cowardly pack,
  Pressed to the wall, dying, but fighting back!

If We Must Die

5 Bananas ripe and green, and ginger-root
    Cocoa in pods and alligator pears,
  And tangerines and mangoes and grape fruit
    Fit for the highest prize at parish fairs.

The Tropics in New York [1920], st. 1

6 Although she feeds me bread of bitterness,
  And sinks into my throat her tiger's tooth,
  Stealing my breath of life, I will confess
  I love this cultured hell that tests my youth!
  Her vigor flows like tides into my blood,
  Giving me strength erect against her hate.
  Her bigness sweeps my being like a flood.

America [1921]

7 I cannot praise, for you have passed from praise,
    I have no tinted thoughts to paint you true;
  But I can feel and I can write the word;
    The best of me is but the least of you.

Heritage [1922]

8 Upon the clothes behind the tenement,
  That hang like ghosts suspended from the lines,
  Linking each flat, but to each indifferent,
  Incongruous and strange the moonlight shines.

A Song of the Moon [1922]

9 Oh, I must keep my heart inviolate,
  Against the potent poison of your hate!

The White House [1922]

1   "Oh them legs!" Jake thought. "Them tantalizing brown legs! "...
Brown girls rouged and painted like dark pansies. Brown flesh draped in soft
colorful clothes. Brown lips full and pouted for sweet kissing. Brown breasts
throbbing with love.   *Home to Harlem [1928]*

2   The deep-dyed color, the thickness, the closeness of it. The noises of
Harlem. The sugared laughter. The honey-talk on its streets. And all night
long, ragtime and "blues" playing somewhere, ... singing somewhere, dancing somewhere! Oh, the contagious fever of Harlem. Burning everywhere
in dark-eyed Harlem.   *Home to Harlem*

A[sa] Phillip Randolph   1889–1979

3   Salvation for a race, nation or class must come from within.
                        The World Crisis and the Negro People Today [1940]

4   Freedom is never granted, it is won. Justice is never given, it is
exacted.   *The World Crisis and the Negro People Today*

5   A community is democratic only when the humblest and the weakest
person can enjoy the highest civil, economic, and social rights that the biggest and most powerful possess.   *Why Should We March? [1942]*

6   Fellow Americans, let the nation and world know the meaning of our
numbers. We are not a pressure group. We are not an organization or a
group of organizations. We are not a mob. We are the advance guard of a
massive moral revolution for jobs and freedom.
                        Opening remarks, March on Washington for Jobs
                        and Freedom [August 28, 1963]

7   Our ancestors were transformed from human personalities into private
property. It falls to us to demand new forms of social planning, to create full
employment, and to put automation at the service of human needs, not at
the service of profits, for we are the worst victims of unemployment.
                        Opening remarks, March on Washington for Jobs and Freedom

8   At the banquet table of nature, there are no reserved seats. You get
what you can take and keep what you can hold. If you can't take anything,
you won't get anything. And if you can't hold anything, you won't keep
anything. And you can't take anything without organization.
                        Inscription on memorial statue, Union Station,
                        Washington, D.C.

Noble Sissle   1889–1975

9   I'm just wild about Harry,
     And Harry's wild about me.

The heavenly blisses of his kisses
Fill me with ecstasy.
He's sweet just like chocolate candy,
And just like honey from the bee.
Oh, I'm just wild about Harry
And he's just wild about,
Cannot do without,
He's just wild about me.

I'm Just Wild About Harry [1921]

Spencer Williams   1889–1965

1   I'm goin' to Tishomingo,
Because I'm sad today.
I wish to linger,
Way down old Dixie way.
Oh my weary heart cries out in pain,
Oh how I wish that I was back again.
With a race,
In a place,
Where they make you welcome all the time.

Tishomingo Blues [1917]

2   Basin Street,
That's the street,
Where the elite
Always meet,
In New Orleans,
The Land of Dreams.

Basin Street Blues [1928]

Mordecai Wyatt Johnson   1890–1976

3   We have the world's problem of race relationships here in crucible, and by strength of our American faith we have made some encouraging progress in its solution. If the fires of this faith are kept burning around that crucible, what comes out of it is able to place these United States in the spiritual leadership of all humanity. When the Negro cries with pain from his deep hurt and lays his petition for elemental justice before the nation, he is calling upon the American people to kindle anew about that crucible of race relationships the fires of American faith.

*The Faith of the American Negro. Commencement speech
at Harvard University [June 1922]*

1   University education is one of the supreme privileges of life. It is not designed primarily to increase one's power to make money, but to enable one, by study and reflection, to arrive at a clear notion of the nature and possibilities of human life in the individual and in the world; and to enable one to choose one's career and to develop one's competence to advance the possibilities of human life with maximum effectiveness and internal satisfaction while at the same time understanding, appreciating and cooperating constructively with the work of others.

Inaugural address, Howard University [June 10, 1927][1]

[Ferdinand Joseph LaMothe] Jelly Roll Morton   1890–1941

2   It is evidently known beyond contradiction that New Orleans is the cradle of jazz and I, myself, happened to be the creator in the year 1902.

Letter to Robert Ripley's Believe It or Not
[March 31, 1938]

3   Jazz is a sort of musical gumbo.

From ALAN LOMAX, *Mister Jelly Roll [1950]*

[Annie Elizabeth] Bessie Delany   1891–1995

4   We loved our country, even though it didn't love us back.

Having Our Say [1993]

5   Today they use this term *African American*. It wouldn't occur to me to use that. I prefer to think of myself as an American, that's all! You see, I think I'm as good as anyone. . . . I'll tell you a secret: I think I'm *better*!

Having Our Say

6   When you get real old, honey, you realize there are certain things that just don't matter anymore. You lay it all on the table. There's a saying: Only little children and old folks tell the truth.

Having Our Say

Zora Neale Hurston   1891–1960

7   I am colored but I offer nothing in the way of extenuating circumstances except the fact that I am the only Negro in the United States whose grandfather on the mother's side was not an Indian chief.

How It Feels to Be Colored Me [1928]

---

[1]From *Education for Freedom* [1979], Howard University Archives, Moorland Spingarn Research Center.

1   I am not tragically colored. There is no great sorrow dammed up in my soul, nor lurking behind my eyes. I do not mind at all. I do not belong to the sobbing school of Negrohood who hold that nature somehow has given them a lowdown dirty deal and whose feelings are all hurt about it.... I have seen that the world is to the strong regardless of a little pigmentation more or less. No, I do not weep at the world—I am too busy sharpening my oyster knife.   *How It Feels to Be Colored Me*

2   The game of keeping what one has is never so exciting as the game of getting.   *How It Feels to Be Colored Me*

3   I have no separate feeling about being an American citizen and colored. I am merely a fragment of the Great Soul that surges within the boundaries. My country, right or wrong.
                                          How It Feels to Be Colored Me

4   Sometimes, I feel discriminated against, but it does not make me angry. It merely astonishes me. How can any deny themselves the pleasure of my company?   *How It Feels to Be Colored Me*

5   Ah's satisfied wid you jes' lak you is, baby. God took pattern after a pine tree and built you noble. Youse a pritty man, and if Ah knowed any way to make you mo' pritty still Ah'd take and do it.
                    The Gilded Six-Bits. Story magazine [August 1933] [Missie May]

6   Don't you love nobody better'n you do yo'self. Do, you'll be dying befo' yo' time is out.   *Jonah's Gourd Vine [1934], ch. 16 [Lucy]*

7   I love myself when I am laughing. And then again when I am looking mean and impressive.
                              Letter to Carl Van Vechten [December 10, 1934]

8   Now me, Ah wouldn't let you fix me no breakfus'. Ah git up and fix mah own and den, whut make it so cool, Ah'd fix *you* some and set it on de back of de cook-stove so you could git it when you wake up.
                                          Mules and Men [1935] [Mr. Pitts]

9   Ships at a distance have every man's wish on board. For some they come in with the tide. For others they sail forever on the horizon, never out of sight, never landing until the Watcher turns his eyes away in resignation, his dreams mocked to death by Time. That is the life of men.
                              Their Eyes Were Watching God [1937], opening lines

10   Now, women forget all those things they don't want to remember, and remember everything they don't want to forget. The dream is the truth. Then they act and do things accordingly.
                                          Their Eyes Were Watching God, ch. 1

1   An envious heart makes a treacherous ear.

Their Eyes Were Watching God, 1 [Pheoby]

2   De nigger woman is de mule uh de world so fur as Ah can see. Ah been prayin' fuh it tuh be different wid you.

Their Eyes Were Watching God, 2 [Nanny]

3   There are years that ask questions and years that answer.

Their Eyes Were Watching God, 3

4   Did marriage end the cosmic loneliness of the unmated? Did marriage compel love like the sun the day?

Their Eyes Were Watching God, 3

5   She didn't read books so she didn't know that she was the world and the heavens boiled down to a drop.   *Their Eyes Were Watching God, 7*

6   No matter how far a person can go the horizon is still way beyond you.   *Their Eyes Were Watching God, 9*

7   He [Tea Cake] drifted off into sleep and Janie looked down on him and felt a self-crushing love. So her soul crawled out from its hiding place.

Their Eyes Were Watching God, 13

8   Gods always behave like the people who make them.

Tell My Horse [1938]

9   There is something about poverty that smells of death.

Tell My Horse

10   A thing is mighty big when time and distance cannot shrink it.

Tell My Horse

11   When one is too old for love, one finds great comfort in good dinners.

Moses, Man of the Mountain [1939], ch. 6

12   Once you wake up thought in a man, you can never put it to sleep again.   *Moses, Man of the Mountain, 10*

13   The present was an egg laid by the past that had the future inside its shell.   *Moses, Man of the Mountain, 29*

14   Happiness is nothing but everyday living seen through a veil.

Moses, Man of the Mountain, 39 [Moses]

15   Mama exhorted her children at every opportunity to "jump at de sun." We might not land on the sun, but at least we would get off the ground.   *Dust Tracks on a Road [1942], ch. 2*

16   Grab the broom of anger and drive off the beast of fear.

Dust Tracks on a Road, 4

17   Truth is a letter from courage.   *Dust Tracks on a Road, 4*

1   Research is formalized curiosity. It is poking and prying with a purpose.
Dust Tracks on a Road, 10

2   Our lives are so diversified, internal attitudes so varied, appearances and capabilities so different, that there is no possible classification so catholic that it will cover us all, except My people! My people!
Dust Tracks on a Road, 12

3   It seems to me that trying to live without friends, is like milking a bear to get cream for your morning coffee. It is a whole lot of trouble, and then not worth much after you get it.
Dust Tracks on a Road, 13

4   Love, I find is like singing. Everybody can do enough to satisfy themselves, though it may not impress the neighbors as being very much.
Dust Tracks on a Road, 14

5   I did not just fall in love, I made a parachute jump.
Dust Tracks on a Road, 14

6   I do not pretend to read God's mind. If He has a plan for the universe worked out to the smallest detail, it would be folly for me to presume to get down on my knees and attempt to revise it.
Dust Tracks on a Road, 15

7   The stuff of my being is matter, ever changing, ever moving, but never lost; so what need of denominations and creeds to deny myself the comfort of all my fellow men?... I am one with the infinite and need no other assurance.
Dust Tracks on a Road, 15

8   I have been in Sorrow's kitchen and licked out all the pots. Then I have stood on the peaky mountain wrapped in rainbows, with a harp and a sword in my hands.
Dust Tracks on a Road, 16

9   Justice, like beauty, is in the eye of the beholder.
Dust Tracks on a Road, 16

10   You who play the zig-zag lightning of power over the world, with the grumbling thunder in your wake, think kindly of those who walk in the dust. And you who walk in humble places, think kindly too, of others. There has been no proof in the world so far that you would be less arrogant if you held the lever of power in your hands.
Dust Tracks on a Road, 16

11   He was top-superior to the whole mess of sorrow. He could beat it all, and what made it so cool, finish it off with a laugh.
High John the Conqueror [1943]

Jomo Kenyatta [Kamau Wa Ngengi]   c. 1891–1978

12   The African is conditioned, by the cultural and social institutions of centuries, to a freedom of which Europe has little conception, and it is not

181

in his nature to accept serfdom forever. He realizes that he must fight unceasingly for his own complete emancipation; for without this he is doomed to remain the prey of rival imperialisms, which in every successive year will drive their fangs more deeply into his vitality and strength.

Facing Mount Kenya: The Tribal Life of the Gikuyu (Kikuyu) [1938], conclusion

1   We must try to trust one another. Stay and cooperate.[1]

Statement, as first president of the Republic of Kenya, to the white settlers [1964]

Nella Larsen   1891–1964

2   For the hundredth time she [Helga Crane] marveled at the gradations within this oppressed race of hers. A dozen shades slid by. There was sooty black, shiny black, taupe, mahogany, bronze, copper, gold, orange, yellow, peach, ivory, pinky white, pastry white. There was yellow hair, brown hair, black hair; straight hair, straightened hair, curly hair, crinkly hair, woolly hair. She saw black eyes in white faces, brown eyes in yellow faces, gray eyes in brown faces, blue eyes in tan faces. Africa, Europe, perhaps with a pinch of Asia, in a fantastic motley of ugliness and beauty, semi-barbaric, sophisticated, exotic, were here.   *Quicksand [1928], ch. 11*

3   And suddenly she was oddly cold. An intimation of things distant, but nonetheless disturbing, oppressed her with a faintly sick feeling. Like a heavy weight, a stone weight, just where she knew, was her stomach.

Quicksand, 14

4   I'm homesick, not for America, but for Negroes.

Quicksand, 16 [Helga Crane]

5   Faith was really quite easy. One had only to yield. To ask no questions. The more weary, the more weak she became, the easier it was.

Quicksand, 23

6   She [Irene] wished to find out about this hazardous business of "passing," this breaking away from all that was familiar and friendly to take one's chances in another environment, not entirely strange, perhaps, but certainly not entirely friendly.

Passing [1929], pt. 1, ch. 2

7   The trouble with Clare was, not only that she wanted to have her cake and eat it too, but that she wanted to nibble at the cakes of other folk as well.   *Passing, 2, 1*

---

[1]Harambee [Swahili for "Let's pull together"]. — *National motto of Kenya*

1   Being a mother is the cruelest thing in the world.

Passing 2, 2 [Clare]

2   She [Irene] was caught between two allegiances, different, yet the same. Herself. Her race. Race! The thing that bound and suffocated her. Whatever steps she took, or if she took none at all, something would be crushed. A person or the race.... For the first time she suffered and rebelled because she was unable to disregard the burden of race. It was, she cried silently, enough to suffer as a woman, an individual, on one's own account, without having to suffer for the race as well. It was a brutality and undeserved.

Passing, 3, 2

Archibald Motley, Jr.   1891–1981

3   I have found that try as I will, I cannot escape the nemesis of my color. I believe, deep in my heart, that the dark tinge of my skin is the thing that has been my making. For you see, I have had to work 100 percent harder to realize my ambition.

Quoted in the New York Times [March 25, 1928]

Haile Selassie I   1891–1975

4   Outside the kingdom of the Lord there is no nation which is greater than any other. God and history will remember your judgment.

Speech to the League of Nations [1936][1]

5   In truth there is no legitimate reason or good cause which justifies war.

Address to American people. BBC [1937][2]

6   Until the philosophy which holds one race superior and another inferior is finally and permanently discredited and abandoned; until there are no longer first-class and second-class citizens of any nation; that until the color of a man's skin is of no more significance than the color of his eyes; until the basic human rights are equally guaranteed to all, without regard to race; until that day, the dream of everlasting peace and world citizenship and rule of international morality will remain but a fleeting illusion, to be pursued, but never attained.

Speech before the United Nations General Assembly,
New York [October 1963]

---

[1]He sought sanctions against Italy, which had invaded Ethiopia.

[2]From *The Autobiography of Emperor Haile Selassie I* [1976], *vol. II.* Translated from Amharic by EDWARD ULLENDORFF.

1   It is from the equity of law that honor and advantage arise; it is from the deficiency of law that distress and damage result; it is through failure to set up law that violence and injury grow.

The Autobiography of Emperor Haile Selassie I [1976], vol. I

2   I am concerned more for the freedom of my soul than for the misery of my body.

The Autobiography of Emperor Haile Selassie I, II

Alma Thomas   1891–1978

3   The use of color in my paintings is of paramount importance to me. Through color I have sought to concentrate on beauty and happiness, rather than on man's inhumanity to man.

Interview in the Art Gallery [April 1970]

Big Bill Broonzy [William Lee Conley Bradley]   1893–1958

4   I got the key to the highway
I'm billed out and bound to go
I'm gonna leave here running,
Because walking is most too slow.

Key to the Highway [1940]

5   They said if you was white, you'd be all right.
If you was brown, stick around.
But as you's black, oh brother, get back, get back, get back.[1]

Black, Brown and White [1945]

Walter White   1893–1955

6   Color prejudice creates certain attitudes of mind on the part of some colored people which form color lines within the color line.

The New Negro [1925]. The Negro and American Tradition

7   If we, as Americans, assure that no man is denied any right of citizenship because he is dark of skin or worships his God in a different place or was born elsewhere, then democracy can never be destroyed. But we also know that human freedom must be in the hearts of men and not solely on paper.

Speech at the NAACP annual convention,
Lincoln Memorial, Washington, D.C. [June, 29, 1947][2]

---

[1]See also Anonymous: American, 572:10; and Joseph Lowery, 274:5.
[2]From *Say It Plain* [2005], edited by CATHERINE ELLIS and STEPHEN DRURY SMITH.

1   In the flickering light the mob swayed, paused, and began to flow toward us. In that instant there opened up within me a great awareness; I knew then who I was. I was a Negro, a human being with an invisible pigmentation which marked me as a person to be hunted, hanged, abused, discriminated against, kept in poverty and ignorance, in order that those whose skin was white would have readily at hand a proof of their superiority, a proof patent and inclusive, accessible to the moron and the idiot, as well as the wise man and the genius.

A Man Called White [1948]

2   There is no difference between the killer and the killed. Black is white and white is black.   *A Man Called White*

3   I am white and I am black, and I know that there is no difference. Each casts a shadow, and all shadows are dark.   *A Man Called White, last lines*

4   Either we must attain freedom for the whole world or there will be no world left for any of us.   *Civil Rights: Fifty Years of Fighting [1950]*

5   All the peoples of the world are in the same boat now. Today, that vessel is unseaworthy because we have not yet mastered the science of living together. Through a major leak caused by color prejudice the waters of hate are rushing in. Our survival may depend on how swiftly and expertly that leak is caulked.   *How Far the Promised Land? [1955]*

Clarence Williams   1893–1965

and

Spencer Williams   1889–1965

6   I Ain't Gonna Give Nobody None o' This Jellyroll   *Song title [1919]*

E[dward] Franklin Frazier   1894–1962

7   Lacking a cultural tradition and rejecting identification with the Negro masses on the one hand, and suffering from the contempt of the white world on the other, the black bourgeoisie has developed a deep-seated inferiority complex. In order to compensate for this feeling of inferiority, the black bourgeoisie has created in its isolation what might be described as a world of make-believe in which it attempts to escape the disdain of whites and fulfill its wish for status in American life.

Black Bourgeoisie [1957], introduction

8   The black bourgeoisie, who have striven to mold themselves in the image of the white man, have not been able to escape from the mark of racial inferiority.   *Black Bourgeoisie*

1   Because of its struggle to gain acceptance by whites, the black bourgeoisie has failed to play the role of a responsible elite in the Negro community.   *Black Bourgeoisie*

Jackie "Moms" Mabley [Loretta Mary Aiken]   1894–1975

2   Never lose your head, not even for a minute—you need your head. Your brain's in it.   *Live at the Greek Theater [1971]*[1]

3   *[On teaching children how to cross the street:]* Damn the lights. Watch the cars. The lights ain't never killed nobody.   *Live at the Greek Theater*

Benjamin E[lijah] Mays   1894–1984

4   We agree that imposed separateness breeds ill-will and hatred, and that it develops in the segregated a feeling of inferiority to the extent that he never knows what his capabilities are. His mind is never free to develop unrestricted. The ceiling and not the sky becomes the limit of his striving. But we seldom realize what discrimination does to the person who practices it. It scars not only the soul of the segregated but the soul of the segregator as well. When we build fences to keep others out, erect barriers to keep others down, deny to them the freedom which we ourselves enjoy and cherish most, we keep ourselves in, hold ourselves down, and the barriers we erect against others become prison bars to our own souls.
     Speech at the Second Assembly of the World Council of Churches, Evanston, Illinois [August 21, 1954]

5   He who starts behind in the great race of life must forever remain behind or run faster than the man in front.
     Speech at Shaw University [November 18, 1966]

6   He was not ahead of his time. No man is ahead of his time. Every man is within his star, each in his time. Each man must respond to the call of God in his lifetime and not in somebody else's lifetime.
     Eulogy for Martin Luther King, Jr., Morehouse College [April 9, 1968]

7   It isn't how long one lives, but how well.
     Eulogy for Martin Luther King, Jr.

8   We, too are guilty of murder. It is time for the American people to repent and make democracy equally applicable to all Americans. What can we do? We, not the assassin, represent America at its best. *We* have the power—not the prejudiced assassin—to make things right.
     Eulogy for Martin Luther King, Jr.

[1]From ELSIE A. WILLIAMS, *The Humor of Jackie Moms Mabley* [1995].

1   If we love Martin Luther King, Jr., and respect him as this crowd
surely testifies, let us see to it that he did not die in vain; let us see to it that
we do not dishonor his name by trying to solve our problems through
rioting in the streets. Violence was foreign to his nature.

Eulogy for Martin Luther King, Jr.

2   It must be borne in mind that the tragedy of life doesn't lie in not
reaching your goal. The tragedy lies in having no goal to reach. It isn't a calamity to die with dreams unfilled, but it is a calamity not to dream. It is not a
disaster to be unable to capture your ideal, but it is a disaster to have no
ideal to capture. It is not a disgrace not to reach the stars, but it is a disgrace
to have no stars to reach for. Not failure, but low aim is sin.

Disturbed about Man [1969]

3   To see a mob of white men bent on lynching Negroes before one is
five years old etches an impression on the mind and soul that only death
can erase.   *Born to Rebel [1971]*

4   To me black power must mean hard work, trained minds, and perfected skills to perform in a competitive society.   *Born to Rebel*

Bessie Smith   c. 1894–1937

5   My mind is like a rowboat out on the stormy sea,
He's with me right now, in the morning, where will he be?

Lonesome Desert Blues [1925]

6   Lord, I went to the gypsy to get my fortune told
She said, "You in hard luck, doggone your bad luck soul."

Baby Doll [1926][1]

7   You can say what you please, you will miss me
There's a lot of things you are bound to see,
When your friends forsake you and your money's gone
Then you'll look around, all your clothes in pawn
Down on your knees, you'll ask for me,
There's no one else you will want to see
Then you'll pray a prayer that men pray everywhere, Lord
When your good woman is gone.   *Hard Time Blues [1926]*[1]

8   No time to marry, no time to settle down
I'm a young woman, and I ain't done running around.

Young Woman's Blues [1926]

---

[1]From Angela Davis, *Blues Legacies and Black Feminism* [1998].

1   When it thunders and lightning, and the wind begin to blow
    There's thousands of people ain't got no place to go
    Backwater blues done caused me to pack my things and go
    'Cause my house fell down and I can't live there no more.

                                          Backwater Blues [1927]

2   Poor man's wife is starvin',
    Your wife's livin' like a queen.   *Poor Man's Blues [1928]*

3   It's a long old road, but I know I'm gonna find the end.

                                              Long Old Road [1931]

Bessie Smith   c. 1894–1937

and

Clarence Williams   1893–1965

4   I don't mind being in jail, but I got to stay there so long,
    When every friend I had is done shook hands and gone.

                                             Jailhouse Blues [1923]

Jean Toomer   1894–1967

5   O can't you see it, O can't you see it,
    Her skin is like dusk on the eastern horizon
    … When the sun goes down.   *Cane [1923]. Karintha*

6   Wind is in the cane. Come along.
    Cane leaves swaying, rusty with talk,
    Scratching choruses above the guinea's squawk,
    Wind is in the cane. Come along.   *Cane. Carma*

7   In time, for though the sun is setting on
    A song-lit race of slaves, it has not set;
    Though late, O soil, it is not too late yet
    To catch thy plaintive soul, leaving, soon gone,
    Leaving, to catch thy plaintive soul soon gone.

                                            Cane. Song of the Son

8   A feast of moon and men and barking hounds,
        An orgy for some genius of the South
        With blood-hot eyes and cane-lipped scented mouth,
    Surprised in making folk songs from soul sounds.

Cane. Georgia Dusk, st. 2

1   Values and meanings, though intangible, are held by everyone consciously or unconsciously as the most real and the most important.

Essentials [1931], no. 1

2   Conscience, the heart of the human world, still beats feebly in our sense of decency. *Essentials, 1*

3   The desire to be has become the desire to belong.

Essentials, 4

4   A symbol is as useful to the spirit as a tool is to the hand.

Essentials, 5

5   We start with gifts. Merit comes from what we make of them.

Essentials, 6

6   The aim is not to measure effort but to make it.

Essentials, 7

7   Growing is a stern taking and eliminating, as relentless as life itself.

Essentials, 8

8   Meet life's terms but never accept them. *Essentials, 9*

9   Men are inclined to either work without hope or to hope without work. *Essentials, 10*

10   Fear is a noose that binds until it strangles. *Essentials, 16*

11   We sleep: who profits by our dreams? *Essentials, 47*

12 Beyond plants are animals,
Beyond animals is man,
Beyond man is the universe.
The Big Light,
Let the Big Light in! *The Blue Meridian [1936]*

13 What use bombs and antibombs,
Sovereign powers, brutal lives, ugly deaths?
Are men born to go down like this?
Violence is violence. *The Blue Meridian*

14 Men,
Men and women —
Liberate! *The Blue Meridian*

15 Unlock the races, Open this pod by outgrowing it,
Free men from this prison and shrinkage,
Not from the reality itself
But from our prejudices and preferences
And the enslaving behavior caused by them,

Eliminate these —
I am, we are, simply of the human race.   *The Blue Meridian*

1   And we are the old people, witnesses
That behind us there extends
An unbroken chain of ancestors,
Ourselves linked with all who ever lived,
Joined with all future generations.   *The Blue Meridian*

Paul R[evere] Williams   1894–1980

2   Planning is thinking beforehand how something is to be made or done, and mixing imagination with the product — which in a broad sense makes all of us planners. The only difference is that some people get a license to get paid for thinking and the rest of us just contribute our good thoughts to our fellow man.

> *The Influence of Planning on Man's Destiny. Speech
> [October 25, 1962]*[1]

Joseph Seamon Cotter, Jr.   1895–1919

3   Why do men sneer when I arise
And stand in their councils,
And look them eye to eye,
And speak their tongue?
Is it because I am black?

> *The Band of Gideon, and Other Lyrics [1918].
> Is It Because I Am Black?*

4   O God, give me words to make my dream-children live.

> *The Band of Gideon, and Other Lyrics. A Prayer*

5   And from their trembling lips shall swell
A song of hope the world can understand.
All this to them shall be a glorious sign,
    A glimmer of that resurrection morn,
When age-long Faith crowned with a grace benign
    Shall rise and from their brows cast down the thorn
Of prejudice. E'en though through blood it be,
There breaks this day their dawn of Liberty.

> *The Band of Gideon, and Other Lyrics.
> Sonnet to Negro Soldiers*

---

[1]From KAREN HUDSON, *Paul R. Williams, Architect* [1993].

Charles Hamilton Houston
1895–1950

1   A lawyer's either a social engineer or he's a parasite on society.

Frequent statement to law students[1]

2   The failure of the Government to enforce democratic practices and to protect minorities in its own capital makes its expressed concern for national minorities abroad somewhat specious, and its interference in the domestic affairs of other countries very premature.

Letter to Harry Truman [December 3, 1945][1]

3   There's no law on our side? Let's make some.

From THURGOOD MARSHALL, *Tribute to Charles H. Houston. Amherst Magazine [Spring 1978]*[2]

Alberta Hunter
1895–1984

4   I may be brown as a berry, but that's only secondary,
You can't tell the difference after dark.

You Can't Tell the Difference After Dark [1935]

Alberta Hunter
1895–1984

and

Lovie Austin [Cora Calhoun]
1887–1972

5   Trouble, trouble, I've had it all my days
It seem like trouble going to follow me to my grave.

Down Hearted Blues [1922]

6   I've got the world in a jug, the stopper's in my hand.

Down Hearted Blues

Hattie McDaniel
1895–1952

7   It has made me feel very, very humble and I shall always hold it as a beacon for anything that I may be able to do in the future. I sincerely hope I shall always be a credit to my race and to the motion picture industry.

Acceptance speech for Academy Award for Best Supporting Actress [February 29, 1940][3]

---

[1]From GENNA RAE McNEIL, *Groundwork: Charles Hamilton Houston and the Struggle for Civil Rights* [1983].

[2]From *Thurgood Marshall: His Speeches, Writings, Arguments, Opinions and Reminiscences* [2001], edited by MARK V. TUSHNET.

[3]McDaniel was the first black woman to win an Academy Award. She won for her role in *Gone with the Wind*.

1   There is only eighteen inches between a pat on the back and a kick in the seat of the pants.   *Quoted in the Denver Post [April 15, 1941][1]*

2   Why should I complain about making $7,000 a week playing a maid? If I didn't, I'd be making $7.00 a week actually being one![2]
         From DONALD BOGLE, Toms, Coons, Mulattoes, Mammies & Bucks [1973]

Andy Razaf   1895–1973

3   Anybody Here Want to Try My Cabbage?   *Song title [1925]*

4   Ain't-cha glad?
     How we get along together?
     Ain't-cha glad?
     We can laugh at "stormy weather"?
     Folks declare
     "What a pair!"
     They can see we're happy
     Ain't-cha glad?   *Ain't-Cha Glad [1929][3]*

5   Ain't misbehavin'
     I'm savin' my love for you!   *Ain't Misbehavin' [1929]*

6   Just 'cause you're black folks think you lack,
     They laugh at you and scorn you too,
     What did I do to be so black and blue?   *Black and Blue [1929]*

7   When you're passing by
     Flowers droop and sigh,
     And I know the reason why,
     You're much sweeter, goodness knows,
     Honeysuckle Rose.   *Honeysuckle Rose [1929][3]*

8   How my heart is singin'
     While the band is swingin',
     Never tired of rompin',
     And stompin' with you
     At the Savoy.   *Stompin' at the Savoy [1936]*

9   This joint is jumpin'
     It's really jumpin'

---

[1]From JILL WATTS, *Hattie McDaniel* [2005].
[2]Also often attributed as "I'd rather play a maid than be a maid" or "I'd rather play a maid than be one."
[3]From BARRY SINGER, *Black and Blue: The Life and Lyrics of Andy Razaf* [1992].

Come in cats and check your hats,
I mean this joint is jumpin'.   *The Joint Is Jumpin' [1937]*[1]

George S[amuel] Schuyler   1895–1977

1   Aside from his color, which ranges from very dark brown to pink, your American Negro is just plain American.

The Negro-Art Hokum. The Nation [June 16, 1926]

2   White at last! Gone was the smooth brown complexion. Gone were the slightly full lips and Ethiopian nose. Gone was the nappy hair that he had straightened so meticulously ever since the kink-no-more lotions first wrenched Aframericans from the tyranny and torture of the comb. There would be no more expenditures for skin whiteners; no more discrimination; no more obstacles in his path. He was free! The world was his oyster and he had the open sesame of pork-colored skin!   *Black No More [1931], ch. 2*

3   As a boy he [Max Disher] had been taught to look up to white folks as just a little less than gods; now he found them little different from the Negroes, except that they were uniformly less courteous and less interesting.   *Black No More, 4*

4   It is clear that the Caucasian problem is painfully real and practically universal. Stated briefly, the problem confronting the colored peoples of the world is how to live in freedom, peace and security without being invaded, subjugated, expropriated, exploited, persecuted and humiliated by Caucasians justifying their actions by the myth of white racial superiority.

The Caucasian Problem[2]

William Grant Still   1895–1977

5   I don't think that it is good for the world of music to have everything come out of the same mold. God didn't place only roses on earth, or only lilies or only violets. He put flowers of many sorts and many colors here, the beauty of each enhancing that of the others.

Horizons Unlimited[3]

Ida [Prather] Cox   1896–1967

6   Oh, the blues ain't nothin' but a slow achin' heart disease.
Just like consumption, it kills you by degrees.

Blues Ain't Nothin' Else But [1924]

---

[1] Music by [Thomas] Fats Waller.
[2] From RAYFORD W. LOGAN, *What the Negro Wants* [1943].
[3] From ROBERT BARTLETT HAAS, *William Grant Still and the Fusion of Cultures in American Music* [1972].

1   Wild women don't worry.
Wild women don't have the blues.

Wild Women Don't Have the Blues [1924]

Amy Jacques Garvey   1896–1973

2   Mr. Black Man, watch your step! Ethiopia's queens will reign again, and her Amazons protect her shores and people! Strengthen your shaking knees, and move forward, or we will displace you and lead on to victory and to glory.   *Women as Leaders. Negro World [October 24, 1925]*

3   The doll-baby type of woman is a thing of the past, and the wide-awake woman is forging ahead prepared for all emergencies, and ready to answer any call, even if it be to face the cannons on the battlefield.

Women as Leaders

Florence [Winfrey] Mills   1896–1927

4   The wide world is my stage and I am my audience.
From BILL EGAN, Florence Mills: Harlem Queen of Jazz [2004]

Ethel Waters   1896–1977

5   Only those who are being burned know what fire is like.
His Eye Is on the Sparrow [1951]

Marian Anderson   1897–1993

6   It is easy to look back, self-indulgently, feeling pleasantly sorry for oneself and saying I didn't have this and I didn't have that. But that is only the grown woman regretting the hardships of a little girl who never thought they were hardships at all.   *My Lord, What a Morning [1956]*

7   There are many persons ready to do what is right because in their hearts they know it is right. But they hesitate, waiting for the other fellow to make the first move — and he, in turn, waits for you.

My Lord, What a Morning

8   *[Speaking about prejudice:]* Sometimes it's like a hair across your cheek. You can't see it, you can't find it with your fingers, but you keep brushing at it because the feel of it is irritating.

From My Life in a White World, Ladies' Home Journal [September 1960]

Sidney Bechet   1897–1959

9   *[On playing music:]* You gotta mean it, and you gotta treat it gentle.
Treat It Gentle [1960]

Lucille Bogan   1897–1948

1   I got a sweet black angel, I like the way he spread his wings.

Black Angel Blues [1929][1]

W[illiam] Herbert Brewster   c. 1897–1987

2   Walk and never get tired,
Fly and never falter
I'm gonna move on up a little higher.   *Move On Up a Little Higher [1946]*

3   Surely, God Is Able   *Song title [1950]*

Blind Lemon [Henry] Jefferson   1897–1929

4   Black snake crawling in my room.   *Black Snake Moan [1926]*

5   This house is lonesome: my baby left me all alone.
I said this house is lonesome, my sugar left me all alone.
If your heart ain't rock, sugar, must be marble stone.

Lonesome House Blues [1927]

6   I'm sittin' here wondering, will a matchbox hold my clothes.

Matchbox Blues [1927]

7   Woman rocks the cradle; I declare she rules the home.

That Crawling Baby Blues [1929]

Hubert Fauntleroy "The Black Eagle" Julian   1897–1983

8   As the pioneer aviator and aeronautical representative of millions of intrepid and cultured Negroes of the world we resent emphatically and without compromise dastardly insult as expressed by the chancellor of the Reich "All Negroes of American and British Empire are half apes and baboons and should be incarcerated in a special camp."... I therefore challenge and defy you Hermann Goering as head of the Nazi air force to meet me... at ten thousand feet above the English Channel to fight an aerial duel to avenge this cowardly insult to the honor of my race.

Cable to Berlin [September 1940][2]

Rayford W[hittingham] Logan   1897–1982

9   Repeal is generally more difficult than original passage.

The Betrayal of the Negro [1965]

---

[1] From ANNA STRONG BOURGEOIS, *Blueswomen* [1996].
[2] From JOHN PEER NUGENT, *The Black Eagle* [1971].

Elijah [Poole] Muhammad   1897–1975

1   The church has failed you. Christianity has failed you. The government of America has failed you. You have not received justice from any quarter. As prophesied, you, my fellow Black men, are as sheep among wolves and, as is to be expected, every wolf is taking a bite at you.

Speech, Washington, D.C. [May 29, 1959]

2   We must realize the difference between integration and separation. To integrate with evil is to be destroyed with evil. What we want — indeed justice for us — is to be set apart. We want and must insist upon an area in this land that we can call our own, somewhere we can hold our heads with pride and dignity without the continuous harassments and indignities of our oppressors.

Speech, Washington, D.C.

3   Don't condemn if you see a person has a dirty glass of water, just show them the clean glass of water that you have. When they inspect it, you won't have to say that yours is better.

From MALCOLM X, The Autobiography of Malcolm X [1965]

4   Not knowing "self" or anyone else, they [black people] are prey in the hands of the white race, the world's archdeceivers (the real devils in person).

Message to the Blackman in America [1965]

5   One of the gravest handicaps among the so-called Negroes is that there is no love for self, nor love for his or her own kind. This not having love for self is the root cause of hate.... How can you be loved if you have not love for self and your own nation and dislike being a member of your own?... What nation will trust your love and membership?

Message to the Blackman in America

6   Black man, you are created Black.... Black man stop trying to be white.

The Fall of America [1973]

Sadie Tanner Mossell Alexander   1898–1989

7   I never looked for anybody to hold the door open for me. I knew well that the only way I could get that door open was to knock it down: because I knocked all of them down.[1]

Interview. Black Women Oral History Project [1977]

---

[1]On becoming the first black woman to earn a Ph.D. in economics and the first black woman to be admitted to the Pennsylvania bar.

Septima Poinsette Clark   1898–1987

1   I never felt that getting angry would do you any good other than hurt your own digestion — keep you from eating, which I liked to do.

Ready from Within [1986]

2   The only thing that's really worthwhile is change. It's coming.

Ready from Within, last lines

Harry Haywood [Haywood Hall, Jr.]   1898–1998

3   The entire Negro world looks up to the American Negro, situated in the center of world reaction, to strip the cloak of false democracy from imperialist vultures and to expose their real predatory aims.

Negro Liberation [1948]

Albert John Luthuli   1898–1967

4   In Africa, as our contribution to peace, we are resolved to end such evils as oppression, white supremacy and racial discrimination, all of which are incompatible with world peace and security.... May the day come soon, when the peoples of the world will rouse themselves, and together effectively stamp out any threat to peace, in whatever quarter of the world it may be found.

An Honor to Africa. Nobel Peace Prize acceptance speech
[December 10, 1961]

5   Our continent has been carved up by the great powers; alien governments have been forced upon the African people by military conquest and by economic domination; strivings for nationhood and national dignity have been beaten down by force; traditional economics and ancient customs have been disrupted, and human skills and energy have been harnessed for the advantage of our conquerors. In these times there has been no peace; there could be no brotherhood between men.

Africa and Freedom. Nobel lecture, Oslo University
[December 11, 1961]

6   Though I speak of Africa as a single entity, it is divided in many ways — by race, language, history and custom; by political, economic and ethnic frontiers. But in truth, despite these multiple divisions, Africa has a single common purpose and a single goal — the achievement of its own independence.

Africa and Freedom

7   Somewhere ahead there beckons a civilization, a culture, which will take its place in the parade of God's history beside other great human

syntheses, Chinese, Egyptian, Jewish, European. It will not necessarily be all black; but it will be African.   *Let My People Go [1962], epilogue*

Queen Mother [Audley] Moore   1898–1997

1   It's past due. The United States will never be able to pay us all they owe us. They don't have the money. But they'll owe it.

From BRIAN LANKER, *I Dream a World [1989]*

Paul Robeson   1898–1976

2   In my music, my plays, my films I want to carry always this central idea: to be African. Multitudes of men have died for less worthy ideals; it is even more eminently worth living for.

What I Want from Life [1934].[1] *I Want to Be African*

3   The artist must take sides. He must elect to fight for freedom or slavery.   *Speech, London [June 24, 1937]*[1]

4   I am not being tried for whether I am a Communist, I am being tried for fighting for the rights of my people, who are still second-class citizens in this United States of America.

Testimony Before the House Committee on Un-American Activities [June 12, 1956]

5   You want to shut up every Negro who has the courage to stand up and fight for the rights of his people, for the rights of workers.

Testimony Before the House Committee on Un-American Activities

6   [Response when asked why he didn't stay in Russia:] My father was a slave, and my people died to build this country, and I am going to stay here, and have a part of it just like you. And no fascist-minded people will drive me from it. Is that clear?

Testimony Before the House Committee on Un-American Activities

7   You are the un-Americans and you ought to be ashamed of yourselves.

Testimony Before the House Committee on Un-American Activities

8   To be free — to walk the good American earth as equal citizens, to live without fear, to enjoy the fruits of our toil, to give our children every

---

[1]From *Paul Robeson Speaks* [1978], edited by PHILLIP S. FONER.

opportunity in life — that dream which we have held so long in our hearts is today the destiny that we hold in our hands.   *Here I Stand [1958]*

Melvin B[eaunorus] Tolson   1898–1966

1   Three hundred years we slaved,
    We slave and suffer yet;
    Though flesh and bone rebel,
    They tell us to forget!

                            Dark Sympathy [1944], III. Andante Sostenuto

2   Into the matrix of the Republic poured
            White gulf streams of Europe,
            Black tidal waves of Africa,
            Yellow neap tides of Asia,
            Niagaras of the little people.

            America?
    America is the Black Man's country
    The Red Man's, the Yellow Man's,
    The Brown Man's, the White Man's.

                            Rendezvous with America [1944], III

3   I judge
    My soul
    Eagle
    Nor mole:
    A man
    Is what
    He saves
    From rot.   *A Song for Myself [1944]*

4   Art
    is not barrel copper easily separated
            from the matrix;
        it is not fresh tissues
        — for microscopic study —
            one may *fix:*
        unique as the white tiger's
        pink paws and blue eyes,
            Art
        leaves her lover as a Komitas
    deciphering intricate Armenian neums,
            with a wild surmise.   *Harlem Gallery [1965]. Delta*

                                                                    199

1   Freedom is the oxygen
of the studio and gallery.

Harlem Gallery. Omega

Marita Bonner   1899–1971

2   If you have never lived among your own, you feel prodigal.
On Being Young — a Woman — and Colored.
The Crisis [December 1925]

3   You wonder and you wonder until you wander out into Infinity, where — if it is to be found anywhere — Truth really exists.

On Being Young — a Woman — and Colored

4   So — being a woman — you can wait.

You must sit quietly without a chip. Not sodden — and weighted as if your feet were cast in the iron of your soul. Not wasting strength in enervating gestures as if two hundred years of bonds and whips had really tricked you into nervous uncertainty.

But quiet; quiet. Like Buddha... Still... "Perhaps Buddha is a woman." So you too. Still; quiet; with a smile, ever so slight, at the eyes so that Life will flow into and not by you. And you can gather, as it passes, the essences, the overtones, the tints, the shadows; draw understanding to yourself.

On Being Young — a Woman — and Colored

5   You have been down on Frye Street. You know how it runs from Grand Avenue and the L to a river, from freckled-faced tow heads to yellow Orientals; from broad Italy to broad Georgia, from hooked nose to square black noses. How it lisps in French, how it babbles in Italian, how it gurgles in German, how it drawls and crawls through Black Belt dialects. Frye Street flows nicely together. It is like muddy water.

Nothing New [1926][1]

6   What's the need of working if it doesn't get you anywhere? What's the use of boring around in the same hole like a worm? Making the hole bigger to stay in?

The Purple Flower [1928][1] [Young Us]

7   No hate has ever unlocked the myriad interlacings — the *front* of love. Hate is nothing.

Hate Is Nothing [1938][1]

Thomas A[ndrew] Dorsey   1899–1993

8   Can't blame nobody, guess I'll have to blame it on the blues.

Blame It on the Blues [1928]

---

[1]*Frye Street and Environs! The Collected Work of Marita Bonner* [1987], edited by JOYCE FLYNN and JOYCE OCCOMY STRICKLIN.

1   Precious Lord, take my hand,
     Lead me on, let me stand,
     I am tired, I am weak, I am worn.
     Though the storm, through the night
     Lead me on to the light,
     Take my hand, Precious Lord,
     Lead me home.   *Take My Hand, Precious Lord [1932]*

2   There'll be peace in the valley for me someday,
     There'll be peace in the valley for me,
     I pray no more sadness, no sorrow, no trouble I'll see,
     There'll be peace in the valley for me.   *Peace in the Valley [1938]*

3   If We Ever Needed the Lord Before, We Sure Do Need Him Now
                                                Song title [1943]

4   I'm Climbing up the Rough Side of the Mountain
                                                Song title [1953]

Aaron Douglas   1899–1979

5   Labor has been one of the most important aspects of our develop-
     ment.... It isn't grand, but it is important and it is a thing that we should
     be proud of, because we have that part of our life that has gone into
     the building of America. Not only of ourselves, but in the building of Amer-
     ican life.
                From The Portable Harlem Renaissance Reader [1994],
                edited by DAVID LEVERING LEWIS

Duke [Edward Kennedy] Ellington   1899–1974

6   Playing "bop" is like playing Scrabble with all the vowels missing.
                        Quoted in Look Magazine [August 10, 1954]

7   Fate is being very kind to me. Fate doesn't want me to be too famous
     too young.
                On being denied a Pulitzer Prize in music at the age of
                sixty-six. New York Times [May 5, 1965]

8   Music is my mistress, and she plays second fiddle to no one.
                                        Music Is My Mistress [1973]

9   Love is supreme and unconditional; like is nice but limited.
                                            Music Is My Mistress

10   My mother told me I was blessed, and I have always taken her word
     for it. Being born of — or reincarnated from — royalty is nothing like being

blessed. Royalty is inherited from another human being, blessedness comes
from God. *Music Is My Mistress*

1   Gray skies are just clouds passing over.

Music Is My Mistress

Howard Thurman   1900–1981

2   There is one overmastering problem that the socially and politically
disinherited always face: Under what terms is survival possible? . . . What
must be the attitude toward the rulers, the controllers of political, social and
economic life? . . . Until he has faced and settled that question, he cannot
inform his environment with reference to his own life, whatever may be his
preparation or his pretensions.   *Jesus and the Disinherited [1949]*

3   Under the general plan of nonresistance one may take the position of
imitation. The aim of such an attitude is to assimilate the culture and the
social behavior-pattern of the dominant group. It is the profound capitulation to the powerful because it means the yielding of oneself to that which,
deep within, one recognizes as being unworthy. . . . The aim is to reduce all
outer or external signs of difference to zero, so that there shall be no osten-
sible cause for active violence or opposition. Under some circumstances it
may involve a repudiation of one's heritage, one's customs, one's faith.

Jesus and the Disinherited

4   Anyone who permits another to determine the quality of his inner life
gives into the hands of the other the keys to his destiny.

Jesus and the Disinherited

5   It is a strange freedom to be adrift in the world of men without a sense
of anchor anywhere. Always there is the need of mooring, the need for the
firm grip on something that is rooted and will not give. The urge to be
accountable to someone, to know that beyond the individual himself there
is an answer that must be given, cannot be denied.

The Inward Journey [1961]

6   Saddle your dreams before you ride them.   *The Inward Journey*

7   Suffering is universal for mankind. There is no one who escapes. It
makes demands alike upon the wise and the foolish, the literate and the illit-
erate, the saint and the sinner. Very likely it bears no relationship to the
character of the individual; it often cannot be assessed in terms of merit
or demerit; reward or punishment. Men have tried to build all kinds of
immunities against it. Much of the meaning of all human striving is to be
found in the desperate effort of the spirit of man to build effective wind-
breaks against the storm of pain that sweeps across the human path. Man

has explored the natural world around him, the heights and depths of his own creative powers, the cumulative religious experience of the race — all in an effort to find some means of escape, but no escape is to be found. Suffering stalks man, never losing his scent, and soon or late seizes upon him to wreak its devastation.   *Disciplines of the Spirit [1963]*

1   A man must be at home somewhere before he can feel at home everywhere.   *The Luminous Darkness [1965]*

2   The burden of being black and the burden of being white is so heavy that it is rare in our society to experience oneself as a human being.... Precisely what does it mean to experience oneself as a human being? In the first place, it means that the individual must have a sense of kinship to life that transcends and goes beyond the immediate kinship of family or the organic kinship that binds him ethnically or "racially" or nationally.... He has a sense of being an essential part of the structural relationship that exists between him and all other men, and between him, all other men and the total external environment. As a human being, then, he belongs to life and the whole kingdom of life that includes all that lives and perhaps, also, all that has ever lived. In other words, he sees himself as a part of a continuing, breathing, living existence. To be a human being, then, is to be essentially alive in a living world.   *The Luminous Darkness*

3   Men may build huge dams, there may be profound disturbances of the earth's surface that throw the river out of its course and force it to cut a new channel across a bed of granite, but at last the river will get to the sea.
Deep River [1969]

4   Liberty can be taken away. But freedom! Freedom is the process by which, standing in my place, where I am, I can so act in that place as to influence, order, alter, or change the future — that time is not frozen, that life is not so fixed that it cannot respond to my own will, my own inner processes.... Freedom is the sense of option, the sense of alternatives which only I can affect.   *America in Search of a Soul [1976]*

5   There is something in every one of you that waits and listens for the sound of the genuine in yourself... the only true guide you'll ever have. And if you cannot hear it, you will all of your life spend your days on the ends of strings that somebody else pulls.   *Speech at Spelman College [1981]*[1]

6   Don't ask yourself what the world needs. Ask yourself what makes you come alive and then go do that. Because what the world needs is people who have come alive.   *From GIL BAILIE, Violence Unveiled [1995]*

---

[1]From MARIAN WRIGHT EDELMAN, *The Measure of Our Success* [1992].

Hale Woodruff
1900–1980

1   Everything the Negro artist does has to do with his image of himself and his aspirations. It involves human as well as racial fulfillment. The Negro artist faces all the "artistic," hence, economic and cultural problems all artists face. But for the Negro artist these problems are aggravated by the fact that the "power structure" of the art world is not altogether prepared to accept him as "just another artist."
Speech [1968][1]

Porter Grainger
Twentieth century

and

Everett Robbins
Twentieth century

2   If I should take a notion
To jump into the ocean
'Tain't nobody's biz-ness if I do.
'Tain't Nobody's Biz-ness [1922]

Mother Pollard
Twentieth century

3   My feets is tired, but my soul is rested.
Response when offered a ride during Montgomery bus boycott [1955]. Quoted by Martin Luther King, Jr., in speech [March 25, 1965]

Louis "Satchmo" Armstrong
1901–1971

4   They would beat Jesus if he was black and marched. . . . My life is my music. They would beat me on the mouth if I marched, and without my mouth I wouldn't be able to blow my horn.
On police violence to civil rights marchers in Selma, Alabama. New York Times [March 10, 1965]

5   All music is folk music. I ain't never heard no horse sing a song.
Obituary. New York Times [July 7, 1971]

6   What we play is life.
Attributed

7   *[Reply when asked "What's new?":]* Nothin' new, white folks still ahead.
Attributed

8   *[Reply when asked what jazz is:]* Man, if you gotta ask you'll never know.
Attributed

[1]From ELSA HONIG FINE, *The Afro-American Artist* [1973].

Sterling A[llen] Brown   1901–1989

1   I don't know which way I'm travelin' —
        Far or near,
     All I knows fo' certain is
        I cain't stay here.   *Long Gone [1931]*[1]

2   Talkinges' guy
     An' biggest liar,
     With always a new lie
     On the fire.   *Slim Greer [1931]*

3   Swing dat hammer — hunh —
     Steady, bo';
     Ain't no rush, bebby,
     Long ways to go.   *Southern Road [1931]*

4   *They dragged you from homeland,*
     They chained you in coffles,
     They huddled you spoon-fashion in filthy hatches.
     They sold you to give a few gentlemen ease.   *Strong Men [1931]*

5   The strong men keep a-comin' on
     The strong men git stronger.   *Strong Men*

6   Honey
     When de man
     Calls out de las' train
     You're gonna ride,
     Tell him howdy.   *Sister Lou [1932]*

7   Brother,
     When, beneath the burning sun
     The sweat poured down and the breath came thick,
     And the loaded hammer swung like a ton
     And the heart grew sick;
     You had what we need now, John Henry.
     Help us get it.
     So if we go down
     Have to go down
     We go like you, brother,
     "Nachal" men...   *Strange Legacies [1932]*

---

[1]From *Caroling Dusk* [1927], edited by COUNTEE CULLEN.

1   The Negro has met with as great injustice in American literature as he has in American life. The majority of books about Negroes merely stereotype Negro character....Those considered important enough for separate classification, although overlappings *do* occur, are seven in number: 1) The Contented Slave, 2) The Wretched Freeman, 3) The Comic Negro, 4) The Brute Negro, 5) The Tragic Mulatto, 6) The Local Color Negro and 7) The Exotic Primitive.

Negro Character As Seen by White Authors [1933]

2   In the broken down car
They jounce up and down
Pretend to be steering
On the way to town.

It's as far as they'll get
For many a year;
Cotton brought them
And will keep them here.

The Young Ones [1938][1]

3   Whippersnapper clerks
Call us out our name
    We got to say mister
    To spindling boys
They make our figgers
Turn somersets
We buck in the middle
    Say, "Thankyuh, sah."
    They don't come by ones
    They don't come by twos
    But they come by tens.

Old Lem [1939]

Beauford Delaney   1901–1978

4   The painting has its own speech.

Interview [September 5, 1970][2]

5   Expatriate? It appears to me that in order to be an expatriate one has to be, in some manner, driven from one's fatherland, from one's native land....One must belong before one may then not belong.

From ELSA HONIG FINE, *The Afro-American Artist*
[1973]

---

[1]From MICHAEL S. HARPER, *Sterling A. Brown: Collected Poems* [1980].
[2]From RICHARD A. LONG, *Beauford Delaney: A Retrospective* [1978].

C[yril] L[ionel] R[ichard] James

1901–1989

1   In the colonies any man who speaks for his country, any man who dares to question the authority of those who rule over him, any man who tries to do for his own people what the Englishmen are so proud that other Englishmen have done for theirs, immediately becomes in the eyes of the colonial Englishman a dangerous person, a wild revolutionary, a man with no respect for law and order, a self-seeker actuated by the lowest motives, a reptile to be crushed at the first opportunity. What at home is the greatest virtue becomes in the colonies the greatest crime.

The Case for West Indian Self-Government [1933][1]

2   Africans and people of African descent, especially those who have been poisoned by British imperialist education, needed a lesson. They have got it. Every succeeding day shows exactly the real motives which move imperialism in its contact with Africa, shows the incredible savagery and duplicity of European imperialism in its quest for markets and raw materials. Let the lesson sink in deep.   *Abyssinia and the Imperialists [1936]*[1]

3   The revolution, precisely because it is a revolution, demands all things for all men. It is an attempt to leap from the realm of objective necessity to the realm of objective freedom.

Dialectical Materialism and the Fate of Humanity
[1947][1]

4   Man is not only what he does but what he thinks and what he aims at.
Dialectical Materialism and the Fate of Humanity[1]

5   Our complete emancipation will mean that we shall see ourselves first as citizens of the world, and only secondarily as colored people who see all history from the point of view of our own deliverance.

Writings from The Nation [February 7, 1959][1]

6   The process of revolution is essentially the process of people finding themselves.   *The People of the Gold Coast [1960]*[1]

7   Great men make history, but only such history as it is possible for them to make. Their freedom of achievement is limited by the necessities of their environment.   *The Black Jacobins [1963], preface*

8   Eminence engenders enemies.   *The Black Jacobins*

9   In revolution, when the ceaseless slow accumulation of centuries bursts into volcanic eruption, the meteoric flares and flights above are a meaningless chaos and lend themselves to infinite caprice and romanticism

---

[1]From *The C. L. R. James Reader* [1992], edited by ANNA GRIMSHAW.

unless the observer sees them always as projections of the sub-soil from which they came. *The Black Jacobins*

1 The patience and forbearance of the poor are among the strongest bulwarks of the rich. *The Black Jacobins*

2 It is from America's urban blacks that many people all over the world have historically gained a consciousness of the problems that black people suffer and their attempts to overcome them. *[1970]*[1]

Edith Spurlock Sampson[2] 1901–1979

3 Some of you may ask, "What does the Negro want?" He wants all he needs in order to become a first-class citizen. He wants an equal chance for education; he wants a chance to develop his abilities, techniques and skills; he wants to be able to seek employment and to secure it despite his color. He wants to support his family, to provide for and educate his children, and he wants to live unmolested and to be free of terror. He does not want to be a ward of anybody. He does want to participate fully in all avenues of American life. He wants, in short, some of the assets of citizenship as well as the liabilities. *Speech, World Security Begins at Home [1950]*[2]

4 Keep America free and make it freer. *World Security Begins at Home*

Jesse Stone 1901–1999

5 Shake, Rattle and Roll *Song title [1954]*

Roy Wilkins 1901–1981

6 We cannot do it, and we shall not do it. We would have no right to be Americans, or to enjoy the respect of our fellows, or to receive the love and honor of our children if we voluntarily accept a lesser status. *Statement on NBC television program [February 8, 1959]*

7 The players in this drama of frustration and indignity are not commas or semicolons in a legislative thesis; they are people, human beings, citizens of the United States of America. *Testimony Before the Senate Commerce Committee regarding the public accommodations component of the civil rights bill [July 22, 1963]*

8 *[On racist violence in the South:]* It is simply incomprehensible to us here today and to millions of others far from this spot that the United States

[1]From *The C. L. R. James Reader* [1992], edited by ANNA GRIMSHAW.
[2]From *Frontiers for Freedom* [1952], edited by R. GORDON HOXIE.

Government, which can regulate the contents of a pill, apparently is power-less to prevent the physical abuse of citizens within its own borders.

March on Washington for Jobs and Freedom
[August 28, 1963]

1   In this long climb, Negroes have had white allies since the first white Southerner violated the law by teaching slaves to read and write.

To Fulfill These Rights. Address, White House conference
[June 2, 1966]

Gwendolyn Bennett   1902–1981

2   I want to breathe the Lotus flow'r
Sighing to the stars
With tendrils drinking at the Nile...

I want to feel the surging
Of my sad people's soul,
Hidden by a minstrel-smile.   *Heritage [1923][1]*

3   I love you for your brownness
And the rounded darkness of your breast.
I love you for the breaking sadness in your voice
And the shadows where your wayward eye-lids rest.

To a Dark Girl [1923][1]

4   Memory will lay its hands
Upon your breast
And you will understand
My hatred.   *Hatred [1926][2]*

5   America where black was black. Wasn't white nowhere black wasn't.

The Wedding Day [1926]

[Arnaud Wendell] Arna Bontemps   1902–1973

6   He [Augie] was a thin, undersized boy, smaller for his years than any other child on the place, and he had round pop-eyes. But he enjoyed a certain prestige among the black youngsters, and older folks as well, because of the legend that he was lucky, a legend that had attended him since birth due to a mysterious veil with which he had entered the world.

God Sends Sunday [1931],[3] ch. 1

---

[1]From *The Book of American Negro Poetry, second edition* [1931], edited by James Weldon Johnson.
[2]From *Caroling Dusk* [1927], edited by Countee Cullen.
[3]This novel was the basis of the 1946 Broadway musical *St. Louis Woman.*

1   Time is not a river. Time is a pendulum.

Black Thunder [1936], introduction

2   Come on in, suh, if you's a-mind to. I'm ready and waiting, me. I ain't been afeared of a nachal man, and I don't know's I mind the old Massa hisself. I ain't been afeared of thunder and lightning, and I don't reckon I'll mind the hurricane. I don't know's I'll mind when the trees bend down and the tombstones commence to bust. Don't reckon I'll mind, suh. Come on in.

Black Thunder, bk. 5, ch. 8 [Gabriel]

3   Yet what I sowed and what the orchard yields
My brother's sons are gathering stalk and root,
Small wonder then my children glean in fields
They have not sown, and feed on bitter fruit.

A Black Man Talks of Reaping [1963], st. 3

4   Yet would we die as some have done:
Beating a way for the rising sun.

The Day-Breakers [1963]

5   *[On the Harlem Renaissance:]* When we were not too busy having fun, we were shown off and exhibited and presented in scores of places, to all kinds of people. And we heard the sighs of wonder, amazement and sometimes admiration when it was whispered and announced that here was one of the "New Negroes."

Personals [1973], introduction

Langston Hughes[1]   1902–1967

6   Hold fast to dreams
For if dreams die
Life is a broken-winged bird
That cannot fly.

Dreams [1923]

7   In a Harlem cabaret
Six long-headed jazzers play.
A dancing girl whose eyes are bold
Lifts high a dress of silken gold.

Jazzonia [1923]

8   To fling my arms wide
In the face of the sun,
Dance! Whirl! Whirl!
Till the quick day is done.
Rest at pale evening . . .
A tall, slim tree . . .

---

[1]From *The Collected Poems of Langston Hughes*, edited by ARNOLD RAMPERSAD.

Night coming tenderly
    Black like me.
                                                 Dream Variations [1924]

1   We have tomorrow
    Bright before us
    Like a flame.
                                                Youth [1924]

2   I, too, sing America.

   I am the darker brother.
   They send me to eat in the kitchen
   When company comes.
   But I laugh,
   And eat well,
   And grow strong.
                                 I, Too [1926]

3   Life for me ain't been no crystal stair.
                 Mother to Son [1926]

4   I am a Negro:
    Black as the night is black,
    Black like the depths of my Africa.
                       Negro [1926]

5   It is the duty of the younger Negro artist...to change through the force of his art that old whispering "I want to be white," hidden in the aspirations of his people, to "Why should I want to be white? I am a Negro—and beautiful!"
        The Negro Artist and the Racial Mountain.
        The Nation [June 23, 1926]

6   We younger artists who create now intend to express our individual dark-skinned selves without fear or shame. If white people are pleased, we are glad. If they are not, it doesn't matter. We know we are beautiful. And ugly too.... If colored people are pleased we are glad. If they are not, their displeasure doesn't matter either. We build our temples for tomorrow, strong as we know how, and we stand on top of the mountain, free within ourselves.   *The Negro Artist and the Racial Mountain*

7   I've known rivers:
   I've known rivers ancient as the world and older than the
      flow of human blood in human veins.
   My soul has grown deep like the rivers.
        The Negro Speaks of Rivers (to W. E. B. Du Bois) [1926]

8   Serve—and hate will die unborn.
   Love—and chains are broken.
        Alabama Earth (at Booker T. Washington's grave) [1928]

1   No matter how belligerent or lewd their talk was, or how sordid the tales they told — of dangerous pleasures and strange perversities — these black men laughed.... No matter how hard life might be, it was not without laughter.

Not Without Laughter [1930]

2   Listen, Christ,
You did alright in your day, I reckon —
But that day's gone now.
They ghosted you up a swell story, too,
Called it Bible —
But it's dead now.

Goodbye Christ [1932]

3   "Besides," Milberry said to himself, "the ways of white folks, I mean some white folks, is too much for me. I reckon they must be a few good ones, but most of 'em ain't good — leastwise they don't treat me good. And Lawd know, I ain't never done nothin' to 'em, nothin' a-tall.

The Ways of White Folks [1933]

4   Let America be America again.
Let it be the dream it used to be.
Let it be the pioneer on the plain
Seeking a home where he himself is free.

(America never was America to me.)

Let America Be America Again [1936]

5   O, let America be America again —
The land that never has been yet —
And yet must be — the land where *every* man is free.
The land that's mine — the poor man's, Indian's, Negro's, ME —
Who made America,
Whose sweat and blood, whose faith and pain,
Whose hand at the foundry, whose plow in the rain,
Must bring back our mighty dream again.   *Let America Be America Again*

6   It was the period when the Negro was in vogue.

The Big Sea [1940]. On the Harlem Renaissance

7   Literature is a big sea full of many fish.   *The Big Sea. Postscript*

8   I dream a world where all
Will know sweet freedom's way.
Where greed no longer saps the soul
Nor avarice blights our day.
A world I dream where black or white,
Whatever race you be,

Will share the bounties of the earth
And every man is free. *I Dream a World [1941]*

1 I swear to the Lord
I still can't see
Why Democracy means
Everybody but me. *Black Man Speaks [1943]*

2 Wear it
Like a banner
For the proud —
Not like a shroud. *Color [1943]*

3 There are words like *Liberty*
That almost make me cry.
If you had known what I know
You would know why. *Words like Freedom [1943]*

4 Sometimes a crumb falls
From the tables of joy,
Sometimes a bone
Is flung. *Luck [1947]*

5 Good morning, daddy!
Ain't you heard
The boogie-woogie rumble
Of a dream deferred? *Dream Boogie [1951]*

6 What happens to a dream deferred?
     Does it dry up
     like a raisin in the sun?
     Or fester like a sore —
     And then run?
     Does it stink like rotten meat?
     Or crust and sugar over —
     like a syrupy sweet?
     Maybe it just sags
     like a heavy load.

   Or does it explode? *Harlem [1951]*

7 You are white —
   yet a part of me, as I am a part of you.
   That's American.
   Sometimes perhaps you don't want to be a part of me.

Nor do I often want to be a part of you.
But we are, that's true!
As I learn from you,
I guess you learn from me —
although you're older — and white —
and somewhat more free.

Theme for English B [1951]

1 Practical man,
He said, Train your head,
Your heart, and your hand.
Your fate is here
Not afar,
So let down your bucket
Where you are.

Ballad of Booker T [1953]

2 Negro blood is sure powerful — because just one drop of black blood
makes a colored man. One drop — you are a Negro! . . . Black is powerful.

Simple Takes a Wife [1953]

3 Saturday and Sunday's
Fun to sport around.
But no use denying —
Monday'll get you down.

Blue Monday [1959]

4 AND THEY ASKED ME RIGHT AT CHRISTMAS
IF MY BLACKNESS WOULD RUB OFF?
I SAID, ASK YOUR MAMA.

Ask Your Mama: 12 Moods for Jazz [1961]. Cultural Exchange

5 AND ONE SHOULD LOVE ONE'S COUNTRY
FOR ONE'S COUNTRY IS YOUR MAMA.

Ask Your Mama. Horn of Plenty

6 TELL ME, MAMA, CAN I GET MY SHOW
TELL ME FARE FROM YOU?
OR DO YOU THINK THAT PAPA'S
GOT CHANGE IN HIS LONG POCKET?
IN THE QUARTER OF THE NEGROES
WHERE THE MASK IS PLACED BY OTHERS
IBM ELECTRIC BONGO DRUMS ARE COSTLY.
TELL ME, MAMA, TELL ME,
STRIP TICKETS STILL ILLUSION?
GOT TO ASK YOU — GOT TO ASK!
TELL ME, TELL ME, MAMA,
ALL THAT MUSIC, ALL THAT DANCING

CONCENTRATED TO THE ESSENCE
OF THE SHADOW OF THE DOLLAR
PAID AT THE BOX OFFICE
WHERE THE LIGHTER IS THE DARKER
IN THE QUARTER OF THE NEGROES
AND THE TELL ME OF THE MAMA
IS THE ANSWER TO THE CHILD.   *Ask Your Mama. Show Fare, Please*

1   The white race drug me over here from Africa, slaved me, freed me, lynched me, starved me during the depression, Jim Crowed me during the war — then they come talking about they is scared of me! Which is why I am glad I have got one spot to call my own where I hold sway — Harlem.
The Best of Simple [1961]

2   I have been worrying as long as I have been black. Since I have to be black a long time yet, what is the sense of so much worriation?
The Best of Simple

3   Harlem, like a Picasso painting in his cubistic period. Harlem — Southern Harlem — the Carolinas, Georgia, Florida — looking for the Promised Land — dressed in rhythmic words, painted in bright pictures, dancing to jazz — and ending up in the subway at morning rush time — *headed downtown.* . . . Melting pot Harlem — Harlem of honey and chocolate and caramel and rum and vinegar and lemon and lime and gall. Dusky dream Harlem rumbling into a nightmare tunnel where the subway from the Bronx keeps right on downtown.
My Early Days in Harlem [Summer 1963]. Freedomways

Wifredo Lam [Wifredo Óscar de la Concepción Lam y Castilla]   1902–1982

4   A true picture has the power to set the imagination to work.
Cahiers d'art [1951]

George Padmore   1902–1959

5   World Imperialism can be divided into two main camps: "The Haves," those who possess colonies, and the "Have-Nots," those who seek to possess.   *Africa and World Peace [1937]*

6   Pan-Africanism looks above the narrow confines of class, race, tribe and religion. In other words, it wants equal opportunity for all. Talent to be rewarded on the basis of merit. Its vision stretches beyond the limited frontiers of the nation-state. Its perspective embraces the federation of

regional self-governing countries and their ultimate amalgamation into a United States of Africa.   *Pan-Africanism or Communism [1956]*

Reyita [Maria de los Reyes Castillo Bueno]   1902–1997

1   I am Reyita, a regular, ordinary person. A natural person, respectful, helpful, decent, affectionate, and very independent. For my mother, it was an embarrassment that I — of her four daughters — was the only black one.
        Reyita: The Life of a Black Cuban Woman in the Twentieth Century [1996], opening lines

Stepin Fetchit [Lincoln Perry]   1902–1985

2   I'm so lazy, even when I walked in my sleep I used to hitchhike.... People say, "How'd you get in pictures?" I say, "Well, when I was a kid I always wanted to be somethin'. Of course I didn't want to do nothin' to be it. I used to go 'round trying to get a job doin' nothin', but everywhere I went they either wanted me to do somethin' or else they didn't wanna give you nothin' for it. So I kept tryin' til I growed up, then I went to see this man in California makin' a picture and I say, "Mr. you want somebody to do nothin?'" and they say, "Yeah." So I been busy working every since. Yeah, and I work up to the place where the less I have to do, the mo' I make. Tryin' to make as much as I can so when I get old I can rest.
        Radio performance and interview [1967][1]

3   It was not Martin Luther King who emancipated the modern Negro, but Stepin Fetchit.... It was Step, who elevated the Negro to the dignity of a Hollywood star. I made the Negro a first-class citizen all over the world.
        Interview. New York Times [July 24, 1968]

4   Now get this — when all the Negroes was goin' around straightening their hair and bleaching theirself trying to be white and thought improvement was white, in them days I was provin' to the world that black was beautiful. Me. I opened so many things for Negroes — I'm so proud today of the things that the Negroes is enjoying because I personally did 'em myself.   *Interview. Film Quarterly [Summer 1971]*

Wallace Thurman   1902–1934

5   More acutely than ever before Emma Lou began to feel that her luscious black complexion was somewhat of a liability, and that her marked color variation from other people in her environment was a decided curse.

---

[1]From Mel Watkins, *Stepin Fetchit: The Life and Times of Lincoln Perry* [2005].

Not that she minded being black, being a Negro necessitated having a colored skin, but she did mind being too black.

The Blacker the Berry... [1929], opening lines

1   She wasn't the only black girl alive. There were thousands on thousands who, like her, were plain, untalented, ordinary, and who, unlike herself, seemed to live in some degree of comfort. Was she alone to blame for her unhappiness? Although this had been suggested to her by others, she had been too obtuse to accept it. She had ever been eager to shift the entire blame on others when no doubt she herself was the major criminal.

The Blacker the Berry...

2   Do you know, Steve, I'm sick of both whites and blacks? I'm sick of discussing the Negro problem, of having it thrust at me from every conversational nook and cranny. I'm sick of whites who think I can't talk about anything else, and of Negroes who think I shouldn't talk about anything else. I refuse to wail and lament... I get it from all sides.

Infants of the Spring [1932] [Raymond]

3   I may get moody and curse my fate, but so does any other human being with an ounce of intelligence.   *Infants of the Spring*

Ella J[osephine] Baker   1903–1986

4   Until the killing of black men, black mothers' sons, becomes as important to the rest of the country as the killing of a white mother's son, we who believe in freedom cannot rest.

Speech, Mississippi Freedom Democratic Party Convention [1964][1]

5   People have to be made to understand that they cannot look for salvation anywhere but to themselves.

*Interview. From GERDA LERNER, Black Women in
White America [1972]*

6   I have always felt it was a handicap for oppressed peoples to depend so largely upon a leader, because unfortunately in our culture, the charismatic leader usually becomes a leader because he has found a spot in the public limelight. It usually means he has been touted through the public media, which means that the media made him, and the media may undo him.

Interview

7   The struggle is eternal. Somebody else carries on.

*Oral history. From ELLEN CANTAROW ET AL.,
Moving the Mountain [1980]*

---

[1]Baker was referring to the murders of civil rights workers James Chaney, Andrew Goodman, and Michael Schwerner.

Countee Cullen

1903–1946

1   We must be one thing or the other, an asset or a liability, the sinew in your wing to help you soar, or the chain to bind you to earth. You cannot go forward unless you take us with you.

             League of Youth address. The Crisis [August 1923][1]

2 She even thinks that up in heaven
    Her class lies late and snores,
  While poor black cherubs rise at seven
    To do celestial chores.   *For a Lady I Know [1925]*

3 One three centuries removed
  From the scenes his fathers loved,
  Spicy grove, cinnamon tree,
  What is Africa to me?   *Heritage [1925]*

4 Now I was eight and very small
    And he was no whit bigger,
  And so I smiled, but he poked out
    His tongue, and called me, "Nigger."   *Incident [1925]*

5 Some are teethed on a silver spoon,
    With the stars strung for a rattle;
  I cut my teeth as the black raccoon—
    For implements of battle.   *Saturday's Child [1925]*

6 Dame Poverty gave me my name,
    And Pain godfathered me.   *Saturday's Child*

7 "Lord, being dark," I said, "I cannot bear
  The further touch of earth, the scented air;
  Lord, being dark, forewilled to that despair
  My color shrouds me in, I am as dirt
  Beneath, my brother's heel; there is a hurt
  In all the simple joys which to a child
  Are sweet; they contaminate, defiled." *The Shroud of Color [1925]*[1]

8 Yet I do marvel at this curious thing:
  To make a poet black, and bid him sing! *Yet I Do Marvel [1925]*

9 We were not made eternally to weep. *From the Dark Tower [1927]*[1]

10 Until I die my burthen be;
  How Cavalry in Palestine,

[1]From *My Soul's High Song: The Collected Writings of Countee Cullen* [1991], edited by GERALD EARLY.

Extending down to me and mine,
Was but the first leaf in a line
Of trees on which a Man should swing
World without end, in suffering
For all men's healing, let me sing. *The Black Christ [1929],[1] I*

1 Your love to me was like an unread book. *Bright Bindings [1929][1]*

Earl "Fatha" Hines 1903–1983

2 I always thought jazz was like the trunk of a tree. After the tree has grown, many branches have spread out. They're all with different leaves and they all look beautiful. But at the end of the season, they fold back up and it's still that tree trunk. *Interview [1976][2]*

[James] Bubber Miley 1903–1932

3 It Don't Mean a Thing If It Ain't Got That Swing
Title of Duke Ellington song [1932][3]

[James Andrew] Jimmy Rushing 1903–1972

and

[Eduard] Eddie Durham 1906–1987

and

Count [William James] Basie 1904–1984

4 Sent for you yesterday, and here you come today.
Sent for You Yesterday [1938][4]

Count [William James] Basie 1904–1984

5 Play like you play. Play like you think, and then you got it, if you're going to get it. And whatever you get, that's you, so that's your story.
*From Good Morning Blues: The Autobiography of
Count Basie [1985]*

---

[1]From *My Soul's High Song: The Collected Writings of Countee Cullen* [1991], edited by GERALD EARLY.

[2]From STUDS TERKEL, *And They Sang* [2005].

[3]"Bubber was the first man I heard use the expression, 'It don't mean a thing if it ain't got that swing.'" From DUKE ELLINGTON, "The Most Essential Instrument," *Jazz Journal,* 18, 12 [December 1965], as reprinted in *The Duke Ellington Reader* [1993], edited by MARK TUCKER. In his memoir *Music Is My Mistress* [1973], Ellington also wrote of Miley, "'It don't mean a thing if it ain't got that swing' was his credo."

[4]Recorded by the Count Basie Orchestra.

Ralph [Johnson] Bunche   1904–1971

1   I have a deep-seated bias against hate and intolerance. I have a bias against racial and religious bigotry. I have a bias against war; a bias for peace. I have a bias which leads me to believe in the essential goodness of my fellow man; which leads me to believe that no problem of human relations is ever insoluble.

Speech at the American Association for the United Nations,
New York [May 9, 1949][1]

2   May there be freedom, equality and brotherhood among all men. May there be morality in the relations among nations. May there be, in our time, at long last, a world at peace in which we, the people, may for once begin to make full use of the great good that is in us.

Nobel Peace Prize acceptance speech
[December 10, 1950]

3   Freedom, democracy, human rights, international morality, peace itself, mean different things to different men. Words, in a constant flow of propaganda — itself an instrument of war — are employed to confuse, mislead, and debase the common man. Democracy is prostituted to dignify enslavement; freedom and equality are held good for some men but withheld from others by and in allegedly "democratic" societies; in "free" societies, so-called, individual human rights are severely denied; aggressive adventures are launched under the guise of "liberation." Truth and morality are subverted by propaganda, on the cynical assumption that truth is whatever propaganda can induce people to believe.

Nobel lecture [December 11, 1950]

4   In his scientific genius, man has wrought material miracles and has transformed his world. He has harnessed nature and has developed great civilizations. But he has never learned very well how to live with himself. The values he has created have been predominantly materialistic; his spiritual values have lagged far behind. He has demonstrated little spiritual genius and has made little progress toward the realization of human brotherhood.   *Nobel lecture*

5   There is the ever-present, simple, but stark truth that though the peoples long primarily for peace, they may be prodded by their leaders and governments into needless war, which may at worst destroy them, at best lead them once again to barbarism.   *Nobel lecture*

---

[1]From Brian Urquhart, *Ralph Bunche: An American Odyssey* [1993].

1   With nationalism per se there may be no quarrel. But narrow, exclusively self-centered nationalism persists as the outstanding dynamic of world politics and is the prime obstacle to enduring peace.

Nobel lecture

2   To suggest that war can prevent war is a base play on words and a despicable form of warmongering. The objective of any who sincerely believe in peace clearly must be to exhaust every honorable recourse in the effort to save the peace. The world has had ample evidence that war begets only conditions which beget further war.

Nobel lecture

Pete Johnson   1904–1967

and

Joe Turner [Joseph Vernon Turner, Jr.]   1911–1985

3   I got a gal, she lives up on the hill
Well, this woman's tryin' to quit me, Lord, but I love her still.

Roll 'Em, Pete [1938]

4   You so beautiful, but you gotta die someday.

Roll 'Em, Pete

5   Roll it, boy, let 'em jump for joy,
Yeah, man happy as a baby boy.

Roll 'Em, Pete

[Dewey] "Pigmeat" Markham   1904–1981

6   Hear ye, hear ye, court is in session...and here come the judge, here come the judge. The judge is higher'n a Gawgia pine!

Here Come the Judge [1969]

[Thomas Wright] "Fats" Waller   1904–1943

7   *[When asked to explain rhythm:]* Lady, if you got to ask, you ain't got it.   *Attributed*

Arthur "Big Boy" Crudup   1905–1974

8   Well, that's all right, mama
That's all right for you
That's all right now, mama
Any way you do.

That's All Right [1943]   221

Lois Mailou Jones   1905–1998

1   The wonderful thing about being an artist is that there is no end to creative expression. Painting is my life; my life is painting.

The Art and Life of Lois Mailou Jones [1994]

Mother [Clara McBride] Hale   1905–1992

2   Being black does not stop you. You can sit out in the world and say, "Well, white people kept me back, and I can't do this." Not so. You can have anything you want if you make up your mind and you want it.

From BRIAN LANKER, I Dream a World [1989]

The Niagara Movement   1905–1909

3   Color-Line: Any discrimination based simply on race or color is barbarous, we care not how hallowed it be by custom, expediency, or prejudice. Differences made on account of ignorance, immorality, or disease are legitimate methods of fighting evil, and against them we have no word of protest; but discriminations based simply and solely on physical peculiarities, place of birth, color of skin, are relics of that unreasoning human savagery of which the world is and ought to be thoroughly ashamed.

Declaration of Principles [1905]

4   Oppression: We repudiate the monstrous doctrine that the oppressor should be the sole authority as to the rights of the oppressed. The Negro race in America, stolen, ravished and degraded, struggling up through difficulties and oppression, needs sympathy and receives criticism, needs help and is given hindrance, needs protection and is given mob-violence, needs justice and is given charity, needs leadership and is given cowardice and apology, needs bread and is given a stone. This nation will never stand justified before God until these things are changed.   *Declaration of Principles*

Josephine Baker   1906–1975

5   You are on the eve of a complete victory. You can't go wrong. The world is behind you.

Speech at the March on Washington for Jobs and Freedom [August 28, 1963][1]

6   Salt and pepper. Just what it should be.

Speech at the March on Washington for Jobs and Freedom[2]

---

[1]From JEAN-CLAUDE BAKER, *Josephine: The Hungry Heart* [1993].

[2]From PHYLLIS ROSE, *Jazz Cleopatra* [1989].

1   I had to succeed. I would never stop trying, never. A violinist had his violin, a painter his palette. All I had was myself. I was the instrument that I must care for.   *Josephine [1976]*

2   My face and rump were famous! I could honestly say that I'd been blessed with an intelligent derrière. Most people's were only good to sit on!
                                                                    Josephine

[William] Waring Cuney   1906–1976

3   She does not know
Her beauty,
She thinks her brown body
Has no glory.

If she could dance
Naked,
Under palm trees.
And see her image in the river
She would know.
But there are no palm trees
On the street,
And dish water gives back no images.   *No Images [1931]*[1]

Richard Bruce Nugent   1906–1987

4   with her beautiful dark body...rosy black...graceful as the tongues of flame she loved to dance around...and pretty...small features...large liquid eyes...over-full sensuous lips...she knew how to dance too... better than any...

                                                              Sahdji [1925][2]

5   Silhouette
On the face of the moon
Am I.
A dark shadow in the light.

                                    Shadow. Opportunity [October 1925]

6   Beauty's cheek felt cool to his arm...his hair felt soft...Alex lay smoking...such a dream...red calla lilies...red calla lilies...and...what could it all mean...did dreams have meanings...

                                    Smoke, Lilies and Jade [November 1926]

[1]From *The Book of American Negro Poetry, second edition* [1931], edited by JAMES WELDON JOHNSON.
[2]From *The New Negro* [1925], edited by ALAIN LOCKE.

Satchel [Leroy] Paige

c. 1906–1982

1   Home plate is home plate regardless where you play. It don't move.

Pitchin' Man [1948]

2   Avoid fried meats which angry up the blood. If your stomach disputes you, lie down and pacify it with cool thoughts. Keep the juices flowing by jangling around gently as you move. Go very light on the vices, such as carrying on in society. The social ramble ain't restful. Avoid running at all times. Don't look back. Something might be gaining on you.

How to Stay Young. Collier's magazine [June 13, 1953]

3   You can't keep swinging when a fight's all over.

Maybe I'll Pitch Forever [1962]

4   There were many Satchels.

On being inducted into the Baseball Hall of Fame [1971]

5   Don't pray when it rains if you don't pray when the sun shines.

From Buck O'Neil, *I Was Right on Time [1996]*

Léopold Sédar Senghor

1906–2001

6   Naked woman, black woman
Dressed in your color that is life, in your form that is beauty!
I grew up in your shadow. The softness of your hands
Shielded my eyes, and now at the height of Summer and Noon,
From the crest of a charred hilltop I discover you, Promised Land
And your beauty strikes my heart like an eagle's lightning flash.

Shadow Songs [1945].[1] *Black Woman*[2]

7   Today is Sunday.
I fear the crowd of my fellows with such faces of stone.
From my glass tower filled with headaches and impatient Ancestors,
I contemplate the roofs and hilltops in the mist.

Shadow Songs. In Memoriam[2]

8   Woman, light the clear-oil lamp. Let the Ancestors
Speak around us as parents do when the children are in bed.

Shadow Songs. Night in Sine[2]

---

[1]*Chants d'Ombre.*

[2]From *The Collected Poetry: Léopold Sédar Senghor* [1991], translated by Melvin Dixon.

1 Masks! O Masks!
Black mask, red mask, you white-and-black masks
Masks of the four cardinal points where the Spirit blows
I greet you in silence!

Shadow Songs. Prayer to the Masks[1]

2 All victory lasts but the blinking of an eye,
Doubly proclaiming the irreparable. In my ancient memory
You were African like me, like the Atlas Mountain snows.

Shadow Songs. Shadow Song[1]

3 I must hide him down in my deepest veins
The Ancestor whose stormy skin
Streaks with lightning and thunder
He is the guardian animal I must hide
Lest I burst the dam of scandal.
He is my loyal blood demanding loyalty,
Protecting my naked pride against myself
And the arrogance of fortunate races...

Shadow Songs. Totem[1]

4 We are all cultural half-castes.

*Address at Le Premier Congrès International des Ecrivains et
Artistes Noirs [1956]*[2]

5 Art is life.

Attributed [1956]

6 In Africa, art for art's sake does not exist. All art is social.

Négro-Africaine [1956][2]

7 Waters of mercy, I invoke you in a rhythmic cry.

Nocturnes [1961]. Elegy of the Waters[1]

8 *Long, so long*, have you held the warrior's black face
Between your hands as if it glowed already with some deadly
Twilight. From the hillside I have seen the sun set
In the bays of your eyes. When will I see my country again,
The pure horizon of your face? When will I sit again
At the table of your dark breasts?

Nocturnes. Songs for Signare[1]

---

[1]From *The Collected Poetry: Léopold Sédar Senghor* [1991], translated by Melvin Dixon.
[2]From *Prose and Poetry: Léopold Sédar Senghor* [1965], translated by John Reed and Clive Wake.

1 *Your face* has the beauty of ancient times! Bring out
The pages perfumed with the music of the past. Memory of times
Without history! The time before our birth.

Nocturnes. Songs for Signare[1]

2 Man is saved since his hope has been maintained. We are now, all of us, of different features, color, languages, customs, stirred and carried by the same movement of life. We are on our way toward the world of tomorrow, the world of the civilization of the universal.

Speech at Fordham University [November 2, 1961]

3 The African is as it were shut up inside his black skin. He lives in primordial night. He does not begin by distinguishing himself from the object, the tree or stone, the man or animal or social event. He does not keep it at a distance. He does not analyze it.

De la Négritude [1962].[2] *Psychologie du Négro-Africaine*

Charles Alston   1907–1977

4 I don't believe there's such a thing as "Black art," though there's certainly been a Black experience. I've lived it. But it's also an American experience.   *Quoted in the New York Times [December 8, 1968]*

Cab[ell] Calloway[3]   1907–1994

5 Folks, now here's a story 'bout Minnie the Moocher
She was a low-down hoochie coocher
She was the roughest, toughest frail
But Minnie had a heart as big as a whale.
Ho de ho de ho (Ho de ho de ho)
Hi de hi de hi (Hi de hi de hi).   *Minnie the Moocher [1931]*

François [Papa Doc] Duvalier   1907–1971

6 Haitians have a destiny to suffer.   *LIFE [March 8, 1963]*

Blind Boy [Fulton Allen] Fuller   1907–1941

7 Keep on truckin'.

Truckin' My Blues Away [1936]

---

[1]From *The Collected Poetry: Léopold Sédar Senghor* [1991], translated by MELVIN DIXON.
[2]From *Prose and Poetry: Léopold Sédar Senghor* [1965], translated by JOHN REED and CLIVE WAKE.
[3]With Irving Mills and Clarence Gaskill.

Jacques Roumain   1907–1944

1   What are we? Since that's your question, I'm going to answer you. We're *this country*, and it wouldn't be a thing without us, nothing at all. Who does the planting? Who does the watering? Who does the harvesting? Coffee, cotton, rice, sugar cane, cacao, corn, bananas, vegetables, and all the fruits, who's going to grow them if we don't? Yet with all that, we're poor, that's true. We're out of luck, that's true. We're miserable, that's true. But do you know why, brother? Because of our ignorance. We don't know yet what a force we are, what a single force — all the peasants, all the Negroes of plain and hill, all united. Some day, when we get wise to that, we'll rise up from one end of the country to the other. Then we'll call a General Assembly of the Masters of the Dew, a great big *coumbite*[1] of farmers, and we'll clear out poverty and plant a new life.

Masters of the Dew [1944],[2] *ch. 5 [Manuel]*

Dorothy West   1907–1998

2   They had been born into a world which took no real notice of their existence. Their leave-takings were as unceremonious. Yet there is no life that does not contribute to history.   *The Living Is Easy [1948], ch. 11*

3   I am no different from other colored women. And colored men will never understand us. They feel mean and low at every slight, at every setback, and want to weep on the world's shoulder. But colored women can't afford self-pity. They're the ones that raise the children. What kind of children would they raise if they let them see their grief and despair? They'd raise humble dogs or mad dogs. They wouldn't raise human beings.

The Living Is Easy, 26 [Cleo]

4   To know how much there is to know is the beginning of learning to live.   *The Richer, the Poorer*[3] *[Bess]*

5   Color was a false distinction; love was not.

The Wedding [1995], ch. 18

Lionel Hampton   1908–2002

6   But it's always jazz. You can put a new dress on her, ... but no matter what kind of clothes you put on her, she's the same old broad.

Hamp [1989]

---

[1]A peasant farming cooperative.

[2]*Gouverneurs de la rosée* [1944, translated 1947]. Translated by Langston Hughes and Mercer Cook.

[3]From *The Best Short Stories* [1967], edited by Langston Hughes.

Louis Jordan

1908–1975

1   Is you is or is you ain't my baby?
    The way you're acting lately makes me doubt.

Is You Is or Is You Ain't (Ma' Baby) [1943]

2   Caldonia! (What?) Caldonia! (What?)
    What makes your big head so hard?   *Caldonia [1945]*

3   Don't let the sun catch you crying,
    Crying at my front door.
    You done your daddy dirty,
    And he don't want you around here no more.

Don't Let the Sun Catch You Cryin' [1945]

4   There ain't nobody here but us chickens
    There ain't nobody here at all.   *Ain't Nobody Here but Us Chickens [1946]*

5   Hey everybody, let's have some fun,
    You only live for once,
    And when you're dead, you're done.
    So let the good times roll,
    Let the good times roll.
    And live a long long time,
    I don't care if you're young or old,
    Get together and let the good times roll.   *Let the Good Times Roll [1946]*

Thurgood Marshall[1]

1908–1993

6   While it may be true that laws and constitutions do not act to right wrong and overturn established folkways overnight, it is also true that the reaffirmation of these principles of democracy build a body of public opinion in which rights and privileges of citizenship may be enjoyed, and in which the more brazen as well as the more sophisticated attempts at deprivation may be halted.

Equal Justice Under Law [July 1939]. The Crisis

7   Racial segregation in public schools reduces the benefits of public education to one group solely on the basis of race and color and is a constitutionally proscribed distinction. Even assuming that the segregated schools attended by appellants are not inferior to other elementary schools in Topeka with respect to physical facilities, instruction and courses of study,

---

[1]All quotes from *Thurgood Marshall: His Speeches, Writings, Arguments, Opinions, and Reminiscences* [2001], edited by MARK V. TUSHNET.

unconstitutional inequality inheres in the retardation of intellectual development and distortion of personality which Negro children suffer as a result of enforced isolation in school from the general public school population.

Initial brief, Brown v. Board of Education [1952]

1   Why of all of the multitudinous groups of people in this country [do] you have to single out Negroes and give them this separate treatment?

Rebuttal argument, Briggs v. Elliot [December 7, 1953]

2   They are graduating every day. That is the one narrow issue involved in this case. When we go from the narrow issue of the individual named plaintiffs involved and get to the class, the class is limited to children of school age. Your school age is something you cannot control and any delay in that is costly.

Argument, Brown v. Board of Education [April 12, 1955]

3   It is interesting to me that the very people that argue for this side [against integration], that would object to sending their white children to school with Negroes are eating food that has been prepared, served, and almost put in their mouths by the mothers of those children; and they do it day in and day out, but they cannot have the child go to school.... The point is as to whether or not, at this late date, with emphasis, this government can any longer tolerate this extreme difference based upon race or color.   *Argument, Brown v. Board of Education*

4   Education is not the teaching of the three R's. Education is the teaching of the overall citizenship, to learn to live together with fellow citizens, and above all to learn to obey the law.

Argument, Cooper v. Aaron [September 11, 1958]

5   Laws not only provide concrete benefits; they can even change the hearts of men — some men, anyway — for good or evil.... The hearts of men do not change themselves.

Speech at the White House Conference on Civil Rights
[June 1, 1966]

6   I have faith in the efficacy of law. Perhaps that is because I am a lawyer and not a missionary.   *Speech at the White House Conference on Civil Rights*

7   Lawlessness is lawlessness and anarchy; neither race, color nor frustration is a sufficient excuse for either lawlessness or anarchy.

Speech at the sixtieth anniversary convention of
Alpha Phi Alpha Fraternity, St. Louis. Sphinx Magazine
[December 1966]

8   Desegregation is not and was never expected to be an easy task.

Dissenting opinion, Milliken v. Bradley [1974]

1   The dream of America as the great melting pot has not been realized for the Negro; because of his skin color he never even made it into the pot.
Judicial opinion, Regents of the University of California v. Bakke [1978]

2   While the Union survived the Civil War, the Constitution did not.
Speech to San Francisco Patent and Trademark Law Association, Maui, Hawaii [May 6, 1987]

Adam Clayton Powell, Jr.   1908–1972

3   Keep the faith, baby.   *Motto*

4   To demand these God-given human rights is to seek black power[1] — what I call audacious power — the power to build black institutions of splendid achievement.   *Speech at Howard University [May 29, 1966]*

5   Black power is the brain power that admonishes. Instead of "Burn, baby, burn," we should be shouting "Learn, baby, learn" and "Earn, baby, earn."   *Keep the Faith, Baby [1967]*

6   Unless man is committed to the belief that all mankind are his brothers, then he labors in vain and hypocritically in the vineyards of equality.   *Keep the Faith, Baby*

7   Press forward at all times, climbing toward that higher ground of the harmonious society that shapes the laws of man to the laws of God.
Inscription on memorial statue, Adam Clayton Powell, Jr., State Office Building, Harlem

Richard Wright   1908–1960

8   Ah cant see white n Ah cant see black, he said. Ah sees rich men n Ah sees po men.
Uncle Tom's Children [1936]. Bright and Morning Star [Johnny-Boy]

9   Goddammit, look! We live here and they live there. We black and they white. They got things and we ain't. They do things and we can't. It's just like living in jail.   *Native Son [1940], bk. I [Bigger Thomas]*

10   Men can starve from a lack of self-realization as much as they can from a lack of bread!   *Native Son, III [Max]*

11   Who knows when some slight shock, disturbing the delicate balance between social order and thirsty aspiration, shall send the skyscrapers in our cities toppling?   *Native Son, III [Max]*

---

[1]See also Kwame Toure and Charles Hamilton, 414:2; Benjamin E. Mays, 187:4; and Walter Rodney, 427:3.

1   If we had been allowed to participate in the vital processes of America's national growth, what would have been the texture of our lives, the pattern of our traditions, the routine of our customs, the state of our arts, the code of our laws, the function of our government! . . . We black folk say that America would have been stronger and greater!

12 Million Black Voices [1941]

2   We black folk, our history and our present being, are a mirror of all the manifold experiences of America. What we want, what we represent, what we endure is what America *is*. If we black folk perish, America will perish.

12 Million Black Voices

3   I had never in my life been abused by whites, but I had already become as conditioned to their existence as though I had been the victim of a thousand lynchings.

Black Boy [1945]

4   Culturally the Negro represents a paradox: Though he is an organic part of the nation, he is excluded by the entire tide and direction of American culture. Frankly it is felt to be right to exclude him, and it is felt to be wrong to admit him freely.

Black Boy

5   Our too-young and too-new America, lusty because it is lonely, aggressive because it is afraid, insists upon seeing the world in terms of good and bad, the holy and the evil, the high and the low, the white and the black, our America is frightened of fact, of history, of processes, of necessity. It hugs the easy way of damning those whom it cannot understand, of excluding those who look different, and it salves its conscience with a self-draped cloak of righteousness. Am I damning my native land? No; for I too share these faults of character! *Black Boy*

6   I wanted to try to build a bridge of words between me and that world outside, that world which was so distant and elusive that it seemed unreal.

    I would hurl words into this darkness and wait for an echo, and if an echo sounded, no matter how faintly, I would send other words to tell, to march, to fight, to create a sense of the hunger for life that gnaws in us all.

Black Boy

7   Negroes, as they enter our culture, are going to inherit the problems we have, but with a difference. They are outsiders and they are going to *know* that they have these problems. They are going to be self-conscious; they are going to be gifted with a double vision, for, being Negroes, they are going to be both *inside* and *outside* of our culture at the same time.

The Outsider [1953]

1   Blue-jazz was the scornful gesture of men turned ecstatic in their state of rejection.

The Outsider

2   Men simply copied the realities of their hearts when they built prisons. They simply extended into objective reality what was already a subjective reality. Only jailors really believe in jails.

The Outsider

3   I had understood nothing. I was black and they were black, but my blackness did not help me.

Black Power! A Record of Reactions in a Land of Pathos [1954]

4   The history of the Negro in America is the history of America written in vivid and bloody terms; it is the history of Western Man writ small. It is the history of men who tried to adjust themselves to a world whose laws, customs, and instruments of force were leveled against them. The Negro is America's metaphor.

White Man, Listen! [1957]

Katherine Dunham   1909–2006

5   You dance because you have to.

From Brian Lanker, *I Dream a World [1989]*

Chester Himes   1909–1984

6   Martyrs are needed to create incidents. Incidents are needed to create revolutions. Revolutions are needed to create progress.

Negro Martyrs Are Needed. The Crisis [May 1944]

7   I dreamed a fellow asked me if I wanted a dog and I said yeah, I'd like to have a dog and he went off and came back with a little black dog with stiff black gold-tipped hair and sad eyes that looked something like a wire-haired terrier. I was standing in front of a streetcar that was just about to start and the fellow led the dog by a piece of heavy stiff wire twisted about its neck and handed me the end of the wire and asked me if I liked the dog. I took the wire and said sure I liked the dog. Then the dog broke loose and ran over to the side of the street trailing the wire behind him and the fellow ran and caught it and brought it back and gave it to me again.

If He Hollers Let Him Go [1945], opening lines

8   Shadows, they are all about me. In the stench-laden corners of my dungeon they are black sentinels at the black gates of death, forbidding me sanctuary. On the slime-encrusted floor they lie motionless, writhing in the eyes of my fear. They hover alive in the space about me, vampires

of thought, drinking the life of my soul. Shadows, flung into space by sharp corners, breaking off at unknown angles, falling on concrete floors, climbing black walls. Shadows, receding before light, racing rapidly off to hide behind bars, making blackness. Shadows of bars swinging out into space to fall with soul-bruising heaviness on shadows of men. Shadows of shadows, no longer men, victims of the night eternal, victims of the shadows....

Cast the First Stone [1952]

1   "Yeah, the Colonel thought the Back-to-Africa movement was as sinful and un-American as bolshevism and should be stamped out at any cost," Coffin Ed added.

"I suppose he thought it was the American thing to do to rob those colored people out of their money," Anderson said sarcastically.

"Well, ain't it?" Coffin Ed said.

Cotton Comes to Harlem [1965]

2   My feelings are too intense. I hate too bitterly, I love too exaltingly, I pity too extravagantly, I hurt too painfully. We American blacks call that "soul."   *The Quality of Hurt [1972]*

Willard Motley   1909–1965

3   Live fast, die young and have a good-looking corpse!

Knock on Any Door [1947], ch. 47 [Nick Romano]

Kwame Nkrumah   1909–1972

4   We prefer self-government with danger to servitude in tranquility.

Motto, Convention People's Party (CPP)

5   From our knowledge of the history of man, from our knowledge of colonial liberation movements, Freedom or Self-government has never been handed over to any colonial country on a silver platter.

What I Mean by Positive Action [1949]

6   As a ship that has been freshly launched, we face the hazards of the high seas alone. We must rely on our own men, on the captain and on his navigation. And, as I proudly stand on the bridge of that lone vessel as she confidently sets sail, I raise a hand to shade my eyes from the glaring African sun, and scan the horizon. There is so much more beyond.

Ghana: The Autobiography of Kwame Nkrumah [1957]

7   No part of Africa is free while any of our national territory remains unliberated.

Africa Day special message [1958]

1   We face neither east nor west; we face forward.

Speech at Accra, Ghana [April 7, 1960]

2   Africa is a paradox which illustrates and highlights neo-colonialism. Her earth is rich, yet the products that come from above and below the soil continue to enrich, not Africans predominantly, but groups and individuals who operate to Africa's impoverishment.

Neo-Colonialism: The Last Stage of Imperialism [1965]

3   You are in Britain not by chance or by choice; you are in Britain for historical reasons; you are in Britain because Britain colonized you and reduced the various countries to which you belong to the level of colonial status. You are in Britain because British neo-colonialism is strangling you in your home countries. Where else can you go to seek survival, except in the "mother country" which has enslaved you?

Message to the Black People of Britain [1968]

4   There is no solution to the race question until all forms of racial discrimination and segregation anywhere are made criminal.

Message to the Black People of Britain

Art[hur] Tatum, Jr.   1909–1956

5   There is no such thing as a wrong note.

Advice to Don Byas. From ARTHUR TAYLOR,
Notes and Tones [1971]

Howlin' Wolf [Chester Burnett]   1910–1976

6   Well, somebody's calling me over my telephone.
Well, keep on calling,
Tell 'em I'm not at home.   *Moanin' at Midnight [1951]*

7   Smokestack lightnin'
shinin' just like gold.

Smokestack Lightnin' [1956]

8   I shoulda quit you a long time ago.

. . .

And I wouldn't a been here
down on the killin' floor.   *Killing Floor [1965]*

Pauli[ne] Murray   1910–1985

9   I spent many hours digging up weeds, cutting grass and tending the family plot. It was only a few feet from the main highway between Durham

and Chapel Hill. I wanted the white people who drove by to be sure to see this banner and me standing by it. Whatever else they denied me, they could not take from me this right and the undiminished stature it gave me. For there at least at Grandfather's grave with the American flag in my hands, I could stand very tall and in proud shoes.

Proud Shoes [1956], last lines

1   Hope is a song in a weary throat.

Dark Testament [1970]

Romare Bearden   1911–1988

2   I believe that art is an expression of what people feel and want. In order for a painting to be "good" two things are necessary: that there be a communion of belief and desire between artist and spectator; that the artist be able to see and say something that enriches the fund of communicable feeling and the medium for expressing it.

Artist's statement [1940]

3   All painting is a kind of talking about life.
Memory and Metaphor: The Art of Romare Bearden [1991]

St. Clair Drake   1911–1990

and

Horace R[oscoe] Cayton, Jr.   1903–1970

4   America is known by her big cities, those amazing congeries of people and houses, offices and factories, which constitute the nerve centers of our civilization, the ganglia of our collective being. America is dominated by her cities as they draw into them the brawn and brain and wealth of the hinterland and give back not only a constant stream of necessities and gadgets, but also a pattern for living. New York, Chicago, San Francisco, New Orleans, Birmingham...the impact of each forces itself upon an ever-widening metropolitan region and filters into a host of tributary small towns and farms by radio and newspaper, book and magazine, and the enthusiastic tales of visitors. Each city, too, has its distinctive reputation in the far corners of the earth, distorted and glamorized, but with a basic element of truth beneath the stereotype.

Black Metropolis [1945], introduction

5   The fate of the people of Black Metropolis — whether they will remain the marginal workers to be called in only at times of great economic activity, or will become an integral part of the American economy and thus lay the

basis for complete social and political integration — depends not so much on what happens locally as on what happens in America and the world.

Black Metropolis

Mahalia Jackson   1911–1972

1   God Put a Rainbow in the Sky   *Song title [1959]*

2   Tell them about your dream, Martin! Tell them about the dream.
*To Martin Luther King, Jr., during his speech at the March
on Washington for Jobs and Freedom [August 28, 1963]*

3   I say this out of my heart — a song must do something for me as well as for the people that hear it. I can't sing a song that doesn't have a message. If it doesn't have the strength it can't lift you.

Movin' On Up [1966]

4   I believe the blues and jazz and even the rock and roll stuff got their beat from the Sanctified Church.   *Movin' On Up*

Robert Johnson   1911–1938

5   You better come on in my kitchen
Well, it's going to be raining outdoors.
The woman I love took from my best friend,
Some joker got lucky,
Stole her back again.   *Come On in My Kitchen [1936]*

6   I'm goin' get up in the morning
I believe I'll dust my broom
'Cause the black man you been loving
Girlfriend, can get my room.

Dust My Broom [1936][1]

7   If I had possession over judgment day
Lord the woman I'm loving
Wouldn't have no right to pray.
If I Had Possession over Judgment Day [1936][1]

8   I got a kind hearted woman, do anything in the world for me
But these evil hearted women, man they will not let me be.
Kind-Hearted Woman Blues [1936]

9   I sent for my baby, and she don't come.   *32-20 Blues [1936]*

---

[1]From *Blues Line: Blues Lyrics from Leadbelly to Muddy Waters* [1969], edited by ERIC SACKHEIM.

1   When I leave this town,
    I'm gonna bid you farewell
    And when I return again,
    You'll have a great long story to tell.   *Four Until Late [1937]*

2   I've got to keep movin',
    Blues falling down like hail.   *Hellhound on My Trail [1937]*

3   Well, it's hard to tell, it's hard to tell,
    When all your love's in vain.   *Love in Vain [1937]*

[John Jordan] Buck O'Neil   1911–2006

4   Give it up. You got to give it up. You got to give people love.
                                          I Was Right on Time [1996]

Eric Williams   1911–1981

5   Slavery was not born of racism: rather, racism was the consequence of
    slavery.   *Capitalism and Slavery [1944]*

6   It takes more than national boundaries, a National Anthem however
    stirring, a National Coat of Arms however distinctive, a National Flag how-
    ever appropriate, a National Flower however beautiful, to make a nation.
                          History of the People of Trinidad and Tobago [1962]

Dorothy I[rene] Height   1912–2010

7   Too many of our young people know only where we are now, not how
    we got here nor where we are going. Too many see doors only recently
    opened and do not appreciate how they got pried ajar.... We must always
    be a strong presence, an unrelenting force working for equality and justice
    until the freedom gates are fully open.   *Open Wide the Freedom Gates [2003]*

8   African-American women seldom do just what we want to do but
    always do what we have to do.
                          Motto inscribed on her Congressional Gold Medal [2004]

Gordon Parks   1912–2006

9   Why does our color make such a difference?... Didn't God know that
    we'd have a lot of trouble if he made us black?
                                          The Learning Tree [1963] [Newt]

10 When the doors of promise open, the trick is to quickly walk through
    them.   *Half Past Autumn [1997]*

Ann Petry

1   God damn white people anyway. I don't want favors. All I want is a job. Just a job. Don't they know if I knew how I'd change the color of my skin?
                                                                    The Street [1946], ch. 2 [Jim]

2   Here she [Lutie] was highly respectable, married, mother of a small boy, and in spite of all that, knowing all that, these people took one look at her and immediately got that now-I-wonder-look. Apparently it was an automatic reaction of white people — if a girl was colored and fairly young, why, it stood to reason she had to be a prostitute. If not that, at least sleeping with her would be just a simple matter, for all one had to do was make the request. In fact, white men wouldn't even have to do the asking because the girl would ask them on sight.
                                                                    The Street, 2

3   She shifted the packages into a more comfortable position, and feeling the hard roundness of the rolls through the paper bag, she thought immediately of Ben Franklin and his loaf of bread. And grinned, thinking, You and Ben Franklin. You ought to take one out and start eating it as you walk along 116th Street. Only you ought to remember while you eat that you're in Harlem and he was in Philadelphia a pretty long number of years ago. Yet she couldn't get rid of the feeling of self-confidence and she went on thinking that if Ben Franklin could live on a little bit of money and prosper, then so could she.
                                                                    The Street, 3

4   She was going to stake out a piece of life for herself. She had come this far poor and black and shut out as though a door had been slammed in her face. Well, she would shove it open; she would beat and bang on it and push against it and use a chisel in order to get it open.
                                                                    The Street, 8

5   Streets like the one she lived on were no accident. They were the North's lynch mobs, she thought bitterly; the method the big cities used to keep Negroes in their place.
                                                                    The Street, 13

6   The snow fell softly on the street. It muffled the sound. It sent people scurrying homeward, so the street was soon deserted, empty, quiet. And it could have been any street in the city, for the snow laid a delicate film over the sidewalk, over the brick of the tired, old buildings; gently obscuring the grime and the garbage and the ugliness.
                                                                    The Street, last lines

7   All life goes in a circle, around and around, you started at one place, and then came right back to it again.
                                                                    The Narrows [1953], ch. 6

8   The Democrats were peevishly blaming the Republicans for the state the country was in; and the Republicans were peevishly blaming the Democrats for the same thing. . . . This was just another case of the pot calling the kettle black; but political parties preferred to hurl the words *venal* and *stupid* at each other.
                                                                    The Narrows, 19

Jo Ann Gibson Robinson

1912–1992

1   Black Montgomery had to go on! They wanted to go on, for the taste of glory was like sweet wine on their lips. For once they were in the driver's seat, and they had made themselves felt. They were "somebody." ... The one day of protest against the white man's traditional policy of white supremacy had created a new person in the Negro. The new spirit, the new feeling did something to blacks individually and collectively.... There was no turning back! There was only one way out — the buses must be changed.

> *On the first day of the 1955–1956 Montgomery bus boycott.*
> *From The Montgomery Bus Boycott and the Women Who*
> *Started It: The Memoir of Jo Ann Gibson Robinson [1987],*
> *edited by* DAVID J. GARROW

Bayard Rustin

1912–1987

2   In all those places where we have a voice, it is our high responsibility to indicate that the Negro can attain progress only if he uses, in his struggle, nonviolent direct action — a technique consistent with the ends he desires.
> *The Negro and Nonviolence [1942]*[1]

3   Conscription for war is inconsistent with freedom of conscience, which is not merely the right to believe, but to act on the degree of truth that one receives, to follow a vocation which is God-inspired.
> *Letter to draft board [1943]*[2]

4   It is very important to have a great sense of racial identity because I believe it is quite impossible for people to struggle creatively if they do not truly believe in themselves. I believe that dignity is first.
> *Radio show with Malcolm X [1960]*[2]

5   The condition of Negro labor is inseparable from that of white labor; the immediate crisis confronting black labor grows out of the unresolved crisis in the national economy.
> *Preamble to the March on Washington [1963]*[2]

6   What is the value of winning access to public accommodations for those who lack money to use them? The minute the movement faced this question, it was compelled to expand its vision beyond race relations to economic relations, including the role of education in modern society.
> *From Protest to Politics. Commentary [February 1965]*

7   Whatever the pace of this technological revolution may be, the direction is clear: the lower rungs of the economic ladder are being lopped off.

---

[1]From *Down the Line: The Collected Writings of Bayard Rustin* [1971].
[2]From *Time on Two Crosses* [2003], edited by DEVON W. CARBADO and DONALD WEISE.

This means that an individual will no longer be able to start at the bottom and work his way up; he will have to start in the middle or on top, and hold on tight.
From Protest to Politics

1   People will never fight for your freedom if you have not given evidence that you are prepared to fight for it yourself.
Interview [1986][1]

2   The New "Niggers" Are Gays
Title of speech [1986][1]

Walter Sisulu   1912–2003

3   The people are our strength. In their service we shall face and conquer those who live on the backs of our people. In the history of mankind it is a law of life that problems arise when the conditions are there for their solution.
Prison essay [1976][2]

4   It is the job, the task of all democrats, wherever we are located, to advance this idea: That nothing short of full freedom will satisfy us.
The Road to Liberation. Speech at the University of Cape Town [October 2, 1990]

Aimé Césaire   1913–2008

5   My name — an offense; my Christian name — humiliation; my status — a rebel; my age — the stone age. [The Rebel]
My race — the human race. My religion — brotherhood. [The Mother]
The Miraculous Weapons [1946][3]

6   At the end of dawn...
Go away, I said, with your mug of a copper,
your mug of a pig, go away. I hate the flunkeys
of order and the beetles of hope. Go away, you
evil charm, little punk of a monk. Then I turned
towards heavens lost to him and his own kind,
heavens more calm than the face of a woman who
lies, and there lulled by the effluvia of endless
thoughts, I fed the wind, I untied the monsters...
Notebook of a Return to My Native Land [1968][4]

7   At the end of dawn, the city — flat,
sprawled, tripped up by its common sense, inert,

---

[1]From *Time on Two Crosses* [2003], edited by DEVON W. CARBADO and DONALD WEISE.
[2]From MAC MAHARAJ, *Reflections in Prison* [2001].
[3]Originally published in French as *les armes miraculeuses*.
[4]Originally published in French as *Cahier d'un retour au pays natal* [1939]. Translated by EMILE SNYDER.

winded under the geometric weight of its eternally
renewed cross, at odds with its fate, mute, baffled,
unable to circulate the pith of this ground, embarrassed,
lopped, reduced, cut off from fauna and flora.

Notebook of a Return to My Native Land

1   Whoever would not comprehend me would not
comprehend the roaring of the tiger.

Notebook of a Return to My Native Land

2   I should come back to this land of mine
and say to it: "Embrace me without fear.... If all
I can do is speak, at least I shall speak for you."

Notebook of a Return to My Native Land

3   Take me as I am. I don't adapt to you!

Notebook of a Return to My Native Land

4   my Negritude is not a stone, its deafness thrown
against the clamor of the day
      my Negritude is not a speak of dead water on
the dead eye of earth
      my Negritude is neither tower nor cathedral.

Notebook of a Return to My Native Land

5   And my original geography also; the map of the
world made for my use, not painted the arbitrary
colors of scientists, but with the geometry of my
shed blood. I accept.

Notebook of a Return to My Native Land

6   A civilization that proves incapable of solving the problems it creates
is a decadent civilization.

      A civilization that chooses to close its eyes to its most crucial problems
is a stricken civilization.

      A civilization that uses its principles for trickery and deceit is a dying
civilization.   *Discourse on Colonialism [1972]*[1]

7   I say that between colonization and civilization there is an infinite distance; that out of all the colonial expeditions that have been undertaken,
out of all the colonial statutes that have been drawn up, out of all the mem-
oranda that have been dispatched by all the ministries, there could not come
a single human value.   *Discourse on Colonialism*

---

[1]Originally published in French as *Discours sur le colonialismè* [1950]. Translated by JOAN PINKHAM.

1   People are surprised, they become indignant. They say: "How strange! But never mind—it's Nazism, it will pass!" And they wait, and they hope; and they hide the truth from themselves, that it is barbarism, the supreme barbarism, the crowning barbarism that sums up all the daily barbarisms...that before they were its victims, they were its accomplices; that they tolerated that Nazism before it was inflicted on them, that they absolved it, shut their eyes to it, legitimized it, because, until then, it had been applied only to non-European peoples.

Discourse on Colonialism

2   No one colonizes innocently.   *Discourse on Colonialism*

3   Colonization = "thingification."   *Discourse on Colonialism*

4   We are not men for whom it is a question of "either-or." For us, the problem is not to make a utopian and sterile attempt to repeat the past, but to go beyond. It is not a dead society that we want to revive.... Nor is it the present colonial society that we wish to prolong, the most putrid carrion that ever rotted under the sun. It is a new society that we must create, with the help of all our brother slaves, a society rich with all the productive power of modern times, warm with all the fraternity of olden days.

Discourse on Colonialism

Carolina Maria de Jesus   1913–1977

5   We are slaves to the cost of living.

Child of the Dark [1962][1]

6   The poor don't rest nor are they permitted the pleasure of relaxation.   *Child of the Dark*

7   I adore my black skin and my kinky hair. The Negro hair is more educated than the white man's hair. Because with Negro hair, where you put it, it stays. It's obedient.... If reincarnation exists I want to come back black.

Child of the Dark

Robert Hayden   1913–1980

8   Quadroon mermaids, Afro angels, black saints
balanced upon the switchblades of that air
and sang. Tight streets unfolding to the eye
like fans of corrosion and elegiac lace
crackled with their singing: Shadow of time. Shadow of blood.

A Ballad of Remembrance [1962], st. 1

[1]Translated by DAVID ST. CLAIR.

1   this man

shall be remembered. Oh, not with statues' rhetoric,
not with legends and poems and wreaths of bronze alone,
but with the lives grown out of his life, the lives
fleshing his dream of the beautiful, needful thing.   *Frederick Douglass [1962]*

2   Middle Passage:

       voyage through death
         to life upon these shores.   *Middle Passage [1962], st. 2*

3   Sundays too my father got up early
and put his clothes on in the blueblack cold,
then with cracked hands that ached
from labor in the weekday weather made
banked fires blaze. No one ever thanked him.
                             Those Winter Sundays [1962], st. 1

4   What did I know, what did I know
of love's austere and lonely offices?   *Those Winter Sundays, st. 3*

5   He X'd his name, became his people's anger,
exhorted them to vengeance for their past;
rebuked, admonished them,

   their scourger who
would shame them, drive them from
the lush ice gardens of their servitude.   *El-Hajj Malik El-Shabazz [1970], III*

6   Naked, he lies in the blinded room
chainsmoking, cradled by drugs, by jazz
as never by any lover's cradling flesh.   *Soledad [1970], st. 1*

7   Killing people to save, to free them?
With napalm lighting routes to the future?
                    Words in the Mourning Time [1970], II

8   here among them   the americans   this baffling
multi people   extremes and variegations   their
noise   restlessness   their almost frightening
energy   *American Journal [1978, 1982]*[1]

9   confess i am curiously drawn   unmentionable   to
the americans   doubt i could exist among them for
long however   psychic demands far too severe

---

[1]From *Collected Poems: Robert Hayden* [1985], edited by FREDERICK GLAYSHER.

much violence   much that repels   i am attracted
none the less   their variousness their ingenuity
their élan vital   and that some thing   essence
quiddity   i cannot penetrate or name   *American Journal [1982]*

Muddy Waters [McKinley Morganfield]   1913–1983

1   Well I'm goin' away to leave,
Won't be back no more.
Goin' back down south, child
Don't you wanna go?

Woman I'm troubled, I be all worried in mind.
Well babe, I just can't be satisfied,
And I just can't keep from cryin'.   *I Can't Be Satisfied [1948]*

2   Now, when I was a young boy,
At the age of five,
My mother said I'd be
The greatest man alive.

…

I'm a man.   *Mannish Boy [1955]*

3   Someday, baby, you ain't gonna trouble poor me no more.
    Trouble No More [1955]

4   That's my religion — blues.   *Attributed*

Jesse [James Cleveland] Owens   1913–1980

5   The battles that count aren't the ones for gold medals. The struggles within yourself — the invisible, inevitable battles inside all of us — that's where it's at. Life is the real Olympics.
    Blackthink [1970]

6   *[On winning four gold medals at the 1936 Berlin Olympics:]* After all those stories about Hitler and his snub, I came back to my native country, and I couldn't ride in the front of the bus. I had to go to the back door. I couldn't live where I wanted. Now what's the difference?
    Quoted in his obituary. New York Times [April 1, 1980]

Rosa Parks   1913–2005

7   *[Recalling her refusal to give up her seat on a Montgomery, Alabama, bus on December 1, 1955:]* I had felt for a long time, that if I was ever told to get up so a white person could sit, that I would refuse to do so.
    From David J. Garrow, Bearing the Cross [1987].

1   People always say that I didn't give up my seat because I was tired, but that isn't true. I was not tired physically, or no more tired than I usually was at the end of a working day. I was not old, although some people have an image of me as being old then. I was forty-two. No, the only tired I was, was tired of giving in.   *Rosa Parks: My Story [1992]*

2   *[To the arresting officer who removed her from the bus:]*
Why do you all push us around?   *Rosa Parks: My Story*

William R[ichard] Tolbert, Jr.   1913–1980

3   We all with faith, goodwill and purpose consider mankind our greatest challenge!
>   *Speech before the General Assembly of the United Nations*
>   *[November 2, 1974]*

4   A world half rich and half exploited is to rational interactions of nations sufficiently a living menace. But a continent half free and half enslaved can become a deadly threat to international peace, security and prosperity.   *Speech, New York [November 4, 1974]*

Daisy Bates   1914–1999

5   Dear Mr. President, Despite repeated bombings, attacks by gunfire and rocks, and other assaults on our home—attacks provoked by the fact that we have stood steadfast for this community's compliance with the federal law—both local and federal authorities have declined to provide the minimum physical protection that we have requested.... I appeal to you, Mr. President, to provide the basic protection that will give us the freedom from fear to which citizens of our free American society are entitled.
>   *Telegram to President Dwight D. Eisenhower [August 13, 1959]*[1]

6   We will join hands with you as women of this country.... We will kneel-in, we will sit-in until we can eat at any counter in the United States. We will walk until we are free, until we can walk to any school and take our children to any school in the United States. And we will sit-in, and we will kneel-in, and we will lie-in if necessary until every Negro in America can vote.
>   *Speech at the March on Washington for Jobs and Freedom*
>   *[August 28, 1963]*

Kenneth B[ancroft] Clark   1914–2005

7   The fact that young Negro children would prefer to be white reflects their knowledge that society prefers white people. White children are

---

[1]From Daisy Bates, *The Long Shadow of Little Rock* [1962].

generally found to prefer their white skin — an indication that they too know that society likes whites better. It is clear, therefore, that the self-acceptance or self-rejection found so early in a child's developing complex of racial ideas reflects the awareness and acceptance of the prevailing racial attitudes in his community.

Prejudice and Your Child [1955]

1   A racist system inevitably destroys and damages human beings; it brutalizes and dehumanizes them, blacks and whites alike.

From Current Biography [1964]

2   The dark ghetto's invisible walls have been erected by the white society, by those who have power, both to confine those who have *no* power and to perpetuate their powerlessness. The dark ghettos are social, political, educational, and — above all — economic colonies. Their inhabitants are subject peoples, victims of the greed, cruelty, insensitivity, guilt, and fear of their masters.

Dark Ghetto [1965]

3   Negroes will not break out of the barriers of the ghetto unless whites transcend the barriers of their own minds, for the ghetto is to the Negro a reflection of the ghetto in which the white lives imprisoned. The poetic irony of American race relations is that the rejected Negro must somehow also find the strength to free the privileged white.   *Dark Ghetto, last lines*

4   Let us make no mistake here: racism is a disease.

The American Revolution [1974]

5   The neoconservatives are formidable adversaries. They say that victims are the cause of their own victimization. "We pulled ourselves up by our bootstraps," they say, and they want us to do the same even though they want to take away our boots.

Quoted in the New York Times [December 27, 1984]

6   Social engineering is no more difficult than space engineering. If a program to get us to the moon didn't work, the engineers would try another program.   *Quoted in the New York Times*

Kenneth B[ancroft] Clark   1914–2005

and

Mamie P[hipps] Clark   1917–1983

7   The discrepancy between identifying one's own color and indicating one's color preference is too great to be ignored. The negation of the color, brown, exists in the same complexity of attitudes in which there also exists

knowledge of the fact that the child himself must be identified with that which he rejects.

Emotional Factors in Racial Identification and Preference
in Negro Children. The Journal of Negro Education
[Summer 1950]

Ernest Crichlow
1914–2005

1   Art says "stop looking at my face or the clothes I wear and look at another important part of me." It's the part of me I can't talk about so I dance it or paint it or compose music about it.

Interview. Stamford Advocate [February 5, 1981]

Owen Dodson
1914–1983

2   Sorrow is the only faithful one:
The lone companion clinging like a season
To its original skin no matter what the variations.

Sorrow Is the Only Faithful One [1943]

3   Now I'm a black mother, Lord I knows that now,
Black and burnin in these burnin times.
I can't hold my peace cause peace ain't fit to mention
When they's fightin right here in our streets
Like dogs — mongrel dogs and hill cats.   *Black Mother Praying [1944]*

4   I'm so black they call me nighttime
When I walk along everyone looks for stars.

Winter Chorus [1946] [Young Boy]

5   The bird is lost,
Dead, with all the music.   *Yardbird's Skull [1963]*

6   Oh my boy: Jesus
my first and only son.
Rock on my breast
my first and only one.

The Confession Stone [1970], Song viii

Ralph [Waldo] Ellison
1914–1994

7   I am an invisible man. . . . I am a man of substance, of flesh and bone, fiber and liquids — and I might even be said to possess a mind. I am invisible, understand, simply because people refuse to see me.

Invisible Man [1952], prologue

1   There are few things in the world as dangerous as sleepwalkers.

Invisible Man, prologue

2   The end is in the beginning and lies far ahead.

Invisible Man, prologue

3   Beware of those who speak of the *spiral* of history; they are preparing a boomerang.   *Invisible Man, prologue*

4   "Now black is ..." the preacher shouted.
"Bloody ..."
"I said black is ..."
"Preach it, brother ..."
"... an' black ain't ..."   *Invisible Man, prologue*

5   It took me a long time and much painful boomeranging of my expectations, to achieve a realization everyone else seems to have been born with: That I am nobody but myself.   *Invisible Man, ch. 1*

6   Live with your head in the lion's mouth. I want you to overcome 'em with yeses, undermine 'em with grins, agree 'em to death and destruction, let 'em swoller you till they vomit or bust wide open.

Invisible Man, 1 [Grandfather]

7   When I discover who I am, I'll be free.   *Invisible Man, 11*

8   Who knows but that, on the lower frequencies, I speak for you?

Invisible Man, last line

9   All novels are about certain minorities: the individual is a minority.

Interview. Paris Review [Spring 1955]

10   One learns by moving from the familiar to the unfamiliar, and while it might sound incongruous at first, the step from the spirituality of the spirituals to that of the Beethoven of the symphonies or the Bach of the chorales is not as vast as it seems. Nor is the romanticism of a Brahms or Chopin completely unrelated to that of Louis Armstrong. Those who know their native culture and love it unchauvinistically are never lost when encountering the unfamiliar.   *Living with Music [1955]*

11   When American life is most American it is apt to be most theatrical.

Shadow and Act [1964]. Change the Joke and Slip the Yoke

12   While one can do nothing about choosing one's relatives one can, as artist, choose one's "ancestors."   *Shadow and Act. The World and the Jug*

13   I know of no valid demonstration that culture is transmitted through the genes.   *Shadow and Act. Some Questions and Some Answers*

14   In the beginning was not the shadow but the act, and the province of Hollywood is not action, but illusion. Actually, the anti-Negro images of the films were (and are) acceptable because of the existence throughout the

United States of an audience obsessed with an inner psychological need to view Negroes as less than men.... The anti-Negro image is a ritual object of which Hollywood is not the creator, but the manipulator.

Shadow and Act. The Shadow and the Act

1   Without the presence of blacks, our political history would have been otherwise. No slave economy, no Civil War; no violent destruction of the Reconstruction, no K.K.K. and no Jim Crow system. And without the disenfranchisement of black Americans and the manipulation of racial fears and prejudices, the disproportionate impact of white Southern politicians upon our domestic and foreign policies would have been impossible. Indeed, it is almost impossible to conceive of what our political system would have become without the snarl of forces — cultural, racial, religious — that makes our nation what it is today.

What America Would Be Like Without Blacks. TIME
[April 6, 1970]

2   Since the beginning of the nation, white Americans have suffered from a deep inner uncertainty as to who they really are. One of the ways that has been used to simplify the answer has been to seize upon the presence of black Americans and use them as a marker, a symbol of limits, a metaphor for the "outsider." Perhaps that is why one of the first epithets that many European immigrants learned when they got off the boat was the term "nigger" — it made them feel instantly American.

What America Would Be Like Without Blacks

Joe Louis [Joseph Louis Borrow]   1914–1981

3   *[On his military service:]* I have only done what any red-blooded American would do. We gonna do our part, and we will win, because we are on God's side.   *Speech at Madison Square Garden [March 10, 1942]*

4   He can run. But he can't hide.
Remark made to reporter before heavyweight title fight with
Billy Conn [June 19, 1946]

Dudley Randall   1914–2000

5   "Mother dear, may I go downtown
Instead of out to play,
And march the streets of Birmingham
In a Freedom March today?"

"No, baby, no, you may not go,
For the dogs are fierce and wild,

And clubs and hoses, guns and jails
Aren't good for a little child."

Ballad of Birmingham [1965]

1 She clawed in bits of glass and brick,
Then lifted out a shoe.
"O, here's the shoe my baby wore
But, baby, where are you?"

Ballad of Birmingham

2 A poet is not a jukebox, so don't tell me what to write.

A Poet Is Not a Jukebox [1981]

Sun Ra [Herman Poole Blount]   1914–1993

3 Imagination is a magic carpet
Upon which we may soar.

Enticement [1957][1]

4 Today is the shadow of tomorrow.   *The Shadow of Tomorrow [1958]*[2]

5 One part of an equation
Is a blueprint/declaration of the other part
Similar
Yet differentially not.

A Blueprint/Declaration [1965][2]

6 Resist me —
Make me strong.
For since I cannot be what you will
I shall always be that much more so
What I will.

Saga of Resistance [1966][3]

7 The city is the Universe.   *The Magic City [1972]*[1]

8 It's after the end of the world. Don't you know that yet?

Space Is the Place [1974]

Elizabeth Catlett   1915–2012

9 Are we here to communicate? Are we here for cultural interchange? Then let us not be narrow. Let us not be small and selfish. Let us aspire to be as great in our communication as were the forefathers of our people, whose struggles made our being here possible.

Speech at the National Conference of Negro Artists
[April 1, 1961][4]

---

[1]From *The Immeasurable Equation: The Collected Poetry and Prose* [2005], compiled and edited by JAMES WOLF and HARTMUT GEERKEN.
[2]From JOHN F. SZWED, *Space Is the Place* [1997].
[3]From *Black Fire* [1968], edited by AMIRI BARAKA and LARRY NEAL.
[4]From SAMELLA LEWIS, *The Art of Elizabeth Catlett* [1984].

1   Advance is difficult and departure from the accepted path is dangerous; but difficulty and danger are old acquaintances.

From SAMELLA LEWIS, The Art of Elizabeth Catlett [1984]

John Henrik Clarke   1915–1998

2   History tells a people where they have been and what they have been, where they are and what they are. Most important, an understanding of history tells a people where they still must go and what they still must be.

African People in World History [1993]

3   It is a story that can never be told in all its gruesome details. Of the countless number of Africans ripped from the villages of Africa—from the Sénegal River to northern Angola—during the nearly four centuries of the slave trade, approximately one third of them died on the torturous march to the ships and one third died in the holding stations on both sides of the Atlantic or on the ships. It is estimated that ten to twenty million arrived in the New World alive, to be then committed to bondage. If the Atlantic were to dry up, it would reveal a scattered pathway of human bones. African bones marking the various routes of the Middle Passage.

From TOM FEELINGS, The Middle Passage [1995], introduction

Willie [William James] Dixon   1915–1992

4   I'm gonna make you girls
Lead me by the hand
Then the world will know
The Hoochie Coochie Man
But you know I'm here
Everybody knows I'm here.

(I'm Your) Hoochie Coochie Man [1954],
Recorded by Muddy Waters

5   On the seventh hour
On the seventh day
On the seventh month
The seventh doctor say
He was born for good luck
And that you'll see
I got seven hundred dollars
Don't you mess with me   *(I'm Your) Hoochie Coochie Man*

6   Men lies about that,
Some of 'em cries about that,
Some of 'em dies about that,

Everybody fightin' about a spoonful,

That spoon, that spoon, that.   *Spoonful [1960], Recorded by Howlin' Wolf*

1   The Blues are the roots; everything else is the fruits.   *Attributed*

C[larence La Vaughn] Franklin[1]   1915–1984

2   My soul is an eagle in the cage that the Lord has made for me. My soul, my soul, my soul is caged in, in this old body, yes it is, and one of these days the man who made the cage will open the door and let my soul go.

The Eagle Stirreth Her Nest [1953]

3   We know what the human problems are, we know men are mean, we know men are prejudiced, we know that men are narrow-minded, and we know they are selfish. We know men are unkind, ruthless, and cruel. We know men are murderers and sinful. But what we don't know is what to do about it.... We have already diagnosed the case, but what we can't do is write a prescription.   *Dry Bones in the Valley [mid-1950s]*

4   When you've got so much religion that you can't mingle with people, and that you're afraid of certain people, let me tell you, you've got too much religion.   *Without a Song [mid-1950s]*

5   Everybody wants justice, everybody wants freedom, everybody wants what's coming to them, but very few of us take the time to think about the price that must be paid for these things and the responsibility that goes along with the achievement of them.   *Moses at the Red Sea [1950s]*

6   Sometimes in the midst of our own crises, the midst of our own life-problems, in the midst of the things that we find ourselves involved in, sometimes the power of our deliverance is in our own power and in our own possession. What you need, my brothers and sisters, is within you.

Moses at the Red Sea

John Hope Franklin   1915–2009

7   Democracy is essentially an act of faith.

History, Weapon of War and Peace [1944]

8   It can hardly be denied that the course of American history has been vitally affected by his presence. At the same time it must be admitted that the effect of acculturation on the Negro in the United States has been so marked that today he is as truly American as any member of other ethnic groups that make up the American population. That is not to say that the story of the Negro is one solely of achievement or success. Too frequently

---

[1]From *Give Me This Mountain: Reverend C. L. Franklin* [1989], edited by JEFF TODD TITON.

the Negro's survival in America has depended on his capacity to adjust —
indeed, to accommodate — himself to the dominant culture and the obstacles have at times been too great to permit him to make significant achievements in the usual sense of the word.

From Slavery to Freedom [1947], preface

1   If the house is to be set in order, one cannot begin with the present; he
must begin with the past.

Rediscovering Black America: A Historical Roundup.
New York Times [September 8, 1968]

2   A color-blind society eludes us. For one reason, we have not sought
diligently and contentiously to pursue it. It is one thing to mouth the words,
but it is quite another to perform the deeds.   *The Color Line [1993]*

3   It was never any different. It has been the same since 1619. That was
when the first ships arrived from West Africa with blacks on them. We got
off to a bad start right then!

New York Times Magazine [September 18, 2005]

4   We must go beyond textbooks, go out into the bypaths and
untrodden depths of the wilderness and travel and explore and tell the world
the glories of our journey.   *Attributed*

Billie Holiday [Eleanora Fagan]   1915–1959

5   I love my man,
I'm a liar if I say I don't.
But I'll quit my man,
I'm a liar if I say I won't.   *Billie's Blues (My Man) [1936]*

6   Love is like a faucet. It turns off and on.
Sometimes when you think it's on, baby,
It has turned off and gone.   *Fine and Mellow [1940]*[1]

7   Them that's got shall get,
Them that's not shall lose
So the Bible says,
And it still is news.
Mama may have, Papa may have,
But God bless the child that's got his own.   *God Bless the Child [1941]*[2]

8   Hush now, don't explain
You're my joy and pain

---

[1]Derived from the classic blues line "Love is like a faucet. It turns off and on."
[2]With Arthur Herzog, Jr., 1927–1983.

My life's yours love
Don't explain.   *Don't Explain [1944]*[1]

1   I can't stand to sing the same song the same way two nights in succession, let alone two years or ten years. If you can, then it ain't music, it's close-order drill or exercise or yodeling or something, not music.
                                             Lady Sings the Blues [1956], ch. 4

2   You can be up to your boobies in white satin, with gardenias in your hair and no sugar cane for miles, but you can still be working on a plantation.   *Lady Sings the Blues, 11*

3   First they hurt me then desert me,
I'm left alone, all alone
There's no house that I can call my home.   *Left Alone [1961]*

Claudia Jones   1915–1964

4   A people's art is the genesis of their freedom.
                              Notting Hill Caribbean carnival slogan [1959]

Memphis Slim [John Peter Chatman, Jr.]   1915–1988

5   Every Day I Have the Blues   *Song title [1948]*

6   Don't care how great you are
Don't care what you worth
When it all ends up
You got to go back to Mother Earth.   *Mother Earth [1960]*

[William Thomas] Billy Strayhorn   1915–1967

7   I want something to live for,
Someone to make my life an adventurous dream
Oh, what I wouldn't give for
Someone who'd take my life and make it seem
As gay as they say as it ought to be.   *Something to Live For [1939]*

8   You must take the "A" Train
To go to Sugar Hill way up in Harlem.   *Take the "A" Train [1941]*

9   Romance is a mush, stifling those who strive,
I'll live a lush life in some small dive.
And there I'll be, while I rot with the rest
Of those whose lives are lonely, too.   *Lush Life [1949]*

---

[1]With Arthur Herzog, Jr., 1927–1983.

Margaret Walker
1915–1998

1   For my People everywhere singing their slave songs repeatedly: their dirges and their ditties and their blues and jubilees, praying their prayers nightly to an unknown god, bending their knees humbly to an unseen power.   *For My People [1937]*

2   Let a new earth rise. Let another world be born.   *For My People*

3   She [Vyry] was only a living sign and mark of all the best that any human being could hope to become. In her obvious capacity for love, redemptive and forgiving love, she was alive and standing on the highest peaks of her time and human personality. Peasant and slave, unlettered and untutored, she was nevertheless the best true example of the motherhood of her race, an ever present assurance that nothing could destroy a people who had come from her loins.   *Jubilee [1966], ch. 57*

4   The black woman has deep wells of spiritual strength. She doesn't know how she's going to feed her family in the morning, but she prays and in the morning, out of thin air, she makes breakfast.

From BRIAN LANKER, I Dream a World [1989]

Harold Cruse
1916–2005

5   Harlem is the black world's key community for historical, political, economic, cultural and/or ethnic reasons.

The Crisis of the Negro Intellectual [1967]

6   Integration is . . . leading to cultural negation.

The Crisis of the Negro Intellectual

7   The Negro intellectual must not be allowed to forget that the integrated intellectual world is not representative of ethnic group aspirations.

The Crisis of the Negro Intellectual

8   The path to more knowledge for the Negro intellectual is through cultural nationalism — an ideology that has made Jewish intellectuals into a social force to be reckoned with in America.

The Crisis of the Negro Intellectual

9   The only real politics for the creative intellectual should be the politics of culture. The activists of race, nationalism, and civil rights will never understand this, hence this dilemma becomes another ramification of the manifold crisis of the Negro intellectual.

The Crisis of the Negro Intellectual

10   Despite the false promises of the civil rights cycle of the Sixties and Seventies, American blacks still represent the most crucial minority group,

the most strategically positioned to impact on the institutional structures of the total society. What is lacking is the quality of black leadership capable of harnessing black potential.   *Plural but Equal [1987]*[1]

Florynce Rae Kennedy   1916–2000

1   Niggerization is the result of oppression — and it doesn't just apply to black people. Old people, poor people, and students can also get niggerized.
        From GLORIA STEINEM, *The Verbal Karate of Florynce R. Kennedy, Esq. [1973]*

2   If men could get pregnant, abortion would be a sacrament.
        From GLORIA STEINEM, *The Verbal Karate of Florynce R. Kennedy, Esq.*

John Oliver Killens   1916–1987

3   Joseph Youngblood, a great fearless black soldier in the army of the Lord, smitten down in the full bloom of life by the Pharisees. And the church said Amen.... And the sun glittering brightly on the stained-glass windows with the pictures of Jesus and the people fanning with paper fans and the black and brown and light skin faces, and the patting of feet and the wiping of eyes all over the church and — Just last Sunday he was sitting over there with the family — and the shaking of heads, and somebody shouted over in the Amen corner and down near the middle of the second aisle. And the congregation said, *Amen.*   *Youngblood [1954], ch. 8*

4   The "Negro Problem" and the "White Man's Burden" are historical misnomers.... The Black Man's Burden, simply stated, was slavery and colonialism.   *Black Man's Burden [1965]*

5   My name is Ben Ali Lumumba, and I'm free, Black and twenty-three. Okay, Lumumba is my given name. Dig. The only name I gave myself, that is.   *Cotillion [1971], foreword*

6   There is no such thing as art for art's sake. All art is propaganda, although there is much propaganda that is not art.
                                        Obituary. New York Times [October 30, 1987]

Edna Lewis   1916–2006

7   Ham held the same rating as the basic black dress. If you had a ham in the meat house any situation could be faced.
                                        The Taste of Country Cooking [1976]

---

[1]From *The Essential Harold Cruse: A Reader* [2002], edited by WILLIAM JELANI COBB.

Albert Murray   1916–2013

1   *American culture, even in its most rigidly segregated precincts, is patently and irrevocably composite. It is, regardless of all the hysterical protestations of those who would have it otherwise, incontestably mulatto.* Indeed, for all their traditional antagonisms and obvious differences, the so-called black and so-called white people of the United States resemble nobody else in the world so much as they resemble each other.   *The Omni-Americans [1970]*

2   It seems altogether likely that white people in the United States will continue to reassure themselves with black images derived from the folklore of white supremacy and the fakelore of black pathology so long as segregation enables them to ignore the actualities.

The Omni-Americans

3   Integrated or not, Negroes have always been in a position to observe almost everything that has been doing and undoing in this country.

The Omni-Americans

4   Going back home has probably always had as much if not more to do with people as with landmarks and place names and locations on maps and mileage charts anyway. Not that home is not a place, for even in its most abstract implications it is precisely the very oldest place in the world.

South to a Very Old Place [1971]

5   *Yes, the also and also of all that also; because the oldness that you are forever going back again by one means or another to is not only of a place and of people, but also and perhaps most often of the promises that exact that haze-blue adventuresomeness from the brown-skinned hometown boy in us all.*   *South to a Very Old Place, epilogue*

6   Improvisation is the ultimate human (i.e., heroic) endowment.

The Hero and the Blues [1973]

7   The Official name of that place (which is perhaps even more of a location in time than an intersection on a map) was Gasoline Point, Alabama, because that was what our post office address was, and it was also the name on the L&N timetable and the road map. But once upon a time it was also the briarpatch, which is why my nickname was then Scooter, and is also why the chinaberry tree (that was ever as tall as any fairy tale beanstalk) was, among other things, my spyglass tree.   *Train Whistle Guitar [1974]*

Frank Yerby   1916–1991

8   That was it, Stephen thought. To live like this — graciously, with leisure to cultivate the tastes and to indulge every pleasure — a man must be

free of labor. Leave the work for the blacks. Breed a new generation of aristocrats.   *The Foxes of Harrow [1946]*

1   There was no wind in all that sweep of sky. Now and again one of the black-gray mountains of cloud, too heavily laden, sank almost to the surface of the Caribbean; but that was where the wind was, and the towering domes and pinnacles of mist were rent into shreds, and sent scudding to leeward to be lost in the white boil of spray where the waves crashed in thunderous fury over the rocks on the Isle de Vaches — Cow Island.

The Golden Hawk [1948], opening lines

2   Oppression is never right, even when it is elegant.
The Devil's Laughter [1953]

3   To dreamers, Truth is an unlovely thing.
Judas, My Brother [1967], prologue

4   He [Hwesu] approached the conviction that all men came to, soon, or late: that *why* is an unanswerable word: that there are no solutions to anything in life. And having almost reached that immense, empty horizon-stretching, utterly barren plateau of always unacceptable truth, he was silent, making of his no answer perhaps the answer. For silence at least has dignity.
The Dahomean [1971], last lines

5   Courage is always admirable, no matter how wrongheaded it is.
Hail the Conquering Hero [1978]

Gwendolyn Brooks   1917–2000

6   Gimme an upsweep, Minnie,
With humpteen baby curls.
'Bout time I got some glamour.
I'll show them girls.   *A Street in Bronzeville [1945]. At the Hairdresser's*

7   Each body has its art.   *A Street in Bronzeville. Gay Chaps at the Bar, st. 2*

8   Abortions will not let you forget.
You remember the children you got that you did not get.
A Street in Bronzeville. The Mother, st. 1

9   Maud went to college.
Sadie stayed at home.
Sadie scraped life
With a fine-tooth comb.

A Street in Bronzeville. Sadie and Maud, st. 1

10   I've stayed in the front yard all my life.
I want a peek at the back

Where it's rough and untended and hungry weed grows.
A girl gets sick of a rose.
A Street in Bronzeville. A Song in the Front Yard, st. 1

1 Exhaust the little moment. Soon it dies.
And be it gash or gold it will not come
Again in this identical disguise.
Annie Allen [1949]. Exhaust the Little Moment

2 Let us combine. There are no magics or elves
Or timely godmothers to guide us. We are lost, must
Wizard a track through our own screaming weed.
Annie Allen. The Womanhood, XV

3 What shall I give my children? who are poor,
Who are adjudged the leastwise of the land.
Annie Allen. The Womanhood, The Children of the Poor, sonnet 2

4 Recipient and benefactor.
It's so good of you.
You're being so good.
Maud Martha [1953]

5 　　Was, perhaps, the whole life of man a dedication to this search for something to lean upon, and was, to a great degree, his "happiness" or "unhappiness" written up for him by the demands or limitations of what he chose for that work? For work it was. Leaning was work.
Maud Martha

6 And remembering...
Remembering, with twinklings and twinges,
As they lean over the beans in their rented back
　　room that is full of beads and receipts and
　　dolls and cloths, tobacco crumbs, vases and
　　fringes.
The Bean Eaters [1960]. The Bean Eaters, st. 3

7 Time upholds or overturns
The many, tight, and small concerns.
*The Bean Eaters. The Chicago Defender Sends a Man
to Little Rock*

8 We real cool. We
Left school. We
Lurk late. We
Strike straight. We
Sing sin. We
Thin gin. We

Jazz June. We
Die soon.
The Bean Eaters. We Real Cool

1   What else is there to say but everything?   *In the Mecca [1968], st. 16*

2   He opened us —
who was a key,
who was a man.   *In the Mecca. After Mecca. Malcolm X*

3   This is the urgency: Live!
and have your blooming in the noise of the whirlwind.
In the Mecca. The Second Sermon on the Warpland, st. 1

4   The time
cracks into furious flower. Lifts its face
all unashamed. And sways in wicked grace.
In the Mecca. The Second Sermon on the Warpland, st. 4

5   A garbageman is dignified
as any diplomat.
Big Bessie's feet hurt like nobody's business,
but she stands — bigly — under the unruly scrutiny, stands
in the wild weed.

In the wild weed
she is a citizen.
In the Mecca. The Second Sermon on the Warpland, pt. 4

6   Beware the easy griefs
that fool and fuel nothing.
Beckonings [1975]. Boys. Black, st. 7

Marie Chauvet   1917–1975

7   The volcano which the colonists had long ignored, pretending it did not exist, was now in full eruption. Masses of slaves poured down from the hills, emerging from the plantations as though they had been spewed up from a crater. Being armed they now struck back savagely in turn, likewise without pity or compassion.

Dance on the Volcano [1959][1]

8   The soul is a millstone, an albatross, it meddles in everything. It creates ties to torture us.   *Love (Amour) [1968]*[2]

---

[1]Translated by SALVATOR ATTANASIO.
[2]From *Daughters of Africa* [1992], edited by MARGARET BUSBY. Translated by BETTY WILSON.

Janet Collins
1917–2003

1   There is no such thing as freedom without discipline. The one who is free is disciplined.

From BRIAN LANKER, I Dream a World [1989]

Ossie [Raiford Chatman] Davis
1917–2005

2   Malcolm was our manhood, our living black manhood! This was his meaning to his people. And, in honoring him, we honor the best in ourselves.... And we shall know him then for what he was and is — a prince, our own black shining Prince! — who didn't hesitate to die, because he loved us so.

Eulogy for Malcolm X. Faith Temple Church of God,
New York City [February 27, 1965]

3   It's not the man, it's the plan.

Speech, Congressional Black Caucus [June 18, 1971]

4   We can't float through life. We can't be incidental or accidental. We must fix our gaze on a guiding star as soon as one comes upon the horizon...we must keep our eyes on it and our hands on the plow. It is the consistency of the pursuit of the highest possible vision that you can find in front of you that gives you...the way to understand where you are and why it's important for you to do what you can do.

Speaking on the Tavis Smiley Show,
National Public Radio [November 8, 2004]

Ella Fitzgerald
1917–1996

5   The only thing better than singing is more singing.

Quoted in the New York Sunday News [August 1, 1954][1]

Dizzy [John Birks] Gillespie
1917–1993

6   The basic thing about jazz music is putting the notes to rhythm, not the other way around.... You can take just one note and put all kinds of different rhythms to the note and with just that one note everybody is clapping their hands and dancing and shouting.

Quoted in the San Francisco Chronicle
[September 30, 1958][2]

7   To Be, or Not...to Bop   *Title of memoir [1979]*

---

[1]From STUART NICHOLSON, *Ella Fitzgerald* [1995].
[2]From DONALD L. MAGIN, *Dizzy: The Life and Times of John Birks Gillespie* [2005].

1   Africa hit me all at once in those little clubs in Spanish Harlem. Got right into my marrow. I found my musical heritage, my roots there. African slaves in America were not allowed to practice their own religions or to use the drum.... The Africa they wouldn't let us have in South Carolina I discovered for myself in East Harlem.   *Interview [1990]*[1]

Fannie Lou Hamer   1917–1977

2   I question America. Is this America, the land of the free and the home of the brave, where we have to sleep with our telephones off the hooks because our lives be threatened daily, because we want to live as decent human beings, in America?
Testimony at Democratic National Convention,
Atlantic City, New Jersey [August 22, 1964]

3   We didn't come all this way for no two seats.
Statement before the Credentials Committee during the
Democratic National Convention[2]

4   I'm sick and tired of being sick and tired.[3]
Speech delivered with Malcolm X at the Williams
Institutional CMA Church, Harlem [December 20, 1964]

5   We have to build our own power. We have to win every single political office we can, where we have a majority of black people.... The question for black people is not, when is the white man going to give us our rights, or when is he going to give us good education for our children, or when is he going to give us jobs—if the white man gives you anything—just remember when he gets ready he will take it right back. We have to take for ourselves.

To Praise Our Bridges [1967]

John Lee Hooker   1917–2001

6   One night I was layin' down
I heard mama and papa talkin'
I heard papa tell mama
Let that boy boogie-woogie
Because it's in him
And it got to come out.   *Boogie Chillen [1948]*

---

[1]From Donald L. Magin, *Dizzy: The Life and Times of John Birks Gillespie* [2005].
[2]Response to Democratic Party leaders' offer of two seats to the Mississippi Freedom Democratic Party delegation, with no power to vote.
[3]Inscribed on her gravestone as "I am sick and tired of being sick and tired."

Lena Horne   1917–2010

1   To some Negroes light color is far from being a status symbol; in fact it's quite the opposite. It is evidence that your image has been corrupted by white people. It was an irony. On the one hand much money was spent on hair straighteners and skin-lighteners, on the other hand you were put down for being naturally closer to the prevailing ideal of beauty. I did not know whether I was supposed to be proud of my color or ashamed of it.

Lena [1965]

2   *[On being a black woman:]* You learn not to depend on anything.... You get into a habit of surviving.

Interview. New York Times [May 3, 1981]

Jacob Lawrence   1917–2000

3   My pictures express my life and experience. I paint the things I know about and the things I have experienced. The things I have experienced extend to my national, racial and class group. So I paint the American scene.

Philosophy of Art. Statement solicited by the Whitney Museum [May 30, 1951][1]

4   The most important function of art is observation.

From Elsa Honig Fine, *The Afro-American Artist: A Search for Identity [1973]*

5   Theirs is a story of African-American strength and courage. I share it now as my parents told it to me, because their struggles and triumphs ring true today. People all over the world are still on the move, trying to build better lives for themselves and for their families.

The Great Migration [1992]

6   And the migrants kept coming.

Text from a panel in the Migration Series [1993]

Thelonious [Sphere] Monk   1917–1982

7   I say, play your own way. Don't play what the public wants — you play what you want, and let the public pick up on what you're doing — even if it does take them fifteen, twenty years.

Interview [1959][2]

---

[1]From Ellen Harkins Wheat, *Jacob Lawrence: American Painter* [1986].

[2]From Grover Sales, *"I Wanted to Make it Better": Monk at the Blackhawk* in *The Thelonious Monk Reader* [2001], edited by Rob van der Bliek.

1   Jazz is my adventure.

Interview. Harper's Magazine [September 1961][1]

2   All you're supposed to do is lay down the sounds.... If you ain't doing that, you just ain't a musician. Nothing more to it than that.

Quoted in TIME [February 28, 1964]

3   All musicians are subconsciously mathematicians.

Interview. Down Beat [October 28, 1971][2]

Oliver Tambo[3]   1917–1993

4   There is no answer to apartheid apart from striking directly at its head. It is so evil and has been condemned so forcibly and so genuinely that the only way to handle it is by destroying it.

Statement at the meeting of the Special Political Committee of the United Nations General Assembly, New York [October 29, 1963]

5   The oppressed people in South Africa must and will settle accounts with their oppressors by any methods and means open to them, the determining consideration being whether they want to achieve their freedom at all costs or to live in bondage forever.

Statement at the Meeting of the United Nations Special Committee Against Apartheid, New York [March 12, 1964]

6   No one can doubt any longer now that life for the African in South Africa is not life. If it is, it is worth nothing. But we promise that in that event no other life in South Africa is worth anything — white or not white. Let the United Nations and the world, therefore, save what it can. What it cannot will either be destroyed or destroy itself.

Statement at the Meeting of the United Nations Special Committee Against Apartheid

7   We who are free to eat and sleep at will, to write, to speak, to travel as we please; we who are free to make or break a revolution, let us use our comparative freedom, not to perpetuate the misery of those who suffer, nor to give indirect aid to the enemy they fight by withholding our own contributions.

New Year's address to the African National Congress External Mission [1971]

---

[1]From Robert Koltowitz, *"Monk Talk,"* in *The Thelonious Monk Reader.*

[2]From Pearl Gonzalez, *"Monk Talk,"* in *The Thelonious Monk Reader.*

[3]From *Preparing for Power: Oliver Tambo Speaks* [1987], complied by Adelaide Tambo.

1   Our watchword must be mobilization, organization, struggle. All our people must be mobilized into action. All our people must be organized for action. All our people must engage in struggle. That must be our reply to the enemy's desperate counteroffensive.

Radio address after the declaration of a state of emergency in response to uprisings in black townships [July 22, 1985]

2   We seek to create a united democratic and nonracial society. We have a vision of South Africa in which black and white shall live and work together as equals in conditions of peace and prosperity. Using the power you derive from the discovery of the truth about racism in South Africa, you will help us to remake our part of the world into a corner of the globe of which all of humanity can be proud.

Speech at Georgetown University [January 27, 1987]

Yosef Ben-Jochannan   1918–

3   It is commonly said in some quarters that "Africa has awakened." This cannot be accepted by conscious Africans, for to have "awakened," one must have been asleep. Africa was not asleep. Africa was wide awake, but her land, as well as her sons and daughters, were subjected to the most barbarous treatment man has ever imposed on man.

The Rape of Africa and the Crisis in Angola [1958]

Elmore James [Elmore Brooks]   1918–1963

4   Shake Your Moneymaker   *Song title [1960]*

John H[arold] Johnson   1918–2005

5   [On starting Ebony magazine in 1945:] If you had relied on the white press of that day, you would have assumed that Blacks were not born, because the White press didn't deal with our births. You would have assumed that we didn't finish school, because the white press didn't deal with our educational achievements. You would have assumed that we didn't get married because the white press didn't print our wedding announcements or pictures of black brides and grooms cutting cakes. You would have assumed we didn't die, because it didn't deal with our funerals.

Succeeding Against the Odds [1989]

6   In a world of despair, we wanted to give hope. In a world of negative Black images, we wanted to provide positive Black images. In a world that said Blacks could do few things, we wanted to say they could do everything.

Succeeding Against the Odds

1   The greater the handicap, the greater the triumph.

Succeeding Against the Odds

Nelson [Rolihlahla] Mandela   1918–

2   The struggle is my life. I will continue fighting for freedom until the end of my days.

Statement to the press [June 26, 1961][1]

3   Government violence can do only one thing and that is to breed counter-violence.

Court address [1962][1]

4   I was made, by the law, a criminal, not because of what I had done, but because of what I stood for, because of what I thought, because of my conscience. Can it be any wonder to anybody that such conditions make a man an outlaw of society?

Court address

5   I have fought against white domination, and I have fought against black domination. I have cherished the ideal of a democratic and free society in which all persons live together in harmony and with equal opportunities. It is an ideal which I hope to live for and to achieve. But if needs be, it is an ideal for which I am prepared to die.

Statement from the dock at the opening of the Rivonia Trial [April 20, 1964][2]

6   Between the anvil of united mass action and the hammer of the armed struggle we shall crush apartheid and white minority racist rule.

Response to Soweto uprising [1976][1]

7   Only free men can negotiate. Prisoners cannot enter into contracts.

Statement from prison [February 10, 1985][1]

8   We have waited too long for our freedom. We can no longer wait.

Speech upon release from twenty-seven years in prison [February 11, 1990][1]

9   The time for the healing of the wounds has come. The moment to bridge the chasms that divide us has come. The time to build is upon us. We have, at last, achieved our political emancipation. We pledge ourselves to liberate all our people from the continuing bondage of poverty, deprivation, suffering, gender and other discrimination.

Inaugural address [May 10, 1994]

---

[1]From NELSON MANDELA, *Nelson Mandela: In His Own Words* [2003].

[2]Also quoted on his release from prison [February 11, 1990].

1   Let there be justice for all. Let there be peace for all. Let there be work, bread, water, and salt for all. Let each know that for each the body, the mind, and the soul have been freed to fulfill themselves. Never, never, and never again shall it be that this beautiful land will again experience the oppression of one by another and suffer the indignity of being the skunk of the world. Let freedom reign. The sun shall never set on so glorious a human achievement! God bless Africa!

Inaugural address

2   I am not truly free if I am taking away someone else's freedom, just as surely as I am not free when my freedom is taken away from me. The oppressed and the oppressor alike are robbed of their humanity.

Long Walk to Freedom [1994]

3   The challenge for every prisoner, particularly every political prisoner, is how to survive prison intact, how to emerge from prison undiminished.

Long Walk to Freedom

4   Any man or institution that tries to rob me of my dignity will lose because I will not part with it at any price or under any pressure.

Long Walk to Freedom

5   I have walked that long road to freedom. I have tried not to falter; I have made missteps along the way. But I have discovered the secret that after climbing a great hill, one only finds that there are many more hills to climb.

Long Walk to Freedom

6   Reconciliation means working together to correct the legacy of past injustice.

Speech [December 16, 1995][1]

7   There is a view that the past is best forgotten. Some criticize us when we say that whilst we can forgive, we can never forget.... The choice of our nation is not whether the past should be revealed, but rather to ensure that it comes to be known in a way which promotes reconciliation and peace.

Address for the Truth and Reconciliation Commission
[February 13, 1996][1]

8   Let us give publicity to H.I.V./AIDS and not hide it, because the only way to make it appear like a normal illness like TB, like cancer, is always to come out and say somebody has died because of H.I.V. And people will stop regarding it as something extraordinary for which people go to hell and not to heaven.

Statement announcing son's AIDS-related death
[January 6, 2005]

---

[1]From NELSON MANDELA, *Nelson Mandela: In His Own Words* [2003].

Professor Longhair [Henry Byrd]   1918–1980

1   Tipitina, tra la la la.   *Tipitina [1953]*

Charles White   1918–1979

2   Paint is the only weapon I have with which to fight what I resent. If I
could write, I would write about it. If I could talk, I would talk about it.
Since I paint, I must paint about it.

Opportunity [1940]

3   The substance of man is such that he has to satisfy the needs of life with
all his senses. His very being cries out for these senses to appropriate the true
riches of life: the beauty of human relationships and dignity, of nature and
art.... Without a history, a culture, without creative art inspiring these
senses, mankind stumbles in a chasm of despair and pessimism.

From Black Artists in America [1972], edited by
EDMUND W. GORDON

Joe Williams [Joseph Goreed]   1918–1999

4   We today have the blues, too, but it is a blues of our day. It's more of
the mind and heart and not of the beating of the back.

Interview [February 21, 1959][1]

Louise Bennett   1919–2006

5   Sun a shine an pot a bwile, but
Things no bright bickle no nuff
Rain a-fall, river dah-flood, but
Wata scarce an dutty tuff!

Dutty Tough (The Ground Is Hard) [1942][2]

6   Back to Africa, Miss Mattie?
Yuh noh wha yuh dah-sey?
Yuh haffe come from some weh fus
Before yuh go back deh!   *Back to Africa [1947]*[2]

7   Miss Jane jus hear from 'Merica,
Her daughta proudly write
Fe sey she fail her exam, but
She passin' dere fe wite!

Pass fe White [1949][2]

---

[1]From *Jazz Singers* [1969], edited by PAUL ROLAND.
[2]From LOUISE BENNETT, *Jamaica Labrish* [1966].

1   Dem half o' dis an half o'dat
     Dem neida dose nor dese —
     So since dem half-an half, dem choice
     Watever side dem please.   *White Pickney [1949]*[1]

2   Independence is we nature
     Born and bred in all we do,
     An she glad fi see dat Government
     Tun independant to.   *Independence [1966]*[2]

3   Once upon a time Anancy tink to himself seh dat if him coulda collect
     up all de common-sense ina de worl an keep it fi himself, den him boun to
     get plenty money an plenty powah, for everybody woulda haffi come to him
     wid dem worries an him woulda charge dem very dear wen him advise dem.
                                              Anancy and Miss Lou [1979]

Art Blakey   1919–1990

4   A name doesn't make the music. Jazz is known all over the world as an
     American musical art form and that's it. No America, no jazz.   *Interview*[3]

Mary Eugenia Charles[4]   1919–2005

5   You can't run a country and be soft.
                                       In the Associated Press [June 11, 1995]

Nat [Nathaniel Adams] King Cole   1919–1965

6   Straighten up and fly right
     Cool down, papa, dont you blow your top.
                                       Straighten Up and Fly Right [1944][5]

7   Madison Avenue is afraid of the dark.
               *Statement following cancellation of his television show because
               of a lack of advertisers [1957]*

Roy DeCarava   1919–2009

8   There's an arc of being. There's a beginning, then the peak is reached
     and then there's the end. It's like the pole vaulter who begins his run, shoots

---

[1]From LOUISE BENNETT, *Jamaica Labrish* [1966].
[2]From *Selected Poems of Louise Bennett* [1982], edited by MERVYN MORRIS.
[3]From ARTHUR TAYLOR, *Notes and Tones* [1977].
[4]As the premier of Dominica, Charles became known as the Iron Lady of the Caribbean.
[5]With Irving Mills.

up, then comes down. At the peak there is no movement. He's neither going up nor going down. It is that moment I wait for.

Roy DeCarava: Photographs [1981]

Jackie [Jack Roosevelt] Robinson

1919–1972

1 *[On hearing racial epithets on the field during first year of integrating baseball:]* I'd get mad. But I'd never let them know it.

TIME [September 22, 1947]

2 I can't speak for any fifteen million people any more than any other person can, but I know that I've got too much invested for my wife and child and myself in the future of this country, and I and other Americans of many races and faiths have too much invested in our country's welfare for any of us to throw it away because of a siren song sung in bass.

Speech regarding Paul Robeson to the House Un-American Activities Committee [July 18, 1949][1]

3 I'm not concerned with your liking or disliking me. All I ask is that you respect me as a human being.

Statement [1954][2]

4 I am convinced that those of us who are earnestly concerned about the problems of civil rights and integration must measure progress not in terms of how much progress we have made recently but how far we have yet to go before we achieve full first class citizenship for the Negro.

Letter to Richard Nixon [February 5, 1958][3]

5 *[Response to a call for patience:]* On hearing you say this, I felt like standing up and saying, "Oh no! Not again." I respectfully remind you, sir, that we have been the most patient of all people. When you said we must have self-respect, I wondered how we could have self-respect and remain patient, considering the treatment accorded us through the years.

Letter to Dwight D. Eisenhower [May 13, 1958][3]

6 Talk is important, especially from the White House. But it isn't enough.

Open letter to John F. Kennedy [May 5, 1962][3]

---

[1] It is unthinkable that American Negroes will go to war in behalf of those who have oppressed us for generations . . . against a country [the Soviet Union] which in one generation has raised our people to full human dignity of mankind. — PAUL ROBESON

Speech at World Congress of Partisans of Peace in Paris [April 20, 1949], from *Paul Robeson Speaks* [1978], edited by ERIC FONER.

[2] From JACKIE ROBINSON, *Baseball Has Done It* [1964].

[3] From *First-Class Citizenship: The Civil Rights Letters of Jackie Robinson* [2007], edited by MICHAEL G. LONG.

1   I cannot stand and sing the national anthem. I cannot salute the flag; I know that I am a black man in a white world.... I know that I never had it made.

I Never Had It Made [1972]

E[dward] R[icardo] Braithwaite   1920–

2   Nothing had really mattered, the teaching, the talking, the example, the patience, the worry. It was all nothing. They, like the strangers on buses and trains, saw only the skins, never the people in those skins.... It was like a disease, and these children whom I loved without caring about *their* skins or *their* backgrounds, they were tainted with the hateful virus which attacked their vision, distorting everything that was not white or English.

To Sir, with Love [1959]

Anatole Broyard   1920–1990

3   Authenticity is difficult to attain. To make it even more difficult, no one seems to know exactly what it consists in. Authenticity, as I take it, would mean stubborn adherence to one's essential self, in spite of the distorting pressures of one's situation. By the Negro's essential self, I mean his innate qualities and developed characteristics as an individual, as distinguished from his preponderantly defensive reactions as a member of an embattled minority.

Portrait of the Inauthentic Negro: How Prejudice Distorts the
Victim's Personality [July 1950], Commentary

4   Like every great tradition, my family had to die before I could understand how much I missed them and what they meant to me. When they went into the flames at the crematorium, all my letters of introduction went with them.

Growing Up Irrational [April 19, 1979]

Alice Childress   1920–1994

5   Everybody can be wrong sometime, and when you wrong you oughta stand up and be wrong right out, and not be hidin and lyin.

A Hero Ain't Nothin' but a Sandwich [1973]
[Benjie]

6   All my life I been hearin bout old folks and, of course, old folks is always somebody else and you can understand that much better than when you might be the one.

A Hero Ain't Nothin' but a Sandwich
[Mrs. Ransom Bell]

1   Thoughts can hurt like real pain.

A Hero Ain't Nothin' but a Sandwich
[Mrs. Ransom Bell]

2   We think of poverty as a condition simply meaning a lack of funds, no money, but when one sees fifth, sixth, and seventh generation poor, it is clear that poverty is as complicated as high finance.

A Hero Ain't Nothin' but a Sandwich
[The Principal]

3   Life is just a short walk from the cradle to the grave.

A Short Walk [1979], ch. 2 [Papa]

4   I am lonesome so regular it's like a job I gotta report to every day.

Rainbow Jordan [1982] [Rainbow]

Declaration of Rights of the Negro Peoples of the World[1]   1920

5   We complain:

1. That nowhere in the world, with few exceptions, are black men accorded equal treatment with white men, although in the same situation and circumstances, but, on the contrary, are discriminated against and denied the common rights due to human beings for no other reason than their race and color.

6. ...Our children are forced to attend inferior separate schools for shorter terms than white children, and the public school funds are unequally divided between the white and colored schools.

13. We believe in the freedom of Africa for the Negro people of the world, and by the principle of Europe for the Europeans and Asia for the Asiatics; we also demand Africa for the Africans at home and abroad.

16. We believe all men should live in peace one with the other, but when races and nations provoke the ire of other races and nations by attempting to infringe upon their rights, war becomes inevitable, and the attempt in any way to free one's self or protect one's rights or heritage becomes justifiable.

17. Whereas the lynching, by burning, hanging or any other means, of human beings is a barbarous practice, and a shame and disgrace to civilization, we therefore declare any country guilty of such atrocities outside the pale of civilization.

39. [We demand] That the colors Red, Black and Green be the colors of the Negro race.

[1]From *Philosophy and Opinions of Marcus Garvey* [1967], edited by AMY JACQUES GARVEY.

James Farmer, Jr.   1920–1999

1   We will not stop, until the dogs stop biting us in the South and the rats stop biting us in the North.

*Message from jail, read at the March on Washington
for Jobs and Freedom [August 28, 1963]*

2   Evil societies always kill their consciences. We, who are the living, possess the past. Tomorrow is for our martyrs.

*On the murders of Chaney, Goodman, and Schwerner.
Lay Bare the Heart [1985]*

Percy Mayfield   1920–1984

3   Just because I'm in misery
I don't beg for no sympathy
But if it's not asking too much
Please send me someone to love.

Please Send Me Someone to Love [1951]

4   Hit the road, Jack, and don't you come back no more.

Hit the Road, Jack [1961]

Charlie Parker   1920–1955

5   Music is your own experience, your thoughts, your wisdom. If you don't live it, it won't come out of your horn. They teach you there's a boundary line to music. But, man, there's no boundary line to art.

*From NAT HENTOFF and NAT SHAPIRO,
Hear Me Talkin' to Ya [1955]*

Percy Sutton   1920–2009

6   Suffer the hurts, but don't show the anger, because if you do, it will block you from being able to effectively do anything to remove the hurts.

From ALFRED DUCKETT, Changing of the Guard [1972]

7   If you could pray for only one thing, let it be for an idea.

*From DENNIS KIMBRO, Daily Motivations for
African-American Success [1994]*

Amos Tutuola   1920–1997

8   I was a palm-wine drunkard since I was a boy of ten years of age. I had no other work more than to drink palm-wine in my life. In those days we did not know other money, except COWRIES, so that everything was very cheap, and my father was the richest man in our town.

The Palm-Wine Drinkard [1953], opening lines

Roy Campanella

1921–1993

1   You have to be a man to be a big-league ballplayer, but you have to have a lot of little boy in you, too.   *Quoted in TIME [August 8, 1955]*

Alex Haley

1921–1992

2   It is rightly said that when a griot dies, it is as if a library has burned to the ground.   *Roots [1976], acknowledgments*

3   Out under the moon and the stars, alone with his son that eighth night, Omoro completed the naming ritual. Carrying little Kunta in his strong arms, he walked to the edge of the village, lifted his baby up with his face to the heavens, and said softly, *"Fend kiling dorong leh warrata ka iteh tee."* (Behold — the only thing greater than yourself.)

Roots, ch. 1

Joseph E[chols] Lowery

1921–

4   *[On the role of the Southern Christian Leadership Conference:]* We've been an umbrella in the 40 years of rain. We saw a fire burning in the souls of Black America. Water hoses couldn't wash it out, billy clubs couldn't beat it out, and jails couldn't lock it out.

Farewell address at SCLC annual meeting,
Atlanta, Georgia [August 1997]

5   Lord, in the memory of all the saints who from their labors rest, and in the joy of a new beginning, we ask you to help us work for that day when black will not be asked to get back, when brown can stick around, when yellow will be mellow, when the red man can get ahead, man; and when white will embrace what is right.[1]

Benediction at the inauguration of President Barack Obama
[January 20, 2009]

Constance Baker Motley

1921–2005

6   A Negro who does not vote is ungrateful to those who have already died in the fight for freedom. . . . Any person who does not vote is failing to serve the cause of freedom — his own freedom, his people's freedom, and his country's freedom.

Keynote address to annual convention of the Southern Christian
Leadership Conference [1965][2]

---

[1]See BIG BILL BROONZY, 184:5, and Anonymous: American, 572:10: If you're white, you're all right, if you're yellow, you're mellow, if you're brown, stick around, but if you're black, get back.

[2]From *The Rhetoric of Struggle* [1992], edited by ROBBIE JEAN WALKER.

1   Something which we think is impossible now is not impossible in another decade.

From BRIAN LANKER, *I Dream a World [1989]*

2   Read the preamble to the Constitution: it is simply unjust to ask the black community to bear all of the consequences of the transition from slavery and a segregated society to a nonsegregated society on the theory that the present-day white majority has little connection to its slaveholding and segregated past and that the sins of its fathers should not be visited upon it today.   *Equal Justice Under Law [1998]*

Sugar Ray Robinson [Walker Smith, Jr.]   1921–1989

3   Mister, it's my business to get him in trouble.

*Reply when asked, at the inquest of opponent
Jimmy Doyle, "Did you intend to get
Doyle in trouble?" [1947]*

4   I never lost. Something just happened to keep me from winning.

Sugar Ray [1970]

[William] Billy Taylor   1921–2010

5   I wish I knew how it would feel to be free
I wish I could break all the chains holding me
I wish I could say all the things that I should say
Say 'em loud say 'em clear
For the whole wide world to hear.

*I Wish I Knew How It Would Feel to Be Free
[1954]*

Mamie Till-Mobley   1921–2003

6   Darling, you have not died in vain. Your life has been sacrificed for something.

*Statement in funeral home upon viewing the body
of her son Emmett Till, who was murdered
and mutilated in Mississippi.
Chicago Defender [September 10, 1955]*

7   *[On why she insisted on an open casket at her son's funeral:]* So all the world can see what they did to my boy.

Jet [September 22, 1955]

8   I knew that I could talk for the rest of my life about what had happened to my baby, I could explain it in great detail, I could describe what

I saw laid out there on that slab . . . one piece, one inch, one body part at a time. I could do all of that and people still would not get the full impact. They would not be able to visualize what had happened unless they were allowed to see the results of what had happened. They had to see what I had seen. The whole nation had to bear witness to this.

From Mamie Till-Mobley *and* Christopher Benson,
Death of Innocence [2003]

Whitney M[oore] Young, Jr.   1921–1971

1   Black is beautiful when it is a slum kid studying to enter college, when it is a man learning new skills for a new job, or a slum mother battling to give her kids a chance for a better life. But white is beautiful, too, when it helps change society to make our system work for black people also. White is ugly when it oppresses blacks — and so is black ugly when black people exploit other blacks. No race has a monopoly on vice or virtue, and the worth of an individual is not related to the color of his skin.

Beyond Racism: Building an Open Society [1969],
ch. 4

Jacques Stephen Alexis   1922–1961

2   Vagabond kids run through the streets like colts. The older people say that *dèye mòn gen mòn;*[1] beyond the mountains, there are also other cities. Those cities are fading. Those mountains are fading too, because the soil is no longer rich and they expose their stony bones, bleached by wind and storm to the sun. Beyond these scorched mountains, there are our cities eaten up by termites, our blackened cities, our cities with dirty, laughing kids running around, carrying new cities in their arms and new hope in their eyes. Other cities at even closer distance. Other cities where everybody will discover the joy and excitements of colts on the plains. But I am getting carried away! I always get carried away when I look at my country.   *General Sun, My Brother [1955]*[2]*, ch. 1*

3   It's impossible for Suffering to continue reigning unchallenged over the kingdom. Suffering will bring the kingdom to ruin or will perish itself. Humanity is beautiful, tender, loving. Look at the striking beauty of that woman's arm, protruding miraculously in the midst of such desolation. Look at the powerful balance of that man's body, standing erect against the sky.   *General Sun, My Brother*

---

[1] Beyond the mountains there are more mountains.
[2] Translated by Carol F. Coates [1999].

Dorothy Dandridge   1922–1965

1   *[On work:]* It's a wonderful therapy. You don't have time to feel sorry
for yourself.   *New York Post [November 7, 1954]*

2   *[On prejudice:]* It's such a waste. It makes you logy and half alive. It
gives you nothing. It takes away.   *New York Post*

Redd Foxx [John Elroy Sanford]   1922–1991

3   Sure, I use the word *nigger* all the time. But I say niggers is holding the
black people back. It don't mean black at all. In the dictionary, *nigger* is
described as a person who is shiftless and lazy. Well, if that's the case, there
must be some white niggers, too.

From Redd Foxx and Norma Miller,
Redd Foxx Encyclopedia of Black Humor [1977]

Lord Kitchener [Aldwyn Roberts]   1922–2000

4   Kitch, come go to bed
I've a small comb to scratch your head
Kitch, don't make me cry
You know I love you, you're playing shy.   *Green Fig [1944]*

5   No you can never get away from the fact
If you're not white you're considered black.   *Black or White [1953]*

6   The sun is descending,
The moon is approaching.
And the crowd is gone.   *Carnival Is Over [1978]*

Floyd McKissick   1922–1991

7   We need not justify any black demands for "separatism" to anybody
white. The real separatists moved to the suburbs long ago.

The Way to a Black Ideology. Black Scholar
[December 1969]

Charles Mingus   1922–1979

8   "In other words, I am three. One man stands forever in the middle,
unconcerned, unmoved, watching, waiting to be allowed to express what
he sees to the other two. The second man is like a frightened animal that
attacks for fear of being attacked. Then there's an over-loving gentle person
who lets people into the uttermost sacred temple of his being and he'll take
insults and be trusting and sign contracts without reading them and get

talked down to working cheap or for nothing, and when he realizes what's been done to him he feels like killing and destroying everything around him including himself for being so stupid. But he can't — he goes back inside himself."

"Which one is real?"

"They're *all* real."

Beneath the Underdog [1971], opening lines

Lloyd Richards   1922–2006

1   What the future will understand about your time and your culture and what you've contributed to it will be influenced by art. That is much more valuable than warships. The rest of the world may be affected by a bomb we drop on them, but their perception of our society will come through the arts.

Interview in American Visions Magazine
[August–September 1998]

Fred Shuttlesworth   1922–2011

2   You have to be prepared to die before you can begin to live.

Quoted in MARTIN LUTHER KING, JR., Why We Can't Wait
[1964]

3   Y'all think it's a fire in here? You know there ain't no fire here. The kind of fire we have in here you can't put out with hoses and axes!

Statement to firemen who forced his congregation to evacuate
St. James Baptist Church [1959][1]

[Ahmed] Sékou Touré   1922–1984

4   We prefer poverty in liberty to riches in slavery.

Response to President Charles de Gaulle's proposal that
Guinea remain tied to France after independence [1958]

5   Culture is a more effective weapon than guns for the purpose of domination. For it was scientific, technical and technological culture which produced the guns. The prerequisite of any domination, exploitation and oppression is the denial to the oppressed man or people of his or their human attributes and therefore, in the first instance, cultural activities.

A Dialectical Approach to Culture. The Black Scholar
[November 1969]

---

[1]From ANDREW M. MANIS, *A Fire You Can't Put Out* [1999].

Harold Washington   1922–1987

1   I hope someday to be remembered by history as the Mayor who cared about people and who was, above all, fair. A Mayor who helped, who really helped, heal our wounds and stood the watch while the City and its people answered the greatest challenge in more than a century. Who saw that City renewed.   *Inaugural address, Chicago [April 29, 1983]*

2   Let's go to work.   *Inaugural address*

3   Bossism is not leadership, and leadership is not bossism.
                                    Second inaugural address [May 4, 1987]

4   A civil society—a civilization—a city that works—requires simply that we behave well toward each other.
                                    Second inaugural address

Cheikh Anta Diop   1923–1986

5   If one wished, the history of humanity could be quite lucid. Despite the repeated acts of vandalism...we still have enough documents left to write a clear history of man. The West today is fully aware of this, but it lacks the intellectual and moral courage required, and this is why textbooks are deliberately muddled. It then devolves on us Africans to rewrite the entire history of mankind for our own edification and that of others.
                                    The African Origin of Civilization [1974][1]

6   A dynamic, modern contact with Egyptian Antiquity would enable Blacks to discover increasingly each day the intimate relationship between all Blacks of the continent and the mother Nile Valley. By this dynamic contact, the Negro will be convinced that these temples, these forests of columns, these pyramids, these colossi, these bas-reliefs, mathematics, medicine, and all this science, are indeed the work of his ancestors and that he has a right and a duty to claim this heritage.
                                    The African Origin of Civilization[1]

Mari Evans   1923–

7   I
     am a black woman
     tall as a cypress
     strong
     beyond all definition still
     defying place

---

[1]Translated by MERCER COOK.   *279*

and time
and circumstance
    assailed
        impervious
            indestructible.

Look
    on me and be
renewed.   *I Am Black Woman [1970]*

Hoyt Fuller   1923–1981

1   The black revolt is as palpable in letters as it is in the streets.
                                        Towards a Black Aesthetic [1968][1]

2   The black writer, like the black artist generally, has wasted much time
and talent denying a propensity every rule of human dignity demands that
he possess, seeking an identity that can only do violence to his sense of self.
Black Americans are, for all practical purposes, colonized in their native
land, and it can be argued that those who would submit to subjection
without struggle deserve to be enslaved. It is one thing to accept the guiding
principles on which the American republic ostensibly was founded; it is
quite another thing to accept the prevailing practices which violate those
principles.   *Towards a Black Aesthetic*

Naomi Long Madgett   1923–

3   (I am not what you see, because you do not look closely enough;
You are too satisfied with a mere glance)
Know me, not as a joke to be laughed at,
Not as a fool of no consequence to be regarded with lifted eyebrow,
Not as a savage to be satiated by primitive rhythms and loud sounds and
        bright colors,
Not as a thief to be distrusted.
Not as a clown to be characterized by thick lips stretched into a grin over
        white teeth.
I am all of these — just as you are all of these.
And I am none of these — just as you are none of these.
                                              A Negro in New York [1946]

4   Wait in the shadows if you choose.
Stand alert to catch
The thunder and first sprinkle of unrest

---

[1]From *The Black Aesthetic* [1971], edited by ADDISON GAYLE.

Your insufficiency demands,
But you will find no comfort.
I will not feed your hunger with my blood
Nor crown your nakedness
With jewels of my elegant pain.   *The Race Question [1965]*

1   This is not what I meant to keep
     I thought of bitter-bright rememberings
     pressed petals of forget — me — nots
     or once-bold daffodils

     not this hardness,
     not
     these bitter stalks of
     weeds   *Connected Islands [2004]. Souvenir*

Louise Meriwether   1923–

2   A number runner is something like Santa Claus and any day you hit
     the number is Christmas.   *Daddy Was a Number Runner [1970]*

3   King James of England wrote the Bible...and he made you niggers
     happy hewers of wood and told you to serve your masters faithfully and
     you'd get your reward in heaven. You all believe that shit and been worship-
     ping a white Jesus ever since. How in the hell could God take the black earth
     and make himself a white man out of it? Answer me that?
                              Daddy Was a Number Runner [Daddy]

Ousmane Sembène   1923–2007

4   We are God's bits of wood, and if you count us out you will bring mis-
     fortune; you will make us die!
                        God's Bits of Wood [1962]. The March of the Women [Seni][1]

5   There is a great rock poised across our path, but together we can
     move it.   *God's Bits of Wood. The Meeting [Bakayoko]*[1]

6   What one hand removes another can put back.   *Xala [1975]*

7   A man who wears trousers full of fat should not approach the fire.
                                                          Ceddo [1976]

8   Our men want to lock up our minds.
        But how do you lock up something invisible?   *Moolaadé [2004]*

9   Africa is a real bitch.   *Moolaadé [Mercenaire]*

---

[1]Translated by FRANCIS PRICE.

1   Father, it is easy to hit a son, but the era of little tyrants is over.

Moolaadé [Doukaré]

James [Arthur] Baldwin   1924–1987

2   When the Negro hates the Jew *as a Jew* he does so partly because the nation does and in much the same painful fashion that he hates himself. It is an aspect of his humiliation, whittled down to a manageable size and then transferred; it is the best form the Negro has for tabulating vocally his long record of grievances against his native land.

The Harlem Ghetto.[1] *Commentary [February 1948]*

3   For while the tale of how we suffer, and how we are delighted, and how we may triumph is never new, it always must be heard. There isn't any other tale to tell, it's the only light we've got in all this darkness.

Sonny's Blues [1948]

4   Boy, ain't it time you was thinking about your soul?

Go Tell It on the Mountain [1952], pt. 1 [Elisha]

5   I'm going to have my baby and I'm going to bring him up to be a man.   *Go Tell It on the Mountain, pt. 2 [Esther]*

6   People are trapped in history and history is trapped in them.

Stranger in the Village [1953][1]

7   This world is white no longer, and it will never be white again.

Stranger in the Village

8   Our passion for categorization, life neatly fitted into pegs, has led to an unforeseen, paradoxical distress, confusion, a breakdown of meaning.

Notes of a Native Son [1955]

9   My life, my *real* life, was in danger, and not from anything other people might do but from the hatred I carried in my own heart.

Notes of a Native Son

10   Harlem had needed something to smash. To smash something is the ghetto's chronic need.   *Notes of a Native Son*

11   They face each other, the Negro and the African, over a gulf of three hundred years—an alienation too vast to be conquered in an evening's good-will, too heavy and too double-edged ever to be trapped in speech. This alienation causes the Negro to recognize that he is a hybrid. Not a physical hybrid merely: in every aspect of his living he betrays the memory of the auction block and the impact of the happy ending. In white Americans

---

[1]From JAMES BALDWIN, *Notes of a Native Son* [1955].

he finds reflected — repeated, as it were, in a higher key — his tensions, his terrors, his tenderness. Dimly and for the first time, there begins to fall into perspective the nature of the roles they have played in the lives and history of each other. Now he is bone of their bone, flesh of their flesh; they have loved and hated and obsessed and feared each other, and his blood is in their soil. Therefore he cannot deny them, nor can they ever be divorced.

Notes of a Native Son. Encounter on the Seine

1   I stand at the window of this great house in the south of France as night falls, the night which is leading me to the most terrible morning of my life.

Giovanni's Room [1956], opening lines

2   My face is like a face you have seen many times.

Giovanni's Room, ch. 1

3   Nothing is more unbearable, once one has it, than freedom.

Giovanni's Room, ch. 1

4   All art is a kind of confession. . . . All artists, if they are to survive, are forced, at last, to tell the whole story, to vomit the anguish up.

Nobody Knows My Name. Partisan Review [Winter 1959][1]

5   Children have never been very good at listening to their elders, but they have never failed to imitate them.

Fifth Avenue, Uptown. Esquire [July 1960]

6   Anyone who has ever struggled with poverty knows how extremely expensive it is to be poor.   *Fifth Avenue, Uptown*

7   Love is a battle, love is a war; love is a growing up.

In Search of a Majority. Speech given at Kalamazoo College [1960][1]

8   The world is before you and you need not take it or leave it as it was when you came in.   *In Search of a Majority*

9   Money, it turned out, was exactly like sex, you thought of nothing else if you didn't have it and thought of other things if you did.

The Black Boy Looks at the White Boy. Esquire [May 1961][1]

10   Not everything that is faced can be changed; but nothing can be changed until it is faced.

As Much Truth As One Can Bear. New York Times [January 14, 1962]

---

[1]From JAMES BALDWIN, *Nobody Knows My Name* [1961].

1   This is the crime of which I accuse my country and my countrymen, and for which neither I nor time nor history will ever forgive them, that they have destroyed and are destroying hundreds of thousands of lives and do not know it and do not want to know it.... It is not permissible that the authors of devastation should also be innocent. It is the innocence which constitutes the crime.

The Fire Next Time [1963]

2   To accept one's past — one's history — is not the same thing as drowning in it; it is learning how to use it. An invented past can never be used; it cracks and crumbles under the pressures of life like clay in a season of drought.

The Fire Next Time

3   Do I really want to be integrated into a burning house?

The Fire Next Time

4   Love takes off the masks that we fear we cannot live without and know we cannot live within.   *The Fire Next Time*

5   When I was very young, and was dealing with my buddies in those wine- and urine-stained hallways, something in me wondered, *What will happen to all that beauty?* For black people, though I am aware that some of us, black and white, do not know it yet, are very beautiful.

The Fire Next Time

6   Color is not a human or a personal reality; it is a political reality.

The Fire Next Time

7   If we do not now dare everything, the fulfillment of that prophecy, re-created from the Bible in song by a slave, is upon us: *God gave Noah the rainbow sign, No more water, the fire next time!*

The Fire Next Time, last lines

8   I do not wish to see Negroes become the equal of their murderers. I wish us to become equal to ourselves. To become a people so free in themselves that they will have no need to — fear — others — and have no need to murder others.

Blues for Mister Charlie [1964], act III
[Meridian Henry]

9   If one can live with one's own pain then one respects the pain of others, and so, briefly, but transcendentally, we can release each other from pain.   *Tell Me How Long the Train's Been Gone [1968]*

10   I'm optimistic about the future, but not about the future of this civilization. I'm optimistic about the civilization which will replace this one.

Interview. Transatlantic Review [1970]

1   If we know, and do nothing, we are worse than the murderers hired in our name. If we know, then we must fight for your life as though it were our own — which it is — and render impassable with our bodies the corridor to the gas chamber. For, if they take you in the morning, they will be coming for us that night.

An Open Letter to My Sister, Angela Y. Davis
[November 19, 1970]

2   People pay for what they do, and, still more, for what they have allowed themselves to become. And they pay for it very simply: by the lives they lead.   *No Name in the Street [1972]*

3   Ignorance, allied with power, is the most ferocious enemy justice can have.   *No Name in the Street*

4   Identity would seem to be the garment with which one covers the nakedness of the self; in which case, it is best that the garment be loose.

The Devil Finds His Work [1976]

5   The white man, someone told me, discovered the Cross by way of the Bible, but the Black man discovered the Bible by way of the Cross.

The Evidence of Things Not Seen [1985]

6   The price the white American paid for his ticket was to become white — and, in the main, nothing more than that, or, as he was to insist, nothing less.

The Price of the Ticket [1985]

7   Our crown has already been bought and paid for. All we have to do is wear it.

Quoted in Toni Morrison, *James Baldwin: His Voice Remembered; Life in His Language. New York Times Book Review [December 20, 1987]*

Amilcar Cabral   1924–1973

8   Always bear in mind that the people are not fighting for ideas, for the things in anyone's head. They are fighting to win material benefits, to live better and in peace, to see their lives go forward, to guarantee the future of their children.

PAIGC directive [1965][1]

9   Tell no lies. Expose lies whenever they are told. Mask no difficulties, mistakes, failures. Claim no easy victories.

PAIGC directive[1]

---

[1]From *Unity and Struggle : Texts Selected by the PAIGC* (Partido Africano da Independência da Guiné e Cabo Verde) [1979]. Translated by Michael Wolfers.

1   The national liberation of a people is the regaining of the historical personality of that people.

> *The Weapon of Theory. Speech, First Solidarity Conference of the Peoples of Africa, Asia, and Latin America, Havana [January 6, 1966]*[1]

2   We Africans, having rejected the idea of begging for freedom, which was contrary to our dignity and our sacred right to freedom and independence, reaffirmed our steadfast decision to end colonial domination of our country, no matter what the sacrifices involved, and to conquer for ourselves the opportunity to achieve in peace our own progress and happiness.

> *Speech. United Nations General Assembly, New York [October 16, 1972]*

Shirley Chisholm   1924–2005

3   Unbought and Unbossed   *Campaign slogan [1967]*

4   We Americans have come to feel that it is our mission to make the world free. We believe we are the good guys everywhere, in Vietnam, in Latin America, wherever we go. We believe we are good guys at home, too.... Unless we start to fight and defeat the enemies in our own country, poverty and racism, and make our talk of equality and opportunity ring true, we are exposed in the eyes of the world as hypocrites when we talk about making people free.

> *Speech [March 1968]*

5   My God, what do we want? What does any human being want? Take away an accident of pigmentation, of a thin layer of our outer skin, and there is no difference between me and anyone else. All we want is for that trivial difference to make no difference.

> *On being asked, What do you Negroes want now? [1969]*[2]

6   It is not heroin or cocaine that makes one an addict, it is the need to escape from a harsh reality. There are more television addicts, more baseball and football addicts, more movie addicts, and certainly more alcohol addicts in this country than there are narcotics addicts.

> *Statement before the House Select Committee on Crime [September 17, 1969]*

7   Health is a human right, not a privilege to be purchased.

> *Speech in the U.S. House of Representatives [1970]*

---

[1]From *Revolution in Guinea: Selected Texts by Amilcar Cabral* [1969]. Translated and edited by RICHARD HANDYSIDE.

[2]From SHIRLEY CHISHOLM, *Unbought and Unbossed* [1972].

1   I hope if I am remembered it will finally be for what I have done, not for what I happen to be. *Unbought and Unbossed [1970]*

2   Of my two "handicaps," being female put many more obstacles in my path than being black. The emotional, sexual, and psychological stereotyping of females begins when the doctor says: It's a girl.
Unbought and Unbossed

3   Racism is so universal in this country, so widespread and deep-seated, that it is invisible because it is so normal. *Unbought and Unbossed*

4   When morality comes up against profit, it is seldom profit that loses. *Unbought and Unbossed*

5   I stand before you today as a candidate for the Democratic nomination for the presidency of the United States. I am not the candidate of black America, although I am black and proud. I am not the candidate of the women's movement of this country, although I am a woman and I'm equally proud of that. I am not the candidate of any political bosses or special interests. I am the candidate of the people.
Speech announcing presidential candidacy [1972]

Celia Cruz
1924–2003

6   Azucar![1] *Trademark phrase*

Ruby Dee [Wallace]
1924–

7   Calling all sisters. Calling all
Righteous sisters.
Calling all women. *My One Good Nerve [1986]. Calling All Women*

Patricia Roberts Harris
1924–1985

8   I am one of them. You do not seem to understand who I am. I am a black woman, the daughter of a dining-car worker....If my life has any meaning at all, it is that those who start out as outcasts can wind up as being part of the system.
In response to being labeled out of touch with poor people. Confirmation hearing, Department of Housing and Urban Development [January 10, 1977]

Michael Manley
1924–1997

9   We know what that system [capitalism and colonialism] has meant for us....And we are not for sale. We are not for sale. And tell them anytime

[1]Sugar! (Sweet!)

they are willing to deal with an honorable Jamaica built on principle, sovereignty, pride and dignity, then we will talk the investment of the money. But if we are to return to our knees, they can keep the money, we will find another way.

Not for Sale [1976]

1   If we look about us we see the lengthening shadows of a thousand small corruptions creeping across the landscape of our nation. This is monstrous, for it is not the evening of our history; it is the morning and the shadows should be forming the other way.

We Are a Country Without a Conscience [1988]

2   Any realistic vision of change must be based on the notion of empowerment of people. The agenda for change must seek to facilitate that empowerment. In the final analysis humankind must develop economic and social institutions which are just in purpose and democratic in form. Otherwise the world will stumble from one disaster to the next.

The Poverty of Nations [1991]

Robert Mugabe   1924–

3   Our votes must go together with our guns. After all, any vote we shall have shall have been the product of the gun. The gun which produces the vote should remain its security officer — its guarantor. The people's votes and the people's guns are always inseparable twins.

Radio broadcast [1976][1]

Max Roach   1924–2007

4   The artist is like a secretary, whether he is a writer, a musician or a painter: He keeps records of his time.

From ARTHUR TAYLOR, Notes and Tones [1971]

Althea Simmons   1924–1990

5   There should be no need for my organization [the National Association for the Advancement of Colored People]. We're trying to work ourselves out of business. . . . I am an incurable activist.

From BRIAN LANKER, I Dream a World [1989]

Sarah Vaughan   1924–1990

6   I just sing. I don't know what I sound like or who I sound like. I don't know what kind of singer I am. I just open my mouth and sing.

From BRIAN LANKER, I Dream a World [1989]

[1]From MARTIN MEREDITH, *Our Votes, Our Guns: Robert Mugabe and the Tragedy of Zimbabwe* [2003].

C[ordy] T[indell] Vivian

1924–

1   People do not choose rebellion, it is forced upon them. Revolution is always an act of self-defense.

Black Power and the American Myth [1970]

2   Blacks have a condition, not a problem. Whites have the problem, racism, that creates our condition.

From STUDS TERKEL, Race [1992]

Dinah Washington [Ruth Jones]

1924–1963

3   There's one heaven, one earth, and one queen, and your Elizabeth is an imposter.

Statement onstage during a 1959 tour of England.
From JAMES HASKINS, Queen of the Blues [1987]

Idi Amin [Dada]

1925–2003

4   I am not a politician, but a professional soldier.

First public words [January 25, 1971][1]

5   In any country there must be people who have to die. They are the sacrifices any nation has to make to achieve law and order.

Statement [1976][2]

6   In warfare, if you do not have food, and your fellow soldier is wounded, you may as well kill him and eat him to survive.

From HENRY KYEMBA, A State of Blood [1977]

[Samuel George] Sammy Davis, Jr.

1925–1990

7   Talent is not an excuse for bad manners.

Referring to Frank Sinatra. Radio interview [1959][3]

8   I'm an outcast. Obviously I'm not white, but now it's gotten so the colored people don't want me either. It's like I'm the man without a country.

Yes I Can [1965]

9   Being a star has made it possible for me to get insulted in places where the average Negro could never hope to go and get insulted.

Yes I Can

---

[1]From HENRY KYEMBA, *A State of Blood* [1977].

[2]From JONATHAN GREEN, *The Cynic's Lexicon* [1984]; "Uganda: Quotes of a Tyrant," Africa News [August 17, 2003].

[3]From RICHARD GEHMAN, *Frank Sinatra and His Rat Pack*, in *The Sammy Davis, Jr. Reader* [2001], edited by GERALD EARLY.

1   I'm Puerto Rican, Jewish, colored and married to a white woman. When I move into a neighborhood, people start running four ways at the same time.   *Interview in Playboy [December 1966]*[1]

2   I know I'm dreadfully ugly, one of the ugliest men you could meet, but ugliness, like beauty, is something you must learn how to use.
                                    From ORIANA FALLACI, *The Egoists [1968]*

3   It was a strange time, the sixties, a strange feeling suddenly being "black." Yet overnight thirty million "colored people" and "Negroes" had become "blacks." It was difficult to think of myself as "black." ... Nobody ever got called "Negro bastard" or "colored motherfucker." It was always "black" and the word was nasty and hard.
                                    Why Me? [1989]

Frantz Fanon   1925–1961

4   In the colonies the economic infrastructure is also a superstructure. The cause is effect: You are rich because you are white, you are white because you are rich.   *The Wretched of the Earth [1961]*[2]

5   When I search for man in the technique and the style of Europe, I see only a succession of negations of man, and an avalanche of murders.
                                    The Wretched of the Earth, conclusion[3]

6   The black man has two dimensions. One with his fellows, the other with the white man. A Negro behaves differently with a white man and with another Negro. That this self-division is a direct result of colonialist subjugation is beyond question.   *Black Skin, White Masks [1967]*[3]

7   To speak ... means above all to assume a culture, to support the weight of a civilization.   *Black Skin, White Masks*[3]

8   When someone else strives and strains to prove to me that black men are as intelligent as white men, I say that intelligence has never saved anyone; and that is true, for, if philosophy and intelligence are invoked to proclaim the equality of men, they have also been employed to justify the extermination of men.   *Black Skin, White Masks*[3]

9   I am black: I am the incarnation of a complete fusion with the world, an intuitive understanding of the earth, an abandonment of my ego in the heart of the cosmos, and no white man, no matter how intelligent he may be, can ever understand Louis Armstrong and the music of the Congo. If I

---

[1] From ALEX HALEY, *The Playboy Interviews* [1993], edited by MURRAY FISHER.
[2] Translated by RICHARD PHILCOX.
[3] Translated by CHARLES LAM MARKHAM.

am black, it is not the result of a curse, but it is because, having offered my skin, I have been able to absorb all the cosmic *effluvia*. I am truly a ray of sunlight under the earth.

Black Skin, White Masks[1]

1   Hate is not inborn; it has to be constantly cultivated, to be brought into being, in conflict with more or less recognized guilt complexes. Hate demands existence, and he who hates has to show his hate in appropriate actions and behavior; in a sense, he has to become hate. That is why the Americans have substituted discrimination for lynching.

Black Skin, White Masks[1]

2   All forms of exploitation are identical because all of them are applied against the same "object": man.

Black Skin, White Masks[1]

Charles Gordone
1925–1995

3   I know what I am by what I see in your faces! You are my mirrors. But unlike a metallic reflection you will not hold my image for very long! Your capacity for attention is very short! Therefore, I must try to provoke you! Provoke your attention. Change my part over and over again. I am rehearsing at the moment. For tomorrow, I will go out amongst you, "The Black Lady in Mourning." I will weep, I will wail, and I will mourn. But my cries will not be heard! No one will wipe away my bitter tears! My black anguish will fall upon deaf ears. I will mourn a passing! Yes. The passing and the ending of a people dying. Of a people dying into that new life. A people whose identity could only be measured by the struggle, the dehumanization and degradation they suffered. Or allowed themselves to suffer perhaps. I will mourn the ending of those years. I will mourn the death of a people dying! Of a people dying into that new life!

No Place to Be Somebody [1969], epilogue [Gabe]

Rosa Guy
1925–2012

4   On that island where rivers run deep, where the sea sparkling in the sun earns it the name Jewel of the Antilles, the tops of the mountains are bare. Ugly scrub brush clings to the sides of their gray stones, giving the peaks a grim aspect that angers the gods and keeps them forever fighting. These terrible battles of the gods affect the lives of all the islanders, rich and poor. But the wealthy towns, protected from the excesses of the gods' furies, claim to be masters of their own destiny. The peasants accept the will of the

---

[1]Translated by CHARLES LAM MARKHAM.

gods as theirs. They pray to the gods when times are hard and give thanks to them when life goes well.

My Love, My Love, or the Peasant Girl [1985], opening lines[1]

Benjamin L[awson] Hooks   1925–2010

1   The train is running toward freedom. We invite you to get on or off at your pleasure, but for God's sake don't stand on the track unless you want to be run down.

Inaugural address to the 68th NAACP Annual Convention, St. Louis [July 1977][2]

2   It looks to me like some folk want to have the bread, the cake, the pie, and all the crumbs that fall from the table and some of us are saying "Hell no, we won't go!" The time has come when all of us must enjoy the goodness and the fruit of this American democracy.   *Speech [April 3, 1978]*[3]

3   All we're asking in this nation is that you give those of us who have planted your corn and picked your cotton and wet-nursed your babies and fought in every war and been loyal to this nation...equal parity and an opportunity. We're not asking you to lower your qualifications...a quota is an artificial ceiling above which one cannot rise. But we do believe in goals and timetables. And if there is to be parity in this nation, goals and timetables must exist.   *Speech*

Bob Kaufman   1925–1986

4   ABOMUNISTS JOIN NOTHING BUT THEIR HANDS OR LEGS, OR OTHER SAME.   *Abomunist Manifesto [1959]*

5   When I die,
I won't stay
Dead.   *Dolorous Echo [1965]*

6   No, I am not anything, that is anything I am not.
I, Too, Know What I Am Not [1965]

7   Variations on a theme by morning,
Two lady birds move in the distance.
Gray jail looming, bathed in sunlight.
Violin tongues whispering.   *Cocoa Morning [1967]*

8   Here, Adam, take back your God damn rib.   *Geneology [1967]*

---

[1] The novel was the basis for the Broadway play *Once on This Island* [1990].
[2] From *African-American Orators* [1996], edited by RICHARD W. LEEMAN.
[3] From *Say It Plain* [2005], edited by CATHERINE ELLIS and STEPHEN DRURY SMITH.

1   Jazz radio on a midnight kick,
     Round about Midnight.

Round About Midnight [1967]

B. B. [Riley] King   1925–

2   Rock me, baby,
     Rock me all night long.

Rock Me, Baby [1964]

3   As long as I'm footin' the bills
     I'm paying the cost to be the boss.

Paying the Cost to Be the Boss [1968]

4   When I first got the blues,
     They brought me over on a ship.
     Men was standing over me,
     And a lot more with a whip.
     And everybody wanna know,
     Why I sing the blues.

Why I Sing the Blues [1969]

Patrice Lumumba[1]   1925–1961

5   All of Africa is irrevocably engaged in a merciless struggle against colonialism and imperialism. We wish to bid farewell to the rule of slavery and
bastardization that has so severely wronged us. Any people that oppresses
another people is neither civilized nor Christian.

Speech at the Ibadan, Nigeria, Conference [March 22, 1959][2]

6   For though this independence of the Congo is today being proclaimed
in a spirit of accord with Belgium, a friendly country with which we are
dealing as one equal with another, no Congolese worthy of the name can ever
forget that we fought to win it, a fight waged each and every day, a passionate
and idealistic fight, a fight in which there was not one effort, not one priva-
tion, not one suffering, not one drop of blood that we ever spared ourselves.
We are proud of this struggle amid tears, fire, and blood, down to our very
heart of hearts, for it was a noble and just struggle, an indispensable struggle
if we were to put an end to the humiliating slavery that had been forced
upon us.   *Speech at the proclamation of independence [June 30, 1960]*

7   We are going to bring peace to the country, not the peace of rifles and
bayonets, but the peace that comes from men's hearts and their good will.

Speech at the proclamation of independence

---

[1]From *Lumumba Speaks* [1972], edited by JEAN VAN LIERDE.
[2]Translated by HELEN R. LANE.

1   History will one day have its say; it will not be the history taught in the United Nations, Washington, Paris or Brussels, however, but the history taught in the countries that have rid themselves of colonialism and its puppets. Africa will write its own history, and both north and south of the Sahara, it will be a history full of glory and dignity.

Last letter to wife Pauline Lumumba [1960]

Malcolm X [El-Hajj Malik El-Shabazz]   1925–1965

2   Who taught you to hate the color of your skin? Who taught you to hate the texture of your hair? Who taught you to hate the shape of your nose and the shape of your lips? Who taught you to hate yourself from the top of your head to the soles of your feet? Who taught you to hate your own kind? Who taught you to hate the race that you belong to so much so that you don't want to be around each other? You know, before you come asking Mr. Muhammad does he teach hate, you should ask yourself who taught you to hate being what God gave you.   *Speech [c. 1962]*[1]

3   If you're born in America with a black skin, you're born in prison.

From KENNETH B. CLARK, *The Negro Protest [1963]*

4   If violence is wrong in America, violence is wrong abroad. If it is wrong to be violent defending black women and black children and black babies and black men, then it is wrong for America to draft us, and make us violent abroad in defense of her. And if it is right for America to draft us, and teach us how to be violent in defense of her, then it is right for you and me to do whatever is necessary to defend our own people right here in this country.

Message to the Grass Roots. Speech [November 1963][2]

5   Our religion teaches us to be intelligent. Be peaceful, be courteous, obey the law, respect everyone; but if someone puts his hand on you, send him to the cemetery.   *Message to the Grass Roots*

6   When you've got some coffee that's too black, which means it's too strong. What do you do? You integrate it with cream, you make it weak. But if you pour too much cream in it, you won't even know you ever had coffee. It used to be hot, it becomes cool. It used to be strong, it becomes weak. It used to wake you up, now it puts you to sleep.

On the inclusion of white people in the March on Washington.
Message to the Grass Roots

---

[1]From *Malcolm X: Make It Plain* [1994], directed by ORLANDO BAGWELL, produced by Blackside, Inc./ PBS, American Experience.

[2]From *Malcolm X Speaks* [1965], edited by GEORGE BREITMAN.

1   We didn't land on Plymouth Rock, the rock was landed on us!

[March 29, 1964][1]

2   I'm not going to sit at your table and watch you eat, with nothing on my plate, and call myself a diner. Sitting at the table doesn't make you a diner, unless you eat some of what's on that plate.

Speech, The Ballot or the Bullet [April 3, 1964]

3   I don't see any American dream; I see an American nightmare.

The Ballot or the Bullet

4   Our people have to be made to see that any time you take your dollar out of your community and spend it in a community where you don't live, the community where you live will get poorer and poorer, and the community where you spend your money will get richer and richer.

The Ballot or the Bullet

5   It'll be the ballot or the bullet. It'll be liberty or it'll be death.

The Ballot or the Bullet

6   Revolution is always based on land. Revolution is never based on begging somebody for an integrated cup of coffee.

Speech, The Black Revolution. New York [April 8, 1964]

7   We are not fighting for integration, nor are we fighting for separation. We are fighting for recognition as human beings. . . . In fact, we are actually fighting for rights that are even greater than civil rights and that is human rights.

Black Revolution

8   There were tens of thousands of pilgrims from all over the world. They were of all colors, from blue-eyed blonds to black-skinned Africans, but were all participating in the same ritual, displaying a spirit of unity and brotherhood that my experiences in America had led me to believe could never exist between white and non-white.

Letter written during pilgrimage to Mecca [April 20, 1964]

9   Time is on the side of the oppressed today, it's against the oppressor. Truth is on the side of the oppressed today, it's against the oppressor. You don't need anything else. *Speech [May 29, 1964]*

10   A race of people is like an individual man; until it uses its own talent, takes pride in its own history, expresses its own culture, affirms its own selfhood, it can never fulfill itself.

Speech at the Organization of Afro-American Unity
[June 28, 1964][2]

---

[1]Frequent statement. Also cited in *MALCOLM X, The Autobiography of Malcolm X [1964]*: "We didn't land on Plymouth Rock, my brothers and sisters, Plymouth Rock landed on us!"

[2]From MALCOLM X, *By Any Means Necessary* [1970].

1   The day that the black man takes an uncompromising step and realizes that he's within his rights, when his own freedom is being jeopardized, to use any means necessary to bring about his freedom or put a halt to that injustice. I don't think he'll be by himself.

Oxford Union Society debate [December 3, 1964][1]

2   Usually when people are sad, they don't do anything. They just cry over their condition. But when they get angry, they bring about a change.

Harlem rally for Fannie Lou Hamer [December 20, 1964][2]

3   Nobody can give you freedom. Nobody can give you equality or justice or anything. If you're a man, you take it.

Harlem rally for Fannie Lou Hamer

4   Our objective is complete freedom, complete justice, complete equality, by any means necessary.

Speech at the Audubon Ballroom [December 20, 1964]

5   You don't have to be a man to fight for freedom. All you have to do is to be an intelligent human being.   *Speech at the Audubon Ballroom*

6   I have no mercy or compassion in me for a society that will crush people, and then penalize them for not being able to stand up under the weight.   *The Autobiography of Malcolm X [1964]*

7   New York was heaven to me. And Harlem was Seventh Heaven!

The Autobiography of Malcolm X

8   *[On the assassination of President John F. Kennedy:]* It was, as I saw it, a case of "the chickens coming home to roost." I said that the hate in white men had not stopped with the killing of defenseless black people, but that hate, allowed to spread unchecked, had finally struck down this country's Chief Magistrate.   *The Autobiography of Malcolm X*

9   The ability to read awoke inside me some long dormant craving to be mentally alive. I certainly wasn't seeking any degree the way a college confers a status symbol upon its students. My homemade education gave me, with every additional book that I read, a little bit more sensitivity to the deafness, dumbness and blindness that was afflicting the black race in America. . . . My alma mater was books, a good library.   *The Autobiography of Malcolm X*

10   I'm for truth no matter who tells it.   *The Autobiography of Malcolm X*

11   I'm a human being first and foremost, and as such I'm for whoever and whatever benefits humanity as a whole.   *The Autobiography of Malcolm X*

---

[1]From MALCOLM X, *By Any Means Necessary* [1970].

[2]From *Malcolm X Speaks* [1965], edited by GEORGE BREITMAN.

1   No man is given but so much time to accomplish whatever is his life's work.
The Autobiography of Malcolm X

2   Thicker each year in these ghettoes is the kind of teen-ager that I was — with the wrong kinds of heroes, and the wrong kinds of influences.
The Autobiography of Malcolm X

3   You can't separate peace from freedom because no one can be at peace unless he has his freedom.
Speech, Prospects for Freedom in 1965 [January 1, 1965][1]

4   You're not supposed to be so blind with patriotism that you can't face reality. Wrong is wrong, no matter who does it or says it.
Speech, Prospects for Freedom in 1965

5   Power never takes a back step — only in the face of more power. Power doesn't back up in the face of a smile, or in the face of a threat, or in the face of some kind of nonviolent loving action. It's not the nature of power to back up in the face of anything but some more power.
Speech, Prospects for Freedom in 1965

6   I believe there will ultimately be a clash between the oppressed and those that do the oppressing. I believe that there will be a clash between those who want freedom, justice and equality for everyone and those who want to continue the systems of exploitation.
Interview [January 19, 1965][1]

7   It is a time for martyrs now. And if I am to be one, it will be in the cause of brotherhood. That's the only thing that can save this country.
Statement two days before he was assassinated
[February 19, 1965][2]

Carl T[homas] Rowan   1925–2000

8   The library is the temple of learning, and learning has liberated more people than all the wars in history.
From RON CHEPESIUK and GALE TEASTER-WOODS, Making a Difference: African-American Leaders Rap About Libraries. American Libraries 26, no. 2 [February 1995]

9   One of the most inflammatory confrontations in the coming race war has been building up for years, and on many battlefields. Americans are brandishing hand grenades over "affirmative action." And some who throughout their lives practiced or tolerated the most egregious racism and discrimination are now waging conflict over their assertion that the victims

---

[1]From *Malcolm X Speaks,* [1965], edited by GEORGE BREITMAN.
[2]From *The Violent End of the Man Called Malcolm* by Gordon Parks. *Life* [March 5, 1965].

of three hundred years of white racism are now the undeserved beneficiaries of "reverse racism."   *The Coming Race War in America [1996]*

John A[lfred] Williams   1925–

1   Most white people I know think it's a great big deal if a Negro compliments them on their tans. It's a large laugh. You have all this volleyball
about color and come summer you can't hold the white folks back from the
beaches, anyplace where they can get some sun. And of course the blacker
they are, the more pleased they are.   *Son in the Afternoon [1959]*

2   All you ever want to do is remind me that I am black. But goddamn it,
I also am.   *The Man Who Cried I Am [1967] [Max Reddick]*

3   A sickness of laughing and giggling hit everyone. The whites were
relieved that blacks at last had joined them, had lost finally that essential
human quality for which they were well known. And his [Blackman's] black
soldiers had been giggling and murdering because they'd come to know
what it felt like to kill without fear of punishment, in broad daylight … had
come to know, like whites who'd done most of it in history, just how
mothafucking easy it was to kill a colored sonofabitch. *Easy!* No, Blackman
told himself, waving his platoon into the choppers. No! We're not joining
them in this shit. We ain't payin *that* price for belonging.

Captain Blackman [1972]

4   My name is Clifford Pepperidge and I am in trouble. I'm an American
Negro and I play piano sometimes, and I'm a vocalist too. I shouldn't be here,
but they didn't pay attention to me when they brought me. Didn't listen when
I was in Berlin either. … As soon as I do get out, I'm hauling ass back home. I
don't care what it's like. They never did this to me in New York, and until I
left Storyville, after they closed it down, I managed not to have anything to
do with the John Laws. That's what back home was all about — playing music
and keeping away from trouble because it was always looking for you. Damn.
I'd even go back to the South to get out of here. Any place but here. It could
be worse. I could be over in the camp. There's a sign on the front gate: *Arbeit
Macht Frei.*   *Clifford's Blues [1999]*

Robert F[ranklin] Williams   1925–1996

5   The Negro in the south cannot expect justice in the courts. He must
convict his attackers on the spot. He must meet violence with violence,
lynching with lynching.

Press conference, Monroe, North Carolina [May 1959]

1   If I'm called a criminal for advocating that people have the right to defend themselves, for telling them to get off their asses and fight for what they deserve. If that's criminal, then I hope that I'll always be a criminal.

Statement made in 1954. Documentary, Negroes with Guns [2005]

Ralph D[avid] Abernathy   1926–1990

2   From the grand action of the Montgomery movement, our lives were filled with the action of doing God's will in village, hamlet and city. We used to talk theology and then we learned to do theology.

A Short Letter to My Dearest Friend in the City Called Heaven. Sermon, West Hunter St. Baptist Church, Atlanta [April 7, 1968]

3   When you are born under a system and see it enforced every day of your life, you get to the point where you can no longer conceive of life being any different.   *And the Walls Came Tumbling Down [1989]*

4   We talked to our people a great deal about the power of redemptive suffering. To suffer, we reminded them, was the experience most typical of the life of Jesus. He suffered the indignities of persecution by secular authority and eventually He suffered the humiliation and final agony of the Cross. We too could suffer, and in doing so share His martyrdom and rejoice in his resurrection. Whatever happened to us would happen to Him. If we were killed, our blood would cry out from the earth for justice.

And the Walls Came Tumbling Down

Chuck Berry [Charles Edward Anderson]   1926–

5   Maybellene, why can't you be true?   *Maybellene [1955]*

6   Roll over Beethoven
     And tell Tchaikovsky the news.   *Roll Over Beethoven [1956]*

7   He never ever learned to read or write so well,
     But he could play the guitar like ringing a bell.

Johnny B. Goode [1958]

Oscar Brown, Jr.   1926–2005

8   Shades of delight, cocoa hue,
     Rich as the night,
     Afro Blue.   *Afro Blue [1959]*

9   I've always lived by this golden rule
     Whatever happens don't blow your cool.   *But I Was Cool [1959]*

1   Been workin' and workin'
    But I still got so terribly long to go.   *Work Song [1960]*

2   Brown baby as years roll by
    I want you to go with your head held high
    I want you to live by the justice code
    I want you to walk down freedom's road.   *Brown Baby [1962]*

3   I want my forty acres and my mule!   *Forty Acres and a Mule [1964]*

4   That sun is hot and plenty bright
    Let's get down to business and get home tonight
    Bid 'em in —
    Auctioning slaves is a real high art.
    Bring that young gal here she's good for a start
    Bid 'em in — Get 'em in
    Now here's a real good buy only 'bout fifteen
    Her great-grandmammy was a Dahomey queen.   *Bid 'Em In [1966]*

John Coltrane   1926–1967

5   That's what music is to me — it's just another way of saying this is a
    big, beautiful universe we live in, that's been given to us, and here's an
    example of just how magnificent and encompassing it is.
                                      Interview. Downbeat [April 12, 1962]

6   No matter what...it is with God. He is gracious and merciful. His
    way is in love, through which we all are. It is truly — A Love Supreme.
                                      A Love Supreme [1964]. Liner notes

7   ELATION, ELEGANCE, EXALTATION — All from God.
                                                      A Love Supreme

Miles [Dewey] Davis   1926–1991

8   If you're not nervous, you're not paying attention   *Attributed*

9   Look, man, all I am is a trumpet player. I can only do one thing —
    play my horn.... I ain't no entertainer and I ain't trying to be one. I am one
    thing, a musician.   *Interview in Playboy [September 1962][1]*

10   In high school I was the best in the music class on the trumpet, but the
    prizes went to the boys with blue eyes. I made up my mind to outdo any-
    body white on my horn.   *Interview in Playboy*

---

[1]From ALEX HALEY, The Playboy Interviews [1993], edited by MURRAY FISHER.

1   The toughest critic I got and the only one I worry about is myself. My music has got to get past me and I'm too vain to play anything I think is bad.
Interview in Playboy

2   I just say what I think, and that bugs people, especially a lot of white people. When they look in my eyes and don't see no fear, they know it's a draw.
Interview in Playboy

3   Listen. The greatest feeling I ever had in my life — with my clothes on — was when I first heard Diz and Bird together in St. Louis, Missouri, back in 1944.
Miles [1989], prologue

4   I've changed music four or five times. What have you done of any importance other than be white?
Response to a white woman who asked what he had done to be invited to the White House [1987][1]

René Depestre   1926–

5   The relationships between consciousness and reality are extremely complex.... It is equally necessary to decolonize our minds, our inner life, at the same time that we decolonize society.
Interview with Aimé Césaire [1967]

6   The lady was not alone;
She had a husband,
A husband who knew everything,
But to tell the truth knew nothing,
For you can't have culture without making concessions.
You concede your flesh and blood to it,
You concede your own self to others;
By conceding your gain
Classicism and Romanticism,
And all that our souls are steeped in.
Face à la Nuit[2]

7   Indian high chiefs were frolicking freely with young Arawak beauties.... Barons and Marquis from the court of Louis XIV were playing leapfrog on the grass.... In the motley crowd, I also saw Simón Bolivar.... The time of masks had assembled three centuries of human history.
Hadriana dans tous mes rêves (Hadriana in All My Dreams) [1988][3]

---

[1]From JOHN SZWED, *So What: The Life of Miles Davis* [2002].
[2]From FRANTZ FANON, *The Wretched of the Earth* [1968]. Translated by CONSTANCE FARRINGTON.
[3]Translated by EDWIDGE DANTICAT, *After the Dance* [2002].

William H[enry] Grier

1926–

and

Price M[ashaw] Cobbs

1928–

1 People bear all they can and, if required, bear even more. But if they are black in present-day America they have been asked to shoulder too much. They have had all they can stand. They will be harried no more. Turning from their tormentors, they are filled with rage.

Black Rage [1968]

Beah Richards

1926–2000

2 What then is this superior thing
that in order to be sustained
must needs feed upon my flesh?
How came this horror to be?
Let's look to history.
They said, the white supremacists said,
that you were better than me.
That your fair brow would never know
the sweat of slavery.
They lied!
White womanhood too is enslaved;
the difference is degree.

A Black Woman Speaks [1974]

3 Being is mortal insistence in a complete and perfect state, lacking no essential characteristic. Everything you need, you got. Perfect. Maybe not yet realized, but perfect, complete.

Beah: A Black Woman Speaks [2003]

Betye Saar

1926–

4 It is my goal as an artist to create works that expose injustice and reveal beauty. The rainbow is literally a spectrum of color while spiritually a symbol of hope and promise.

Colored: Consider the Rainbow [2002]

[Willie Mae] "Big Mama" Thornton

1926–1984

5 Sitting by my window, baby
I was looking out at the rain.
You know something struck me, honey

Clamped onto me
Like a ball and chain.   *Ball 'n' Chain [1968]*

Hank Ballard [John Henry Kendricks]   1927–2003

1   Work with Me, Annie   *Song title [1954]*

2   Come on baby, let's do the twist.

The Twist [1958]

3   If you're looking for youth, you're looking for longevity, just take a
dose of rock 'n' roll. It keeps you going, just like the caffeine in your coffee.
Rock 'n' roll is good for the soul, for the well-being, for the psyche, for your
everything.
Radio interview [1996], quoted in obituary,
Associated Press [March 4, 2003]

Harry Belafonte   1927–

4   You can cage the singer but not the song.
Quoted in the International Herald Tribune
[October 3, 1988]

5   Songs are celebration and they're an articulation for hope and
freedom.   *Interview. American Legacy [2002]*

David N[orman] Dinkins   1927–

6   We are all foot soldiers on the march to freedom.
Inaugural speech, New York City [January 1, 1990]

7   One does not have to be a nuclear scientist to understand what fair is.
Fair is, if you got a pie, you say we're going to divide it, and if you take a
great big piece and leave me a little-bitty piece — that ain't fair. Fair is when
you cut it down the middle.
Speech following deaths and racial strife in Crown Heights,
Brooklyn [August 25, 1991]

Althea Gibson   1927–2003

8   I always wanted to be somebody.... If I made it, it's half because I was
game enough to take a lot of punishment along the way and half because
there were a lot of people who cared enough to help me.
I Always Wanted to Be Somebody [1958]

9   Being a champ is all well and good, but you can't eat a crown.
So Much to Live For [1968]

Nathan Irvin Huggins

1927–1989

1   Within that tyranny, looking beyond the acts of defiance, rebellion, and escape, we will find a quality of courage still unsung. It is in the triumph of the human spirit over unmitigated power. It raised no banners. It gained no vengeance. It was only the pervasive and persistent will among Afro-Americans to hold together through deep trauma and adversity.

Black Odyssey [1977]

2   The shadows and ghosts of the past remind us that those who would be tyrants cannot be called free men.

Black Odyssey, epilogue

Coretta Scott King

1927–2006

3   How many men must die before we can really have a free and true and peaceful society? How long will it take? If we can catch the spirit and the true meaning of this experience, I believe that this nation can be transformed into a society of love, of justice, peace, and brotherhood where all men can really be brothers.

Speech on the day before the funeral of Martin Luther King, Jr., Memphis City Hall [April 8, 1968][1]

4   *[On Martin Luther King, Jr.'s speech at the 1963 March on Washington:]* At that moment it seemed as if the Kingdom of God appeared. But it only lasted for a moment.

From A Testament of Hope [1986], edited by James M. Washington

5   I don't believe you can stand for freedom for one group of people and deny it to others.

Speech, Washington, D.C. [June 23, 1994]

Eartha Kitt [Eartha Mae Keith]

1927–2008

6   I am learning all the time. The tombstone will be my diploma.

Playbill [1978]

George Lamming

1927–

7   I am always feeling terrified of being known; not because they really know you, but simply because their claim to this knowledge is a concealed attempt to destroy you. That is what knowing means. As soon as they know you they will kill you, and thank God that's why they can't kill you. They can

---

[1]From Coretta Scott King, *My Life with Martin Luther King, Jr.* [1969].

never know you.... The likenesses will meet and make merry, but they won't never know you. They won't know the you that's hidden somewhere in the castle of your skin.

In the Castle of My Skin [1953]

Babatunde Olatunji
1927–2003

1   I'm the drum. You're the drum. We're the drum. Where I come from, we say that rhythm is the soul of life. The whole universe revolves in rhythm. When we get out of rhythm, that's when we get into trouble. We are in rhythm or we are not in rhythm — the rhythm of life, the rhythm of relationships. Because of its rhythmic nature, because it helps keep us in rhythm, the drum, next to the human voice, is our most important, most sacred instrument.   *The Beat of My Drum [2005]*

Sidney Poitier
1927–

2   It has been a long journey to this moment.

Acceptance speech, Academy Award for best actor in a leading role [April 13, 1964]

3   We're all of us a little greedy. We're all somewhat courageous, and we're all considerably cowardly. We're all imperfect, and life is simply a perpetual, unending struggle against those imperfections.

The Measure of a Man [2000]

Leontyne Price
1927–

4   [*On her farewell performance:*] I prefer to leave standing up, like a well-mannered guest at a party.

Quoted in the New York Times [December 31, 1984]

5   Art is the only thing you cannot punch a button for. You must do it the old-fashioned way. Stay up and really burn the midnight oil. There are no compromises.

From BRIAN LANKER, I Dream a World [1989]

6   Accomplishments have no color.   *From I Dream a World*

Maya Angelou [Marguerite Johnson]
1928–

7   If growing up is painful for the Southern Black girl, being aware of her displacement is the rust on the razor that threatens the throat. It is an unnecessary insult.

I Know Why the Caged Bird Sings [1969]

8   I discovered that to achieve perfect personal silence all I had to do was to attach myself leechlike to sound. I began to listen to everything. I

probably hoped that after I had heard all the sounds, really heard them and packed them deep down, deep in my ears, the world would be quiet around me. I walked into rooms where people were laughing, their voices hitting the walls like stones, and I simply stood still — in the midst of the riot of sound. *I Know Why the Caged Bird Sings*

1   You're Africa to me
         At brightest dawn.
       The Congo's green and
         Copper's brackish hue,
       A continent to build
         With Black Man's brawn.
       I sit at home and see it all
         Through you.

To a Husband [1971][1]

2   Sixty years in these white folks' world
       The child I works for calls me girl
       I say "Yes ma'am" for working's sake
       Too proud to bend
       Too poor to break,
       I laugh until my stomach ache,
       When I think about myself.

When I Think About Myself [1971][1]

3   The mixture of arrogance and insecurity is as volatile as the much-touted alcohol and gasoline. The difference is that with the former there is a long internal burning usually terminating in self-destroying implosion.
Gather Together in My Name [1974]

4   I lay down in my grave
       and watch my children
       grow
       Proud blooms
       above the weeds of death.
Elegy for Harriet Tubman and Frederick Douglass [1975][1]

5   They've laughed to shield their crying
         then shuffled through their dreams
         and stepped 'n fetched a country
       to write the blues with screams.
       I understand their meaning

[1]From MAYA ANGELOU, *Maya Angelou: Poems* [1981].

it could and did derive
from living on the edge of death
They kept my race alive.

Song for the Old Ones [1975][1]

1   Shadows on the wall
Noises down the hall
Life doesn't frighten me at all.
Bad dogs barking loud
Big ghosts in a cloud
Life doesn't frighten me at all.

Life Doesn't Frighten Me [1978]

2   When my bones are stiff and aching
And my feet won't climb the stair,
I will only ask one favor:
Don't bring me no rocking chair.

On Aging [1978]

3   Pretty women wonder where my secret lies.
I'm not cute or built to suit a fashion model's size
But when I start to tell them,
They think I'm telling lies.
I say,
It's in the reach of my arms,
The span of my hips,
The stride of my step,
The curl of my lips.
I'm a woman
Phenomenally.
Phenomenal woman,
That's me.

Phenomenal Woman [1978]

4   You may write me down in history
With your bitter, twisted lies,
You may trod me in the very dirt
But still, like dust, I'll rise.

Still I Rise [1978], st. 1

5   Bringing the gifts that my ancestors gave,
I am the dream and the hope of the slave.

---

[1]From Maya Angelou, *Maya Angelou: Poems* [1981].

> I rise
>
> I rise
>
> I rise.
>
> *Still I Rise, st. 9*

1   If one is lucky, a solitary fantasy can totally transform one million realities.

The Heart of a Woman [1981]

2   Tragedy, no matter how sad, becomes boring to those not caught in its addictive caress.

All God's Children Need Traveling Shoes [1986]

3   History, despite its wrenching pain,
Cannot be unlived, but if faced
With courage, need not be lived again.

*On the Pulse of Morning, inaugural poem for
President William Jefferson Clinton [1993]*

4   Here on the pulse of this new day
You may have the grace to look up and out
And into your sister's eyes,
And into your brother's face,
Your country,
And say simply
Very simply
With hope—
Good morning.

On the Pulse of Morning

5   I have found that among its other benefits, giving liberates the soul of the giver.

Wouldn't Take Nothing for My Journey Now [1993]

Lerone Bennett, Jr.   1928–

6   For the human chattel involved, the slave trade was a stupendous roulette wheel.... Around and around the wheel went, stopping here and there, sealing, wherever it stopped, the fate of mothers and fathers and their children to the nth generation. It made a great deal of difference to the slaves where the dice of fate fell — whether they landed, for example, in a country where *the* word was the Spanish *yo* or the French *je* or the English *I*. Slavery, to be sure, was a form of hell wherever it existed.

Before the Mayflower [1962]

7   Negro men and women came here long before the Mayflower and they cleared the forests, drained the swamps, and cultivated the grain. The wealth of this country was founded on what Abraham Lincoln called "the

250 years of unrequited toil" of Negro men and women. From the muted wail of slaves going in chains to American plantations came the gold that made capitalism possible; from black brawn came tobacco; from black blood, white sugar.

The Negro Mood and Other Essays [1964]

1   The first challenge of blackness is the challenge of defining it.

Speech [1969][1]

2   We hear people say, "We tried integration and it failed." That isn't so. Integration has never been tried in this country. It has not even been defined. What is integration? If you put two, three blacks in an all-white institution, it's not integrated. It requires a complete change in the way you think as an institution. Real integration involves a change in values.

From Studs Terkel, Race [1992]

Thornton Dial   1928–

3   Art ain't about paint. It ain't about canvas. It's about ideas.

Thornton Dial, Strategy of the World [1990]

Bo Diddley [Ellas McDaniel]   1928–2008

4   I'm a man
I spell M-A-N.
Man.   *I'm a Man [1955]*

5   I opened the door for a lot of people and they just ran through and left me holding the knob.

On having his style appropriated. Interview in Melody Maker [December 18, 1971][2]

[Antoine] Fats Domino   1928–

6   Ain't that a shame?
You're the one to blame.

Ain't That a Shame [1955]

7   I'm walkin', yes indeed
And I'm talkin' 'bout you and me
I'm hopin'
That you'll come back to me.

I'm Walkin' [1957]

---

[1]From Lerone Bennett, Jr., *The Challenge of Blackness* [1972].
[2]From Robert Ford, *A Blues Bibliography* [2007].

James Forman

1928–2005

1   We are demanding $500,000,000 from the Christian white churches and the Jewish synagogues. This total comes to 15 dollars per nigger. This is a low estimate for we maintain there are probably more than 30,000,000 black people in this country. $15 a nigger is not a large sum of money and we know that the churches and synagogues have a tremendous wealth and its membership, white America, has profited and still exploits black people. We are also not unaware that the exploitation of colored peoples around the world is aided and abetted by the white Christian churches and synagogues. This demand for $500,000,000 is not an idle resolution or empty words. Fifteen dollars for every black brother and sister in the United States is only a beginning of the reparations due us as people who have been exploited and degraded, brutalized, killed and persecuted. Underneath all of this exploitation, the racism of this country has produced a psychological effect upon us that we are beginning to shake off.

The Black Manifesto adopted by the National Black Economic Conference [1969]

2   We are not born revolutionary. Revolutionaries are forged through constant struggle and the study of revolutionary ideas and experiences.... As some of my generation were unaware of much that influenced our development, so there will be future generations unaware of all the forces of resistance that have determined their actions. In the years ahead, more and more people will be forced to become revolutionary, for the repression and decay of United States society leaves few options.

The Making of Black Revolutionaries [1972]

3   We will be carrying on the work of all the black sons and daughters who have died in every corner of Africa and the Americas under the whiplash of racism, colonialism, capitalism, and imperialism. And we shall win without a doubt.   *The Making of Black Revolutionaries, last lines*

Édouard Glissant

1928–2011

4   We know ourselves as part and as crowd, in an unknown that does not terrify. We cry our cry of poetry. Our boats are open, and we sail them for everyone.   *Poetics of Relation [1997]*[1]

5   Sameness is sublimated difference; Diversity is accepted difference.

Caribbean Discourse [1989][2]

[1]Translated by BETSY WING.
[2]Translated by J. MICHAEL DASH.

1   We know what threatens Caribbeanness: the historical balkanization of the islands, the inculcation of different and often "opposed" major languages, the umbilical cords that maintain in a rigid or flexible way, many of these islands within the sphere of influence.... This isolation postpones in each island the awareness of a Caribbean identity and at the same time it separates each community from its own true identity.

Caribbean Discourse

2   *When one knows* the tremendous *strength of their roots*, and the arid fraternity among them, *their conventional exotic image* fades away.... In this place of acceptance and denial, this line of trees contains the essentials of wisdom: it teaches moderation and at the same time inspires audacity.

The Ripening [1985][1]

Cheikh Hamidou Kane
1928–

3   I should like to ask you: can one learn *this* without forgetting *that*, and is what one learns worth what one forgets?

Ambiguous Adventure [1962][2]*, ch. 3 [The Chief]*

4   At the heart of the moment, behold man as immortal, for the moment is infinite, when it is. The purity of the moment is made from the absence of time. Life of the moment, life without age of the moment which reigns, in the luminous arena of your duration man unfurls himself into infinity.

Ambiguous Adventure, ch. 10[2]

A[loyisus] Leon Higginbotham, Jr.
1928–1998

5   The poisonous legacy of legalized oppression based upon the matter of color can never be adequately purged from our society if we act as if slave laws never existed.

In the Matter of Color [1978], epilogue

6   When I think of your appointment to the Supreme Court, I see not only the result of your own ambition, but also the culmination of years of heartbreaking work by thousands who preceded you. I know you may not want to be burdened by the memory of their sacrifices. But I also know that you have no right to forget that history. Your life is very different from what it would have been had these men and women never lived.

*An Open Letter to Justice Clarence Thomas
[November 29, 1991]*[3]

---

[1] Translated by J. MICHAEL DASH; originally published in 1958.
[2] *L'Aventure ambigue*, translated by KATHERINE WOODS.
[3] From *Race-ing Justice, En-gendering Power [1992]*, edited by TONI MORRISON.

1   Developing a racist precept is very much like colonizing a nation or, perhaps more to the point, enslaving its people. One needs to go about these tasks with the enthusiastic devotion and single-minded determination of a zealot. One must hear only the call of one's crusade and not the cries of one's victims. In short, one needs to be totally convinced of the righteousness of one's task, while not being too troubled by one's own conscience or the reasoning of those who disagree.

Shades of Freedom [1996], ch. 4

2   I sometimes feel as if I am watching justice die.

Breaking Thurgood Marshall's Promise. New York Times [January 18, 1998]

Ted Joans   1928–2003

3   Bird Lives!

Slogan written in chalk on NYC sidewalks after Charlie Parker's death [1955]

4   JAZZ is my religion   and it alone I do dig   the jazz clubs are my houses of worship   *Jazz Is My Religion [1967]*

5   Africa I live and study for thee
And through you I shall be free
Someday I'll come back and see
Land of my mothers, where a black god made me
My Africa, your Africa, a free continent to be.   *Afrodisia [1970]. Africa*

6   Jazz music is our natural
Black anthem.

Proposition for a Black Power Manifesto [1971]

7   Don't let the minute spoil the hour.   *Trademark phrase*

Camara Laye   1928–1980

8   Did you not know that I was waiting for you?

The Radiance of the King [1971], last line [The King]

Magnificent [Nathaniel] Montague   1928–

9   Burn, baby! Burn!

Trademark phrase [1963][1]

---

[1]As a DJ in New York and California, Montague used this phrase on air while playing music that was particularly "hot." This refrain took on another meaning when it was uttered during the 1965 riots in the Watts section of Los Angeles, California.

Andrew Salkey   1928–1995

1   Anancy is a spider
     Anancy is a man;
     Anancy's West Indian
     And West African.

     Sometimes, he wears a waistcoat;
     Sometimes, he carries a cane;
     Sometimes, he sports a top hat;
     Sometimes, he's just a plain,
     Ordinary, black, hairy spider.

     Anancy is vastly cunning,
     Tremendously greedy,
     Excessively charming,
     Hopelessly dishonest,
     Warmly loving,
     Firmly confident,
     Fiercely wild,
     A fabulous character,
     Completely out of our mind
     And out of his, too.

                                              Anancy [1970]

2   An a so de rain a-fall
     An a so de snow a-rain

     An a so de fog a-fall
     An a so de sun a-fail

     An a so de seasons mix
     An a so de bag-o' tricks

     But a so me understand'
     De misery o' de Englishman.   *A Song for England [1970]*

3   Sameness may be dull but reassuring. Difference is usually difficult. Its
     acceptance does not always come easily.

                                       Breaklight [1973], introduction

4   You did know say
     that none o' them
     know how much history
     under them skin,

coil up inside, there so,
like baby hold back from born?

Jamaica [1973]

1   Culture come when you buck up
on you'self.
It start when you' body make shadow
on the lan',
an' you know say
that you standin' up into mirror
underneat' you.

Jamaica

2   Is the lan' I want
an' is the lan'
I out to get.

Jamaica

3   you and Caribbea are one in us.
you are Caribbea!

Jamaica

Norma Sklarek

1928–2012

4   Architecture should be working on improving the environment of people in their homes, in their places of work and their places of recreation. It should be functional and pleasant, not just in the image of the architect's ego.

From BRIAN LANKER, *I Dream a World* [1989]

Piri Thomas [John Peter Thomas]

1928–2011

5   Man! How many times have I stood on the rooftop of my broken-down building at night and watched the bulb-lit world below.

Like somehow it's different at night, this my Harlem.

There ain't no bright sunlight to reveal the stark naked truth of garbage-lepered streets.

Gone is the drabness and hurt, covered by a friendly night.

It makes clean the dirty-faced kids.

Down These Mean Streets [1967], *prologue*

6   The worlds of home and school were made up of rules laid down by adults who had forgotten the feeling of what it means to be a kid but expected a kid to remember to be an adult — something he hadn't gotten to yet. The world of street belonged to the kid alone.

Down These Mean Streets

7   Our children are beauty
with the right to be born.
Born anew at each a.m.

Like a child out of twilight,
flying toward sunlight,
Born anew at each a.m.   *Born Anew at Each A.M. [1994]*

1   We must learn words can be bullets or butterflies.
     30th Anniversary Edition of
     Down These Mean Streets [1997], afterword

Berry Gordy, Jr.   1929–

and

Janie Bradford   1939–

2   The best things in life are free
     But you can keep 'em for the birds and bees
     Now give me money, that's what I want.   *Money [1959]*

Eloise Greenfield   1929–

3   I went all the way to Africa
     In a dream one night
     I crossed over the ocean
     In a slow, smooth jump
     And landed in Africa
     Long-ago Africa.   *Africa Dream [1977]*

4   I love a lot of things, a whole lot of things
     Like
     My cousin comes to visit and you know he's from the South
     'Cause every word he says just kind of slides out of his mouth
     I like the way he whistles and I like the way he walks
     But honey, let me tell you that I LOVE the way he talks
                                                Honey, I Love [1978]

5   A childtime is a mighty thing.   *Childtimes [1979]*

Martin Luther King, Jr.   1929–1968

6   If it falls your lot to be a street sweeper, sweep streets like Michelangelo
     painted pictures, like Shakespeare wrote poetry, like Beethoven composed
     music; sweep streets so well that all the host of Heaven and earth will have
     to pause and say, "Here lived a great street sweeper who swept his job well."
                        Speech, Montgomery, Alabama [December 1956][1]

---

[1]From *A Testament of Hope* [1986], edited by JAMES M. WASHINGTON.

1   There is nothing in all the world greater than freedom. It is worth paying for; it is worth losing a job; it is worth going to jail for. I would rather be a free pauper than a rich slave. I would rather die in abject poverty with my convictions than live in inordinate riches with the lack of self-respect.

Speech, Montgomery, Alabama

2   Violence is immoral because it thrives on hatred rather than love. It destroys community and makes brotherhood impossible. It leaves society in monologue rather than dialogue. Violence ends by defeating itself. It creates bitterness in the survivors and brutality in the destroyers.

Stride Toward Freedom [1958]

3   We have come a long, long way. We have a long, long way to go. I close, if you will permit me, by quoting the words of an old Negro slave preacher. He didn't quite have his grammar right, but he uttered some words in the form of prayer with great symbolic profundity and these are the words he said: "Lord, we ain't what we want to be; we ain't what we ought to be; we ain't what we gonna be, but thank God, we ain't what we was."

Address to House of Representatives of the first Legislature of Hawaii [September 17, 1959][1]

4   Time is neutral. It can be used destructively or constructively.

Speech at the annual meeting of the Fellowship of the Concerned [November 16, 1961][1]

5   The problem of race and color prejudice remains America's greatest moral dilemma. When one considers the impact it has upon our nation, internally and externally, its resolution might well determine our destiny.... The price that America must pay for the continued oppression of the Negro is the price of its own destruction.

Ethical Demands for Integration. Speech [December 27, 1962][2]

6   Injustice anywhere is a threat to justice everywhere.

Letter from Birmingham City Jail [April 16, 1963]

7   For years now I have heard the word "Wait!" It rings in the ear of every Negro with a piercing familiarity. This "Wait" has almost always meant "Never." *Letter from Birmingham Jail*

8   Freedom is never voluntarily given by the oppressor; it must be demanded by the oppressed.

Letter from Birmingham City Jail

---

[1]From *The Papers of Martin Luther King, Jr.* [2005], edited by CLAYBORNE CARSON, RALPH LUKER, and PENNY A. RUSSELL.

[2]From *A Testament of Hope* [1986], edited by JAMES M. WASHINGTON.

1   The Negro's great stumbling block...is not the White Citizen's Counciler or the Ku Klux Klanner, but the white moderate who is more devoted to "order" than to justice; who prefers a negative peace which is the absence of tension to a positive peace which is the presence of justice...; who paternalistically believes that he can set the timetable for another man's freedom.   *Letter from Birmingham City Jail*

2   We must come to see that human progress never rolls in on wheels of inevitability. It comes through the tireless efforts and persistent work of men willing to be co-workers with God, and without this hard work time itself becomes an ally of the forces of social stagnation.
                        Letter from Birmingham City Jail

3   The question is not whether we will be extremist but what kind of extremist we will be. Will we be extremists for hate or will we be extremists for love?   *Letter from Birmingham City Jail*

4   Nonviolence demands that the means we use must be as pure as the ends we seek.   *Letter from Birmingham City Jail*

5   If a man hasn't discovered something that he will die for, he isn't fit to live.   *Speech in Detroit [June 23, 1963]*

6   The Negro is still languishing in the corners of American society and finds himself an exile in his own land.
                        Speech at the March on Washington for Jobs and Freedom
                        [August 28, 1963]

7   When the architects of our republic wrote the magnificent words of the Constitution and the Declaration of Independence, they were signing a promissory note to which every American was to fall heir. This note was a promise that all men — yes, black men as well as white men — would be guaranteed the "unalienable rights of life, liberty, and the pursuit of happiness." It is obvious today that America has defaulted on this promissory note insofar as her citizens of color are concerned. Instead of honoring this sacred obligation, America has given the Negro people a bad check, a check which has come back marked "insufficient funds."
                        Speech at the March on Washington for Jobs and Freedom

8   Let us not seek to satisfy our thirst for freedom by drinking from the cup of bitterness and hatred.
                        Speech at the March on Washington for Jobs and Freedom

9   There are those who are asking the devotees of civil rights, "When will you be satisfied?" We can never be satisfied as long as the Negro is the victim of the unspeakable horrors of police brutality. We can never be satisfied as long as our bodies, heavy with the fatigue of travel, cannot gain lodging in

the motels of the highways and the hotels of the cities. We cannot be satisfied as long as the Negro's basic mobility is from a smaller ghetto to a larger one. We can never be satisfied as long as our children are stripped of their selfhood and robbed of their dignity by signs stating: "for whites only." We cannot be satisfied as long as a Negro in Mississippi cannot vote and a Negro in New York believes he has nothing for which to vote. No, no, we are not satisfied, and we will not be satisfied until justice rolls down like waters, and righteousness like a mighty stream.[1]

Speech at the March on Washington for Jobs and Freedom

1   I have a dream that one day on the red hills of Georgia the sons of former slaves and the sons of former slave-owners will be able to sit down together at the table of brotherhood.

Speech at the March on Washington for Jobs and Freedom

2   I have a dream that my four little children will one day live in a nation where they will not be judged by the color of their skin, but by the content of their character.

Speech at the March on Washington for Jobs and Freedom

3   When we allow freedom to ring, when we let it ring from every village and every hamlet, from every state and every city, we will be able to speed up that day when all of God's children, black men and white men, Jews and Gentiles, Protestants and Catholics, will be able to join hands and sing in the words of the old Negro spiritual, "Free at last! Free at last! Thank God Almighty, we are free at last!"[2]

Speech at the March on Washington for Jobs and Freedom

4   Rarely do we find men who willingly engage in hard, solid thinking. There is an almost universal quest for easy answers and half-baked solutions. Nothing pains some people more than having to think.

Strength to Love [1963]

5   Science gives man knowledge which is power; religion gives man wisdom which is control. Science deals mainly with facts; religion deals mainly with values. The two are not rivals.   *Strength to Love*

6   The ultimate measure of a man is not where he stands in moments of comfort and convenience, but where he stands at times of challenge and controversy.   *Strength to Love*

7   Darkness cannot drive out darkness: only light can do that. Hate cannot drive out hate: only love can do that.   *Strength to Love*

---

[1]But let justice roll down as waters, and righteousness as a mighty stream. — *Amos 5:24*

[2]King's epitaph in South View Cemetery, Atlanta, Georgia.

1   Love is the only force capable of transforming an enemy into a
friend.   *Strength to Love*

2   Nonviolence is the answer to the crucial political and moral questions
of our time; the need for man to overcome oppression and violence without
resorting to oppression and violence. Man must evolve for all human conflict a method which rejects revenge, aggression and retaliation. The foundation of such a method is love.
             Speech accepting the Nobel Peace Prize [December 11, 1964]

3   The tortuous road which has led from Montgomery to Oslo is a road
over which millions of Negroes are traveling to find a new sense of dignity.
It will, I am convinced, be widened into a superhighway of justice.
                        Speech accepting the Nobel Peace Prize

4   I refuse to accept despair as the final response to the ambiguities of
history. I refuse to accept the idea that the "isness" of man's present nature
makes him morally incapable of reaching up for the eternal "oughtness"
that forever confronts him.   *Speech accepting the Nobel Peace Prize*

5   I refuse to accept the cynical notion that nation after nation must
spiral down a militaristic stairway into the hell of nuclear destruction.
I believe that unarmed truth and unconditional love will have the final word
in reality.   *Speech accepting the Nobel Peace Prize*

6   The Negro was willing to risk martyrdom in order to move and stir
the social conscience of his community and the nation.... he would force
his oppressor to commit his brutality openly, with the rest of the world
looking on.... Nonviolent resistance paralyzed and confused the power
structures against which it was directed.   *Why We Can't Wait [1964]*

7   How long? Not long, because the arc of the moral universe is long, but
it bends toward justice.[1]
                        Our God Is Marching On. Sermon
                        [March 25, 1965]

8   If America's soul becomes totally poisoned, part of the autopsy must
read Vietnam.
                        Sermon on the Vietnam War. Riverside Church,
                        New York [April 4, 1967]

9   We must rapidly begin the shift from a "thing-oriented" society to a
"person-oriented" society. When machines and computers, profit motives
and property rights are considered more important than people, the giant

---

[1]I do not pretend to understand the moral universe, the arc is a long one ... but ... it bends toward
justice. — THEODORE PARKER, theologian and abolitionist.

triplets of racism, materialism and militarism are incapable of being conquered. *Sermon on the Vietnam War*

1   True compassion is more than flinging a coin to a beggar; it is not haphazard and superficial. It comes to see that an edifice which produces beggars needs restructuring. *Sermon on the Vietnam War*

2   Now let us begin. Now let us rededicate ourselves to the long and bitter — but beautiful — struggle for a new world.

Sermon on the Vietnam War

3   As long as the mind is enslaved the body can never be free. Psychological freedom, a firm sense of self-esteem, is the most powerful weapon against the long night of physical slavery.... The Negro will only be truly free when he reaches down to the inner depths of his own being and signs with the pen and ink of assertive selfhood his own emancipation proclamation. *Where Do We Go from Here? [1967]*

4   A riot is at bottom the language of the unheard.

Where Do We Go from Here?

5   Today's despair is a poor chisel to carve out tomorrow's justice.

Where Do We Go from Here?

6   We are bound together in a single garment of destiny.

Where Do We Go from Here?

7   Life's piano can only produce the melodies of brotherhood when it is recognized that the black keys are as basic, necessary and beautiful as the white keys. *Where Do We Go from Here?*

8   We have inherited a large house, a great world house in which we have to live together — black and white, Easterner and Westerner, Gentile and Jew, Catholic and Protestant, Muslim and Hindu — a family unduly separated in ideas, culture, and interest, who, because we can never again live apart, must learn somehow to live with each other in peace.

Where Do We Go from Here?

9   Justice is indivisible. *The Trumpet of Conscience [1967]*

10   Everybody can be great because everybody can serve.... You only need a heart full of grace.

The Drum Major Instinct. Sermon, Ebenezer Baptist Church [February 4, 1968]

11   We must come to see that the roots of racism are very deep in our country, and there must be something positive and massive in order to get rid of all the effects of racism and the tragedies of racial injustice.

Remaining Awake Through a Great Revolution. Speech, Washington, D.C. [March 31, 1968]

1   We must face the sad fact that at eleven o'clock on Sunday morning when we stand to sing. . . . we stand in the most segregated hour of America.
Remaining Awake Through a Great Revolution

2   It is a crime for people to live in this rich country and receive starvation wages.
Speech to striking sanitation workers, Memphis, Tennessee [March 18, 1968]

3   A man can't ride your back unless it is bent.
Address to sanitation workers, Memphis, Tennessee, the night before he was assassinated [April 3, 1968]

4   Like anybody, I would like to live a long life. Longevity has its place. But I'm not concerned about that now. I just want to do God's will. And He's allowed me to go up to the mountain. And I've looked over, and I've seen the promised land. I may not get there with you, but I want you to know tonight that we as a people will get to the promised land. . . . So I'm happy tonight. I'm not worried about anything. I'm not fearing any man.
Address to sanitation workers, Memphis, Tennessee

5   The comfortable, the entrenched, the privileged cannot continue to tremble at the prospect of change in the status quo.
A Testament of Hope. Playboy [January 1969]

6   Ultimately, one's sense of manhood must come from within.
A Testament of Hope

Paule Marshall   1929–

7   In the somnolent July afternoon the unbroken line of brownstone houses down the long Brooklyn street resembled an army massed at attention. They were all one uniform red-brown stone. All with high massive stone stoops and black iron-grille fences staving off the sun. All draped in ivy as though mourning. Their somber facades, indifferent to the summer's heat and passion, faced a park while their backs reared dark against the sky.
Brown Girl, Brownstones [1959], opening lines

8   It's a terrible thing to know that you gon be poor all yuh life, no matter how hard you work. You does stop trying after a time. People does see you so and call you lazy. But it ain laziness. It just that you does give up. You does kind of die inside.
Brown Girl, Brownstones, bk. 3, ch. 1 [Silla]

9   She died and I lived, but always, to this day even, within the shadow of her death.   *To Da-duh, In Memoriam [1967]*

1   Once a great wrong has been done, it never dies. People speak the words of peace, but their hearts do not forgive. Generations perform ceremonies of reconciliation, but there is no end.

From the Tiv of West Africa, The Chosen Place,
The Timeless People [1969], epigraph

2   Sometimes a person has to go back, really back — to have a sense, an understanding of all that's gone to make them — before they can go forward.   *The Chosen Place, The Timeless People, ch. 11 [Merle]*

3   A person can run for years but sooner or later he has to take a stand in the place which, for better or worse, he calls home, do what he can to change things there.   *The Chosen Place, The Timeless People, ch. 11 [Merle]*

4   I grew up among poets. Now they didn't look like poets — whatever that breed is supposed to look like. Nothing about them suggested that poetry was their calling. They were just a group of ordinary housewives and mothers, my mother included, who dressed in a way (shapeless house dresses, dowdy felt hats and long, dark, solemn coats) that made it impossible for me to imagine they had ever been young.

From the Poets in the Kitchen. New York Times Book Review
[January 9, 1983]

5   They just turned, my gran' said, all of 'em and walked on back down to the edge of the river here. Every las' man, woman and chile. And they wasn't taking they time no more. They had seen what they had seen and those Ibos was stepping! And they didn't bother getting back into the small boats drawed up here — boats take too much time. They just kept walking right on out over the river.   *Praisesong for the Widow [1983], ch. 3*

6   We live surrounded by white images, and white in this world is synonymous with the good, light, beauty, success, so that, despite ourselves sometimes, we run after that whiteness and deny our darkness, which has been made into the symbol of all that is evil and inferior.   *Reena [1983] [Reena]*

Chinua Achebe [Albert Chinualumogu Achebe]   1930–2013

7   Okonkwo was well known throughout the nine villages and even beyond.   *Things Fall Apart [1959], opening line*

8   Among the Ibo the art of conversation is regarded very highly, and proverbs are the palm-oil with which words are eaten.

Things Fall Apart, ch. 1

9   A proud heart can survive a general failure because such a failure does not prick its pride. It is more difficult and more bitter when a man fails *alone.*   *Things Fall Apart, ch. 3 [Unoka]*

1   The white man is very clever. He came quietly and peaceably with his religion. We were amused at his foolishness and allowed him to stay. Now he has won our brothers, and our clan can no longer act like one. He has put a knife on the things that held us together and we have fallen apart.

Things Fall Apart, ch. 20

2   The impatient idealist says: "Give me a place to stand and I shall move the earth." But such a place does not exist. We all have to stand on the earth itself and go with her at her pace.   *No Longer at Ease [1960]*

3   The writer cannot expect to be excused from the task of reeducation and regeneration that must be done. In fact, he should march right in front.   *The Novelist as Teacher. New Statesman [1965]*

4   In such a regime, I say, you died a good death if your life had inspired someone to come forward and shoot your murderer in the chest — without asking to be paid.   *A Man of the People [1966], last line*

5   Belief in superior and inferior races; belief that some people who live across our frontiers or speak a different language from ourselves are the cause of all the trouble in the world, or that our own particular group or class or caste has a right to certain things which are denied to others; the belief that men are superior to women, and so on — are all fictions generated by the imagination.

Convocation lecture, University of Ife [1978]

6   I don't lay down the law for anybody else. But I think writers are not only writers, they are also citizens. . . . Serious and good art has always existed to help, to serve, humanity. Not to indict.

Interview. Paris Review [Winter 1994]

7   Man is a story-making animal.
The Empire Fights Back. Lecture,
Harvard University [1998]

8   The psychology of the dispossessed can be truly frightening.

The Empire Fights Back

Benny Andrews   1930–2006

9   Whatever it is I do or do not do in the paintings I paint really are attempts by me to communicate to the "Folks." While I could write yards on who the "Folks" are, just let it suffice to say for this time, they are "Us." The next question is automatically, who are "Us"? The answer to that automatic question at this moment is, "Us" are the "Folks," and I am one of them.

From SAMELLA S. LEWIS and RUTH G. WADDY,
Black Artists on Art [1969]

Derrick Bell   1930–2011

1   Black people are the magical faces at the bottom of society's well. Even the poorest whites, those who must live their lives only a few levels above, gain their self-esteem by gazing down on us. Surely, they must know that their deliverance depends on letting down their ropes. Only by working together is escape possible. Over time, many reach out, but most simply watch, mesmerized into maintaining their unspoken commitment to keeping us where we are, at whatever cost to them or to us.

Faces at the Bottom of the Well [1992]

2   We rise and fall less as a result of our efforts than in response to the needs of a white society that condemns all blacks to quasi-citizenship as surely as it segregated our parents and enslaved their forebears. The fact is that, despite what we designate as progress wrought through struggle over many generations, we remain what we were in the beginning: a dark and foreign presence, always the designated "other." Tolerated in good times, despised when things go wrong, as a people we are scapegoated and sacrificed as distraction or catalyst for compromise to facilitate resolution of political differences or relieve economic adversity.

Faces at the Bottom of the Well

Edward Kamau Brathwaite   1930–

3   Drum skin whip
lash, master's sun's
cutting edge of
heat, taut
surfaces of things
I sing
I shout
I groan
I dream
about.   *Rites of Passage [1967]. Prelude to I, Work Songs and Blues*

4   Memories are smoke
lips we can't kiss
hands we can't hold
will never be
enough for us.   *Rites of Passage. Prelude to II, The Spades*

5   Where then is the nigger's
home?
In Paris Brixton Kingston

Rome?
Here?
Or in Heaven?   *Rites of Passage. Postlude/Home*

1   So the god,
     mask of dreamers,
     hears lightnings
     stammer, hearts
     rustle their secrets,
     blood shiver like leaves
     on his branches. Will
     the tree, god
     of path-
     ways, still
     guide us? Will
     your wood lips speak
     so we see?   *Masks [1968]*

2   My mother said I'd be alone
     and when I cried (she said)
     I'd be Columbus of my ships
     and sail the garden round
     the tears that fell into my hand.   *Islands [1969]. The Cracked Mother*

3   I return,
     expecting nothing;
     my name burnt out.   *Islands. Homecoming*

4   And as he worked within his
     shattered Sunday shop, the wood took shape: dry shuttered
     eyes, slack anciently everted lips, flat
     ruined face, eaten by pox, ravaged by rat
     and woodworm, dry cistern mouth, cracked
     gullet crying for the desert, the heavy black
     enduring jaw; lost pain, lost iron;
     emerging woodwork image of his anger.   *Islands. Ogun*

5   When the stone fall that morning out of the johncrow sky
     it was not dark at first . that opening on to the red sea humming
     but something in my mouth like feathers . blue like bubbles
     carrying signals & planets & the sliding curve of the
     world like a water pic. ture in a raindrop when the pressure. drop
                         Middle Passages [1992]. Stone

1   How to make sense
     of all this. all this pain. this drought
     scramble together vowels jewels that will help
     you understand will help you understand these rain.
     these rain. these rain. less
     words. need love. love too   *Words Need Love Too [1998]*

Betty Carter [Lillie Mae Jones]   1930–1998

2   There are all different shades of blues. There's all different shades of
     singer.
                                    From *Jazz Voices, [1983], edited by* Kitty Grime

Ray Charles [Robinson]   1930–2004

3   I got a woman, way over town
     That's good to me.
     She gives me money when I'm in need
     Yeah she's a kind of friend indeed.   *I Got a Woman [1954]*

4   My friends don't come around me
     Because I've been so blind,
     I can't even borrow a nickel
     Now I've almost lost my mind.   *Blackjack [1955]*

5   Hallelujah I Love Her So   *Song title [1956]*

6   Tell me what'd I say?
     Tell me what'd I say right now?

                                                    What'd I Say? [1959]

7   Genius + Soul = Jazz   *Title of album [1960]*

8   It's like electricity; we don't really know what it is, do we? But it's a
     force that can light a room. Soul is like electricity.
                                        Quoted in Life [July 29, 1966]

9   *[On music:]* It was a necessity for me — like food or water.
                                                    Brother Ray [1992]

Ornette Coleman   1930–

10   Many people apparently don't trust their reactions to art or to music
     unless there is a verbal explanation for it. In music the only thing that mat-
     ters is whether you feel it or not.
                                    Change of the Century [1959], liner notes

Dorothy Cotton

1930–

1 If a house is burning, and a bucket of water is thrown on the blaze and doesn't extinguish the fire, this doesn't mean that water won't put out fire. It means we need more water. And so with nonviolence.

Interview. The Other Side [January 1, 1998]

2 Black folk, a lot of us lived as victims in a certain part of our history. And we had to really erase that tape. We're not victims. We are citizens.

Interview. The Tavis Smiley Show [January 2007]

Sam Greenlee

1930–

3 Had his mask become him? He would find out soon now.... They had never felt he had either the guts or intelligence to function in the field and he had reinforced their thoughts on that score. He smiled to himself. He had conned them all and in his own way had been the best of the spooks and they might never know it. For five years he had been the CIA nigger and his job had been to sit by the door.   *The Spook Who Sat by the Door [1969]*

Lorraine Hansberry

1930–1965

4 In my mother's house there is still God.

A Raisin in the Sun [1958], act 1 [Mama]

5 Children see things very well sometimes — and idealists even better.

A Raisin in the Sun, act 3 [Asagai]

6 I didn't make this world! It was given to me this way.

A Raisin in the Sun, act 3 [Walter]

7 Child, when do you think is the time to love somebody the most? When they done good and made things easy for everybody? Well then, you ain't through learning, because that ain't the time at all. It's when he's at his lowest and can't believe in hisself 'cause the world done whipped him so! When you starts measuring somebody — measure him right, child. Measure him right. Make sure you done taken into account what hills and valleys he come through before he got to wherever he is.

A Raisin in the Sun, act 3 [Mama]

8 I wish to live because life has within it that which is good, that which is beautiful and that which is love. Therefore, since I have known all of these things, I have found them to be reason enough and — I wish to live. Moreover, because this is so, I wish others to live for generations and generations and generations and generations.   *Speech [March 1, 1959][1]*

---

[1]From *To Be Young, Gifted and Black* [1969], adapted by ROBERT NEMIROFF.

1   Eventually it comes to you: the thing that makes you exceptional, if you are at all, is inevitably that which must also make you lonely.

Journal entry [May 1, 1962]

2   Though it be a thrilling and marvelous thing to be merely young and gifted in such times, it is doubly so — doubly dynamic — to be young, gifted and *black.*

Speech at awards ceremony, United Negro College
Fund writing contest [May 1964][1]

3   I am simply saying that a device is a device, but that it also has consequences: once invented it takes on a life, a reality of its own. So, in one century men invoke the device of religion to cloak their conquests. In another, race. Now, in both cases you and I may recognize the fraudulence of the device, but the fact remains that a man who has a sword run through him because he refuses to become a Moslem or a Christian — or who is shot in Zatembe or Mississippi because he is black — is suffering the utter reality of the device. And it is pointless to pretend that it doesn't exist — merely because it is a lie!

Les Blancs [1969], act 2 [Tshembe]

4   *[Sidney responding to being called a fool:]* Always have been. A fool who believes that death is waste and love is sweet and that the earth turns and men change every day and that rivers run and that people want to be better than they are and that flowers smell good and that I hurt terribly today, and that hurt is desperation and desperation is — energy and energy can *move* things.

The Sign in Sidney Brustein's Window [1965], act 3, sc. 2

5   In order to create the universal, you must pay very great attention to the specific.

To Be Young, Gifted and Black [1969]

Abbey Lincoln [Anna Marie Wooldridge]   1930–2010

6   For some this road is smooth and easy
Travelin' high without a care
But if you got to use the backroads
Straight ahead can lead nowhere.

Straight Ahead [1961]

7   Who will revere the Black woman? Who will keep our neighborhoods safe for Black innocent womanhood? Black womanhood is outraged and humiliated. Black womanhood cries for dignity and restitution and salvation. Black womanhood wants and needs protection, and keeping, and holding. Who will assuage her indignation? Who will keep her precious and pure? Who will glorify and proclaim her beautiful image? To whom will she cry rape?

Who Will Revere the Black Woman? Negro Digest [September 1966]

---

[1]From *To Be Young, Gifted and Black* [1969], adapted by ROBERT NEMIROFF.

1   Throw it away
    Throw it away
    Give your love, live your life
    Each and every day.

    And keep your hand wide open
    And let the sun shine through
    'Cause you can never lose a thing
    If it belongs to you.   *Throw it Away [1980]*

2   I am the first instrument. I am the voice. I do not imitate other instruments. Other instruments imitate *me*.

                    From Jazz Voices [1983], edited by KITTY GRIME

3   Bird alone,
    Flying low
    Over where the grasses grow
    Swingin' low, then out of sight
    You'll be singing in the night.

                                            Bird Alone [1991]

Odetta [Holmes]   1930–2008

4   *[On why prison and work songs are liberation songs:]* You're walking down life's road, society's foot is on your throat, every which way you turn you can't get from under that foot. And you reach a fork in the road and you can either lie down and die, or insist upon your life.

                                Interview. New York Times [2007]

Charles B[ernard] Rangel   1930–

5   We see a different kind of slavery today. Guest-workers, lured from third world countries with false promises, are forced to work in hazardous work conditions with very little wages in countries where oftentimes they do not even speak the language. They have virtually no rights as foreign workers and are sometimes forbidden by law to form unions. These modern-day slaves have no recourse but to follow the directives of their employers to exploit their helplessness.

                    Speech, U.S. House of Representatives [July 19, 2006]

Faith Ringgold   1930–

6   Sleeping on Tar Beach was magical. Lying on the roof in the night, with stars and skyscraper buildings all around me, made me feel rich, like I owned all that I could see.   *Tar Beach [1991]*

1   It's very easy, anyone can fly. All you need is somewhere to go that you can't get to any other way. The next thing you know, you're flying among the stars.

Tar Beach

Thomas Sowell   1930–

2   Discussions of ethnic minorities tend to drift toward the *problems* of ethnic minorities, or the problems that ethnic minorities cause other people. Both kinds of problems deserve serious attention. However, the history of American ethnic minorities is not exclusively a history of problems.

Race and Economics [1975]

3   Individualism as a philosophic value cannot change the historical fact of group discrimination and group conditioning, both of which severely limit the opportunities facing any particular individual in a disadvantaged group.

Race and Economics

4   Race is a biological concept but it is a social reality.

Race and Culture [1994], preface

Derek Walcott   1930–

5   I who am poisoned with the blood of both,
Where shall I turn, divided to the vein?
I who have cursed
The drunken officer of British rule, how choose
Between this Africa and the English tongue I love?

A Far Cry from Africa [1962][1]

6   The starved eye devours the seascape for the morsel
Of a sail.

The Castaway [1965][1]

7   Something inside is laid wide like a wound,

some open passage that has cleft the brain,
some deep, amnesiac blow. We left
somewhere a life we never found,

customs and gods that are not born again,
some crib, some grille of light
clanged shut on us in bondage, and withheld

---

[1]From DEREK WALCOTT, *Collected Poems: 1948–1984 [1986]*.

us from that world below us and beyond,
and in its swaddling cerements we're still bound.

Laventille (for V. S. Naipaul) [1965][1]

1   The time will come
when, with elation,
you will greet yourself arriving
at your own door, in your own mirror,
and each will smile at the other's welcome,

and say, sit here. Eat.   *Love after Love [1976]*

2   My race began as the sea began,
with no nouns, and with no horizon.   *Names [1976], I*[1]

3   These palms are greater than Versailles,

for no man made them.   *Names [1976]. II*[1]

4   Then after Eden,
was there one surprise?
O yes, the awe of Adam
at the first bead of sweat.   *Sea Grapes [1976]. New World*[1]

5   The tourist archipelagoes of my South
are prisons too, corruptible, and though
there is no harder prison than writing verse,
what's poetry, if it is worth its salt,
but a phrase men can pass from hand to mouth?   *Forest of Europe [1979]*[1]

6   I have Dutch, nigger, and English in me,
and either I'm nobody or I'm a nation   *The Schooner Flight [1979], 1*[1]

7   I had no nation now but the imagination.   *The Schooner Flight [1979], 1*[1]

8   The Caribbean was borne like an elliptical basin
in the hands of acolytes, and a people were
absolved
of a history which they did not commit.   *The Star-Apple Kingdom [1979]*[1]

9   I thought, who cares how many million starve?
Their rising souls will lighten the world's weight
and level its gull-glittering waterline.

The Fortunate Traveller (for Susan Sontag) [1981], I[2]

---

[1]From DEREK WALCOTT, *Collected Poems: 1948–1984* [1986].
[2]From DEREK WALCOTT, *Fortunate Traveller* [1981].

1   Now I have come to where the phantoms live,
    I have no fear of phantoms, but of the real.

The Fortunate Traveller (for Susan Sontag), II

2   I am tired of words,
    and literature is an old couch stuffed with fleas.

North and South [1981][1]

3   No language is neutral.   *Midsummer [1984],*[2] *LII*

4   and O was the conch-shell's invocation, *mer* was
    both mother and sea in our Antillean patois,
    os, a grey bone, and the white surf as it crashes.

Omeros [1990], ch. II, iii

5   Change lay in our silence. We had come to that bend
    where the trees are warped by wind, and the cliffs, raw,
    shelve surely to foam
                    "Is right here everything end."   *Omeros, XLV, iii*

Douglas Turner Ward   1930–

6   Factories standing idle from the loss of non-essential workers. Stores shuttered from the absconding of un-crucial personnel. Uncollected garbage threatening pestilence and pollution...dozens of decrepit old men and women usually tended by faithful nurses and servants are popping off like flies — abandoned by sons, daughters and grandchildren.... But most critically affected of all by this complete drought of Afro-American resources are policemen and other public safety guardians denied their daily quota of Negro arrests.   *Day of Absence [1966] [Announcer]*

Alvin Ailey   1931–1989

7   I believe the dance came from the people and that it should be delivered back to the people.   *Interview, An Evening with Alvin Ailey [1986]*

8   For many years, I felt that no matter what I did, what ballet I made, how beautifully I danced, it was not good enough.... That's one of the worst things about racism, what it does to young people. It tears down your insides so that no matter what you achieve, no matter what you write or choreograph, you feel it's not quite enough. You're not quite up to snuff.

Revelations [1995]

---

[1]From Derek Walcott, *Fortunate Traveller [1981]*.
[2]From Derek Walcott, *Collected Poems: 1948–1984 [1986]*.

1   The creative process is not controlled by a switch you can simply turn
     on or off; it's with you all the time.   *Revelations*

Otis Blackwell   1931–2002

2   I'm daddy rolling stone.   *Daddy Rollin' Stone [1953]*

3   You give me fever when you kiss me
     Fever when you hold me tight
     Fever in the morning
     Fever all through the night.   *Fever [1956]*

4   Don't be cruel to a heart that's true.   *Don't Be Cruel [1956]*

5   I'm in love,
     I'm all shook up.   *All Shook Up [1957]*

6   You shake my nerves and you rattle my brain
     Too much love drives a man insane
     You broke my will, but what a thrill
     Goodness gracious, great balls of fire!   *Great Balls of Fire [1957]*

7   I gave a letter to the postman
     He put it in his sack
     Bright and early next morning
     He brought my letter back.   *Return to Sender [1962]*

James Cleveland   1931–1991

8   Call him up, call my Jesus up
     Tell him what you want!
                Call Him Up and Tell Him What You Want [1954]

9   Walk on by faith each day.   *Walk On by Faith [1962]*

Sam Cooke   1931–1964

10   You Send Me   *Song title [1957]*

11   Don't know much about history
     Don't know much biology
     Don't know much about a science book
     Don't know much about the French I took
     But I do know that I love you
     And I know that if you love me, too
     What a wonderful world this would be.

                                              Wonderful World [1959]   333

1   Uh!
That's the sound of the men workin' on the chain gang.   *Chain Gang [1960]*

2   I was born by the river
In a little tent
And just like the river
I've been running ever since
It's been a long time coming
But I know a change is gonna come.   *A Change Is Gonna Come [1964]*

3   Bring It on Home to Me   *Song title [1962]*

J[oan] California Cooper

c. 1931[1]–

4   Life is more like rain. The river and the lake lay down for you. All you got to do is learn how to swim fore you go where they are and jump in.... You don't go to the rain, the rain comes to you.

Homemade Love [1986]. Swimming to the Top of the Rain [Aunt Ellen]

5   Cause all these people livin are brothers and sisters and cousins. All these beautiful different colors! We!...We the human Family. God said so! FAMILY!   *Family [1991]*

6   Some people say it takes courage to face the matter of death. I believe it takes more courage to face Life.

The Matter Is Life [1991]. Author's note

Herbert Daughtry, Sr.

1931–

7   There are many who may lay claim to the dubious distinction of being the world's number one sufferer. In the competing foray, we sufferers must learn to hear one another.... Sufferers who struggle for justice, freedom, and dignity must be vigilant lest they become one with the image of those they struggle against.... Sufferers must resist the temptation of exacting tribute for their pain from everyone.... Sufferers must resist the urge, however strong, to argue for preeminence in suffering. All sufferers believe they have suffered more than others, just as those who carry a burden believe theirs heaviest. Those who strive for monopoly on suffering will never create space to hear one another.

No Monopoly on Suffering: Blacks and Jews in Crown Heights (and Elsewhere) [1997]

---

[1]According to the U.S. Copyright Office database, a birth date of 1931 was indicated for the writer of *The Unintended*, a playwright Joan "California" Cooper. Claimant: Joan M. Cooper [1978].

1   Given the immense wealth made from the African, both from his person and his labor, one would have thought that when liberation came there would have been a special financial consideration accorded them, at the least, humane treatment. Neither occurred: Africans were never paid reparations nor treated humanely even to the present.

My Beloved Community [2001]. History of Racism and Color Prejudice

David Driskell   1931–

2   The black community must come to realize that art can have intrinsic value, and act accordingly. Otherwise, it will limit its artists to reproducing when they could define and reveal.... Only when we recognize the historical patterns of isolation and accept the responsibility of supporting those artists who express themselves in a universal language of form will black American artists be seen as major contributors to the art of this country.

Two Centuries of Black American Art [1976]. The Evolution of a Black Aesthetic, 1920–1950

Lonne Elder III   1931–1996

3   Who the hell ever told every Black woman she was some kind of god damn savior!   *Ceremonies in Old Dark Men [1965], act 2, sc. 1 [Adele]*

4   Be a dancer — any kind of dancer you wanta be — but dance it! Be a singer — sing any song you wanta sing, but sing! And you've got enough trouble to take you to the graveyard! But think of all that life you had before they buried you.   *Ceremonies in Old Dark Men, act 2, sc. 2 [Mr. Parker]*

Vincent Harding   1931–

5   We may sense that the river of black struggle is people, but it is also the hope, the movement, the transformative power that humans create and that create them, us, and makes them, us, new persons.   *There Is a River [1981]*

James Earl Jones   1931–

6   I'm convinced that racism is a form of psychosis. And black people can catch it like anybody else.

Quoted in the Washington Post [December 20, 1995]

Adrienne Kennedy   1931–

7   It is my father. He is arriving again for the night. He comes through the jungle to find me. He never tires of his journey.

Funnyhouse of a Negro [1969] [Victoria]

Don King

1   Only in America!   *Trademark phrase*

Etheridge Knight

1931–1991

2   The fears of years, like a biting whip,
     Had cut deep bloody grooves
     Across our backs.

> *Hard Rock Returns to Prison from the Hospital for the Criminal*
> *Insane [1968]*

3   Taped to the wall of my cell are 47 pictures: 47 black
     faces: my father, mother, grandmothers (1 dead), grand-
     fathers (both dead), brothers, sisters, uncles, aunts,
     cousins (1st and 2nd), nieces, and nephews. They stare
     across the space at me sprawling on my bunk. I know
     their dark eyes, they know mine. I know their style,
     they know mine. I am all of them, they are all of me;
     they are farmers, I am a thief, I am me, they are thee.

> *The Idea of Ancestry [1968]*

Willie Mays

1931–

4   Say hey!   *Trademark phrase*

John S[amuel] Mbiti

1931–

5   I am because we are; and since we are, therefore I am.

> *African Religions & Philosophy [1969]*

Toni Morrison [Chloe Anthony Wofford]

1931–

6   Quiet as it's kept there were no marigolds in the fall of 1941. We
     thought, at the time, that it was because Pecola was having her father's baby
     that the marigolds did not grow. A little examination and much less melan-
     choly would have proved to us that our seeds were not the only ones that
     did not sprout; nobody's did.

> *The Bluest Eye [1970], prologue*

7   There is really nothing more to say — except why. But since why is
     difficult to handle, one must take refuge in how.   *The Bluest Eye, prologue*

8   A little black girl yearns for the blue eyes of a little white girl, and
     the horror at the heart of her yearning is exceeded only by the evil of
     fulfillment.   *The Bluest Eye. Summer*

1   What was taken by outsiders to be slackness, slovenliness or even generosity was in fact a full recognition of the legitimacy of forces other than good ones. They did not believe doctors could heal — for them, none ever had done so. They did not believe death was accidental — life might be, but death was deliberate.
                                                          Sula [1973], pt. 2, 1937

2   I don't want to make somebody else. I want to make myself.
                                                          Sula, pt. 2, 1937 [Sula]

3   Nothing in this world loves a black man more than another black man. You hear of solitary white men, but niggers? Can't stay away from one another a whole day. So. It looks to me like you the envy of the world.
                                                          Sula, pt. 2, 1937 [Sula]

4   In a way, her strangeness, her naiveté, her craving for the other half of her equation was the consequence of an idle imagination. Had she paints, or clay, or knew the discipline of the dance, or strings; had she anything to engage her tremendous curiosity and her gift for metaphor, she might have exchanged the restlessness and preoccupation with whim for an activity that provided her with all she yearned for. And like any artist with no art form, she became dangerous.
                                                          Sula, pt. 2, 1939

5   I know what every colored woman in this country is doing.... Dying. Just like me. But the difference is they dying like a stump. Me, I'm going down like one of those redwoods. I sure did live in this world.
                                                          Sula, pt. 2, 1940 [Sula]

6   When am I happy and when am I sad and what is the difference? What do I need to know to stay alive? What is true in the world? Her [Pilate's] mind traveled crooked streets and aimless goat paths, arriving sometimes at profundity, other times at the revelations of a three-year-old.
                                                          Song of Solomon [1977], pt. 1, ch. 5

7   Wanna fly, you got to give up the shit that weighs you down.
                                                          Song of Solomon, pt. 1, ch. 8 [Guitar]

8   When you know your name, you should hang on to it, for unless it is noted down and remembered, it will die when you do.
                                                          Song of Solomon, pt. 2, ch. 15

9   For now he knew what Shalimar knew: If you surrendered to the air, you could *ride* it.   *Song of Solomon, last line*

10 At some point in life the world's beauty becomes enough. You don't need to photograph, paint or even remember it. It is enough. No record of it needs to be kept and you don't need someone to share it with or tell it to. When that happens — that letting go — you let go because you can.
                                                          Tar Baby [1981], ch. 8

1   Access to knowledge is the superb, the supreme act of truly great civilizations.

Speech at the New York Public Library
[October 2, 1986][1]

2   If a Negro got legs he ought to use them. Sit down too long, somebody will figure out a way to tie them up.   *Beloved [1987], pt. 1 [Paul D]*

3   I got a tree on my back and a haint in my house, and nothing in between but the daughter I am holding in my arms. No more running—from nothing. I will never run from another thing on this earth. I took one journey and I paid for the ticket, but let me tell you something, Paul D Garner: it cost too much!   *Beloved, pt. 1 [Sethe]*

4   A man ain't nothing but a man.... But a son? Well now, that's *somebody.*   *Beloved, pt. 1 [Baby Suggs]*

5   No matter what all your teeth and wet fingers anticipated, there was no accounting for the way that simple joy could shake you.

Beloved, pt. 1

6   Some things go. Pass on. Some things just stay. I used to think it was my rememory. You know. Some things you forget. Other things you never do. But it's not. Places, places are still there. If a house burns down, it's gone, but the place — the picture of it — stays, and not just in my rememory, but out there, in the world.   *Beloved, pt. 1 [Sethe]*

7   Grown don't mean nothing to a mother. A child is a child. They get bigger, older, but grown? What's that supposed to mean? In my heart it don't mean a thing.   *Beloved, pt. 1 [Sethe]*

8   Can't nothing heal without pain, you know.

Beloved, pt. 1 [Amy]

9   Here...in this here place, we flesh; flesh that weeps, laughs; flesh that dances on bare feet in grass. Love it. Love it hard. Yonder they do not love your flesh. They despise it. They don't love your eyes; they'd just as soon pick em out. No more do they love the skin on your back. Yonder they flay it. And O my people they do not love your hands. Those they only use, tie, bind, chop off and leave empty. Love your hands! Love them. Raise them up and kiss them. Touch others with them, pat them together, stroke them on your face 'cause they don't love that either. *You* got to love it, *you!* ... Love your heart. For this is the prize.   *Beloved, pt. 1 [Baby Suggs]*

10   I am Beloved and she is mine.   *Beloved, pt. 2*

[1]Engraved in the Humanities and Social Sciences Library, New York Public Library.

1   The future was sunset; the past something to leave behind. And if it didn't stay behind, well, you might have to stomp it out. Slave life; freed life — every day was a test and a trial. Nothing could be counted on in a world where even when you were a solution you were a problem.   *Beloved, pt. 3*

2   She is a friend of my mind. She gather me, man. The pieces I am, she gather them and give them back to me in all the right order. It's good, you know, when you got a woman who is a friend of your mind.

Beloved, pt. 3 [Sixo]

3   There is a loneliness that can be rocked. Arms crossed, knees drawn up; holding, holding on, this motion, unlike a ship's, smooths and contains the rocker. It's an inside kind — wrapped tight like skin. Then there is a loneliness that roams. No rocking can hold it down. It is alive, on its own.

Beloved, pt. 3

4   This is not a story to pass on.   *Beloved, pt. 3*

5   I really think the range of emotions and perceptions I have had access to as a black person and as a female person are greater than those of people who are neither. . . . So it seems to me that my world did not shrink because I was a black female writer. It just got bigger.

Quoted in the New York Times [August 26, 1987]

6   I envy them their public love. I myself have only known it in secret, shared it in secret and longed, aw longed to show it — to be able to say out loud what they have no need to say at all: *That I have loved only you, surrendered my whole self reckless to you and nobody else. That I want you to love me back and show it to me. That I love the way you hold me, how close you let me be to you. I like your fingers on and on, lifting, turning. I have watched your face for a long time now, and missed your eyes when you went away from me. Talking to you and hearing you answer — that's the kick.*   *Jazz [1992]*

7   Deep within the word "American" is its association with race. . . . American means white, and Africanist people struggle to make the term applicable to themselves with ethnicity and hyphen after hyphen after hyphen.

Playing in the Dark: Whiteness and the Literary Imagination [1992]

8   Oppressive language does more than represent violence; it is violence; does more than represent the limits of knowledge; it limits knowledge.

Nobel lecture [December 7, 1993]

9   We die. That may be the meaning of life. But we do language. That may be the measure of our lives.   *Nobel Lecture*

10   Language alone protects us from the scariness of things with no names.   *Nobel Lecture*

1   Whose house is this?
    Whose night keeps out the light
    In here?
    Say, who owns this house?
    It's not mine.
    I dreamed another, sweeter, brighter
    With a view of lakes crossed in painted boats;
    Of fields wide as arms open for me.
    This house is strange.
    Its shadows lie.
    Say, tell me, why does its lock fit my key?

    Honey and Rue [1993]. Whose House Is This?[1]

2   They shoot the white girl first. With the rest they can take their time.
    No need to hurry out here. They are seventeen miles from a town which has
    ninety miles between it and any other. Hiding places will be plentiful in the
    Convent, but there is time and the day has just begun.

    Paradise [1998], opening lines

3   Love is divine only and difficult always. If you think it is easy you are a
    fool. If you think it is natural you are blind. It is a learned application
    without reason or motive except that it is God.

    Paradise. Divine [Reverend Senior Pulliam]

4   [On love:] It is easily the most empty cliché, the most useless word, and
    at the same time the most powerful human emotion—because hatred is
    involved in it, too.   *Interview. O, the Oprah Magazine [November 2003]*

5   Only unharnessed hearts
    Can survive a locked-down life.   *Margaret Garner [2005]. A Quality Love*

6   When sorrow is deep,
    The secret soul keeps
    Its weapon of choice:
    The love of all loves.   *Margaret Garner. A Quality Love*

7   You can think what I tell you a confession, if you like, but one full of
    curiosities familiar only in dreams and during those moments when a dog's
    profile plays in the steam of a kettle. Or when a corn-husk doll sitting on a
    shelf is soon splaying in the corner of a room and the wicked of how it got
    there is plain. Stranger things happen all the time everywhere. You know. I
    know you know.   *A Mercy [2008], opening lines*

---

[1]Epigraph for *Home [2012]*

1   Misery don't call ahead. That's why you have to stay awake — otherwise it just walks on in your door.   *Home [2012]*

Flora Nwapa [Florence Nwanzuruahu Nkiru]   1931–1993

2   They saw each other fairly often and after a fortnight's courting she
agreed to marry him. But the man had no money for the dowry. He had just
a few pounds for the farm and could not part with that. When the woman
saw that he was unable to pay anything, she told him not to bother about
the dowry. They were going to proclaim themselves married and that was
that.   *Efuru [1966], opening lines*

3   What arrogance, what stupidity led us to this desolation, to this madness, to this wickedness, to this war, to this death? When this cruel war was
over, there will be no more war. It will not happen again, never again.
NEVER AGAIN, never again.   *Never Again [1975]*

Ike Turner   1931–2007

4   You women have heard of jalopies,
You've heard the noise they make,
But let me introduce my new Rocket '88.
Yes it's great, just won't wait,
Everybody likes my Rocket '88.   *Rocket 88 [1951]*

Desmond Tutu   1931–

5   When two persons are engaged in conflict and one of them is considerably stronger than the other, to be neutral is not just and fair and impar-
tisan, because to be neutral is in fact to side with the powerful.
                Hope and Suffering [1983]. Politics and Religion

6   History, like beauty, depends largely on the beholder, so when you
read that, for example, David Livingstone discovered the Victoria Falls, you
might be forgiven for thinking that there was nobody around the Falls until
Livingstone arrived on the scene.
                Hope and Suffering. Fortieth Anniversary of the Republic?

7   There is no peace in Southern Africa. There is no peace because there
is no justice.   *Nobel lecture [December 11, 1984]*

8   When will we learn that human beings are of infinite value because
they have been created in the image of God, and that it is a blasphemy to
treat them as if they were less than this and to do so ultimately recoils on
those who do this? In dehumanizing others, they are themselves dehumanized. Perhaps oppression dehumanizes the oppressor as much as, if not

more than, the oppressed. They need each other to become truly free, to become human.   *Nobel lecture*

1   We must confess, sadly and humbly, that Africa has one of the worst records of violations of human rights. Africa has a spate of military dictatorships. In many places, all that has changed for the people who suffer is the complexion of the oppressor. In colonial times the oppressor was of a different complexion. Sadly, today the complexion of the oppressor is the same as the complexion of the oppressed.   *The Rainbow People of God [1994]*

2   We are beautiful because we are the rainbow people of God.
The Rainbow People of God

3   Having looked the beast of the past in the eye, having asked and received forgiveness and having made amends, let us shut the door on the past — not in order to forget it but in order not to allow it to imprison us.
Report of South Africa's Truth and Reconciliation
Commission [1998], foreword

4   Without forgiveness, without reconciliation, we have no future.
No Future Without Forgiveness [1999][1]

L[awrence] Douglas Wilder   1931–

5   We mark today not a victory of party or the accomplishments of an individual, but the triumph of an idea — an idea as old as America: as old as the God who looks out for us all. It is the idea expressed so eloquently from this great Commonwealth by those who gave shape to the greatest nation ever known, Jefferson, Madison, Mason and their able colleagues. The idea that all men and women are created equal, that they are endowed by their Creator with certain inalienable rights, the right to life, liberty and the pursuit of happiness.
On becoming the first black governor to be elected since
Reconstruction. Inaugural address, Richmond, Virginia
[January 13, 1990]

Addison Gayle, Jr.   1932–1991

6   The question for the black critic today is not how beautiful is a melody, a play, a poem, or a novel, but how much more beautiful has the poem, melody, play, or novel made the life of a single Black man? How far has the work gone in transforming an American Negro into an African-American or a Black man? The Black Aesthetic then...is a

---

[1]From *The Impossible Will Take a Little While* [2004], edited by PAUL LOEB.

corrective—a means of helping black people out of the polluted mainstream of Americanism. *The Black Aesthetic [1971]*

[Richard Claxton] Dick Gregory 1932–

1   Last time I was down South I walked into this restaurant and this white waitress came up to me and said, "We don't serve colored people here." I said, "That's all right. I don't eat colored people. Bring me a whole fried chicken."
Performance at the Playboy Club, Chicago [January 1961]

2   Let me tell you about this daughter of mine.... She said, "I don't believe in Santa Claus." I said, "What in the world you mean you don't believe in Santa Claus?...Why?" She said, "Because you know darn good and well there ain't no white man coming into our neighborhood after midnight."
Performance in Birmingham, Alabama [May 20, 1963]

3   Any clown knows that if you want to segregate somebody and keep them down forever, you put them up front. They made the great mistake of putting us in the back; we've been watching them for 300 years.
Performance in Birmingham, Alabama

4   Keep me a second-class citizen, but just don't make me pay first-class taxes. *Performance in Birmingham, Alabama*

5   Dear Momma—Wherever you are, if ever you hear the word "nigger" again, remember they are advertising my book.
Nigger [1964], dedication

6   Poor is a state of mind you never grow out of, but being broke is just a temporary condition. *Nigger*

7   I never learned hate at home, or shame. I had to go to school for that. *Nigger*

8   We used to root for the Indians against the cavalry, because we didn't think it was fair in the history books that when the cavalry won it was a great victory, when the Indians won it was a massacre. *Nigger*

9   Just being a Negro doesn't qualify you to understand the race situation any more than being sick makes you an expert on medicine.
The Back of the Bus [1962]

10   Those of us who weren't destroyed got stronger, got calluses on our souls. And now we're ready to change a system, a system where a white man can destroy a black man with a single word. Nigger. *Nigger, last lines*

11   If a man calls me a nigger, he is calling me something I am not. The nigger exists only in his own mind; therefore his mind is the nigger. I must feel sorry for such a man. *The Shadow That Scares Me [1968]*

Stuart Hall
1932–

1   Cultural identity is a matter of "becoming" as well as of "being." It belongs to the future as much as to the past. It is not something which already exists, transcending place, time, history and culture. Cultural identities come from somewhere, have histories. But, like everything which is historical, they undergo constant transformation. Far from being eternally fixed in some essentialized past, they are subject to the continuous "play" of history, culture and power. Far from being grounded in a mere "recovery" of the past, which is waiting to be found, and which, when found, will secure our sense of ourselves into eternity, identities are the names we give to the different ways we are positioned by, and position ourselves within, the narratives of the past.

Cultural Identity and Diaspora [1990]

Little Richard [Richard Wayne Penniman]
1932–

2   Keep a knockin' but you can't come in.   *Keep a Knockin' [1957]*

3   I am the originator. I am the emancipator. I am the architect of Rock and Roll.

Speech. Award of Merit, American Music Awards [1997]

Little Richard [Richard Wayne Penniman]
1932–

and

Dorothy LaBostrie
1928–2007

4   Awop-bop-a-loo-mop alop-bam-boom!   *Tutti Frutti [1955]*

5   I'm gonna rock it up!
I'm gonna shake it up!
I'm gonna ball it up!
I'm gonna Rip it Up!   *Rip It Up [1956]*

Little Richard [Richard Wayne Penniman]
1932–

and

Robert "Bumps" Blackwell
1918–1985

and

Enotris Johnson
Twentieth century

6   Well, long tall Sally, she's built for speed.   *Long Tall Sally [1956]*

Miriam Makeba
1932–2008

1   *[On being onstage:]* This is the one place where I am most at home,
where there is no exile.   *Makeba: My Story [1988]*

Christopher Okigbo
1932–1967

2   Before you, mother Idoto,
        naked I stand;
before your watery presence,
        a prodigal.   *Labyrinths [1961]. The Passage*

3   Eye open on the sea,
        eyes open, of the prodigal;
upward to heaven shoot
where stars will fall from.   *Watermaid [1961]*

4   Out of the solitude, the fleet,
Out of the solitude,
Intangible like silk thread of sunlight,
The eagles ride low,
Resplendent...resplendent;
And small birds sing in shadows,
Wobbling under their bones.   *Fragments of the Deluge [1962], VIII*

5   Is there...Is certainly there...
For as in sea-fever globules of fresh anguish
immense golden eggs empty of albumen
sink into our balcony...

How does one say NO in thunder?   *Lament of the Silent Sisters [1962], I*

6   I see many colours in the salt teeth of foam
Which is no where to face under the half-light
The rainbow they say is full of harmonies
We shall make a grey turn to face it.   *Lament of the Silent Sisters, IV*

7   Silences are melodies
Heard in retrospect.   *Lament of the Silent Sisters, V*

8   One dips one's tongue in the ocean;
Camps with the choir of inconstant
Dolphins, by shallow sand banks
Sprinkled with memories;
Extends one's branches of coral,
The branches extends in the senses'

Silence; this silence distills
in yellow melodies. *Lament of the Silent Sisters, V*

1   I was the sole witness to my homecoming. *Distances [1964], I*

Melvin Van Peebles   1932–

2   Come on feet
cruise for me
trouble aint no place to be
come on feet
do your thing
come on legs
come on run. *Sweet Sweetback's Baadasssss Song [1971]*

3   Black aint only beautiful its bad too.
Ain't Supposed to Die a Natural Death [1972]

Charles S[tevenson] Wright   1932–2008

4   Do not the auburn-haired gain a new sense of freedom as a blonde (see Miss Clairol)? Who can deny the madness of a redesigned nose (see Miami Beach)? Yes, indeed. A wild excitement engulfed me. My mirrored image reflected, in an occult fashion, a magnificent future.... The texture of my hair had changed. *The Wig [1966]*

5   All vanity is fear. *The Wig [Madame X]*

Andrew Young   1932–

6   Nothing is illegal if one hundred businessmen decide to do it.
From PAUL DICKSON, The Official Explanations [1980]

7   People who think education is expensive have never counted the cost of ignorance. *An Easy Burden [1996]*

8   The struggle to eliminate racism, war, and poverty is a burden, but in America, with all the freedom and opportunity afforded us under our Constitution, in the most productive society in human history, it is an easy burden if we undertake it together. *An Easy Burden, afterword*

Unita Blackwell   1933–

9   You don't have to think about courage to have it.... Courage is the most hidden thing from your eye or mind until after it's done. There's some inner something that tells you what's right. You know you have to do it to survive as a human being. You have no choice. *Barefootin' [2006]*

James Brown   1933–2006

1   Papa's Got a Brand New Bag   *Song title [1965]*

2   It's a Man's, Man's, Man's World   *Song title [1966]*

3   I feel good, I knew that I would, now.   *I Feel Good (I Got You) [1966]*

4   Say it loud: "I'm Black and I'm Proud."
    Some people say we've got a lot of malice,
    Some say it's a lot of nerve.
    But I say we won't quit moving
    Until we get what we deserve.
                    Say It Loud: I'm Black and I'm Proud [1968]

5   I don't want nobody to give me nothing.
    Open up the door, I'll get it myself.   *I Don't Want Nobody [1969]*

6   Stay on the scene
    Like a sex machine.   *Get Up (I Feel Like Being a) Sex Machine [1970]*[1]

7   Sometimes I feel so nice, good God!
    I jump back, I wanna kiss myself
    I've got soul, and I'm superbad.   *(Call Me) Super Bad [1970]*

8   Of course, once we — meaning Black performers — crossed the line, we
    could see our remnant shadows in the best of them! Elvis Presley, Mick Jagger,
    and Bruce Springsteen for openers, and then all the thousands who followed
    in their wake who emerged from the great encompassing Black Shadow of
    American culture.   *I Feel Good: A Memoir of a Life of Soul [2005]*

Joycelyn Elders [Minnie Lee Jones]   1933–

9   In regard to masturbation, I think that it is something that is a part of
    human sexuality and it's a part of something that perhaps should be taught.
    But we've not even taught our children the very basics. And I feel we have
    tried ignorance for a very long time and it's time we try education.
                Statement at United Nations World AIDS Day
                [December 1, 1994]

10   If I could be the "condom queen" and get every young person who is
    engaged in sex to use a condom in the United States, I would wear a crown
    on my head with a condom on it!
                Interview in the New York Times [January 30, 1994]

---

[1]With Bobby Byrd and Ronald Lenhoff.

1   We really need to get over this love affair with the fetus and start worrying about children.

Interview in the New York Times [January 30, 1994]

Myrlie Evers-Williams   1933–

2   Somewhere in Mississippi lives the man who murdered my husband. Sometimes at night when my new house in Claremont, California, is quiet and the children are in bed I think about him and wonder how he feels. I have never seriously admitted the possibility that he has forgotten what I can never forget, though I suppose that hours and even days may go by without his thinking of it. Still, it must be there, the memory of it, like a giant stain in one part of his mind, ready to spring to life whenever he sees a Negro, whenever his hate rises like a bitterness in the throat. He cannot escape it completely.

For Us the Living [1967][1]

3   We ask, too, Almighty, that where our paths seem blanketed by throngs of oppression and riddled by pangs of despair, we ask for your guidance toward the light of deliverance and that the vision of those who came before us and dreamed of this day, that we recognize that their visions still inspire us. They are a great cloud of witnesses unseen by the naked eye, but all around us, thankful that their living was not in vain.

Invocation delivered at the second presidential inauguration of Barack Obama [January 21, 2013]

Louis Farrakhan [Louis Eugene Walcott]   1933–

4   Only those who wish to be led to hell, or to their doom, will follow Malcolm. The die is set, and Malcolm shall not escape, especially after such evil, foolish talk about his benefactor [Elijah Muhammad] in trying to rob him of the divine glory which Allah has bestowed upon him. Such a man as Malcolm is worthy of death, and would have met with death if it had not been for Muhammad's confidence in Allah for victory over the enemies.

Malcolm — Muhammad's Biggest Hypocrite. Muhammad Speaks [December 4, 1964]

5   The current American way of life can only produce an apparent unity among Caucasians, because it negates the diversity and beauty of the non-white population. You can never achieve unity, or E Pluribus Unum, in this country under the doctrine of white supremacy.

A Torchlight for America [1993]

---

[1]In 1964, Byron De la Beckwith was acquitted of the murder of Medgar W. Evers. He was retried and found guilty of murder in 1994 and sentenced to life in prison.

1   We are standing on the blood of our ancestors. We are standing on the blood of those who died in the middle passage, who died in the fields and swamps of America, who died hanging from trees in the South, who died in the cells of their jailers, who died on the highways and who died in the fratricidal conflict that rages within our community. We are standing on the sacrifice of the lives of those heroes, our great men and women, that we today may accept the responsibility that life imposes upon each traveler who comes this way.

Speech at the Million Man March on Washington
[October 16, 1995]

2   Black men, we got to stop what we're doing where it is. We cannot continue the destruction of our lives and the destruction of our community. But that change can't come until we feel sorry.

Speech at the Million Man March on Washington

3   I pledge that from this day forward I will strive to love my brother as I love myself. I, from this day forward will strive to improve myself spiritually, morally, mentally, socially, politically, and economically for the benefit of myself, my family, and my people.

Pledge, Million Man March on Washington

4   We've kneeled-in, crawled-in, prayed-in, lied-in, slept-in, but still we're out. If you want to get what you want, we've got to start with a contract...a covenant, with us.

State of the Black Union. Speech [February 26, 2005]

Ernest J[ames] Gaines   1933–

5   He did not like the way he was feeling. He was feeling empty — unable to recognize things, unable to associate himself with things. He did not like being unable to recognize the graves. He did not like being unable to associate with the people. He did not like being unable to go to church with his aunt, or to drink in the sideroom with Brother. What then? Was it to be there? No, that was not it either. If neither there nor here, neither the living nor the dead, then what?

Catherine Carmier [1964], ch. 38

6   Question everything. Every stripe, every star, every word spoken. Everything.   *Bloodline [1968]. The Sky Is Gray*

7   There will always be men struggling to change, and there will always be those who are controlled by the past.   *Interview [1972]*[1]

---

[1]From *Conversations with Ernest Gaines* [1995], edited by John Lowe.

1   This earth is yours and don't let that man out there take it from you. It's yours because your people's bones lays in it; it's yours because their sweat and their blood done drenched this earth.

The Autobiography of Miss Jane Pittman [1973], bk. II,
Reconstruction [Ned]

2   There's an old oak tree up in the quarters.... and it has seen much much, and it knows much much. And I'm not ashamed to say I have talked to it, and I'm not crazy either. It's not necessary craziness when you talk to trees and rivers. But a different thing when you talk to ditches and bayous. A ditch ain't nothing, and a bayou ain't too much either.... But when you talk to an oak tree that's been here all these years, and knows more than you'll ever know, it's not craziness; it's just the nobility you respect.

The Autobiography of Miss Jane Pittman, bk. III,
The Plantation

3   Anytime a child is born, the old people look in his face and ask him if he's the One.

The Autobiography of Miss Jane Pittman, bk. IV, The Quarters

4   I was paralyzed. Paralyzed. Yes, I had a mouth, but I didn't have a voice. I had legs, but I couldn't move. I had arms, but I couldn't lift them up to you. It took a man to do these things, and I wasn't a man. I was just some other brutish animal who could cheat, steal, rob, kill — but not stand.... They had branded that in us from the time of slavery.

In My Father's House [1978] [Phillip]

5   I did it for them back there under them trees. I did it 'cause that tractor is getting closer and closer to that graveyard, and I was scared if I didn't do it, one day that tractor was go'n come in there and plow up them graves, getting rid of all the proof that we ever was. Like now they trying to get rid of all proof that black people ever farmed this land with plows and mules — like if they had nothing from the starten but motor machines. Sure, one day they will get rid of the proof that we ever was, but they ain't go'n do it while I'm still here.

A Gathering of Old Men [1983] [Johnny Paul]

6   Sometimes you got to hurt something to help something. Sometimes you have to plow under one thing in order for something else to grow.

A Gathering of Old Men [Russ]

7   What justice would there be to take this life? Justice, gentlemen? Why, I would just as soon put a hog in the electric chair as this.

A Lesson Before Dying [1993], ch. 1
[court appointed attorney]

1   good by mr wigin tell them im strong tell them im a man.

A Lesson Before Dying, ch. 29 [Jefferson]

2   Why is it that, as a culture, we are more comfortable seeing two men holding guns than holding hands?[1]

Quincy Jones   1933–

3   Check your egos at the door.

Sign posted outside "USA for Africa" recording studio [1985]

4   When I was young, I lived on the run, trying to make sure I wasn't missing anything. But I kept running into myself coming from the opposite direction — and he didn't know where he was going either.

Interview. Playboy [July 1990]

Samora Machel[2]   1933–1986

5   Solidarity is not an act of charity but mutual aid between forces fighting for the same end.

Speech, National Conference of Solidarity [March 25, 1973][3]

6   Divesting ourselves of the exploitative ideology and culture and adopting and living, in each detail of everyday life, the ideology required for the revolution is the essence of the fight to create the new man. It is not the personal fight of one man wrapped up in himself. It is a mass struggle in which we accept criticism and do self-criticism, purifying ourselves in their fire, which makes us conscious of the path to be followed and fills us with hatred for the negative values of the old society.

Speech, Conkary [January 1973]

7   The exploiters' power is to oppress the people. Our power is the power of the people.   *Speech [1974]*

8   We are declaring war on the enemy within.

Speech, Maputo [March 18, 1980]

James H[oward] Meredith   1933–

9   I am making this move in what I consider the interest of and for the benefit of: (1) my country, (2) my race, (3) my family, and (4) myself. I am familiar with the probable difficulties involved in such a move as I am

---

[1]From *Conversations with Ernest Gaines* [1995], edited by JOHN LOWE.

[2]From *Samora Machel: African Revolutionary* [1985], edited by BARRY MUNSLOW. Translated by MICHAEL WOLFERS.

[3]*The African Liberation Reader: The Strategy of Liberation*, edited by AQUINO DE BRAGANÇA and IMMANUEL MAURICE WALLERSTEIN.

undertaking and I am fully prepared to pursue it all the way to a degree from the University of Mississippi.

> *Letter to Thurgood Marshall requesting legal representation*
> *in his fight for admission to the University of Mississippi*
> *[January 29, 1961][1]*

[Bonny] Mack Rice

1933–

1   Mustang Sally, think you better slow your Mustang down.
You been running all over town now,
I'm a have to put your flat feet on the ground.   *Mustang Sally [1965]*

[Bonny] Mack Rice

1933–

and

Luther Ingram

1937–2007

2   If you disrespect everybody that you run into
How in the world do you think anybody's supposed to respect you?
Respect Yourself [1971]

Nina Simone [Eunice Waymon]

1933–2003

3   I want a little sugar in my bowl,
I want a little sweetness down in my soul.
I Want a Little Sugar in My Bowl [1962]

4   Alabama's got me so upset
Tennessee made me lose my rest
And everybody knows about Mississippi Goddam.
Mississippi Goddam [1964]

5   You don't have to live next to me
Just give me my equality.   *Mississippi Goddam*

6   My skin is black
My arms are long
My hair is wooly
My back is strong.   *Four Women [1965]*

7   I'm awfully bitter these days,
Because my parents were slaves.   *Four Women*

8   An artist's duty, as far as I'm concerned, is to reflect the times.
Unreleased video interview [c.1970], Definition of an Artist,
Protest Anthology [2008]

---

[1]From CONSTANCE BAKER MOTLEY, *Equal Justice Under the Law* [1998].

Cicely Tyson
1933–

1   I did not set out to become a role model. I did set out to become the best possible actress I could be.

From Brian Lanker, *I Dream A World [1989]*

[Clerow] Flip Wilson
1933–1998

2   The devil made me do it.   *Trademark phrase*

[Henry Louis] Hank Aaron
1934–

3   I'm not trying to make anyone forget Babe Ruth. I just want them to remember Henry Aaron.   *Quoted in TIME [September 23, 1973]*

4   It's the only way I've ever had of dealing with things like fastballs and bigotry — keep swinging at them.   *I Had a Hammer [1991]*

5   I never doubted my ability, but when you hear all your life that you're inferior, it makes you wonder if the other guys have something you've never seen before. If they do, I'm still looking for it.   *I Had a Hammer*

6   *[On Jackie Robinson:]* I don't know how he withstood the things he did without lashing back. I've been through a lot in my time, and I consider myself to be a patient man, but I know I couldn't have done what Jackie did. I don't think anybody else could have done it. Somehow, though, Jackie had the strength to suppress his instincts, to sacrifice his pride for his people's.

Essay in TIME [June 14, 1999]

Amiri Baraka [LeRoi Jones]
1934–

7   The idea of "a revolution" had been foreign to me. It was one of those inconceivably "romantic" and/or hopeless ideas that we Norteamericanos have been taught since public school to hold up to the cold light of "reason." That reason being whatever repugnant lie our usurious "ruling class" had paid their journalists to disseminate. The reason that allows that voting, in a country where the parties are exactly the same, can be made to assume the gravity of actual moral engagement.

Cuba Libre [1961]

8   Saturday mornings we listened to *Red Lantern* &
        his undersea folk.
At 11, *Let's Pretend*/& we did/& I, the poet, still
        do, Thank God!   *In Memory of Radio [1961]*

9   It's so diffuse
being alive. Suddenly one is aware
        that nobody really gives a damn.

Look for You Yesterday, Here You Come Today [1961]

1   Lately, I've become accustomed to the way
The ground opens up and envelops me
Each time I go out to walk the dog.

Preface to a Twenty-Volume Suicide Note [1961]

2   Blues as a verse form has as much social reference as any poetry, except for the strict lyric, and that also is found in blues. Love, sex, tragedy in interpersonal relationships, death, travel, loneliness, etc., are all social phenomena. And perhaps these are the things which actually create a poetry, as things, or ideas: there can be no such thing as poetry (or blues) exclusive of the matter it proposes to be about.

Blues People [1963]

3   A whole people of neurotics, struggling to keep from being sane. And the only thing that would cure the neurosis would be your murder. Simple as that. I mean if I murdered you, then other white people would begin to understand me. You understand? No. I guess not. If Bessie Smith had killed some white people she wouldn't have needed that music. She could have talked very straight and plain about the world. No metaphors. No grunts. No wiggles in the dark of her soul. Just straight two and two are four. Money. Power. Luxury. Like that.

Dutchman [1964] [Clay]

4   We are unfair, and unfair
We are black magicians, black art
s we make in black labs of the heart.

The fair are
fair, and death
ly white

The day will not save them
and we own
the night.   *State/Meant* [1965][1]

5   In America, black is a country.   *Home* [1966]

6   We are beautiful people
with african imaginations
full of masks and dances and swelling chants
with african eyes, and noses, and arms,
though we sprawl in gray chains in a place
full of winters when what we want is sun.   *Ka 'Ba* [1969][2]

---

[1]From *The Amiri Baraka Reader* [1991].

[2]From *Amiri Baraka/Le Roi Jones, Selected Poetry* [1979].

1   Time to get
together
time to be one strong fast black energy space
        one pulsating positive magnetism, rising
time to get up and
be
come
be
come.   *It's Nation Time [1970]*[1]

2   Walk it slow
where you go
walk it slow ...
We in the world
Poor as dirt
Don't get some rhythm
Somebody'll get hurt
the world is black
the world is green
the world is red, yellow, brown
the world is mean.   *3rd World Blues [1979]*

3   The name change seemed fitting to me ... and not just the meaning of the name Blessed Prince, but the idea that I was now literally being changed into a blacker being. I was discarding my "slave name" and embracing blackness.

                         The Autobiography of LeRoi Jones [1984]

4   Who own them buildings
Who got the money
Who think you funny
Who locked you up
Who own the papers
Who owned the slave ship
Who run the army
Who the fake president
Who the ruler
Who the banker

      Who/ Who/ Who/

                      Somebody Blew Up America [2001]

---

[1]From *The Amiri Baraka Reader [1991]*.

Willie [Lewis] Brown, Jr. 1934–

1 Give me back my delegation!
Speech demanding seating of California delegates supporting
George McGovern, Democratic National Convention [1972]

2 *[On American politics:]* A lie unanswered becomes the truth within twenty-four hours. *Interview. New York Times [October 31, 1988]*

Austin Clarke 1934–

3 Money and love flow past us, like the waves on that beach with that inner tube that drowned at sea; or was lost. And no man came to put the voiceless conch-shell to his lips. *The Origin of Waves [1997]*

4 I find that I live the past as if it is the present. They mean the same to me. *The Origin of Waves [Tim]*

5 My name is Mary. People in this Village call me Mary-Mathilda. Or Tilda, for short. To my mother I was Mary-girl. My names I am christen with are Mary Gertrude Mathilda, but I don't use Gertrude, because my maid has the same name. My surname that people 'bout-here uses, is either Paul, or Bellfeels, depending who you speak to . . .
The Polished Hoe [2002], opening lines

Roberto Clemente 1934–1972

6 Accomplishment is something you can't buy. If you have a chance and don't make the most of it, you are wasting your time on this earth.
Speech [October 1971]

Henry Dumas 1934–1968

7 If an eagle be imprisoned
On the back of a coin
And the coin is tossed into the sky,
That coin will spin,
That coin will flutter,
But the eagle will never fly. *America [1974][1]*

8 Beloved,
I have to adore the earth:
The wind must have heard
your voice once.
It echoes and sings like you. *Love Song [1974][1]*

[1]From *Knees of a Natural Man: The Selected Poetry of Henry Dumas* [1989].

1   On hands and knees, the ocean begs up the beach,
       And falls at your feet
   I have to adore
   the mirror of the earth
   You have taught her well
   how to be beautiful.   *Love Song*[1]

2   Hold it people, I see a flying saucer comin
       guess I wait and see
   Yeah, a spaceship comin
       guess I wait and see
   All I know they might look just like me.   *Outer Space Blues [1974]*[1]

3   One of the greatest roles
   ever created by Western man
   has been the role of "Negro."
   One of the greatest actors
   to play the role has been
   the "Nigger."   *Thought [1974]*[1]

4   Son, you are in the house of generations. Every African who lives in America has a part of his soul in this ark. God has called you, and I shall anoint you.
       Goodbye Sweetwater: New & Selected Stories [1988].
       Ark of Bones [Old Man]

Audre[y] Lorde   1934–1992

5   If you come as softly
   as wind within the trees
   you may hear what I hear
   see what sorrow sees.   *The First Cities [1968]. If You Come Softly*

6   I is the total black
   being spoken
   from the earth's inside.   *Coal [1962]. Coal*

7   when we speak we are afraid
   our words will not be heard
   nor welcomed
   but when we are silent
   we are still afraid

---

[1]From *Knees of a Natural Man: The Selected Poetry of Henry Dumas* [1989].

So it is better to speak
remembering
we were never meant to survive.
> *The Black Unicorn [1978]. A Litany for Survival*

1   When we look away from the importance of the erotic in the development and sustenance of our power, or when we look away from ourselves as we satisfy our erotic needs in concert with others, we use each other as objects of satisfaction rather than share our joy in the satisfying.
> *Uses of the Erotic as Power. Paper delivered at the Berkshire Conference on the History of Women, Mount Holyoke College [August 25, 1978]*

2   The Master's Tools Will Never Dismantle the Master's House.
> *Title of essay [1979]*

3   The master's tools will never dismantle the master's house. They may allow us temporarily to beat him at his own game, but they will never enable us to bring about a genuine change.
> *Comments at Second Sex Conference, New York [September 29, 1979]*

4   When I dare to be powerful, to use my strength in the service of my vision, then it becomes less important whether or not I am unafraid.
> *The Cancer Journals [1980]*

5   I have always wanted to be both man and woman, to incorporate the strongest and richest parts of my mother and father within/into me — to share valleys and mountains upon my body the way the earth does in hills and peaks.
> *Zami: A New Spelling of My Name: A Biomythography [1982], prologue*

6   The white fathers told us: I think, therefore I am. The Black mother within each of us — the poet — whispers in our dreams: I feel, therefore I can be free.
> *Sister Outsider [1984]. Poetry Is Not a Luxury*

7   Your silence will not protect you.
> *Sister Outsider. The Transformation of Silence into Language and Action*

8   Unity does not require that we be identical to each other. Black women are not one great vat of homogenized chocolate milk.
> *I Am Your Sister [1985]*

9   Racism. Cancer. In both cases, to win the aggressor must conquer, but the resisters need only survive.
> *A Burst of Light [1988]*

1   I am a Black Lesbian Feminist Warrior Poet Mother, stronger for all
my identities, and I am indivisible.
Speech at the Bill Whitehead Award Ceremony [May 15, 1990]

Alvin F[rancis] Poussaint   1934–

2   Through systematic oppression, the black American has been effec-
tively castrated by white America.
A Negro Psychiatrist Explains the Negro Psyche.
New York Times [August 20, 1967]

3   It is as if in a sheer mood of desperation, blacks seek to become a part
of the white mainstream and obtain so-called manhood by turning to physical brutality and petty crimes against one another. Violence can be a
potent drug for the oppressed person.   *Why Blacks Kill Blacks [1972]*

Sonia Sanchez [Wilsonia Driver]   1934–

4   i have returned
leaving behind me
all those hide and
seek faces peeling
with freudian dreams.
this is for real.
         black
      niggers
         my beauty.   *Homecoming [1969]*

5   i am a blk /wooOOOOMAN
my face.
         my brown
      bamboo/colored
blk/berry/face
will spread itself over
this western hemisphere and
be remembered.   *We a BaddDDD People [1970], introduction*

6   blues ain't culture
         they sounds of
oppression
         against the white man's
shit.   *We a BaddDDD People. liberation/poem*

7   it's america's
most famous past time

> and the name
> of the game
> ain't baseball.
>
> *We a BaddDDD People. on watching a world series game*

1   forgive me if i laugh
     you are so sure of love
     you are so young
     and i too old to learn of love.   *Homegirls & Handgrenades [1984]. Ballad*

2   let me wear the day
     well so when it reaches you
     you will enjoy it.   *Homegirls & Handgrenades. Haiku*

3   we must learn to suckle life not
     bombs and rhetoric.
>   *Homegirls & Handgrenades. Reflections after the
>   June 12th March for Disarmament*

4   how does one scream in thunder?
>   *Under a Soprano Sky [1987]. Elegy (for MOVE and Philadelphia)*

5   And a new earth will rise. For we have endured and we are in
     spite of our wounds. In spite of our sorrow songs. We are. And shall be.
>   *Under a Soprano Sky. For Black History Month/February 1986*

6   under a soprano sky, a woman sings,
     lovely as chandeliers.   *Under a Soprano Sky. Title poem*

7   I shall become a collector of me.
     AND PUT MEAT ON MY SOUL.
>   *Wounded in the House of a Friend [1995]*

Wole Soyinka [Akinwande Oluwole Soyinka]   1934–

8   Child, your hand is pure as sorrow
     Free me of the endless burden,
     Let this gourd, let this gourd
     Break, beyond my hearth.   *A Dance of the Forests [1960] [Dead Woman]*

9   Trouble me no further. The fooleries of beings whom I have fashioned
     closer to me weary and distress me. Yet I must persist, knowing that nothing
     is ever altered. My secret is my eternal burden — to pierce the encrustations
     of soul-deadening habit, and bare the mirror of original nakedness —
     knowing full well, it is all futility.

A Dance of the Forests [Forest Head]

1   But the skin of progress
Masks, unknown, the spotted wolf of sameness.

The Lion and the Jewel [1963]. Night [Baroka]

2   Suddenly the world has run amok and left you alone and sane behind.

Kongi's Harvest [1965] [Danlola]

3   The artist has always functioned in African society, as the record of the mores and experiences of his society *and* as the voice of vision in his own time. It is time for him to respond to this essence of himself.

Speech, The Writer in a Modern African State [1967]

4   Books and all forms of writing have always been objects of terror to those who seek to suppress truth.

The Man Died [1972]

5   The man dies in all who keep silent in the face of tyranny.

The Man Died

6   You think you've stamped it all out but it's always lurking under the surface somewhere.   *Death and the King's Horseman [1975], act 2 [Pilkings]*

7   The sprawling, undulating terrain is all of Aké. More than mere loyalty to the parsonage gave birth to a puzzle, and a resentment, that God should choose to look down on his own pious station, the parsonage compound, from the profane heights of Itoko.

Aké [1981], opening lines

8   Every act of racial terror, with its vastly increasing sophistication of style and escalation in human loss, is itself an acknowledgement of improved knowledge and respect for the potential of what is feared, an acknowledgement of the sharpening tempo of triumph by the victimized.

Nobel lecture [December 8, 1986]

9   The purpose is not really to indict the past, but to summon it to the attention of a suicidal, anachronistic present. To say to that mutant present: you are a child of those centuries of lies, distortion and opportunism in high places, even among the holy of holies of intellectual objectivity. But the world is growing up, while you willfully remain a child, a stubborn, self-destructive child, with certain destructive powers, but a child nevertheless. And to say to the world, to call attention to its own historic passage of lies — as yet unabandoned by some — which sustains the evil precocity of this child. . . . Demand that it rescues itself, by concrete acts, from the stigma of being the willful parent of a monstrosity, especially as that monstrous child still draws material nourishment, breath, and human recognition from the strengths and devises of that world, with an umbilical cord which stretches across oceans, even across the cosmos via so-called programs of technological co-operation. We are saying very simply but urgently: Sever that cord.

Nobel Lecture

Diahann Carroll [Carol Diann Johnson]

1935–

1   [*Advice to black actresses:*] If you want to be an actor move to New York City. Don't go to Los Angeles. They have a machine out there, it makes little blonde girls, with long stringy hair, and they have wonderful careers.

The HistoryMakers. Interview with Diahann Carroll broadcast on public television [May 7, 2005]

[Leroy] Eldridge Cleaver

1935–1998

2   I became a rapist. To refine my technique and modus operandi, I started out by practicing on black girls in the ghetto . . . and when I considered myself smooth enough, I crossed the tracks and sought out white prey. . . . Rape was an insurrectionary act.   *Soul on Ice [1968]. On Becoming*

3   The price of hating other human beings is loving oneself less.

Soul on Ice. On Becoming

4   All the gods are dead except the god of war.

Soul on Ice. Four Vignettes, The "Christ" and His Teachings

5   You're either part of the solution or you're part of the problem.

Speech, San Francisco [1968]

Ron[ald] Dellums

1935–

6   Everything we have struggled for remains under attack — and in some measure it always will. Some will always reject equality as a first principle and will do no more than pay lip service to the ideal that the common good means including everybody. They will persist in the belief that individualism is a paramount virtue, and that government should not seek to level the playing field or break down the walls against opportunity. Some will always believe that war is the inevitable solution to international affairs, and will refuse to commit to strategies that avoid militarism and conflict as early or first options. Some will always seek to consume rather than preserve the environment, indifferent to our responsibility to be careful stewards of the planet for subsequent generations. And so it will go.   *Lying Down with the Lions [2000]*

James A[lexander] Forbes, Jr.

1935–

7   We must listen to the black folk, the white folk, the poor folk, the rich folk. We need to know what marginal folk are saying, what corporate rulers are saying. You can't preach if you don't know what the folks are saying, not only with their mouths, but with the conditions of their lives.

The Holy Spirit & Preaching [1989]

8   Every human being is a researcher and we are all researching with our lives the issue of whether, when the umbilical cord was severed, that was a

friendly gesture or not. The way we live our lives is our report on our research. And your spirituality is your report on your research as to whether that was a fortuitous moment or the beginning of deep tragedy for us.

Interview, Riverside Church, New York [December 18, 1996][1]

1   Oh, how foolish it is to become so attached to our things that we think that will satisfy us. To trust in things as adequate to keep us happy.

No Time for Foolishness

Earl Graves, Sr.   1935–

2   Business was the white man's game. Well, basketball was once a white man's game, too.   *How to Succeed in Business Without Being White [1997]*

3   Money makes people listen. When you have it, then you have something others want and need. When you don't, you become invisible.

How to Succeed in Business Without Being White

Richard Hunt   1935–

4   Art does not succeed in time by being more personal, different, or even original than any other. It succeeds by remaining intact, and... containing within its form ideas and associations, which can continue to stimulate people who view it.   *Artist's statement [1967]*

Vernon Jordan   1935–

5   My view on all this business about race is never to get angry, no, but to get even. You don't take it out in anger; you take it out in achievement.

Interview. New York Times [July 16, 2000]

6   Black people have done wonderful things for this country (saved its soul, in fact), and we have been an example to the world in the process. That should never be forgotten, even as we continue to press ahead, in our many and varied ways, toward our future. If we did so much when we had so little, think of what we can do now that we have so much more.

Vernon Can Read [2001]

Earl Lovelace   1935–

7   Look, and feel anger building within you, bulging your neck veins, bristling your neck hairs, feel the blood of anger thumping in your ears—this is your city too. On those hills there, it is not only poverty. It is disorder; it is crime; it is a kind of fear, and a way of thinking; it is as if there is a special, narrow meaning to life, as if life has no significance beyond the primary

---

[1]From CORNEL WEST, *Restoring Hope* [1997].

struggles for a bed to sleep in, something to quiet the intestines, and moments of sexual gratification: indeed, it is as if all Gods have fallen and there is nothing to look up to, no shrine to worship at, and man is left only bare flesh and naked passions. *While Gods Are Falling [1965], ch. 1*

[Eugene] Gene [Booker] McDaniels 1935–2011

1   Possession is the motivation
That's hanging up the goddamn nation
Looks like we always end up in a rut.
Trying to make it real
But compared to what? *Compared to What [1969]*

Mighty Sparrow [Slinger Francisco] 1935–

2   Jean and Dinah, Rosita and Clementina
'Round the corner posing,
Bet your life is something they selling
And if you catch them broken
You can get it all for nothing
Don't make no row.
The Yankees gone and Sparrow take over now. *Jean and Dinah [1956]*

3   But if they know they didn't want Federation
And they know they don't want to unite as one
Independence was at the door, why didn't they speak before
This is no time to say you ain't Federating no more. *Federation [1959]*

4   Hoo-de, hoo de oh! *Congo Man [1965]*

5   Drunk and disorderly
Always in custody
Drunk and disorderly
Friends and family
All dem fed up with me cause I
drunk and disorderly. *Drunk and Disorderly [1972]*

Bob [Robert Parris] Moses 1935–

6   This is Mississippi, the middle of the iceberg. "Michael row the boat ashore, Alleluia; Christian brothers don't be slow, Alleluia; Mississippi next to go, Alleluia." This is a tremor from the middle of the iceberg—from a stone the builders rejected.

Letter from jail to the Student Nonviolent Coordinating Committee [November 1, 1961]

1   The questions that we think face the country are questions which in one sense are much deeper than civil rights. They're questions which go very much to the bottom of mankind and people. They're questions which have repercussions in terms of a whole international affairs and relations. They're questions which go to the very root of our society. What kind of society will we be?
Speech, Stanford University [April 24, 1964][1]

2   The most urgent social issue affecting poor people and people of color is economic access. In today's world, economic access and full citizenship depend crucially on math and science literacy. I believe that the absence of math literacy in urban and rural communities throughout this country is an issue as urgent as the lack of registered Black voters in Mississippi was in 1961.
Radical Equations [2001]

Floyd Patterson   1935–2006

3   It's easy to do anything in victory. It's in defeat that a man reveals himself.
The Loser. Esquire [March 1964][2]

Reverend Ike [Frederick Eikerenkoetter]   1935–2009

4   Nothing is free, not even the air you breathe. Before you receive another breath, you must give up the one you have.
Rev. Ike's Secrets for Health, Happiness, and Prosperity — for You! [1982]

5   If it's that difficult for a rich man to get into heaven think how terrible it must be for a poor man to get in. He doesn't even have a bribe for the gatekeeper.
Quoted in obituary. New York Times [July 29, 2009]

6   The best thing you can do for the poor is not be one of them.
Attributed

Ivan Van Sertima   1935–2009

7   The African presence in America before Columbus is of importance not only to African and American history but to the history of world civilizations. It provides further evidence that all great civilizations and races are heavily indebted to one another and that no race has a monopoly on enterprise and inventive genius.
They Came Before Columbus [1976]

---

[1]From *African-American Orators* [1996], edited by Richard W. Leeman.
[2]From Gay Talese, *The Gay Talese Reader* [2003].

William Julius Wilson   1935–

1   In the economic sphere, class has become more important than race in determining black access to privilege and power.

The Declining Significance of Race [1978]

2   A history of discrimination and oppression created a huge black underclass, and the technological and economic revolutions have combined to insure it a permanent status.   *The Declining Significance of Race*

3   The person who scored well on an SAT will not necessarily be the best doctor or the best lawyer or the best businessman. These tests do not measure character, leadership, creativity, perseverance.

Interview. Mother Jones [September/October 1996]

Marion Barry, Jr.   1936–

4   Why should black people feel elated when we see men eating on the moon when millions of blacks and poor whites don't have enough money to buy food here on earth?

Statement published in the Baltimore Afro-American [July 22, 1969]

5   Bitch set me up.

On discovering he was under surveillance while smoking crack cocaine [January 18, 1990][1]

6   [On being reelected for a fourth term as Mayor:] Get over it. I'm the best person for Washington.

Quoted in the Washington Post [September 15, 1994]

Sonny Carson [Mwlina Imiri Abubadika]   1936–2002

7   [On his first day of school:] Certainly not then, but years later, I began to perceive of this as the beginning of the most magnificent kind of programming that's ever been devised by any system in the history of mankind. For then it begins. White, white, white, white.... white, white, white, all through the years: a succession of the Washingtons, the Lincolns, the Jeffersons, the Shermans, the Lees — and, occasionally a Booker T. Washington and a George Washington Carver.... This, then, was the beginning of my miseducation.

The Education of Sonny Carson [1974]

8   No justice, no peace. You don't give us any justice, then there ain't going to be no peace.   *Quoted in the New York Times [July 6, 1987]*

[1]Barry was then serving his third term as mayor of Washington, D.C.

Wilt[on Norman] Chamberlain
1936–1999

1   Nobody roots for Goliath.

Reply when asked if winning the championship would gain him public support [1967][1]

2   If I had to count my sexual encounters, I would be closing in on twenty thousand women. Yes, that's correct — twenty thousand different ladies.
A View from Above [1991]

Lucille Clifton
1936–2010

3   these hips have never been enslaved,
they go where they want to go
they do what they want to do.
these hips are mighty hips.
these hips are magic hips.
i have known them
to put a spell on a man and
spin him like a top!
homage to my hips [1980]

4   listen,
you a wonder.
you a city
of a woman.
you got a geography
of your own.
What the Mirror Said [1980]

5   they ask me to remember
but they want me to remember
their memories
and i keep on remembering
mine.
Why Some People Be Mad at Me Sometimes [1988]

6   may the tide
that is entering even now
the lip of our understanding
carry you out
beyond the face of fear.
Blessing the Boats [1991]

7   i wish them cramps.
i wish them a strange town
and the last tampon.
i wish them no 7-11.
Wishes for Sons [1991]

[1]From *Bartlett's Book of Anecdotes* [2000], edited by CLIFTON FADIMAN and ANDRÉ BERNARD.

1 loaded like spoons
into the belly of Jesus
where we lay for weeks for months
in the sweat and stink
of our own breathing
Jesus

Slaveships [1996]

2 to be alive.   i am alive and furious
Blessed be even this?

Dialysis [2000]

Johnnetta B[etsch] Cole   1936–

3 Soul is the ability to feel oneness with all black people.
*Culture: Negro, Black and Nigger. The Black Scholar
[June 1970]*

4 Although the ideologies of racism and sexism are to a great degree
inherited, they are not genetic.   *Conversations [1993]*

5 In advocating education as the most viable means of empowerment,
I mean much more than our people's ability to read and write. I mean a
process of intellectual development that should last as long as there is life
within us.   *Conversations*

Marva Collins   1936–

6 If you raise your fist and yell at someone today, he may give you something because he feels sorry for you or is frightened of you, but what are you
going to do tomorrow and the next day and ten years from now? I am convinced that the real solution is education.   *The Marva Collins Way [1982]*

7 The one question that ought to be asked on a teaching application is:
do you love children?   *The Marva Collins Way*

Jayne Cortez   1936–2012

8 i am new york city
of the brown spit and soft tomatoes
give me my confetti of flesh
my marquee of false nipples
my sideshow of open beaks
in my nose of soot
in my ox bled eyes
in my ears of saturday night specials.   *I Am New York City [1973]*[1]

---

[1]From JAYNE CORTEZ, *Coagulations: New and Selected Poems* [1984].

1   And if we don't fight
if we don't resist
if we don't organize and unify and
get the power to control our own lives
Then we will wear
the exaggerated look of captivity
the stylized look of submission
the bizarre look of suicide
the dehumanized look of fear
and the decomposed look of repression
forever and ever and ever
And there it is.

There It Is [1982][1]

2   if the drum is a woman
don't abuse your drum.

If the Drum Is a Woman [1984][1]

3   To breathe clean air
to drink pure water to plant new crops
to soak up the rain to wash off the stink
to hold this body and soul together in peace
that's it
Push back the catastrophes.

Push Back the Catastrophes [1990]

Frankétienne [Franck Étienne]

1936–

4   The night is thick, the night is tough. But still our hope
is kept safe in the depths of our hearts.

Dezafi (Cockfight Marathon) [1975][2]

5   Unemployment is like a curse. The gangrene of empty hours. The wounds of bad luck. The leprosy of insomnia. Boredom, grief, depression, melancholy, paranoia, financial difficulties, economic problems, unsuspected hazards and all misfortune accumulate suddenly in the cracks of everyday life.

Gun Blesse America [1995][3]

6   The only thing not chaotic is death.

Quoted in the New York Times [April 30, 2011]

7   Every day I use the dialect of lunatic hurricanes.
I speak the madness of clashing winds.

---

[1]From JAYNE CORTEZ, *Coagulations: New and Selected Poems* [1984].

[2]From *Open Gate: An Anthology of Haitian Creole Poetry* [2001], edited by PAUL LARAQUE and JACK HIRSCHMAN. Translated by JACK HIRSCHMAN and BOADIBA.

[3]Translated by TRACY ELIZABETH ROBEY, NATALIE HAMPSHIRE, ALISON DYKMAN, MIKE BUTH, BEAU PLATTE, and SOFIA OHLMAN under the supervision of Professor ISABELLE CATA, Grand Valley State University; revised and edited by JEAN JONASSAINT. From *Journal of Haitian Studies* [Spring 2008].

Every evening I use the patois of furious rains.
I speak the fury of waters in flood.   *Ripe to Burst [2013]*[1]

1   Fundamentally, life is tension. Towards something. Towards someone. Towards oneself. Towards the point of maturity where the old and the new, death and birth untangle. And every being is realized in part in the search for its double, a search which may, in a sense, merge with the intensity of a need, a desire, and an infinite quest.   *Ripe to Burst*

Donald Goines   1936–1974

2   The white powder looked innocent as it lay there in the open, but this was the drug of the damned, the curse of mankind. Heroin, what some call smack, others junk, snow, stuff, poison, horse — it had different names, but it still had the same effect. To all of its users — to all of the dopefiends in the Detroit ghetto — it was slow death.   *Dopefiend [1971]*

3   Most of the prisoners who came out of the wards seemed happy to be going. . . . All of them had something in common: they were either smiling or laughing loudly. A passerby who didn't know would have thought the men were going home. He would never guess that they were all on their way to the state prison. But that was the way the county jail affected a man. After staying there any length of time, the men were glad to go to prison, just to get away from the sorry food, the sorry sleeping conditions, the unwholesome closeness of a lot of men shoved inside a small ward with nothing to occupy their minds.   *White Man's Justice, Black Man's Grief [1973]*

Virginia Hamilton   1936–2002

4   The highest law for us is to live for one another.
                    The Planet of Junior Brown [1971] [Buddy]

5   All others of his family were asleep in the house. To be by himself in the perfect quiet was reason enough for him to wake up way early. Alone for half an hour, he could believe he had been chosen to remain forever suspended, facing the hills. He could pretend there was nothing terrible behind him, above his head. Arms outstretched, picture-framed by pine uprights supporting the gallery roof, he was M. C. Higgins, higher than everything.
                    M. C. Higgins the Great [1974]

6   They say the people could fly. Say that long ago in Africa, some of the people knew magic. And they would walk up on the air like climbing up on a gate. And they flew like blackbirds over the fields.
                    The People Could Fly [1985]

[1]Translated by ANDRÉ NAFFIS-SAHELY.

Barbara C[harline] Jordan
1936–1996

1   "We, the people." It is a very eloquent beginning. But when that document was completed on the seventeenth of September in 1787, I was not included in that "We, the people." I felt somehow for many years that George Washington and Alexander Hamilton just left me out by mistake. But through the process of amendment, interpretation and court decision I have finally been included in "We, the people."
Statement at debate on articles of impeachment, Judiciary Committee, House of Representatives [July 25, 1974]

2   Many seek only to satisfy their private work wants. To satisfy their private interests. But this is the great danger America faces. That we will cease to be one nation and become instead a collection of interest groups: city against suburb, region against region, individual against individual. Each seeking to satisfy private wants. If that happens, who then will speak for America? Who then will speak for the common good?
Democratic National Convention keynote address [July 12, 1976][1]

3   What the people want is simple. They want an America as good as its promise.   *Commencement address. Harvard University [June 16, 1977]*

June Jordan
1936–2002

4   I am black, alive and looking back at you.   *Who Look at Me [1969]*[2]

5   No one should feel peculiar living
as they do.   *Not a Suicide Poem [1971]*[2]

6   I will no longer lightly walk behind
a one of you who fear me:
Be afraid.
I Must Become a Menace to My Enemies [1977][2]

7   be-
cause what I wanted was
to braid my hair/bathe and bedeck my
self so fully be-
cause what I wanted was
your love

---

[1]From *The Rhetoric of Struggle* [1992], edited by ROBBIE JEAN WALKER.
[2]From *Directed by Desire: The Collected Poems of June Jordan* [2005], edited by JAN HELLER LEVI and SARA MILES.

not pity
be-
cause what I wanted was
your love
your love

The Talking Back of Miss Valentine Jones [1977]. Poem #One[1]

1   These poems
    they are things that I do
    in the dark
    reaching for you
    whoever you are
    and
    are you ready?   *These Poems [1977]*[1]

2   A democratic state is not proven by the welfare of the strong but by
    the welfare of the weak.   *For the Sake of People's Poetry [1980]*

3   We are the ones we have been waiting for.

                          Poem for South African Women [1980][1]

4   There oughta be a woman can break down
    Sit down, break down, sit down.   *Oughta Be a Woman [1980]*

5   A way outa no way is flesh outa flesh,
    Bravery kept out of sight.   *Oughta Be a Woman*

6   If we lived in a democratic state our language would have to hurtle,
    fly, curse and sing, in all the common American names, all the undeniable
    and representative participating voices of everybody here. We would not
    tolerate the language of the powerful and thereby lose all respect for words,
    per se. We would make our language conform to the truth of our many
    selves and we would make our language lead us into the equality of power
    that a democratic state must represent.

                 Problems of Language in a Democratic State [1982]

7   We do not sweat and summon our best in order to rescue the killers; it
    is to comfort and empower the possible victims of evil that we do tinker and
    daydream and revise and memorize and then impart all that we can of our
    inspired, our inherited humanity.

               *Of Those So Close Beside Me, Which Are You? Commencement
               address. University of California, Berkeley [May 17, 1986]*

---

[1]From *Directed by Desire: The Collected Poems of June Jordan* [2005], edited by Jan Heller Levi and Sara Miles.

1   If you are free you are not predictable and you are not controllable.
                              Technical Difficulties [1992]. A New Politics of Sexuality

Clarence Major   1936–

2   We are the kind of short-
                    term visitors who
        each engage the heart
                of each
                        others lives, one
        anothers bodies;
                sometimes forever yet
        so brief the
        sad distance
                of
                        our all-night transit
        leaves us
                        numb: to love.   *All-Night Visitors [1969]*

3   *All* alive art is rebellious, and *all* alive speech, slang or otherwise, is
        rebellious, rebellious in the healthy sense that they challenge the stale and
        the conventional. . . . Black slang is a living, breathing form of expression,
        that changes so quickly no researcher can keep up with it. . . . The need for
        secrecy is part of the reason for the rapid change. Since the days of slavery,
        this secrecy has served as a form of cultural self-defense against exploitation
        and oppression.   *From Juba to Jive [1994], introduction*

Winnie [Madikizela] Mandela   1936–

4   I have ceased a long time ago to exist as an individual. The ideals, the
        political goals that I stand for, those are the ideals and goals of the people in
        this country. They cannot just forget their own ideals. My private self
        doesn't exist. Whatever they do to me, they do to the people in this
        country.   *Part of My Soul Went with Him [1984]*

5   We have no guns — we have only stones, boxes of matches and petrol.
        Together, hand in hand, with our boxes of matches and our necklaces we
        shall liberate this country.   *Speech [April 13, 1986]*

[Rainford] Lee "Scratch" Perry   1936–

6   You take people for fools
    And use them as tools . . .
    I told you once to run
    But you take it all in fun

I am the upsetter
You'll never get away from me.

I Am the Upsetter [1966]

1   When you were down and out
I used to help you out
But now that you win jackpot
You don't remember that.

People Funny Boy [1968]

[Robert] Bobby Seale 1936–

2   *[On the Vietnamese:]* They have never called us nigger.
Black Soldiers as Revolutionaries to Overthrow the Ruling Class.
The Black Panther [September 20, 1969]

3   We look around the world today, and we look around at home right now, and we see that oppression exists. We know that the workers are exploited, and that most of the people in this country are exploited, in one way or another. We know that as a people, we must seize our time.

Seize the Time [1970]

Betty [Sanders] Shabazz 1936–1997

4   When we say "Peace on earth," we can sing about it, preach about it, or pray about it, but if we have not internalized the mythology to make it happen inside of us, then it will not be.

From BRIAN LANKER, I Dream a World [1989]

Sugarhill Gang
Sylvia Robinson 1936–2011

and

Big Bank Hank [Henry Jackson] 1956–

and

Wonder Mike [Michael Wright] 1957–

and

Master Gee [Guy O'Brien] 1962–

5   I said a hip hop
the hibbie, the hibbie

to the hip hip hop, you don't stop the rockin
To the bang bang boogie, say up jumped the boogie
To the rhythm of the boogedy beat.   *Rapper's Delight [1979]*

Robert Jackey Beavers   1937–2008

and

Johnny Bristol   1939–2004

and

Harvey Fuqua   1929–2010

1   Someday We'll Be Together   *Song title [1961]*

Claude Brown   1937–2002

2   The children of these disillusioned colored pioneers inherited the total lot of their parents — the disappointments, the anger. To add to their misery, they had little hope of deliverance. For where does one run to when he's already in the promised land?

Manchild in the Promised Land [1965]

Johnnie Cochran, Jr.   1937–2005

3   If it doesn't fit, you must acquit.
    Closing argument for the defense in murder trial, referring to glove introduced as evidence, which did not fit defendant O. J. Simpson [September 27, 1995][1]

4   What we have in this country is the appearance of justice.
    A Lawyer's Life [2002]

Maryse Condé   1937–

5   Segu is a garden where cunning grows. Segu is built on treachery. Speak of Segu outside Segu, but do not speak of Segu in Segu.
    Segu [1987][2], ch. 1

6   Friendship between women can resemble love. It has the same possessiveness as love, the same jealousies and lack of restraint. But the complicities

---

[1]In *A Lawyer's Life*, Cochran writes, "Not only was this the most memorable line in the entire trial, it's the line that eventually will be cited in *Bartlett's Familiar Quotations*, the line endlessly quoted to me by people, the line by which I'll be remembered, and I suspect it will probably be my epitaph."

[2]Translated by BARBARA BRAY.

of friendship are more durable than those of love, for they are not based on the language of the body. *Tree of Life [1992]*[1]

1   Without love, a woman's heart hardens. It becomes a desolate savanna where only cacti grow. *Crossing the Mangrove [1995]*[2]

[William H.] Bill Cosby   1937–

2   Human beings are the only creatures on earth that allow their children to come back home. *Fatherhood [1986]*

3   I guess the real reason that my wife and I had children is the same reason that Napoleon had for invading Russia: it seemed like a good idea at the time. *Fatherhood*

4   Parents are not really interested in justice. They just want quiet.
Fatherhood

5   "Don't worry about senility," my grandfather used to say. "When it hits you, you won't know it." *Time Flies [1987]*

6   I do want to die before my wife and the reason is this: if it is true that when you die, your soul goes up to judgment, I don't want my wife up there ahead of me to tell them things. *Cosbyology [2001]*

7   The lower-economic people are not holding up their end in this deal. These people are not parenting. They are buying things for kids — $500 sneakers for what? And won't spend $200 for Hooked on Phonics.
Speech commemorating the fiftieth anniversary of Brown v. Board of Education *[May 17, 2004]*

8   Your dirty laundry gets out of school at 2:30 every day, it's cursing and calling each other nigger as they're walking up and down the street. They can't read; they can't write. They're laughing and giggling, and they're going nowhere.
Speech. Annual conference of Rainbow/PUSH Coalition & Citizenship Education Fund [July 1, 2004]

Leon Forrest   1937–1997

9   Why pose and posture a self that is other than you, when I know your true name. *There Is a Tree More Ancient than Eden [1973]. The Dream*

10   Generations have to pay for the bloodshed, avarice and madness of their forefathers. *There Is a Tree More Ancient than Eden. The Dream*

---

[1]Translated by VICTORIA REITER.
[2]Translated by RICHARD PHILCOX.

1   Is there no Balm in Gilead? Is that Tomorrow grieving and slouching in a Windstorm? For still our ancient enemy employs his woe; his craft and power are great, and mighty with avenging hate, on earth is not his equal for menace without mercy, for sabbath without soul, for fire without warmth.

There Is a Tree More Ancient than Eden. Transformation

2   Sleep for me is great and the deeper the better, for there I often dream and dreams awaken me to the crisis of living.   *Divine Days [1992], ch. 15*

Morgan Freeman   1937–

3   *[On Black History Month:]* Ridiculous. You're going to relegate my history to a month? I don't want a Black History Month. Black history is American history.

Television interview. 60 Minutes [2005]

Bessie Head   1937–1986

4   People who hoard little bits of things cannot throw out and expand, and, in doing so, keep in circulation a flowing current of wealth.

The Woman from America [1966]

5   The woman from America loves both Africa and America, independently. She can take what she wants from both and say: "Dammit." It is a most strenuous and difficult thing to do.

The Woman from America

6   In Botswana they say: Zebras, Lions, Buffalo and Bushmen live in the Kalahari Desert. If you can catch a Zebra, you can walk up to it, forcefully open its mouth and examine its teeth. The Zebra is not supposed to mind because it is an animal. Scientists do the same to Bushmen and they are not supposed to mind, because there is no one they can still turn round to and say, "At least I am not a —" Of all things that are said of oppressed people, the worst things are said and done to the Bushmen.

Maru [1971]

7   It is preferable to change the world on the basis of love of mankind. But if that quality be too rare, then common sense seems the next best thing.   *Maru*

8   Love is so powerful, it's like unseen flowers under your feet as you walk.   *A Question of Power [1973]*

9   If the things of the soul are really a question of power, then anyone in possession of power of the spirit could be Lucifer.

A Question of Power [Sello]

Isley Brothers

O'Kelly Isley   1937–1986

and

Ronald Isley   1941–

and

Rudolph Isley   1939–

1   You know you make me wanna shout!   *Shout [1959]*

2   It's your thing: Do what you wanna do.   *It's Your Thing [1969]*

William Melvin Kelley   1937–

3   I hit him all right, but the African just stood there, and then finally
sunk to his knees, and then forward on his hands. He seemed to be melting
away, and then suddenly he looked up with shock on his face, like he'd just
remembered something and had to do it before he passed on.

A Different Drummer [1962]

Walter Dean Myers   1937–

4   You ever have an idea that really sounds good until you do it and find
out how stupid it was?   *Young Landlords [1979], opening line*

5   "My father used to call all soldiers angel warriors," he [Lieutenant
Carroll] said. "Because usually they get boys to fight wars."

Fallen Angels [1988]

6   The war was not a long way from where we were; we were in the
middle of it, and it was deeply within us.   *Fallen Angels*

7   If somebody starts messing with my game it's like they're getting into
my head. But if I've got the ball it's okay, because I can take care of the situation. That's the word and I know it the same way I know my tag, Slam.
Yeah, that's it. Slam. But without the ball, without the floorboards under
my feet, without the mid-court line that takes me halfway home, you can get
to me.   *Slam! [1996]*

8   The best time to cry is at night, when the lights are out and someone is
being beaten up and screaming for help.   *Monster [1999]*

9   Sometimes I feel like I have walked into the middle of a movie. It is a
strange movie with no plot and no beginning. . . . I have seen movies of
prisons but never one like this. This is not a movie about bars and locked

doors. It is about being alone when you are not really alone and about being
scared all the time.   *Monster*

Larry Neal   1937–1981

1   The Black Arts Movement believes that your ethics and your aesthetics
are one. That the contradictions between ethics and aesthetics in Western
society is symptomatic of a dying culture.   *The Black Arts Movement [1968]*

2   We are beautiful — but there is more work to do, and just being beautiful is not enough.
                        *From Black Fire: An Anthology of Afro-American Writing
                        [1968], edited by* AMIRI BARAKA *and* LARRY NEAL

3   Our nightmares are tight compacted
whitenesses, smotherings of babies,
jammed into drunken limits.
our souls are open skies and children
zooming across green places;
sea-shell prisons; are things heard
in between tropical blasts of wind;
are ancestor-wisdom making itself
known in every black face born or about to be.
                              The Middle Passage and After [1969]

4   I remember the faces
the soft and the hard
faces scarred, wailing
for the song and the moan
digging the gardenia thing
she was into.   *Lady's Days [1972]*

5   Remember me baby in my best light,
lovely and hip style and all;
all laid out in my green velour
stashing on corners
in my boxcar coat —
so sure of myself, too cool for words,
and running down a beautiful game.
                        Poppa Stoppa Speaks from His Grave [1974]

Eleanor Holmes Norton   1937–

6   If women were suddenly to achieve equality with men tomorrow,
black women would continue to carry the entire array of utterly oppressive

handicaps associated with race. Racial oppression of black people in America has done what neither class oppression nor sexual oppression, with all their perniciousness, has ever done: destroyed an entire people and their culture. The difference is between exploitation and slavery. Slavery partakes of all the worst excesses of exploitation — and more — but exploitation does not always sink people to the miserable depths of slavery.

For Sadie and Maud [1970][1]

1   You can't win what you don't fight for.   *Fire in My Soul [2003]*

Colin Powell   1937–

2   African Americans have come too far and we have too far yet to go to take a detour into the swamp of hatred. Never let the dying hand of racism rest on your shoulder, weighing you down. Let racism always be someone else's burden to carry.

Commencement speech. Howard University [May 14, 1994]

3   American blacks sometimes regard Americans of West Indian origin as uppity and arrogant. The feeling, I imagine, grows out of an impressive record of accomplishment by West Indians. What explains that success?... My black ancestors may have been dragged to Jamaica in chains, but they were not dragged to the United States. Mom and Pop chose to emigrate to this country for the same reason that Italians, Irish, and Hungarians did, to seek better lives for themselves and their children. That is a far different emotional and psychological beginning than that of American blacks, whose ancestors were brought here in chains.   *My American Journey [1995]*

4   I have lived in and risen in a white-dominated society and white-dominated profession, but not by denying my race, not by seeing it as a chain holding me back or an obstacle to overcome. Others may use my race against me, but I will never use it against myself.   *My American Journey*

5   There can be no doubt that Saddam Hussein has biological weapons and the capability to rapidly produce more, many more.

Security Council Address to the United Nations
[February 5, 2003]

6   It's a blot. I'm the one who presented it on behalf of the United States to the world, and [it] will always be a part of my record. It was painful. It's painful now.

On encouraging the United States to go to war in Iraq based on bad intelligence. Interview, 20/20 [September 8, 2005]

---

[1]From *Sisterhood Is Powerful* [1970], edited by Robin Morgan.

1   The country is changing demographically. And if the Republican Party does not change along with that demographic, they're going to be in trouble. And so, when we see that in one more generation, the minorities of America, African-Americans, Hispanic Americans, and Asian Americans will be the majority of the country, you can't go around saying we don't want to have a solid immigration policy. We're going to dismiss the 47 percent. . . . There's also a dark vein of intolerance in some parts of the Party. What I do mean by that? What I mean by that is they still sort of look down on minorities.

Television appearance [January 13, 2013]

Eugene B[enjamin] Redmond   1937–

2   As the drum stands at the crossroads of traditional African and Afro-American culture, so the poet should stand at the center of the drum. . . . And poetry is music's twin. Both the metaphysical and the metaphorical word stem from and return to the drum: life, love, birth, and death labored out in measured rumble or anxious cacophony.

Drumvoices [1976]

3   Consider loneliness as a weaver of want,
As a giver of needs undefined,
As some ancestral repository
For a personal mythic tablet;
As a nerve, nudged overgently —
Or laced with worry;
As a womb, wailing out its
Liquid waifs, its tight lips waiting,
Waiting . . .
As a tyrant, timeless and elastic —
Consider loneliness.

The Eye in the Ceiling [1991]. Consider Loneliness as These Things

4   You sit snug in my ceiling
Staring at the room
While insects worship you.

But I can hide you in the night
And your body like a corpse
Loses its heat in seconds.

The Eye in the Ceiling. Title poem, st. 1–2

1   Mechanical oracles
Dot the sky,
Casting shadows on the sun.
Instead of manna
Leaflets fall
To resurrect coals, dead
From the week's bombing.

The Eye in the Ceiling. Gods in Vietnam

2   *River of time:*
Vibrant vein,
Bent, crooked,
Older than the Red Men
Who named you;
Ancient as the winds
That break on your
Serene and shining face;
One time western boundary of America
From whose center
Your broad shoulders now reach
To touch sisters
On the flanks.

*The Eye in the Ceiling. River of Bones and Flesh and Blood
(Mississippi), st. 1*

Barbara Ann Teer   1937–2008

3   We are beautiful, imaginative and gifted people, and we owe it to our-selves and to our future generations to restore, to recreate this beauty. We must begin building cultural centers where we can enjoy being free, open and black, where we can find out how talented we really are, where we can be what we were born to be, and not what we were brainwashed to be.

We Can Be What We Were Born to Be.
New York Times [July 7, 1968]

Kofi Annan   1938–

4   The most effective interventions are not military. It is much better, from every point of view, if action can be taken to resolve or manage a con-flict before it reaches the military stage.

Speech. Ditchley Park, United Kingdom [June 26, 1998]

5   Sovereignty implies responsibility, not just power.

Speech. Ditchley Park, United Kingdom

1   No government has the right to hide behind national sovereignty in order to violate the human rights or fundamental freedoms of its peoples.

Address to the United Nations Commission on Human Rights, Geneva [April 7, 1999]

2   Today's real borders are not between nations, but between powerful and powerless, free and fettered, privileged and humiliated. Today, no walls can separate humanitarian or human rights crises in one part of the world from national security crises in another.

Nobel lecture, Oslo [December 10, 2001]

3   A genocide begins with the killing of one man — not for what he has done, but because of who he is.   *Nobel lecture*

4   Most nations have monuments or memorials to war, bronze salutations to heroic battles, archways of triumph. But peace has no parade, no pantheon of victory.   *Nobel lecture*

5   We can love what we are, without hating what — and who — we are not.   *Nobel lecture*

6   The obstacles to democracy have little to do with culture or religion, and much more to do with the desire of those in power to maintain their position at any cost.   *Nobel lecture*

7   A world where many millions of people endure brutal oppression and extreme misery will never be fully secure, even for its most privileged inhabitants.

Address to the United Nations General Assembly [September 23, 2003]

8   Climate change does not respect national borders. We are all in the same boat; a hole at one end will sink us all.

Statement at the United Nations Copenhagen Climate Change Conference. Quoted in the Guardian [December 10, 2009]

Mary Frances Berry   1938–

9   When it comes to the cause of justice, I take no prisoners and I don't believe in compromising.   *From* BRIAN LANKER, *I Dream a World [1989]*

Shirley Caesar [Shirley Ann Caesar-Williams]   1938–

10   You're Next in Line for a Miracle   *Song title [1997]*

Joe [Louis] Clark   1938–

11   Discipline is the ultimate tenet of education. Discipline establishes the format, the environment for academic achievement to occur.

Quoted in TIME [February 1, 1988]

Vertamae Grosvenor   1938–

1   Food changes into blood, blood into cells, cells change into energy which changes up into life...food is life.

Vibration Cooking [1970]

2   Soul food is more than chitlins and collard greens, ham hocks and black-eyed peas. Soul food is about a people who have a lot of heart and soul.   *Vibration Cooking*

Michael S[teven] Harper   1938–

3   Those four black girls blown up
in that Alabama church
remind me of five hundred
middle passage blacks,
in a net, under water
in Charleston harbor
so *redcoats* wouldn't find them.
Can't find what you can't see
can you?   *American History [1970]*

4   Black man:
I'm a black man;
I'm black; I am —
A black man; black —
I'm a black man;
I'm a black man;
I'm a man; black —
I am —   *Brother John [1970]*

5   Why you so black?
cause I am.   *Dear John, Dear John Coltrane [1970]*

6   The birds flit
in the blue palms,
the cane workers wait,
the man hangs
twenty feet above;
he must come down.   *Village Blues [1970]*

Maynard Jackson   1938–2003

7   Our Democratic Party is not an end; it is a means to an end. The end is a greater America — where individual worth is valued and no person is

left out; where every vote counts; and where "inclusion" is not a catchword,
but is a passion.   *Quoted. New York Times [February 25, 2001]*

Etta James [Jamesetta Hawkins]   1938–2012

1   You gotta roll with me, Henry,
All right, baby
Roll with me, Henry
Don't mean maybe.   *Wallflower (Dance with Me, Henry) [1955]*

2   Let me tell you now, I've never felt like this before
Something's got a hold on me that won't let go
I believe I'd die if I only could
I feel so strange, but it sure is good.   *Something's Got a Hold on Me [1962]*

3   I wanted to be rare, I wanted to be noticed, I wanted to be glamorous,
I wanted to be exotic as a Cotton Club chorus girl, and I wanted to be
obvious as the most flamboyant hooker on the street. I just wanted to *be*.
                    Rage to Survive [1995]

Keorapetse Kgositsile[1]   1938–

4   Blessed are the dehumanized
for they have nothing to lose
but their patience.   *Spirits Unchained [1969]. Mandela's Sermon*

5   deep in your cheeks
your specific laughter owns
all things south of the ghosts
we once were.   *For Melba [1970]. Origins*

6   All things come to pass
When they do, if they do
All things come, to their end
When they do, as they do.   *My Name Is Afrika [1971]. Title poem*

7   This wind you hear is the birth of memory
when the moment hatches in time's womb
there will be no art talk. the only poem
you will hear will be the spearpoint pivoted
in the punctured marrow of the villain; the
timeless native son dancing like crazy to
the retrieved rhythms of desire
fading

---

[1]From KEORAPETSE KGOSITSILE, *If I Could Sing: Selected Poems* [2002].   *385*

in-
to
memory.   *My Name Is Afrika. Towards a Walk in the Sun*

1   The circle continues
    time will always be
    in spite of minutes that know no life.
    Lives change in life
    at times even rot
    or be trampled underfoot
    as the back of a slave
    There are cycles in the circle
    I may even moan my deadness
    or mourn your death.

                The Present Is a Dangerous Place to Live [1975]. In the Mourning

2   Or should I just plead
    like the blues singer
    hit me in the eye
    maybe then maybe then
    I'll see better
    because when I search the crevices of my voice
    I do not want to say anything unreal
    as the ancients say
    when the clouds clear
    we shall know the color of the sky.

                              When the Clouds Clear [1990]. Title poem

Ben[jamin] E[arl Nelson] King   1938–

3   When the night has come
    And the land is dark
    And the moon is the only light we'll see
    No I won't be afraid, no I won't be afraid
    Just as long as you stand, stand by me.   *Stand by Me [1961]*

Fela [Anikulapo] Kuti   1938–1997

4   Black people we no know ourselves.   *Why Black Man Dey Suffer [1971]*[1]

5   Zombie O zombie
    Zombie no go unless you tell am to go

---

[1]From TEJUMOLA OLANIYAN, *Arrest the Music!* [2004].

Zombie no go stop unless you tell am to stop
Zombie no go turn unless you tell am to turn
Zombie no go think, unless you tell am to think.   *Zombie [1976]*

1   Suffer, suffer, suffer, suffer for the world
na your fault be that (that is your own fault)
Me I say:
na your fault be that.   *Shuffering and Shmiling [1978][1]*

2   Perambulator
every morning
6 in the morning
going to work
6 in the evening
coming back home
every month
small salary
for 55 years
him go tire
if he no tire
dem go tire am.   *Perambulator [1983][1]*

3   United Nations get name for us
Dem go call us "Underdeveloped Nations."
We must be "underdeveloped" to dey
stay 10-10 in one room
First and second day dem go call us
"Third World."   *Beasts of No Nation [1989][1]*

Diane Nash   1938–

4   Sir, you should know, we all signed our last wills and testaments last night before they left. We know someone will be killed. But we cannot let violence overcome non-violence.

> *Statement in response to urging of John Seigenthaler, assistant to Attorney General Robert F. Kennedy, that the Freedom Riders cancel their ride from Nashville, Tennessee, to Alabama [1961][2]*

---

[1]From Tejumola Olaniyan, *Arrest the Music!* [2004].

[2]"That's virtually a direct quote of the words that came out of that child's mouth. Here I am, an official of the United States government, representing the President and the Attorney General, talking to a student at Fisk University. And she in a very quiet but strong way gave me a lecture." Interview with John Seigenthaler for the documentary film *Freedom Riders* [2011]. Interviewed for the same documentary, Diane Nash said, "The attitude became, 'Well, kill us if that's what you're going to do.' But we were going to be rid of segregation."

1   The movement had a way of reaching inside me and bringing out things that I never knew were there. Like courage, and love for people. It was a real experience to be seeing a group of people who would put their bodies between you and danger. And to love people that you work with enough that you would put your body between them and danger.

From Juan Williams, *Eyes on the Prize:*
America's Civil Rights Years, 1954–1965 [1987]

Ngugi wa Thiong'o [James Ngugi]   1938–

2   That day for the first time, he wept with fear and guilt. And he did not pray.   *Weep Not, Child [1966], ch. 15*

3   The morning itself was so dull we feared the day would not break into life. But the rain had stopped. The air was soft and fresh, and an intimate warmth oozed from the pregnant earth to our hearts.

A Grain of Wheat [1967], ch. 14

4   He took the children out into the field to study nature, as he put it. He picked flowers and taught them the names of the various parts.... One child cried out:

"Look. A flower with petals of blood."

It was a solitary red beanflower in a field dominated by white, blue and violet flowers. No matter how you looked at it, it gave you the impression of a flow of blood. Munira bent over it and with a trembling hand plucked it. It had probably been the light playing upon it, for now it was just a red flower.

"There is no color called blood. What you mean is that it is red. You see?"   *Petals of Blood [1977], pt. 1, ch. 1*

5   WARNING! THIS PROPERTY BELONGS TO A WIZARD WHOSE POWER BRINGS DOWN HAWKS AND CROWS FROM THE SKY. TOUCH THIS HOUSE AT YOUR PERIL. SGD. WIZARD OF THE CROW.

Wizard of the Crow [2006], bk. 2, ch. 7

Ishmael Reed   1938–

6   do not resist this poem
this poem has yr eyes
this poem has his head
this poem has his arms
this poem has his fingers
this poem has his fingertips.

Conjure [1972]. Beware: Do Not Read This Poem

1   I am a cowboy in the boat of Ra,
sidewinders in the saloons of fools
bit my forehead   like   O
the untrustworthiness of Egyptologists
who do not know their trips. Who was that
dog-faced man? they asked, the day I rode
from town.   *Conjure. I Am a Cowboy in the Boat of Ra*

2   Neo-HooDoo is a "Lost American Church" updated. Neo-HooDoo is the music of James Brown without the lyrics and ads for Black Capitalism. Neo-HooDoo is the 8-basic dances of 19th-century New Orleans' *Place Congo*...modernized into the Philly Dog, the Hully Gully, the Funky Chicken, the Popcorn, the Boogaloo.   *Conjure. Neo-HooDoo Manifesto*

3   Neo-HooDoo believes that every man is an artist and every artist a priest.   *Conjure. Neo-HooDoo Manifesto*

4   We learn about one another's cultures the same way we learn about sex: in the streets.   *Writin' Is Fightin' [1988]. Hymietown Revisited*

5   Are there black racists? Of course there are, and the media, which serve as the chief arm of white nationalist propaganda, joyfully reward the blacks who make anti-white and anti-Semitic statements with considerable coverage, as a way of attracting viewers to their vile products and providing whites with entertainment, while embarrassing blacks.
                          Another Day at the Front [2003], introduction

6   All: Our God is a walking God
He is not one still in stone
Our God is a walking God
He moves through the towns and cities
Through mountains and valleys
He roams.
        New and Collected Poems, 1964–2006 [2006].
        Chorus, Gethsemane Park

7   I want to be a right wing
family values type of man
preach that the drug laws
shouldn't bend
But you'd find me in Georgetown
snorting coke
any weekend.
        New and Collected Poems, 1964–2006.
        I Want to Be a Right-Wing Family Values Type of Man

Simone Schwarz-Bart

1938–

1   A man's country may be cramped or vast according to the size of his heart.   *The Bridge of Beyond [1974],[1] opening line*

2   Sorrow is a wave without end. But horse musn't ride you, you must ride it.   *The Bridge of Beyond [Queen Without a Name]*

3   All rivers, even the most dazzling, those that catch the sun in their streams, all rivers go down to and are drowned in the sea. And life awaits man as the sea awaits the river.   *The Bridge of Beyond*

4   The sun never tires of rising, but it sometimes happens that man is weary of being under the sun.   *The Bridge of Beyond*

Ellen Johnson Sirleaf

1938–

5   I would like to talk to the women, the women of Liberia, the women of Africa — and the women of the world. . . . My Administration shall thus endeavor to give Liberian women prominence in all affairs of our country. My Administration shall empower Liberian women in all areas of our national life. We will support and increase the writ of laws that restore their dignities and deal drastically with crimes that dehumanize them.

Inaugural address [January 16, 2006]

6   We are moving forward. Our best days are coming. The future belongs to us because we have taken charge of it. We have the resources. We have the resourcefulness.   *Inaugural address*

7   Women have demonstrated considerable leadership at the family level, in the community and informal organizations, in high levels of international organizations, and are now boldly stepping up the highest mantle of state authority in public life, and we are convinced that with good guidance, commitment, dedication to change, with a vision that carries forward equality and social equity, women, through their leadership role, will help to make the world a safer, peaceful, more progressive place for themselves and their children.

Address, International Women's Day [March 8, 2006]

Wallace Terry

1938–2003

8   There were no flags waving or drums beating upon the return of any Vietnam veterans, who were blamed by the right in our society for losing the war, and by the left for being the killers of the innocent. But what can be said about the dysfunction of Vietnam veterans in general can be doubled in its

[1]Translated by BARBARA BRAY.

impact upon most blacks; they hoped to come home to more than they had before; they came home to less.   *Bloods [1984], introduction*

Askia Touré [Rolland Snellings]   1938–

1   Ambush the Silver Screen. Rob it of its victims —
frightened coons and screeching Aunt Jemimas.
Kidnap Birmingham/Stepin/ Fetchit/Beaulah/Butterfly.
Nature them to life with the love-cry echoes
of your soul.   *The Birth of a Nation [1972]*

2   We, poet and magic myth-making Giant of Song, wander on.
Holy the bones of our ancestors wrapped in Pyramids
          resting 'til the end of Time
Holy the Magi, priests and Myth-scientists of Africa
          for sending him to us.   *Juju (for John Coltrane, The Joy) [1972]*

3   Make your vital Circle,
you pain-wracked, whip-scarred
hordes. You sun-scorched saints
of myriad bondage seasons;
You Mande, Ibo, Bakongo,
Dogon.   *Transformations [1990]*

Allen Toussaint   1938–

4   Now I'm a happy fella
Well I'm married to the fortune teller
We're happy as we can be
And I get my fortune told for free.   *Fortune Teller [1962]*

5   I know we can make it, I know that we can
I know darn well we can work it out
Oh yes we can, I know we can can
Yes we can can, why can't we
If we wanna get yes we can can.   *Yes We Can [1970]*[1]

6   Everything I Do Gonna Be Funky   *Song title [1971]*

7   Play something sweet, play something mellow
Play something I can sink my teeth in like jello
Play something I can understand
Play me some brickyard blues.   *Play Something Sweet (Brickyard Blues) [1974]*

---

[1]See also Barack Obama, 522:5.

1   Southern nights,
Have you ever felt a southern night?
Free as a breeze
Not to mention the trees
Whistling tunes that you know and love so.   *Southern Nights [1977]*

Maxine Waters   1938–

2   I like to laugh. I like to have a great time. But I also have the right to
my anger, and I don't want anybody telling me I shouldn't be, that it's not
nice to be and that something is wrong with me because I get angry.

From Brian Lanker, *I Dream a World [1989]*

Bill Withers   1938–

3   Ain't no sunshine when she's gone.   *Ain't No Sunshine [1971]*

4   Grandma's hands clapped in church on Sunday morning.
Grandma's hands played the tambourine so well.
Grandma's hands used to issue out a warning,
She'd say, "Billy, don't you run so fast,
might fall on a piece of glass,
might be snakes there in that grass."   *Grandma's Hands [1971]*

5   Lean on me when you're not strong.
And I'll be your friend
I'll help you carry on.
For, it won't be long 'til
I'm gonna need somebody to lean on.   *Lean on Me [1972]*

6   We look for love
No time for tears
Wasted water's all that is
And it don't make no flowers grow.
Good things might come to those who wait
Not for those who wait too late
We gotta go for all we know.   *Just the Two of Us [1981]*[1]

Camille Yarbrough   1938–

7   Little girl, little boy,
with the cornrowed style

---

[1]Cowritten with Ralph MacDonald and William Salter.

let me see your pretty face,
let me see your handsome smile. *Cornrows [1979]*

Ayi Kwei Armah 1939–

1   The banister had originally been a wooden one, and to this time it was still possible to see in the deepest of the cracks between the swellings of other matter, a dubious piece of deeply aged brown wood.... The wood underneath would win and win till the end of time. Of that there was no doubt possible, only the pain of hope perennially doomed to disappointment.... Of course it was in the nature of the wood to rot with age. The polish, it was supposed, would catch the rot. But of course in the end it was the rot which imprisoned everything in its effortless embrace. It did not really have to fight. Being was enough.   *The Beautyful Ones Are Not Yet Born [1968]*

2   It should be easy now to see there have never been people to save anybody but themselves, never in the past, never now, and there will never be any saviors if each will not save himself.

The Beautyful Ones Are Not Yet Born

3   Each thing that goes away returns and nothing in the end is lost. The great friend throws all things apart and brings all things together again. That is the way everything goes and turns round. That is how all living things come back after long absences, and in the whole great world all things are living things. All that goes returns.   *Fragments [1969]*

4   I am here against the last of my veils. Take me. I am ready. You are the end. The beginning. You who have no end. I am coming.

Fragments, last lines

5   Remember this: against all that destruction some yet remained among us unforgetful of origins, dreaming secret dreams, seeing secret visions, hearing secret voices of our purpose. Further: those yet to appear, to see, hear, to utter and to make — little do we know what changes they will come among. Idle then for us to presume despair on their behalf; foolish when we have no knowledge how much closer to the way their birth will come, how much closer than our closet hopes.   *Two Thousand Seasons [1973]*

[Miltona Mirkin] Toni Cade Bambara 1939–1995

6   We are involved in a struggle for liberation: liberation from the exploitive and dehumanizing system of racism, from the manipulative control of a corporate society; liberation from the constrictive norms of "mainstream" culture, from the synthetic myths that encourage us to fashion ourselves rashly from without (reaction) rather than from within (creation).

The Black Woman [1970], preface

1   If you say Gorilla, My Love you suppose to mean it. Just like when you say you goin to give me a party on my birthday, you gotta mean it....I mean even gangsters in the movies say My word is my bond. So don't nobody get away with nothing far as I'm concerned.

Gorilla, My Love [1972]. Title story

2   The only proper mask to wear in life is your own damn face.

Gorilla, My Love. The Johnson Girls

3   Where we are is who we are, Miss Moore always pointin out. But it don't necessarily have to be that way, she always adds then waits for somebody to say that poor people have to wake up and demand their share of the pie and don't none of us know what kind of pie she talkin about in the first damn place.

Gorilla, My Love. The Lesson

4   He ain't my man, mind you, just a nice ole gent from the block that we all know cause he fixes things and the kids like him. Or used to fore Black Power got hold their minds and mess em around till they can't be civil to ole folks. So we at this benefit for my niece's cousin who's runnin for something; with this Black party somthin or other behind her. And I press up close to dance with Bovanne who blind and I'm hummin and he hummin, chest to chest like talkin. Not jammin my breasts into the man. Wasn't bout tits. Was bout vibrations.

Gorilla My Love. My Man Bovanne

5   We stand there with this big smile of respect between us. It's about as real a smile as girls can do for each other, considering we don't practice real smiling every day, you know, cause maybe we too busy being flowers or fairies or strawberries instead of something honest and worthy of respect...you know...like being people.   *Gorilla, My Love. Raymond's Run*

6   For sometimes a person held on to sickness with a fiercesomeness that took twenty hard-praying folk to loosen. So used to being unwhole and unwell, one forgot what it was to walk upright and see clearly, breathe easily, think better than was taught, be better than one was programmed to believe — so concentration was necessary to help a neighbor experience the best of herself or himself. For people sometimes believed that it was safer to live with complaints, was necessary to cooperate with grief, was all right to become an accomplice in self-ambush.   *The Salt Eaters [1980], ch. 5*

7   Not all wars have casualties....Some struggles between old and new ideas, some battles between ways of seeing have only victors. Not all dying is the physical self.   *The Salt Eaters [1980], ch.10 [Sophie]*

Barbara Chase-Riboud   1939–

8   How could she have known that her vision of the perfect slave would coincide with his vision of the perfect woman? And Sally Hemings loved

Thomas Jefferson. That was the tragedy. Love, not slavery. And God knew how much slavery there was in love. *Sally Hemings: A Novel [1979], ch. 1*

James H[al] Cone
1939–

1   God is black.... There is no place in black theology for a colorless God in a society where human beings suffer precisely because of their color. The blackness of God means that God has made the oppressed condition God's own condition. *A Black Theology of Liberation: Second Edition [1986]*

2   Anger and humor are like the left and right arm. They complement each other. Anger empowers the poor to declare their uncompromising opposition to oppression, and humor prevents them from being consumed by their fury. *Malcolm and Martin in America [1991]*

Marian Wright Edelman
1939–

3   Service is the rent we pay for living.
The Measure of Our Success [1992]

4   It is utterly exhausting being Black in America — physically, mentally and emotionally. While many minority groups and women feel similar stress, there is no respite or escape from your badge of color.
The Measure of Our Success

5   The question is not whether we can afford to invest in every child; it is whether we can afford not to. *The Measure of Our Success*

6   Children — all children — are the world. Children are hope and life. Children are our immortality. Children are the seeds and the molders of history and the transmitters of our values — good and bad.
Standing Up for Children [2003][1]

Charles Fuller
1939–

7   They call me Zoo-man! That's right. Z-O-O-M-A-N! From the Bottom! I'm the runner down thea'. When I knuck with a dude, I fight like a panther. Strike like a cobra! Stomp on mothafuckas' like a whole herd of Bi-son! *Zooman and the Sign [1980], act I, sc.1 [Zooman]*

8   They'll still hate you! They still hate you!...They still hate you!
A Soldier's Play [1981], act 1 [Waters]

9   Do you know the damage one ignorant Negro can do?
A Soldier's Play, act 2 [Waters]

[1]From *The Impossible Will Take a Little While* [2004], edited by PAUL LOEB.

1   You got to be like them! And I was — but the rules are fixed. It doesn't make any difference.

A Soldier's Play, act 2 [Waters]

2   Oh you'll get used to it — you can bet your ass on that. Captain — you will get used to it.

A Soldier's Play, act 2, last lines [Davenport]

Marvin Gaye [Marvin Pentz Gay, Jr.]   1939–1984

3   There'll be singing, swaying, and records playing
     Dancing in the street.   *Dancing in the Street [1964]*[1]

4   If this world were mine
     I would place at your feet
     All that I own.   *If This World Were Mine [1967]*

5   It makes me wanna holler
     And throw up both my hands.   *Inner City Blues [1971]*

6   Oh, mercy, mercy me,
     Oh, things ain't what they used to be, no, no.
     Where did all the blue skies go?
     Poison is the wind that blows,
     From the north, and south and east.

Mercy, Mercy Me (The Ecology) [1971]

7   Let's Get It On   *Song title [1973]*

8   When I get that feeling
     I want sexual healing.   *Sexual Healing [1982]*

Marvin Gaye [Marvin Pentz Gay, Jr.]   1939–1984

and

Renauldo Benson   1937–2005

and

Al[fred] Cleveland   1930–1996

9   Mother, Mother, there's too many of you crying
     Brother, brother, brother, there's far too many of you dying.

What's Going On [1970]

---

[1]With Ivy Jo Hunter and William Mickey Stevenson.

[Edward] Eddie Holland

1939–

and

Norman Whitfield

1943–2008

1   I know flowers grow from rain,
but how can love grow from pain?
Now ain't that peculiar,
a peculiarity?
      Ain't That Peculiar? [1965]

2   If you're lookin' for a lover
don't judge a book by its cover.
      Beauty Is Only Skin Deep [1965]

3   If I have to beg and plead for your sympathy,
I don't mind 'cause you mean that much to me.
Ain't too proud to beg and you know it
Please don't leave me, girl.
      Ain't Too Proud to Beg [1966]

Julius Lester

1939–

4   To be a slave was to be a human being under conditions in which humanity was denied. They were not slaves. They were people. Their condition was slavery.
      To Be a Slave [1968]

E[dward] A[rchibald] Markham

1939–2008

5   Patience is a visit from another age.
      Crossfire [1972]. Patience

6   Chase him down the alley
put him behind bars
in a basement and charge him rent.
      A Mugger's Game [1984]

7   Grandmother, grandmother, her bath, over, smelling of bay rum &
    bible
knows how bad habits, like long years abroad, and the profession of
    maleness,
lead to ugly bumps on the head. So men must cover theirs.
In my hat, in a foreign garden, when the leaf is about to fall from its
    tree,
grandmother appears to speak to me.
      Grandmotherpoem [1989]

8   I have
Explored the world, tasted its strangeness,
Resisted and colluded out of strength,
Out of weakness, failed to colonize it
With family, tongue or name.
      Hinterland [1989]

Hugh Masekela

1939–

1   It's not my music. I got it from the people and I will be paying interest
on that loan for the rest of my life.   *Radio interview [2006]*

Quincy Troupe

1939–

2   so get on up & fly away duke, bebop
slant & fade on in, strut, dance swing, riff
& float & stroke those tickling, gri-gri keys
those satin ladies taking the A train up
to harlem, those gri-gri keys
of birmingham, breakdown
sophisticated ladies, mood indigo
get on up & strut across, gri-gri
raise on up, your band's waiting   *The Day Duke Raised [1979]*

3   take it to the hoop "magic" johnson,
take the ball dazzling down the open lane
herk & jerk & raise your six foot nine inch
frame into the air sweating screams of your neon name.
A Poem for "Magic" [1984]

4   so where do the tumbling words spend themselves after they have spent
all meaning residing in the warehouse of language, after they have slipped
from our lips, like skiers on ice slopes, strung together words linking
themselves through smoke, where do the symbols they carry
stop everything, put down roots, cleanse themselves of everything
but clarity — though here eye might be asking a little too much of any
poet's head, full as it were with double-entendres
Poem Reaching Towards Something [1984]

5   up from new orleans, on riverboats
from the gulf of mexico, memory carries
sweet legacy of niggerland speech, brown tongue bluesing
muddy water
underbottomed spirits crawling, nightmares
of shipwrecked bones, bones gone home to stone, to stone
bones gone home to stone, to stone
riverbottomed, underbellied spirits   *Skulls Along the River [1984]*

6   father, it was an honor to be there, in the dugout
with you, the glory of great black men swinging their lives
as bats, at tiny white balls
burning in at unbelievable speeds, riding up & in & out

a curve breaking down wicked, like a ball falling off a table
moving away, snaking down, screwing its stitched magic
into chitlin circuit air, its comma seams spinning
again toward breakdown, dipping, like a hipster
bebopping a knee-dip stride in the charlie parker forties
wrist curling like a swan's neck
behind a "slick" black back
cupping an invisible ball of dreams

Poem for My Father [1991]

Tina Turner [Anna Mae Bullock]   1939–

1   We never ever do nothing nice and easy. We always do it nice and
rough.

Spoken introduction to a recording of "Proud Mary" [1971]

2   I will never give in to old age until I *become* old. And I am *not* old yet!

I, Tina [1986]

Al[bert] Young   1939–

3   I turned to poetry & to singing by choice,
        reading everyone always & listening, listening for a
            silence deep enough
        to make out the sound of my own background music.

A Little More Traveling Music [1969]

4   Genius does not grow on trees.   *Dance of the Infidels [1993]*

Al Bell [Alvertis Isbell]   1940–

5   I know a place
Ain't nobody crying
Ain't nobody worried
Ain't no smiling faces
Lying to the races
I'll take you there.

I'll Take You There [1972]

John W[esley] Blassingame   1940–2000

6   If scholars want to know the hearts and secret thoughts of slaves, they
must study the testimony of the blacks. But, since the slaves did not know
the hearts and secret thoughts of masters, historians must also examine the
testimony of whites. Neither the whites nor the blacks had a monopoly on

399

truth, had rended the veil cloaking the life of the other, or had seen clearly the pain and joy bounded by color and caste.

Slave Testimony: Two Centuries of Letters, Speeches,
Interviews and Autobiographies [1977], introduction

Julian Bond

1940–

1 Once, we thought that segregation and racism were the same thing, and that when segregation was done away with, racism would be done away with, too. We enjoyed the community of segregation and it conflated all the differences among us into one undifferentiated mass. This unfortunate luxury blinded us to the reality of the diversity of our "community," and the prospect that after segregation that diversity would spread and increase.

Interview. New Yorker [April 29/May 6, 1996]

2 Affirmative action really isn't about preferential treatment for blacks. It is about removing preferential treatment whites have received through history.

Speech at the 89th NAACP Convention, Atlanta [August 1998]

3 Sadly, today much of *Brown*'s promise is lost in fantasyland. The Magic Kingdom remains closed to many children of color in America.

The Broken Promise of Brown. Speech [2004]

John Lewis

1940–

4 What political leader can stand up and say "My party is a party of principles"? ... Where is our party? Where is the political party that will make it unnecessary to march on Washington? Where is the political party that will make it unnecessary to march in the streets of Birmingham?

Speech. March on Washington for Jobs and Freedom
[August 28, 1963]

5 To those who have said, "Be patient and wait," we must say that "patience" is a dirty and nasty word. We cannot be patient; we do not want to be free gradually. We want our freedom, and we want it now.

Speech. March on Washington for Jobs and Freedom

6 We will march through the South, through the Heart of Dixie, the way Sherman did.... And I say to you, Wake up, America! Wake up, for we cannot stop and we will not and cannot be patient.

Speech. March on Washington for Jobs and Freedom

7 Our future is in the hands of the young, as it always has been. One generation hands off to the next, and each new generation has its own

vision, its own ideals, its own beliefs. That is what it means to be young: you believe.
Walking with the Wind [1999]

1   Sometimes I hear people saying nothing has changed, but for someone to grow up the way I grew up in the cotton fields of Alabama to now be serving in the United States Congress makes we want to tell them come and walk in my shoes. Come walk in the shoes of those who were attacked by police dogs, fire hoses and nightsticks, arrested, and taken to jail.
Speech on 50th anniversary of the March on Washington [August 28, 2013]

2   Fifty years later we can ride anywhere we want to ride, we can stay where we want to stay. Those signs that said "white" and "colored" are gone. And you won't see them anymore — except in a museum, in a book, on a video. But there are still invisible signs buried in the hearts in humankind that form a gulf between us. Too many of us still believe our differences define us instead of the divine spark that runs through all of human creation.
Speech on 50th anniversary of the March on Washington [August 28, 2013]

Frankie Lymon   1940–1968

3   Why Do Fools Fall in Love?   *Song title [1956]*[1]

Wangari Maathai   1940–2011

4   Let us embrace democratic governance, protect human rights and protect our environment. I am confident that we shall rise to the occasion. I have always believed that solutions to most of our problems must come from us.
Nobel lecture, Oslo [December 10, 2004]

5   When the environment is destroyed, plundered or mismanaged, we undermine our quality of life and that of future generations.
Nobel lecture

6   In the course of history, there comes a time when humanity is called to shift to a new level of consciousness, to reach a higher moral ground. A time when we have to shed our fear and give hope to each other. That time is now.
Nobel lecture

7   Trees are living symbols of peace and hope. A tree has roots in the soil yet reaches to the sky. It tells us that in order to aspire we need to be grounded and that no matter how high we go it is from our roots that we draw sustenance.
Unbowed [2006]

---

[1]With Morris Levy.

[Essie Mae] Anne Moody

1940–

1   Before Emmett Till's murder, I had known the fear of hunger, hell, and the Devil. But now there was a new fear known to me — the fear of being killed just because I was black.... I was fifteen years old when I began to hate people. I hated the white men who murdered Emmett Till and I hated all the other whites who were responsible for the countless murders.... But I also hated Negroes. I hated them for not standing up and doing something about the murders. In fact, I think I had a stronger resentment toward Negroes for letting the whites kill them than toward the whites.   *Coming of Age in Mississippi [1968]*

2   After the sit-in all I could think of was how sick Mississippi whites were. They believed so much in the segregated Southern way of life, they would kill to preserve it. I sat there in the NAACP office and thought of how many times they had killed when this way of life was threatened.... I knew that the killing had just begun. Before the sit-in, I had always hated the whites in Mississippi. Now I knew it was impossible for me to hate sickness. The whites had a disease, an incurable disease in its final stage.

Coming of Age in Mississippi

Orlando Patterson

1940–

3   We should drop the terms *black* and *white*.... Not only are the terms *black* and *white* denotatively loaded in favor of Euro-Americans — as a check in *The Oxford English Dictionary* will attest in lurid detail — but by their emphasis on the somatic, they reinforce and legitimize precisely that biological notion of "race" that we claim we want to be rid of.

The Ordeal of Integration [1997]

Pelé [Edson Arantes do Nascimento]

1940–

4   *[Describing football/soccer:]* The beautiful game.

My Life and the Beautiful Game [1977]

Sterling D[ominic] Plumpp

1940–

5   Be-Bop is precise clumsiness
        Awkward lyricism
        under a feather's control.
A world in a crack.

Be-Bop [1995]

Richard Pryor

1940–2005

6   I was a nigger for twenty-three years. I gave it up — no room for advancement.   *Live and Smokin' [1971]*

1   You all know how black humor started? It started on slave ships. Cat was on his way over here — rowing — and dude says, "What you laughing about?" He said, "Yesterday I was a king."

Bicentennial Nigger [1976]

2   I'm just so thrilled to be over here. Over here in America. I'm so glad you all took me out of Dahomey. I used to could live to be a hundred and fifty, now I die of the high blood pressure by the time I'm fifty-two. That thrills me to death. I'm just so pleased America's gon' last. They brought me over here in a boat. There was four hundred of us come over here. Three hundred sixty of us died on the way over here. I love that. That just thrills me so.

Bicentennial Nigger

3   Racism is a bitch.... It's hard enough being a human being.

Live on the Sunset Strip [1982]

4   *[On ceasing to use the word* nigger *in his act:]* When I was in Africa, this voice came to me and said, "Richard, what do you see?" I said, "I see all types of people." The voice said, "But do you see any niggers?" I said, "No." It said, "Do you know why? Cause there aren't any."

Live on the Sunset Strip

[William] Smokey Robinson   1940–

5   Don't you know I sit around
With my head hanging down.
And wonder who is lovin' you.

Who's Lovin' You[1960]

6   You've Really Got a Hold on Me   *Song title [1962]*

7   I'm telling you from the start
I can't be torn apart from my guy.

My Guy [1964]

8   Well I wouldn't be doggone,
I'd be long gone.

I'll Be Doggone [1965]

9   I'm gonna make you love me, too
So get ready, get ready, cause here I come.

Get Ready [1971]

[William] Smokey Robinson   1940–

and

Al[fred] Cleveland   1930–1996

10   I Second That Emotion   *Song title [1967]*   403

[William] Smokey Robinson

1940–

and

Henry Cosby

1928–2002

and

Ronald White

1939–1995

> 1 I've got sunshine on a cloudy day
> When it's cold outside
> I've got the month of May
> I guess you'd say
> What can make me feel this way?
> My girl, my girl, my girl
> Talkin' 'bout my girl.

My Girl [1964]

[William] Smokey Robinson

1940–

and

Berry Gordy, Jr.

1929–

> 2 My mama told me, you better shop around.

Shop Around [1960]

[William] Smokey Robinson

1940–

and

Warren Moore

1939–

> 3 I'm cryin'
> Ooo, baby baby.

Ooo, Baby Baby [1965]

[William] Smokey Robinson

1940–

and

Warren Moore

1939–

and

Marv Tarplin

1941–2011

> 4 So take a good look at my face.
> You'll see my smile looks out of place
> If you look closer it's easy to trace
> The tracks of my tears.

The Tracks of My Tears [1965]

[William] Smokey Robinson
1940–

and

[Robert Edward] Bobby Rogers
1940–2013

1   Well, you could've been anything that you wanted to
And I can tell, the way you do the things you do.

The Way You Do the Things You Do [1964]

[William] Smokey Robinson
1940–

and

Stevie Wonder [Stevland Morris]
1950–

2   Now there's some sad things known to man
But ain't too much sadder than
The tears of a clown
When there's no one around.

Tears of a Clown [1967]

Wilma Rudolph
1940–1994

3   It took sheer determination to be able to run a hundred yards and remember all of the mechanics that go along with it. It takes steady nerves and being a fighter to stay out there.

From BRIAN LANKER, *I Dream a World [1989]*

Pharoah [Ferrell] Sanders
1940–

and

Leon Thomas
1937–1999

4   The creator has a master plan,
Peace and happiness for every man.

Karma [1968]. The Creator Has a Master Plan

Nick Ashford
1941–2011

and

Valerie Simpson
1946–

5   There ain't no mountain high enough
Ain't no valley low enough
Ain't no river wide enough
To keep me from getting to you, babe.

Ain't No Mountain High Enough [1967]

1 Ain't Nothing Like the Real Thing, Baby   *Song title [1967]*

2 Like an eagle protects his nest
   For you I'll do my best
   Stand by you like a tree
   Dare anybody to try and move me.

   You're All I Need to Get By [1968]

3 Reach out and touch somebody's hand,
   Make this world a better place if you can.

   Reach Out and Touch Somebody's Hand [1970]

4 I'm every woman, it's all in me.

   I'm Every Woman [1978]

5 Thought I could turn my emotions on and off
   I was sure, so sure,
   But love taught me who was the boss.

   The Boss [1979]

Melba Pattillo Beals   1941–

6 Thank you, I can take that too.
   *Response when slapped in the face by a white girl
   on her first day of high school as one of the
   Little Rock Nine [September 1957]*

7 My eight friends and I paid for the integration of Central High with
   our innocence. During those years when we desperately needed approval
   from our peers, we were victims of the most harsh rejection imaginable. The
   physical and psychological punishment we endured profoundly affected all
   our lives. It transformed us into warriors who dared not cry even when we
   suffered intolerable pain.   *Warriors Don't Cry [1994]*

Simi Bedford   1941–

8 How we danced. The music poured through our veins and we flowed
   with the beat. The wheel had come full circle. We wound and unwound our
   bodies seamlessly as if we had no bones. Is there a sight more beautiful, the
   older women said, than a Yoruba girl dancing?

   Yoruba Girl Dancing [1991], last lines

Ed[ward] Bradley   1941–2006

9 *[On broadcast journalism:]* You can shine a light in a dark corner and
   make life better for people living there in the dark.

Interview. Archive of American Television [May 12, 2000]

Ronald H[armon] Brown

1941–1996

1   Indeed, free trade can be described as democracy in the marketplace. And just as we have pushed forward on many fronts to nurture and encourage democracy around the world, so we must work to expand economic freedom. We must not settle for an uneven playing field: free trade for some, protection for others.

Speech [March 26, 1993]

2   The common thread of Democratic history.... has been an abiding faith in the judgment of hardworking American families, and a commitment to helping the excluded, the disenfranchised and the poor strengthen our nation by earning themselves a piece of the American Dream. We remember that this great land was sculpted by immigrants and slaves, their children and grandchildren.

From Alan Colmes, *Red, White & Liberal [2003]*

George Clinton

1941–

3   Free your mind and your ass will follow
The kingdom of heaven is within.

Free Your Mind ... and Your Ass Will Follow [1970].
Recorded by Funkadelic

4   A chocolate city is no dream
It's my piece of the rock and I dig you, CC
God bless Chocolate City and its vanilla suburbs.

Chocolate City [1975]. Recorded by Parliament

5   Everybody's got a little light under the sun.

Flashlight [1977]. Recorded by Parliament

6   One Nation Under a Groove   *Song title [1978]. Recorded by Funkadelic*

Desmond Dekker

1941–2006

7   Dem a loot, dem a shoot, dem a wail
A Shanty Town
Dem rude boys out on probation
A Shanty Town
Dem a rude when dem come up to town
A Shanty Town   *007 (Shanty Town) [1967]*

Toi Derricotte

1941–

8   There is no perfect
past to go back to.

Tender [1997]. Exits from Elmina Castle: Cape Coast, Ghana,
The Journey

1 Maybe one day we will have
written about this color thing
until we've solved it.   *Tender. After a Reading at a Black College*

2   All my life I have passed invisibly into the white world, and all my life
I have felt that sudden and alarming moment of consciousness when
I remember I am black.   *The Black Notebooks [1997]*

Ernest Green   1941–

3   *[On being one of the Little Rock Nine:]* It's just the price we've got to
pay. And for what is involved, I think it is cheap at the price.
Interview. Chicago Defender [November 21, 1957]

Brian Holland   1941–

4 Wait! Oh, yes, wait a minute, Mr. Postman.
Please Mr. Postman [1961][1]

Brian Holland   1941–

and

Lamont Dozier   1941–

and

Edward Holland, Jr.   1939–

5 Could it be a devil in me
Or is this the way love's supposed to be
It's like a heat wave burnin' in my heart.   *Heat Wave [1963]*

6 Baby love, my baby love
I need you, oh how I need you.   *Baby Love [1964]*

7 Baby, I Need Your Loving   *Song title [1964]*

8 How Sweet It Is to Be Loved by You   *Song title [1964]*

9 Where Did Our Love Go?   *Song title [1964]*

10 Sugar pie, honey bunch, you know that I love you
I can't help myself, I love you and nobody else.   *I Can't Help Myself [1965]*

11 Whenever you're near
I hear a symphony.   *I Hear a Symphony [1965]*

[1]With William Garrett, Georgia Dobbins, and Robert Bateman.

1   It's the same old song but with a different meaning,
Since you've been gone.   *It's the Same Old Song [1965]*

2   Nowhere to run to, baby.
Nowhere to hide.   *Nowhere to Run [1965]*

3   Stop! In the name of love, before you break my heart.
        Stop! In the Name of Love [1965]

4   Reach out, reach out
I'll be there with a love that will shelter you.
I'll be there, with a love that will see you through.
        Reach Out, I'll Be There [1966]

5   Standing in the shadows of love,
I'm getting ready for the heartaches to come.
        Standing in the Shadows of Love [1966]

6   You can't hurry love,
No, you just have to wait.   *You Can't Hurry Love [1966]*

7   Reflections of the way life used to be
Reflections of the love you took from me.   *Reflections [1967]*

George Jackson
1941–1971

8   Being born a slave in a captive society and never experiencing any objective basis for expectation had the effect of preparing me for the progressively traumatic misfortunes that lead so many blackmen to the prison gate. I was prepared for prison. It required only minor psychic adjustments.
        Soledad Brother [1970]

9   Patience has its limits. Take it too far, and it's cowardice.
        Soledad Brother

Jesse [Louis] Jackson
1941–

10   When we're unemployed, we're called lazy; when the whites are unemployed, it's called a depression.
        From DAVID FROST, *The Americans [1970]*

11   We say that we may be in the slum, but the slum is not in us.
        WattStax [August 1972]

12   We are shifting from burn baby burn, to learn baby learn.   *WattsStax*

13   Tears will get you sympathy, but sweat will get you change.
        Quotations from a Spellbinder. TIME [July 10, 1978]

1   You can't plant the seed and pick the fruit the next morning.

Quotations from a Spellbinder

2   We must convince New Generation Blacks that if they can conceive it and believe it, they can achieve it. They must know that it is not their *aptitude* but their *attitude* that will determine their *altitude*. . . . We must teach our children that their minds are pearls and they can learn anything in the world.   *A Challenge to the New Generation. Ebony [August 1978]*

3   My constituency is the desperate, the damned, the disinherited, the disrespected, and the despised.

Speech at the Democratic National Convention, San Francisco
[July 17, 1984]

4   When I look out at this convention, I see the face of America, red, yellow, brown, black and white. We are all precious in God's sight — the real rainbow coalition.

Speech at the Democratic National Convention, Atlanta
[July 19, 1988]

5   My right and my privilege to stand here before you has been won — won in my lifetime — by the blood and the sweat of the innocent.

Speech at the Democratic National Convention, Atlanta

6   Keep hope alive.

Speech at the Democratic National Convention

7   I am somebody.   *Slogan*

Maulana Karenga [Ronald Everett]   1941–

8   1. Umoja (Unity): To strive for and maintain unity in the family, community, nation and race.

2. Kujichagulia (Self-determination): To define ourselves, name ourselves, create for ourselves and speak for ourselves instead of being defined, named, created for and spoken for by others.

3. Ujima (Collective Work and Responsibility): To build and maintain our community together and make our sister's and brother's problems our problems and to solve them together.

4. Ujamaa (Cooperative Economics): To build and maintain our own stores, shops and other businesses and to profit from them together.

5. Nia (Purpose): To make our collective vocation the building and developing of our community in order to restore our people to their traditional greatness.

6. Kuumba (Creativity): To do always as much as we can, in the way we can, in order to leave our community more beautiful and beneficial than we inherited it.

> 7. Imani (Faith): To believe with all our heart in our people, our parents, our teachers, our leaders and the righteousness and victory of our struggle.
> *Nguzo Saba (The Seven Principles) of Kwanzaa*[1]
> *[September 7, 1965]*

Aaron Neville
1941–

1   In New Orleans you're born into music and you die into music and music all in between.   *Make It Funky! [2005]*

Wilson Pickett
1941–2006

2   I'm gonna wait 'til the midnight hour.   *In the Midnight Hour [1966]*

3   Ninety-Nine and a Half (Won't Do)   *Song title [1966]*[2]

David Porter
1941–

and

Isaac Hayes
1942–2008

4   I'm a soul man.   *Soul Man [1967]*

Martin Puryear
1941–

5   I value the referential quality of art, the fact that a work can allude to things or states of being without in any way representing them.
Wall text, Museum of Modern Art [2007]

Otis Redding
1941–1967

6   These arms of mine are lonely
They are lonely and feeling blue
These arms of mine are yearning
Yearning from wanting you.   *These Arms of Mine [1962]*

7   I've been loving you too long to stop now.
I've Been Loving You Too Long [1965]

8   What you want,
Honey, I got
What you need

---

[1]Derived from the Swahili term *matunda ya kwanza*, meaning "first fruits." — MAULANA KARENGA, *Kwanzaa: Origin, Concepts, Practice* [1977].

[2]With Steve Cropper.

You know I got it
All I'm askin' for
Is a little respect when I come home.   *Respect [1965]*

1   You got to hold her, squeeze her, never leave her.
                              Try a Little Tenderness [1966][1]

2   Sittin' on the dock of the bay
Watching the tide roll away
Sittin' on the dock of the bay wastin' time.

                              Dock of the Bay [1968][2]

Randall Robinson   1941–

3   What exactly is hate, and has it to be returned in kind? Can it afflict its
victim with a muted form? The kind that doesn't preoccupy, past which one
can smile and function civilly? Can the tumor, enlarged and hardened over
time by a weather of ceaseless slights, be benign? . . . White-hot hatred would
seem the proper reflex. But there is no survival there.

                              Defending the Spirit [1998]

4   I have come to know race as a sealed dwelling with windows but no
doors. One can look out but never leave.   *Defending the Spirit*

5   Like slavery, other human rights crimes have resulted in the loss of
millions of lives. But only slavery, with its sadistic patience, asphyxiated
memory, and smothered cultures, has hulled empty a whole race of people
with inter-generational efficiency. . . . It is a human rights crime without par-
allel in the modern world. For it produces its victims *ad infinitum*, long after
the active stage of the crime has ended.   *The Debt [2000]*

6   [On reparations:] The appeal here is not for affirmative action but,
rather, for just compensation as an entitlement for the many years of hei-
nous U.S. government-embraced wrongs and the stolen labor of our forebears. We make only the claims that other successful group complainants
have made in the world. Put simply, we too are *owed*.   *The Debt*

7   The faces are adolescent but too knowing, old from unnatural experience, at once expressionless and quietly menacing. The eyes, empty of light,
evidence the dissociation of battered souls that had given up and left home
long ago. Floppy caps turned backward over black rags, pants bagging low
over haute hood sneakers. . . . Man-boys. . . . They are the children of long-

---

[1]Written by Harry Woods, Jimmy Campbell, and Reg Connelly [1965]. The lyrics were substantially
changed by Redding; this became his signature song.

[2]With Steve Cropper.

sown seed, old burned Civil War canisters packed with live grapeshot, marked: DANGEROUS IF NOT TREATED. They are slavery's harvest.

Quitting America [2004]

1   America. America. Land of my birth and erstwhile distress. Hypocrite immemorial. My heart left long ago. At long last, I have followed it. Trying my very best, how could I, in good conscience, remain *for* a country that has never ever, at home or abroad, been *for* me or *for* mine?

Quitting America

Ken[ule] Saro-Wiwa   1941–1995

2   I saw the people who were singing. Young young boys like myself, all of them with gun and uniform. It is that uniform that I like very much. When I see how they are all marching, prouding and singing, I am very happy. But when I see all their uniform shining and very very nice to see, I cannot tell you how I am feeling. Immediately I know that this soza is wonderful thing.

Sozaboy [1985]

3   Trouble no dey ring bell.

Sozaboy

4   And I was thinking how I was prouding before to go to soza and call myself Sozaboy. But now if anybody say anything about war or even fight, I will just run and run and run and run and run. Believe me yours sincerely.

Sozaboy

5   I recall, many years ago as a young child, reading in a newspaper of an African leader who stood on the grave of a dead lieutenant and through his tears said: "Africa kills her sons." I don't know what he meant by that, and though I've thought about it long enough, I've not been able to unravel the full mystery of those words. Now, today, this moment, they come flooding back to me. And I want to borrow from him. I'd like you to put this on my gravestone as an epitaph: "Africa Kills Her Sun." A good epitaph, eh? Cryptic. Definite. A stroke of genius, I should say. I'm sure you'll agree with me. "Africa Kills Her Sun!" That's why she's been described as the Dark Continent? Yes?   *Adaku and Other Stories [1989]. Africa Kills Her Sun*

Kwame Toure [Stokely Carmichael]   1941–1998

6   The only position for women in SNCC[1] is prone.

Interview [November 1964][2]

---

[1]Student Nonviolent Coordinating Committee.

[2]From *Sisterhood Is Powerful* [1970], edited by Robin Morgan. Toure contended that his comment was a joke, as did the interviewer, Mary E. King, in a letter to the editor in the *New York Times*: "He Said It, Sisters, but It's Not What He Meant" [April 20, 1996].

1   We must recognize that black people, whether we are in Durham, North Carolina; San Francisco, California; Jamaica, Trinidad, Brazil, Europe, or on the mother continent, that we are all an African people, we are Africans, there can be no question about that.   *Speech [October 1969]*

Kwame Toure [Stokely Carmichael]   1941–1998

and

Charles V[ernon] Hamilton   1929–

2   Black power[1] ... is a call for black people in this country to unite, to recognize their heritage, to build a sense of community. It is a call for black people to begin to define their own goals, to lead their own organizations and to support those organizations. It is a call to reject the racist institutions and values of this society.   *Black Power! [1967], ch. 2*

3   Before a group can enter the open society, it must first close ranks.
    Black Power!

Maurice White   1941–

and

Philip Bailey   1951–

and

Larry Dunn   1953–

4   You're a shining star
No matter who you are
Shining bright to see
What you can truly be.   *Shining Star [1975]*

Maurice White   1941–

and

Charles Stepney   1931–1976

and

Verdine White   1951–

5   That's the way of the world
Plant your flower and you grow a pearl

---

[1]Toure first used this term in a Greenwood, Mississippi, speech: "What we are going to start saying now is 'Black Power!'" [June 16, 1966].

Child is born with a heart of gold
The way of the world makes his heart so cold.

That's the Way of the World [1975]

John Edgar Wideman   1941–

1   Stories are letters. Letters sent to anybody or everybody. But the best kind are meant to be read by a specific somebody. When you read that kind you know you are eavesdropping.   *Damballah [1981], dedication*

2   They're killing us faster now. And beating down the ones they can't kill. Our boys over there supposed to be dying equal. It's a crying shame how they do us.   *Sent for You Yesterday [1983] [Samantha]*

3   Brother could be in both places at once. A Brother in the sky. A Brother humping down Finance Street. In one place he had no color, he could not speak or play. In another place he watches and waits.

Sent for You Yesterday

4   No one does time outside of time. . . . Since a person can't be removed from time unless you kill him, what prison does to its inmates is make time as miserable, as unpleasant as possible. Prison time must be hard time, a metaphorical death, a sustained twilight condition of death-in-life. The prisoner's life is violently interrupted, enclosed within a parenthesis. The point is to create the fiction that he doesn't exist. Prison is an experience of death by inches, minutes, hours, days.   *Brothers and Keepers [1984]*

5   I still can't believe it. Eleven people murdered. Babies, women, didn't make no nevermind to the cops. Eleven human beings dead for what? Tell me for what. Why did they have to kill my brothers and sisters? Burn them up like you burn garbage?   *Philadelphia Fire [1990]*

6   What should open now in response to the tragedy of a city burning is the vista of your heart. But you run away every time. You'll turn your back every time. Philadelphia's on fire.   *Philadelphia Fire*

7   If a certain kind of camera, yet to be invented, achieved the capacity to record the instantaneous give-and-take between two black people meeting in the street, looking at the artifact this "camera" produces you would see the shared sense of identity, the bloody secrets linking us and setting us apart, the names flapping in the air — black, negro, african american, colored, etc., etc. — we sometimes answer to but never internalize completely because they are inadequate to describe the sense of common ground we exchange at this moment.   *Fatheralong [1994]*

8   Teach me who I might be, who you might be — without it [race].

Fatheralong   415

1   The stories must be told. Ideas of manhood, true and transforming, grow out of private, personal exchanges between fathers and sons. Yet for generations of black men in America this privacy, this privilege has been systematically breached in a most shameful and public way. Not only breached, but brutally usurped, mediated by murder, mayhem, misinformation.

Fatheralong

2   Tell me, finally, what is a man. What is a woman. Aren't we lovers first, spirits sharing an uncharted space, a space our stories tell, a space chanted, written upon again and again, yet one story never quite erased by the next, each story saving the space, saving itself, saving us. If someone is listening.   *The Cattle Killing [1996], pt. 2*

3   I imagine my mother dreaming the streets and her dreams are what happens in the streets below, the way she used to dream me home safely by sitting up and waiting for me to stumble in, no matter how late the hour.   *Sitting*[1]

Jeremiah A[lvesta] Wright, Jr.   1941–

4   Have the audacity to hope for that child of yours. Have the audacity to hope for that home of yours. Have the audacity to hope for that church of yours. For whatever it is you've been praying for, keep on praying.

The Audacity to Hope. Sermon [1990]

5   It's easy to hope when there are evidences all around of how good God is. But to have the audacity to hope when that love is not evident . . . that is a true test. . . . To take the one string you have left and to have the audacity to hope — make music and praise God on and with whatever it is you've got left, even though you can't see what God is going to do.

The Audacity to Hope

6   The government gives them the drugs, builds bigger prisons, passes a three-strike law and then wants us to sing "God Bless America." No, no, no, God damn America, — that's in the Bible — for killing innocent people. God damn America for treating our citizens as less than human. God damn America for as long as she acts like she is God and she is supreme.

Sermon [2003]

Ama Ata Aidoo   1942–

7   Our people say a bad marriage kills the soul. Mine is fit for burial.

No Sweetness Here [1970]

---

[1]From *Dream Me Home Safely* [2003], edited by Susan Richards Shreve.

1   Old yam has to rot in order that new yam can grow. Where is the earth? Who is going to do the planting?

No Sweetness Here. For Whom Things Did Not Change

2   Negativism is malign, like cancer. It chokes all life within its reach as it grows.

Our Sister Killjoy [1977]

Muhammad Ali [Cassius Marcellus Clay, Jr.]   1942–

3   I am the greatest.   *Slogan, inspired by wrestler Gorgeous George*

4   Float like a butterfly, sting like a bee.

Boxing credo, devised by aide Drew "Bundini" Brown

5   Not only do I knock 'em out, I pick the round.

Statement [December 1962]

6   Ain't never been another fighter like me. Ain't never been no nothing like me.   *Interview. Playboy [October 1964]*

7   I ain't got no quarrel with them Viet Cong.

On the draft [February 1966]

8   I am America. Only, I'm the part you won't recognize. But get used to me. Black, confident, cocky; my name, not yours; my religion, not yours; my goals, my own — get used to me!   *The Greatest [1975]*

9   Me, Wheee![1]

Speech at Harvard University [June 4, 1975]

10 Champions aren't made in gyms. Champions are made from something they have deep inside — a desire, a dream, and a vision. They have to have the skill and the will. But the will must be stronger than the skill.

The Soul of a Butterfly [2004][2]

Molefi Kete Asante [Arthur Smith]   1942–

11 Afrocentricity is the belief in the centrality of Africans in postmodern history. It is our history, our mythology, our creative motif and our ethos exemplifying our collective will.

Afrocentricity [1988]

12 It is not unity that we must seek but collective consciousness. In Afrocentricity, there is a remarkable surge of consciousness that transcends the current emphasis on unity; this is the next act in our drama.... Consciousness precedes unity.

Afrocentricity

---

[1]Often referred to as the shortest poem ever written, this is also quoted as "Me. We."
[2]*The Harvard Crimson Online* [June 9, 1975] and MUHAMMAD ALI, *The Soul of a Butterfly* [2004].

Samuel R[ay] Delany
1942–

1 We have to name ourselves first. And you don't know who you are.

Babel-17 [1966] [Butcher]

2 Imagine, a great web that spreads across the galaxy, as far as man. That's the matrix in which history happens today.... Each individual is a junction in that net, and the strands between are the cultural, the economic, the psychological threads that hold individual to individual.

Nova [1968] [Katin]

3 to wound the autumnal city.
So howled out for the world to give him a name.
The in-dark answered with wind.   *Dhalgren [1974], opening lines*

4 It would be as naive to think that all forgettings are random as it would be to think thus of all dreams: the first things to go are, systematically, the incidents confirming our own weaknesses which, because we are lucky enough not to *have* to talk about, there's no particular reason to recall. The incidents we will, likewise, retain are among those that tell of a certain strength.

Atlantis: Model 1924 [1995]

Aretha Franklin
1942–

5 R-E-S-P-E-C-T
Find out what it means to me
R-E-S-P-E-C-T
Take care—TCB.
     Refrain added in 1967 to Otis Redding's 1965 song "Respect"[1]

6 Rock steady, baby!

Rock Steady [1971]

Aretha Franklin
1942–

and

Ted White
Twentieth century

7 Don't send me no doctor
Fillin' me up with all those pills

---

[1] Aretha Franklin's interpretation of "Respect" overshadowed Redding's and became her signature song and anthem.

I got a man named Dr. Feelgood,
That man takes care of all my pains and ills.   *Dr. Feelgood [1967]*

1   You better think,
Think about what you're trying to do to me
Think, let your mind go and let yourself be free.   *Think [1968]*

Peter J[ohn] Gomes   1942–2011

2   Fear denies change. . . . And simple justice, the moral fuel of progress, makes change inevitable.
Op-ed in the New York Times [May 22, 1993]

3   One of the great paradoxes of race in America is that the religion of the oppressor, Christianity, became the religion of the oppressed and the means of their liberation.   *The Good Book [1996]*

4   "Judicial tyranny" is a phrase usually heard from those whose prejudices have not been sustained by a court's decision.
Op-ed in the Boston Globe [February 8, 2004]

Chris Hani [Martin Thembisile]   1942–1993

5   Many sacrifices are going to be exacted before we finally defeat De Klerk and his government. More and more atrocities will be committed by the erstwhile admirers of Hitler and dictators of Latin America. But for us, there is no other choice but to engage them in a struggle, not just once but more than a million times.
Speech delivered less than one year before assassination [1992]

Isaac Hayes   1942–2008

6   Hot Buttered Soul   *Title of album [1969]*

7   Who's the black private dick
That's a sex machine to all the chicks?
Shaft!
You're damn right.   *Shaft [1971]*

[James Marshall] Jimi Hendrix   1942–1970

8   Have you ever been experienced?   *Are You Experienced? [1967]*

9   I have only one burning desire
Let me stand next to your fire!   *Fire [1967]*

419

1   Hey Joe, where you going with that gun in your hand?

Hey Joe [1967]

2   I'm gonna wave my freak flag high.

If 6 Was 9 [1967]

3   'Scuse me while I kiss the sky.

Purple Haze [1967]

4   Will the wind ever remember
The names it has blown in the past?
And with this crutch, its old age, and its wisdom
It whispers, "No, this will be the last."
And the wind cries, Mary.   *The Wind Cries Mary [1967]*

5   I'm bold as love.   *Bold As Love [1968]*

6   And so castles made of sand melts into the sea, eventually.

Castles Made of Sand [1968]

7   Well she's walking through the clouds
With a circus mind that's running wild.

Little Wing [1968]

8   I'm a voodoo chile, baby.

Voodoo Chile [1968]

David Hilliard   1942–

9   The ideology of the Black Panther Party is the historical experiences of
Black people in America translated through Marxism-Leninism. When we
review the past history of Black people in this country, we realize that after
four hundred years we are victims of the oppressive machinery that gags,
binds, and chains Black men who speak out in defense of their alleged constitutional rights.

The Ideology of the Black Panther Party. The Black Panther
[November 8, 1969][1]

10   We ain't here for no goddamned peace, because we know that we
can't have no peace because this country was built on war. And if you want
peace you got to fight for it.

If You Want Peace You Got to Fight for It. The Black Panther
[November 19, 1969][1]

[1]From *Black Panthers Speak* [1970], edited by PHILLIP S. FONER.

Leon Huff   1942–

and

Gene McFadden   1948–2006

and

John Whitehead   1948–2004

1   They're smiling in your face,
All the time they wanna take your place.
The backstabbers.

Back Stabbers [1972]

Charlayne Hunter-Gault   1942–

2   You have to assess every situation that you're in and you have to decide, is this happening because I'm black? Is this happening because I'm a woman? Or is this happening because this is how it happens?

From BRIAN LANKER, I Dream a World [1989]

3   If people are informed they will do the right thing. It's when they are not informed that they become hostages to prejudice.   *I Dream a World*

4   When I walked onto the campus of the University of Georgia and they were saying, "Nigger, go home!" I was looking around for the nigger. I mean I knew who I was. I was a queen.

On the "suit of armor" given to her by her parents' generation.
Interview. Cambridge, Massachusetts [May 7, 1997][1]

Reginald F[rancis] Lewis   1942–1993

5   Why Should White Guys Have All the Fun?

Title of autobiography [1995]

Haki R. Madhubuti [Don Luther Lee]   1942–

6   BLACK PEOPLE THINK—
THINK BLACK.

Awareness [1966]

7   I
seek
integration
of
negroes

---

[1]From CORNEL WEST, *Restoring Hope* [1997].

with
black
people.   *The New Integrationist [1968]*

1   ever wonder where the circle came from
    or who were the first people to use the triangle?
    who were the original cultivators of the earth, who used
    water of the nile to power minds and machines? what people
    created music from instrument and voice and viewed the
    building of cities as art and science? who were the
    first to love because love contained the secrets of tomorrow?
    look at yourselves.   *Seeking Ancestors [1987]*

2   The most prevailing consciousness among Black people today is one
    of survival. And this survival is not of a collective nature, in which indivi-
    duals, communities and institutes work together to solve problems. Black
    survival, especially in the urban areas, is more Darwinism, a "survival of the
    fittest" attitude.
                        Black Men: Obsolete, Single, Dangerous? [1990]. Were Corners
                        Made for Black Men to Stand On?

3   soft. strong. not afraid to take the lead. creative father. organized and orga-
    nizer. a brother to brothers. a brother to sisters. understanding. patient. a
    winner. maintainer of the i can, i must, i will attitude toward Black struggle
    and life. a builder of the necessary.
                        Black Men. Black Manhood: Toward a Definition [1991]

Curtis Mayfield   1942–1999

4   From nowhere, through a caravan around the campfire light,
    A lovely woman in motion with hair as dark as night.
    Her eyes were like that of a cat in the dark that hypnotized me with love.
    She was a gypsy woman.   *Gypsy Woman [1961]*

5   Keep on pushin', keep on pushin'
    I can't stop now.   *Keep On Pushin' [1964]*

6   People get ready
    There's a train a-coming
    You don't need no baggage
    You just get on board
    All you need is faith to hear the diesels humming
    Don't need no ticket, you just thank the Lord.   *People Get Ready [1964]*

7   There'll be no more Uncle Tom.
    At last that blessed day has come and we're a winner.

And everybody knows the truth
We just keep on pushin' like Martin Luther told you to
And I don't mind leavin' here to show the world we have no fear,
'Cause we're movin' on up, movin' on up.
Lord have mercy, we're movin' on up.   *We're a Winner [1967]*

1   Some people think we don't have the right
To say it's my country
Before they give in they'd rather fuss and fight
Than say it's my country
I've paid three hundred years or more
Of slave-driving sweat and welts on my back
This is my country.   *This Is My Country [1968]*

2   Hush now child, and don't you cry
Your folks might understand you by and by.   *Move On Up [1970]*

3   Freddie's dead, that's what I said.   *Freddie's Dead [1972]*

4   Why can't we brothers protect one another?
No one's serious and it makes me furious.   *Freddie's Dead*

5   I'm your mama, I'm your daddy
I'm that nigger in the alley.
I'm your doctor, when you need.
Want some coke? Have some weed.   *Pusherman [1972]*

6   Superfly, you're gonna make your fortune by and by,
but if you lose don't ask no questions why,
the only game you know is do or die.   *Superfly [1972]*

Thabo Mbeki   1942–

7   All they had been saying was — give a chance for the curtains to part,
so that we can see the world beyond, the world of progress and human dignity, in a country which truly belongs to all who live in it, both black and
white, both women and men! If all of us stand tall today, as all of us surely
do, it is only because we are borne aloft by the firm hands of the ordinary
people of our country who, through the generations, have said all they want
is peace, progress and liberty.
            Address following his election as president of South Africa
            [June 14, 1999][1]

---

[1]From THABO MBEKI, *Africa Define Yourself* [2002].

1   The full meaning of liberation will not be realized until our people are freed both from oppression and from the dehumanizing legacy of deprivation we inherited from our past.   *Inaugural address [June 16, 1999]*[1]

2   *[Response when asked "Are you prepared to acknowledge that there is a link between HIV and AIDS?":]* I am saying that you cannot attribute immune deficiency solely and exclusively to a virus.[2]

Interview. TIME [September 11, 2000]

3   There is a new dawn on the African horizon. I know this as a matter of fact that this new beginning is not a mirage. It portends a rebirth of Africa that can and must occur. It imposes an obligation on all of us to join together as midwives of Africa's Renaissance.

Address at the twenty-fifth meeting of the Association of African Central Bank Governors [August 16, 2001]

Robbie McCauley   1942–

4   Survival is luck. Or unlucky.   *Sally's Rape [1991]*

Huey P[ercy] Newton   1942–1989

5   A people who have suffered so much for so long at the hands of a racist society must draw the line somewhere.

Executive Mandate Number One [May 2, 1967][3]

6   Men weren't created in order to obey laws. Laws were created to obey men.   *In Defense of Self-Defense, I [June 20, 1967]*[3]

7   The oppressor must be harassed until his doom. He must have no peace day or night. The slaves have always outnumbered the slavemasters. The power of the oppressor rests on the submission of the people.

In Defense of Self-Defense, I

8   An unarmed people are slaves or are subject to slavery at any given moment. If a government is not afraid of the people it will arm the people against foreign aggression. Black people are held captive in the midst of their oppressors. There is a world of difference between thirty million unarmed submissive Black people and thirty million Black people armed with freedom and defense, guns, and the strategic methods of liberation.

In Defense of Self-Defense, I

---

[1]From THABO MBEKI, *Africa Define Yourself* [2002].

[2]Several months earlier, Mbeki delivered a speech at the 13th International AIDS Conference held in Durban, South Africa [July 9, 2000], in which he said, "The world's biggest killer and the greatest cause of ill-health and suffering across the globe, including South Africa, is extreme poverty." Mbeki's speech prompted a declaration and plan of action signed by five thousand scientists, including Nobel Prize winners, reaffirming the science of the HIV/AIDS epidemic.

[3]From HUEY P. NEWTON, *Essays from the Minister of Defense* [1968].

1   When a mechanic wants to fix a broken-down car engine, he must have the necessary tools to do the job. When the people move for liberation, they must have the basic tool of liberation: the gun.

In Defense of Self-Defense, I

2   Abstractions come only with leisure.

In Defense of Self-Defense, II [July 3, 1967][1]

3   Politics is merely the desire of individuals and groups to satisfy their basic needs first: food, shelter, and clothing and security for themselves and their loved ones.

In Defense of Self-Defense, II

4   The prison cannot be victorious because walls, bars and guards cannot conquer or hold down an idea.

To Prisons [July 12, 1969][2]

5   The terms "faggot" and "punk" should be deleted from our vocabulary, and especially we should not attach names normally designed for homosexuals to men who are enemies of the people.... Homosexuals are not enemies of the people.

The Women's Liberation and Gay Liberation Movements
[August 15, 1970][2]

6   To die for the . . . racists . . . is lighter than a feather. But to die for the people . . . is heavier than any mountain and deeper than any sea.

To Die for the People [1972], epigraph

7   There is an old African saying. "I am we." If you met an African in ancient times and asked him who he was, he would reply "I am we." This is revolutionary suicide: I, we, all of us are the one and the multitude.

To Die for the People

8   By having no family,
I inherited the family of humanity.
By having no possessions,
I have possessed all.
By rejecting the love of one,
I received the love of all.
By surrendering my life to the revolution,
I found eternal life.
Revolutionary Suicide.

Revolutionary Suicide [1973], epigraph

---

[1]From Huey P. Newton, *Essays from the Minister of Defense* [1968].
[2]From *To Die for the People* [1972].

Huey P[ercy] Newton

1942–1989

and

[Robert] Bobby Seale

1936–

1   We Want Freedom. We Want Power to Determine the Destiny of Our Black Community.

We believe that Black and oppressed people will not be free until we are able to determine our destinies in our own communities ourselves, by fully controlling all the institutions which exist in our communities.

Black Panther Party: Ten-Point Program [1967–1972], No. 1

2   We Want an End to the Robbery by the CAPITALIST of our Black Community.

We believe that this racist government has robbed us and now we are demanding the overdue debt of forty acres and two mules.... We will accept the payment in currency which will be distributed to our many communities.... The American racist has taken part in the slaughter of over fifty million Black people; therefore we feel that this is a modest demand that we make.

Black Panther Party: Ten-Point Program, No. 3

3   We Want Education for Our People That Exposes the True Nature of This Decadent American Society.

We Want Education That Teaches Us Our True History and Our Role in the Present-Day Society.

We believe in an educational system that will give to our people knowledge of the self. If you do not have knowledge of yourself and your position in the society and in the world, then you will have little chance to relate to anything else.

Black Panther Party: Ten-Point Program, No. 5

Bernice Johnson Reagon

1942–

4   They are falling all around me
The strongest leaves of my tree.

They Are Falling All Around Me [1978]

5   Sometime day breaks in my life
Sometime the sun shines in my life
Sometime things work right in my life
You are my sometime.   *Sometime [1981]*

6   The older I get, the better I know that the
secret of my going on

Is when the reins are in the hand of the
young, who dare to run against the storm.

Ella's Song [1983]

1   We will not bow down to racism
We will not bow down to injustice
We will not bow down to exploitation
I'm gon' stand.

I'm Gon' Stand [1983]

2   We all, everyone of us,
must come home again.

We All ... Everyone of Us [1983]

Walter Rodney   1942–1980

3   Black Power is a doctrine about black people, for black people,
preached by black people. I'm putting it to my black brothers and sisters
that the color of our skin is the most fundamental thing about us.... I am
not saying that is the way things ought to be, I am simply recognizing the
real world — that is the way things are. Under different circumstances, it
would have been nice to be color blind, to choose my friends solely because
their social interests coincided with mine — but no conscious black man
can allow himself such luxuries in the contemporary world.

The Groundings with My Brothers [1969], ch. 2

4   All of the countries named as "underdeveloped" in the world are
exploited by others; and the underdevelopment with which the world is
now preoccupied is a product of capitalist, imperialist and colonialist
exploitation.

How Europe Underdeveloped Africa [1972]

Jamil Abdullah Al-Amin [H. Rap (Hubert Gerold) Brown]   1943–

5   Violence is as American as cherry pie.

Press conference [July 27, 1967]

6   America is the ultimate denial of the theory of man's continuous
evolution.

Die, Nigger, Die [1969]

7   What better way to enslave a man than give him the vote and call him
free? What does it profit a man to be able to vote when he has to choose
between a Democrat and a Republican — Tweedledee and Tweedledum?

Quoted in the New Yorker [April 29–May 6, 1996]

Arthur Ashe

1943–1993

1   True heroism is remarkably sober, very undramatic. It is not the urge to surpass all others at whatever cost, but the urge to serve others at whatever cost.

Commencement speech, Ohio Wesleyan University
[May 12, 1991]

2   Race is for me a more onerous burden than AIDS. My disease is the result of biological factors over which we, thus far, have no control. Racism, however, is entirely made by people, and therefore it hurts and inconveniences infinitely more.   *Days of Grace [1993]*

3   From what we get, we can make a living; what we give, however, makes a life.   *Days of Grace*

4   Racism and sexism must never be an excuse for not doing your best. Racism and sexism will probably always exist but you must always try to rise above them.   *Letter to his daughter. Days of Grace*

Cecil Brown

1943–

5   Life is a lie. But people don't know that, see. Only smart people like me know that.

The Life and Loves of Mr. Jiveass Nigger [1969].
The Tale [George Washington]

Elaine Brown

1943–

6   I have all the guns and all the money. I can withstand challenge from without and from within.

Speech as first and sole female chairman of the Black Panthers
[August 1974]

7   The answer was love — the love that was inside the madness. It was about not forgetting. It was about living and about dying for freedom.

A Taste of Power [1992]

8   When I was a little girl, I wanted to be white. My mother sent me to schools dominated by rich white children where I learned that I was a "nigger." Oh that wasn't because anybody called me that, but because I saw I was poor and black.... By the time I realized there was no place in America for a black girl, I discovered another trick. Even if I had been able to be white, there were no paths out of the powerlessness. The keys to the kingdom were gripped in the hands of a few white men — and *only* men. I could work for those men, if I "behaved," but I could never be them, have what they had, be master of my own ship.... What I saw was that my

oppression and my freedom were *umbilically* tied to the oppression and freedom of all my people. So I became a Black Panther.

A Taste of Power

1   They [the male leadership of the Black Panther Party] wanted so little from our revolution; they had lost sight of it. Too many of them seemed satisfied to appropriate for themselves the power the party was gaining, measured by the shiny illusion of cars and clothes and guns.

On the downfall of the Black Panther Party.
A Taste of Power

Kenneth Gamble   1943–

and

Leon Huff   1942–

2   If you don't know me by now,
      You will never, never, never know me.

If You Don't Know Me by Now [1972]

3   People all over the world, join hands,
      Start a love train.   *Love Train [1972]*

4   Am I Black Enough for You?   *Song title [1972]*

5   I'll always love my mama,
      She's my favorite girl.
      I'll always love my mama,
      She brought me in this world.   *I'll Always Love My Mama [1973]*

6   For the love of money,
      People will steal from their mother
      For the love of money,
      People will rob their own brother.   *For the Love of Money [1974]*

7   For a small piece of paper it carries a lot of weight.

For the Love of Money

8   When will I see you again?
      When will our hearts beat together?
      Are we in love or just friends?
      Is this my beginning or is this the end?

When Will I See You Again? [1974]

9   It's so nice to see
      All the folks you love together.   *Family Reunion [1975]*

Kenneth Gamble
1943–

and

Leon Huff
1942–

and

Jerry Butler
1939–

1   Only the strong survive, only the strong survive.
Hey, you gotta be strong, you'd better hold on.

Only the Strong Survive [1969]

[Yolande Cornelia] Nikki Giovanni, Jr.
1943–

2   i just wanta say just gotta say something
bout those beautiful beautiful beautiful outasight
black men
with they afros
walking down they street
is the same ol danger
but a brand new pleasure.

Beautiful Black Men [1968]

3   Death is a slave's freedom.   *The Funeral of Martin Luther King, Jr. [1968]*[1]

4   Childhood remembrances are always a drag
if you're Black.

Nikki-Rosa [1968]

5   I really hope no white person ever has cause
to write about me
because they never understand
Black love is Black wealth and they'll
probably talk about my hard childhood
and never understand that
all the while I was quite happy.

Nikki-Rosa

6   Where are your heroes, my little Black ones?   *Poem for Black Boys [1968]*

7   you my children of battle, are your heroes
You must invent your own games and teach us old ones
how to play

Poem for Black Boys

8   it's a sex object if you're pretty
and no love
or love and no sex if you're fat

Woman Poem [1968]

---

[1]From *The Collected Poetry of Nikki Giovanni: 1968–1998* [2003].

1   joy is finding a pregnant roach
     and squashing it

Woman Poem

2   I was born in the congo.
     I walked to the fertile crescent and built
        the sphinx.
     I designed a pyramid so tough that a star
        that only glows every one hundred years falls
     into the center giving divine perfect light
        I am bad.

Ego-Tripping [1970]

3   Mistakes are a fact of life
     It is the response to error that counts.

Of Liberation [1970]

4   show me someone not full of herself
     and i'll show you a hungry person

Poem for a Lady Whose Voice I Like [1970], last line

5   I can walk ten paces behind a dog. It means nothing to me, but if that's
     what the black man needs, I'll never get far enough behind him for him to
     be a man. I'll never walk that slowly.

A Dialogue: Nikki Giovanni and James Baldwin [1971]

6   if i am imprisoned in my skin let it be a dark world
     with a deep bass walking a witch doctor to me for spiritual
     consultation
     let my world be defined by my skin and the skin of my people
     for we spirit to spirit   will embrace
     this world

Poem (for Nina) [1972]

7   and if ever I touched a life I hope
     that life knows that I know that touching was and still is and will always
        be the true
     revolution

When I Die [1972]

8   i would not reject
     my strength
     though its source
     is not choice
     but responsibility

Boxes [1978]

9   If loneliness were a grape
        the wine would be vintage
     If it were a wood
        the furniture would be mahogany

But since it is life   it is
    Cotton Candy
    on a rainy day
The sweet soft essence
    of possibility
Never quite maturing   *Cotton Candy on a Rainy Day [1978]*

1   We are not friends
because of the laughs
we spend
but the tears
we save   *A Poem of Friendship [1978]*

2   The very fact...that something has
been done...over and over again...
is one reason...to change...   *Charting the Night Winds [1983]*

3   I think hands must be very important...
Hands: plait hair...knead bread...spank
bottoms...wring in anguish...shake the
air in exasperation...wipe tears, sweat,
and pain from faces...are at the end
of arms which hold...   *Hands: For Mother's Day [1983]*

4   I wrote a good omelet...and ate a hot poem...
after loving you
Buttoned my car...and drove my coat home...in the
rain...
after loving you   *I Wrote a Good Omelet [1983]*

5   I wish we had been enslaved...at the same rate we are being set...free.
             Lorraine Hansberry: An Emotional View [1983]

6   We love because it's the only true adventure.
                 Love: Is a Human Condition [1983]

7   No one said a word...in 1776...
to us about Freedom   *But Since You Finally Asked [1993]*

8   We didn't write a constitution...we live one...
We didn't say "We the People"...we are one...
We didn't have to add...as an afterthought...
"Under God"...We turn our faces to the
rising sun...knowing...a New Day...
is always...beginning   *But Since You Finally Asked*

Weldon J[onathan] Irvine, Jr.
1943–2002

1   To be young, gifted and black.
Oh what a lovely precious dream.
To be young, gifted and black,
Open your heart to what I mean.
In the whole world you know
There are a billion boys and girls
Who are young, gifted and black,
And that's a fact.
                    To Be Young, Gifted and Black [1969]

Judith Jamison
1943–

2   Dance is bigger than the physical body. Think bigger than that. When you extend your arm, it doesn't stop at the end of your fingers, because you're dancing bigger than that; you're dancing spirit.   *Dancing Spirit [1993]*

3   I feel like an ordained minister; I was supposed to preach here. Through dance, we're as close to God as we're going to get — until he calls us home.   *Quoted in the New York Times [July 5, 2006]*

Sindiwe Magona
1943–

4   What I do remember has never left my recall. On the other hand, what I have forgotten, I forgot with amazing swiftness: inside a week, and it was all gone. Moreover, it has remained safely tucked away. It doesn't haunt me. And for that, I am truly grateful.
          Living, Loving and Lying Awake at Night [1991].
          It Was Easter Sunday the Day I Went to Netreg

James Alan McPherson
1943–

5   I discovered that nothing really matters except not being old and being alive and having potential to dream about, and not being alone.
                         Gold Coast [1968]

6   No one will believe that I like country music. Even my wife scoffs, when told such a possibility exists. "Go on!" Gloria tells me. "I can see blues, bebop, maybe even a little buckdancing. But not bluegrass." Gloria says, "Hillbilly stuff is not just music. It's like the New York Stock Exchange. The minute you see a sharp rise in it, you better watch out."
                Elbow Room [1977]. Why I Like Country Music

7   While the two of us are black, the distance between us is sometimes as great as that between Ibo and Yoruba.
                  Elbow Room. Why I Like Country Music

433

1   "I'm black. I've accepted myself as that. But didn't I make some elbow room, though?" She tapped her temple with her forefinger. "I mean up here?"

Elbow Room [Virginia]

Alphonso Mizell

1943–2011

and

Frederick Perren

1943–2004

and

Deke Richards

1944–2013

and

Berry Gordy, Jr.

1929–

2   ABC, easy as 123.

ABC [1970]

3   Stop! The love you save may be your own!
Darling, take it slow,
Or someday you'll be all alone.

The Love You Save [1970]

Eric Monte [Kenneth Williams]

1943–

4   This is for the brothers who ain't here. *Cooley High [1975] [Cochise]*

Ebele Oseye [Ellease Southerland]

1943–

5   It seemed that somewhere the whole earth was vibrant and bleeding. Sun soaked her shining body. Soft-black-mystery. To bleed and not die.... A woman. She was a woman now. *Let the Lion Eat Straw [1979]*

6   It is God who lies under the thoughts of man. He is cartilage. Memory. The spinning of this earth and a thousand other earths. Sound. Distance. God forms our blue songs. Creates the stammering tongue and leaves motherless children crying. It is God in the house when the curtains lift gently at windows and a young child sucks her itching gums. We do not understand the mysteries of God. God the winter. Summer. Septembers. Moody dark tones of fathers dying. The splash and laughter. Children playing.

Let the Lion Eat Straw

Calvin Peete

1943–

7   The things I knew I could do, I tried to master. The things I knew I couldn't do, I never tried.

Quoted in the New York Times [May 14, 1990]

Sly Stone [Sylvester Stewart]   1943–

1   I am everyday people.   *Everyday People [1969]*

2   Don't Call Me Nigger, Whitey   *Song title [1969]*

3   Stand.
     In the end you'll still be you.   *Stand [1969]*

4   One child grows up to be
     Somebody that just loves to learn.
     And another child grows up to be
     Somebody you'd just love to burn.
     Mom loves the both of them
     you see it's in the blood.
     Both kids are good to Mom
     Blood's thicker than the mud.
     It's a family affair.   *Family Affair [1971]*

Mildred D[eLois] Taylor   1943–

5   White is something just like black is something. Everybody born on
     this earth is something, and nobody, no matter what color, is better than
     anybody else.   *Roll of Thunder, Hear My Cry [1976] [Mama]*

6   What had happened to T.J. in the night I did not understand, but I
     knew that it would not pass. And I cried for those things which had hap-
     pened in the night and would not pass. I cried for T.J. For T.J. and the land.
                          Roll of Thunder, Hear My Cry, last lines

7   Gonna go to register.... I'm gonna do this thing. I know don't none
     of y'all like the idea, but that's too bad. Now, I knows what could happen,
     but I jus' gotta do it. Gotta stand up once in this life, and that's jus' what
     I'm gonna do.   *Let the Circle Be Unbroken [1981] [Mrs. Lee Annie]*

[Alyce] Faye Wattleton   1943–

8   Many teenagers spend more time in front of the television than they
     do in the classroom, and their sexual behavior in part reflects what they have
     learned from this thoroughly unreliable teacher. Nowhere is it more
     apparent than on television that America suffers from sexual schizophrenia:
     We exploit sex, and at the same time we try to repress it.
                                          Teenage Pregnancy [1990][1]

9   The only safe ship in a storm is leadership.   *Attributed*

---

[1]From *The Black Women's Health Book* [1990], edited by EVELYN C. WHITE.

Norman Whitfield   1943–2008

and

Barrett Strong   1941–

1   I heard it through the grapevine
    Not much longer would you be mine.
                            I Heard It Through the Grapevine [1967]

2   No matter how hard you try
    You can't stop me now.   *Message from a Black Man [1969]*

3   Segregation, determination, demonstration, integration, aggravation,
    humiliation, obligation to our nation,
    Ball of confusion, that's what the world is today.
                                          Ball of Confusion [1970]

4   It was just my imagination
    Running away with me.   *Just My Imagination [1970]*

5   War! What is it good for?
    Absolutely nothing!   *War [1970]*

6   Smiling faces — sometimes they don't tell the truth.
                                     Smiling Faces Sometimes [1971]

7   Papa was a rollin' stone
    Wherever he laid his hat was his home.
    And when he died all he left us was alone.
                                   Papa Was a Rollin' Stone [1972]

Charles Burnett   1944–

8   You are not a child anymore. You will soon be a goddamn man. Start
    learning what life is about now, son.
                       Killer of Sheep [1977], opening scene [Stan's father]

9   Man, I ain't poor. Look, I give away stuff to the Salvation Army. You
    can't give nothing away to Salvation Army if you poor.
                                        Killer of Sheep [Stan]

10 Don't you know it's more to it than just with your fist? You think
    you're still in the bush some goddamn where? You're here. You use your
    brains.   *Killer of Sheep [Stan's wife]*

11 If you are made to feel half a man, what do you think the other half is?
                                   To Sleep with Anger [1989] [Harry]

Angela Y[vonne] Davis   1944–

1   We are never assured of justice without a fight.

If They Come in the Morning [1971]

2   In the heat of our pursuit of fundamental human rights, Black people have been continually cautioned to be patient. We are advised that as long as we remain faithful to the existing democratic order, the glorious moment will eventually arrive when we will come into our own as full-fledged human beings.

Political Prisoners, Prisons & Black Liberation,
Marin County Jail [1971]

3   Our very survival has frequently been a direct function of our skill in forging effective channels of resistance. In resisting we have sometimes been compelled to openly violate those laws which directly or indirectly buttress our oppression.... There is a distinct and qualitative difference between one breaking a law for one's own individual self-interest and violating it in the interests of a class or a people whose oppression is expressed either directly or indirectly through that particular law.

Political Prisoners, Prisons & Black Liberation,
Marin County Jail

4   Jails and prisons are designed to break human beings, to convert the population into specimens in a zoo — obedient to our keepers but dangerous to each other.   *Angela Davis: An Autobiography [1974]*

5   Black women could hardly strive for weakness; they had to become strong, for their families and their communities needed their strength to survive.... Harriet Tubman, Sojourner Truth, Ida Wells and Rosa Parks are not exceptional Black women as much as they are epitomes of Black womanhood.   *Women, Race and Class [1981]*

6   It is both humiliating and humbling to discover that a single generation after the events that constructed me as a public personality, I am remembered as a hairdo.   *Afro Images: Politics, Fashion and Nostalgia [1994][1]*

Buchi Emecheta   1944–

7   Every girl born in Ibuza after Aku-nna's death was told her story, to reinforce the old taboos of the land. If a girl wished to live long and see her children's children, she must accept the husband chosen for her by her people, and the bride price must be paid. If the bride price was not paid, she would never survive the birth of her first child. It was a psychological hold

---

[1]From *The Angela Y. Davis Reader* [1998], edited by JOY JAMES.

over every young girl that would continue to exist, even in the face of every modernization, until the present day. Why this is so is, as the saying goes, anybody's guess. *The Bride Price [1976], last lines*

1   You want a husband who has time to ask you if you wish to eat rice, or drink corn pap with honey? Forget it. Men here are too busy being white men's servants to be men. We women mind the home. Not our husbands. Their manhood has been taken away from them. The shame of it is that they don't know it. All they see is the money, shining white man's money.
The Joys of Motherhood [1979], ch. 4 [Cordelia]

2   Nnu Ego realized that part of the pride of motherhood was to look a little unfashionable and be able to drawl with joy: "I can't afford another outfit, because I am nursing him, so you see I can't go anywhere to sell anything." One usually received the answer, "Never mind, he will grow soon and clothe you and farm for you, so that your old age will be sweet."
The Joys of Motherhood, ch. 7

3   Poor Nnu Ego, even in death she had no peace! Still, many agreed that she had given her all to her children. The joy of being a mother was the joy of giving all to your children, they said. And her reward? Did she not have the greatest funeral Ibuza had ever seen? *The Joys of Motherhood, ch. 18*

Joe Frazier   1944–2011

4   The truth hurts… and I'm the truth.   *Said to Muhammad Ali [1967]*

5   I want you like a hog wants slop.
Said to Muhammad Ali [July 2, 1975]

6   As a champion, you carry an air of invincibility… folks see you as bigger than life. When you lose, though, they feel as though they'd been fooled, suckered into thinking so highly of you; that's why folks jump off that bandwagon quick as can be, and then throw stones at it.
Smokin' Joe [1996]

7   Boxing is the only sport you can get your brain shook, your money took, and your name in the undertaker book.   *Attributed*[1]

Marcia Ann Gillespie   1944–

8   I've often felt like a would-be farmer trying to plant a vital crop in hilly, rocky soil. At first I scattered my ideas, like seeds, over my body ground. Some took, most withered. Till finally I made a decision and began the

---

[1]Also quoted as: Your brains get shook, your money gets took and your name ends up in the undertaker's book. — *The New York Post* [December 21, 1999]

inevitable process of dragging away from my ground the rocks that kept my fertile seeds from thriving. It was not the overnight transformation I had first thought—rather, backbreaking, painful labor as bigger or sharper stones were still left to be unearthed.   *Editor's letter, Essence [September 1975]*

Bernie [Bernard] Grant   1944–2000

1   The colonization and exploitation of Africa and the enslavement of African people must be the biggest crime in the whole of history, and one from which we still suffer, both materially and psychologically. Yet we never had even an apology, let alone any form of compensation.
                    Op-ed in New Statesman & Society [October 15, 1993]

Merle Hodge   1944–

2   Hm! You see the family I got! Spend my life teaching my children to be decent, teaching them what is important, and then they forget who it was that got them where they are.   *Crick Crack Monkey [1970] [Aunt Beatrice]*

3   Everything was changing, unrecognizable, pushing me out. This was as it should be, since I had moved up and no longer had any place here. But it was painful, and I longed all the more to be on my way. . . . I desired with all my heart that it were the next morning and a plane were lifting me off the ground.   *Crick Crack Monkey*

Willie Hutch   1944–2005

4   Brother's Gonna Work It Out   *Song title [1973]*

Jack Mapanje   1944–

5   No, your grace, I am no alarmist nor banterer, I am
Only a child surprised how you broadly disparage me
Shocked by the tedium of your continuous palaver. I
Adore your majesty. But paramountcy is like a raindrop
On a vast sea. Why should we wait for the children to
Tell us about our toothless gums or our showing flies?
                    Of Chameleons and Gods [1981].
                    On His Royal Blindness Paramount Chief Kwangala

6   Those ticks in the cracks of cement floors
Still testify here; the fleas in the pores
Of your desert skin, those hyenas yapping
Worse than leprous midnight dogs, those
Scorpions whose sting sings like brain

Tumour, the swarming mosquitoes and bats;
What, who won't you find here, welcome
To these Chattering wagtails of Mikuyu Prison.

The Chattering Wagtails of Mikuyu Prison [1993], V

1   I will, skip without your rope
    Since you say I should not.

Skipping Without Ropes [1998]

Nancy Morejón   1944–

2   the heart of the city has not yet died
    for us need never die.

Where the Island Sleeps Like a Wing [1985].[1]
Amor, Ciudad Atribuida [Love, Attributed City]

3   My mother had the handkerchief and the song
    to cradle my body's deepest faith,
    and hold her head high,
    banished queen —
    She gave us her hands, like precious stones,
    before the cold remains of the enemy.

Where the Island Sleeps Like a Wing.[1] Madre

4   This is the land where I suffered
    mouth-in-the-dust and the lash.
    I rode the length of all its rivers.
    Under its sun I planted seeds, brought in the crops,
    but never ate those harvests.
    A slave barracks was my house,
    built with stones that I hauled myself.
    While I sang to the pure beat of native birds.
        I rose up.

Where the Island Sleeps Like a Wing. Mujer Negra [Black Woman]

5   I am at the window.
    I know there is someone.
    I know that a woman is flaunting my flesh and bones;
    That she has sought me in her weary bosom
    And that she finds me lost and in constant movement.
    The night is buried under our skins.

Persona [1999][2]

---

[1]Translated by KATHLEEN WEAVER.
[2]Translated by DAVID FRYE.

1   Daughter of ocean waters
asleep in that womb
I am reborn.

> *Where the Island Sleeps Like a Wing. Renacimiento*
> *[Rebirth]*

Elizabeth Nunez   1944–

2   She had never thought of murder. The seed the Chinaman jarred out of its quiet place was not bred out of thoughts of murder. Of death, yes, but not of brutality. Of wishing he would no longer be there to torment her. But then, at that moment when the slits that were his eyes narrowed to a sliver of black light, and spit jettisoned from between his teeth, stained from years of tobacco smoke and much, much more, she conceived it: his murder. The Chinaman's murder. Man-woman business.

> *Bruised Hibiscus [2000], ch. 1*

3   Slaveowners in America were torturing the Africans they enslaved for reading, but the British had discovered the hard way of truth of the maxim — *Nature abhors a vacuum. Fill their minds with your stories and they will adore you; leave their minds free to roam and they will hatch plans to destroy you.*   *Boundaries [2011]*

Pat Parker   1944–1989

4   The first thing you do is to forget that I'm Black.
Second, you must never forget that I'm Black.

> *For the White Person Who Wants to Know How to*
> *Be My Friend [1978]*

5   I am the Black woman
I am the child of the sun
the daughter of dark
I carry fire to burn the world
I am water to quench its throat
I am the product of slaves
I am the offspring of queens
I am still as silence
I flow as the stream.

> *Movement in Black [1978]*

Diana Ross   1944–

6   It's taken me a lifetime to get here. I'm not going anywhere.

> *Secrets of a Sparrow [1993]*

Charlie Smalls

1943–1987

1 Believe in yourself, right from the start
Believe in the magic that's inside your heart
Believe what you see
Not what life told you to.

. . .

Just believe in yourself
As I believe in you.

The Wiz [1974]. Believe in Yourself

2 Come on,
Ease on down, ease on down the road.
Don't you carry nothin',
That might be a load.

The Wiz. Ease on Down the Road

3 When I think of home, I think of a place
Where there's love overflowing.

The Wiz. Home

Tommie Smith

1944–

4 My raised right hand stood for the power in black America. Carlos' raised left hand stood for the unity of black America.[1] Together, they formed an arch of unity and power. The black scarf around my neck stood for black pride. The black socks with no shoes stood for black poverty in racist America. The totality of our effort was the regaining of black dignity.

Television interview regarding his giving the black power salute after winning an Olympic gold medal [October 16, 1968]

5 My silent gesture was designed to speak volumes.   *Silent Gesture [2007]*

Alice Walker

1944–

6 "To hell with dying," my father would say.

To Hell with Dying [1967]

7 then there was
the
picture of
the
bleak-eyed
little black
girl
waving the

[1]John Carlos won the bronze.

american
flag
holding it
gingerly
with
the very
tips
of her
fingers
Once [1968], st. 14

1   Nobody's as powerful as we make them out to be.
The Third Life of Grange Copeland [1970] [Grange]

2   How to teach a barren world to dance? It is a contradiction that divides the world.
In Love and in Trouble [1973]. The Diary of an African Nun

3   "Always respect the word of God,"
she said on her way to she didn't
know where, except it would be by
electric chair, and she continued
"Don't y'all forgit to *water*
my purple petunias."
Revolutionary Petunias [1973]

4   Womanist is to feminist as purple is to lavender.
In Search of Our Mothers' Gardens [1974], epigraph

5   Our mothers and grandmothers have, more often than not anonymously, handed on the creative spark, the seed of the flower they themselves never hoped to see; or like a sealed letter they could not plainly read.
In Search of Our Mothers' Gardens

6   Guided by my heritage of a love of beauty and a respect for strength—in search of my mother's garden, I found my own.
In Search of Our Mothers' Gardens

7   there is a magic
lingering after people
to whom success is merely personal.
Light Baggage [1975]

8   Looking down into my father's
dead face
for the last time
my mother said without
tears, without smiles
without regrets

but with *civility*
"Good night, Willie Lee, I'll see you in the morning."
Good Night, Willie Lee, I'll See You in the Morning [1975]

1   There was in Meridian's chest a breaking as if a tight string binding her lungs had given way, allowing her to breathe freely. For she understood, finally, that the respect she owed her life was to continue, against whatever obstacles, to live it, and not to give up any particle of it without a fight to the death, preferably *not* her own.   *Meridian [1976]. Camara*

2   It is the song of the people, transformed by the experiences of each generation, that holds them together, and if any part of it is lost the people suffer and are without soul.   *Meridian. Camara*

3   there is water in the world for us
brought by our friends
though the rock of mother and god
vanishes into sand
and we, cast out alone
to heal
and re-create
ourselves.   *Meridian. Pilgrimage*

4   Time moves slowly, but passes quickly.   *The Color Purple [1982]*

5   I think it pisses God off if you walk by the color purple in a field somewhere and don't notice it.   *The Color Purple [Shug]*

6   People think pleasing God is all God care about. But any fool living in the world can see it always trying to please us back.
                      The Color Purple [Shug]

7   I'm pore, I'm black, I may be ugly and can't cook, a voice say to everything listening. But I'm here.   *The Color Purple [Celie]*

8   Some colored people so scared of whitefolks they claim to love the cotton gin.   *The Color Purple [Sofia]*

9   If a mule could tell folks how it's treated, it would.[1]
                      The Color Purple [Mr. —]

10   I realized I had never been given the opportunity to appreciate my hair for its true self. That it did, in fact, have one. I remembered years of enduring hairdressers—from my mother onward—doing missionary work on my hair. They dominated, suppressed, controlled. . . . Eventually I knew *precisely* what my hair wanted: it wanted to grow, to be itself, to attract

---

[1]De nigger woman is de mule uh de world so fur as Ah can see. — ZORA NEALE HURSTON

lint, if that was its destiny, but to be left alone by anyone, including me, who did not love it as it was.

> *Oppressed Hair Puts a Ceiling on the Brain. Founder's Day speech, Spelman College [April 11, 1987]*

1   After thousands and thousands of years of women and men living apart, the Ababa had, with great trepidation, experimented with the two tribes living, a couple to a household, together. Each person must remain free, they said. That is the main thing. And so they had designed a dwelling shaped like a bird.   *The Temple of My Familiar [1989]*

2   I knew I wanted my own suffering, the suffering of women and little girls, still cringing before the overpowering might and weapons of the torturers, to be the subject of a sermon. Was woman herself not the tree of life? And was she not crucified? Not in some age no one even remembers, but right now, daily, in many lands on earth?

> *Possessing the Secret of Joy [1992] [Tashi-Evelyn-Mrs. Johnson]*

3   Healing begins where the wound was made.

> *The Way Forward Is with a Broken Heart [2000]*

4   Though War is Old
It has not
Become wise.   *Why War Is Never a Good Idea [2007]*

Barry [Eugene Carter] White   1944–2003

5   I'm never, never gonna quit
'Cause quittin' just ain't my shtick.

> *Never, Never Gonna Give You Up [1973]*

6   Can't Get Enough of Your Love, Babe   *Song title [1974]*

7   You're the First, the Last, My Everything   *Song title [1974]*

Sherley Anne Williams   1944–1999

8   Wasn't no "death do us part" in slavery; wasn't even no "dead or sold" less'n two peoples made it that. Far as two peoples loving with each other, it was any handy place if you was willing — and sometimes if you wasn't; or you jumped the broom if the masters let you marry. But you couldn't help dreaming. Dreams was one of the reasons you got up the next day.

> *Dessa Rose [1986]. The Negress*

[Robert Dwayne] Bobby Womack   1944–

9   I used to love her, but it's all over now.   *It's All Over Now [1964]*

1   The family on the other side of town,
Would catch hell without a ghetto around.
In every city you find the same thing going down,
Harlem is the capital of every ghetto town.   *Across 110th Street [1972]*

Kathleen Cleaver   1945–

2   The right-wing fascist element of this mother country madness has one outstanding political drawback: it cannot produce any charismatic or brilliant orators to advance its cause.... The bullet has been called in to silence the oratory of the political leaders from the white liberal to black revolutionary arenas as well as destroy their political work. The price of speaking the truth, or even beautiful, inspiring lies, has become murder. These are political decisions made and implemented with the bullet.
Liberation and Political Assassination. The Black Panther
[May 18, 1968][1]

3   I think it is important to place the women who fought oppression as Black Panthers within the longer tradition of freedom fighters like Sojourner Truth, Harriet Tubman, Ida Wells Barnet [Wells-Barnett], who took on an entirely oppressive world and insisted that their race, their gender, and their humanity be respected all at the same time. Not singled out, each one separate, but all at the same time. You cannot segregate out one aspect of our reality and expect to get a clear picture of what this struggle is about.
Liberation, Imagination and the Black Panther Party [2001].
Women, Power and Revolution

Stanley Crouch   1945–

4   Jazz musicians symbolize . . . a freedom from the taste-making of mass media and an embracing of a vision that has much more to do with aesthetic satisfaction than the gold-rush culture of popular entertainment, where one takes the clichés of adolescent narcissism into the side of the mountain rather than a pickaxe, some pans, and a burro.
The All-American Skin Game, or The Decoy of Race [1995].
Blues Rebellion Breakdown

5   We can never forget that our fate as Americans is, finally, collective, and that we fail our mission as a democratic nation whenever we submit

---

[1]Cleaver made these statements after the assassinations of John F. Kennedy, Malcolm X, and Martin Luther King, Jr., after the police shooting of her then husband, Eldridge Cleaver. From *Black Panthers Speak* [1970], edited by PHILLIP S. FONER.

to any sort of segregation that would remake the rules and distort the truth in the interest of creating or satisfying a constituency unwilling to assert the tragic optimism so intrinsic to the blues and to the Constitution.

The All-American Skin Game. Do the Afrocentric Hustle

1   If there's an intellectual highway, there's also an intellectual subway.

Interview. The American Enterprise [March 2001]

Ja'net DuBois   1945–

and

Jeff Barry   1937–

2   Well, we're movin' on up, to the East Side.
To a deluxe apartment in the sky.
Movin' on up, to the East Side.
We finally got a piece of the pie.

Movin' On Up [1976], theme song for television show The Jeffersons

Nuruddin Farah   1945–

3   You exist, you think, the way the heavenly bodies exist, for although one does not extend one's fingers and point at the heavens, one knows, yes that's the word, one knows that that is not the heavens. Unless…unless there are, in a sense, as many heavens as there are thinking beings; unless there are as many heavens as there are pointing fingers.

Maps [1987], ch. 1

4   Annoy a child and you'll discover the adult in him. Please an adult with gifts and the child therein re-emerges.   *Maps, ch.1*

5   Overwhelmed as I am with the magnitude of the crisis, I say this: Somalia is an open sore, a wound gaping as wide as a gate on broken hinges, a mouth toothless and without a tongue, ugly in the extreme, cavernous, tomblike.   *Op-ed in the New York Times [December 28, 1992]*

6   Every gift has a personality—that of its giver.   *Gifts [1993]*

7   Secrets define us, they mark us, they set us apart from all the others. The secrets which we preserve provide a key to who we are, deep down.

Secrets [1998]

8   Motherhood is the off-and-on light in the darkness of night, a firefly in joyous dizziness and rejoicing, now here, now there, and everywhere. Our problem as a society is that we pay mothers only lip service, nothing else. In fact, the crisis that is coming to a head in the shape of civil strife would not be breaking on us if we'd offered women-as-mothers their due worth,

respect and affection, a brightness celebrating motherhood, a monument erected in a worship of women. *Secrets [Nonno]*

1 Guns lack the body of human truths! *Links [2003]*

Floyd H[arold] Flake 1945–

2 Regardless of what color you are, regardless of what background you come from, you can't spend your life talking like a victim, acting like a victim, walking like a victim.

Speech commemorating Martin Luther King, Jr. Day, New York Times [January 19, 1999]

3 Today's actions create tomorrow's legacy.

The Way of the Bootstrapper [1999]. Practical Values

Donny Hathaway 1945–1979

and

Leroy Hutson 1945–

4 The ghetto, talkin' 'bout the ghetto.

The Ghetto [1969]

5 Tryin' times, what the world is talkin' about
You got confusion all over the land,
You got mother against daughter, you got father against son
You know the whole thing is getting out of hand.

But maybe folks wouldn't have to suffer
If there was more love for your brother
But these are tryin' times. *Tryi*

Donny Hathaway

and

Nadine McKinnor 1941–

6 Hang all the mistletoe
I'm gonna get to know you better
This Christmas. *This Christmas [1978]*

Bob Herbert 1945–

7 Fantasy must always genuflect before reality.

From Dream to Nightmare. New York Times [April 30, 2004]

Bob Marley   1945–1981

1   One good thing about music
When it hits you
You feel no pain.   *Trench Town Rock [1971]*

2   Get up, stand up, stand up for your rights.
Get up, stand up, don't give up the fight.   *Get Up, Stand Up [1973]*

3   I shot the sheriff
But I did not shoot the deputy.   *I Shot the Sheriff [1973]*

4   Every day the bucket a go a well
One day the bottom a go drop out.   *I Shot the Sheriff*

5   Slave driver, the table is turn.
Catch a fire so you can get burn.   *Slave Driver [1973]*

6   And hey Mr. Cop
Ain't got no birth certificate on me now
Rebel Music (3 O'Clock Roadblocks) [1974]

7   No Woman No Cry   *Song title [1975]*

8   Them belly full but we hungry
A hungry mouth is an angry mob   *Them Belly Full [1975]*

9   Until the color of a man's skin
Is of no more significance
Than the color of his eyes
Is a war.   *War [1976]*[1]

10   Don't gain the world and lose your soul
Wisdom is worth more than silver or gold.   *Jammin' [1977]*

11   We're leaving Babylon
We're going to our Father's land.
Exodus!   *Movement of Jah People [1977]*

12   One love, one heart
Let's get together and feel all right.   *One Love [1977]*

13   Don't worry about a thing.
'Cause every little thing gonna be all right.   *Three Little Birds [1977]*

14   Could you be loved and be loved?   *Could You Be Loved? [1980]*

---

[1] Adapted from a speech by HAILE SELASSIE I [October 1963].

1 Emancipate yourselves from mental slavery;
None but ourselves can free our minds.   *Redemption Song [1980]*

2 How long shall they kill our prophets,
While we stand aside and look?   *Redemption Song*

Bob Marley   1945–1981

and

Noel Williams   1943–

3 Buffalo Soldier, Dreadlock Rasta
There was a Buffalo Soldier
In the heart of America
Stolen from Africa, brought to America
Fighting on arrival, fighting for survival.   *Buffalo Soldier [1983]*

Jessye Norman   1945–

4 Pigeonholing is interesting only for pigeons.
Interview. LIFE [March 1985]

Carolyn M[arie] Rodgers   1945–2010

5 My mother, religious-negro, proud of
having waded through a storm, is very obviously,
a sturdy Black bridge that I
crossed over, on.   *Song of a Blackbird [1969]. It Is Deep*

6 me?
I never could keep my edges and kitchen
straight
even after
supercool/straighterPerm had burned
whiteness onto my scalp
my edges and kitchen didn't
ever get the message that they
was not supposed to go back home.
Song of a Blackbird [1969]. For Sistuhs Wearin Straight Hair

7 i felt a spiritual transformation
a root revival of love
and i knew that many things
were over
and some me of — beauty —
was about to begin . . .   *How I Got Ovah [1975]. Some Me of Beauty*

1 the Revolution aint dead
   its tired,
          and jest resting.   *The Revolution Is Resting [1975]*

August Wilson [Frederick August Kittel]   1945–2005

2 They're tearing everything down around here. All along Wylie there. You see they done tore everything down. They gonna tear this building down.... We're gonna have to move. Either that or split up. We can't stay here no more.   *Jitney [1983], act I, sc. iv [Turnbo]*

3 As long as the colored man look to white folks to put the crown on what he say ... as long as he looks to white folks for approval ... then he ain't never gonna find out who he is and what he's about.
                    Ma Rainey's Black Bottom [1984], act I [Toledo]

4 White folks don't understand about the blues. They hear it come out, but they don't know how it got there. They don't understand that's life's way of talking. You don't sing to feel better. You sing 'cause that's a way of understanding life.   *Ma Rainey's Black Bottom, act II [Ma Rainey]*

5 Life ain't shit. You can put it in a paper bag and carry it around with you. It ain't got no balls. Now death ... death got some style! Death will kick your ass and make you wish you never been born! That's how bad death is! But you can rule over life. Life ain't nothing!
                    Ma Rainey's Black Bottom, act II [Levee]

6 Ain't nothing wrong with talking about death. That's part of life.
                    Fences [1986], act I, sc. i [Troy]

7 I took all my feelings, my wants and my needs, my dreams ... and I buried them inside you. I planted a seed and watched and prayed over it. I planted myself inside you and waited to bloom. And it didn't take me no eighteen years to find out the soil was hard and rocky and it wasn't never gonna bloom.   *Fences, act II, sc. i [Rose]*

8 I come to this place ... to this water that was bigger than the whole world. And I looked out ... and I seen these bones rise up out of the water. Rise up and begin to walk on top of it.
                    Joe Turner's Come and Gone [1988], act I, sc. iv [Loomis]

9 It got so I used all of myself up in the making of that song. Then I was the song in search of itself. That song rattling in my throat and I'm looking for it.   *Joe Turner's Come and Gone, act II, sc. ii*

10 You ain't taking that piano out of my house. Look at this piano. Look at it. Mama Ola polished this piano with her tears for seventeen years. For seventeen years she rubbed on it till her hands bled. Then she rubbed the

blood in.... Every day that God breathed life into her body she rubbed and cleaned and polished and prayed over it. "Play something for me, Berniece. Play something for me, Berniece." Every day.... You always talking about your daddy, but you ain't never stopped to look at what his foolishness cost your mama. Seventeen years' worth of cold nights and an empty bed. For what? For a piano? For a piece of wood? To get even with somebody? I look at you and you're all the same... you're all alike. All this thieving and killing and thieving and killing. And what it ever lead to? More killing and more thieving. I ain't never seen it come to nothing. People getting burned up. People getting shot. People falling down their wells. It don't never stop.

The Piano Lesson [1989] act I, sc. ii [Berniece]

1   Aunt Esther give you more than money. She make you right with yourself. You ain't got to go far. She live at 1839 Wylie. In the back. Go up there and you'll see a red door. Go up there and knock on that.

Two Trains Running [1992], act I, sc. i [Holloway]

2   He gonna give me my ham. I want my ham!

Two Trains Running, act I, sc. i [Hambone]

3   All I want is you to get out of my way. I got somewhere to go. See, everybody can't say that. Some people ain't got nowhere to go. They don't wanna go nowhere. If they wanted to go somewhere they would have been there.

Seven Guitars [1995], act I, sc. iv [Floyd]

4   That place where you live in your own special life... I would be happy to be big there.

Seven Guitars, act II, sc. i [Hedley]

5   I had seven ways to go. They cut that down to six. I say "Let me try one of them six." They cut it down to five. Every time I push... they pull. They cut it down to four. I say "What's the matter? Everything can't go wrong all the time." They cut it down to three. I say "Three is better than two, I really don't need but one." They cut it down to two.... I don't want to live my life without. Everybody I know live without. I don't want to do that. I want to live with.

Seven Guitars, act. II, sc. iii [Floyd]

6   The term black or African-American not only denotes race, it denotes condition, and carries with it the vestige of slavery and the social segregation and abuse of opportunity so vivid in our memory.

The Ground on Which I Stand [1996]

7   Colorblind casting is an aberrant idea that has never had any validity other than as a tool of the Cultural Imperialists who view their American culture, rooted in the icons of European culture, as beyond reproach in its perfection. It is inconceivable to them that life could be lived and enriched without knowing Shakespeare or Mozart. Their gods, their manners, their

being, are the only true and correct representations of humankind. They refuse to recognize black conduct and manners as part of a system that is fueled by its own philosophy, mythology, history, creative motif, social organization and ethos.... To cast us in the role of mimics is to deny us our own competence. *The Ground on Which I Stand*

1   I ain't sorry for nothing I done. And I ain't gonna be sorry. I'm gonna see to that. 'Cause I'm gonna do the right thing. Always. It ain't in me to do nothing else. We might disagree about what that is. But I know what is right for me. *King Hedley II [2001], act I, sc. iii [King]*

2   Jazz or blues: you can't disregard that part of the African-American experience, or even try to transcend it. They are affirmations and celebrations of the value and worth of the African-American spirit. And young people would do well to understand them as the roots of today's rap, rather than some antique to be tossed away. *Interview. Literature Film Quarterly [2002]*

3   You see, Mr. Caesar, you can put the law on the paper, but that don't make it right. That piece of paper say I was property. Say anybody could buy or sell me. The law say I need a piece of paper to say I was a free woman. But I didn't need no piece of paper to tell me that. Do you need a piece of paper, Mr. Caesar? *Gem of the Ocean [2004], act II, sc. iv [Aunt Ester]*

4   Negroes got blindyitis. A dog knows it's a dog. A cat knows it's a cat. But a Negro don't know he's a Negro. He thinks he's a white man. *Radio Golf [2005], act II [Sterling]*

Ysaye M[aria] Barnwell   1946–

5   We bring more than a paycheck
to our loved ones and family.
We bring home asbestosis, silicosis,
brown lung, black lung disease.
And radiation hits the children
before they've even been conceived.

More Than a Paycheck [1981]

6   When I die, you can bury me on a mountain top.
But when I die, let my spirit breathe.
Let it soar like an eagle
to its highest peak
when I die.

When I Die [1992]

7   There were no mirrors in my Nana's house,
No mirrors in my Nana's house.

And the beauty that I saw in everything
was in her eyes.   *No Mirrors* [1993]

[Howard] Frankie Beverly   1946–

1 Joy and pain,
   Like sunshine and rain.   *Joy and Pain* [1980]

[Stephen Bantu] Steve Biko[1]   1946–1977

2   What we want is not black visibility but real black participation.
                        Speech, Durban, South Africa [December 1969]

3   At the heart of true integration is the provision for each man, each
group to rise and attain the envisioned self. Each group must be able to
attain its style of existence without encroaching on or being thwarted by
another. Out of this mutual respect for each other and complete freedom
of self-determination there will obviously arise a genuine fusion of the
life-styles of the various groups. This is true integration.
                              Black Souls in White Skins? [August 1970]

4   A people without a positive history is like a vehicle without an
engine.   *We Blacks* [September 1970]

5   The most potent weapon in the hands of the oppressor is the mind of
the oppressed.   *White Racism and Black Consciousness* [January 1971]

6   The basic tenet of black consciousness is that the black man must
reject all value systems that seek to make him a foreigner in the country of
his birth and reduce his basic human dignity.
                                     Statement as witness [May 3, 1976][2]

Michelle Cliff   1946–

7   NO TELEPHONE TO HEAVEN. No Voice to God. A waste to try.
Cut off. No way of reaching out or up. Maybe only one way. Not God's way.
No matter if him is Jesus or him is Jah. Him not gwan like dis one lickle bit.
NO TELEPHONE TO HEAVEN.   *No Telephone to Heaven* [1987]

Wanda Coleman   1946–

8   its music comes out the radio
   drives beside me in my car. strolls along with me

---

[1]From *Steve Biko, I Write What I Like: Selected Writings* [1978], edited by AELRED STUBBS.
[2]From *Black Consciousness in South Africa* [1979], edited by MILLARD ARNOLD.

down supermarket aisles
it's on television
and in the streets even when my walk is casual/undefined
it's overhead flashing lights
i find it in my mouth
when i would speak of other things.   *the ISM [1983]*

1   usta be young usta be gifted — still black.
                                   American Sonnet [1994]. Sonnet 35

Danny Glover   1946–

2   Living on the creative edge means daring every day to dream of
a world beyond the socially constructed barriers that imprison and
divide us.   *Interview. O, the Oprah Magazine [April 2008]*

Al[bert] Green   1946–

and

[Mabon] Teenie Hodges   1945–

3   Love and happiness,
     Something that can make you do wrong, make you do right.
                                        Love and Happiness [1972]

4   Take me to the river
     And wash me down
     Won't you cleanse my soul
     Put my feet on the ground.   *Take Me to the River [1974]*

Chester Higgins, Jr.   1946–

5   We are Africans not because we are born in Africa, but because Africa
     is born in us.   *Feeling the Spirit [1994]*

Gregory Hines   1946–2003

6   Everything I do . . . comes out of tap dancing. When I take a European
     flight and fill out a landing card I put down tap dancer as my occupation.
                               Interview. New York Times [July 6, 1988]

[Reginald Martinez] Reggie Jackson   1946–

7   I'm the straw that stirs the drink.
                    *On his importance to the New York Yankees. Quoted in Sport
                    Magazine [June 1977]*

Barbara Lee

1946–

1   We must be careful not to embark on an open-ended war with neither an exit strategy nor a focused target. We cannot repeat past mistakes.[1]

Speech to the House of Representatives before making sole dissenting vote against allowing President George W. Bush to use "all necessary and appropriate force" in response to the terrorist attacks of September 11, 2001 [September 14, 2001]

Marilyn Nelson

1946–

2   I've always pictured my own death
as a closed door,
a black room,
a breathless leap from the mountain top
with time to throw out my arms, lift my head,
and see, in the instant my heart stops,
a whole galaxy of blue.
I imagined I'd forget,
in the cessation of feeling,
while the guilt of my lifetime floated away
like a nylon nightgown,
and that I'd fall into clean, fresh forgiveness.   *Mama's Promise [1985]*

3   Juneteenth: when the Negro telegraph
reached the last sad slave...   *Juneteenth [1990]*

4   Being black in America
was the Original Catch,
so no one was surprised
by 22.   *Lonely Eagles [1990]*

5   Miracles happen all the time.
We're here, aren't we?   *Abba Jacob and Miracles [1994]*

Barbara Smith

1946–

6   Black women's existence, experience and culture and the brutally complex systems of oppression which shape these are in the "real world" of white and/or male consciousness beneath consideration, invisible, unknown.   *Toward a Black Feminist Criticism [1977]*[2]

---

[1]Lee was referring to the Vietnam War.
[2]From *But Some of Us Are Brave* [1982], edited by GLORIA T. HULL, PATRICIA BELL SCOTT, and BARBARA SMITH.

1   If we have to wait for racism to be obliterated before we can begin to address sexism, we will be waiting for a long time.

Homegirls [1983], introduction

2   Rape is a national pastime, a form of torture visited upon all girls and women, from babies to the aged.   *Homegirls*

3   I never believe white people when they tell me they aren't racist. I have no reason to.... It is neither possible nor necessary to be morally exempt in order to stand in opposition to oppression.

The Truth That Never Hurts [2000]

Shelby Steele   1946–

4   In the deepest sense, the long struggle of blacks in America has always been a struggle to retrieve our full humanity. But now the reactive stance we adopted to defend ourselves against oppression binds us to the same racial views that oppressed us in the first place. Snakelike, our defense has turned on us. I think it is now the last barrier to the kind of self-possession that will give us our full humanity, and we must overcome it ourselves.

The Content of Our Character [1990]

Susan L. Taylor   1946–

5   We each have a finite number of heartbeats, a finite amount of time. But we have enough heartbeats and enough time to do what is important.

Passage. In the Spirit [column]. Essence [October 1991]

6   Having faith doesn't mean sitting back and waiting for miracles. Life is the miracle. You are the miracle.   *In the Spirit [1993]*

7   Motherlove is unfailing love. Tough stuff. It never gives up.

In the Spirit

André Watts   1946–

8   Some people will think I'm great even if I play like an idiot and some people will think I'm an idiot even if I'm great.

Interview. New York Times [January 13, 1988]

Kareem Abdul-Jabbar [Ferdinand Lewis Alcindor]   1947–

9   *[On the hero worship of athletes:]* We are more visible, but not more valuable.   *Giant Steps [1983]*

10   Black kids all want to go out and play basketball or football, and they should be thinking that there's an easier way to make a living.... Unfortunately, you have kids hoping for careers that hinge on their physical abilities

and that's not going to make it. You know how many jobs there are in pro basketball? . . . It's so redundant and depressing. It's the only thing these kids talk about. It's part of the vicious cycle much of the black community has lived with.   *Interview. Playboy [June 1986]*

1   You won't win until you learn how to lose.   *Kareem [1990]*

2   It's the mind that makes everything else work.   *Kareem*

3   More people have to start spending as much time in the library as they do on the basketball court.   *Kareem*

Ai [Florence Anthony]   1947–2010

4   Again and again, I play memory games
        in the casino of the past.
        Yes, half a chance,
        I'd do it all the same.   *Fate [1991]. Jimmy Hoffa's Odyssey*

5   I know the difference between
        what it is and what it isn't.
        Just because I can't touch it
        doesn't mean it isn't real.
        All I have to do is smash the screen,
        reach in and take what I want.
        Break out of prison.
        South Central homey's newly risen
        from the night of living dead,
        but this time he lives,
        he gets to give the zombies
        a taste of their own medicine.   *Greed [1993]. Riot Act, April 29, 1992*

6   Memory is a highway,
        where a car is speeding into the sunset.   *Vice [1999]. Rapture: A Fiction*

Patrick Bellegarde-Smith   1947–

7   [On the earthquakes in Haiti:] Every corpse is mine; every body is mine. Their spirit fuses with mine and that of all Haitians. Spirits live beyond death — and before birth. The dead are not dead, but alive in new dimensions.   *www.blog.speakingoffaith.org [January 24, 2010]*

Carol Moseley Braun   1947–

8   The imprimatur that is being sought here today sends a sign out to the rest of this country that the peculiar institution has not been put to bed for

once and for all; that indeed, like Dracula, it has come back to haunt us time and time and time again; and that, in spite of the fact that we have made strides forward, the fact of that matter is that there are those who would keep us slipping back into the darkness of division, into the snake pit of racial hatred.

> *Speech to the U.S. Senate during vote on patenting the*
> *Confederate flag [July 22, 1993][1]*

1   It's time to take the "Men Only" sign off the White House door.

> *Speech announcing her candidacy during the 2004 presidential*
> *election [February 18, 2003]*

Octavia E[stelle] Butler   1947–2006

2   I had seen people beaten on television and in the movies. I had seen the too-red substitute streaked across their backs and heard their well-rehearsed screams. But I hadn't lain nearby and smelled their sweat or heard them pleading and praying, shamed before their families and themselves. I was probably less prepared for the reality than the child crying not far from me. In fact, she and I were reacting very much alike. My face too was wet with tears. And my mind was darting from one thought to another, trying to tune out the whipping.

> *Kindred [1979]. The Fire*

3   My last night of childhood began with a visit home.

> *Bloodchild [1984]*

4   Beware:
All too often,
We say
What we hear others say.
We think
What we're told that we think.
We see
What we're permitted to see.
Worse!
We see what we're told that we see.

> *Parable of the Talents [1998], ch. 18*

5   Tolerance, like any aspect of peace, is forever a work in progress, never completed, and, if we're as intelligent as we like to think we are, never abandoned.   *Essay for National Public Radio online [2001]*

---

[1]From JOHN CLAY SMITH, *Rebels in Law: Voices in History of Black Women Lawyers* [1998].

Cheryl Clarke[1]   1947–

1   For a woman to be a lesbian in a male-supremacist, capitalist, misogynist, racist, homophobic, imperialist culture, such as that of North America, is an act of resistance.   *Lesbianism: An Act of Resistance [1981]*

2   Being given a lover's key is an intimate gesture: without it
one can figure what course the relationship will take; with it
trust is a temptation.   *Vicki and Daphne [1986]*

Paula Giddings   1947–

3   Black women survived the rigors of slavery to demand the rights of their race and of their sex. They rose above the most demeaning forms of labor and demanded to be called by their last names. Black women forged humane communities out of rough settlements. They converted the rock of double oppression into a steppingstone.   *When and Where I Enter [1984]*

Lorna Goodison   1947–

4   The welcome turns sour
she finds a woman's tongue
and clacks curses at the wind
for taking advantage

box her about this way
and that is the reason

wait is the reason

Tamarind Season.   *Tamarind Season [1980]*

5   Believe, believe
and believe this
the eye know how far
Heartease is.   *Heartease [1989]*

6   My mother raises rare blooms
and waters them with tea
her birth waters sang like rivers
my mother is now me.   *I Am Becoming My Mother [1989]*

7   There is everywhere here.
There is Alps and Lapland and Berlin.

---

[1]From *The Days of Good Looks: The Prose and Poetry of Cheryl Clarke, 1980–2005* [2006].

Armagh, Carrick Fergus, Malvern
Rhine and Calabar, Askenish
where freed slaves went to claim
what was left of the Africa within,
staging secret woodland ceremonies.   *To Us, All Flowers Are Roses [1995]*

1   But there is blood, red blood in the fields
of our lives, blood the bright banner flowing
over the order of cane and our history.

To Us, All Flowers Are Roses

Carolivia Herron   1947–

2   Johnnie, thereafter, forever, because as I have told you of this last image of
the city, now she is a light
a light
alight.   *Thereafter Johnnie [1991], last lines*

3   Them some willful intentional naps you
got all over your head.
   Sure enough.
Your hair intended to be nappy.
   Indeed it did.   *Nappy Hair [1997]*

Cathy Hughes   1947–

4   It's critical for us to tell our story from our perspective. When the
company is Black-owned, you have Black decision makers, a Black perspective and Black employees.   *Interview. Essence [October 1998]*

Geronimo ji-Jaga [Elmer Pratt]   1947–2011

5   You may call me crazy [but I believe] that because of our socioeco-
nomic conditions, every Black man and woman in prison is, in fact, a political prisoner. Every one, bar none.
        *Interview following release after twenty-seven years of wrongful
        imprisonment. Essence [November 1997]*

Yusef Komunyakaa [James William Brown, Jr.]   1947–

6   My black face fades,
hiding inside the black granite.
I said I wouldn't
dammit: No tears.
I'm stone. I'm flesh.   *Facing It [1988]*   461

1   Weeks of lifting & grunting
Never added up to much,
But we couldn't stop
Believing in iron.
Abandoned trucks & cars
Were held to the ground
By thick, nostalgic fingers of vines
Strong as a dozen sharecroppers.   *Believing in Iron [1992]*

2   How can love heal
the mouth shut this way?
Say something worth breath.   *Safe Subjects [1993]*

3   Redemptive as a straight razor
against a jugular vein—
unacknowledged & unforgiven.
It's truth we're after here,
hurting for, out in the streets
where my brothers kill each other,
each other's daughters & guardian angels
in the opera of dead on arrival.   *Safe Subjects*

4   I told my brothers I heard
You & mother making love,
Your low moans like blues
Bringing them into the world.   *Songs for My Father [1993]*

5   Unearthly
desire makes man & woman
God's celestial wishbone
to snap at midnight.   *What Counts [1998]*

6   For weeks, for months,
I could taste him in the dusty air.
        Do you know how it feels
to have your tongue shaped
        from a dead man's name?
Suppose that grenade
        hadn't fallen like jackfruit
from a heavy branch,
        & Oliver walked in here
today, took a seat beside
        Nancy, & began to talk
Autobiography of My Alter Ego [2002]

1
When deeds splay before us
precious as gold & unused chances
stripped from the whine-bone,
we know the moment kindheartedness
walks in.

Kindness [2003]

Nathaniel Mackey   1947–

2
The way we lay
we mimed a body
of water. It was
this or that way
with
the dead and we
were them.

Splay Anthem [2006]. Eye of the Scarecrow

3
Asked his name, he said,
"Stra, short for Stranger."

Splay Anthem. Song of the Andoumboulou: 40

Assata Shakur [JoAnne Chesimard]   1947–

4
We had been completely brainwashed and we didn't even know it. We accepted white value systems and white standards of beauty and, at times, we accepted the white man's view of ourselves.... From when I was a tot, I can remember Black people saying, "Niggas ain't shit." "You know how lazy niggas are." "Give a nigga an inch and he'll take a mile." Everybody knew what "niggas" like to do after they eat: sleep. Everybody knew "niggas" couldn't be on time; that's why there was c.p.t. (colored people's time). "Niggas don't take care of nothin'." "Niggas don't stick together." The list could go on and on. To varying degrees we accepted these statements as true. And, to varying degrees, we each made them true within ourselves because we believed them.

Assata [1987]

5
Nobody in the world, nobody in history, has ever gotten their freedom by appealing to the moral sense of the people who were oppressing them.   *Assata*

6
Revolution is about change, and the first place the change begins is in yourself.

Assata

7
Any community seriously concerned with its own freedom has to be concerned about other people's freedom as well. The victory of oppressed people anywhere in the world is a victory for Black people. Each time one of imperialism's tentacles is cut off we are closer to liberation.   *Assata*

463

O[renthal] J[ames] Simpson

1947–

1   Don't feel sorry for me. I've had a great life, great friends. Please think of the real O.J. and not this lost person.

Apparent suicide note discovered shortly before his arrest for the murder of his ex-wife and her friend [June 17, 1994]

2   Absolutely, 100 percent not guilty.

Plea entered in the arraignment for the murder [July 22, 1994]

3 If I Did It

Title of book [2007]

Sylvester [James, Jr.]

1947–1988

4 You Make Me Feel (Mighty Real)

Song title [1978]

Pearl Cleage

1948–

5   What looks like *crazy* on an ordinary day looks a lot like *love* if you catch it in the moonlight. *What Looks like Crazy on an Ordinary Day [1997]*

Jimmy Cliff [James Chambers]

1948–

6 As sure as the sun will shine
I'm going to get it, what's mine
And then the harder they come
The harder they fall,
One and all.

The Harder They Come [1970]

7 Many rivers to cross,
But I can't seem to find my way over. *Many Rivers to Cross [1970]*

8 You can get it if you really want,
But you must try, try and try, try and try.

You Can Get It If You Really Want [1970]

Jewelle Gomez

1948–

9   I think the most important thing for you to do in the meantime is live. It is a very involving job, which takes much concentration and practice.

The Gilda Stories [1991]

Fred Hampton

1948–1969

10   You can murder a liberator, but you can't murder liberation.

Speech [April 27, 1969][1]

---

   [1]From *Black Panthers Speak* [1970], edited by PHILLIP S. FONER.

Charles R[ichard] Johnson
1948–

1   The wretchedness of being colonized was not that slavery created feelings of guilt and indebtedness . . . ; nor that it created a long, lurid dream of multiplicity and separateness, which it did indeed create, but the fact that men had epidermalized *Being*.

Oxherding Tale [1982], ch. 3

2   Was sorcery a gift given to a few, like poetry? Did the Lord come, lift you up, then drop you forever?

The Sorcerer's Apprentice [1986]

3   Of all the things that drive men to sea, the most common disaster, I've come to learn, is women.

Middle Passage [1990], opening line

4   He was traveling light again, for the long, lurid dream of multiplicity and separateness, the very belief in an "I" that suffered and strained to affect the world, dissolved, and for the first time he felt like a dreamer gently roused from sleep and forgetfulness.   *Dreamer [1998], ch. 4*

Zakes Mda
1948–

5   "Tears are very close to my eyes," says Bhonco, son of Ximiya. "Not for pain . . . no . . . I do not cry because of pain. I cry only because of beautiful things."   *The Heart of Redness [2000], opening lines*

6   The Unbelievers like to explore various strategies in pursuit of happiness. Whereas Believers have a tendency of wanting to stay ignorant of the things that could make them unhappy, the Unbelievers like to induce sadness in order to attain happiness.   *The Heart of Redness, ch. 8*

Adrian Piper
1948–

7   Dear Friend,

I am black.

I am sure you did not realize this when you made/laughed at/agreed with that racist remark. In the past, I have attempted to alert white people to my racial identity in advance. Unfortunately, this invariably causes them to react to me as pushy, manipulative or socially inappropriate. Therefore, my policy is to assume that white people do not make these remarks, even when they believe there are no black people present, and to distribute this card when they do.

I regret any discomfort my presence is causing you, just as I am sure you regret the discomfort your racism is causing me.

My Calling Card #1 [1986]

Phylicia Rashād   1948–

1   Often I've wondered what it takes for this to happen. And now
I know. It takes effort and grace.

> *Speech, on becoming the first black woman to win a Tony*
> *Award for best performance by a leading actress in a play*
> *[January 6, 2004]*

Ntozake Shange [Paulette Williams]   1948–

2   we gotta dance to keep from cryin

> *For Colored Girls Who Have Considered Suicide When the*
> *Rainbow Is Enuf [1975] [Lady in Yellow]*

3   layin in water
she became herself
ordinary
brown braided woman
with big legs & full lips
reglar...
& now she stood a
reglar colored girl

> *For Colored Girls Who Have Considered Suicide When the*
> *Rainbow Is Enuf [Lady in Red]*

4   nice is such a rip-off

> *For Colored Girls Who Have Considered Suicide When the*
> *Rainbow Is Enuf [Lady in Blue]*

5   ever since i realized there waz
someone callt
a colored girl an evil woman a
bitch or a nag
i been tryin not to be that & leave
bitterness
in somebody else's cup

> *For Colored Girls Who Have Considered Suicide When the*
> *Rainbow Is Enuf [Lady in Orange]*

6   my love is too delicate to have thrown back on my face

> *For Colored Girls Who Have Considered Suicide When the*
> *Rainbow Is Enuf [Lady in Yellow]*

7   somebody almost walked off wid alla my stuff
like a kleptomaniac workin hard & forgettin while stealin
this is mine/this ain't yr stuff

> *For Colored Girls Who Have Considered Suicide When the*
> *Rainbow Is Enuf [Lady in Green]*

1   i found god in myself.
    & i loved her/i loved her fiercely
        For Colored Girls Who Have Considered Suicide When the
        Rainbow Is Enuf

2   nappy edges
    the roots of your hair/what
    turns back when we sweat, run,
    make love, dance, get afraid, get
    happy: the tell-tale sign of living   *nappy edges [1978]*

3   yes yes yes   3 wishes is all you get
      scarlet ribbons for yr hair
      a farm in Mississippi
      a someone to love you madly
    all things are possible
    but aint no colored magician in his right mind
    gonna make you white
    cuz this is blk magic you lookin at
    & i'm fixin you up good/fixin you up good & colored
    & you gonna be colored all yr life
    & you gonna love it/bein colored/all yr life
    colored & love it/love it/bein colored   *spell #7 [1979] [Lou]*

4   Where there is a woman there is magic.
                        Sassafrass, Cypress and Indigo [1982]

5   Love kisses were the best kind. There was no denying that a kiss from
someone you loved was different from any other kind of kiss and should be
studied up on and looked at carefully, so you could recognize it when love
came down on you. That's what love did. It came down on you like rain
or sunshine.   *Betsy Brown [1985]*

Sekou Sundiata [Robert Franklin Feaster]   1948–2007

6   People be droppin' revolution like it was a pick-up line.
You wouldn't use that word if you knew what it meant.
It ain't pretty
It's bloody
It overturns things.

                        Droppin' Revolution [2000]

7   I had taken it for granted that the most important part of the body
was located front and center. This is what I mean about the body being
a sneak.

It'll let you believe things like that until it's ready to tell you the truth.
It ain't the heart or the lungs or the brain.
The biggest, most important part of the body is the part that hurts.

Blessing the Boats [2002]

Charles [Ghankay] Taylor   1948–

1   He killed my ma, he killed my pa, but I will vote for him.

Campaign slogan [1997][1]

2   I can no longer see you suffer. The suffering is enough for you are
good people. I will always remember you wherever I am and I say to you,
God willing, I will be back.

*Statement following exile from Liberia prompted by indictment
by the Special Court for Sierra Leone and United Nations
efforts to stabilize Liberia [August 2003]*[2]

Luisah Teish   1948–

3   Birth is the beginning of physical life and death is the end of it. But the
essential energy of existence (Da) continues beyond physical life. Both life
and death simply exist and are two sides of the same coin of existence.

Jambalaya [1985]

Clarence Thomas   1948–

4   This is a circus. It is a national disgrace. And from my standpoint, as a
black American, as far as I am concerned, it is a high-tech lynching for uppity
blacks who in any way deign to think for themselves, to do for themselves, to
have different ideas, and it is a message that, unless you kow-tow to an old
order, this is what will happen to you. You will be lynched, destroyed, carica-
tured by a committee of the U.S. Senate, rather than hung from a tree.

*Statement concerning Professor Anita Hill's allegations
of sexual harassment, made to the U.S. Senate Judiciary
Committee [October 11, 1991]*

5   I think it is important for judges not to have agendas or to have strong
ideology or ideological views. That is baggage.

*Statement at his nomination hearing, U.S. Senate Judiciary
Committee*

---

[1]From MEREDITH MARAN, *The Fate of Africa* [2006].

[2]Taylor was the first former head of state in Africa to face trial in a war crimes court at the Hague and the
first head of state convicted of war crimes and crimes against humanity since the Nuremberg trials after
World War II.

1   Arguments should not sneak around in disguise, as if dissent were somehow sinister.

> *Speech to the American Enterprise Institute, Washington, D.C.*
> *[February 13, 2001]*

John Whitehead
1948–2004

and

Gene McFadden
1948–2006

2   Ain't No Stoppin' Us Now
Song title [1979]

Johnny Ray Youngblood
1948–

3   Christ forces me to confess that even when you've got the Lord, every now and then you need somebody else. That is not against the Lord. But sometimes you need another mortal. You need another piece of flesh and blood talking to you. It doesn't mean the Lord is absent, but y'all, we're just not sure angels and divinities go through what we go through.... And while "just having Jesus is enough" is a great-sounding statement, you better speak it with caution, because you may find yourself with just Him and need somebody else.

> *From* Samuel G. Freedman, *Upon This Rock [1993]*

4   God's will is not that we be confined to ghettos and ghetto thinking.
Upon This Rock

5   If Jesus came back this morning to check on our discipleship, to see what we have done, right here in our very midst, he would find failures that do not have to be. We have failed in terms of black men. And if you really want to go into the lion's den, we have failed our children.... Accept, first of all, we have failed.
Sermon. Upon This Rock

John Agard
1949–

6   First rape a people
simmer for centuries

bring memories to boil
foil voice of drum

add pinch of pain
to rain of rage

stifle drum again
then mix strains of blood

over slow fire
watch fever grow   *Man to Pan [1982]. Pan Recipe*

Arrow [Alphonsus Cassell]   1949–2010

1   Feeling hot, hot, hot!   *Hot, Hot, Hot [1982]*

Calvin O[tis] Butts III   1949–

2   *[On 9/11:]* Don't tell us about terror! We know terror. Oh, yes, we
know terror. And don't allow people to go off on some tangent about
Islamic terrorism or militant terrorism from Islam. Oh, religion is not the
cause of this! Let me tell you about the terror we know. We know the terror
that was called the Christian Knights of the Ku Klux Klan. No, we did not
have World Trade Towers. We did not have a multi-trillion-dollar financial
district. All we had was our homes and our churches. But the terror used to
ride by night. They would rape our women, lynch our men, kill our children, burn our churches. We know terror! And the terror did not come with
a star and a crescent. The terror was a burning cross on our front lawn.

Manage Your Fear[1]

George Foreman   1949–

3   Life is like boxing. You've only got so many punches to throw and you
can only take so many.   *By George [1991]*

Gayl Jones   1949–

4   When I'm telling you something don't you ever ask if I'm lying.
Because they didn't want to leave no evidence of what they done — so it
couldn't be held against them. And I'm leaving evidence. And you got to
leave evidence too. And your children got to leave evidence. And when it
come time to hold up the evidence, we got to have evidence to hold up.

Corregidora [1975] [Great Gram]

5   I am Ursa Corregidora. I have tears for eyes. I was made to touch my
past at an early age.   *Corregidora*

6   Some people think before they talk. Some people talk before they
think. Some people make you say things you don't want to say. I don't know
how they do it. I wish I knew someone who could make you say what you
do want to say. I suppose that is only yourself.

White Rat [1977]. Your Poems Have Very Little Color

---

[1]From *9.11.01: African American Leaders Respond to an American Tragedy* [2001], edited by MARTHA SIMMONS and FRANK A. THOMAS.

1   When you tell a story you automatically talk about traditions, but they're never separate from the people, the human implications.... You're talking about all your connections as a human being.

From Chant of Saints [1979], edited by MICHAEL S. HARPER and ROBERT B. STEPTOE

2   Seem like most people turn they own flaws of character into virtues. They see other people's flaws, but they own flaws, they turn into virtues.

The Healing [1998]

Tom Joyner   1949–

3   Fighting the power is good, but becoming the power is even better.

I'm Just a DJ but . . . It Makes Sense to Me
[2005]

Jamaica Kincaid [Elaine Potter Richardson]   1949–

4   I stood above the land and the sea, and I felt that I was not myself as I had once known myself to be: I was not made up of flesh and blood and muscles and bones and tissue and cells and vital organs but was made up of my will, and over my will I had complete dominion.

At the Bottom of the River. The New Yorker
[May 3, 1982]

5   For a short while during the year I was ten, I thought only people I did not know died.   *Annie John [1985], opening line*

6   When I got home, my mother came toward me, arms outstretched, concern written on her face. My whole mouth filled up with a bitter taste, for I could not understand how she could be so beautiful even though I no longer loved her.   *Annie John, ch. 3*

7   An ugly thing, that is what you are when you become a tourist, an ugly, empty thing, a stupid thing, a piece of rubbish pausing here and there to gaze at this and taste that, and it will never occur to you that the people who inhabit the place in which you have just paused cannot stand you.

A Small Place [1988]

8   Most natives in the world cannot go anywhere. They are too poor. They are too poor to go anywhere. They are too poor to escape the reality of their lives; and they are too poor to live properly in the place where they live, which is the very place you, the tourist, want to go — so when the natives see you, the tourist, they envy you, they envy your ability to leave your own banality and boredom, they envy your ability to turn their own banality and boredom into a source of pleasure for yourself.

A Small Place   471

1   Do you know why people like me are shy about being capitalists? Well, it's because we, for as long as we have known you, *were* capital, like bales of cotton and sacks of sugar.   *A Small Place*

2   As for what we were like before we met you, I no longer care. No periods of time over which my ancestors held sway, no documentation of complex civilizations, is any comfort to me. Even if I really came from people who were living like monkeys in trees, it was better to be that than what happened to me, what I became after I met you.   *A Small Place*

3   I was always being told I should be something, and then my whole upbringing was something I was not: it was English.

                                              Interview. Callaloo [Spring 1989]

4   I was then at the height of my two-facedness: that is, outside I seemed one way, inside I was another; outside false, inside true.   *Lucy [1990]*

5   I had come to feel that my mother's love for me was designed solely to make me into an echo of her; and I didn't know why, but I felt that I would rather be dead than become just an echo of someone.   *Lucy*

6   History is full of great events; when the great events are said and done, there will always be someone, a little person, unhappy, dissatisfied, discontented, not at home in her own skin, ready to stir up a whole new set of great events again.   *Lucy*

7   Friendship is a simple thing, and yet complicated; friendship is on the surface, something natural, something taken for granted, and yet underneath one could find worlds.   *Lucy*

8   My mother died at the moment I was born, and so for my whole life there was nothing standing between myself and eternity; at my back was always a bleak, black wind. I could not have known at the beginning of my life that this would be so; I only came to know this in the middle of my life, just at the time when I was no longer young and realized that I had less of some of the things I used to have in abundance and more of some of the things I had scarcely had at all.

                          The Autobiography of My Mother [1996], opening lines

9   I shall never have the garden I have in my mind, but that for me is the joy of it; certain things can never be realized and so all the more reason to attempt them. A garden, no matter how good it is, must never completely satisfy. The world as we know it, after all, began in a very good garden, a completely satisfying garden — Paradise — but after a while the owner and the occupants wanted more.   *My Favorite Plant [1998], introduction*

10   The present will be a now then and the past is now then and the future will be a now then.   *See Now Then [2013]*

Lionel Richie
1949–

1 I'm easy like Sunday morning.   *Easy [1977]*

2 You're once, twice, three times a lady.

Three Times a Lady [1978]

3 Father, help your children and don't let them fall by the side of the road.

Jesus Is Love [1980]

4 Lady, I'm your knight in shining armor and I love you.
   You have made me what I am and I am yours.   *Lady [1980]*

5 You will always be my endless love.   *Endless Love [1981]*

6 Believe in who you are, you are a shining star.   *Say You, Say Me [1985]*

Thomas Sankara[1]
1949–1987

7   Women suffer doubly from all the scourges of neocolonial society. First, they experience the same suffering as men. Second, they are subjected to additional suffering by men.

A New Society Free from Social Justice and Imperialist Domination [October 2, 1983]

8   The revolution and women's liberation go together. We do not talk of women's emancipation as an act of charity or because of a surge of human compassion. It is a basic necessity for the triumph of the revolution. Women hold up the other half of the sky.

A New Society Free from Social Justice and Imperialist Domination

9   The quest for peace goes hand and hand with the firm application of the right of countries to independence, of peoples to liberation, and of nations to self-determination.

Freedom Is Won. Speech at the United Nations General Assembly [October 4, 1984]

10   Ours is the blood that nourished the rise of capitalism. . . . The truth can no longer be concealed by doctoring numbers. For every black brought to the plantations at least five others died or were mutilated.

Freedom Is Won. Speech at the United Nations General Assembly

11   Imperialism is the arsonist setting fire to our forests and savannah.

Speech to the First International Tree and Forest Conference, Paris [February 5, 1986]

---

[1]From THOMAS SANKARA, *We Are Heirs of the World's Revolutions: Speeches from the Burkina Faso Revolution, 1983–87* [2002].

Gil Scott-Heron   1949–2011

1   You will not be able to stay home, brother.
    You will not be able to plug in, turn on, and cop out.
                                        The Revolution Will Not Be Televised [1970]

2   The revolution will not be televised
                    will not be televised
            not be televised
                    be televised
    The revolution will be no re-run, brothers.
    The revolution will be LIVE.   *The Revolution Will Not Be Televised*

3   A junkie walking through the twilight,
    I'm on my way home.
    I left three days ago,
            but no one seems to know I'm gone.
    Home is where the hatred is.
    Home is filled with pain and it
    Might not be such a bad idea if I never,
            never went home again.   *Home Is Where the Hatred Is* [1971]

4   With the help of those educators who are intelligent enough to recog-
    nize the need for drastic reconstruction there will be a new era of Black
    thought and Black thinkers who enter the working world from colleges aware
    of the real problems that will face them and not believing that a piece of paper
    will claim a niche for them in the society-at-large [*sic*]. The education process
    will not whitewash them into thinking that their troubles are over. They will
    come out as Black people.   *The Nigger Factory* [1972]. *Author's Note*

Joan Armatrading   1950–

5   With a friend
    I can smile
    But with a lover
    I could hold my head back
    I could really laugh
    Really laugh.   *Love and Affection* [1976]

6   I had somebody say once I was way too black,
    And someone answers she's not black enough for me.   *How Cruel* [1979]

7   I wanna be by myself
    I came in this world alone
    Me myself I.   *Me Myself I* [1980]

David Bradley, Jr.　　　　　　　　　　　1950–

1　　Probably he [the white historian] thinks it has something to do with economics, or with greed, or with lust; most likely he thinks the effects of the Trade can be seen in the shifts of the worldwide balance of power.... To an extent, he will be correct. But he will also believe that the African Slave Trade is over, that whatever its effects were, they are existing now in and of themselves, waves spreading across a pond, the stone that caused them having long ago come to rest. He will think this because to understand otherwise involves dealing with something so basic, so elemental, so fundamental that it can be faced only if one is forced to face it: death. For that is what the Slave Trade was all about. Not death from poxes and musketry and whippings and malnutrition and melancholy and suicide; death itself.

The Chaneysville Incident [1981]

[Elizabeth] Bebe Moore Campbell　　　　　1950–2006

2　　My father took to his grave the short-sleeved, beer-swilling men of summer, big bellies, raucous laughter, pipe smoke and the aroma of cigars. My daddy is really gone and his vacant place is my cold, hard border. As always, my life is framed by his absence.　*Sweet Summer [1989]*

3　　The music was as much a gift as sunshine, as rain, as any blessing ever prayed for.　*Your Blues Ain't Like Mine [1992], opening line*

4　　In life, the trick is just to do what's necessary to keep on living.

Your Blues Ain't Like Mine, ch. 26 [Willow]

5　　The flames of April came out of season.

There is a time for burning in Los Angeles, months when devastation is expected and planned for, and blazes attack with the power and cruelty of old enemies. August. September. These are the city's appointed months of conflagration. But the fires of April were not weather. They chose their own time, creating destruction that spared no one. Long after the flames were quelled, the city was still smoldering, and even those whose lives were cooled by ocean breezes felt the heat.　*Brothers and Sisters [1994], prologue*

6　　Mental illness is a kind of slavery.　*72 Hour Hold [2005] [Brad]*

Melvin Dixon　　　　　　　　　　　　1950–1992

7　　I'll be somewhere listening for my name.[1]... You, then, are charged by the possibility of your good health, by the broadness of your vision, to remember us.　*Keynote address at OutWrite [1992]*

---

[1]Refers to the spiritual *I'll Be Somewhere Listening.*

1   Today? Tonight?
     It waits. For me.   *Heartbeats*[1]

Dr. J [Julius Erving]   1950–

2   *[Reply when asked about dunking:]* It's easy, once you learn how to fly.
                                                                 Attributed

Henry Louis Gates, Jr.   1950–

3   Censorship is to art what lynching is to justice.
               2 Live Crew Decoded. Op-ed in the New York Times
               [June 19, 1990]

4   I rebel at the notion that I can't be part of other groups, that I can't
     construct identities through elective affinity, that race must be the most
     important thing about me. Is that what I want on my gravestone: Here lies
     an African American? So I'm divided. I want to be black, to know black, to
     luxuriate in whatever I might be calling blackness at any particular time —
     but to do so in order to come out the other side, to experience a humanity
     that is neither colorless nor reducible to color. Bach *and* James Brown. Sushi
     and fried catfish.   *Colored People [1994]*

5   All human civilization wears Africa on its face. . . . And until the
     West — and the rest of us — knows Africa, we can never truly know
     ourselves.   *Wonders of the African World [1999]*

6   Memories . . . form the building blocks of family history. They are the
     stories that survive in our kitchens and in our living rooms. Stories that tell
     it like it is about the way it was, the way it used to be. Some are humorous,
     others are painful, even embarrassing, but all of them make up the essence
     of African American history.   *African American Lives [2006]*

7   We will never know even a tiny fraction of the names of our ancestors
     who were taken from Africa. We will never see their faces, never read their
     words. They are lost to us forever, because of the devastatingly effective way
     the slave trade worked in its attempt to erase the past from the present of a
     slave.   *In Search of Our Roots [2009]*

Marita Golden   1950–

8   After a season of fitful migration, I had come home. To rest against
     the bedrock inside myself. I had wandered. Will wander still . . . and will take
     home with me wherever I go.   *Migrations of the Heart [1983], last lines*

---

[1]From *Every Shut Eye Ain't Sleep* [1994], edited by MICHAEL S. HARPER.

1   A legacy is a contract that obligates the recipient to rise to meet the best that the legacy symbolizes.

> *Gumbo: An Anthology of African American Writing [2002], introduction*

[Carol] Lani Guinier   1950–

2   In a racially divided society, majority rule is not a reliable instrument of democracy.

> *Second Proms and Second Primaries: The Limits of Majority Rule. Boston Review [September–October 1992]*

3   The tyranny of The Majority is just as much a problem of silencing minority viewpoints as it is of excluding minority representatives or preferences. We cannot all talk at once, but that does not mean only one group should get to speak. We can take turns.

> *The Tyranny of the Majority [1994]*

Edward P[aul] Jones   1950–

4   It could be winter, it could be summer, but the most she ever got was something she called pigeon silence. Sometimes she had the urge to unlatch the door and go into the coop, or, at the very least, to try to reach through the wire and the wooden slats to stroke a wing or a breast, to share whatever the silence seemed to conceal. But she always kept her hands to herself, and after a few minutes, as if relieved, she would go back to her bed and visit the birds again in sleep.

> *Lost in the City [1992]. The Girl Who Raised Pigeons*

5   She was eighty-six years old, and had learned that life was all chaos and painful uncertainty and that the only way to get through it was to expect chaos even in the most innocent of moments. Offer a crust of bread to a sick bird and you often drew back a bloody finger.   *Lost in the City. Marie*

6   Henry had always said that he wanted to be a better master than any white man he had ever known. He did not understand that the kind of world he wanted to create was doomed before he had even spoken the first syllable of the word *master*.   *The Known World [2003], ch. 3*

7   The hitter can never be the judge. Only the receiver of the blow can tell you how hard it was, whether it would kill a man or make a baby just yawn.   *The Known World, ch. 6 [Fern]*

8   It is a map of life made with every kind of art man has ever thought to represent himself. Yes, clay. Yes, paint. Yes, cloth.... It is what God sees when He looks down.   *The Known World [Calvin]*

1   It's a shame before God, the way they do all Aunt Hagar's children.
>   *All Aunt Hagar's Children [2006]. All Aunt Hagar's Children*
>   *[Aunt Penny]*

2   Remember, every happy birthday boy is headed for his grave.
>   *All Aunt Hagar's Children. All Aunt Hagar's Children [Mother]*

3   They were the children of once-upon-a-time slaves, born into a kind of freedom, but they had traveled down through the wombs with what all their kind had been born with — the knowledge that God had promised next week to everyone but themselves.
>   *All Aunt Hagar's Children. In the Blink of God's Eye*

4   The heart can be cruel, the heart can be wicked, the heart can give joy . . . but it is always an instrument we can never understand.
>   *All Aunt Hagar's Children. Tapestry [Anne]*

[Robert] Bobby McFerrin, [Jr.]   1950–

5   In your life expect some trouble
     When you worry you make it double.   *Don't Worry, Be Happy [1988]*

Ronald E[rwin] McNair   1950–1986

6   The true courage of space flight is not sitting aboard 6 million pounds of fire and thunder as one rockets away from this planet. True courage comes in enduring . . . persevering, the preparation and believing in oneself.
>   *Speech [1984]*[1]

E[ugene] Ethelbert Miller   1950–

7   tomorrow
     i will take the
     journey back
     sail
     the
     middle passage
     it
     would be better
     to be packed
     like spoons again
     than
     to continue to

---

[1]Reprinted in *TIME* magazine [February 10, 1986].

live among
knives and forks   *First Light: New and Selected Poems [1994]. Tomorrow*

1   I am the land
I am the grass growing.
I am the trees.
I am the wind, the voice calling.
I am the poor.
I am the hungry.
             I Am the Land: A Poem in Memory of Oscar Romero [1994][1]

2   Night as dark as the inside
of a catcher's mitt
There are blows I can take
head on and never step back
from. When Jackie made the news
I knew I would have a chance
to play ball in the majors.
Ten years ago I put the number
39 on my back and tonight God
tries to steal home.   *Roy Campanella: January, 1958 [1998]*

Gloria Naylor   1950–

3   Brewster Place became especially fond of its colored daughters as they
milled like determined spirits among its decay, trying to make it a home.
Nutmeg arms leaned over windowsills, gnarled ebony legs carried groceries
up double flights of steps, and saffron hands strung out wet laundry on
back-yard lines. Their perspiration mingled with the steam from boiling
pots of smoked pork and greens, and it curled on the edges of the aroma
of vinegar douches and Evening in Paris cologne that drifted through the
street.... They were hard-edged, soft-centered, brutally demanding, and
easily pleased, these women of Brewster Place. They came, they went, grew
up, and grew old beyond their years. Like an ebony phoenix, each in her
own time and with her own season had a story.
                          The Women of Brewster Place [1982]. Dawn

4   Sometimes being a friend means mastering the art of timing. There
is a time for silence. A time to let go and allow people to hurl themselves
into their own destiny. And a time to prepare to pick up the pieces when it's
all over.   *The Women of Brewster Place. Etta Mae Johnson*

---

[1]Romero, the archbishop of El Salvador, was assassinated in 1980 while saying mass.

1   Black isn't beautiful, and it isn't ugly — black is! It's not kinky hair and it's not straight hair — it just is.

The Women of Brewster Place. Kiswana Browne [Mrs. Browne]

2   No one cries when a street dies. There's no line of mourners to walk behind the coffin wheeled on the axis of the earth and lidded by the sky. No organ-piped dirges, no whispered prayers, no eulogy.

The Women of Brewster Place. Dusk

3   Really listen this time: the only voice is your own.   *Mama Day [1988]*

4   Everybody wants to be right in a world where there ain't no right or wrong to be found.   *Mama Day*

Grace Nichols   1950–

5   Not every skin-teeth
is a smile "Massa"

if you see me smiling
when you pass

if you see me bending
when you ask

Know that I smile
know that I bend
only the better
to rise and strike
again.   *I Is a Long Memoried Woman [1984]. Skin-Teeth*

6   I come from web of kin
from sacred new yam reapings.   *I Is a Long Memoried Woman. Web of Kin*

7   Fat is
as fat is
as fat is.   *Fat Black Woman's Poems [1985]. . . . And a Fat Poem*

8   I have crossed an ocean
I have lost my tongue
from the root of the old one
a new one has sprung.   *Fat Black Woman's Poems, epilogue*

William C[lay] Rhoden   1950–

9   In the antebellum South, the slave and the plantation described tangible circumstances; today the slave and the plantation describe a state of mind and the conditioning of the mind. In an era of multimillion-dollar

salaries, slavery remains the model for the power relationship between athletes and their owners. *Forty Million Dollar Slaves [2006]*

Sapphire [Ramona Lofton] 1950–

1   There has always been something wrong wif the tesses. The tesses paint a picture of me wif no brain. The tesses paint a picture of me an' my muver — my whole family, we more than dumb, we invisible.
Push [1996]

2   "I'm tired," I says. She [Ms. Rain] says, "I know you are, but you can't stop now Precious, you gotta push." And I do. *Push*

Anna Deavere Smith 1950–

3   Speaking teaches us what our natural "literature" is. In fact, everyone, in a given amount of time, will say something that is like poetry.
Fires in the Mirror [1993], introduction

4   In America, identity is always being negotiated.
Fires in the Mirror, introduction

5   Those in the margins are always trying to get to the center, and those at the center, frequently in the name of tradition, are trying to keep the margins at a distance. *Fires in the Mirror, introduction*

Stevie Wonder [Stevland Morris] 1950–

6   My cherie amour
Lovely as a summer day
My cherie amour
Distant as the Milky Way. *My Cherie Amour [1968]*

7   You Are the Sunshine of My Life *Song title [1972]*

8   Very superstitious, writing's on the wall.
Very superstitious, ladder's 'bout to fall. *Superstition [1972]*

9   Don't you worry 'bout a thing, mama
'Cause I'll be standing on the side when you check it out.
Don't You Worry 'Bout a Thing [1973]

10   A boy is born in hard time Mississippi
Surrounded by four walls that ain't so pretty. *Living for the City [1973]*

11   Living just enough, just enough for the city. *Living for the City*

12   Isn't she lovely,
Isn't she wonderful?

Isn't she precious?
Less than one minute old.   *Isn't She Lovely [1976]*

1   Music is a world within itself,
With a language we all understand.   *Sir Duke [1976]*

2   Love's in Need of Love Today   *Song title [1976]*

3   There's a ribbon in the sky for our love.   *Ribbon in the Sky [1982]*

4   I Just Called to Say I Love You   *Song title [1984]*

Stevie Wonder [Stevland Morris]   1950–

and

Syreeta Wright   1946–2004

and

Lee Garrett   1948–

and

Lula Mae Hardaway   1930–2006

5   Signed, Sealed, Delivered, I'm Yours   *Song title [1970]*

Paul Boateng   1951–

6   We have won a great victory here tonight.... For 400 years we have
waited to go to that place of our independence and I say this, we went before
as humble petitioners — Never again! We go now as Socialist Tribunes of all
the people, black and white.[1]   *Speech on election night [June 11, 1987][2]*

Ellis Cose   1951–

7   Despite its very evident prosperity, much of America's black middle
class is in excruciating pain. And that distress — although most of the
country does not see it — illuminates a serious American problem: the
problem of the broken covenant, of the pact ensuring that if you work hard,
get a good education, and play by the rules, you will be allowed to advance
and achieve to the limits of your ability.   *Rage of a Privileged Class [1993]*

8   Racial discussions tend to be conducted at one of two levels — either
shouts or whispers. The shouters are generally so twisted by pain or

---

[1]Four black MPs were elected to the British Parliament on June 11, 1987.
[2]From Terri A. Sewell, *Black Tribunes* [1993].

ignorance that spectators tune them out. The whisperers are so afraid of the sting of truth that they avoid saying much of anything at all.

Rage of a Privileged Class

1   Weak as its scientific foundation may be, race is an essential part of who we are (and how we see others) that is no more easily shed than un-pleasant memories. Few of us would choose to be rendered raceless — to be suddenly without a tribe.   *Colorblind [1997]*

2   Black men are not "endangered species," not in the sense of, say, the peregrine falcon or the bog turtle, whose long-term existences on Earth are in question. We stand nearly seventeen million strong, an ever-growing extended family of black boys and men.

The Envy of the World [2002]

Arthur [A. R.] Flowers   1951–

3   The zombie have long been with us. Souldead casualties of our long years of defeat. But now they sprout like weeds, evidence of our genocide.

De Mojo Blues [1985]

Eric [Himpton] Holder   1951–

4   Though this nation has proudly thought of itself as an ethnic melting pot, in things racial we have always been and continue to be, in too many ways, essentially a nation of cowards. Though race related issues continue to occupy a significant portion of our political discussion, and though there remain many unresolved racial issues in this nation, we, average Americans, simply do not talk enough with each other about race.

Speech at a Department of Justice African American History Month Program [February 18, 2009]

Terry [Lynn] McMillan   1951–

5   A man's mind is about the strongest thing he got going for him.

Disappearing Acts [1989] [Franklin]

6   Instead of wasting my time wishing and hoping, sleeping with self-pity and falling in love over and over again with ghosts, I'm going to stop con-centrating so hard on what's missing in my life and be grateful for what I've got.... And if there's a man out there who's willing to ride or walk or run or even fly with me, he'll show up. Probably out of nowhere. I'm just not going to hold my breath.   *Disappearing Acts [Zora]*

7   I worry about if and when I'll ever find the right man, if I'll ever be able to exhale.   *Waiting to Exhale [1992] [Savannah]*

1   I have pretty much come to the conclusion that marriage itself is a dead-end institution. I'm not doing it again. All I want is a little companion. No ring. No "I do till death do us part," because I said that once and we're both still very much alive.   *How Stella Got Her Groove Back [1996]*

2   Being a lifetime wife and mother has afforded me the luxury of having multiple and even simultaneous careers: I've been a chauffeur. A chef. An interior decorator. A landscape architect, as well as a gardener. I've been a painter. A furniture restorer. A personal shopper. A veterinarian's assistant and sometimes the veterinarian. I've been an accountant, a banker, and on occasion, a broker. I've been a beautician. A map. A psychic. Santa Claus. The Tooth Fairy. The T.V. Guide. A movie reviewer. An angel. God. . . . For a long time I have felt like I inadvertently got my master's in How to Take Care of Everybody Except Yourself and then a Ph.D. in How to Pretend Like You Don't Mind.

   But I do mind.
                        The Interruption of Everything [2006] [Marilyn Grimes]

Luther Vandross   1951–2005

3   I can't fool myself.
      I don't want nobody else
      to ever love me.
      You are my shining star,
      my guiding light, my love fantasy.   *Never Too Much [1981]*

4   It's so amazing to be loved
      I'd follow you to the moon in the sky above.   *So Amazing [1983]*

Luther Vandross   1951–2005

and

Marcus Miller   1959–

5   And everybody feels alone without any love, any love.   *Any Love [1988]*

Afaa Michael Weaver [Michael S. Weaver]   1951–

6   At a phone looking to Africa over the Mediterranean,
      I called my father, and, missing me, he said,
      "You almost home boy. Go on cross that sea!"

                                    My Father's Geography [1992]

7   Composition for White Critics Who Think African-American Poets Cannot Work in Contexts of Pure Concerns for Language and Post-Post Modern

Twentyfirst Century Inventiveness in Lyric Expression Due to Their Self-Limiting Concerns With Language as a Means of Self-Expression and Racial/Cultural Identity in Poetry That Is Ultimately Perhaps Beautiful However Too Trite and Too Folksy to Be Post [II] Theorist Efficacy

Title of poem [2000]

1 To die sweetly in the night is to die
   as men should die when corralled,
   when hustled by hate to such peevish
   ways of prospering. To die is to die.   *Baltimore*[1]

Patricia J[oyce] Williams   1951–

2   That life is complicated is a fact of great analytic importance. Law too often seeks to avoid this truth by making up its own breed of narrower, simpler, but hypnotically powerful rhetorical truths. Acknowledging, challenging, playing with these as rhetorical gestures is, it seems to me, necessary for any conception of justice. Such acknowledgment complicates the supposed purity of gender, race, voice boundary; it allows us to acknowledge the utility of such categorizations for certain purposes and the necessity of their breakdown on other occasions.

Alchemy of Race and Rights [1991]

3   I am so many of the things that many people seemed to think were antifamily—"unwed," "black," "single," everything but "teenage." Add "mother" and it began to sound like a curse.

The Rooster's Egg [1995]

Geoffrey Canada   1952–

4   Violence has always been around, usually concentrated amongst the poor.... The nature of the violent act has changed from the fist, stick, and knife to the gun.   *Fist, Stick, Knife, Gun [1995], preface*

5   If I could get the mayors, and the governors, and the president to look into the eyes of the five-year-olds of this nation, dressed in old raggedy clothes, whose zippers are broken but whose dreams are still alive, they would know what I know—that children need people to fight for them.

Fist, Stick, Knife, Gun

6   I promise to always dream out loud. To lift my head and be proud. And never end up a face in the crowd.   *Promise Academy creed*[2]

---

[1]From *Beyond the Frontier* [2002], edited by E. Ethelbert Miller.
[2]From Paul Tough, *Whatever It Takes* [2009].

Victor Carstarphen   1952–

and

John Whitehead   1948–2004

and

Gene McFadden   1949–2006

1   Wake up everybody no more sleeping in bed.
     No more backward thinking time for thinking ahead
     The world has changed so very much from what it used to be
     There is so much hatred, war and poverty.   *Wake Up Everybody [1975]*

Julie Dash   1952–

2   The ancestors and the womb, they're one, they're the same.
                                    Daughters of the Dust [1991] [Nana Peazant]

3   I love you 'cause you're mine. You're the fruit of an ancient tree.
                                           Daughters of the Dust [Nana Peazant]

4   There gonna be all kind of road to take in life. Let's not be fraid to take
         'em. We deserve 'em. Because we all good woman. Do you understand?
         Who we are and what we become? We the daughters of all those dusty
         things Nana carries around in her tin can. We carry too many scars from the
         past. Our past owns us. We wear our scars like armor.... For protection....
         Thick and hard, ugly scars that no one can pass through to ever hurt us
         again. Let's live our lives without living in the fold of old wounds.
                                            Daughters of the Dust [Eula Peazant]

Rita Dove   1952–

5   You start out with one thing, end
     up with another, and nothing's
     like it used to be, not even the future.
                           The Yellow House on the Corner [1980]. Title poem

6   In water-heavy nights behind grandmother's porch
     We knelt in the tickling grasses and whispered:
     Linda's face hung before us, pale as a pecan,
     And it grew wise as she said:
             "A boy's lips are soft,
             As soft as baby's skin."

The Yellow House on the Corner. Adolescence I

1   There is a parrot imitating spring
in the palace, its feathers parsley green.
Out of the swamp the cane appears
to haunt us, and we cut it down.

Museum [1983]. Parsley: The Cane Fields

2   The general remembers the tiny green sprigs
men of his village wore in their capes
to honor the birth of a son. He will
order many, this time, to be killed
for a single, beautiful word.   *Museum. Parsley: The Palace*

3   Twelve years to the day
he puts the blue worry bead into his mouth.
The trick is to swallow your good luck, too.
Last words to a daughter . . .
and a wink to remember him by.

Thomas and Beulah [1986]. Anniversary

4   Every day a wilderness — no
shade in sight. Beulah
patient among knickknacks,
the solarium a rage
of light, a grainstorm
as her gray cloth brings
dark wood to life.   *Thomas and Beulah. Dusting*

5   The hat on the table
in the dining room
is no pet trained
to sit still. Three
pearl-tipped spears and Beulah
maneuvering her shadow
to the floor. The hat
is cold. The hat
wants more.   *Thomas and Beulah. Headdress*

6   Each hurt swallowed
is a stone.   *Thomas and Beulah. Promises*

7   Here's a riddle for Our Age: when the sky's the limit,
how can you tell you've gone too far?   *Grace Notes [1989]. And Counting*

8   If you can't be free, be a mystery.   *Grace Notes. Canary*

1   How she sat there,
    the time right inside a place
    so wrong it was ready.

On the Bus with Rosa Parks [1999]. Rosa

2   I didn't notice
    how still you'd become until
    we had done it
    (for two measures?
    four?)—achieved flight,
    that swift and serene
    magnificence,
    before the earth
    remembered who we were
    and brought us down.

American Smooth [2004]

bell hooks [Gloria Watkins]   1952–

3   At a time in American history when black women in every area of the country might have joined together to demand social equality for women and recognition of the impact of sexism on our social status, we were by and large silent. Our silence was not merely a reaction against white women liberationists or a gesture of solidarity with black male patriarchs. It was the silence of the oppressed—that profound silence engendered by resignation and acceptance of one's lot. Contemporary black women could not join together to fight for women's rights because we did not see "womanhood" as an important aspect of our identity. Racist, sexist socialization had conditioned us to devalue our femaleness and to regard race as the only relevant label of identification. In other words, we were asked to deny a part of ourselves—and we did.   *Ain't I a Woman [1981], introduction*

4   As people of color, our struggle against racial imperialism should have taught us that wherever there exists a master/slave relationship, an oppressed/oppressor relationship, violence, mutiny, and hatred will permeate all elements of life. There can be no freedom for black men as long as they advocate subjugation of black women. There can be no freedom for patriarchal men of all races as long as they advocate subjugation of women. Absolute power for patriarchs is not freeing....Freedom...can only be a complete reality when our world is no longer racist or sexist.

Ain't I a Woman. The Imperialism of Patriarchy

5   Moving from silence into speech is for the oppressed, the colonized, the exploited, and those who stand in struggle side by side a gesture of defiance that heals, that makes new life and new growth possible. It is that act of

speech, of "talking back" that is no mere gesture of empty words, that is the expression of our movement from object to subject — the liberated voice.

Talking Back: Thinking Feminist, Thinking Black [1989]

1   Good hair — that's the expression. We all know it, begin to hear it when we are small children.... Good hair is hair that is not kinky, hair that does not feel like balls of steel wool, hair that does not take hours to comb, hair that does not need tons of grease to untangle, hair that is long. Real good hair is straight hair, hair like white folks' hair. Yet no one says so. No one says Your hair is so nice, so beautiful because it is like white folks' hair. We pretend that the standards we measure our beauty by are our own invention.   *Bone Black [1996]*

Linton Kwesi Johnson   1952–

2   rituals of blood on the burning
served by a cruel in-fighting
five nights of horror an of bleeding
                    broke glass
cold blades as sharp as the eyes of hate
and the stabbings
it's war amongst the rebels
madness...madness...war.   *Five Nights of Bleeding [1975]*

3   Shock-black-bubble doun-beat bouncing
rock-wise tumble-doun sound music;
foot-drop find drum, blood story,
bass history is a moving
        is a hurting black story.   *Reggae Sounds [1975]*

4   Inglan Is a Bitch   *Title of poem [1980]*

5   evrybady claim dem demacratic
but some a wolf an some a sheep
an dat is prablematic   *Mi Revalueshanary Fren [1991]*

6   I woodah write a poem
soh dyam deep
dat it bittah-sweet
like a precious
memari
whe mek yu weep
whe mek yu feel incomplete   *If I Woz a Tap-Natch Poet [1998]*

7   some polece inna Inglan gat liesense fi kill.   *Liesense Fi Kill [1999]*

489

1 there are sufferers with guns movin breeze through the
    trees
there are people waging war in the heat and hunger
    of the streets. *Mi Revalueshanary Fren [2002]. Song of Blood*

[William] Bill T[ass] Jones 1952–

2 My mother's praying was the first theater I ever saw — and the truest. *Last Night on Earth [1995]*

3 All dance exists in memory.... It leaves no physical evidence.
Last Night on Earth

Dambudzo Marechera 1952–1987

4 I couldn't have stayed on in that House of Hunger where every morsel of sanity was snatched from you the way some kinds of bird snatch food from the very mouths of babes. And the eyes of that House of Hunger lingered upon you as though some indefinable beast was about to pounce upon you. *House of Hunger [1978]*

Walter Mosley 1952–

5 I was surprised to see a white man walk into Joppy's bar. It's not just that he was white but he wore an off-white linen suit and shirt with a Panama straw hat and bone shoes over flashing white silk socks.... He stopped in the doorway, filling it with his large frame, and surveyed the room with pale eyes; not a color I'd ever seen in a man's eyes. When he looked at me I felt a thrill of fear, but that went away quickly because I was used to white people by 1948.
Devil in a Blue Dress [1990], opening lines

6 Because in L.A. people don't have time to stop; anywhere they have to go they go there in a car. The poorest man has a car in Los Angeles; he might not have a roof over his head but he has a car.
Devil in a Blue Dress, ch. 7

7 Defeat goes down hard with black people; it's our most common foe. *White Butterfly [1992], ch. 1*

8 Tell me how a healthy boy ain't wrong when he kills his black brother who sick.
Always Outnumbered, Always Outgunned [1998].
Crimson Shadow [Socrates Fortlow]

9 In prison, studying for survival was the only real pastime.
Always Outnumbered, Always Outgunned. The Thief

1   Being challenged by the law was a rite of passage for any Negro who wanted to better himself or his situation.   *Fearless Jones [2001], ch. 1*

2   The best thing about Fearless was the attribute he was named for; he didn't fear anything, not death or pain or any kind of passion.

Fearless Jones, ch. 5

3   You think that you can have the easy life of TV and gasoline without someone suffering and dying somewhere?

The Man in My Basement [2001], ch. 28 [Anniston Bennet]

4   "A man's bookcase will tell you everything you'll ever need to know about him," my father had told me more than once. "A business-man has business books and a dreamer has novels and books of poetry. Most women like reading about love and a true revolutionary will have books about the minutiae of overthrowing the oppressor. A person with no books is inconsequential in a modern setting, but a peasant that reads is a prince in waiting."   *The Long Fall [2009]*

5   The older you get the more you live in the past.

The Last Days of Ptolemy Grey [2010] [Coy]

6   Many and most moments go by with us hardly aware of their passage. But love and hate and fear cause time to snag you, to drag you down like a spider's web holding fast to a doomed fly's wings.

When the Thrill Is Gone [2011]

Jill Nelson
1952–

7   I was looking for the authentic Negro experience, which of course my own wasn't, since being bourgeois somehow negated being black.

Volunteer Slavery [1993]

8   Not that there's anything inherently horrible about making a mistake, but when you're a Negro in America it's usually not just you who's making the mistake. It's y'all, the race, black folks in toto.   *Volunteer Slavery*

Michele Wallace
1952–

9   There has been a growing distrust, even hatred, between black men and black women. It has been nursed along not only by racism on the part of whites but also by an almost deliberate ignorance on the part of blacks about the sexual politics of their experiences in this country.

Black Macho and the Myth of the Superwoman [1979].
Black Macho

10   From the intricate web of mythology which surrounds the black woman, a fundamental image emerges. It is of a woman of inordinate

strength, with an ability for tolerating an unusual amount of misery and heavy, distasteful work. This woman does not have the same fears, weaknesses, and insecurities as other women, but believes herself to be and is, in fact, stronger emotionally than most men. Less of a woman in that she is less "feminine" and helpless, she is really *more* of a woman in that she is the embodiment of Mother Earth, the quintessential mother with infinite sexual, life-giving and nurturing reserves. In other words, she is a superwoman.

> *Black Macho and the Myth of the Superwoman.*
> *The Myth of the Superwoman*

1   The imperative is clear: Either we will make history or remain the victims of it.

> *Black Macho and the Myth of the Superwoman.*
> *The Myth of the Superwoman*

2   How one is seen (as black) and therefore what one sees (in a white world) is always already crucial to one's existence as an Afro-American. The very markers that reveal you to the rest of the world, your dark skin and your kinky/curly hair, are visual. However, *not* being seen by those who don't want to see you because they are racist...often leads racists to the interpretation that *you are unable* to see.

> *Modernism, Postmodernism and the Problem of the Visual in*
> *Afro-American Culture [1990]*[1]

Diane Abbott   1953–

3   The concerns which black people voice about service delivery, housing, unemployment and security are important to white people as well. I don't think that providing good education and decent housing are marginal issues. The black agenda is not a marginal agenda.

> *From* TERRI A. SEWELL, *Black Tribunes [1993]*

Jean-Bertrand Aristide   1953–

4   The rich of my country, a tiny percentage of our population, sit at a vast table covered in white damask and overflowing with good food, while the rest of my countrymen and countrywomen are crowded under that table, hunched over in the dirt and starving. It is a violent situation, and one day the people under that table will rise up in righteousness, and knock the table of privilege over, and take what rightfully belongs to them.

> *In the Parish of the Poor [1990]*[2]

---

[1] From *Out There: Marginalization and Contemporary Culture* [1990], edited by RUSSELL FERGUSON ET AL.
[2] Translated by AMY WILENTZ.

1   Haiti is the parish of the poor. In Haiti, it is not enough to heal wounds, for every day another wound opens up. It is not enough to give the poor food one day, to buy them antibiotics one day, to teach them to read a few sentences or to write a few words. Hypocrisy. The next day they will be starving again, feverish again, and they will never be able to buy the books that hold the words that might deliver them.

In the Parish of the Poor

2   Hiding the truth is like trying to bury water. It seeps out every-where.   *In the Parish of the Poor*

3   The people do not buy liberty and democracy at the market.

Dignity [1996].[1] *Justice*

4   There will never be enough money to give each person the house, the job, the school fees that they need, but we always have enough humanity to treat one another with the respect and dignity that we all deserve.

Eyes of the Heart [2000][2]

Dionne Brand   1953–

5   what is the
political position of stars?

Primitive Offensive [1982]. Canto II

6   Grace. Is Grace, yes. And I take it, quiet, quiet, like thiefing sugar.

In Another Place, Not Here [1996]

Patrick Chamoiseau   1953–

7   Upon his entrance to Texaco, the Christ was hit by a stone — an aggression that surprised no one.

Texaco [1997],[3] *opening line*

Jawanza Kunjufu   1953–

8   The conspiracy to destroy Black boys is very complex and inter-woven.... Those people who adhere to the doctrine of white racism, imperi-alism, and white male supremacy are easier to recognize. Those people who actively promote drugs and gang violence are active conspirators and easier to identify. What makes the conspiracy more complex are those people who do not plot together to destroy Black boys, but through their indifference,

---

[1]Translated by CAROL F. COATES.
[2]Edited by LAURA FLYNN.
[3]Translated by ROSE-MYRIAM RÉJOUIS and VAL VINOKUROV.

perpetuate it. This passive group of conspirators consists of parents, educators, and white liberals who deny being racists, but through their silence allow institutional racism to continue.

Countering the Conspiracy to Destroy Black Boys [1985]

Andrea Lee   1953–

1   Sometimes the suspicion crossed my mind that all adults belonged to a species completely different from my own. One was never quite sure what they cared about, just as it was hard to tell why they laughed, and what kind of laughter it was. The eye of a grownup, like that of a cat or a praying mantis, seemed to admit a different spectrum of light. Compared to my world — a place of flat, brilliant colors, where every image was literal, and a succession of passions grabbed my soul with forthright violence — the atmosphere in which my parents existed seemed twilit, full of tricky nuance.

Sarah Phillips [1984]

Harryette Mullen   1953–

2   Retiring to the canopy of the bedroom, turning on the bedside light, taking the big dictionary to bed, clutching the unabridged bulk, heavy with the weight of all the meanings between these covers, smoothing the thin sheets, thick with accented syllables — all are exercises in the conscious regimen of dreamers, who toss words on their tongues while turning illuminated pages.

Sleeping with the Dictionary [2002]

Iyanla Vanzant [Rhonda Harris]   1953–

3   The stress began the day you learned you were expected to please other people.

Acts of Faith [1993]

4   When we acknowledge our errors and face up to our shortcomings, no one can use them against us.   *Acts of Faith*

Carrie Mae Weems   1953–

5   It was clear, I was not Manet's type. Picasso — who had a way with women — only used me & Duchamp never even considered me.

Text from Not Manet's Type [1997]

Cornel West   1953–

6   As long as black people are viewed as "them," the burden falls on blacks to do all the "cultural" and "moral" work necessary for healthy race

relations. The implication is that only certain Americans can define what it means to be American—and the rest must simply "fit in."

Race Matters [1993], introduction

1   The major enemy of black survival in America has been and is neither oppression nor exploitation but rather the nihilistic threat—that is, loss of hope and absence of meaning. For as long as hope remains and meaning is preserved, the possibility of overcoming oppression stays alive. . . . Without hope there can be no future, without meaning there can be no struggle.[1]

Race Matters. Nihilism in Black America

2   Black people have always been in America's wilderness in search of a promised land.   *Race Matters. Nihilism in Black America*

3   The blues is not simply a music to titillate; it is a hard-fought way of life, and as such should unsettle and unnerve whites about the legacy of white supremacy.   *Democracy Matters [2004]*

4   The ugly terrorist attacks on innocent civilians on 9/11 plunged the whole country into the blues. Never before have Americans of all classes, colors, regions, religions, genders, and sexual orientations felt unsafe, unprotected, subject to random violence, and hated. Yet to have been designated and treated as a nigger in America for over 350 years has been to feel unsafe, unprotected, subject to random violence, and hated.

Democracy Matters

5   We have seen that there are two opposing tendencies in American democracy—toward imperialism and toward democratization—and we are in a period of intense battle between the two.   *Democracy Matters*

6   I have always marveled at how such an unfree people as blacks in America created the freest forms in America, such as blues and jazz.

Democracy Matters

7   The niggerization of black people tried to make black love a crime, black history a curse, black hope a joke, and black freedom a pipe dream.

Hope on a Tightrope [2012]

Mumia Abu-Jamal [Wesley Cook]   1954–

8   You will find a blacker world on death row than anywhere else. African-Americans, a mere 11 percent of the national population, compose about 40 percent of the death row population. There, too, you will find this writer.   *Live from Death Row [1996]*

---

[1]If there is no struggle, there is no progress. — FREDERICK DOUGLASS

K[wame] Anthony Appiah   1954–

1   "Race" disables us because it proposes as a basis for common action
the illusion that black (and white and yellow) people are fundamentally
allied by nature and, thus, without effort; it leaves us unprepared, therefore,
to handle the "interracial" conflicts that arise from the very different situations of black (and white and yellow) people in different parts of the
economy and of the world.   *In My Father's House [1992]*

2   There are no races: there is nothing in the world that can do all we ask
race to do for us.   *In My Father's House*

3   Cultures are made of continuities and changes, and the identity of a
society can survive through these changes. Societies without change aren't
authentic; they're just dead.   *Cosmopolitanism [2006]*

Joseph F. Beam   1954–1988

4   We are Black men who are proudly gay. What we offer is our lives, our
love, our visions. We are risin' to the love we all need. We are coming home
with our heads held up high.   *In the Life [1986], introduction*

Ruby Bridges   1954–

5   Please God, try to forgive those people.
Because even if they say those bad things,
They don't know what they're doing.
So You could forgive them,
Just like You did those folks a long time ago,
When they said terrible things about You.
            Prayer for the angry white mob opposing the six-year-old's
            integration of a New Orleans school [1960][1]

Stephen L[isle] Carter   1954–

6   We are measured by a different yardstick: *first black, only black, best*
black. The best black syndrome is cut from the same cloth as the implicit and
demeaning tokenism that often accompanies racial preferences: "Oh we'll tolerate so-and-so at our hospital or in our firm or on our faculty because she's
the best black."   *Reflections of an Affirmative Action Baby [1991]*

7   You draw a line.... Put the past on one side, the future on the other,
and decide which side you want to live on.
            The Emperor of Ocean Park [2002] [Judge Oliver Garland]

---

[1]From Robert Coles, *The Ruby Bridges Story* [1995].

Cornelius Eady   1954–

1   As a favor to me
     Let's not talk any more about old dances.
     I have an entire world on the tip of my tongue.

Victims of the Latest Dance Craze [1985]

2   You can actually hear it in his voice:
     Sometimes the only way to discuss it
     Is to grip a guitar as if it were
     Somebody's throat
     And pluck.

Leadbelly [1991]

3   I think that every hymn is a flare of longing, that the key to any heaven is
     language.

Paradiso [1995]

Randall Kennedy   1954–

4   The experience of racial oppression provides no inoculation against
     complacency. Nor does it inoculate its victims against their own versions
     of prejudice and tyranny.

Radical Critiques of Legal Academia. Harvard Law Review [1989]

5   Over the years, *nigger* has become the best known of the American
     language's many racial insults, evolving into the paradigmatic slur. It is the
     epithet that generates epithets. That is why Arabs are called "sand niggers,"
     Irish "the niggers of Europe," and Palestinians "the niggers of the Middle
     East"; why black bowling balls have been called "nigger eggs," games of
     craps "nigger golf," watermelons "nigger hams," rolls of one-dollar bills
     "nigger rolls," bad luck "nigger luck," gossip "nigger news," and heavy boots
     "nigger stompers."

Nigger [2002]

6   For bad or good, *nigger* is destined to remain with us for many years
     to come — a reminder of the ironies and dilemmas, the tragedies and glories
     of the American experience.

Nigger

7   Many Americans talk of wanting to create a society in which
     racial boundaries have disappeared and race no longer matters to anyone.
     At the same time, though, many of these same people either organize them-
     selves implicitly or explicitly around racial signposts or support others
     who do.

Interracial Intimacies [2003]

Janet McDonald   1954–2007

8   I know where my heart is, and I can go home again, whenever I like.
     Mother likes to say, "You can take the girl out the projects, but you can't

take the projects out the girl." That may not apply to everyone, but in my case it's true. And I would have it no other way.

Project Girl [1999], last lines

David A[lexander] Paterson   1954–

1   We don't know the path yet. But that's because we haven't blazed the trail. And I think you all know that I know a little bit about finding one's way through the dark.   *Inaugural speech [March 17, 2008][1]*

Condoleezza Rice   1954–

2   If your first reaction to failure is that prejudice is to blame — if your first thought when you or another minority succeeds is that race or gender or physical disability must have been the patron — if when someone disagrees with you or stands in your way, you immediately suspect that the person is a bigot . . . bigotry and prejudice are winning because their mere existence has begun to define your successes, your failures and your relationship to others. You have become part of the pernicious dismissal of individual will.   *Speech, Stanford University [June 1988][2]*

3   I don't think anybody could have predicted that these people would take an airplane and slam it into the World Trade Center, take another one and slam it into the Pentagon; that they would try to use an airplane as a missile, a hijacked airplane as a missile.

Press briefing [May 16, 2002]

4   The problem here is that there will always be some uncertainty about how quickly he [Saddam Hussein] can acquire nuclear weapons. But we don't want the smoking gun to be a mushroom cloud.

Television interview, CNN [September 8, 2002]

5   I believe that while race neutral means are preferable, it is appropriate to use race as one factor among others in achieving a diverse student body.   *Statement [January 17, 2003]*

6   Our own history should remind us that the union of democratic principle and practice is always a work in progress. When the founding fathers said "We the people," they did not mean the people in this room. Our ancestors were three-fifths of a man.

Statement before the National Association of Black Journalists convention [August 8, 2003]

---

[1] Paterson became the first black and first blind governor of New York State.
[2] From MARCUS MABRY, *Twice As Good* [2007].

Paul Rusesabagina
1954–

1   *[On genocide:]* Never Again. We all know these words. But we never seem to hear them.... Unless the world community can stop finding ways to dither in the face of this monstrous threat to humanity, those words, Never Again, will persist in being one of the most abused phrases in the English language and one of the greatest lies of our time.   *An Ordinary Man [2006]*

Al[fred] Sharpton
1954–

2   It is true that Mr. Lincoln signed the Emancipation Proclamation, after which there was a commitment to give forty acres and a mule. That's where the argument, to this day, of reparations starts. We never got the forty acres.... We didn't get the mule. So we decided we'd ride this donkey as far as it would take us.   *Speech at the Democratic National Convention [2004]*

3   There's a difference between peace and quiet. Quiet means shut up. Quiet means suffer in silence. Peace means justice. We want peace, but we won't get quiet until we get justice.

Speech at the funeral of Sean Bell [December 1, 2006][1]

Denzel Washington
1954–

4   It's just acting. All you're doing is showing off. It's not brain surgery.
Interview. Interview magazine [May 1990]

5   When I was in college first starting out as an actor, they asked each one of us what we wanted to do. I said, "I want to be the best actor in the world." All the students in the classroom looked at me like I was a nut.

Acceptance speech for an Academy Award for best leading actor [March 24, 2002]

Oprah Winfrey
1954–

6   It has just stopped me cold from eating another burger!

On learning that some American cattle were eating ground-up livestock, which can lead to mad cow disease. Oprah Winfrey Show [April 1996]

7   I come from a people who struggled and died to use their voice in this country, and I refuse to be muzzled.

Statement after a Texas federal jury ruled against the Texas Cattlemen's suit alleging that Winfrey's comment had caused the cattle market to plunge [February 26, 1998]

---

[1]The twenty-three-year-old Bell was killed by fifty shots fired by New York City police officers.

1   It's up to each of us to get very still and say, "This is who I am." No one else defines your life. Only you do.

What I Know for Sure. Column, O, the Oprah Magazine [October 2000]

2   Failure is just a way for our lives to show us we're moving in the wrong direction.   *What I Know for Sure [February 2001]*

3   If you don't know what your passion is, realize that one reason for your existence on earth is to find it.

What I Know for Sure [September 2001]

4   My grandmother was a maid and she worked for white folks her whole life. And her idea of having a big dream was to have white folks who at least treated her with some dignity, who showed her a little bit [of] respect. And she used to say, I hope you get some good white folks that are kind to you. And I regret that she didn't live past 1963 to see that I did grow up and get some really good white folks working for me.

Commencement speech, Howard University [May 12, 2007]

George C[ostello] Wolfe   1954–

5   God created black people and black people created style.

The Colored Museum [1988]. The Gospel According to Miss Roj

6   I have no history, I have no past. I can't. It's too much. It's much too much. I must be able to smile on cue and watch the news with an impersonal eye. I have no stake in the madness. Being Black is too emotionally taxing, therefore I will be Black only on weekends and holidays.

The Colored Museum [The Man]

7   I'm not what I was ten years ago or ten minutes ago. I'm all of that and then some.

The Colored Museum [Topsy/Everybody]

8   N' it came to pass that a messenger was called
Who came to believe that the message was him.
Yes, he of diamond tooth n' flashy threads;
Yes, he who drinks from the vine of syncopation
But denies the black soil from which
this rhythm was born.

Jelly's Last Jam [1991] [Chimney Man]

9   I pride myself on being available to as many people's stories as I possibly can.

On directing. Quoted in the New York Times [April 23, 1995]

Afrika Bambaataa and the Soulsonic Force
Arthur Henry Baker
1955–

and

Ellis Williams
1961–

and

Robert Darrell Allen
1961–

and

John Miller
1961–

and

Afrika Bambaataa [Kevin Donovan]
1957–

1   Rock rock to the planet rock, don't stop.

Planet Rock [1982]

Whoopi Goldberg [Caryn Elaine Johnson]
1955–

2   This is my long, luxurious blond hair. Ain't it pretty? . . . Okay, let me
get it off my shoulder. Wait. See look? And look now it's in my eyes. And my
mother made me go to my room 'cause she said that wasn't nothing but a
shirt on my head and I said, "Nuh-uh, this is my long, luxurious blond
hair." And she said, "Nuh-uh, fool, that's a shirt." And I said, "You a fool,
it's my hair." And she made me go to my room.

Whoopi [1985].[1] Girl with the Long Blond Hair

3   I want to thank everybody who makes movies. As a little kid, I lived in
the projects, and you're the people I watched. You're the people who made
me want to be an actor.

*Acceptance speech for Academy Award for best supporting
actress [March 1991]*

4   I am not an African American. I'm not from Africa. I'm from New
York. My roots run a whole lot deeper than most of the people who don't
have anything in front of the word *American*. I can trace my family tree back
to the *Mayflower*. We may not have been on it, but we were under it, and
that counts too.

Book [1997]

---

[1]From *Extreme Exposure* [2000], edited by Jo Bonney.

E[verette] Lynn Harris

1955–2009

1　　When men dealt with men, they knew the risk they were taking, most women did not. Though some women were convinced they could spot a gay man, I was not persuaded. Many of us *passed* in and out of their worlds. Asking the questions and hoping for the truth was the only certainty.

Invisible Life [1991], ch. 21

2　　I was in love for the first time and it was like the sun had dropped down from the sky and kissed me.　*If This World Were Mine [1997]*

3　　A tough-guy swagger looks just as dumb as a robe and halo.

Not a Day Goes By [2000], pt. 1

4　　I've learned that you have to be able to flow. Any way the wind blows is cool with me.　*Any Way the Wind Blows [2001], last lines*

5　　I wanted to be released from all the loneliness, feelings of shame and despair. The pain I felt but couldn't describe. . . . Was it because I was a black man living in America? Was it because I was gay? Or was it because I was a gay black man who was living in a world that had a problem with both?

What Becomes of the Brokenhearted [2003]

Gwen Ifill

1955–

6　　Every time a young black girl shyly approaches me for an autograph or writes or calls or stops me on the street to ask how she can become a journalist, I feel an enormous responsibility. It's more than simply being a role model. I know I have to be a voice for them as well.

Op-ed. New York Times [April 10, 2007]

Iman [Mohamed Abdulmajid]

1955–

7　　Since I've been in America, I've always been intrigued by one phrase: "She is beautiful, like the girl next door." I have always wondered whose neighborhood they were talking about.

I Am Iman [2001]

Kerry James Marshall

1955–

8　　What's excellent is always beautiful.

Kerry James Marshall [2000]

Nathan McCall

1955–

9　　A lot of young brothers . . . were so fed up with the white man they were willing to risk prison, and even death, to get away from him.

Makes Me Wanna Holler [1994]

1
    For those who'd like answers, I have no pithy social formulas to end black-on-black violence. But I do know that I see a younger, meaner generation out there now — more lost and alienated than we were, and placing even less value on life. We were at least touched by role models; this new bunch is totally estranged from the black mainstream.... I've come to fear that of the many things a black man can die from, the first may be rage — his own or someone else's.

Makes Me Wanna Holler

Cynthia McKinney 1955–

2
    Why aren't the hard questions being asked?...What did this administration know and when did it know it about the events of September 11? Who else knew and why did they not warn the innocent people of New York who were needlessly murdered?

Radio interview [March 25, 2002]

3
    September 11 erased the line between "over there" and "over here." The American people can no longer afford to be detached from the world, as our actions abroad will have a direct impact on our lives at home. In Washington, D.C., decisions affecting home and abroad are made, and too many of us leave the responsibility of protecting our freedoms to other people whose interests are not our own.... What our government does in our name is important. It is now also clear that our future, our security, and our rights depend on our vigilance.

Radio interview [March 25, 2002]

Lorene Cary 1956–

4
    I had no option but to succeed and no doubt that I could will my success.   *Black Ice [1991]*

5
    In the aftermath of Black Is Beautiful, I began to feel black and blue.

Black Ice

6
    Black ice is the smoothest naturally occurring ice there is, as if nature were condescending to art.   *Black Ice*

Percival Everett 1956–

7
    I have dark brown skin, curly hair, a broad nose, some of my ancestors were slaves and I have been detained by pasty white policemen in New Hampshire, Arizona and Georgia and so the society in which I live tells me I am black; that is my race. Though I am fairly athletic, I am no good at basketball. I listen to Mahler, Aretha Franklin, Charlie Parker and Ry Cooder on vinyl records and compact discs. I graduated *summa cum laude*

from Harvard, hating every minute of it. I am good at math. I cannot dance. I did not grow up in any inner city or the rural south.

Erasure [2001], opening lines

Arsenio Hall   1956–

1   Let's get busy!
> *Trademark phrase used on eponymous late-night talk show [1989–1994]*

Steve Harvey   1956–

2   Act Like a Lady, Think Like a Man   *Title of book [2009]*

Anita [Faye] Hill   1956–

3   It would have been more comfortable to remain silent. I took no initiative to inform anyone. But when I was asked by a representative of this committee to report my experience, I felt that I had to tell the truth. I could not keep silent.
> *Statement before the Senate Judiciary Committee regarding the nomination of Clarence Thomas to the Supreme Court [October 11, 1991]*

Mae Jemison   1956–

4   Space belongs to all of us. There is science in dance and art in science.
> *Interview. Essence [April 1993]*

Andrea Levy   1956–

5   There are some words that once spoken will split the world in two.
> *Small Island [2004], ch. 55*

C[larence] Ray Nagin, Jr.   1956–

6   Don't tell me 40,000 people are coming here. They're not here. It's too doggone late. Now get off your asses and do something, and let's fix the biggest goddamn crisis in the history of this country.
> *Plea to the U.S. government to respond to the aftermath of Hurricane Katrina. Radio interview [September 1, 2005]*

7   This city will be chocolate at the end of the day. This city will be a majority African-American city. It's the way God wants it to be. You can't have New Orleans no other way.
> *Speech referring to the rebuilding of New Orleans after Hurricane Katrina [January 16, 2006]*

Deval Patrick

1956–

1   Our founders came on the *Mayflower,* the *Arabella,* and the early clipper ships. But there were other boats, too. There was the *Amistad* and her cargo of kidnapped Africans, who commandeered the ship to sail home to Africa, but who were seized in Long Island Sound and imprisoned in New Haven. . . . I am descended from people once forbidden their most basic and fundamental freedoms, a people desperate for a reason to hope and willing to fight for it. And so are you. So are you. Because the *Amistad* was not just a Black man's journey; it was an American journey. This commonwealth — and the nation modeled on it — is at its best when we show we understand a faith in what's possible, and the willingness to work for it.

Inaugural speech as governor of Massachusetts
[January 4, 2007]

Malidoma Patrice Somé

1956–

2   As long as we are not ourselves, we will try to be what other people are.   *Of Water and the Spirit [1994]*

Phil Wilson

1956–

3   AIDS in America today is a black disease. Nobody wants to talk about that, and nobody wants to own that. That silence is killing us.

Interview. Associated Press [June 22, 2007]

4   Watching people be shunned for their "otherness," every one of us begins to feel a little doubt about ourselves. You may want to deny that part of yourself that doesn't measure up, and not speak up. If we are serious about stopping AIDS, we have to end the silence and stigma around homosexuality — and in the process rethink our beliefs about what it means to be Black and male in America.

In the Fight of Our Lives: Notes on the AIDS Crisis
in the Black Community [2002][1]

Suzan Johnson Cook

1957–

5   In the park, the seesaw is more than a piece of wood that goes up and down. It teaches children that if a balance isn't struck, they will not have a smooth and successful ride. Too much weight on either side causes one end to go up and the other down. This is true in life as well. . . . Our lives require balance.   *Live Like You're Blessed [2006]*

---

[1]From *Race and Resistance* [2002], edited by HERB BOYD.

Joy DeGruy   1957–

1   Post Traumatic Slave Syndrome is a condition that exists when a
population has experienced multigenerational trauma resulting from centuries of slavery and continues to experience oppression and institutionalized
racism today. Added to this condition is a belief (real or imagined) that the
benefits of the society in which they live are not accessible to them.

Post Traumatic Slave Syndrome [2005]

Nikky Finney [Lynn Carol]   1957–

2   in full we are paid
we owe nothing
on a bill that's never existed
the final payment is in
and for the next one thousand years
we are paid in full

On Wings Made of Gauze [1985].
For the Next One Thousand Years

3   He does not hesitate The coral bed of my
afterlife is washed into the drain Without comment
The highest bidder raises her hand I am tossed into
the icy silver bowl A lifetime of waiting Hungering
to be called Delicious

Head Off & Split. Title poem

4   People who outlived bullwhips & Bull Connor, historically afraid of water
and routinely fed to crocodiles, left in the sun on the sticky tar-heat of roofs
to roast like pigs, surrounded by forty feet of churning water, in the summer
of 2005, while the richest country in the world played the old observation
game, studied the situation: wondered by committee what to do; counted,
in private, by long historical division; speculated whether or not some
people are surely born ready, accustomed to flood, famine, fear.

My mother said to pick
The very best one
And you are not it!

Head Off & Split. Left

5   A fastened woman
can be messed with, one too many times.

Head Off & Split [2011]. Red Velvet (for Rosa Parks)

6   The ones who longed to read and write, but were forbidden, who lost
hands and feet, were killed, by laws written by men who believed they

owned other men. Their words devoted to quelling freedom and insurgency, imagination, all hope; what about the possibility of one day making a poem?...Tonight these forbidden ones move around the room as they please, they sit at whatever table they want, wear camel-colored field hats, tomato-red kerchiefs....Some have just climbed out of the cold, wet Atlantic just to be here. We shiver together. If my name is ever called out I promised my girl poet self, so too would I call out theirs.

Acceptance speech, National Book Award for Poetry
[November 16, 2011]

Nelson George   1957–

1   There is something missing in black America, and symptoms of the illness are in its music.   *Death of Rhythm and Blues [1988]*

Essex Hemphill   1957–1995

2   If one of these thick-lipped,
     wet, black nights
     while I'm out walking,
     I find freedom in this village.
     If I can take it with my tribe
     I'll bring you here.
     And you will never notice
     the absence of rice
     and bridesmaids.   *In the Life [1986]*

3   When my brother fell
     I picked up his weapons
     and never once questioned
     whether I could carry
     the weight and grief,
     the responsibility
     he shouldered.
     I never questioned
     whether I could aim
     or be as precise as he.
     I only knew he had fallen
     and the passing ceremonies
     marking his death
     did not stop the war.   *When My Brother Fell (for Joseph Beam) [1991]*

4   I live in a town
     where pretense and bone structure

prevail as credentials
of status and beauty —
a town bewitched
by mirrors, horoscopes,
and corruption.

Family Jewels (for Washington, D.C.) [1992]

T[homas] D[exter] Jakes, Sr.   1957–

1   Jesus said, "Woman, thou art loosed." He did not call her by name. He wasn't speaking to her just as a person. He spoke to her femininity. He spoke to the song in her. He spoke to the lace in her. Like a crumbling rose, Jesus spoke to what she could, and would, have been.

Woman, Thou Art Loosed! [1993]

2   It has been said that love is a many-splendored thing. If that is true, then one of those splendors should be directed inward.

The Lady, Her Lover, and Her Lord [2000]

3   Restoration is more than observation. It's more than looking from the safety of our television into the lives of other people, and assessing their situation from the comfort of our own luxuries and lives. We can no longer be a nation that overlooks the poor and the suffering and continues past the ghetto on our way to the Mardi Gras.

*Sermon at National Cathedral for victims of
Hurricane Katrina [September 16, 2005]*

4   If someone else's apology is a prerequisite for your healing, you may never get well.

Essay. Essence [November 2006]

[Shelton] Spike Lee   1957–

5   Please, baby, please baby, please baby, baby, baby please!

She's Gotta Have It [1986] [Mars Blackmon]

6   Wake up![1]

School Daze [1988]

7   Always try to do the right thing.

Do the Right Thing [1989] [Da Mayor]

8   How come you ain't got no brothers up on the wall?

Do the Right Thing [Buggin' Out]

9   Not every black person is a pimp, murderer, prostitute, convict, rapist or drug addict, but that hasn't stopped Hollywood from writing these roles for African-Americans. Negative images of black people are presented on

[1]See John Lewis, 400:6; Toni Cade Bambara, 394:3; and Victor Carstarphen et al., 486:1.

film and television every day and there's no great uproar. It's sad, but most film critics don't even recognize these images when they come across them. They surely don't write about it.
I Am Not an Anti-Semite. New York Times *[August 22, 1990]*

1   I don't know what causes the upset when it's stated that for the most part people of Jewish ancestry run the entertainment industry. This is not an indictment, and it's not a moral judgment. It's like saying the National Basketball Association is made up mostly of African Americans.
Five for Five [1991]

James McBride   1957–

2   As a boy, I never knew where my mother was from — where she was born, who her parents were. When I asked she'd say, "God made me." When I asked if she was white, she'd say, "I'm light-skinned," and change the subject. She raised twelve black children and sent us all to college and in most cases graduate school. Her children became doctors, professors, chemists, teachers — yet none of us even knew her maiden name until we were grown. It took me fourteen years to unearth her remarkable story — the daughter of an Orthodox Jewish rabbi, she married a black man in 1942 — and she revealed it more as a favor to me than out of any desire to revisit her past.   *The Color of Water [1996], opening lines*

3   "What color is God's spirit?"
"It doesn't have a color," she [Mommy] said. "God is the color of water. Water doesn't have a color."   *The Color of Water*

4   Everybody got something to do with everything.
Miracle at St. Anna [2002]

Marlon Riggs   1957–1994

5   Behind the Sambo and the SNAP! Queen lies a social psyche in torment, a fragile psyche threatened by deviation from its egocentric/ethnocentric construct of self and society....Hence: blacks are inferior because they are not white. Black gays are unnatural because they are not straight. Majority representations of both affirm the view that blackness and gayness constitute a fundamental rupture in the order of things, that our very existence is an affront to nature and humanity.
Black Macho Revisited: Reflections of a Snap! Queen [1991]

6   Cornered
by identities I never wanted to claim,
I ran.

Fast.
Hard
Deep
Inside myself. *Tongues Untied [1991]*

Russell Simmons 1957–

1   Hip-hop is the only real description of the suffering of our people.
Quoted in the New York Times [March 1, 2006]

2   Spit truth to power.[1] *Do You! [2007]*

Angela Bassett 1958–

3   This is a career about images. It's celluloid; they last forever. I'm a black woman from America. My people were slaves in America, and even though we're free on paper and in law, I'm not going to allow you to enslave me on film, in celluloid, for all to see.
Interview, the Guardian [February 11, 2009]

Michael Eric Dyson 1958–

4   Gangsta rap often reaches higher than its ugliest, lowest common denominator. Misogyny, violence, materialism and sexual transgression are not its exclusive domain. At its best, this music draws attention to complex dimensions of ghetto life ignored by many Americans.
Between God and Gangsta Rap [1996]

5   There are millions of black women from every walk of life who simply want, like every other group of women alive, to be wanted and loved by the men who issued from their mother's wombs. To dishonor that wish is the seed of our destruction. *Why I Love Black Women [2003]*

6   Black urban fashion constantly reminds young folk of just how culturally durable they are, since they are among the most imitated and appropriated people on the globe, though often without footnotes, copyrights or royalties.
Is Bill Cosby Right? Or Has the Black Middle Class Lost Its Mind? [2005]

Annette Gordon-Reed 1958–

7   These African Americans, whom he [Thomas Jefferson] had sentimentalized as having the best hearts of any people in the world, had given

---

[1]A play on "Speak Truth to Power," a Quaker slogan central to the civil rights movement.

their lives to him — followed him about, cleaned up after him, no doubt worried about him, for his sake and their own — slept with him, and borne him children. He had held them as chattel, trying, in the case of the Hemingses, to soften a reality that could never be made soft. While he claimed to know and respect the quality of their hearts, he could never truly see them as human beings separate from him and his own needs, desires, and fears. . . . The world they shared twisted and perverted practically everything it touched, made entirely human feelings and connections difficult, suspect, and compromised. What could have been in the hearts of any human beings living under the power of that system was inevitably complicated, inevitably tragic.   *The Hemingses of Monticello [2008]*

Ice-T [Tracy Marrow]   1958–

and

Afrika Islam [Charles Andre Glenn]   1967–

1   Freedom of speech!
    Just watch what you say.   *Freedom of Speech [1989]*

Michael Jackson   1958–2009

2   I wanna rock with you.   *Rock with You [1979]*

3   Don't Stop 'Til You Get Enough   *Song title [1979]*

4   They told you don't you ever come around here
    Don't wanna see your face you better disappear.
    The fire's in their eyes and their words are really clear.
    So beat it, just beat it.   *Beat It [1982]*

5   Billie Jean is not my lover.
    She's just a girl who claims that
    I am the one,
    But the kid is not my son.   *Billie Jean [1982]*

6   I said you wanna be startin' somethin'
    You got to be startin' somethin'
    It's too high to get over
    Too low to get under
    You're stuck in the middle
    And the pain is thunder.   *Wanna Be Startin' Somethin' [1982]*

7   We're sending out our major love
    And this is our message to you

The planets are lining up
We're bringing brighter days
They're all in line waiting for you.   *Another Part of Me [1987]*

1   You know I'm bad, I'm bad, you know it.   *Bad [1987]*

2   Who's bad?   *Bad [1987]*

3   Leave me alone. Stop it!
Just stop doggin' me around.   *Leave Me Alone [1987]*

4   It's black, it's white, it's tough for you to get by.

    Black or White [1991]

5   Heal the world
Make it a better place
For you and for me
And the entire human race.
There are people dying
If you care enough for the living
Make a better place for you and for me.   *Heal the World [1991]*

6   Hold me
Like a River Jordan
And I will then say to thee
You are my friend.
Carry me
Like you are my brother
Love me like a mother
Will you be there?   *Will You Be There [1991]*

Michael Jackson   1958–2009

and

Lionel Richie   1949–

7   We are the world,
We are the children,
We are the ones
To make a better day.   *We Are the World [1985]*

Nega Mezlekia   1958–

8   The dark blanket of night did not hide the scars of war. No hyenas came to visit us during the night. Instead, gunfire descended from the

desolate mountains, convincing people that the war was being waged in their own living rooms. We made fortresses around our bedrooms with sandbags and heavy stones, and slept under our beds. But soon we realized that the enemy was not under our dining-room table, but outside.

Notes from the Hyena's Belly: An Ethiopian Boyhood [2000]

Euzhan Palcy   1958–

1   Justice and law are often distant cousins.

A Dry White Season [1989][1] [McKenzie]

Caryl Phillips   1958–

2   The treachery of these white men, even towards one such as I who esteemed their values, tore at my heart with great passion. That I, a virtual Englishman, was to be treated as base African cargo caused me such hurtful pain as I was barely able to endure. To lose my dear wife, fair England and now liberty in such rapid succession!

Cambridge [1991], pt. 2

3   A desperate foolishness. The crops failed. I sold my children.

Crossing the River [1993], opening line

4   There are no paths in water. No signposts. There is no return.

Crossing the River

5   My friend, an African river bears no resemblance to a Venetian canal. Only the strongest spirit can hold both together. Only the most powerful heart can endure the pulse of two such disparate life-forces.

The Nature of Blood [1997]

6   Belonging is a contested state. Home is a place riddled with vexing questions.   *A New World Order [2001]*

Prince [Prince Rogers Nelson]   1958–

7   I guess I should have known
By the way you parked your car sideways
That it wouldn't last.   *Little Red Corvette [1982]*

8   I was dreaming when I wrote this,
Forgive me if it goes astray
But when I woke up this morning
I could have sworn it was judgment day.   *1999 [1982]*

---

[1]Screenplay written with Colin Welland.

1   I'm not a woman
I'm not a man
I am something that you'll never understand.   *I Would Die 4 U [1984]*

2   Let's go crazy, let's get nuts.   *Let's Go Crazy [1984]*

3   I never meant to cause you any sorrow
I never meant to cause you any pain
I only wanted to one time see you laughing
I only want to see you laughing in the purple rain.   *Purple Rain [1984]*

4   Why do we scream at each other?
This is what is sounds like when doves cry.   *When Doves Cry [1984]*

5   You don't have to be rich to be my girl.
You don't have to be cool to rule my world.
Ain't no particular sign I'm more compatible with
I just want your extra time and your . . . kiss.   *Kiss [1986]*

6   It's silly no? When a rocket ship explodes
And everybody still wants to fly?
Some say a man ain't happy
Unless a man truly dies.   *Sign o' the Times [1987]*

7   They don't care where they kick
Just as long as they hurt you.   *Thieves in the Temple [1990]*

Neil deGrasse Tyson   1958–

8   I see the universe not as a collection of objects, theories and phenomena, but as a vast stage of actors driven by intricate twists of story line and plot.   *Death by Black Hole [2007]*

9   The only people who still call hurricanes "acts of God" are the people who write insurance forms.   *Death by Black Hole*

Kurtis Blow [Kurt Walker]   1959–

10   These are the breaks
Break it up, break it up, break it up.   *The Breaks [1980]*[1]

Juanita Bynum   1959–

11   I find it very difficult to listen to anybody preach to me about being single when they've got a pair of thighs in their bed every night. You're

---

   [1]With J. B. Moore, Robert Ford, and Russell Simmons.

telling me, "Hold on, honey, sanctify yourself," and you're going home to biceps and triceps, and big old muscles and thighs.

No More Sheets [1997]. Sermon

1   Many of us are rich in our pockets, but we are bankrupt in our spirits.

The Threshing Floor [2005]

Tsitsi Dangarembga   1959–

2   Quietly, unobtrusively and extremely fitfully, something in my mind began to assert itself, to question things and refuse to be brainwashed, bringing me to this time when I can set down this story. It was a long and painful process for me, that process of expansion.

Nervous Conditions [1988], lines from last paragraph

[Earvin] Magic Johnson   1959–

3   I'm not a hero because I got HIV. And I didn't get HIV because I was a "bad" person or a "dirty" one or someone who "deserved" it. . . . No one "deserves" to get HIV. I got HIV because I had unprotected sex. I got HIV because I thought HIV could never happen to someone like me.

My Life [1992]

4   *[On his reception by other players when he returned from retirement to an All-Star game:]* It was the first game ever called on account of hugs.

[1992][1]

Ben Okri   1959–

5   The world is full of riddles that only the dead can answer.

The Famished Road [1991], bk. 2, ch. 1

6   We are the miracles that God made to taste the bitter fruits of time. We are precious, and one day our suffering will turn into wonders of the earth. The sky is not our enemy. There are things that burn me now which turn golden when I am happy. Do you not see the mystery of our pain? That we bear our poverty, are able to sing and dream sweet things, and that we never curse the air when it is warm, or the fruit when it tastes so good, or the lights that bounce gently on the waters. We bless things even in our pain. We bless them in silence. That is why our music is sweet. It makes the air remember.

The Famished Road, 5, 2 [Dad]

7   A dream can be the highest point of a life.

The Famished Road, last line

---

[1] www.NBA.com.

Carl Phillips

1959–

1 This is the black, shot with blue, of my dark
daddy's knuckles, that do not change, ever.
Which is to say they are no more pale
in anger than at rest, or when, as
I imagine them now, they follow
the same two fingers he has always used
to make the rim of every empty blue
glass in the house sing.
Always, the same
blue-to-black sorrow
no black surface can entirely hide.

Blue [1992]

2 What will happen to the memory of his
body, if one of us doesn't hurry now
and write it down fast? Will it be
salt or late light that it melts like?

As from a Quiver of Arrows [1998]

3   The difference between
God and luck is that luck, when it leaves,
does not go far: the idea is to believe
you could almost touch it.

If a Wilderness [2004]

Sade [Helen Folasade Adu]

1959–

4 No need to ask
He's a smooth operator.

Smooth Operator [1984][1]

5 Your love is king
Crown you with my heart.

Your Love Is King [1984]

6 Reach for the top
And the sun is gonna shine
Every winter was a war she said
I want to get what's mine.

Jezebel [1985]

7 Sometimes it comes and it goes
You take it ever so slow
And then you lose it, then it flows right to you
So we rely on the past
Special moments that last

---

[1]With Ray St. John.

Were they as tender as we dare to remember?
Such a fine time as this
What could equal the bliss?
The thrill of the first kiss
It'll blow right to you
It's never as good as the first time.

Never As Good As the First Time [1985]

1   You give me the sweetest taboo
That's why I'm in love with you
You give me the sweetest taboo
Sometimes I think you're just too good for me.   *The Sweetest Taboo [1985]*

2   I won't pretend that I intend to stop living
I won't pretend I'm good at forgiving
But I can't hate you
Although I have tried
I still really really love you
Love is stronger than pride.   *Love Is Stronger Than Pride [1988]*

3   As I reveal my shame to you
I wear it like a tattoo.   *Like a Tattoo [1992]*

4   When you're on the outside baby and you can't get in
I will show you you're so much better than you know
When you're lost and you're alone and you can't get back again
I will find you darling and I will bring you home.   *By Your Side [2000]*

Jean-Michel Basquiat   1960–1988

5   SAMO as an end to bogus pseudo intellectual. My mouth, therefore
an error. Plush safe...he think.   *[1978]¹*

6   I wanted to be a star, not a gallery mascot.
Quoted in the New York Times [February 10, 1985]

7   Every line means something.   *Motto*

Chuck D [Carlton Douglas Ridenhour]   1960–

8   Here is a land that never gave a damn
About a brother like me and myself
Because they never did.   *Black Steel in the Hour of Chaos [1988]*

---

¹Basquiat's art career began with graffitied phrases signed SAMO (Same Old Shit).

1 Turn it up! Bring the noise!   *Bring the Noise [1988]*

2 The minute they see me, fear me
   I'm the epitome — a public enemy
   Used, abused without clues
   I refused to blow a fuse
   They even had it on the news
   Don't believe the hype!   *Don't Believe the Hype [1988]*

3 Rap is black America's TV station.   *Interview. Spin [September 1988]*

Chuck D [Carlton Douglas Ridenhour]   1960–

and

Keith Schocklee [Keith Matthew Boxley]   1962–

4 Yo! Bum rush the show
   You gotta go for what you know
   To make everybody see, in order to
   Fight the powers that be!   *Fight the Power [1989]*

5 Most of my heroes don't appear on no stamps.   *Fight the Power*

6 All I got is genes and chromosomes
   Consider me Black to the bone
   All I want is peace and love
   On this planet.
   (Ain't that how God planned it?)   *Fear of a Black Planet [1990]*

Fred D'Aguiar   1960–

7 The future is just more of the past waiting to happen.
                                         The Longest Memory [1994]. Remembering

8 Forget. Memory is pain trying to resurrect itself.
                                              The Longest Memory. Forgetting

Isaac Julien   1960–

9 In this Western culture we have all grown up as snow queens —
   straights, as well as white queers — Western culture is in love with its own
   (white) image.   *Confessions of a Snow Queen [1994]*

Mark [Johannes] Mathabane   1960–

10 The white man of South Africa certainly does not know me. He certainly does not know the conditions under which I was born and had to live

for eighteen years. So my story is intended to show him with words a world he would otherwise not see...and make him feel what I felt when he contemptuously called me a "Kaffir boy."

Kaffir Boy [1986], ch. 1

Lorna Simpson   1960–

1   Is she as pretty as a picture
Or clear as crystal
Or pure as a lily
Or black as coal
Or sharp as a razor?   *Text from Twenty Questions (A Sampler) [1986]*

2   She saw him disappear by the river, they asked her to tell what happened, only to discount her memory.

Text from Waterbearer [1986]

Student Nonviolent Coordinating Committee (SNCC)   1960–1976

3   Through nonviolence, courage displaces fear. Love transcends hate. Acceptance dissipates prejudice; hope ends despair. Faith reconciles doubt. Peace dominates war. Mutual regards cancel enmity. Justice for all overthrows injustice. The redemptive community supersedes immoral social systems.

By appealing to conscience and standing on the moral nature of human existence, nonviolence nurtures the atmosphere in which reconciliation and justice become actual possibilities.   *Founding Statement [1960]*

Hilton Als   1961–

4   I have always hated to observe things, always, because to observe anything has meant I will remember it.   *The Women [1996]*

5   What the Negress has always been: a symbol of America's by now forgotten strain of puritanical selflessness. The Negress is a perennial source of "news" and interesting "copy" in the newspapers and magazines she does not read because she is a formidable character in the internal drama most Americans have with the issue of self-abnegation. The Negress serves as a reminder to our sentimental nation that what its countrymen are shaped by is a nonverbal confusion about and, ultimately, abhorrence for the good neighbor policy. Most Americans absorb the principles of the good neighbor policy through the language-based tenets of Judaism and Christianity. These laws lead to a deep emotional confusion about the "good"

since most Americans are suspicious of language and spend a great deal of time and energy on Entertainment and Relaxation in an attempt to avoid its net result: Reflection.   *The Women*

1   For black people, being around white people is sometimes like taking care of babies you don't like, babies who throw up on you again and again, but whom you cannot punish, because they're babies. Eventually, you direct that anger at yourself — it has nowhere else to go.

A Pryor Love. The New Yorker [September 13, 1999]

2   "Nigger" is a slow death.   *GWTW (Gone with the Wind)*[1]

3   What they want generally speaking is for an audience to validate their body's breath, they kiss us, each and every one of us, then they close the show, those performers, taking our hearts with them when they use phrases like "Good night," or "This is our last song," creating longing in the process, their long and short goodbye being part of who they are, and what they can give until they breathe on us again.

The Last Interview. Believer [July/August 2009]

Eric Jerome Dickey   1961–

4   Sometimes grasping words sounded desperate, or expecting, and ruined a damn good thing. Let it ride.   *Milk in My Coffee [1998]*

5   She [Michelle] was giving me the same motions and moans she had been giving somebody else. I wasn't loving her, I was stabbing her. She accepted the pain. We finished and lay next to each other like strangers.

Cheaters [1999]

Grandmaster Melle Mel [Melvin Glover]   1961–

and

Edward "Duke Bootee" Fletcher   1951–

6   Don't push me 'cause I'm close to the edge.
I'm tryin' not to lose my head.
It's like a jungle sometimes, it makes me wonder
How I keep from going under.   *The Message [1982]*

7   A child is born with no state of mind
Blind to the ways of mankind
God is smiling on you but He's frowning too
Because only God knows what you'll go through.   *The Message*

[1]From *Without Sanctuary* [2000], edited by JAMES ALLEN.

Grandmaster Melle Mel [Melvin Glover] 1961–

1 A million magic crystals
Painted pure and white
A multimillion dollars
Almost over night
Twice as sweet as sugar
Twice as bitter as salt
And if you get hooked, baby
Ain't nobody else's fault
So don't do it!

White Lines [1983]

Wynton Marsalis 1961–

2 Jazz is the nobility of the race put into sound; it is the sensuousness of romance in our dialect; it is the picture of the people in all their glory.
Why We Must Preserve Our Jazz Heritage.
Ebony magazine [February 1986]

3 *[Definition of jazz:]* A swinging dialogue between concerned parties whose philosophy is "Let's try to work it out."
Sweet Singing Blues on the Road [1994]

4 I don't need what you hate. Give me what you love. And if that costs you too much, at least give me what you like.
Jazz in the Bittersweet Blues of Life [2001]

5 In music and life serious listening forces you to recognize others. Emphatic listeners almost always have more friends than other people, and their counsel is more highly valued. A patient, understanding listener lives in a larger world than a nonlistening know-it-all.... The humanity in a sound ... comes from understanding the soft and hard parts of life.
Moving to Higher Ground: How Jazz Can
Change Your Life [2008]

6 I believe that to know the essence of a thing requires returning as closely as possible to the origin of that thing. The passage of time tends to quietly erode meaning and enthusiasm. The farther you move away from the sun, the colder it gets.
Moving to Higher Ground: How Jazz Can Change Your Life

Eddie Murphy 1961–

7 I have some ice cream and I'm gonna eat it all. You don't have no ice cream. You didn't get none 'cause you are on the welfare. You can't afford it.
Delirious [1983]

1   If you're starving and somebody throw you a cracker you gonna be like this: goddamn that's the best cracker I ever ate in my life!

Raw [1987]

Barack [Hussein] Obama   1961–

2   I decided to become a community organizer.... Change won't come from the top, I would say. Change will come from a mobilized grass roots.

Dreams from My Father [1995]

3   How far do our obligations reach? How do we transform mere power into justice, mere sentiment into love? The answers I find in law books don't always satisfy me.... And yet, in the conversation itself, in the joining of voices, I find myself modestly encouraged, believing that so long as the questions are still being asked, what binds us together might somehow, ultimately, prevail.

Dreams from My Father

4   I don't oppose all wars. And I know that in this crowd today, there is no shortage of patriots, or of patriotism. What I am opposed to is a dumb war. What I am opposed to is a rash war.

Speech to antiwar rally in Chicago [October 2, 2002]

5   Yes, we can![1]

Slogan [2004 Illinois senate campaign and 2008 presidential campaign]

6   The pundits like to slice-and-dice our country into Red States and Blue States; Red States for Republicans, Blue States for Democrats. But I've got news for them, too. We worship an awesome God in the Blue States, and we don't like federal agents poking around our libraries in the Red States. We coach Little League in the Blue States and have gay friends in the Red States. There are patriots who opposed the war in Iraq and patriots who supported it. We are one people, all of us pledging allegiance to the stars and stripes, all of us defending the United States of America.

Keynote address at Democratic National Convention [2004]

7   Hope in the face of difficulty. Hope in the face of uncertainty. The audacity of hope![2] In the end, that is God's greatest gift to us.

Keynote address at Democratic National Convention

---

[1]Cf. the slogan of United Farm Workers: Si se puede (Yes, it can be done).
[2]See also Jeremiah A. Wright, Jr., 416:4–5.

1   I stand here today, grateful for the diversity of my heritage, aware that my parents' dreams live on in my precious daughters. I stand here knowing that my story is part of the larger American story, that I owe a debt to all of those who came before me, and that, in no other country on earth, is my story even possible.

Keynote address at Democratic National Convention

2   If you will join me in this improbable quest, if you feel destiny calling, and see, as I see, a future of endless possibility stretching before us; if you sense, as I sense, that the time is now to shake off our slumber, and slough off our fear, and make good on the debt we owe past and future generations, then I'm ready to take up the cause, and march with you, and work with you. Together, starting today, let us finish the work that needs to be done, and usher in a new birth of freedom on this Earth.

Speech announcing candidacy for president of the
United States [February 10, 2007]

3   The civil rights movement wasn't just a fight against the oppressor; it was also a fight against the oppressor in each of us.

Speech at the Selma Voting Rights March Commemoration
[March 4, 2007]

4   The criminal justice system is not colorblind. It does not work for all people equally, and that is why it's critical to have a president who sends a signal that we are going to have a system of justice that is not just us, but is everybody.

Third presidential Democratic primary debate, Howard
University, Washington, D.C. [June 28, 2007]

5   One of the things I think I can bring to the presidency is to make government and public service cool again.

Interview. TIME magazine [November 29, 2007]

6   I'm asking you to believe. Not just in my ability to bring about real change in Washington. . . . I'm asking you to believe in yours.

Campaign slogan [2007]

7   We are choosing hope over fear. We're choosing unity over division and sending a powerful message that change is coming to America.

Speech after winning Iowa caucuses, Des Moines, Iowa
[January 3, 2008]

8   Nothing can stand in the way of the power of millions of voices calling for change.

Speech after the New Hampshire primary
[January 8, 2008]

1   It was a creed written into the founding documents that declared the destiny of a nation: Yes we can.[1] It was whispered by slaves and abolitionists as they blazed a trail towards freedom through the darkest of nights: Yes we can. It was sung by immigrants as they struck out from distant shores and pioneers who pushed westward against an unforgiving wilderness: Yes we can. It was the call of workers who organized, women who reached for the ballot, a president who chose the moon as our new frontier, and a King who took us to the mountaintop and pointed the way to the Promised Land.

Speech after the New Hampshire primary

2   Change will not come if we wait for some other person or if we wait for some other time. We are the ones we've been waiting for.[2] We are the change that we seek.

Speech on Super Tuesday, Chicago, Illinois [February 5, 2008]

3   Of course, the answer to the slavery question was already embedded within our Constitution — a Constitution that had at its very core the ideal of equal citizenship under the law; a Constitution that promised its people liberty, and justice, and a union that could be and should be perfected over time.[3]

And yet words on a parchment would not be enough to deliver slaves from bondage, or provide men and women of every color and creed their full rights and obligations as citizens of the United States. What would be needed were Americans in successive generations who were willing to do their part — through protests and struggle, on the streets and in the courts, through a civil war and civil disobedience and always at great risk — to narrow that gap between the promise of our ideals and the reality of their time.

Speech, Philadelphia, Pennsylvania [March 18, 2008]

---

[1]Obama first used "Yes we can" as the campaign slogan for his successful 2004 bid for the United States Senate. During a January 5, 2008, Democratic presidential debate with Hillary Clinton, John Edwards, and Bill Richardson, then Senator Obama said: "When the American people are determined that something is going to happen, then it happens. And if they are disaffected and cynical and fearful and told that it can't be done, then it doesn't. I'm running for president because I want to tell them 'Yes we can.'" President Obama reprised this signature phrase in his victory speech: "This is our chance to answer that call. This is our moment. This is our time — to put our people back to work and open doors of opportunity for our kids; to restore prosperity and promote the cause of peace; to reclaim the American dream and reaffirm that fundamental truth that out of many, we are one; that while we breathe, we hope; and where we are met with cynicism and doubt and those who tell us that we can't, we will respond with that timeless creed that sums up the spirit of a people: Yes, we can" [November 4, 2008]. See also Allen Toussaint, 391:5.

[2]See also June Jordan, 372:3.

[3]Refers to the preamble of the Constitution of the United States of America: "We the People of the United States, in Order to form a more perfect Union, establish Justice, insure domestic Tranquility, provide for the common defense, promote the general Welfare, and secure the Blessings of Liberty to ourselves and our Posterity, do ordain and establish this Constitution for the United States of America."

1   The anger [of black people] is real; it is powerful; and to simply wish it away, to condemn it without understanding its roots, only serves to widen the chasm of misunderstanding that exists between the races.

Speech, Philadelphia, Pennsylvania

2   Working together we can move beyond some of our old racial wounds... in fact we have no choice if we are to continue on the path of a more perfect union.   *Speech, Philadelphia, Pennsylvania*

3   In the white community, the path to a more perfect union means acknowledging that what ails the African-American community does not just exist in the minds of black people; that the legacy of discrimination — and current incidents of discrimination, while less overt than in the past — are real and must be addressed. Not just with words, but with deeds.

Speech, Philadelphia, Pennsylvania

4   You go into some of these small towns in Pennsylvania, a lot like a lot of small towns in the Midwest, the jobs have been gone now for twenty-five years and nothing's replaced them. And they fell through the Clinton administration, and the Bush administration, and each successive administration has said that somehow these communities are gonna regenerate and they have not. So it's not surprising then that they get bitter, they cling to guns or religion or antipathy towards people who aren't like them or anti-immigrant sentiment or anti-trade sentiment as a way to explain their frustrations.   *Speech at a San Francisco fundraiser [April 6, 2008]*

5   I come to Berlin as so many of my countrymen have come before. Tonight, I speak to you not as a candidate for president, but as a citizen — a proud citizen of the United States, and a fellow citizen of the world.

Speech, Berlin, Germany [July, 24 2008]

6   The walls between old allies on either side of the Atlantic cannot stand. The walls between the countries with the most and those with the least cannot stand. The walls between races and tribes, natives and immigrants, Christian and Muslim and Jew cannot stand. These now are the walls we must tear down.

Speech, Berlin, Germany

7   Four years ago, I stood before you and told you my story — of the brief union between a young man from Kenya and a young woman from Kansas who weren't well-off or well-known, but shared a belief that in America, their son could achieve whatever he put his mind to.

It is that promise that has always set this country apart — that through hard work and sacrifice, each of us can pursue our individual dreams but still come together as one American family, to ensure that the next generation can pursue their dreams as well. That's why I stand here tonight. Because for 232 years, at each moment when that promise was in jeopardy, ordinary men and women — students and soldiers, farmers and teachers, nurses and janitors — found the courage to keep it alive.

Speech at the Democratic National Convention [August 28, 2008]

1   It's been a long time coming, but tonight, because of what we did on this day, in this election, at this defining moment, change has come to America.

Presidential victory speech, Grant Park, Chicago
[November 4, 2008]

2   I will never forget who this victory truly belongs to. It belongs to you.   *Presidential victory speech*

3   And to all those watching tonight from beyond our shores, from parliaments and palaces to those who are huddled around radios in the forgotten corners of the world, our stories are singular, but our destiny is shared, and a new dawn of American leadership is at hand. To those who would tear the world down: we will defeat you. To those who seek peace and security: we support you. And to all those who have wondered if America's beacon still burns as bright: tonight we proved once more that the true strength of our nation comes not from the might of our arms or the scale of our wealth, but from the enduring power of our ideals — democracy, liberty, opportunity and unyielding hope. That's the true genius of America, that America can change. Our union can be perfected. And what we have already achieved gives us hope for what we can and must achieve tomorrow.

Presidential victory speech

4   My fellow citizens: I stand here today humbled by the task before us, grateful for the trust you have bestowed, mindful of the sacrifices borne by our ancestors.

Inaugural address, Washington, D.C. [January 20, 2009]

5   We remain a young nation, but in the words of scripture, the time has come to set aside childish things. The time has come to reaffirm our enduring spirit; to choose our better history; to carry forward that precious gift, that noble idea, passed on from generation to generation: the God-given promise that all are equal, all are free, and all deserve a chance to pursue their full measure of happiness.   *Inaugural address*

6   The nation cannot prosper long when it favors only the prosperous. The success of our economy has always depended not just on the size of our gross domestic product, but on the reach of our prosperity; on the ability to extend opportunity to every willing heart — not out of charity, but because it is the surest route to our common good.   *Inaugural address*

1   We know that our patchwork heritage is a strength, not a weakness. We are a nation of Christians and Muslims, Jews and Hindus, and nonbelievers. We are shaped by every language and culture, drawn from every end of this Earth. And because we have tasted the bitter swill of civil war and segregation and emerged from that dark chapter stronger and more united, we cannot help but believe that the old hatreds shall someday pass; that the lines of tribe shall soon dissolve; that as the world grows smaller, our common humanity shall reveal itself; and that America must play its role in ushering in a new era of peace.   *Inaugural address*

2   Our challenges may be new, the instruments with which we meet them may be new, but those values upon which our success depends — honesty and hard work, courage and fair play, tolerance and curiosity, loyalty and patriotism — these things are old. These things are true. They have been the quiet force of progress throughout our history. What is demanded, then, is a return to these truths. What is required of us now is a new era of responsibility — a recognition, on the part of every American, that we have duties to ourselves, our nation and the world, duties that we do not grudgingly accept but rather seize gladly, firm in the knowledge that there is nothing so satisfying to the spirit, so defining of our character than giving our all to a difficult task. This is the price and the promise of citizenship.   *Inaugural address*

3   With hope and virtue, let us brave once more the icy currents, and endure what storms may come. Let it be said by our children's children that when we were tested we refused to let this journey end, that we did not turn back nor did we falter; and with eyes fixed on the horizon and God's grace upon us, we carried forth that great gift of freedom and delivered it safely to future generations.[1]   *Inaugural address*

4   We lose ourselves when we compromise the very ideals that we fight to defend. And we honor those ideals by upholding them not when it's easy, but when it is hard.

Nobel lecture, Oslo [December 10, 2009]

5   The absence of hope can rot a society from within.   *Nobel lecture*

6   We can acknowledge that oppression will always be with us, and still strive for justice. We can admit the intractability of deprivation, and still strive for dignity. Clear-eyed, we can understand that there will be war, and still strive for peace. We can do that — for that is the story of human

---

[1] "Let it be told to the future world that in the depth of winter, when nothing but hope and virtue could survive, that the city and the country, alarmed at one common danger, came forth to meet it." — THOMAS PAINE. Read to George Washington's troops in Valley Forge.

progress; that's the hope of all the world; and at this moment of challenge, that must be our work here on Earth.   *Nobel lecture*

1   Our troops come from every corner of this country — they are black, white, Latino, Asian, and Native American. They are Christian and Hindu, Jewish and Muslim. And, yes, we know that some of them are gay. Starting this year, no American will be forbidden from serving the country they love because of who they love.

State of the Union speech [January 25, 2011]

2   Today, at my direction, the United States launched a targeted operation against that compound in Abbottabad, Pakistan. A small team of Americans carried out the operation with extraordinary courage and capability. No Americans were harmed. They took care to avoid civilian casualties. After a firefight, they killed Osama bin Laden and took custody of his body.   *Speech [May 2, 2011]*

3   The American people did not choose this fight. It came to our shores, and started with the senseless slaughter of our citizens.

Speech [May 2, 2011]

4   Democracy in a nation of 300 million can be noisy and messy and complicated. We have our own opinions. Each of us has deeply held beliefs. And when we go through tough times, when we make big decisions as a country, it necessarily stirs passions, stirs up controversy. That won't change after tonight — and it shouldn't. These arguments we have are a mark of our liberty, and we can never forget that as we speak, people in distant nations are risking their lives right now just for a chance to argue about the issues that matter, the chance to cast their ballots like we did today.

Victory speech, Chicago, Illinois [November 7, 2012]

5   The freedom which so many Americans have fought for and died for comes with responsibilities as well as rights. And among those are love and charity and duty and patriotism.

Victory speech, Chicago, Illinois

6   This is our first task — caring for our children. It's our first job. If we don't get that right, we don't get anything right. That's how, as a society, we will be judged.

Remarks at prayer vigil, Sandy Hook, Connecticut [December 16, 2012]

7   We do not believe that in this country freedom is reserved for the lucky, or happiness for the few. We recognize that no matter how responsibly we live our lives, any one of us at any time may face a job loss, or a sudden illness, or a home swept away in a terrible storm. The commitments

we make to each other through Medicare and Medicaid and Social Security, these things do not sap our initiative, they strengthen us. They do not make us a nation of takers; they free us to take the risks that make this country great.

Second inaugural address [January 21, 2013]

1   We will defend our people and uphold our values through strength of arms and rule of law. We will show the courage to try and resolve our differences with other nations peacefully — not because we are naïve about the dangers we face, but because engagement can more durably lift suspicion and fear.

Second inaugural address

2   Our journey is not complete until our wives, our mothers and daughters can earn a living equal to their efforts. Our journey is not complete until our gay brothers and sisters are treated like anyone else under the law — for if we are truly created equal, then surely the love we commit to one another must be equal as well. Our journey is not complete until no citizen is forced to wait for hours to exercise the right to vote. Our journey is not complete until we find a better way to welcome the striving, hopeful immigrants who still see America as a land of opportunity — until bright young students and engineers are enlisted in our workforce rather than expelled from our country. Our journey is not complete until all our children, from the streets of Detroit to the hills of Appalachia, to the quiet lanes of Newtown, know that they are cared for and cherished and always safe from harm.

Second inaugural address

3   Progress does not compel us to settle centuries-long debates about the role of government for all time, but it does require us to act in our time.

Second inaugural address

4   Let us, each of us, now embrace with solemn duty and awesome joy what is our lasting birthright. With common effort and common purpose, with passion and dedication, let us answer the call of history and carry into an uncertain future that precious light of freedom.

Second inaugural address

5   Our faith in each other, our love for each other, our love for country, our common creed that cuts across whatever superficial differences there may be — that is our power. That's our strength.

That's why a bomb can't beat us. That's why we don't hunker down. That's why we don't cower in fear. We carry on. We race. We strive. We build, and we work, and we love — and we raise our kids to do the same.

Speech at an interfaith prayer service in Boston
[April 18, 2013]

1   There are very few African American men in this country who haven't had the experience of being followed when they were shopping in a department store. That includes me. There are very few African American men who haven't had the experience of walking across the street and hearing the locks click on the doors of cars. That happens to me — at least before I was a senator. There are very few African Americans who haven't had the experience of getting on an elevator and a woman clutching her purse nervously and holding her breath until she had a chance to get off. That happens often.

And I don't want to exaggerate this, but those sets of experiences inform how the African American community interprets what happened one night in Florida. And it's inescapable for people to bring those experiences to bear. The African American community is also knowledgeable that there is a history of racial disparities in the application of our criminal laws — everything from the death penalty to enforcement of our drug laws. And that ends up having an impact in terms of how people interpret the case.

Now, this isn't to say that the African American community is naive about the fact that African American young men are disproportionately involved in the criminal justice system, that they are disproportionately both victims and perpetrators of violence. It's not to make excuses for that fact — although black folks do interpret the reasons for that in a historical context.

They understand that some of the violence that takes place in poor black neighborhoods around the country is born out of a very violent past in this country, and that the poverty and dysfunction that we see in those communities can be traced to a very difficult history.

Remarks on the trial of George Zimmerman for the fatal
shooting of Trayvon Martin [July 19, 2013]

2   In families and churches and workplaces, there's the possibility that people are a little bit more honest, and at least you ask yourself your own questions about, am I wringing as much bias out of myself as I can? Am I judging people as much as I can, based on not the color of their skin, but the content of their character?[1] . . .

Each successive generation seems to be making progress in changing attitudes when it comes to race. It doesn't mean we're in a post-racial society. It doesn't mean that racism is eliminated. . . .

We have to be vigilant and we have to work on these issues. And those of us in authority should be doing everything we can to encourage the

---

[1]See Martin Luther King, Jr., 318:2.

better angels of our nature[1] as opposed to using these episodes to heighten
divisions.   *Remarks on the trial of George Zimmerman*

1   The arc of the moral universe may bend towards justice, but it doesn't
bend on its own.

Speech on 50th anniversary of the March on Washington
[August 28, 2013]

Stew [Mark Stewart]   1961–

2   In the end we're just two brothers passing. Like your high yellow
grandma back in the day, only we're passing for black folks.

Passing Strange [2006] [Mr. Franklin]

Elizabeth Alexander   1962–

3   I am called "Venus Hottentot."
I left Capetown with a promise
of revenue: half the profits
and my passage home: A boon!
Master's brother proposed the trip;
the magistrate granted me leave
I would return to my family
a duchess, with watered-silk
dresses and money to grow food.   *The Venus Hottentot (1825) [1990], st. 2*

4   Since my own genitals are public
I have made other parts private.   *The Venus Hottentot (1825)*

5   Life is only momentarily fearless; life is only for a moment
full of cures; the body, as always, tells the round, bald truth
when my stomach grips to say, no cure in sight.   *Body of Life [1996]*

6   Giving birth is like jazz, something from silence, then all of it.
Antebellum Dream Book [2001]. Neonatology

7   What a strange thing is "race," and family, stranger still.
Antebellum Dream Book. Race

8   Poetry is what you find
in the dirt in the corner,
overhear on the bus, God

---

[1]"We are not enemies, but friends. We must not be enemies. Though passion may have strained, it must
not break our bonds of affection. The mystic chords of memory, stretching from every battlefield and
patriot grave to every living heart and hearthstone all over this broad land, will yet swell the chorus of
the Union, when again touched, as surely they will be, by the better angels of our nature." — ABRAHAM
LINCOLN, First Inaugural Address [March 4, 1861]

in the details, the only way
to get from here to there.

American Sublime [2005]. Ars Poetica #100: I Believe

1   Say it plain: that many have died for this day.
Sing the names of the dead who brought us here,
who laid the train tracks, raised the bridges,

picked the cotton and the lettuce, built
brick by brick the glittering edifices
they would then keep clean and work inside of.

Praise Song for the Day [January 20, 2009][1]

2   In today's sharp sparkle, this winter air,
any thing can be made, any sentence begun.
On the brink, on the brim, on the cusp,
praise song for walking forward in that light.   *Praise Song for the Day*

Kwame Dawes   1962–

3   The propellers undress the sea;
the pattern of foam like a broken zip
opening where the bow cuts the wave
and closing in its wake.   *Progeny of Air [1994]*

4   Let us gather around the legend of faith,
truth of our lives in this crude foment of days.
We are so afraid to look to the sky, so cowed, we whisper
of straight paths while a nation grows fat on its own flesh.

Holy Dub [2001], st. 1

5   We have come this way before, I am certain,
but the landmarks are not exactly what they were.   *Map Maker [2001], st. 3*

6   We carve out our generations in stained ivory,
totems. Oh, to be able
to plant a tree that bears fruit,
like fat ancestors that tell their story.   *Staff [2004]*

Trey Ellis   1962–

7   I know we're not supposed to say this after civil rights and all, but do
you ever feel different just because you're black?

Platitudes [1988] [Dorothy]

[1]Read at the inauguration of President Barack Obama.

1   Just as a genetic mulatto is a black person of mixed parents who can often get along fine with his white grandparents, a cultural mulatto, educated by a multiracial mix of cultures, can also navigate easily in the white world.   *The New Black Aesthetic. Callaloo [Winter 1989]*

[Jacqueline] Jackie Joyner-Kersee   1962–

2   I don't think being an athlete is unfeminine. I think of it as a kind of grace.   *Interview. TIME magazine [September 19, 1988]*

Charles Barkley   1963–

3   You might listen to black music, and you might watch black athletes, but that doesn't mean you'll be willing to talk to that black guy who just moved down the street.   *Interview. Boston Globe [January 17, 1992]*[1]

4   If the only qualification for being a role model is that you have to be able to dunk a basketball, then I know millions of people who could become role models. That's not enough. Hell, I know drug dealers who can dunk. Can drug dealers be role models, too?   *Associated Press [June 19, 1992]*[1]

5   This is my new shoe. It's a good shoe. It won't make you dunk like me. It won't make you rich like me. It won't make you rebound like me. It definitely won't make you handsome like me. It'll only make you have shoes like me.   *Nike commercial [1993]*[1]

6   When you're the top dog, everybody want to put you in the pound.
                    Quoted in the Los Angeles Times [March 24, 1993][1]

Malcolm Gladwell   1963–

7   Three characteristics — one, contagiousness; two, the fact that little causes can have big effects; and three, that change happens not gradually but at one dramatic moment — are the same three principles that define how measles moves through a grade-school classroom or the flu attacks every winter. Of the three, the third trait — the idea that epidemics can rise or fall in one dramatic moment — is the most important, because it is the principle that makes sense of the first two and that permits the greatest insight into why modern change happens the way it does. The name given to that one dramatic moment in an epidemic when everything can change all at once is the Tipping Point.   *The Tipping Point [2000]*

8   Look at the world around you. It may seem like an immovable, implacable place. It is not. With the slightest push — in just the right place — it can be tipped.   *The Tipping Point*

---

[1]From *Sir Charles: The Wit and Wisdom of Charles Barkley* [1994].

1   Decisions made very quickly can be every bit as good as decisions made cautiously and deliberately.

Blink [2005]

2   We have, as human beings, a storytelling problem. We're a bit too quick to come up with explanations for things we don't really have an explanation for.

Blink

3   Superstar lawyers and math whizzes and software entrepreneurs appear at first blush to lie outside ordinary experience. But they don't. They are products of history and community, of opportunity and legacy. Their success is not exceptional or mysterious. It is grounded in a web of advantages and inheritances, some deserved, some not, some earned, some just plain lucky — but all critical to making them who they are. The outlier, in the end, is not an outlier at all.

Outliers [2008]

Whitney Houston
1963–2012

4   I don't know how to sing Black — and I don't know how to sing white, either. I know how to sing. Music is not a color to me.

Interview. Essence [December 1990]

Michael Jordan
1963–

5   Fear is an illusion. You think something is standing in your way, but nothing is really there. What is there is an opportunity to do your best and gain some success.

I Can't Accept Not Trying [1994]

6   I can accept failure. Everyone fails at something. But I can't accept not trying.

I Can't Accept Not Trying

7   Talent wins games, but teamwork and intelligence win championships.

I Can't Accept Not Trying

Randall Kenan
1963–

8   What does it mean to be black? . . . The culture of being black, great or small for some, but present for practically all, remains fascinating and elusive, multifaceted and ever-changing, problematic and profound. Despite its Old World origins, black American culture, the language, the art, the music, the customs, ad nauseam, is a New World creation, as varied as the geography of the Americas, and belonging to all. It is a part of America.

Walking on Water [1999]

Kool Moe Dee [Mohandas Dewese]
1963–

9   Guns, we don't like to use 'em
Unless our enemies choose 'em

We prefer to fight you on like a man and
Beat you down with our hands, and bodyslam you
At the wild, wild west.   *Wild Wild West [1987]*

March on Washington for Jobs and Freedom   1963

1   I will pledge my heart and my mind and my body unequivocally and without regard to personal sacrifice, to the achievement of social peace through social justice.   *From Marchers' Pledge [August 28, 1963]*

Suzan-Lori Parks   1963–

2   You will write it down because if you dont write it down then we will come along and tell the future that we did not exist.
The Death of the Last Black Man in the Whole Entire World [1989], final chorus [Yes and Black-Eyed Peas Cornbread]

3   He digged the hole and the whole held him.
The America Play [1992], act I
[The Founding Father as Abraham Lincoln]

4   When death met Love Death deathd Love
and left Love tuh rot
au naturel end for thuh Miss Hottentot.
Loves soul, which was tidy, hides in heaven, yes, thats it
Loves corpse stands on show in museum. Please
visit.   *Venus [1997] [Venus]*

5   My *inheritance*. You stole my *inheritance*, man. That aint right. That aint right and you know it. You had yr own. And you blew it. You *blew it* motherfucker! I saved mines and you blew yrs.
Topdog/Underdog [2001], sc. vi [Booth]

6   At the start theres always energy. Sometimes joy. Sometimes fear. By the end, youll be so deep into the habit of continuing on, youll pray that youll never stop. Happens all the time. But dont take my word for it. Lets go and youll see for yrself.   *365 Days/365 Plays [2006]. Start Here [Krishna]*

Vanessa Williams   1963–

7   *[On losing the Miss America title after publication of nude photos:]* The past just came up and kicked me.
Interview. People magazine [August 6, 1984]

8   If situations arose where I could get revenge, I absolutely would. But at this point, success is the best revenge.   *Interview. Ebony [April 1990]*

Jacqueline Woodson

1963–

1   I'm on the outside of things. I wish it didn't matter so much. But it does, doesn't it? Difference matters.   *Melanin Sun [1995]*

2   I sewed stars and roads
into quilts and curtains and clothes because Mama said,
*All the stuff that happened before you were born
is your own kind of Show Way.
There's a road, girl,* my mama said. *There's a road.*   *Show Way [2005]*

3   Time comes to us softly, slowly. It sits beside us for a while. Then, long before we are ready, it moves on.   *If You Come Softly [2006]*

4   No matter how big you get, it's still okay to cry if you need to because everybody's got a right to their own tears.

Peace, Locomotion [2009] [Miss Edna]

Tracy Chapman

1964–

5   Don't you know
They're talkin' about a revolution
It sounds like a whisper.   *Talkin' Bout a Revolution [1982]*

6   Last night I heard the screaming
Loud voices behind the wall
Another sleepless night for me
It won't do no good to call
The police
Always come late
If they come at all.   *Behind the Wall [1983]*

7   Why are the missiles called peace keepers
When they're aimed to kill
Why is a woman still not safe
When she's in her home?   *Why? [1986]*

9   You got a fast car
I want a ticket to anywhere
Maybe we can make a deal
Maybe together we can get somewhere
Anyplace is better
Starting from zero, got nothing to lose.   *Fast Car [1987]*

10   And I was born to fight
I ain't been knocked down yet

I was born to fight
I'm the surest bet.

Born to Fight [1989]

Denyce Graves

1964–

1   Music brings a stability to humanity in an uncivilized time.
On singing at a prayer service days after 9/11.
USA Weekend [October 28, 2001]

Lynn Nottage

1964–

2   It 'bout who we be today,
And in our fabulating way
'Bout saying that we be
Without a-pology.
It's a circle that been run.
That ain't no one ever won.
It that silly rabbit grin,
'Bout running from your skin.

Fabulation [2004], act II, sc. vi [Flow]

3   My mother taught me that you can follow behind everyone and walk in the dust, or you can walk ahead through the unbroken thorny brush. You may get blood on your ankles, but you arrive first and not covered in the residue of others.

Ruined [2009], act I, sc. v [Mama Nadi]

4   But they still took me from my home. They took me through the bush — raiding thieves. Fucking demons! "She is for everyone, soup to be had before dinner," that is what someone said. They tied me to a tree by my foot, and the men came whenever they wanted soup. I make fires, I cook food, I listen to their stupid songs, I carry bullets, I clean wounds, I wash blood from their clothing, and, and, and...I lay there as they tore me to pieces, until I was raw...five months. Five months. Chained like a goat. These men fighting...fighting for our liberation. Still I close my eyes and I see such terrible things. Things I cannot stand to have in my head. How can men be this way?

Ruined, act II, sc. ii [Salima]

5   You will not fight your battles on my body anymore.

Ruined, act II, sc. vi [Salima]

Michelle [LaVaughn Robinson] Obama

1964–

6   We have lost the understanding that in a democracy, we have a mutual obligation to one another. That we cannot measure the greatness

of our society by the strongest and richest of us, but we have to measure our greatness by the least of these.[1]

Speech at the University of California, Los Angeles
[February 3, 2008]

1   For the first time in my adult life I am proud of my country, because it feels like hope is finally making a comeback.

Speech, Milwaukee, Wisconsin [February 18, 2008]

2   My first job in all honesty is going to continue to be mom-in-chief.

Interview. Ebony [September 2008]

3   The physical and emotional health of an entire generation and the economic health and security of our nation are at stake. This isn't the kind of problem that can be solved overnight, but with everyone working together, it can be solved. So, let's move.

Statement at the launch of the Let's Move! Initiative to fight childhood obesity [February 9, 2010]

4   Being president doesn't change who you are — it reveals who you are.

Speech at the Democratic National Convention [September 4, 2012]

5   Just as each seed we plant has the potential to become something extraordinary, so does every child.   *American Grown [2012]*

Susan E[lizabeth] Rice   1964–

6   Full, sustained, and universal democracy and respect for human rights are our guideposts. On these we do not compromise.

U.S. Policy in Africa: A Partnership for the 21st Century.
Keynote address at the Brookings Institution
[March 12, 1998]

Run-DMC
Run [Joseph Simmons]   1964–

and

DMC [Darryl McDaniels]   1964–

7   Unemployment at a record high
People coming, people going
People born to die

---

[1]Inasmuch as ye have done it unto one of the least of these my brethren, ye have done it unto me. — *Matthew 25:40*

Don't ask me because I don't know why
But it's like that and that's the way it is.   *It's Like That [1983]*

1   The rhymes have to make a lot of sense.
      You got to know when to start when the beats commence.
                                                                 Sucker MCs [1983]

2   For all you sucker MCs perpetrating a fraud
      Your rhymes are cold whack and keep the crowd cold bored
      You're the kind of guy that girls ignore
      I'm drivin' a Caddy, you're fixin' a Ford.   *Rock Box [1984]*

3   It's tricky to rock a rhyme, to rock a rhyme that's right on time.
                                                                 It's Tricky [1986]

4   My Adidas walk through concert doors
      And roam all over coliseum floors.   *My Adidas [1986]*[1]

5   You Be Illin'   *Song title [1986]*[1]

Sister Souljah [Lisa Williamson]   1964–

6   *[On the Los Angeles riots:]* If black people kill black people every day,
      why not have a week and kill white people? . . . In other words, white people,
      this government, and that mayor were well aware of the fact that black
      people were dying every day in Los Angeles under gang violence. So if you're
      a gang member and you would normally be killing somebody, why not kill a
      white person? Do you think that somebody thinks that white people are
      better, or above and beyond dying, when they would kill their own kind?
                               Interview in the Washington Post [May 13, 1992]

7   Brooklyn-born I don't have no sob stories for you about rats and roa-
      ches and pissy-pew hallways. I came busting out of my momma's big coo-
      chie on January 28, 1977, during one of New York's worst snowstorms. So
      my mother named me Winter.   *The Coldest Winter Ever [1999]*

8   It might be hard to believe, but the air in prison is different. There's
      like one thousand people sucking on the one little piece of fresh air until
      it turns stale.   *The Coldest Winter Ever*

Tavis Smiley   1964–

9   There is no "them"; there is only "us." Remember "us"? We the
      people? . . . We the people say that in the most multicultural, multiracial and

---

[1]With Rick Rubin; all other songs with Lawrence Smith.

multiethnic America ever, now is the time to make real the promises of our democracy.... Now is the time to stop talking about our pain and to start talking about our plan.

The Covenant with Black America [2006], introduction

Yvonne Vera

1964–2005

1   There is a severe moment one wishes to retreat from because the time before, in its not-knowing, its not-tragedy, is preferable and consoling, and good.

Butterfly Burning [1998], ch. 21

Keith Boykin

1965–

2   Only when African Americans, the lesbian and gay community, and families accept black homosexuals and love them for who they are will these now separate families regain many of their members. In doing so, they will help some to find their way back home and discover that many others are already there.

One More River to Cross [1996], last lines

3   You don't have to be black, you don't have to be male, you don't have to be HIV positive, and you don't even have to be in a relationship to be on the down low. The down low is everything and nothing.... It can mean whatever the user wants it to mean. For closeted black gay and bisexual men, the down low is a way to validate their masculinity. For straight black women, the down low is a way to avoid the difficult issues of personal responsibility. For white America, the down low is a way to pathologize black lives.

Beyond the Down Low [2005]

Eric B[arrier]

1965–

and

Rakim [William Griffin]

1968–

4   Thinkin' of a master plan
'Cause ain't nuthin but sweat inside my hand
So I dig into my pocket, all my money is spent
So I dig deeper but still comin' up with lint
So I start my mission, leave my residence
Thinkin' how could I get some dead presidents?

Paid in Full [1986]

5   Hit the studio, 'cause I'm paid in full.

Paid in Full

6   In this journey you're the journal, I'm the journalist.
Am I eternal or an eternalist?

Follow the Leader [1988]

1   Since you was tricked, I have to raise ya
     From the cradle to the grave
     But remember, you're not a slave.   *Follow the Leader*

2   Rap is rhythm and poetry.   *Follow the Leader*

3   I was a fiend before I became a teen
     I melted microphones instead of cones of ice cream
     Music orientated so when hip-hop was originated
     Fitted like pieces of puzzles — complicated.   *Microphone Fiend [1988]*

Thelma Golden   1965–

4   Post-black was the new black.   *Freestyle [2001], introduction*

Jazzy Jeff [Jeffrey Townes]   1965–

and

Will[ard Christopher] "The Fresh Prince" Smith [Jr.]   1968–

5   Parents Just Don't Understand   *Song title [1988]*

Rodney [Glen] King   1965–2012

6   I just want to say, you know, can we all get along?
                        Response to the Los Angeles riots [May 1, 1992]

KRS-One [Laurence Parker]   1965–

7   Cocaine business controls America
     Ganja business controls America
     KRS-One come to start some hysteria
     Illegal business controls America.   *Illegal Business [1988]*

8   Some MCs be talkin' and talkin'
     Tryin' to show how black people are walkin
     But I don't walk this way to portray
     Or reinforce stereotypes of today
     Like all my brothas eat chicken and watermelon
     Talk broken English and drug sellin'
     See I'm tellin, and teaching real facts
     The way some act in rap is kind of wack
     And it lacks creativity and intelligence
     But they don't care 'cause the company's sellin' it.

                                        My Philosophy [1988]   541

1   Maybe I should write some songs like Mozart
'Cause many people don't believe rap is an art.

House Niggas [1991]

2   Rap is something you do, hip-hop is something you live.

Interview. Rap Pages [October 1995]

John McWhorter   1965–

3   More and more of us are realizing that the enshrinement of victimhood as an identity and a focus upon tribalism over hybridicity has fallen
out of step with our historical moment and become an obstacle to progress,
and more and more of us are saying this out loud. There will remain those
who can only see us as "sell-outs," but as barriers to black achievement continue to fall away by the month, we're going to keep coming, more every
year, and I do not mean only a few black academics, but black people from
all walks of life.... To those black Americans out there who are tired of
being told that to be black one must be a provincial, anti-intellectual
underdog, I beseech you all to join in reviving the Struggle and getting back
to making our way up the last few steps to the mountaintop. Don't be
afraid. The ones calling the tune today will be curiosities in the history books
tomorrow. We are the future. It's time for *us* to STAND UP!!!

Losing the Race [2000]

N.W.A. [Niggas with Attitude]
Dr. Dre [Andre R. Young]   1965–

and

Ice Cube [O'Shea Jackson]   1969–

and

MC Ren [Lorenzo Patterson]   1969–

4   Fuck tha police
Comin' straight from the underground
A young nigga got it bad 'cause I'm brown
And not the other color so police think
They have the authority to kill a minority.   *Fuck tha Police [1988]*

John Ridley   1965–

5   I have no qualm about using the word *nigger*. It is a word. It is in the
English lexicon, and no amount of political correctness, no amputation into

"the *n*-word" — as if by the castration of a few letters we should then be able to conceptualize its meaning without feeling its sting — will remove it from reality.

> *The Manifesto of Ascendancy for the Modern American Nigger.*
> *Esquire [December 2006]*

Slick Rick [Richard Walters]   1965–

1   Sirens sounded, he seemed astounded,
and before long the little boy got surrounded.
He dropped his gun, so went the glory,
and this is the way I have to end this story,
He was only seventeen, in a madman's dream,
the cops shot the kid, I still hear him scream.
This ain't funny so don't ya dare laugh,
just another case about the wrong path,
Straight and narrow or your soul gets cast.

> *Children's Story [1988]*

David Adjaye   1966–

2   Buildings are deeply emotive structures which form our psyche. People think they're just things they maneuver through, but the makeup of a person is influenced by the nature of spaces.

> *Interview. The Guardian [February 8, 2003]*

Halle Berry   1966–

3   This moment is so much bigger than me. This moment is for Dorothy Dandridge, Lena Horne, Diahann Carroll. It's for the women that stand beside me, Jada Pinkett, Angela Bassett, Vivica Fox. And it's for every nameless, faceless woman of color that now has a chance because this door tonight has been opened.

> *Speech on becoming the first black woman to win an Academy*
> *Award for best performance by an actress in a leading role*
> *[March 24, 2002]*

Majora Carter   1966–

4   Economic degradation begets environmental degradation, which begets social degradation.

> *Green the Ghetto. Speech at the TED (Technology,*
> *Entertainment, Design) conference [February 2006]*

Doug E. Fresh [Douglas E. Davis] 1966–

1 My word is my sword
And I use my vocal cords.[1]

The Greatest Entertainer [1988]

Sybrina Fulton 1966–

2 Today it was my son. Tomorrow it might be yours.
*Statement regarding not-guilty verdict in the murder trial
of George Zimmerman, who shot and killed her
17-year-old son, Trayvon Martin [July 20, 2013]*

Chris[topher Julius] Rock [III] 1966–

3 Everything white people don't like about black people, black people really don't like about black people. It's like a civil war going on with black people and there's two sides: there's black people and there's niggers. And niggers have got to go.... I love black people, but I hate niggers.

Bring the Pain [1996]

4 White people don't know how to tell the difference between one black man and another.... They see two black men together and it's a crowd. A dangerous mob. *Rock This! [1997]*

5 You don't need no gun control. We need some bullet control.... I think all bullets should cost $5,000.... You know why? Cause if a bullet cost $5,000 there'd be no more innocent bystanders. *Bigger and Blacker [1999]*

6 A man is basically as faithful as his options.

Bigger and Blacker

7 When you're white the sky's the limit. When you're black the limit's the sky. *Bigger and Blacker*

8 We need a new leader. We ain't had a black leader in a while.... We had Martin Luther King and Malcolm X and ever since then a bunch of substitute teachers. *Bigger and Blacker*

9 People hate America; the number one reason is because of our religion. Americans worship money, we worship money. Separate God from school; separate God from work; separate God from government, but on your money it says in God we trust. All my life I've been looking for God and He's right in my pocket. *Never Scared [2004]*

---

[1]Doug E. Fresh, the first "human beat box," uses his vocals to imitate the sounds of drums and other instruments.

Natasha Trethewey   1966–

1   *Goodbye . . .*
    is the waving map of your palm, is
    a stone on my tongue.

                        Bellocq's Ophelia [2002]. Letter Home

2   All the grave markers, all the crude headstones —
    water-lost. Now fish dart among their bones,
    and we listen for what the waves intone.
    Only the fort remains, near forty feet high,
    round, unfinished, half open to the sky,
    the elements — wind, rain — God's deliberate eye.

                Native Guard [2006]. Elegy for the Native Guards

3   Death stops the body's work, the soul's a journeyman.

                        Native Guard. Graveyard Blues

4   That home-going road's always full of holes;
    Though we slow down, time's wheel still rolls.

                        Native Guard. Graveyard Blues

5   You can get there from here, though
    there's no going home.   *Native Guard. Theories of Time and Space*

Mike [Michael Gerard] Tyson   1966–

6   I am many things. I am an animal. I am a convicted rapist, a hell-
    raiser, a loving father, a semi-good husband. You don't know me.

                Statement at press conference [September 14, 2000]

7   Everyone has a plan until they get punched in the mouth.   *Attributed*

8   I know at times I come across like a Neanderthal or a babbling idiot,
    but I like that person. I like to show you that person because that's who you
    all come to see. I'm Tyson. I'm a tyrannical titan. And sometimes I say,
    "God, it would be good to be a fake somebody rather than a real nobody."

                Statement during a conversation with a group of reporters.
                Quoted in the New York Times [May 21, 2002]

Michelle Alexander   1967–

9   In the era of colorblindness, it is no longer socially permissible to use
    race, explicitly, as a justification for discrimination, exclusion, and social
    contempt. So we don't. Rather than rely on race, we use our criminal justice
    system to label people or color "criminals" and then engage in all the prac-
    tices we supposedly left behind. Today it is perfectly legal to discriminate

against criminals in nearly all the ways that it was once legal to discriminate against African Americans. . . . As a criminal, you have scarcely more rights, and arguably less respect, than a black man living in Alabama at the height of Jim Crow. We have not ended racial caste in America; we have merely redesigned it.

The New Jim Crow [2010], introduction

Jamie Foxx [Eric Bishop] 1967–

1   My grandmother's name is Estelle Marie Talley. She's not here tonight. And this is going to be the toughest part. But she was my first acting teacher. She told me to stand up straight. Put your shoulders back. Act like you got some sense. . . . She still talks to me now. Only now, she talks to me in my dreams. And I can't wait to go to sleep tonight because we got a lot to talk about.

Acceptance speech for Academy Award for best actor in a leading role [February 27, 2005]

Marie NDiaye 1967–

2   So many women here are ruled by their bodies. All buxom or bony and I don't want a confused woman or a careless woman or a depressed woman, Franck, I want a woman who is entirely under control. How can a woman look after my house and my children if she can't even look after her own body?

Hilda [2002], act I, sc. i[1] [Mrs. Lemarchand]

3   Khady was so hungry she bit violently into the bread. . . . Her gums were bleeding. They left traces of blood on the bread. But her heart was beating gently, calmly, and she felt the same way: gentle and calm, beyond reach, shielded by her unshakable humanity.

Three Strong Women [2012], pt. 3[2]

Diran Adebayo 1968–

4   The games that white folk play on blacks are straightforward enough and well documented; the games that black folk play on whites are equally obvious. But the games that black folk play on one another! Well, that's something else again.

Some Kind of Black [1996]

---

[1]Translation by SARAH WOODS.

[2]Translation by JOHN FLETCHER.

That now was still something she never doubted: that she was indivisible and precious and could only ever be herself. — MARIE NDIAYE, *Three Strong Women*, pt. 3

Big Daddy Kane [Antonio Hardy]   1968–

1   So full of action, my name should be a verb.
     My voice will float on every note
     When I clear my throat, that's all she wrote.

                                        Raw [1988]

Sean Combs [P. Diddy] [Puff Daddy]   1968–

2   It's all about the Benjamins, baby.   *It's All About the Benjamins [1997]*[1]

De La Soul
Trugoy the Dove [David Jolicoeur]   1968–

and

Prince Paul [Paul Huston]   1967–

and

Maseo [Vincent L. Mason, Jr.]   1970–

and

Posdnuos [Kelvin Mercer]   1969–

3   Mary had a little lamb — that's a fib
     She had two twins though, and one crib
     Now she's only fourteen — what a start
     But this effect is found common in these parts
     Now life in this world can be such a bitch
     And dreams are often torn and shattered and hard to stitch
     Negative the attitude that runs the show
     When the stage is the g-h-e-t-t-o.   *Ghetto Thang [1988]*

4   Mirror mirror on the wall
     Tell me mirror what is wrong?
     Can it be my De La Clothes
     Or is it just my De La Song?
     What I do ain't make believe
     People say I sit and try
     But when it comes to being De La
     It's just me myself and I.   *Me, Myself and I [1988]*

---

[1]With Lil' Kim [Kimberly Jones], Jason Phillips, David Styles, Notorius B.I.G. [Christopher Wallace], Sean Jacobs, and Deric Angelettie.

[Anthony Kapel] Van Jones 1968–

1   We want to build a green economy strong enough to lift people out of poverty. We want to create green pathways out of poverty and into great careers for America's children. We want this "green wave" to lift all boats. This country can save the polar bears and poor kids too.

The Green Collar Economy [2008]

LL Cool J [James Todd Smith] 1968–

2   L.L. Cool J. is hard as hell
Battle anybody I don't care who you tell.   *Rock the Bells [1985]*

3   I Can't Live Without My Radio   *Song title [1985]*

4   I want a girl with extensions in her hair
Bamboo earrings
At least two pair.   *Around the Way Girl [1990]*

Meshell Ndegeocello [Johnson] 1968–

5   If That's Your Boy Friend (He Wasn't Last Night)   *Song Title [1993]*

6   The capitalistic hand around my throat
Shoot'n' up dope just to cope,
In this dehumanizing society.   *Shoot'n' Up and Gett'n High [1993]*

7   Illusions of her virginal white beauty,
Dancing in your head
You let my sisters go by
Your soul's on ice.   *Soul on Ice [1993]*

Chris Ofili 1968–

8   *[On use of elephant dung in controversial pieces such as "Holy Virgin Mary":]* It's what people really want from black artists. We're the voodoo king, the voodoo queen, the witch doctor, the drug dealer, the *magicien de la terre*. The exotic, the decorative. I'm giving them all of that, but it's packaged slightly differently.   *Interview [March 23, 1995]*[1]

John Singleton 1968–

9   Remember this: Any fool with a dick can make a baby, but only a real man can raise children.   *Boyz n the Hood [1991] [Furious]*

[1]From *Brilliant!* [1995], edited by STUART MORGAN ET AL.

1   Well, how do you think the crack rock gets into the country? We don't own any planes. We don't own no ships. We are not the people who are flying and floating that shit in here. I know every time you turn on a TV that's what you see: black people, selling the rock, pushing the rock. Yeah, I know, but that wasn't a problem as long as it was here. It wasn't a problem until it was in Iowa and it showed up on Wall Street where there are hardly any black people.   *Boyz n the Hood [Furious]*

2   Turned on the TV this morning. Had this shit on about living in a violent world. Showed all these foreign places foreigners live and all. I started thinking, man. Either they don't know, don't show, or don't care about what's going on in the 'hood.   *Boyz n the Hood [Doughboy]*

3   You still got one brother left, man.   *Boyz n the Hood [Tre]*

Will[ard Christopher] "The Fresh Prince" Smith [Jr.]   1968–
and

[Harold] Hype Williams   1970–

4   Gettin' Jiggy wit It   *Song title [1997]*

Farai Chideya   1969–

5   "Nigger" is the all-American trump card, the nuclear bomb of racial epithets.   *The Color of Our Future [1999]*

Cory Booker   1969–

6   There is a boundless reservoir of power in all of our communities, a power not conferred by the powerful but at ready access to anyone willing to claim it. Nothing is beyond the capacity of a unified community, people acting on a moral imperative.

The Reformer. Esquire [December 2002]

7   The real test of leadership has never been who can get people to follow them. We've got charismatic leaders who get followed a lot. The real test of leadership is to motivate people to be leaders themselves and to carry the burden.

Quoted in GWEN IFILL, *The Breakthrough:*
Politics and Race in the Age of Obama [2009]

Edwidge Danticat   1969–

8   Tante Atie once said that love is like rain. It comes in a drizzle sometimes. Then it starts pouring and if you're not careful it will drown you.

Breath, Eyes, Memory [1994], ch. 9

1 I come from a place where breath, eyes, and memory are one, a place from which you carry your past like the hair on your head. Where women return to their children as butterflies or as tears in the eyes of statues that their daughters pray to. My mother was as brave as stars at dawn. She too was from this place. My mother was like that woman who could never bleed and then could never stop bleeding, the one who gave in to her pain, to live as a butterfly. Yes, my mother was like me. *Breath, Eyes, Memory, ch. 35*

2 When you write, it's like braiding your hair. Taking a handful of coarse unruly strands and attempting to bring them unity. Your fingers have still not perfected the task. Some of the braids are long, others are short. Some are thick, others are thin. Some are heavy. Others are light.
Krik? Krak! [1995]

3 Me, I have no paper in my palms to say where I belong. My son, this one who was born here in this land, has no papers in his palms to say where he belongs. Those who work in the cane mills, the owners keep their papers, so they have this as a rope around their necks. Papers are everything. You have no papers in your hands, they do with you what they want.
The Farming of Bones [1998], ch. 14

4 Misery won't touch you gentle. It always leaves its thumbprints on you; sometimes it leaves them for others to see, sometimes for nobody but you to know of. *The Farming of Bones, ch. 31*

5 When you hear that someone has died whom you've not seen in a long time, it's not too difficult to pretend that it hasn't really happened, that the person is continuing to live just as she has before, in your absence, out of your sight. *Brother, I'm Dying [2008]*

Jay Z [Shawn Carter] 1969–

6 I'm from the school of the hard knocks,
We must not let outsiders violate our blocks, and my plot
Let's stick up the world and split it fifty-fifty
Let's take the dough and stay real jiggy.
Hard Knock Life (Ghetto Anthem) [1998]

7 Now all the teachers couldn't reach me and my momma couldn't beat me
Hard enough to match the pain of my pop not seein' me
So with that disdain in my membrane
Got on my pimp game, fuck the world, my defense came.
December 4th [2003]

8 You gotta get, that, dirt off your shoulder.
Dirt off Your Shoulder [2003]

1   I'm not afraid of dying
     I'm afraid of not trying.   *Beach Chair [2006]*

Wyclef Jean   1969–

2   Every time I make a run, girl, you turn around and cry
     I ask myself why, oh why
     See you must understand, I can't work a 9 to 5
     So I'll be gone 'til November.
                                                    Gone 'til November [1997]

3   Lifestyles of the rich and famous
     Some die with a name, some die nameless.   *Gone 'til November*

Dambisa Moyo   1969–

4   The trouble with the aid-dependency model is, of course, that Africa is
     fundamentally kept in its perpetual childlike state.
                      *Dead Aid: Why Aid Is Not Working and How There Is
                      Another Way for Africa [2009]*

Naughty by Nature
DJ Kay Gee [Kier Gist]   1969–

and

Vin Rock [Vincent Brown]   1970–

and

Treach [Anthony Criss]   1970–

5   A ghetto bastard, born next to the projects,
     Livin' in the slums with bums, I said, "Now why Treach,
     Do I have to be like this?"
     Mama said I'm priceless
     So why am I worthless?
     Starving — it's just what being nice gets.
                      *Ghetto Bastard, Everything's Gonna Be All Right
                      [1991]*

6   If you ain't never been to the ghetto
     Don't ever come to the ghetto
     'Cause you wouldn't understand the ghetto
     So stay the fuck outta the ghetto.

                      Ghetto Bastard, Everything's Gonna Be All Right

Tyler Perry
1969–

1   Love is stronger than any addiction, baby; hell, it is one.

Diary of a Mad Black Woman [2005] [Madea]

2   Everybody's got skeletons in the closet. Every once in a while, you've got to open up the closet and let the skeletons breathe.

Don't Make a Black Woman Take Off Her Earrings: Madea's Uninhibited Commentaries on Love and Life [2006]

3   I tell people, don't go out there trying to get no relationship when you ain't ready. Hell, sit back and work on yourself. How are you going to offer something to somebody else if you ain't been to visit *you* yet?

Don't Make a Black Woman Take Off Her Earrings

4   Speak your mind or lose it!

Don't Make a Black Woman Take Off Her Earrings

Kara Walker
1969–

5   I often compare my method of working to that of a well-meaning freed woman in a Northern state who is attempting to delineate the horrors of Southern slavery but with next to no resources, other than some paper and a pen knife and some people she'd like to kill.

Interview [July 21, 1996][1]

6   The story that has interested me is the story of Muck.

After the Deluge [2006]

Colson Whitehead
1969–

7   This need to rise is biological, transcending the vague physics of department store architecture. We choose the escalator, we choose the elevator, and these choices say much about who we are.

The Intuitionist [1999], pt. 2

8   After the killing is over, after the gunman has slid to the ground, after the gunsmoke has dissipated into the invisible, the witnesses rouse themselves into this world again, find themselves waking in warm huddles, reinforcing each other's humanity; they blink at their surroundings to squeeze violence from their eyes.... The witnesses thank God. The witnesses share what they have seen and fit their perspectives into one narrative through a system of sobbing and barter. In these first few minutes a thousand different stories collide; this making of truth is violence too, out of which facts are formed.

John Henry Days [2001], pt. 1

---

[1]From *Kara Walker: Pictures from Another Time* [2002], edited by ANNETTE DIXON.

1   No matter how long you have been here, you are a New Yorker the first time you say, That used to be Munsey's, or That used to be the Tic Toc Lounge.... You are a New Yorker when what was there before is more real and solid than what is here now.   *The Colossus of New York [2004]*

2   Colored, Negro, Afro-American, African American . . . Every couple of years someone came up with something that got us an inch closer to the truth. Bit by bit we crept along. As if that thing we believed to be approaching actually existed.   *Apex Hides the Hurt [2006]*

3   We never see other people anyway, only the monsters we make of them.   *Zone One [2011]*

Lydia R. Diamond   1970–

4   Look baby, you just have to look at everyone like they're bugs under a microscope. Like ants. Figure out the patterns.
         Stick Fly [2008], act II, sc. iii [Taylor]

The Jungle Brothers
Afrika Baby Bam [Nathaniel Hall]   1970–

and

Mike Gee [Michael Small]   1969–

5   Listen please to this fact:
      Black is black is black is black.   *Black Is Black [1988]*

Queen Latifah [Dana Owens]   1970–

6   It's time to teach the def, the dumb, the blind
      That black-on-black crime only shackles and binds.
               The Evil That Men Do [1989]

7   U.N.I.T.Y. that's a unity. (You gotta let him know)
      U.N.I.T.Y., Love a black woman from (You gotta let him know)
      infinity to infinity (You ain't a bitch or a ho)   *U.N.I.T.Y. [1993]*

8   The key is not to rule others but to reign over yourself.
               Ladies First: Revelations of a Strong Woman [1999]

Marcus Samuelsson [Kassahun "Joar" Tsegie]   1970–

9   Through food we express love. We bring comfort and hope. We forge new relationships and strengthen old bonds. Food reaffirms not only our humanity but the joy of being alive.   *The Meaning of Food [2004]*

1   A hundred years ago, black men and women had to fight to get out of
the kitchen. These days, we have to fight to get *in*.

Yes, Chef [2012]

Kevin Young   1970–

2   The day folds up like money
if you're lucky.

Jelly Roll [2003]. *Busking*

3   In the Africa
of your eyes — my

lost tribe —
I am safari

this stumbling
shooting off

foolishly. Apologies —
you are no country.

Jelly Roll. Tune

4   I showed up for jury duty —
turns out the one on trial was me.

Paid me for my time & still
I couldn't make bail.

Black Cat Blues. From The Best American Poetry 2005,
edited by PAUL MULDOON [2005]

5   In my movie there are no
horses, no heroes
only draftees fleeing

into the pines, some few
who survive, gravely
wounded, lying

burrowed beneath the dead —
silent until the enemy
bayonets what is believed
to be the last of the breathing.

For the Confederate Dead [2007]

Erykah Badu [Erica Wright]   1971–

6   Peace and blessings manifest with every lesson learned
If your knowledge were your wealth then it would be well earned.

On and On [1997]

1   They play it safe, are quick to assassinate what they do not understand.
     They move in packs ingesting more and more fear with every act of hate on
          one another.
     They feel most comfortable in groups, less guilt to swallow.
     They are us.   *Window Seat [2010]*[1]

MC Lyte [Lana Moorer]   1971–

2   I am a Rock and you are just a pebble.   *Lyte as a Rock [1988]*

The Roots
Black Thought [Tariq Collins Trotter]   1971–

and

Questlove [Ahmir Thompson]   1971–

3   Pretend-to-be cats don't seem to know they limitation
     Exact replication and false representation
     You wanna be a man, then stand your own
     To MC requires skills, I demand some shown.

                                                 What They Do [1996][2]

4   Yo, you need to walk straight, master your high
     Son you missin' out on what's passing you by
     I done seen the streets suck a lot of cats dry
     But not you and I my nigga
     We got to get, over, over the water.   *Water [2002]*

5   Between the greenhouse gases and earth spinnin' off its axis
     Got mother nature doin' back flips
     The natural disasters
     It's like 80 degrees in Alaska
     You in trouble if you not an Onassis
     It ain't hard to tell that the conditions is drastic
     Just turn on the telly check for the news flashin'
     How you want it bagged, paper or plastic?
     Lost in translation or just lost in traffic?
     Yo, I don't wanna floss I done lost my passion
     And I aint trying to climb, Yo, I lost my traction.

                                                    Rising Down [2008]

---

[1]With James Poyser.
[2]With Leonard Hubbard and Raphael Saadiq.

THE ROOTS — SNOOP DOGG

1 Out on the streets, where I grew up
  First thing they teach us, not to give a fuck
  That type of thinking can't get you nowhere
  Someone has to care.   *How I Got Over [2010]*[1]

Tupac Shakur   1971–1996

2 Much love to my brothers in the pen
  See ya when I free ya if not when they shove me in.
          Holler If Ya Hear Me [1993]

3 I wonder why we take from our women
  Why we rape our women, do we hate our women?
  I think it's time to kill for our women
  Time to heal our women, be real to our women
  And if we don't we'll have a race of babies
  That will hate the ladies that make the babies
  And since a man can't make one
  He has no right to tell a woman when and where to create one
  So will the real men get up
  I know you're fed up, ladies, but keep your head up.
          Keep Ya Head Up [1993]

4 They got money for wars, but can't feed the poor
  Say there ain't no hope for the youth and the truth is
  It ain't no hope for the future
  And then they wonder why we crazy. *Keep Ya Head Up*

5 I was given this world, I didn't make it. *Keep Ya Head Up*

6 Everything will be alright if ya hold on
  It's a struggle everyday, gotta roll on
  And there's no way I can pay you back
  But my plan is to show you that I understand
  You are appreciated.   *Dear Mama [1995]*

7 If I die, I wonder if heaven got a ghetto.
       I Wonder If Heaven Got a Ghetto [1997]

Snoop Dogg [Calvin Broadus, Jr.]   1971–

8 Ain't nuthin' but a G thang, baby.
        Nuthin' but a "G" Thang [1992]

   [1]With Dice Raw.

Touré [Neblett] 1971–

1 To be born Black is an extraordinary gift bestowing access to an unbelievably rich legacy of joy. It'll lift you to ecstasy and give you pain that can make you stronger than you imagined possible. To experience the full possibilities of Blackness, you must break free of the strictures sometimes placed on Blackness from outside the African-American culture and also from within it. These attempts to conscript the potential complexity of Black humanity often fly in the face of the awesome breadth of Black history. . . . Some Blacks may see the range of Black identity as something obvious but I know there are many who are unforgiving and intolerant of Black heterogeneity and still believe in concepts like "authentic" or "legitimate" Blackness. There is no such thing.   *Who's Afraid of Post-Blackness?* [2011]

The Notorious B.I.G. [Christopher Wallace] 1972–1997

2 I don't wanna live no more
Sometimes I hear death knocking at my front door
Ready to Die [1994]. Everyday Struggle

3 Mo Money, Mo Problems
Song title [1997]

Shaquille "Shaq" O'Neal 1972–

4 *[On basketball:]* It's ballet, hip-hop, and kung fu. The ballet is grace, the hip-hop is cool, and the kung fu is kill the opponent.
Interview. New York Magazine [February 15, 2010]

Tracy K[athleen] Smith 1972–

5 They defy gravity to feel tugged back.
The clatter, the mad slap of landing.

Duende [2007], st. 1

6 Time never stops, but does it end? And how many lives
Before take-off, before we find ourselves
Beyond ourselves, all glam-glow, all twinkle and gold?
Life on Mars [2011]. Don't You Wonder, Sometimes?, st. 2

7 Perhaps the great error is believing we're alone,
That the others have come and gone — a momentary blip —
When all along, space might be choc-full of traffic,
Bursting at the seams with energy we neither feel
Nor see, flush against us, living, dying, deciding.
Life on Mars. My God, It's Full of Stars, st. 3

Dave Chappelle [David Khari Webber] 1973–

1   *[On walking away from a $50 million television deal:]* I want to make sure I'm dancing and not shuffling.

Interview. TIME.com [May 2005]

2   A lot of white kids, you got things accessible to you like therapy. We don't have that. We have liquor stores and weed.

Interview. Inside the Actor's Studio [2006]

3   The worst thing to call somebody is crazy. It's dismissive. "I don't understand this person, so they're crazy." That's bullshit.

Interview. Inside the Actor's Studio

4   Every black American is bilingual. We speak street vernacular and job interview.

Interview. Inside the Actor's Studio

5   You can get infamous, but you can't get unfamous.

Interview. Inside the Actor's Studio

Staceyann Chin 1973–

6   Imagination is the bridge between
the things we know for sure
and the things we need to believe
When our world becomes unbearable.

Def Poetry Jam on Broadway [2003].
And These Are Only Some of the Things I Believe

Savion Glover 1973–

7   I want to bring in 'da noise. I want to bring in 'da funk.

Bring In 'da Noise, Bring In 'da Funk [1996]

Benjamin T[odd] Jealous 1973–

8   The right to vote is the right upon which all of our rights are leveraged and without which none can be protected.

Keynote address at the annual convention of the National
Association for the Advancement of Colored People, Los Angeles
[July 25, 2011]

9   I stand here as a son, father, uncle who is tired of being scared for our boys. I'm tired of telling our young men how they can't dress, where they can't go and how they can't behave.

Statement at town hall meeting calling for arrest in the fatal
shooting of unarmed seventeen-year-old Trayvon Martin,
Sanford, Florida [March 20, 2012]

1   Stop-and-frisk is the most massive local racial profiling program in
the country. All children, of every color, should feel protected by our police,
not threatened, harassed or intimidated.

> *Statement regarding Silent Father's Day March against the*
> *New York City Police Department's "stop-and-frisk" practices*
> *disproportionately aimed at black and Latino men [June 17, 2012]*

Sarah Jones   1973–

2   Your revolution will not happen between these thighs.

> *Your Revolution [1999]*

3   Here in America we have freedom to say what we want, be what we
want, to decide what happens in our country. We even get to decide what
happens in other people's countries.

> *Bridge and Tunnel [2004] [Lorraine Levine]*

Mos Def [Yasiin Bey] [Dante Smith]   1973–

4   My restlessness is my nemesis
It's hard to really chill and sit still.   *Hip Hop [1999]*

Mos Def [Yasiin Bey] [Dante Smith]   1973–

and

Talib Kweli [Greene]   1975–

5   I find it's distressin', there's never no in-between
We either niggas or kings, we either bitches or queens
The deadly ritual seems immersed in the perverse
Full of short attention spans, short tempers, and short skirts
Long barrel automatics released in short bursts
The length of black life is treated with short worth.

> *Thieves in the Night [1998]*

Nas [Nasir Jones]   1973–

6   Street's disciple, my raps are trifle
I shoot slugs from my brain just like a rifle.   *Live at the BBQ [1991]*

7   Hip Hop Is Dead   *Song title [2006]*

Kiese Laymon   1974–

8   Faster. Slower...Easy remedies like eating your way out of sad, or
fucking your way out of sad, or lying your way out of sad, or slanging your
way out of sad, or robbing your way out of sad, or gambling your way out of

sad, or shooting your way out of sad, are just slower, more acceptable ways for desperate folks, and especially paroled black boys in our country, to kill ourselves and others close to us in America.

How to Slowly Kill Yourself and Others in America: A Remembrance. gawker.com [July 28, 2012]

Syreeta McFadden
1974–

1   Only in America can a dead black boy go on trial for his own murder.

Statement in response to national discussion of the trial of George Zimmerman, who shot and killed Trayvon Martin, an unarmed 17-year-old. Twitter [July 12, 2013]

André 3000 [André Lauren Benjamin]
1975–

2   Shake it like a Polaroid picture.

Hey Ya! [2003]

50 Cent [Curtis James Jackson III]
1975–

3   Go shorty, it's your birthday.

In Da Club [2003]

4   Get Rich or Die Tryin'

Title of debut album [2003]

The Fugees
Lauryn Hill
1975–

and

Wyclef Jean
1969–

and

Pras [Praskazrel Michel]
1972–

5   Oooh la la la,
It's the way that we rock when we're doing our thing
Oooh la la la,
It's the natural la that the Refugees bring.   *Fu-Gee-La [1996][1]*

Lauryn Hill
1975–

6   You might win some but you just lost one.

The Miseducation of Lauryn Hill [1998]. Lost Ones

7   Everything is everything
What is meant to be will be.

---

[1]With Salaam Remi Gibbs.

After winter, must come spring
Change, it comes eventually.

The Miseducation of Lauryn Hill. Everything Is Everything

India.Arie [India Arie Simpson] 1975–

1 I'm not the average girl from your video,
And I ain't built like a supermodel
But I learned to love myself unconditionally,
Because I am a queen. *Video [2001]*[1]

2 I Am Not My Hair *Song title [2006]*[2]

Marion Jones 1975–

3 It's hard to have a bad hair day when you're famous.

Interview. Ebony [March 2001]

4 It is with a great amount of shame that I stand before you and tell you that I have betrayed your trust. I want you to know that I have been dishonest and you have the right to be angry with me. I have let them [my family] down, I have let my country down and I have let myself down.

Press conference to admit to using steroids [October 5, 2007]

Zadie Smith 1975–

5 Greeting cards routinely tell us everybody deserves love. No. Everybody deserves clean water. Not everybody deserves love all the time.

White Teeth [2000], ch. 17

6 But surely to tell these tall tales and others like them would be to spread the myth, the wicked lie, that the past is always tense and the future, perfect. *White Teeth, ch. 20*

7 The greatest lie ever told about love is that it sets you free.

On Beauty [2005]

8 Any woman who counts on her face is a *fool*.

On Beauty [Kiki]

9 Tell the truth through whichever veil comes to hand — but tell it. Resign yourself to the lifelong sadness that comes from never being satisfied.
*Ten Rules for Writing Fiction. The Guardian
[February 19, 2010]*

10 I am the sole author of the dictionary that defines me. *NW [2013]*

---

[1]With Carlos Broady and Shannon Sanders.
[2]With Shannon Sanders and Andrew Ramsey.

[Eldrick] Tiger Woods 1975–

1   *[On his Caucasian, Black American, American Indian, Thai, and Chinese ancestry:]* Growing up, I came up with this name: I'm a "Cablinasian."

Interview. Oprah Winfrey Show [April 24, 1997]

Chimamanda Ngozi Adichie 1977–

2   There are people . . . who think that we cannot rule ourselves because the few times we tried, we failed, as if all the others who rule themselves today got it right the first time. It is like telling a crawling baby who tries to walk, and then falls back on his buttocks, to stay there. As if the adults walking past him did not all crawl, once.   *Purple Hibiscus [2003]*

3   There are some things that happen for which we can formulate no whys, for which whys simply do not exist and, perhaps, are not necessary.

Purple Hibiscus

4   Master was a little crazy; he had spent too many years reading books overseas, talked to himself in his office, did not always return greetings, and had too much hair. Ugwu's aunty said this in a low voice as they walked on the path. "But he is a good man," she added. "And as long as you work well, you will eat well. You will even eat meat every day."

Half a Yellow Sun [2006], opening lines

5   My point is that the only authentic identity for the African is the tribe. . . . I am Nigerian because a white man created Nigeria and gave me that identity. I am black because the white man constructed *black* to be as different as possible from his *white*. But I was Igbo before the white man came.   *Half a Yellow Sun [Master]*

6   This was love: a string of coincidences that gathered significance and became miracles.

Half a Yellow Sun

7   You can't write a script in your mind and then force yourself to follow it. You have to let yourself be.

Half a Yellow Sun [Kainene]

8   "You must never behave as if your life belongs to a man. Do you hear me?" Aunty Ifeka said. "Your life belongs to you and you alone."

Half a Yellow Sun

9   The single story creates stereotypes, and the problem with stereotypes is not that they are untrue, but that they are incomplete. They make one story become the only story. . . . The consequence of the single story is this: it robs people of dignity.

TED Talks [2009]

Terius "The-Dream" Nash   1977–

1   If you like it then you should've put a ring on it.[1]

Single Ladies (Put a Ring on It) [2008]

Kanye West   1977–

2   We at war with terrorism, racism, and most of all we at war with ourselves.

Jesus Walks [2004]

3   I ain't saying she a gold digger
     But she ain't messing with no broke niggas.   *Gold Digger [2005]*

4   George Bush doesn't care about black people.

*On the federal government's inaction in New Orleans following
Hurricane Katrina. Telethon appearance [September 2, 2005]*

Taiye Selasi   1979–

5   We are Afropolitans: not citizens, but Africans of the world.

*Bye-Bye, Babar (Or: What Is an Afropolitan?). Essay
[March 2005]*

Venus Williams   1980–

6   It's strange. I always dream I win a grand slam. When I wake up, it's a
nightmare. Now that I've got it, I don't have to wake up like that anymore.

*Statement after becoming first black woman to win at
Wimbledon since Althea Gibson [July 8, 2000]*

Katori Hall   1981–

7   You gone have to pass off that baton, little man. You in a relay race, albeit
     the fastest runner we done ever seen't. But you 'bout to burn out,
     superstar. You gone need to pass off that baton.

The Mountaintop [2011] [Camae]

8   Some say it take a village to raise a chile. Some time the child gotsta raise
     they goddamn self.   *Hurt Village [2011], epilogue [Cookie]*

Serena Williams   1981–

9   I want to go out in my peak. That's my goal. But have I peaked yet?

*Statement after winning her sixteenth Grand Slam title
[June 8, 2013]*

---

[1]When The-Dream (born Terius Nash) came up with the "put a ring on it" hook to "Single Ladies," he
told himself, "All I have to do is write around that. I'd have to be a fool to f — this up." It was 2008, and he
was in the studio with Beyoncé for the first time. Quoted in the *Wall Street Journal* [August 13, 2010].

African-American Women in Defense of Ourselves   1991

1   Throughout U.S. history Black women have been sexually stereotyped as immoral, insatiable, perverse, the initiators of all sexual contacts — abusive or otherwise. The common assumption in legal proceedings as well as in the larger society has been that Black women cannot be raped or otherwise sexually abused....

We pledge ourselves to continue to speak out in defense of one another, in defense of the African-American community and against those who are hostile to social justice, no matter what color they are. No one will speak for us but ourselves.

Excerpt from advertisement in the New York Times in support of Anita Hill [November 1991]

Anonymous: African

2   In the time when Dendid created all things,
He created the sun,
And the sun is born, and dies, and comes again.   *Old Song (Dinka)*

3   He created man,
And man is born, and dies, and does not come again.   *Old Song (Dinka)*

4   Somewhere the Sky touches the Earth, and the name of that place is the End.   *Saying (Wakamba)*

5   Everything has an end.   *Saying (Masai)*

6   When elephants fight it is the grass that suffers.   *Proverb (Kikuyu)*

7   Haste, haste has no blessing.   *Proverb (Swahili)*

8   To the person who seizes two things, one always slips from his grasp!
Proverb (Swahili)

9   The lie has seven endings.   *Proverb (Swahili)*

10   Goodness sold itself, badness flaunted itself about.
Proverb (Swahili)

11   Speak silver, reply gold.   *Proverb (Swahili)*

12   Thunder is not yet rain.   *Proverb (Kenya)*

13   The prayer of the chicken hawk does not get him the chicken.
Proverb (Swahili)

14   Wisdom is not bought.   *Proverb (Akan)*

15   Not even God is wise enough.   *Proverb (Yoruba)*

16   Leave a log in the water as long as you like: it will never be a crocodile.
Proverb (Guinea-Bissau)

1   He who is being carried does not realize how far the town is.

Proverb (Nigeria)

2   He who conceals his disease cannot expect to be cured.

Proverb (Ethiopia)

3   When the mouse laughs at the cat there is a hole nearby.

Proverb (Nigeria)

4   Don't insult the crocodile until you cross the water.

Proverb (West Africa)

5   Rats don't dance in the cat's doorway.   *Proverb (West Africa)*

6   No matter how full the river, it still wants to grow.   *Proverb (Congo)*

7   Love is like a baby: it needs to be treated tenderly.

Saying (West Africa)

8   Children are the reward of life.   *Saying (West Africa)*

9   Being well dressed does not prevent one from being poor.

Saying (Congo)

10   Rain beats a leopard's skin, but it does not wash out the spots.

Proverb (Ashanti, Ghana)

11   One falsehood spoils a thousand truths.   *Proverb (Ashanti, Ghana)*

12   The lion that roars catches no prey.   *Proverb (Uganda)*

13   By the time the fool has learned the game, the players have dispersed.   *Proverb (Ashanti, Ghana)*

14   Fire and gunpowder do not sleep together.   *Proverb (Ashanti)*

15   If you are in hiding, don't light a fire.   *Proverb (Ashanti)*

16   It is the calm and silent water that drowns a man.   *Saying (Ashanti)*

17   No one tests the depth of a river with both feet.   *Saying (Ashanti)*

18   The ruin of a nation begins in the homes of its people.

Proverb (Ashanti)

19   There is no medicine to cure hatred.   *Saying (Ashanti)*

20   When you are rich, you are hated; when you are poor, you are despised.   *Saying (Ashanti)*

21   He who upsets a thing should know how to rearrange it.

Saying (Sierra Leone)

22   If you do not step on the dog's tail, he will not bite you.

Proverb (Cameroon)

23   Knowledge is better than riches.   *Saying (Cameroon)*

1   He who learns, teaches.   *Saying (Ethiopia)*

2   Evil enters like a needle and spreads like an oak tree.

                                       Proverb (Ethiopia)

3   A close friend can become a close enemy.

                                       Saying (Ethiopia)

4   When spiderwebs unite, they can tie up a lion.   *Proverb (Ethiopia)*

5   A too modest man goes hungry.   *Saying (Ethiopia)*

6   A fool and water will go the way they are diverted.

                                       Saying (Ethiopia)

7   The house roof fights with the rain, but he who is sheltered ignores it.

                                       Proverb (Wolof)

8   He is patient, he is not angry.
He sits in silence to pass judgment.
He sees you even when he is not looking.
He stays in a far place — but his eyes are on the town.

                                 Oriki Obatala (Yoruba)[1]

9   Having thrown a stone yesterday — he kills a bird today.
Lying down, his head hits the roof.
Standing up, he cannot look into the cooking pot.
Eshu turns right into wrong, wrong into right.   *Oriki Eshu (Yoruba)*[1]

10   Esu, do not undo me,
Do not falsify the words of my mouth,
Do not misguide the movements of my feet.
You who translates yesterday's words
Into novel utterances,
Do not undo me,
I bear you sacrifice.   *Oriki Esu*[2]

11   Shango is the death that drips to, to, to
Like indigo dye dripping from a cloth.   *Oriki Shango (Yoruba)*[1]

12   We call her and she replies with wisdom.
She can cure those whom the doctor has failed.
She cures the sick with cold water.
When she cures the child, she does not change the father.
We remain in the world without fear.   *Oriki Oshun (Yoruba)*[1]

---

[1]From *Yoruba Poetry* [1959], collected and translated by Bakare Gbadamosi and Ulli Beier.

[2]From Henry Louis Gates, *The Signifying Monkey* [1989].

1   Ogun kills the thief and the owner of the stolen goods.
    Ogun kills the owner of the slave — and the slave runs away.

                                                Oriki Ogun (Yoruba)[1]

2   Ogun is the needle that pricks at both ends.   *Oriki Ogun (Yoruba)*[1]

3   The lizard cannot pretend to be a boa.

            The Oriki of Kings: Oriki of the Ogoga of Ikere (Yoruba)[1]

4   Lies travel for twenty years and never arrive.

                                                Odu Ifa (Yoruba)[1]

5   Wisdom is the finest beauty of a person.   *Odu Ifa (Yoruba)*[1]

6   Four times
            Listen Zulus.
    Listen to the people talking
    About your country.
    We hear the clans are gossiping
    Gossiping about you.   *Like Birds*[2]

7   Go round the rocks
    We are going soon.   *Jikele 'Maweni (Go Round the Rocks)*[3]

8   Come, love,
    Let us live happily.   *Woza (Come)*[3]

9   Unite.
    There is no more time for crying.
    Restore Africa. Right now. Mayibuye.   *Restore Africa to Its Owners*[3]

10 A man who pays respect to the great, paves the way for his own
    greatness.   *Proverb (Igbo)*

11 Do not look where you fell, but where you slipped.

                                                Proverb (Yoruba)

12 Until lions have their historians, tales of the hunt shall always glorify
    the hunter.   *Proverb (West Africa)*

13 A luta continua. *[The struggle continues.]*
            Slogan, African Liberation Movement [c. 1960]

14 Amandla! Awethu! *[Power is ours!]*
            Slogan, South African Liberation Movement

---

[1]From *Yoruba Poetry* [1959], collected and translated by BAKARE GBADAMOSI and ULLI BEIER.
[2]From *Lalela Zulu* [1948], edited by TRACEY HUGH.
[3]From MIRIAM MAKEBA, *The World of African Song* [1971].

Anonymous: American

1   John Henry, he was a steel-drivin' man.
He died wid a hammer in his han'.
O come long boys, an' line up de track,
For John Henry, he hain't never comin' back.[1]

John Henry told his captain,
Says, "A man ain't nothin' but a man,
And before I'd let your steam drill beat me down, Lord,
I'd die with this hammer in my hand."

John Henry [1873]

2   Stagolee, Stagolee was a man an' they killed Stagolee.

Stagolee[1]

3   Stackolee was a bad man.

Stackolee

4   Tell Me How Long the Train's Been Gone

Traditional song

5   They tell me Joe Turner's come and gone
(Oh Lordy) Got my man and gone.

Blues song

6   Love is jes a thing o' fancy,
Beauty's jes a blossom;
If you wants to git you' finger bit,
Stick it at a 'possum.[1]

Folklore

7   I went down to de river an' I couldn't get 'cross,
So I give a whole dollar fer a ole blin' hoss.[1]

Folklore

8   Juba dis, an' Juba dat,
Juba skin dat Yaller Cat. Juba! Juba![1]

Song

9   Stand back, black man,
You cain't shine.[1]

Song game

10   My ole Missus promise me,
W'en she died she'd set me free.
She lived so long dat 'er head got bal',
An' she give out'n de notion a dyin' at all.[1]

Folklore

11   Run, Nigger, run! De Patter-rollers'll ketch you.
Run, Nigger, run! It's almos' day.[1]

Folklore

---

[1]From *Thomas W. Talley's Negro Folk Tales: A New, Expanded Edition, with Music* [1991], edited by CHARLES K. WOLFE.

1   Hey Shoo-fly

     Ladies' bowtie, gentleman's necktie, hey.[1]   *Song game*

2   Shoo fly, don't bother me.   *Song game*

3   Mammy's little baby loves short'nin', short'nin',

     Mammy's little baby loves short'nin' bread.[1]   *Song*

4   I would rather be a Negro than a poor white man.   *Song*

5   De boll-weevil's in de cotton,

     De cut-worm's in de corn,

     De Devil's in de white man;

     An' de war's a-gwine on.

     Poor Nigger hain't got no home!   *Song*

6   You gotta jump down, turn around, pick a bale o' cotton

     Jump down, turn around, pick a bale a day.   *Work song*

7   Follow the North Star.   *Underground Railroad instruction*

8   Follow the drinking gourd.

                          Underground Railroad instruction

9   Can it be contended that a difference of color alone can constitute a difference of species? — If not, in what single circumstance are we different from the rest of mankind? What variety is there in our organization? What inferiority of art in the fashioning of our bodies? What imperfection in the faculties of our minds?   *Anonymous [1789]*

10   Has not a Negro eyes? Has not a Negro hands, organs, dimensions, senses, affections, passions? — fed with the same food; hurt with the same weapons; subject to the same diseases; healed by the same means; warmed and cooled by the same summer and winter as a white man?

                               Anonymous [1789][2]

11   We do not believe that things will always continue the same. The time must come when the Declaration of Independence will be felt in the heart, as well as uttered from the mouth, and when the rights of all shall be properly acknowledged and appreciated. God hasten that time. This is our home, and this is our country. Beneath its sod lie the bones of our fathers; for it, some of them fought, bled, and died. Here we were born, and here we will die.

         An address to the citizens of New York [January 25, 1831]

---

[1]Transcription by JOHN W. WORK from *Lost Delta Found* [2005], edited by ROBERT GORDON and BRUCE NEMEROV.

[2]Hath not a Jew eyes? Hath not a Jew hands, organs, dimensions, passions? — WILLIAM SHAKESPEARE, *The Merchant of Venice*

1   I thought that there was not a man to be known by his colour under the British flag and we left the United States because we were in hopes that prejudice was not in this land, and I came to live under your Government if my God would be my helper and to be true to the Government. I am sorry to annoy you by allowing this thing but we are grieved much, we are imposed on much and if it pleases your Excellency to attend to this grievance if you please sire.

The colored people of Hamilton (Canada) to Charles
T. Metcalfe [October 15, 1843][1]

2   Let none but him dat makes de thunder,
Put dis he-male an' dis she-male asunder.

Slave marriage invocation (Jumping the Broom)

3   Got one mind for white folk to see
'Nother for what I know is me.   *Slave saying*

4   Hello, Massa, bottom rail on top dis time.
Former enslaved man to imprisoned Confederate former master

5   If you lie down with dogs you get up with fleas.   *Saying*

6   You don't have to eat a peck of dirt before you die.   *Saying*

7   Last hired, first fired.   *Saying*

8   Study long, study wrong.   *Saying*

9   Hard times will make a monkey eat cayenne pepper.   *Saying*

10   It's the pot calling the kettle black.   *Saying*

11   Different strokes for different folks.   *Saying*

12   Don't trouble trouble until trouble troubles you.   *Saying*

13   Let every tub sit on its own bottom.   *Saying*

14   An empty wagon rattles.   *Saying*

15   Each one teach one.   *Reconstruction Era motto*

16   Dem what eats can say grace.   *Slave proverb*[2]

17   Mole don't see what his naber doing.   *Slave proverb*[2]

18   Jaybird don't rob his own nes'.   *Slave proverb*[2]

19   You can hide de fire, but what you gwine do wid the smoke?

Slave proverb[2]

---

[1]From *The Black Abolitionist Papers* [1986], *vol. II, Canada*, edited by C. Peter Ripley et al.

[2]From Anand Prahlad, *African American Proverbs in Context* [1996], and *The Book of Negro Folklore* [1958], edited by Langston Hughes and Arna Bontemps.

1   Rise, Sally. Rise!
     Wipe your weeping eyes.
     Put your hand on your hip.
     Let your backbone slip.
     Shake it to the east,
     Shake it to the west,
     Shake it to the one you love the best.   *Song game*

2   The blacker the berry, the sweeter the juice.   *Saying*

3   Beauty is only skin deep but ugly is to the bone.   *Saying*

4   Hambone, Hambone, where you been?
     'Round the world and back again.   *Song*

5   I'm dangerous and blue, can't stay here no more.
     Here come my train, folks, I have to go.   *Traveling Blues*

6   You don't miss your water till your well runs dry.   *Blues song*

7   See, see rider, see what you done done,
     Made me love you, now your gal done come.   *Blues song*

8   Love is like a hydrant, it turns on and off.   *Blues song*

9   Love, oh love, oh careless love.   *Careless Love*

10   Lifting As We Climb
              Motto, National Association of Colored Women's Clubs [c. 1896]

11   If you can't bear no cross, you can't wear no crown.
                                                              Saying

12   Make a way out of no way.   *Saying*

13   The unjust discriminations which are imposed upon Negro travelers
     I believe are due largely to our own failure to ward off such.
                                                Letter. The Crisis [1910]

14   Shine, Shine, save poor me. I'll give you more money than any
          black man see.
     Shine said to the Captain, "Money is good on land and on sea
     Get your ass in the water and swim like me."
     And Shine swam on . . .   *Shine and the Titanic*

15   Monkey in the tree,
     Lion on the ground.
     Monkey kept on signifying
     But he didn't come down.

                                              The Signifying Monkey   571

1   If blood be the price of liberty,
     Lord God, we have paid in full.[1]
                    Appeared above lynching statistics in early issues of Crisis [1910]

2   He lifted the veil of ignorance from his people and pointed the way to
     progress through education and industry.
                    Inscription on Tuskegee University Monument to Booker
                    T. Washington [1922]

3   Not alms, but opportunity
                    Motto, National Urban League's Opportunity magazine [1923]

4   I went down to St. James Infirmary,
     Saw my baby there,
     She was stretched out on a long white table,
     So cold, so sweet, so fair.
     Let her go, let her go, God bless her,
     Wherever she may be,
     She can look this wide world over,
     But she'll never find a sweet man like me.   *St. James Infirmary*

5   One monkey don't stop no show.   *Saying*

6   Every goodbye ain't gone.   *Saying*

7   Nothing comes to a sleeper but a dream.   *Saying*

8   Fool me once, shame on you.
     Fool me twice, shame on me.   *Saying*

9   Pay me, oh pay me,
     Pay me my money down.   *Song*

10   If you're white, you're all right,
     If you're yellow, you're mellow,
     If you're brown, stick around,
     If you're black, get back.   *Saying*

11   I know one thing we did right
     Was the day we started to fight,
     Keep your eyes on the prize,
     Hold on.   *Civil rights–era song*

12   I Am a Man
                    Slogan of Memphis sanitation workers' strike [1968]

---

[1]If blood be the price of Admiralty, Lord God, we ha' paid in full. — RUDYARD KIPLING, *Song of the Dead, The Collected Poems of Rudyard Kipling* [1999]

1   The people are the ultimate source of power.

The Black Panther [October 26, 1968]

2   Black is beautiful.   *Saying [1960s]*

3   Power to the People!   *Saying*

4   All Power to the People   *Black Panther slogan*

5   Freedom Now!   *Saying*

6   A mind is a terrible thing to waste.

Advertising slogan, United Negro College Fund [1972]

7   Black men have no country, but they are a country in their hearts.

Joseph Langstaff, retired carpenter and mason[1]

8   I don't have to do anything but stay black and die.   *Saying*

9   Blackness is a state of mind.   *Saying*

10   We may not know what the future holds, but we know who holds the
future.   *Saying*

11   Good black don't crack.   *Saying*

12   No justice!
No peace!   *Common call and response at demonstrations and rallies*

13   Buy Black
Slogan used to encourage support of black businesses

14   We believe that sexual politics under patriarchy is as pervasive in
Black women's lives as are the politics of class and race. We also find it difficult to separate race from class from sex oppression because in our lives
they are most often experienced simultaneously.

Statement, Combahee River Collective [April 1977][2]

15   African American is a contradiction in terms.   *Saying*

16   Being black in America is like being forced to wear ill-fitting shoes.
Some people adjust to it. It's always uncomfortable on your foot, but you've
got to wear it because it's the only shoe you've got.... Some people can
block it from their minds, some can't. When you see some acting docile
and some acting militant, they have one thing in common: the shoe is
uncomfortable.

Middle-aged male caller to radio program[3]

---

[1]From John Langston Gwaltney, *Drylongso* [1975].

[2]This Boston-based Black feminist group took its name from a military plan executed by Harriet
Tubman in 1863 that freed more than 750 slaves.

[3]From Studs Terkel, *Race* [1992].

1   I am not what you call me. I am what I respond to.   *Saying*

2   Don't hate the player, hate the game.   *Saying*

3   It takes a village to raise a child.[1]   *Saying*

4   It's a black thing—you wouldn't understand.   *Saying*

Anonymous: Caribbean

5   Shut mouth, catch fly.   *Saying (Antigua)*

6   All rope got two end.   *Saying (Guyana)*

7   Great gods ride little horses.   *Saying (Haiti)*

8   Dutty water can put out fire.   *Saying (Jamaica)*

9   Never buy puss in a bag.   *Saying (Jamaica)*

10   Duppy know who to frighten.   *Saying*

11   Skin, skin, ya na know me?[2]

    West Indian folktale

12   Brown girl in the ring,
Tra la la la la,
There's a brown girl in the ring,
Tra la la la la.   *Song game[3]*

13   Jane and Louisa will soon come home,
Soon come home, soon come home.
Jane and Louisa will soon come home,
Into this beautiful garden.   *Song game[3]*

14   Afouyéké,
Dou man, dou man-man,
Afouyéké,
Oh my sweet ma-ma.   *Song game[3]*

15   Look at a fine, fine girl,
    You lie, you lie,
Look at she up and down,
    You lie, you lie
Look at she wish no mind,
    You lie, you lie,

[1]Often attributed as an African proverb, this is a modern interpretation of the African philosophy that holds that children are central to family, community, and country.

[2]From LORENE CAREY, *Black Ice* [1991], *epigraph.*

[3]From *Brown Girl in the Ring* [1997], collected and documented by ALAN LOMAX, J. D. ELDER, and BESS LOMAX HAWES.

    Oh, let me know,
        You lie, you lie.   *Song game*[1]

1   Day — O, Day-O,
     Daylight come and me wan' go home.   *Banana Boat Song*[2]

2   In 1891 before I'd work,
     I'd rather be hung.   *Calypso song*

3   Mama Don't Want No Peas an' Rice an' Coconut Oil

                                 Calypso song title

4   Brown skin gal, stay home and mind baby.   *Brown Skin Gal*

5   This long time gal me never see yuh,
     Come mek me hold yuh hand.
     Peel head John Crow sit upon the tree top,
     Pick out the blossom,
     Mek me hold yuh hand gal,
     Mek me hold yuh hand.   *Long Time Gal (Jamaica)*

6   When you pray for rain, you've got to deal with the mud, too.

                                   Saying

7   Time longer dan a rope.   *Saying*

8   After fish spoil 'e spoil. (What's done is done.)   *Saying*[3]

9   All crave, all lost.

                                   Saying[3]

10   Big blanket mek man sleep late.

                                   Saying[3]

11   Big ship need da wata.

                                   Saying[3]

12   Cut eye don't kill.   *Saying*

13   When belly full, heart glad.   *Saying*

14   Full belly tell hungry belly "Take heart."   *Saying (Jamaica)*

15   De older de moon, de brighter it shine.   *Saying*[3]

16   New broom sweep clean, but ole broom know corner best.   *Saying*[3]

---

[1]From *Brown Girl in the Ring* [1997], collected and documented by ALAN LOMAX, J. D. ELDER, and BESS LOMAX HAWES.

[2]This song is most closely associated with Harry Belafonte, whose 1956 version remains the best-known rendition.

[3]From JOY LAWRENCE, *Colors and Rhythms* [2003]; LITO VALLS, *Ole Time Sayin's* [1983].

1. Every fish eena sea no shark. *Saying*[1]

2. Come see me one thing, come live with me another. *Saying*

3. Jack Mandora me no choose none.

    Last line of all Anancy Tales[2]

4. Once upon a time, Anancy, feeling very greedy for power and wealth, decided to collect all the commonsense there was in the world.... He collected and he collected, and all that he found he put in a large calabash. When he could find no more commonsense, he sealed the calabash with a roll of dry leaves. Then he decided to hide all the commonsense, at the top of a very high tree, so that no one else could get at it. *Folktale*[3]

Anonymous: Spirituals

5. Nobody knows the trouble I've seen,
    Nobody knows but Jesus. *Nobody Knows the Trouble I've Seen*

6. Joshua fit the battle of Jericho,
    And the walls come tumbling down. *Joshua Fit the Battle of Jericho*

7. Sometimes I feel like a motherless child,
    A long ways from home,
    A long ways from home. *Motherless Child*

8. Go tell it on the mountain,
    Over the hills and everywhere;
    Go tell it on the mountain,
    That Jesus Christ is born. *Go Tell It on the Mountain*

9. Follow the drinking gourd
    For the old man is a-waitin' for
    To carry you to freedom. *Follow the Drinking Gourd*

10. Go down, Moses,
    Way down in Egypt land,
    Tell old Pharaoh,
    Let my people go. *Go Down, Moses*

11. Free at last, free at last,
    Thank God Almighty, we're free at last. *Free at Last*[4]

---

[1]From JOY LAWRENCE, *Colors and Rhythms* [2003]; LITO VALLS, *Ole Time Sayin's* [1983].

[2]Variations: Jack Mandora me no choose one; Jack Mandora me no choose any. From *Jamaican Song and Story* [1907], edited by WALTER JEKYLL.

[3]As told by Louise Bennett in ANDREW SALKEY, *Caribbean Folk Tales and Legends* [1980].

[4]See Martin Luther King, Jr. 318:3.

1   I looked over Jordan, and what did I see? . . .
A band of angels coming after me,
Coming for to carry me home.   *Swing Low, Sweet Chariot*

2   Swing low, sweet chariot,
Coming for to carry me home.   *Swing Low, Sweet Chariot*

3   Michael row the boat ashore,
Hallelujah!   *Michael Row the Boat Ashore*

4   Rise and shine and give God the glory
For the year of Jubilee.   *Rise and Shine*

5   My Lord, what a morning,
When the stars begin to fall.   *My Lord, What a Morning*

6   One more river,
And that's the river of Jordan,
One more river,
There's one more river to cross.   *One More River*

7   Oh, freedom! Oh, freedom!
Oh, freedom over me!
And before I'd be a slave, I'll be buried in my grave,
And go home to my Lord and be free.   *Oh, Freedom!*

8   Get on board, little children,
There's room for many a more.   *Get on Board, Little Children*

9   The Gospel train's a-coming.   *Get on Board, Little Children*

10   Just like a tree that's standing by the water,
We shall not be moved.   *We Shall Not Be Moved*

11   Woke up this morning with my mind set on freedom.
         Traditional

12   O Lord, I want to be in that number,
When the saints go marching in.
         When the Saints Go Marching In

13   I got a robe, you got a robe,
All o' God' s chillun got a robe.
I got a crown, you got a crown
all God's chillun got a crown.   *All God's Chillun Got Wings*

14   And my soul looked back and wondered,
How I got over, my Lord.   *How I Got Over*

1   Guide my feet while I run this race,
     For I don't want to run this race in vain!   *Guide My Feet*

2   Every time I feel the spirit moving in my heart,
     I will pray.   *Every Time I Feel the Spirit*

3   No more auction block for me,
     No more, no more.
     No more auction block for me,
     Many thousand gone.   *Many Thousand Gone*

4   In that great gettin' up morning.   *Traditional*

5   Oh Mary don't you weep, don't you moan
     Pharaoh's army got drownded
     Oh Mary, don't you weep.   *Oh Mary, Don't You Weep*

6   Steal away to Jesus,
     Steal away, steal away home,
     I ain't got long to stay here.   *Steal Away*

7   I've been 'buked and I been scorned,
     Children, I've been 'buked and I been scorned.
     I've been talked about sure's you born.   *I've Been 'Buked and I Been Scorned*

8   There is trouble all over this world.
                        I've Been 'Buked and I Been Scorned

9   Rock-a my soul in the bosom of Abraham.   *Rock-a My Soul*

10   Wade in the water, children.
     God's a-gonna trouble the water.
                        God's A-Gonna Trouble the Water

11   I'm gonna lay down my sword and shield,
     Down by the riverside,
     Ain't gonna study war no more.   *Down by the Riverside*

12   Walk together, children,
     Don't you get weary.   *Walk Together, Children*

13   Didn't my lord deliver Daniel?
     And why not every man?   *Didn't My Lord Deliver Daniel?*

14   Soon I will be done with the troubles of the world.   *Soon I Will Be Done*

15   Oh, deep in my heart, I do believe,
     That we shall overcome someday.   *We Shall Overcome*

1   This little light of mine,
    I'm gonna let it shine.   *This Little Light of Mine*

2   Ain't gonna let nobody turn me around,
    I'm gonna keep on a-walkin', keep on a-talkin',
    Marchin' up to freedom land!
                            Ain't Gonna Let Nobody Turn Me Around

3   There is a balm in Gilead,
    To make the wounded whole.   *There Is a Balm in Gilead*

4   I'm going to eat at the welcome table,
    Some of these days.   *I'm Going to Eat at the Welcome Table*

5   We've Come This Far by Faith   *Song title*

6   When I'm in trouble,
    Do Lord remember me.   *Do Lord Remember Me*

7   I sing because I'm happy,
    I sing because I'm free.
    For His eye is on the sparrow,
    And I know He watches me.   *His Eye Is on the Sparrow*

8   Oh, don't feel no ways tired.
    I've come too far from where I started from.   *No Ways Tired*

9   Just a Closer Walk with Thee   *Song title*

10 Come by here, my Lord, come by here.[1]   *Come by Here*

---

[1]As sung by H. Wylie in Georgia [1926]. More popularly known as "Kumbaya," from a later folksong adaptation.

Index

Accomplish, time to a. life's work, 297:1

Accomplished, jealous of good not themselves a., 68:6

Accomplishment by West Indians, 380:3
  is something you can't buy, 356:6

Accomplishments have no color, 305:6

Account, duty to render a. of my conduct, 68:1

Accountable, urge to be a. to someone, 202:5

Acculturation, effect of a. on the Negro, 252:8

Accuse, do not a. me before the great god, 2:6

Aches an' pains an' troubles all, 149:3

Achieve, advance and a. to limits of ability, 482:7
  can and must a. tomorrow, 526:3
  conceive it believe it a. it, 410:2
  conquer opportunity to a., 286:2
  freedom at all costs, 264:5
  ideal I hope to a., 266:5
  law and order, 289:5

Achieved political emancipation, 266:9

Achievement, academic a., 383:11
  barriers to black a., 542:3
  institutions of splendid a., 230:4
  responsibility goes with a., 252:5
  story of Negro a., 252:8

Acknowledge errors, 494:4

Acquaintances, difficulty and danger are old a., 251:1

Acquainted them and all country, 62:2

Acquit, if it doesn't fit you must a., 375:3

Acres, forty a. and my mule, 300:3
  forty a. and a mule, 499:2
  never got the forty a., 499:2

Across, grooves a. our backs, 336:2

Act, guilty of a. detested in others, 66:2
  helps not men who will not a., 46:n2
  in bounties unconfin'd, 72:1
  Like a Lady Think Like a Man, 504:2
  of speech of talking back, 488:5

Acting, it's just a., 499:4

Action, anvil of united mass a., 266:6
  grand a. of Montgomery, 299:2
  men grow strong in a., 114:4
  mobilized into a., 265:1
  nonviolent direct a., 239:2
  organized for a., 265:1
  public sentiment demands a., 138:6
  want of unity in a., 96:1

Actions, today's a. tomorrow's legacy, 448:3

Activist, incurable a., 288:5

Activities, denial of cultural a., 278:5

Actor, want to be best a. in the world, 499:5

Actors, greatest a. to play role of Negro, 357:3

Actress, become best a. I could be, 353:1

Adam, a deep sleep to fall upon A., 6:11
  awe of A., 331:4
  called his wife's name Eve, 7:1
  created from whole earth, 59:5
  in A. all die, 40:4
  never had no Mammy, 156:1
  take back your God damn rib, 292:8

Adapt, I don't a. to you, 241:3

Addict, escape from reality makes an a., 286:6
  not every black person is an a., 508:9

Addiction, love is an a., 552:1

Address, Gasoline Point post office a., 257:7

Adidas walk through concert doors, 539:4

Adjudged the leastwise of the land, 259:3

Adjust, Negro's capacity to a., 252:8

Admiration, accomplishes elevation a. increased, 96:2
  from hearts of savages, 139:5

Admit, wrong to a., 231:4

Adolescent, faces are a. but too knowing, 412:7

Adopted, receives us as a. children, 94:3

Adore my black skin kinky hair, 242:7
  the mirror of the earth, 357:1

Adores, sighing for what one a., 67:5

Adoring, Innocence is its own a., 164:6

Adornment, wealth and children are a. of life, 55:2

Adrift without a sense of anchor, 202:5

Adult, annoy a child discover the a., 447:4

Adultery, committed a. in his heart, 26:14
  thou shall not commit a., 10:8

Adults a different species, 494:1
  as if a. did not all crawl once, 562:2

Advance achieve to limits of ability, 482:7
  is difficult, 251:1

Advancement, no room for a., 402:6
  of free colored people, 96:1

Advantage, honor and a. arise from equity of law, 184:1
  superior a. of being white, 97:7

Adventure, jazz is my a., 264:1
  love is the only true a., 432:6

Adventures, had a. that my race never had, 159:1

Adventurous, make my life a. dream, 254:7

Adversity, faint in the day of a., 19:3
  hold together through a., 304:1
  uses of a. is a worn theme, 119:1

Aerial, fight a. duel to avenge race, 195:8

Aesthetic, the Black A. is a corrective, 342:6

Aesthetics, ethics and a. are one, 379:1

Affair, it's a family a., 435:4

Affected, zealously a. in a good thing, 41:5

Affection, divine passion without a., 64:5
  on things above, 41:15
  renewing of a., 47:n4

Affectioned, be kindly a., 38:17

Affections were not dead, 72:2

Affiliation, lack of brotherly a., 136:3

Affirmative action about removing preferential treatment, 400:2
  hand grenades over a. action, 297:9

Afflicted, I have been grievously a., 61:4
  oppress not the a., 18:24
  succour man's a. son, 72:1

Affluence from our labors, 65:1

Against (*continued*)
   forgive those who trespass a. us, 27:*n*1
   he not with me is a. me, 28:9
   I tell the truth though a. myself, 68:1
   if God for us who can be a. us, 38:14
   means employed a. me, 68:2
   nation shall rise a. nation, 30:3
   sword a. his fellow, 13:6
   who a. hope believed in hope, 38:7
Age, flower of their a., 13:1
   in a good old a., 8:3
   school a. you cannot control, 229:2
Aged may look with gladness, 96:2
Agenda, black a. is not a marginal a., 492:3
Agendas, judges not to have a., 468:5
Ages, shaking the dust of a., 85:8
Aggression that surprised no one, 493:7
Agitate, a. a. a., 104:5
Agitated, nations a. for freedom, 64:3
Agonies of centuries crowd my soul, 127:2
Ahead, no man a. of his time, 186:6
   white folks still a., 204:7
Aid, demand your sympathy and a., 116:3
   lend a. in bursting fetters, 100:1
   to the worker God lends a., 46:*n*2
   you in the fight for Liberty, 172:7
AIDS in America is a black disease, 505:3
   race more burden than A., 428:2
   serious about stopping A., 505:4
Ails, if alive what a. you, 65:4
Aim, not failure but low a. is sin, 187:2
   one God one A. one Destiny, 170:5
   to make effort not measure it, 189:6
Aims, expose their predatory a., 197:3
Ain't gonna let nobody turn me around, 579:2
   gonna study war no more, 578:11
   got long to stay here, 578:6
   is or is you a. my baby, 228:1
   misbehavin', 192:5

Ain't (*continued*)
   no fire here, 278:3
   no mountain high enough, 405:5
   No Stoppin' Us Now, 469:2
   nobody here but us chickens, 228:4
   Nothing Like the Real Thing Baby, 406:1
   that a shame, 309:6
   that peculiar, 397:1
   too proud to beg, 397:3
   well a. it, 233:1
Air in prison is different, 539:8
   makes the a. remember, 515:6
   surrendered to the a., 337:9
   unfit for respiration, 69:3
   walk up on the a., 370:6
Airplane, hijacked a. as a missile, 498:3
Aké, sprawling terrain is all of A., 361:7
Alabama, Gasoline Point A., 257:7
Alabama's got me so upset, 352:4
Albatross, soul is an a., 260:8
Alcohol, volatile as a. gasoline, 306:3
Alert white people to racial identity, 465:7
Alex lay smoking such a dream, 223:6
Alexander asked what they dreaded most, 47:*n*9
Alien governments forced upon African people, 197:5
   I am a. and citizen, 51:3
   nothing human is a., 47:6
   peculiar a. creature, 86:3
Alienation too vast to be conquered, 282:11
Alike, darkness and light are a., 18:6
Alive and furious, 368:2
   ask what makes you come a., 203:6
   be cheerful while you are a., 2:2
   dead and a. again, 34:11
   food affirms joy of being a., 553:9
   how shall I be brought forth a., 55:3
   if a. what ails you, 65:4
   in Christ all a., 40:4
   is it not burying a man a., 68:3
   makes you half a., 277:2
   no man should take me a., 111:2
   rap upon box see if he's a., 100:2
   said that once and we're both a., 484:1

Alive (*continued*)
   to be human is to be a., 203:2
   to our responsibilities, 96:3
   to tell the tale, 130:5
All about the Benjamins, 547:2
   appear to love liberty for a., 68:5
   are equal a. are free, 526:5
   Christ is a. and in a., 41:16
   for one one for a., 88:2
   get it a. for nothing, 364:2
   God's chillun got a crown, 577:13
   having nothing yet possessing a., 40:13
   high and yet the servant of a., 133:2
   I am a. of these, 280:3
   I am made a. things to men, 39:11
   I heard I never forgot, 98:6
   I'm a. of that and then some, 500:7
   man hath will he give for his life, 108:*n*1
   men eligible to all employment, 67:8
   men regardless of color, 67:8
   men should live in peace, 272:5
   moderation in a. things, 47:2
   my letters of introduction, 271:4
   of them a. of me, 336:3
   one event happeneth to a., 19:15
   Power to the People, 573:4
   same for a. in punishment and protection, 67:8
   sheep have gone astray, 23:1
   shook up, 333:5
   that goes returns, 393:3
   that I have is thine, 34:12
   that I own, 396:4
   that I would do I cannot, 116:4
   the days of my life, 16:10
   things come to pass, 385:6
   things come to their end, 385:6
   things lawful not expedient, 39:13
   things must come to pass, 30:3
   we have to do is wear it, 285:7
   ye that are heavy laden, 28:8
   you are a. of these, 280:3
Allah, Muhammad's confidence in A., 348:4
All-American trump card, 549:5
All-commanding question for nation to solve, 106:3
Allegiance to stars and stripes, 522:6
Allegiances, two a. herself her race, 183:2

Alleluia, Mississippi next to go A., 364:6

Alley, chase him down the a., 397:6

Allies, white a., 209:1

Alligator, cocoa pods and a. pears, 175:5

All-night transit, 373:2

Allowed, if black folk a. to participate, 231:1

not a. to resist the blow, 98:7

Allude to things without representing them, 411:5

All-white, two blacks in a. institution, 309:2

Ally, time becomes a. of stagnation, 317:2

Alms, not a. but opportunity, 572:3

Alone, being a. when not really a., 378:9

believing we're a., 557:7

each must make his way a., 162:1

escaped a. to tell thee, 14:18

I one who alone exists, 51:6

it is not good that man be alone, 6:10

leave me a. stop it, 512:3

left a. all a., 254:3

left you a. and sane behind, 361:2

let him a., 106:4

not being a., 433:5

when you're lost and a., 517:4

without any love, 484:5

Along, can we all get a., 541:6

Alpha, I am A. and Omega, 45:7

Alright, everything will be a., 556:5

Also, the a. and a. of all that a., 257:5

Altar of nation's avarice, 83:7

Altered, nothing is ever a., 360:9

Alternatives, freedom is the sense of a., 203:4

Altitude, attitude will determine a., 410:2

Always bear in mind, 285:8

I am with you a., 32:5

I'll a. love my mama, 429:5

ye have the poor a., 30:13

Am, black cause I a., 384:5

I a. because we are, 336:5

I a. what I a., 40:3

I a. what I respond to, 574:1

I Black Enough for You, 429:4

I my brother's keeper, 7:4

Amandla Awethu, 567:14

Amantium irae amoris integratio est, 47:n4

Amassed, what your hearts have a., 53:11

Amazing, so a. to be loved, 484:4

Ambassadors from Celtae, 47:n9

what a. dreaded most, 47:n9

Ambiguities of history, 319:4

Ambition, every colored man and woman who has a., 163:6

result of your own a., 311:6

work harder to realize a., 183:3

Ambush, Indians did in a. lay, 65:9

Amen, congregation said A., 256:3

Amend your ways, 23:10

America, AIDS in A. is a black disease, 505:3

as good as its promise, 371:3

being a colored man inconvenient in A., 156:4

Black and male in A., 505:4

black in A. was Original Catch, 456:4

born A. with black skin, 294:3

building of A., 201:5

can change, 526:3

castrated by white A., 359:2

change is coming to A., 523:7

defaulted on note, 317:7

destiny bound with A., 91:5

destiny of A., 106:2

enriched A. with blood and tears, 78:3

exhausting being Black in A., 395:4

experiences in A. believe, 295:8

face of A. red yellow brown black white, 410:4

for Americans all colors, 162:9

frightened of history, 231:5

God damn A., 416:6

greater A., 384:7

here in A., 559:3

hugs the easy way, 231:5

I am A., 417:8

I question A., 262:2

I too sing A., 211:2

identity always negotiated in A., 481:4

if A. breaks we break, 91:5

illegal business controls A., 541:7

in A. black is a country, 354:5

is false to past present future, 105:1

is the Black Man's country, 199:2

America (continued)

is the denial of man's evolution, 427:6

keep A. free and make it freer, 208:4

known by her big cities, 235:4

land of my birth and distress, 413:1

let A. be A. again, 212:4, 212:5

loves both Africa and A., 377:5

mirror of experiences in A., 231:2

must play its role, 527:1

Negro race in A. stolen ravished, 222:4

Negro's survival in A., 252:8

never was A. to me, 212:4

no A. no jazz, 269:4

no place in A. for a black girl, 428:8

not candidate of black A., 287:5

only in A., 336:1

only in A. dead black boy on trial, 560:1

segregated hour of A., 321:1

slavery in A. was debasing, 130:6

souls of Black A., 274:4

the dream of A., 230:1

the great danger A. faces, 371:2

the woman from A., 377:5

thrilled to be here in A., 403:2

true genius of A. that A. can change, 526:3

too-young too-new A., 231:5

violence wrong in A., 294:4

wake up A., 400:6

what we want is what A. is, 231:2

where black was black, 209:5

white A. still exploits black, 310:1

who will speak for A., 371:2

whose bodies A. owns, 90:3

without her Negro people, 144:5

would A. have been A., 144:5

would have been stronger, 231:1

wrong for A. to draft us, 294:4

America's beacon burns bright, 526:3

famous past time, 359:7

from A. urban blacks, 208:2

Negro is A. metaphor, 232:4

rap is black A. TV station, 518:3

so pleased A. gon' last, 403:2

soul poisoned, 319:8

wilderness in search of promised land, 495:2

Angels *(continued)*
  with A. share, 63:2
Anger, also have the right to my a., 392:2
  and humor like left and right arm, 395:2
  at yourself nowhere else to go, 520:1
  don't show the a., 273:6
  empowers the poor, 395:2
  God slow to a., 14:13
  grab the broom of a., 180:16
  is a weed, 53:1
  look and feel a. building within you, 363:7
  of black people is real, 525:1
  of lovers renews love, 47:*n*4
  of lovers renews strength of love, 47:*n*4
  provoke not your children to a., 41:17
  without cause, 64:5
Anglo-Saxon, affinity with A. race worked for my escape, 99:2
Angry, get a. bring change, 296:2
  getting a. never do you good, 197:1
  never get a. get even, 363:5
Anguish, black a. will fall upon deaf ears, 291:3
  vomit the a. up, 283:4
Animal, because it is an an., 377:6
  guardian a. I must hide, 225:3
  I am many things I am an an., 545:6
  just some brutish a., 350:4
  man is an absurd a., 64:5
  story-making a., 323:7
Animosity, hold no a. towards any man, 160:2
Ankle, chain about a. of fellow man, 106:9
Ankles, blood on your a., 537:3
Annie, Work with Me A., 303:1
Anoint, I shall a. you, 357:4
Anointest my head with oil, 16:10
Another, love one a., 38:23
Answer a fool according to his folly, 19:4
  beyond individual an a. given, 202:5
  no a. perhaps the a., 258:4
  the a. was love, 428:7
  the call of history, 529:4
  the tell me of the mama is the a., 214:6

Answer *(continued)*
  years that a., 180:3
Answers, universal quest easy a., 318:4
Ant, weight of an a., 54:5
Antebellum South, little difference between A. and New South, 138:5
Anthem, jazz music our black a., 312:6
  more than National A. to make a nation, 237:6
  sing the national a., 271:1
Antifamily unwed black single, 485:3
Anti-intellectual underdog, 542:3
Antilles, Jewel of the A., 291:4
Anti-Negro images of films, 248:14
Anti-Semitic statements, 389:5
Anti-white statements, 389:5
Anvil of mass action, 266:6
Anxiety, banquet partaken in a., 46:1
Anxious cacophony, 381:2
Anybody Want to Try My Cabbage, 192:3
Anyone could be Lucifer, 377:9
  no one make war on a., 58:1
Anything, I am not a. I am not, 292:6
  nobody can give you a., 296:3
  you don't need a. else, 295:9
Apart, divided and kept a., 170:6
  justice for us is to be set a., 196:2
  secrets setting us a., 415:7
  we have fallen a., 323:1
Apartheid, crush a., 266:6
  no answer to a., 264:4
Apartment in the sky, 447:2
Apologies you are no country, 554:3
Apology a prerequisite for healing, 508:4
  I have no a. to make, 129:7
  no a. for African enslavement, 439:1
  we be without a., 537:2
Apostles, I am least of the a., 40:3
Appear to love liberty for all, 68:5
  whenever you a. I will hide, 51:1
  whenever you hide I will a., 51:1
  you have hidden and a., 51:1
Appearance, judge not according to a., 36:1
  looketh on outward a., 13:7
Appearances are deceiving, 45:9
Applause, easy to win a. and approval, 166:4

Apple, he'd a let dat a. be, 156:1
  of the eye, 16:4
Apples, comfort me with a., 21:6
Apply our hearts unto wisdom, 17:19
Appointment, your a. to Supreme Court, 311:6
Appreciated, you are a., 556:5
Apprehension, consume oneself in a., 156:7
Approach slowly and quickly turn away, 67:4
Approval, looks to white folks for a., 451:3
Arabs of the desert say We believe, 56:11
Arawak, frolicking A. beauties, 301:7
Arbeit Macht Frei, 298:4
Arc of being, 269:8
  of moral universe, 319:7, 319:*n*1, 531:1
Archdeceivers, white race world's a., 196:4
Architect of Rock and Roll, 344:3
Architect's, architecture in image of a. ego, 314:4
Architects of republic, 317:7
Architecture, department store a., 552:7
  in image of architect's ego, 314:4
Are, and you don't know who you a., 418:1
  love what we a., 383:5
  there black racists, 389:5
  we a. and shall be, 360:5
  we a. therefore I am, 336:5
  we men, 78:1
  we now smitten, 47:*n*1
  without hating what we a. not, 383:5
  you ready, 372:1
Aren't I a woman, 82:6
Argue, to a. to discredit effects of slavery, 132:3
Argument, reinforce a. with results, 133:4
  without punishment, 60:1
Arguments are a mark of liberty, 528:4
  should not sneak in disguise, 469:1
Arise and walk, 32:7
  Barak, 12:14
  day star a. in your hearts, 43:11
  from this dust, 100:6
  shine for thy light is come, 23:5

Arise *(continued)*
  why men sneer when I a., 190:3
Aristocrats, breed new generation of
    a., 257:8
Ark of the covenant, 12:7
  two of every sort bring into the a.,
    7:10
Arm, seal upon thine a., 21:14
Arm's, grapple with slavery not at a.
    length, 79:5
  too short to box with God, 148:4
  yo' a. too short to box with God,
    147:n1
Armageddon, gathered them into A.,
    44:20
Armed they now struck back, 260:7
  with freedom defense and guns,
    424:8
Armenian, intricate A. neums,
    199:4
Armor, put on a. of God, 41:11
  we wear our scars like a., 486:4
Arms, consciousness of Everlasting
    A., 125:5
  everlasting a., 12:6
  fling my a. wide, 210:8
  new cities in their a., 276:2
  of prayer and faith, 72:3
  these a. of mine are lonely, 411:6
  tries everything before a., 48:9
Army, Freedom's a. crowned with
    laurels, 102:5
  of the Lord, 256:3
  Pharaoh's a. got drownded, 578:5
  terrible as an a. with banners,
    21:11
  who run the a., 355:4
Arose, a hope a. in my heart, 74:4
  a mother in Israel, 12:13
  Deborah a., 12:13
  people a. as one man, 12:18
  there a. a new king over Egypt,
    8:20
Around, ain't done running a.,
    187:8
Arouse justice from its slumbers,
    127:5
Arrests, daily quota of Negro a.,
    332:6
Arrival, opera of dead on a., 462:3
Arrive, lies travel years and never a.,
    567:4
Arriving again for the night, 335:7
  at own door own mirror, 331:1

Arrogance, mixture of a., 306:3
  of fortunate races, 225:3
Arrogant, do not be a., 1:4
  no proof less a., 181:10
Arrow feathered with plumes, 47:1
Arsonist, imperialism is the a.,
    473:11
Art, acquired great skill in the a., 71:1
  ain't about paint, 309:3
  all a. is propaganda, 256:6
  all alive a. is rebellious, 373:3
  American musical a. form, 269:4
  as if nature were condescending to
    a., 503:6
  auctioning slaves is high a., 300:4
  cannot punch a button, 305:5
  change through a. that old
    whispering, 211:5
  each body has its a., 258:7
  expression of belief and desire,
    235:2
  for art's sake, 225:6, 256:6
  function of a. is observation, 263:4
  future influenced by a., 278:1
  good a. to serve humanity, 323:6
  is a kind of confession, 283:4
  is life, 225:5
  is not barrel copper, 199:4
  is the genesis, 254:4
  leaves her lover as a Komitas,
    199:4
  map of life made with a., 477:8
  mastering a. of timing, 479:4
  measure of greatness is a.
    produced, 147:9
  Negros' second career in a., 168:2
  no boundary line to a., 273:5
  Our Father which a. in heaven,
    27:2
  power structure of the a. world,
    204:1
  referential quality of a., 411:5
  says stop looking at my face,
    247:1
  science in dance and a. in science,
    504:4
  succeeds by remaining intact,
    363:4
  the quintessence of meaning,
    157:6
  there will be no a. talk, 385:7
Articulation for hope freedom,
    303:5
Artificial, quota a. ceiling, 292:3

Artist, black a. has wasted time,
    280:2
  communion between a. and
    spectator, 235:2
  duty of younger Negro a., 211:5
  every a. a priest, 389:3
  is like a secretary, 288:4
  keeps records of his time, 288:4
  less an a. who gives attention,
    136:6
  must take sides, 198:3
  Negro a. not just another a., 204:1
  one can as a. choose, 248:12
  respond to this essence of himself,
    361:3
  to see and say something that
    enriches, 235:2
Artist's duty is to reflect the times,
    352:8
Artists, black a. contributors to art,
    335:2
  express universal language, 335:2
  if they are to survive, 283:4
  people want from black a. the
    exotic, 548:8
  pioneer American Negro a., 168:2
  younger a. express without fear,
    211:6
Arts, Black A. Movement, 379:1
Ascending, angels a. and descending,
    35:12
  behold angels a. and descending,
    8:8
Ascetics, haunt of saints and a., 60:3
Ashamed, I am a., 49:3
  ought to be a. of yourselves, 198:7
  proud of my color or a., 263:1
  they were both naked and not a.,
    6:13
  whom you have been a., 50:3
  workman that needeth not to be
    a., 42:12
Ashes, slaves to dust and a., 78:1
  speak upon the a., 83:6
Ashore, row the boat a., 577:3
Ask and it shall be given, 27:7
  bread will give him a stone, 27:9
  don't a. me I don't know why,
    538:7
  got to a. you got to a., 214:6
  if you got to a. you ain't got it,
    221:7
  if you gotta a. you'll never know,
    204:8

Ask *(continued)*
  love has nothing more to a. to give, 169:4
  no favors but plead for justice, 101:6
  of him they will a. more, 34:7
  of the world a free Africa, 171:1
  that we be treated as well as those, 107:3
  they a. me to remember, 367:5
  what makes you come alive, 203:6
  ye shall receive, 36:20
  your mama, 214:4
Asked if my blackness would rub off, 214:4
  on a teaching application, 368:7
Asking for a little respect, 411:8
  if it's not a. too much, 273:3
Asleep, Africa was not a., 265:3
  some think God is a., 77:5
Aspiration, social order and thirsty a., 230:11
Aspirations, ethnic group a., 255:7
Aspire, to a. we need to be grounded, 401:7
Ass, free your mind and your a. will follow, 407:3
  get your a. in the water, 571:14
  hauling a. back home, 298:4
  shalt not covet neighbor's a., 10:8
Assassin, prejudiced a., 186:8
Asses, get off your a. and do something, 504:6
  off their a. and fight, 299:1
Asset, we must be an a. or a liability, 218:1
Assets and liabilities of citizenship, 208:3
Assistance, couldn't move without man's a., 129:5
  thee we worship and beg a., 53:7
Assume all is well, 127:3
Assumption that law-abiding Negroes, 145:5
Astonishment among all nations, 12:3
Astray, all sheep have gone a., 23:1
Asunder, let not man put a., 29:13
  put he-male an' she-male a., 570:2
Aten, O living A., 4:6
  shine as A. of daytime, 5:1
Athlete, being an a. a kind of grace, 533:2

Athletes, slavery model for power relationship a. and owners, 480:9
Atlantic, climbed out of the cold wet A., 506:6
  if A. were to dry up, 251:3
Atlas Mountain snows, 225:2
Atmosphere, prejudice is like the a., 84:3
Atom's weight of evil, 57:7
  weight of good, 57:7
Attached to things that will satisfy us, 363:1
Attack, do not a. him, 2:3
  everything struggled for remains under a., 362:6
Attackers, convict a. on the spot, 298:5
Attacks for fear of being attacked, 277:8
Attained, equally desired equally a., 166:2
Attainments, habits fixed for higher a., 109:2
  no limits to the a. of the Negro, 133:3
Attempt, die if make a. die if not, 89:2
  to destroy you, 304:7
Attend inferior separate schools, 272:5
Attention, not nervous not paying a., 300:8
  pay a. to the specific, 328:5
  provoke your a., 291:3
Attitude, charging failures to white people's a., 160:3
  negative a. that runs the show, 547:3
  of the i can i must i will a., 422:3
  survival of the fittest a., 422:2
  will determine altitude, 410:2
Attitudes, color prejudice creates a., 184:6
Attracted, much that repels i am a., 243:9
Auction, betrays memory of a. block, 282:11
  Clotel on the a. block, 97:1
  no more a. block, 578:3
  not one escaped the a. block, 94:8
Auctioning slaves is high art, 300:4
Audacious power, 230:4

Audacity, inspires a., 311:2
  of hope, 522:7
  to hope, 416:4, 416:5
Audi partem alteram, 52:n2
Audience, I am my a., 194:4
  to validate their breath, 520:3
August 'twas the twenty-fifth, 65:9
Aunt Hagar's, all A. children, 478:1
Aunt Jemimas, screeching A., 391:1
Aurora hail and thousand dies, 71:6
Authentic Blackness there is no such thing, 557:1
  identity for the African, 562:5
  Negro experience, 491:7
Authenticity difficult to attain, 271:3
Author of dictionary that defines me, 561:10
Authority, dares to question colonial a., 207:1
  of Church moved me, 52:11
  pass through with My a., 57:1
  persecution by a., 299:4
  to kill a minority, 542:4
  whites seeking power and a., 78:2
Authors of devastation, 284:1
Automatic reaction of white people, 238:2
Automobile, kind of a. one drives, 142:5
Autopsy read Vietnam, 319:8
Autumn's house where dreams grow thin, 158:1
Available to as many people's stories, 500:7
Avalanche of murders, 290:5
Avarice, altar of this nation's a., 83:7
  victim of a. and hatred, 101:2
  victims to the improvident a., 69:3
Avenge, fight aerial duel to a. race, 195:8
Avenger, enemy and a., 15:22
Avoid running at all times, 224:2
Awake, Africa was wide a., 265:3
  and sing, 22:11
  be a., 103:1
  Deborah utter a song, 12:14
  millions of voices are calling, 100:6
  new spirit a. in the masses, 167:6
  O north wind, 21:9
Awakened one must have been asleep, 265:3
Awakening of Afro-American woman, 138:4

Awareness I was a Negro, 185:1

Away, accepted the peoples cast a., 59:2

approach slowly and quickly turn a., 67:4

each thing that goes a. returns, 393:3

learned running a. to perfection, 98:6

pass not a. I pray thee, 8:5

Awop-bop-a-loo-mop alop-bamboom, 344:4

Axes, can't put out with a., 278:3

Axis, wheeled on the a. of earth, 480:2

Azucar, 287:6

B

Babel, the name of it called B., 8:1

Babes, out of the mouth of b., 15:22

Babies, hate the ladies that make the b., 556:3

like taking care of b., 520:1

wet-nursed your b., 292:3

Baby, any fool with a dick can make a b., 548:9

brown b. years roll by, 300:2

burn b. burn, 230:5, 312:9, 409:12

going to have my b., 282:5

hold back from born, 313:4

I Need Your Loving, 408:7

is you is or is you ain't my b., 228:1

keep the faith b., 230:3

learn b. learn, 409:12

lifted b. to the heavens, 274:3

love my b. love, 408:6

Mammy's little b. loves short'nin bread, 569:3

ooo b. b., 404:3

Pecola having father's b., 336:6

please b. b. b. please, 508:5

sent for my b. and she don't come, 236:9

stay home mind b., 575:4

the shoe my b. wore, 250:1

Babylon is fallen, 22:6, 44:18

we're leaving B., 449:11

Bach and James Brown, 476:4

of the chorales, 248:10

Back, beating of the b., 268:4

can't ride b. unless bent, 321:3

Back *(continued)*

come b. to you one of these days, 171:6

don't you come b. no more, 273:4

go b. before go forward, 322:2

had to go to b. door, 244:6

my b. is strong, 352:6

of de cook-stove, 179:8

pat on the b., 192:1

talking b., 488:5

to Africa Miss Mattie, 268:6

to this land of mine, 241:2

white man will take it b., 262:5

you go b. to Mother Earth, 254:6

Backhold, grapple with slavery with a b., 79:5

Backroads, if you got to use the b., 328:6

Backs, bloody grooves across b., 336:2

dark against sky, 321:7

on the b. of our people, 240:3

Backstabbers smiling in your face, 421:1

Back-to-Africa movement, 233:1

Backwater blues caused me to go, 188:1

Bad, black aint only beautiful its b. too, 346:3

check, 317:7

hair day, 561:3

I am b., 431:2

into a world of b. spirits, 69:2

just as b. as it was before, 83:5

luck soul, 187:6

off to a b. start, 253:3

you know I'm b. I'm b., 512:1

Badge, no escape from b. of color, 395:4

Badness flaunted itself, 564:10

Bag, Papa's Got a Brand New B., 347:1

Bail, couldn't make the b., 554:4

Bakongo, you Mande Ibo B. Dogon, 391:3

Balance, disturbing the delicate b., 230:11

of man's body, 276:3

our lives require b., 505:5

Bale, jump down turn around pick a b. a day, 569:6

Balkanization of the islands, 311:1

Ball, cupping an invisible b. of dreams, 398:6

if I've got the b. it's okay, 378:7

it up, 344:5

of confusion, 436:3

take the b. dazzling down, 398:3

without the b. you can get to me, 378:7

Ballet hip-hop and kung fu, 557:4

is grace, 557:4

Ballot, believed in that small white b., 139:5

cheated him out of his b., 138:5

or the bullet, 295:5

using b. in promoting interests, 168:5

Ballot-box, going to the b., 106:4

Ballots, chance to cast their b. like we did, 528:4

Ballplayer, to be a big-league b., 274:1

Balls, great b. of fire, 333:6

life it ain't got no b., 451:5

Balm in Gilead, 23:12, 579:3

is there no B. in Gilead, 377:1

Bamboo earrings at least two pair, 548:4

Bananas ripe and ginger-root, 175:5

Band of angels coming after me, 577:1

Band's, raise on up your b. waiting, 398:2

Bandage removed from other eye, 135:10

Bands of bondage were strong, 74:4

Bandwagon, jump off b. throw stones at it, 438:6

Bang bang boogie, 374:5

Banished queen, 440:3

Banishment, slavery or b., 113:4

Banjo, my ol' b. f'om de wall, 149:3

Banker, who the b., 355:4

Bankrupt in our spirits, 515:1

Banner, blood the bright b. flowing, 461:1

his b. over me was love, 21:6

star-spangled b. millions of slaves, 112:5

Banners, no victory to crown her b., 113:5

terrible as an army with b., 21:11

Banquet partaken in anxiety, 46:1

table of nature, 176:8

Baptizing them in name of the Father, 32:4

Barak, arise B., 12:14

Barbarian among barbarians, 50:3

Barbarians, judgment of Greeks and b., 50:3

knowledge of b., 50:3

no image among b., 50:3

Barbarism, cruelty and b. of men, 66:1

it is b. supreme b. the crowning b., 242:1

lynch law last relic of b., 139:1

war at best may lead to b., 220:5

Barbarisms, sums up all the daily b., 242:1

Barbarity, sign of b. and immorality, 87:1

Barbarous, Color-Line b., 222:3

Bards, oh black and unknown b., 147:8

Bare the mirror of nakedness, 360:9

Barley, land of wheat and b., 11:15

Barons playing leap-frog, 301:7

Barren one and many sons, 49:1

Barrier to self-possession, 457:4

Barriers, breaking the b. of virtue, 69:4

of the ghetto, 246:3

that imprison and divide us, 455:2

to black achievement, 542:3

we erect against others, 186:4

Barristers, Caucasian b. not to blame, 135:2

Bars, behind b. in a basement, 397:6

prison b. cannot hold down an idea, 425:4

Baseball, name of the game ain't b., 359:7

Basement, behind bars in a b., 397:6

Basin, borne like elliptical b., 331:8

Basin Street where elite meet, 177:2

Basis of race and color, 228:7

Basketball, as much time in library as on b. court, 458:3

black kids want to play b., 457:10

once a white man's game, 363:2

Baskets, twelve b. full, 28:21

Bas-reliefs mathematics science, 279:6

Bass, siren song sung in b., 270:2

Bastard, ghetto b., 551:5

Bastardization, bid farewell to b., 293:5

Bathe and bedeck my self, 371:7

Baton, pass off that b., 563:7

Bats, swinging their lives as b., 398:6

Battle between imperialism and democratization, 495:5

last b. is with ourselves, 97:5

love is a b., 283:7

not to the strong, 20:9

of Jericho, 576:6

prepare himself to b., 40:1

spirits engaged in b., 87:5

Battle-cry, songs to stir like a b., 115:8

Battlefield, face cannons on the b., 194:3

world is one great b., 128:3

Battles aren't for gold medals, 244:5

not fight your b. on my body, 537:5

Battling billows while shrouds rattling, 85:5

Bayonets, not peace of b., 293:7

Bayou ain't too much, 350:2

life of the b., 153:9

Be a dancer, 353:4

afraid, 467:2

an intelligent human being, 296:5

and it is, 54:9

awake, 103:1

cannot b. what you will, 250:6

cheerful while you are alive, 2:2

desire to b. desire to belong, 189:3

do not b. ignorant of me, 49:1

fruitful and multiply, 6:5

I just wanted to b., 385:3

like them and I was, 396:1

make ourselves what we want to b., 172:10

not afraid, 28:23, 64:4

not afraid of sudden fear, 18:12

not deceived, 41:8

not forgetful to entertain strangers, 42:19

not righteous over much, 20:4

not troubled, 30:3

of good cheer, 28:23, 36:21

on the down low, 540:3

on your guard, 50:2

shall b. what I will, 250:6

Be *(continued)*

sober b. vigilant, 43:10

still and know that I am God, 17:2

time will always b., 386:1

To B. or Not to Bop, 261:7

we are and shall b., 360:5

what they still must b., 251:2

what we were born to b., 382:3

will try to b. what other people are, 505:2

Beaches, white folks from the b., 298:1

Beacon, America's b. burns bright, 526:3

Bead, blue worry b. into mouth, 487:3

Beads dolls cloths vases, 259:6

Beale Street, if B. could talk, 151:8

Beale Street's done gone dry, 151:9

Beams of heaven as I go, 128:6

Beans, over b. in their back room, 259:6

Beanstalk, tall as fairy tale b., 257:7

Bear all the consequences, 275:2

fruit throughout eternity, 115:3

hardest thing to b., 67:5

his own burden, 41:7

I am the midwife who does not b., 49:1

I could b. the lash, 82:6

infirmities of the weak, 39:2

milking a b. to get cream, 181:3

no cross wear no crown, 571:11

Beareth, charity b. all things, 39:16

Bears, polar b. and poor kids too, 548:1

Beast about to pounce upon you, 490:4

drive off the b. of fear, 180:16

every b. is mine, 17:3

first b. like a lion, 44:3

fourth b. like a flying eagle, 44:3

kind of rare b., 86:3

mark of the b., 44:16

righteous man regardeth life of b., 18:16

second b. like a calf, 44:3

slavery treats him as b., 101:2

third b. had face as a m., 44:3

Beasts browse on their herbs, 5:2

cheweth the cud among the b., 10:13

four b. had each six wings, 44:3

shall teach thee, 15:8

591

Beat, billy clubs couldn't b. it out, 274:4

drum lak in de Affica soil, 124:6

from the Sanctified Church, 236:4

him at his own game, 358:3

it, 511:4

rhythm of the boogedy b., 374:5

swords into plowshares, 22:1

they would b. Jesus if he was black, 204:4

Beats, when to start when the b. commence, 539:1

Beautiful, being b. is not enough, 379:2

black aint only b. its bad too, 346:3

black is b., 276:1, 573:2

Black Is B., 503:5

black people are very b., 284:5

cry only because of b. things, 465:5

excellent is always b., 502:8

how she could be so b., 471:6

humanity is b., 276:3

just seen a b. thing, 161:5

needful thing, 243:1

Negro and b., 211:5

outasight black men, 430:2

people with african imaginations, 354:6

proclaim her b. image, 328:7

provin' to world black was b., 216:4

taught her how to be b., 357:1

the b. game, 402:4

white is b., 276:1

you b. but you gotta die someday, 221:4

Beauty, accepted white standards of b., 463:4

ancient and new, 52:8

becomes enough, 337:10

black niggers my b., 359:4

children are b., 314:7

create works reveal b., 302:4

credentials of status and b., 507:4

does not know her b., 223:3

in everything in her eyes, 453:7

in the eye of beholder, 181:9

laws of b., 116:5

motley of ugliness and b., 182:2

of ancient times, 226:1

of each enhancing the others, 193:5

of Nature, 167:2

of woman's arm, 276:3

Beauty *(continued)*

skin deep ugly to the bone, 571:3

some me of b. about to begin, 450:7

standards are our own invention, 489:1

strikes my heart, 224:6

to restore recreate this b., 382:3

what will happen to all that b., 284:5

wisdom is finest b. of a person, 567:5

Beauty's cheek felt cool, 223:6

sun goes down, 81:4

Bebop slant and fade on in, 398:2

Be-Bop is precise clumsiness, 402:5

Became, what I b. after I met you, 472:2

Because, different just b. you're black, 532:7

forbidden b. of who they love, 528:1

happening b. I'm a woman, 421:2

happening b. I'm black, 421:2

I am queen, 561:1

I was a black man, 502:5

I was a gay man, 502:5

is it b. I'm black, 190:3

not straight, 509:5

not white, 509:5

their skins are dark, 117:4

Become, what I might have b., 141:3

Becoming, cultural identity is matter of b., 344:1

the power is better, 471:3

Bed, pair of thighs in their b. every night, 514:11

take up thy b., 32:7

taking big dictionary to b., 494:2

Bedrock inside myself, 476:8

Bedrooms with sandbags and stones, 512:8

Bee, sting like a b., 417:4

Beethoven, like B. composed music, 315:6

of the symphonies, 248:10

roll over B., 299:6

Beetles of hope, 240:6

Before he got to wherever he is, 327:7

nothing said has not been said b., 48:4

yuh go back deh, 268:6

Beg, ain't too proud to b., 397:3

nor stoop to b. for my rights, 121:4

worship and b. assistance, 53:7

Beggar, dependent from king to the b., 66:4

flinging a coin to b., 320:1

Beggarly, weak and b. elements, 41:4

Begging for freedom, 286:2

revolution never based on b., 295:6

Begin, now let us b., 320:2

Beginning, different b. than that of American blacks, 380:3

fear of the Lord is b. of wisdom, 18:3

I am the b. and end, 45:7

in b. was the Word, 35:5

in the b. God created heaven and earth, 5:4

is this my b. or the end, 429:8

New Day is always b., 432:8

of deep tragedy for us, 362:8

of learning to live, 227:4

of my miseducation, 366:7

the end is in the b., 248:2

was the act, 248:14

we remain in the b., 324:2

you are the end the b., 393:4

Begotten, gave his only b. Son, 35:18

not b. and has not been b., 57:8

Begun, the day has just b., 340:2

Behave, gods b. like people, 180:8

how they can't b., 558:9

well toward each other, 279:4

yourself up here, 142:8

Behaves differently with white man, 290:6

Behavior, enslaving b. caused by prejudices, 189:15

Behind, get thee b. me Satan, 29:9

go forward or be left b., 106:7

Behold a pale horse, 44:7

a virgin with child, 25:17

angels of God ascending and descending, 8:8

his conscience, 81:7

I come quickly, 45:6

I stand at the door, 44:2

only thing greater than yourself, 274:3

the hour is at hand, 31:10

the Lamb of God, 35:10

the man, 37:1

this dreamer cometh, 8:13

woman b. thy son, 37:2

Beholder, history depends on the b., 341:6

Being black does not stop you, 221:2

black in America like ill-fitting shoes, 573:16

Black is emotionally taxing, 500:6

born of royalty, 201:10

cultural identity is matter of b., 344:1

every b. in search for its double, 370:1

food affirms joy of b. alive, 553:9

is complete perfect, 302:3

Lord of all B., 53:7

men had epidermalized B., 465:1

part of the system, 287:8

the stuff of my b., 181:7

there's an arc of b., 269:8

too black, 216:5

was enough, 393:1

Beings, most degraded b. since world began, 77:4

signs for all living b., 56:3

what business have such b., 64:5

Belief, art is expression of b. and desire, 235:2

committed to the b., 230:6

in superior inferior races, 323:5

true knowledge of this b., 56:9

Beliefs, rethink our b., 505:4

Believe, all b. that shit, 281:3

Arabs of the desert say We b., 56:11

asking you to b. in yours, 523:6

cannot b. history sacred or profane, 77:5

conceive it b. it achieve it, 410:2

deep in my heart I b., 578:15

don't b. the hype, 518:2

in freedom of Africa, 272:5

in goals and timetables, 292:3

in God b. in me, 36:13

in who you are, 473:6

in yourself as I b. in you, 442:1

not b. doctors heal, 337:1

not what life told you to, 442:1

profess to b. men love one another, 105:4

things we need to b., 558:6

this nation transformed, 304:3

truly b. in themselves, 239:4

Believe *(continued)*

truth is whatever propaganda people b., 220:3

we are good guys, 286:4

we b. in God, 53:9

we who b. in freedom cannot rest, 217:4

who b. stand firm by His Word, 54:8

will they not then b., 55:4

you b. love another yet hate, 105:4

Believed, as if thing b. actually existed, 553:2

blessed they have not seen yet b., 37:5

not b. the gospel, 52:11

what is uncommon is rarely b., 68:7

who against hope b. in hope, 38:7

Believers, true b., 56:10

Believeth, charity b. all things, 39:16

he b. in me shall never die, 36:10

he that b. on me shall never thirst, 35:23

whosoever b. should not perish, 35:18

Believing, couldn't stop b. in iron, 462:1

prevented men from b., 54:14

slave better than an idolater, 53:10

true courage comes in b. in oneself, 478:6

Bell, play guitar like ringing a b., 299:7

the cat, 46:11

trouble no dey ring b., 413:3

Belligerent, no matter how b. their talk, 212:1

Belly, full b. tell hungry b. take heart, 575:14

full but we hungry, 449:8

in the b. of the fish, 24:10

upon thy b. shalt thou go, 6:17

when b. full heart glad, 575:13

Belong, desire to b., 189:3

one must b. before one may not b., 206:5

Belonged, deprive that which b. to us, 170:7

Belonging is a contested state, 513:6

payin price for b., 298:3

Beloved, I am B. and she is mine, 338:10

Luke the b. physician, 41:18

this is my b. and friend, 21:10

this is my b. Son, 26:9

Beloved's, I am my b., 21:13

Belt, trusty guns in my b., 130:3

Ben Franklin, if B. could live on little so could she, 238:3

Bend, too proud to b., 306:2

Benefactor, recipient and b., 259:4

Beneficent mother of gods and men, 4:5

Beneficiaries of reverse racism, 297:9

Benefits, fighting to win material b., 285:8

laws provide concrete b., 229:5

whatever b. humanity, 296:11

Benjamins, all about the B., 547:2

Bent, can't ride back unless b., 321:3

Berlin, listen in B. either, 298:4

Berniece, play something for me B., 451:10

Berry, blacker the b. sweeter the juice, 571:2

brown as a b., 191:4

Beside, Paul thou art b. thyself, 38:1

still waters, 16:10

Bessie's, Big B. feet hurt, 260:5

Best black syndrome tokenism, 496:6

get over it I'm the b. person, 366:6

of me is the least of you, 175:7

pick the b. one and you are not it, 506:4

remember me in my b. light, 379:5

that the legacy symbolizes, 477:1

things in life free, 315:2

time to cry is at night, 378:8

Bethlehem, Jesus was born in B., 25:18

Betray, one of you shall b. me, 31:3

Betrayed by some of my own complexion, 73:2

Son of man is b., 31:10

Betrays memory of auction block, 282:11

Better angels of our nature, 530:2

death b. than day of birth, 20:2

enemies get the b. of us, 127:3

good name b. than precious ointment, 20:2

himself or situation, 491:1

in a state of servitude, 74:5

Better *(continued)*
is a neighbor near, 19:6
is thy love than wine, 21:8
no b. thing under the sun, 20:8
nobody b. than anybody else,
435:5
place for you and me, 512:5
so much b. than you know, 517:4
tell you a secret I'm b., 178:5
than a brother far off, 19:6
than themselves, 56:10
they are no b. than you, 79:4
to be packed like spoons, 478:7
to have good opinion when dead,
166:3
to make a b. day, 512:7
to rise and strike again, 480:5
to save brother's house on fire,
66:3
understand it b. by and by, 128:4
white people b. or above dying,
539:6
Between us a gulf, 34:14
Beulah patient among knickknacks,
487:4
Beware false prophets, 27:11
of punishing wrongfully, 2:4
of those who speak, 248:3
the easy griefs, 260:6
Beyond all definition defying place,
279:7
horizon still way b. you, 180:6
individual an answer given, 202:5
old racial wounds, 525:2
scorched mountains, 276:2
so much more b. horizon, 233:6
the face of fear, 367:6
the mountains are mountains,
276:n1
Bias, wringing as much b. out, 530:2
Bible by way of the Cross, 285:5
says it still is news, 253:7
story called B. but it's dead now,
212:2
Bid 'em in Get 'em in, 300:4
farewell to rule of slavery, 293:5
Bidder, highest b. raised her hand,
506:3
Big Bessie's feet hurt, 260:5
let the B. Light in, 189:12
sea full of fish, 212:7
world as b. as you make it, 169:5
would be happy to be b. there,
452:4

Bigger, making hole b. to stay in,
200:6
my world got b., 339:5
than life, 438:6
Big-league, to be a b. ballplayer,
274:1
Bigness, her b. sweeps my being,
175:6
Bigotry and prejudice are winning,
498:2
bias against racial b., 220:1
fastballs and b., 353:4
Bilingual, every black American is b.,
558:4
Billie Jean is not my lover, 511:5
Bills, as long as I'm footin' the b.,
293:3
Billy clubs couldn't beat it out, 274:4
Binds, what b. us together might
prevail, 522:3
Biological, Saddam Hussein has b.
weapons, 380:5
this need to rise is b., 552:7
Bird alone flying low, 329:3
Diz and B. together, 301:3
dwelling shaped like a b., 445:1
is lost dead, 247:5
life is a broken-winged b., 210:6
little b. must you scold me, 3:5
Lives, 312:3
rise at the voice of the b., 20:11
snatch food from mouths of
babes, 490:4
why the caged b. sings, 150:4
Birds, bitter as the gall of b., 3:4
caught in the snare, 20:9
fine feathers make fine b., 46:3
fly from their nests, 5:2
I sang to the beat of native b.,
440:4
in the blue palms, 384:6
sing in shadows, 345:4
two lady b., 292:7
visit the b. again in sleep, 477:4
Birmingham, march the streets of B.,
249:5
Birth, common destiny in land of
our b., 111:9
death better than day of b., 20:2
despise the land of my b., 122:1
gave b. to a puzzle, 361:7
giving b. is like jazz, 531:6
got no b. certificate, 449:6
honor the b. of a son, 487:2

Birth *(continued)*
new b. of freedom, 523:2
of memory, 385:7
spirits live beyond death before b.,
458:7
time before b., 226:1
waters sang like rivers, 460:6
Birthday boy headed for grave,
478:2
go shorty it's your b., 560:3
party on my b., 394:1
Birthright, justice every man's b.,
103:5
sold his b. unto Jacob, 147:n1
sold my b. for pottage, 147:7
Births, press didn't deal with our b.,
265:5
Bitch, Africa is a b., 281:9
Inglan Is a B., 489:4
racism is a b., 403:3
set me up, 366:5
you ain't a b. or a ho, 553:7
Bitches, we either b. or queens, 559:5
Bite, every wolf taking a b. at you,
196:1
step on dog's tail he will b. you,
565:22
Biting, dogs stop b. in the South,
273:1
Bitter as the gall of birds, 3:4
because my parents were slaves,
352:7
children feed on b. fruit, 210:3
fate turns up the b. cup, 149:5
fruits of time, 515:6
mouth filled with a b. taste, 471:6
stalks of weeds, 281:1
swill of civil war, 527:1
they get b. they cling to guns,
525:4
when man fails alone, 322:9
with b. herbs they shall eat, 9:9
woes of a race b. reality, 127:2
Bitter-bright rememberings, 281:1
Bitterness, bread of b., 175:6
cup of b., 317:8
in somebody else's cup, 466:5
in the throat, 348:2
life too short to hold b., 160:2
Bittersweet like a precious memari,
489:6
Black, a world where b. or white,
212:8
accepted myself as b., 434:1

Black *(continued)*

access to privilege and power, 366:1

ads for B. Capitalism, 389:2

Aesthetic is a corrective, 342:6

agenda is not a marginal agenda, 492:3

AIDS is a b. disease, 505:3

ain't had a b. leader in a while, 544:8

aint only beautiful its bad too, 346:3

alive and looking back at you, 371:4

although I am b. and proud, 287:5

Am I B. Enough for You, 429:4

America is the B. Man's country, 199:2

America where b. was b., 209:5

America's b. middle class, 482:7

American castrated by white America, 359:2

American culture is a New World creation, 534:8

Americans are colonized, 280:2

and blue, 192:6

and burnin in burnin times, 247:3

and male in America, 505:4

and unfair we are b. magicians, 354:4

and white as equals, 265:2

anguish fall upon deaf ears, 291:3

are filled with rage, 302:1

are there b. racists, 389:5

artist has wasted time, 280:2

artists contributors to art, 335:2

Arts Movement, 379:1

as a b. female writer, 339:5

as the night is b., 211:4

beautiful outasight b. men, 430:2

began to feel b. and blue, 503:5

being b. does not stop you, 222:2

being b. in America, 573:16

being b. in America was Original Catch, 456:4

being spoken from earth's inside, 357:6

being too b., 216:5

Belt dialects, 200:5

best b. troops of our Army, 142:6

blood came white sugar, 308:7

born with b. skin, 294:3

bourgeois negated being b., 491:7

Black *(continued)*

bourgeoisie failed to play role, 186:1

bourgeoisie has inferiority complex, 185:7

bourgeoisie in image of the white man, 185:8

brides and grooms cutting cakes, 265:5

burden of being b., 203:2

Buy B., 573:13

call for b. people to unite, 414:2

cant see b., 230:8

cause I am, 384:5

cherubs rise at seven, 218:2

childhood always a drag if you're B., 430:4

coffee that's too b., 294:6

colored persons more white than b., 134:2

consciousness, 454:6

conspiracy to destroy B. boys, 493:8

criminal prey on his own, 145:5

day b. man takes step, 296:1

dead b. boy on trial for murder, 560:1

destroy a b. man with single word, 343:10

didn't God know if he made us b., 237:9

different just because you're b., 532:7

distrust between b. men b. women, 491:9

domination, 266:5

don't know how to sing B., 534:4

don't mean b. at all, 277:3

don't want a B. History Month, 377:3

drop the terms b. and white, 402:3

every b. face born, 379:3

every house built by b. men, 104:6

exhausting being B. in America, 395:4

experience an American experience, 226:4

fakelore of b. pathology, 257:2

fast b. energy space, 355:1

fifteen dollars for every b. brother, 310:1

finger pointing upwards, 161:5

first b. only b. best b., 496:6

first thing is forget I'm B., 441:4

Black *(continued)*

folk are a mirror, 231:2

folk lived as victims, 327:2

folk say America would have been stronger, 231:1

folks in toto, 491:8

four b. girls blown up, 384:3

free B. and twenty-three, 256:5

games b. folk play on one another, 546:4

gates of death, 232:8

gay b. man living in a world, 502:5

generations of b. men, 416:1

get back get back get back, 184:5

girl yearns blue eyes, 336:8

God is b., 395:1

god made me, 312:5

God take the b. earth, 281:3

good b. don't crack, 573:11

great b. men swinging their lives, 398:6

growing up Southern B. girl, 305:7

happening because I'm b., 421:2

Harlem is b. world's community, 255:5

harnessing b. potential, 255:10

he was half b. half white, 74:2

her b. complexion a liability, 216:5

history is American history, 377:3

History Month, 377:3

homosexuals and love them, 540:2

how b. humor started, 403:1

how one is seen as b., 492:2

hurting b. story, 489:3

I am a b. woman, 279:7, 287:8

I am a b. wooooooooman, 358:5

I am b. but comely, 21:3

I am black the incarnation, 290:9

I am the B. woman, 441:5

I am white and I am b., 185:3

I remember I am b., 407:8

I'm a b. mother, 247:3

I'm B. I'm Proud, 347:4

ice is the smoothest, 503:6

if b. folk allowed to participate, 231:1

if you're b. get back, 572:10

images from folklore, 257:2

in America b. is a country, 354:5

innocent womanhood, 328:7

is b. is b. is b., 553:5

is beautiful, 276:1

Is Beautiful, 503:5

Black *(continued)*
is beautiful, 573:2
is it because I'm b., 190:3
is not a curse, 290:9
is powerful, 214:2
is something, 435:5
is ugly, 276:1
is white and white is b., 185:2
it just is, 480:1
it's a b. thing, 574:4
it's b. it's white it's tough to get by, 512:4
jazz music our b. anthem, 312:6
keys beautiful as white keys, 320:7
Lady in Mourning, 291:3
Lesbian Feminist Warrior, 359:1
liberty equally precious to B. as to white, 70:5
life treated with short worth, 559:5
like me, 210:8
like the depths of Africa, 211:4
little b. dog with sad eyes, 232:7
love a b. woman, 553:7
love b. people hate niggers, 544:3
love is B. wealth, 430:5
magic you lookin at, 467:3
make a poet b. and bid him sing, 218:8
make b. men American citizens, 145:8
male patriarchs, 488:3
man discovered Bible, 285:5
man has two dimensions, 290:6
man I'm a b. man I'm b., 384:4
man in white world, 271:1
man sitting down to eat, 99:4
man stop trying to be white, 196:6
man you are created B., 196:6
man you cain't shine, 568:9
Man's Burden, 256:4
man's journey, 505:1
men accorded equal treatment, 272:5
men are a country, 573:7
men are most men, 164:8
men are not endangered species, 483:2
men once great shall be great again, 172:2
men proudly gay, 496:4
men sheep among wolves, 196:1
Montgomery had to go on, 239:1
more obstacles than being b., 287:2

Black *(continued)*
mother within each of us, 358:6
Mr. B. Man watch your step, 194:2
my countenance, 91:2
my face is b. not my fault, 138:2
mythology surrounds b. woman, 491:10
naked woman b. woman, 224:6
negative B. images, 265:6
niggers holding b. back, 277:3
niggers my beauty, 359:4
no b. surface can entirely hide, 516:1
no place in America for a b. girl, 428:8
not all b. but it will be African, 197:7
not b. enough, 474:6
not candidate of b. America, 287:5
not that she minded being b., 216:5
now b. is the preacher shouted, 248:4
of that b. land, 175:2
only on weekends and holidays, 500:6
outside or b. inside, 74:1
people are an African people, 414:1
people are very beautiful, 284:5
people armed with freedom defense and guns, 424:8
people around white people, 520:1
people catch it, 353:6
people created style, 500:5
people exploit blacks, 276:1
people have done wonderful things, 363:6
people in America's wilderness, 495:2
people magical faces, 324:1
people of B. Metropolis, 235:5
people saved this country's soul, 363:6
people viewed as them, 494:6
people want from b. artists the exotic, 548:8
people we no know, 386:4
poor and b. and shut out, 238:4
positive B. images, 265:6
post-black was the new b., 541:4
pot calling the kettle b., 570:10
power is a call, 414:2
Power is about black people, 427:3
power is the brain power, 230:5

Black *(continued)*
power must mean hard work, 187:4
Power, 414:n1
private dick, 419:7
provin' to world b. was beautiful, 216:4
quality of b. leadership, 255:10
question for b. critic today, 342:6
race not a race of criminals, 128:1
rap is b. America's TV station, 518:3
Red B. Green colors, 272:5
reincarnation I want to come back b., 242:7
remind me I am b., 298:2
respect B., 122:2
revolt palpable in letters, 280:1
ruling over white and b., 110:4
saints sang, 242:8
second never forget that I'm B., 441:4
seek b. power, 230:4
seize upon b. Americans, 249:2
sexual politics in B. women's lives, 573:14
Shadow of American culture, 347:8
shining Prince, 261:2
shiny curls, 174:8
show you my b. bottom, 169:8
skin is b. arms are long, 352:6
skins wooly heads, 107:5
slang, 373:3
so b. they call me nighttime, 247:4
so-called b. people, 257:1
society tells me I am b., 503:7
socks stood for b. poverty, 442:4
soil this rhythm was born, 500:8
soldiers giggling, 298:3
sons and daughters, 310:3
sooty b. shiny b., 182:2
soul is to feel oneness with b. people, 368:3
souls of B. America, 274:4
spirit of service in b. man, 120:1
stay b. and die, 573:8
strange suddenly being b., 290:3
sturdy B. bridge I crossed over, 450:5
subjugation of b. women, 488:4
survival in America, 495:1
survival in the urban areas, 422:2
sweet b. angel, 195:1

Black *(continued)*

talk to b. guy down the street,
533:3

the term b. denotes condition,
452:6

the white b. man, 74:1

the word b. nasty and hard, 290:3

there's b. people and there's
niggers, 544:3

they will come out as B. people,
474:4

they would beat Jesus if he was b.,
204:4

think b., 421:6

this is the b. shot with blue, 516:1

tidal waves of Africa, 199:2

to ask b. community, 275:2

to be born b., 557:1

to be young gifted and b., 328:2

to the bone, 518:6

tolerate so-and-so because best b.,
496:6

two b. men a dangerous mob,
544:4

underclass, 366:2

urban fashion, 510:6

usta be young usta be gifted still b.,
455:1

wall of my cell 47 b. faces, 336:3

war is at us my b. skins, 108:7

warrior's b. face, 225:8

wasn't the only b. girl, 217:1

wasn't white nowhere b. wasn't,
209:5

way too b., 474:6

we b. and they white, 230:9

we want b. participation, 454:2

when b. the limit's the sky, 544:7

where b. deeds are done, 175:2

while the two of us are b., 433:7

white America still exploits b.,
310:1

white and b., 64:2

white man constructed b., 562:5

white people constantly talk of b.
people, 107:6

who told B. woman she was savior,
335:3

who will revere B. woman,
328:7

why you so b., 384:5

will not be asked to get back,
274:5

woman wells of strength, 255:4

Black *(continued)*

women are not homogenized
chocolate milk, 358:8

women carry the handicaps,
379:6

women sexually stereotyped,
564:1

women's existence, 456:6

world b. green red yellow, 355:2

you're considered b., 277:5

young gifted and b., 433:1

Black Panther, so I became a B.,
428:8

Black Panthers, women B. as
freedom fighters, 446:3

Blackbirds, they flew like b., 370:6

Blacker, changed into a b. being,
355:3

than a hundred midnights, 148:2

the berry sweeter the juice, 571:2

they are the more pleased, 298:1

world on death row, 495:8

Blackness a rupture in the order of
things, 509:5

asked if my b. would rub off, 214:4

authentic or legitimate B., 557:1

challenge of b. is defining it, 309:1

did not help me, 232:3

embracing b., 355:3

is a state of mind, 573:9

possibilities of B., 557:1

Black-on-black crime, 553:6

violence, 503:1

Blacks, America's urban b., 208:2

American b. call that soul, 233:2

among the b. is not poetry,
66:*n*1

crucial minority, 255:10

dehumanizes b. and whites alike,
246:1

different beginning than American
b., 380:3

have a condition not problem,
289:2

inferior because not white, 509:5

middle passage b. in a net, 384:3

New Generation B., 410:2

nor whites had monopoly on
truth, 399:6

of the continent, 279:6

presence of b., 249:1

sick of both whites and b., 217:2

slavery a curse to whites b., 95:3

to quasi-citizenship, 324:2

Blacks *(continued)*

two b. in all-white institution,
309:2

unemployed we're called lazy,
409:10

Vietnam impact on b., 390:8

whites relieved b. joined, 298:3

Black-skinned Africans, 295:8

Blame, eager to shift b. on others,
217:1

it on the blues, 200:8

leader on whom b. or praise falls,
84:4

prejudice is to b., 498:2

Blanket, big b. mek man sleep late,
575:10

Blaze, hope then burn and b. forever,
81:3

water on the b., 327:1

Bleached by wind and storm, 276:2

poor white in a sudsy tub, 165:1

Bleed, to b. and not die, 434:5

Bleeding, earth was vibrant and b.,
434:5

five nights of b., 489:2

tracked my b. countrymen, 127:2

Bless, God b. Africa, 267:1

God b. child, 253:7

God b. you make haste, 82:4

Lord b. thee and keep thee, 11:5

them that curse you, 27:1

things even in our pain, 515:6

Blessed are the dead, 44:19

are the dehumanized, 385:4

are the meek, 26:12

are the merciful, 26:12

are the peacemakers, 26:12

are the poor in spirit, 26:12

are the pure in heart, 26:12

are they that mourn, 26:12

are they which are persecuted,
26:12

are they which hunger and thirst,
26:12

are ye when men revile you, 26:12

art thou among women, 32:17

be even this, 368:2

be Lord God of Israel, 33:1

be name of the Lord, 14:19

be the Lord God of Shem, 7:16

generations shall call us b., 171:2

is the fruit of thy womb, 32:19

Jesus Heavenly Dove, 63:2

Jesus took bread and b. it, 31:6

Blessed *(continued)*
    more b. to give than receive, 37:14
    mother told me I was b., 201:10
    Prince, 355:3
    the man that endureth
        temptation, 43:1
    they have not seen yet believed,
        37:5
    whom thou blessest is b., 11:7
    whose precinct We have b., 54:10
    with intelligent derrière, 223:2
Blessedness comes from God, 201:10
Blessing aid white more than Negro,
    124:2
    as any b. ever prayed for, 475:3
    of the Brahmins while you live,
        166:3
    upon the President, 70:2
Blessings, every individual enjoy the
        b., 66:1
    peace and b. manifest, 554:6
Blind, dollar fer a ole b. hoss, 568:7
    eyes to the b., 15:19
    have the sense of hearing acute,
        77:2
    I was b. now I see, 36:6
    I've been so b., 326:4
    if b. lead the b., 29:3
    leaders of the b., 29:3
    love is b., 86:4
    men must be willfully b., 74:3
    to the ways of mankind, 520:7
    with patriotism, 297:4
Blindness afflicting the black race,
    296:9
Blindyitis, Negroes got b., 453:4
Blinking of an eye, 225:2
Bliss, deprived of b., 81:2
    glory life and b. unknown, 71:5
    what could equal the b., 516:7
Block, betrays memory of auction b.,
    282:11
    Clotel on the auction b., 97:1
Blocks, outsiders violate our b.,
    550:6
Blond, long luxurious b. hair, 501:2
Blonde girls with stringy hair,
    362:1
Blood and sweat of the innocent,
    410:5
    brother's b. crieth from the
        ground, 7:5
    created man of a b. clot, 57:6
    created of a b. clot, 55:5

Blood *(continued)*
    cry for justice, 299:4
    cup is new testament in my b.,
        39:15
    Drink this is my b., 31:6
    enriched America with b. and
        tears, 78:3
    flower with petals of b., 388:4
    fried meats angry up the b., 224:2
    geometry of my shed b., 241:5
    God made all of the same b., 79:4
    hatred would demand b., 123:7
    his b. is in their soil, 282:11
    I am innocent of the b., 31:16
    if b. the price of liberty, 572:1
    loyal b. demanding loyalty, 225:3
    made of one b. all nations, 37:13
    made white in b. of the lamb,
        44:11
    man who will enslave own b.,
        105:7
    Negro b. flowing in his veins,
        108:5
    of an outcast race, 113:3
    of our ancestors, 349:1
    of the lamb, 44:11
    of the new testament, 31:6
    on us and our children, 31:17
    on your ankles, 537:3
    one drop of b. we spared, 293:6
    one drop of black b., 136:4, 214:2
    ours is the b. that nourished,
        473:10
    poisoned b. of both, 330:5
    red b. in the fields, 461:1
    restoring his b. to free course, 80:2
    rituals of b. on the burning, 489:2
    rivers of tears lakes of b., 118:4
    shadow of b., 242:8
    shed for the remission of sins, 31:6
    shiver like leaves, 325:1
    sweat and b. done drenched this
        earth, 350:1
    tears and b. sacrificed, 83:7
    two races are of one b., 136:5
    washed robes in b., 44:11
    where is b. of your fathers, 100:6
    whoso sheddeth man's b., 7:13
Blood's thicker than the mud,
    435:4
Bloodhounds, pursued with guns
    and b., 99:1
Blood-red, both sides of b. waters,
    100:4

Bloodshed of their forefathers,
    376:10
Bloody, revolution it's b., 467:6
Bloom, full b. of life, 256:3
    waited to b., 451:7
    wasn't never gonna b., 451:7
Blooming in the noise, 260:3
Blooms above weeds, 306:4
    mother raises rare b., 460:6
Blossom in time, 115:3
Blot, it's a b., 380:6
    out his name, 44:1
Blow, deep amnesiac b., 330:7
    don't b. your top, 269:6
    my horn, 204:4
    the trumpet against evil, 75:1
    your shells roll your drums, 108:7
Blue above brown under, 157:8
    began to feel black and b., 503:5
    black and b., 192:6
    black girl yearns for b. eyes, 336:8
    boys with b. eyes, 300:10
    dangerous and b., 571:5
    glass in the house sing, 516:1
    like bubbles, 325:5
    lonely and feeling b., 411:6
    rich as night Afro B., 299:8
    States for Democrats, 522:6
    this is the black shot with b., 516:1
    Vein Society, 134:2
Blue-eyed blonds, 295:8
    full b. Summer, 128:7
Blue-jazz gesture in state of rejection,
    232:1
Blueprint/declaration of the other,
    250:5
Blues ain't nothin' but a heart
    disease, 193:6
    all night ragtime and b., 176:2
    American music derives from b.,
        148:7
    are the roots, 252:1
    as much social reference as poetry,
        354:2
    as roots of today's rap, 453:2
    backwater b. caused me to go,
        188:1
    beat from Sanctified Church,
        236:4
    blame it on the b., 200:8
    brickyard b., 391:7
    different shades of b., 326:2
    Every Day I Have the B., 254:5
    falling down like hail, 237:2

Boredom, turn their b. into pleasure for yourself, 471:8

Born a slave I was prepared for prison, 409:8

anew at each a.m., 314:7

anytime a child is b., 350:3

baby hold back from b., 313:4

be what we were b. to be, 382:3

being b. of royalty, 201:10

black skin b. in prison, 294:3

but I was free b., 37:15

by the river, 334:2

daughters b. to pamper lusts, 100:6

every black face b., 379:3

every one is b. of the Spirit, 35:16

for good luck, 251:5

good if he had not been b., 31:5

had I been b. white, 153:5

hard luck started when b., 155:7

here we were b. here will die, 569:11

I was b. in slavery, 67:7

in hard time Mississippi, 481:10

in the congo, 431:2

in the days of Herod, 25:18

into music die into music, 411:1

Jesus Christ is b., 576:8

Jesus was b. in Bethlehem, 25:18

King of the Jews, 25:18

let another world be b., 255:2

live and die free and French, 67:8

man b. and dies, 564:3

man b. unto trouble, 15:6

man be b. again, 35:15

of his spiritual genius, 120:1

Queen must live like Queen, 59:6

sun b. and dies, 564:2

there is none b. wise, 1:3

this day a Savior, 33:4

time to be b., 19:17

to be b. black, 557:1

to draw to our end, 25:6

to fight, 536:9

to go down like this, 189:13

to wear this chain, 81:2

under a system, 299:3

with no state of mind, 520:7

Borne the burden, 29:16, 148:6

Borrowed plumes, 46:2

Borrower is servant to the lender, 18:23

Bosom, carry them in his b., 22:15

in the b. of Abraham, 578:9

Boss, love taught me who was the b., 406:5

paying the cost to be the b., 293:3

Bossism is not leadership, 279:3

Boston, I found my way to B., 121:2

Bottom a go drop out, 449:4

every tub on its own b., 570:13

faces at the b., 324:1

light fire at b. of the pile, 166:2

rail on top dis time, 570:4

show you my black b., 169:8

start at b. and work way up, 239:6

Bought and sold like an ox, 98:7

and sold, 122:6

crown b. and paid for, 285:7

wisdom is not b., 564:14

Bound in bundle of humanity, 114:2

in chains hand and foot, 98:7

single garment of destiny, 320:6

utmost b. of the everlasting hills, 8:19

with fetters of brass, 12:16

Boundaries, more than national b. make a nation, 237:6

racial b. disappeared, 497:7

Boundary line to music, 273:5

Bounties, act in b. unconfin'd, 72:1

share the b. of the earth, 212:8

Bourgeois negated being black, 491:7

Bourgeoisie, black b. failed to play role, 186:1

black b. has inferiority complex, 185:7

black b. in image of the white man, 185:8

mistreated by no b., 174:3

Bovanne, dance with B., 394:4

Bow, my fame makes great ones b. down, 4:1

Bowl, sugar in my b., 352:3

tossed into the icy silver b., 506:3

Bowtie, ladies' b. gentleman's necktie, 569:1

Box, arm's too short to b. with God, 148:4

break open the b., 100:2

rap upon b. see if he's alive, 100:2

shutting myself in a b., 100:1

yo' arm's too short to b. wid God, 148:n1

Boxing is only sport get your brain shook, 438:7

Boy ain't it time, 282:4

brown-skinned hometown b., 257:5

cried wolf, 45:15

healthy b. ain't wrong when he kills his brother, 490:8

let that b. boogie-woogie, 262:6

lot of little b. in you, 274:1

what they did to my b., 275:7

Your B. Friend He Wasn't Last Night, 548:5

Boy's lips are soft as baby's skin, 486:6

Boys, scared for our b., 558:9

they get b. to fight wars, 378:5

wine-flushed bold-eyed b., 174:8

with blue eyes, 300:10

with gun and uniform, 413:2

Bracelets on my wrists iron and steel, 121:3

Brahmins, blessing of the B. while you live, 166:3

Braid my hair, 371:7

Braiding, write it's like b. hair, 550:2

Brain, black power is the b. power, 230:5

come from heart as well as b., 153:6

get your b. shook your money took, 438:7

it's not b. surgery, 499:4

soothes my thumpin' bumpin' b., 156:2

you rattle my b., 333:6

Brains, use your b., 436:10

Brainwashed and we didn't know it, 463:4

not what we were b. to be, 382:3

refuse to be b., 515:2

Branches of coral, 345:8

Brand, last foul chain and slavish b., 116:6

Branded from the time of slavery, 350:4

Brass, feet like unto fine b., 43:18

fetters of b., 12:16

Brass Ankles bear the prejudice, 154:3

Brave, come if you are b. enough, 84:7

fortune favors the b., 48:n4

Brave *(continued)*
fortune helps the b., 48:12
men or women do not stand by, 140:3
the icy currents, 527:3
Braver, words are b. than fighting, 2:3
Bravery, does color impair my b., 68:2
kept out of sight, 372:5
Bravest, education which b. men followed, 109:5
Brawn, Black Man's b., 306:1
Bread and pottage of lentils, 147:*n*1
ask b. will give him a stone, 27:9
cast thy b. upon the waters, 20:10
eat b. without scarceness, 11:15
folk want b. cake pie crumbs, 292:2
give us our daily b., 27:2
I am the b. of life, 35:23
Jesus gave b. to the disciples, 31:6
Jesus took b. and blessed it, 31:6
lack of b., 230:10
Mammy's little baby loves short'nin' b., 569:3
neither eat b. nor drink water, 10:12
not live by b. only, 11:14
of bitterness, 175:6
prepare b. and mind, 51:4
roast with fire and unleavened b., 9:9
seven days shall ye eat unleavened b., 9:12
to the wise, 20:9
water salt for all, 267:1
Break all the chains holding me, 275:5
down sit down, 372:4
if America breaks we b., 91:5
it up b. it up, 514:10
open the box, 100:2
time to b. down, 19:17
too poor to b., 306:2
Breakdown of meaning, 282:8
Breakfast, fix me no b., 179:8
out of thin air, 255:4
Breaking the barriers of virtue, 69:4
wrestled a man until the b. day, 8:11
Breaks, if America b. we break, 91:5
on the sheltering bars, 169:3
these are the b., 514:10

Breast, rounded darkness of your b., 209:3
Breastplate of faith, 42:1
Breasts, brown b. throbbing, 176:1
table of dark b., 225:8
Breath, crumble before the b. of time, 158:2
eyes and memory are one, 550:1
giveth to all life and b., 37:13
God breathed the b. of life, 6:7
hot and cold with same b., 46:12
I my b. resign, 92:2
not going to hold my b., 483:6
say something worth b., 462:2
Breathe, until they b. on us again, 520:3
Breathing, last of the b., 554:5
Breathless breath come through, 165:2
Breed new generation of aristocrats, 257:8
violence can b. counter-violence, 266:3
Breeds, familiarity b. contempt, 45:14
Brethren, free my b. fetter'd slaves, 91:1
least of these my b., 30:12
my b. my kinsmen, 72:3
Brewster, women of B. Place, 479:3
Briarpatch, once upon a time the b., 257:7
Bribe for the gatekeeper, 365:5
Brick, clawed in glass and b., 250:1
Brickyard blues, 391:7
Bride, I am b. and bridegroom, 49:1
Jerusalem as b. adorned, 45:3
price must be paid, 437:7
Bridegroom, I am bride and b., 49:1
virgins went to meet the b., 30:7
Brides, black b. and grooms cutting cakes, 265:5
Bridesmaids, the absence of rice and b., 507:2
Bridge, build a b. of words, 231:6
imagination is the b., 558:6
sturdy Black b. I crossed over, 450:5
the chasms that divide, 266:9
Bridle, put on b. with such trembling, 82:4
Bright, America's beacon burns b., 526:3
Eye of Horus comes, 3:1

Bright *(continued)*
I have made b. the truth, 4:1
Brighter days, 511:7
Brightness celebrating motherhood, 447:8
I eat of its b., 4:1
Brilliant wit will shine, 90:2
Bring back our mighty dream, 212:5
every work into judgment, 21:1
fatted calf, 34:10
in 'da noise b. in 'da funk, 558:7
It on Home to Me, 334:3
Judgment Day, 174:*n*2
the noise, 518:1
Bringer of good tidings, 54:1
Bringest God and angels as a surety, 54:14
Brink, on the b. on the brim the cusp, 532:2
Britain, in B. because B. colonized you, 234:3
spleen that scourge of B., 85:4
British, known by colour under B. flag, 569:12
neo-colonialism strangling your countries, 234:3
Broad is the way, 27:10
new dress same old b., 227:6
Broadcasting, think of nature as b. stations, 142:4
Broke, being b. a temporary condition, 343:6
Broken, I am like a b. vessel, 16:14
the bands of slavery, 98:6
this is my body b. for you, 39:14
unto the ground, 22:6
Broken-winged bird that cannot fly, 210:6
Bronze, taupe mahogany b., 182:2
Brooklyn-born don't have no sob stories, 539:7
Broom, grab the b. of anger, 180:16
I'll dust my b., 236:6
ole b. know corner best, 575:16
Brother, better than a b. far off, 19:6
carry me like you are my b., 512:6
every man's sword against his b., 23:22
fifteen dollars for every black b., 310:1
help of our b. slaves, 242:4
I am the darker b., 211:2
in both places at once, 415:3

Brother *(continued)*
    lend hand to b. in distress, 66:3
    like me and myself, 517:8
    love God in words hate b. in
        works, 92:4
    still got one b. left, 549:3
    strive to love my b., 349:3
    too many of you dying, 396:9
    when my b. fell, 507:3
Brother's, am I my b. keeper, 7:4
    better to save b. house on fire, 66:3
    blood crieth from the ground, 7:5
    Gonna Work It Out, 439:4
Brotherhood among all men, 220:2
    in the cause of b., 297:7
    little progress toward b., 220:4
    love the b., 43:7
    melodies of b., 320:7
    my religion the b., 240:5
    no peace no b. between men, 197:5
    society of peace and b., 304:3
    spirit of b., 295:8
    table of b., 318:1
    true sense of b., 126:4
Brotherly, let b. love continue, 42:19
    love, 38:17
    spirit of b. love, 170:6
Brothers, all mankind are his b., 230:6
    Christian b. don't be slow, 364:6
    for the b. who ain't here, 434:4
    in Christ, 144:7
    in the pen, 556:2
    kill each other, 462:3
    men black brown white are b.,
        144:6
    no b. up on the wall, 508:8
    protect one another, 423:4
    sisters cousins, 334:5
    so fed up with white man, 502:9
    two b. passing, 531:2
    where men can be b., 304:3
    why kill my b. and sisters, 415:5
Brought forth her firstborn son,
    33:3
Brow, fair b. would never know,
    302:2
Brown, America is the B. Man's
    country, 199:2
    as a berry, 191:4
    baby years roll by, 300:2
    can stick around, 274:5
    girl in the ring, 574:12
    girls rouged and painted, 176:1
    gone was the b. complexion, 193:2

Brown *(continued)*
    if you're b. stick around, 572:10
    skin gal stay home mind baby,
        575:4
    stick around, 184:5
    world black red yellow b., 355:2
Brown's promise is lost in
    fantasyland, 400:3
Brownness, I love you for your b.,
    209:3
Browns, pretty B. in beautiful gowns,
    151:8
Brownstone, unbroken line of b.,
    321:7
Brussels, not history taught in B.,
    294:1
Brutality, police b., 317:9
Brute, sell in shambles like a b., 112:1
    slavery to make man b., 101:2
Brutish, just some b. animal, 350:4
Bubbles, blue like b., 325:5
Buck, we b. in the middle, 206:3
Bucket a go a well, 449:4
    cast down your b., 131:5
    drop of a b., 22:16
    let down your b., 214:1
    water is thrown, 327:1
Buddies in wine-stained hallways,
    284:5
Buddy Bolden, thought I heard B.
    say, 157:3
Buffalo Soldier, 450:3
Bugs people especially white, 301:2
    under a microscope, 553:4
Build a body of public opinion,
    228:6
    a green economy strong, 548:1
    a store of your own, 89:1
    fences to keep others out, 186:4
    men may b. dams, 203:3
    my people died to b. this country,
        198:6
    our power, 262:5
    our temples for tomorrow, 211:6
    they b. houses we rent them, 93:5
    time to b. is upon us, 266:9
    time to b. up, 19:17
    upon this rock b. my church, 29:8
    we b. and work and love, 529:5
Builder of the necessary, 422:3
Building blocks of family history,
    476:6
    engaged in nation b., 171:3
    of American life, 201:5

Building *(continued)*
    somebody else's civilization, 173:7
Buildings, who own them b., 355:4
Built, God b. you noble, 179:5
Bullet, ballot or the b., 295:5
    called in to silence the oratory,
        446:2
    control, 544:5
Bullets, words can be b., 315:1
Bullies are cowards, 135:8
Bullwhips, outlived b. and Bill
    Connor, 506:4
Bulwarks of the rich, 208:1
Burden, bear his own b., 41:7
    Black Man's B., 256:4
    borne the b., 29:16
    disregard the b. of race, 183:2
    easy b., 346:8
    falls on the blacks, 494:6
    let racism be someone else's b.,
        380:2
    my b. is light, 28:8
    of being black, 203:2
    of being white, 203:2
    of the desert of the sea, 22:5
    White Man's B., 256:4
Burdens, lay b. on men's shoulders,
    101:5
Burger, stopped cold from eating
    another b., 499:6
Buried, life you had before b., 353:4
    long my b. heart is lain, 85:5
    people dead haven't been b., 164:4
    them inside you, 451:7
Buries all sentiments in ruins, 69:4
Burn, 'bout to b. out superstar, 563:7
    baby b., 230:5, 312:9
    did not our heart b. within us,
        35:3
    hope then b. and blaze forever,
        81:3
    shifting from b. baby b., 409:12
    the midnight oil, 305:5
Burned, library b. to the ground,
    274:2
    the bush b. with fire, 8:22
    those being b. know fire, 194:5
    whiteness onto my scalp, 450:6
Burning, black and b. in b. times,
    247:3
    in Los Angeles, 475:5
    integrated into a b. house, 284:3
    long internal b., 306:3
    shining light, 35:19

Cane appears to haunt us and we cut it, 487:1
leaves swaying, 188:6
no sugar c. for miles, 254:2
over order of c. and history, 461:1
spread out c. along the steep, 128:7
wind is in the c., 188:6
workers wait, 384:6
Canisters packed with grapeshot, 412:7
Cannons, face c. on the battlefield, 194:3
Cannot, all that I would do I c., 116:4
be first in everything, 46:7
himself he c. save, 32:1
Canvas, art ain't about c., 309:3
Capetown, left C. with promise of revenue, 531:3
Capital, Harlem c. of every ghetto, 446:1
we were c. likes bales of cotton, 472:1
Capital punishment, only excuse c. attempts to find, 139:8
Capitalism, ads for Black C., 389:2
blood that nourished c., 473:10
gold that made c., 308:7
whiplash of c., 310:3
Capitalist class use women to reduce wages, 129:4
end the Robbery by the C., 426:2
underdevelopment a product of c. exploitation, 427:4
Capitalistic hand around throat, 548:6
Capitalists, shy about being c., 472:1
Capitulation to the powerful, 202:3
Caprice, infinite c. and romanticism, 207:9
Captive, lead thy captivity c., 12:14
Captivity, detaining brethren under c., 66:2
lead thy c. captive, 12:14
rivers of tears shed in c., 118:4
Captured and taken to extreme South, 99:1
Car, have to go they go in c., 490:6
in the broken down c., 206:2
no roof over head but he has a c., 490:6
speeding into the sunset, 458:6
way you parked c. sideways, 513:7
you got a fast c., 536:8

Caramel, Harlem of c. and rum, 215:3
Caravan around the campfire light, 422:4
Caravans, meeting place of c. and boats, 60:3
Care, don't c. how great you are, 254:6
don't c. one straw, 48:7
don't c. who you tell, 548:2
live this long taken better care, 165:5
nor do they c. a straw, 48:n2
of this world, 28:14
someone has to c., 556:1
take c. say with presence of mind, 48:8
Careers, luxury of multiple c., 484:2
they have wonderful c., 362:1
Careless, oh c. love, 571:9
Cares more than for a lame horse, 79:1
Caress, caught in addictive c., 308:2
Cargo, Englishman treated as African c., 513:2
Caribbea, you are C., 314:3
Caribbean born in hands of acolytes, 331:8
identity, 311:1
Caribbeanness, what threatens C., 311:1
Caring, first task is c. for our children, 528:6
without c. about their skins, 271:2
Carpenter's, is not this the c. son, 28:17
Carpet, imagination a magic c., 250:3
Carried away as with a flood, 17:17
getting c. away, 276:2
His servant by night, 54:10
to the throne of grace, 72:3
who is c. does not realize how far town is, 565:1
Carries, somebody else c. on, 217:7
Carry forward noble idea, 526:5
he may c. away in hand, 20:1
me back to old Virginny, 130:1
me home, 577:1
nothing out, 42:8
old man a-waitin' to c. you, 576:9
precious light of freedom, 529:4
them in his bosom, 22:15

Cars, damn the lights watch the c., 186:3
Carthage, to C. I came, 52:3
Carve out that future that destiny, 171:5
Case is closed, 53:3
plead c. before whites, 89:4
we have diagnosed the c., 252:3
Cast, do not c. nor turn away, 51:2
down but not destroyed, 40:10
down thorn of prejudice, 190:5
down your bucket, 131:5
dragon was c. out, 44:15
first stone, 36:3
forth upon earth, 51:4
God accepted the peoples c. away, 59:2
it before Pharaoh, 9:5
like a net c. into the sea, 28:16
pearls before swine, 27:6
pluck it out and c. from thee, 26:14
thy bread upon the waters, 20:10
time to c. away stones, 19:17
time to c. away, 19:17
whole body not be c. into hell, 26:14
Caste, redesigned racial c., 545:9
Castest, why c. thou off my soul, 17:16
Casteth, perfect love c. out fear, 43:15
Castle of your skin, 304:7
Castles made of sand, 420:6
Castrated by white America, 359:2
Casts, white black c. dark shadows, 185:3
Casualties, not all wars have c., 394:7
souldead c. of our defeat, 483:3
Cat, bell the c., 46:11
Juba skin dat Yaller C., 568:8
mouse laughs at c. there is hole nearby, 565:3
Cat's, rats don't dance in c. doorway, 565:5
Catastrophes, push back the c., 369:3
Catch a fire so you can get burn, 449:5
don't let sun c. you crying, 228:3
if you c. it in the moonlight, 464:5
it like anybody else, 353:6
shut mouth c. fly, 574:5
the spirit, 304:3

Catch (continued)
   the thunder, 280:4
   thy plaintive soul, 188:7
Catched, swallow gudgeons ere
   they're c., 45:n2
Catchword, inclusion is not a c.,
   384:7
Categorization, passion for c.,
   282:8
Catfish, sushi and fried c., 476:4
Cats, come in c. check your hats,
   192:9
Cattle upon a thousand hills, 17:3
Caucasian barristers not to blame,
   135:2
   problem is real and universal,
   193:4
Caucasians, apparent unity among
   C., 348:5
Caught between two allegiances,
   183:2
Cause, anger without c., 64:5
   black c. I am, 384:5
   no good c. justifies war, 183:5
   no love for self root c. of hate,
   196:5
   of freedom c. of humankind,
   135:9
   of freedom, 274:6
   plead our own c., 80:1
   ready to take up the c., 523:2
   slavery is not a just c., 72:5
   that's the c. of it, 47:n3
   them to be sold, 57:10
   white people who take up our c.,
   165:6
Cavalry, root for Indians against the
   c., 343:8
Cayenne, hard times make monkey
   eat c., 570:9
Cease, grinders c., 20:11
   have independence or c. to live,
   75:5
   let education c. enslave the mass,
   99:3
   to be one nation, 371:2
Ceases to be a man, 104:4
Ceasing, pray without c., 42:2
Ceiling, quota artificial c., 292:3
   snug in my c., 381:4
Celebration, your c. is a sham,
   105:3
Celestial, black cherubs do c. chores,
   218:2

Cell taped to wall of cell, 336:3
Celluloid, enslave me in c., 510:3
Celtae, ambassadors from C., 47:n9
Cemetery, send him to the c., 294:5
Censorship is to art what lynching is
   to justice, 476:3
Center, in c. trying keep margins at
   distance, 481:5
Centuries, agonies of c. crowd my
   soul, 127:2
   burst into volcanic eruption, 207:9
   four c. slave trade, 251:3
   of lies, 361:9
Cerements, swaddling c. bound,
   330:7
Ceremonies, staging secret
   woodland c., 460:7
Certain man from Jerusalem, 34:1
Certainty, hoping for the truth the
   only c., 502:1
Certificate, got no birth c., 449:6
Chain about ankle of fellow man,
   106:9
   born to wear this c., 81:2
   fastened about own neck, 106:9
   feel the c. galling us, 84:3
   forever wear galling c., 117:4
   last foul c. and slavish brand, 116:6
   right is mightier than the c.,
   117:1
   to bind you to earth, 218:1
   unbroken c. of ancestors, 190:1
   workin' on the c. gang, 334:1
Chained, black people c. together,
   69:2
   five months c. like a goat, 537:4
   you in coffles, 205:4
Chainless Liberty, 117:5
Chains, bound in c. hand and foot,
   98:7
   break the c. holding me, 275:5
   dare death than endure c., 100:1
   deliverance from c., 104:1
   do not make the slave, 129:1
   galling of the c., 69:3
   love and c. are broken, 211:8
   rattling of c., 73:1
   release him from his c., 80:2
   wail of slaves in c., 308:7
Chair, don't bring no rocking c.,
   307:2
   put a hog in the electric c., 350:7
Challenge for every prisoner, 267:3
   of blackness is defining it, 309:1

Challenge (continued)
   where man stands times of c.,
   318:6
   withstand c. from without and
   within, 428:6
Challenged by the law rite of passage,
   491:1
Champ, being c. well and good,
   303:9
Champion, air of invincibility as a c.,
   438:6
Championed the cause of colored
   people, 124:1
Champions aren't made in gyms,
   417:10
Championship, colored man was
   holding the c., 159:2
Championships, teamwork and
   intelligence win c., 534:7
Chance, equal c. in battle of life,
   124:5
   for the curtains to part, 423:7
   in Britain not by c., 234:3
   knock and ask for equal c.,
   140:5
   time and c. happeneth to all,
   20:9
   to cast their ballots like we did,
   528:4
   to pursue happiness, 526:5
   to stand on own legs, 106:4
Chandeliers, woman sings lovely as
   c., 360:6
Change, ability to bring about real c.,
   523:6
   always be men struggling to c.,
   349:7
   based on empowerment, 288:2
   begins in yourself, 463:6
   bring about genuine c., 358:3
   can Ethiopian c. his skin, 23:13
   can't come until we feel sorry,
   349:2
   everything can c. all at once,
   533:7
   fear denies c., 419:2
   get angry bring c., 296:2
   has come to America, 526:1
   hearts of men for good or evil,
   229:5
   if Republican Party does not c.,
   381:1
   in the status quo, 321:5
   is coming to America, 523:7

605

Change *(continued)*
  it comes eventually, 560:7
  it's coming, 197:2
  justice makes c. inevitable, 419:2
  knew how I'd c. the color, 238:1
  know c. gonna come, 334:2
  lay in our silence, 332:5
  leopard c. his spots, 23:13
  millions of voices calling for c.,
    523:8
  my part over and over, 291:3
  one reason to c., 432:2
  only thing worthwhile is c., 197:2
  revolution is about c., 463:6
  societies without c. are dead, 496:3
  sweat will get you c., 409:13
  through art that old whispering,
    211:5
  tremble at c., 321:5
  we are the c. that we seek, 524:2
  will come from grass roots, 522:2
Changed into a blacker being, 355:3
  not all sleep but all be c., 40:7
  not everything can be c., 283:10
  nothing c. until faced, 283:10
  nothing has c., 401:1
Changes, God c. not people, 54:6
Changing, everything was c. pushing
    me out, 439:3
Channels of resistance, 437:3
Chaos, expect c. in innocent
    moments, 477:5
  meteoric flares are meaningless c.,
    207:9
Chaotic, only thing not c. is death,
    369:6
Character, a good c. is remembered,
    2:5
  defining of our c., 527:2
  flaws of c. into virtues, 471:2
  judged content of c., 318:2
  judging people on content of c.,
    530:2
  SAT tests do not measure c.,
    366:3
  share these faults of c., 231:5
  stereotype Negro c., 206:1
Charge, give his angels c. over thee,
    33:9
  him rent, 397:6
  not soul save to its ability, 55:6
Chariot of fire, 14:4
  of Israel, 14:5
  swing low sweet c., 577:2

Charismatic leader in the limelight,
    217:6
Charity beareth all things, 39:16
  begins at home, 47:5
  believeth all things, 39:16
  edifieth, 39:10
  endureth all things, 39:16
  greatest of these is c., 39:17
  hopeth all things, 39:16
  now abideth c., 39:17
  rejoiceth in truth, 39:16
  shall cover multitude of sins, 43:8
  solidarity is not act of c., 351:5
Charles Town, I determined to go to
    C., 75:2
Charleston, under water in C.
    harbor, 384:3
Charm, go away you evil c., 240:6
Chase him down the alley, 397:6
Chasm of despair and pessimism,
    268:3
  that exists between the races, 525:1
  yawns wide and deep, 140:7
Chasms, bridge the c. that divide,
    266:9
Chasteneth, he that loveth him c.
    him, 18:17
Chastity, give me c. and continence,
    52:6
Chattel, wreckage of c. slavery, 146:7
Chattering wagtails of Mikuyu
    Prison, 439:6
Cheap at the price, 408:3
  talked down to working c., 277:8
Check, given Negro bad c., 317:7
  your egos at the door, 351:3
Cheek, beauty's c. felt cool, 223:6
  like a hair across your c., 194:8
Cheeks, mask that hides our c., 150:2
Cheer, be of good c., 28:23, 36:21
  men c. in the heart, 108:7
Cheerful, be c. while you are alive,
    2:2
Cheerfully, obey c. and freely, 63:6
Cheerfulness, put on face of c.,
    109:1
Cherie amour, 481:6
Cherish, guardians of the liberty you
    c., 73:4
Cherry, as American as c. pie,
    427:5
Cherub, he rode upon a c., 16:5
Cherubims, east of the garden of
    Eden c., 7:2

Cherubs, black c. rise at seven, 218:2
Chest, in Meridian's c. a breaking,
    444:1
Cheweth the cud among the beasts,
    10:13
Chicken, bring a whole fried c., 343:1
  prayer of c. hawk not get c.,
    564:13
Chickens coming home to roost,
    296:8
  count c. before hatched, 45:10
  nobody here but us c., 228:4
Chief, grandfather not an Indian c.,
    178:7
  hate struck down C. Magistrate,
    296:8
Child, a c. is a c., 338:7
  anytime a c. is born, 350:3
  behold a virgin with c., 25:17
  born with no state of mind,
    520:7
  calls me girl, 306:2
  condition of mother determines
    c., 94:2
  don't you cry, 423:2
  flying toward sunlight, 314:7
  forsake wife c. or die a slave,
    99:1
  God bless c., 253:7
  gotsta raise they self, 563:8
  has potential to become
    extraordinary, 538:5
  I feel like a motherless c., 576:7
  I'm a voodoo c., 420:8
  imitate the growing c., 73:3
  invest in every c., 395:5
  of the sun, 91:2, 441:5
  of those centuries of lies, 361:9
  out of twilight, 314:7
  please an adult the c. therein
    re-emerges, 447:4
  saw the c. with Mary, 26:1
  spake as a c., 39:17
  takes a village to raise a c., 574:3
  the tell me is the answer to the c.,
    214:6
  thought as a c., 39:17
  understood as a c., 39:17
  you're not a c. anymore, 436:8
Child's developing complex, 245:7
Childhood always a drag if you're
    Black, 430:4
  last night of c. began a visit home,
    459:3

Childish, put away c. things, 39:17
  set aside c. things, 526:5
Childlike, Africa kept in c. state,
  551:4
Children, all Aunt Hagar's c., 478:1
  all c. should feel protected by
    police, 559:1
  all God's c. got a crown, 577:13
  allow c. to come back home, 376:2
  and old folks tell the truth, 178:6
  are beauty, 314:7
  are our immortality, 395:6
  are reward of life, 565:8
  attend inferior schools, 272:5
  borne thirteen c., 82:6
  come and beg weeping, 161:4
  crops failed sold my c., 513:3
  do you love c., 368:7
  father help your c., 473:3
  feed on bitter fruit, 210:3
  first task is caring for our c., 528:6
  freed c. see no clouds, 123:3
  get on board little c., 577:8
  give our c. opportunity, 198:8
  guarantee future of c., 285:8
  his blood on us and our c., 31:17
  I and my c. are free, 95:5
  lead c. in path of virtue, 75:1
  like the c. of Israel, 100:4
  listening to elders, 283:5
  mothers weeping for c., 97:2
  my four little c., 318:2
  need people to fight for them,
    485:5
  Negro c. suffer, 228:7
  of battle are your heroes, 430:7
  of disillusioned colored pioneers,
    375:2
  of Israel went into the midst, 9:16
  of light, 41:21
  of long-sown seed, 412:7
  of once-upon-a-time slaves, 478:3
  of school age, 229:2
  of the day, 41:21
  of the magistrates, 1:3
  of the sun, 173:5
  only a real man can raise c., 548:9
  provoke not your c. to anger,
    41:17
  Rachel weeping for her c., 26:3
  reason my wife and I had c., 376:3
  receives us as adopted c., 94:3
  regard such c. as property, 95:2
  remember c. you did not get, 258:8

Children *(continued)*
  Return ye c. of men, 17:17
  see things very well, 327:5
  splash and laughter c. playing,
    434:6
  start worrying about c., 348:1
  suffer the little c., 32:14
  they shall be called c. of God,
    26:12
  wade in the water c., 578:10
  walk together c., 578:12
  watch my c. grow, 306:4
  we are the c., 512:7
  we have no C., 61:2
  wealth and c. adornment of life,
    55:2
  what shall I give my c., 259:3
  when c. are in bed, 224:8
  white c. to school with Negroes,
    229:3
  whom I loved, 271:2
  why wait for the c. to tell us, 439:5
  wisdom exalteth her c., 25:8
  wisdom justified of c., 28:7
  would they raise, 227:3
  young c. prefer to be white, 245:7
Children's, weakness of c. limbs
    innocent, 52:2
Childtime is a mighty thing, 315:5
Chinaberry Tree became a Temple,
    164:1
  tree my spyglass tree, 257:7
Chinaman's, the C. murder, 441:2
Chisel, despair a poor c., 320:5
Chitlin, magic into c. circuit air,
    398:6
Chitlins, soul food is more than c.,
    384:2
Chivalry can command no respect,
    139:7
Chocolate City and its vanilla
    suburbs, 407:4
  homogenized c. milk, 358:8
  sweet like c. candy, 176:9
  this city will be c., 504:7
Choice, no right so sacred as c., 117:2
  not c. but responsibility, 431:8
Choir of dolphins, 345:8
Chondria, Russia's c. for short,
    85:4
Choose Africa and English tongue,
    330:5
  American people did not c. this
    fight, 528:3

Choose *(continued)*
  between Tweedledee and
    Tweedledum, 427:7
  Jack Mandora me no c. none,
    576:3
  one's ancestors, 248:12
  wait in shadows if you c., 280:4
Choosing hope over fear, 523:7
Chords, living c. of my heart, 113:1
Chores, black cherubs do celestial c.,
    218:2
Chorus, exotic as a c. girl, 385:3
Choruses above the guinea's squawk,
    188:6
Chosen, I have c. you, 36:19
  many called few c., 29:21
  Mary hath c. that part, 34:5
  people of Ethiopia were c., 59:2
  to be special people, 11:13
  vessel, 37:11
  ye have not c. me, 36:19
Christ, brothers in C., 144:7
  come from God and a woman,
    83:1
  in C. all alive, 40:4
  is all and in all, 41:16
  joint-heirs with C., 38:13
  kingdoms of our Lord and his C.,
    44:13
  our Passover is sacrificed, 39:8
  risen from the dead, 40:4
  Savior C. the Lord, 33:4
  separate us from the love of C.,
    38:15
  Son of the living God, 29:7
  to live is C. to die is gain, 41:12
  was hit by a stone, 493:7
  you did alright in your day, 212:2
Christian brothers don't be slow,
    364:6
  demanding from C. white
    churches, 310:1
  neither civilized nor C., 293:5
Christianity has failed you, 196:1
  religion of the oppressor C., 419:3
Christians in style of the Egyptians,
    58:1
  Negroes join angelic train, 71:4
Christmas, asked me right at C.,
    214:4
  this C., 448:6
Chromosomes, genes and c., 518:6
Chronicles, monk will transcribe my
    c., 85:8

Church, authority of C. moved me,
52:11
  beat from the Sanctified C., 236:4
  Lost American C., 389:2
  ruling over C. and State, 110:4
  said Amen, 256:3
  the c. has failed you, 196:1
  upon this rock build my c., 29:8
Churches, abetted by white Christian
c., 310:1
CIA, five years C. nigger, 327:3
Cicero, book of a certain C., 52:5
Cigars, pipe smoke and aroma of c.,
475:2
Circle, cycles in the c., 386:1
  life goes in a c., 238:7
  make your vital C., 391:3
  wheel had come full c., 406:8
  where the c. came from, 422:1
Circumstances, accomplished under
adverse c., 125:5
  force of c. keep us down, 119:3
  reverse the c., 99:3
Circus mind that's running wild,
420:7
  this is a c. a national disgrace,
468:4
Cities eaten by termites, 276:2
  in their arms, 276:2
  Lot dwelled in the c. of the plain,
8:2
  method the big c. used, 238:5
  two c. formed by two loves, 53:6
Citizen, alien and c., 51:3
  American c. and colored, 179:3
  fellow c. of the world, 525:5
  first-class c., 208:3
  in the wild weed she is c., 260:5
  Negro is an American c., 128:2
  proud c. of the United States,
525:5
  second-class c. don't pay first-class
taxes, 343:4
Citizens, ask our white fellow c.,
125:1
  attempt to make black men c.,
145:8
  first-class and second-class c.,
183:6
  of the United States of America,
208:7
  of the world, 207:5
  rights as men and c., 79:3
  second-class c., 198:4

Citizens *(continued)*
  senseless slaughter of our c., 528:3
  we are c., 327:2
Citizenship and sentiments innate in
me, 67:3
  assets and liabilities of c., 208:3
  dream of world c., 183:6
  economic access and full c., 365:2
  education is the teaching of c.,
229:4
  equal c. under the law, 524:3
  exemplifying manhood dying for
c., 139:5
  first class c. for the Negro, 270:4
  foolish to give up c. for Africa,
162:9
  Negro c. is a fiction, 154:4
  price and promise of c., 527:2
  proofs of my good c., 67:3
  responsibilities of c., 168:5
  rights of c. enjoyed, 228:6
City affords information, 107:4
  and its people, 279:1
  continuing c. we seek to come,
42:21
  did not grow up in any inner c.,
503:7
  each c. has distinctive reputation,
235:4
  glorious c. of God, 53:5
  heart of the c. has not yet died,
440:2
  how doth the c. sit solitary,
23:16
  in the c. of David, 33:4
  induces profitable reflections,
107:4
  is the Universe, 250:7
  living just enough for the c., 481:11
  of a woman, 367:4
  renewed, 279:1
  this c. will be chocolate, 504:7
  this is your c. too, 363:7
  unsullied by worship of idols, 60:3
  we have no C., 61:2
Civil, activists of c. rights, 255:9
  bitter swill of c. war, 527:1
  greater than c. rights is human
rights, 295:7
  rights cycle of the Sixties, 255:10
Civil War canisters packed with
grapeshot, 412:7
  Constitution did not survive C.,
230:2

Civilization, between colonization
and c., 241:7
  chooses to close its eyes, 241:6
  incapable of solving problems,
241:6
  lynching disgrace to c., 272:5
  of the universal, 226:2
  optimistic about c., 284:10
  our boasted c. a fraud, 126:1
  outside pale of c., 272:5
  part and parcel of American c.,
166:1
  support weight of c., 290:7
  that uses trickery and deceit,
241:6
  that works requires simply, 279:4
  tired of building somebody else's
c., 173:7
  wears Africa on its face, 476:5
Civilizations, great c. indebted to
one another, 365:7
Civilized, in the vocabulary of the c.,
95:6
  nations term themselves c., 95:6
  neither c. nor Christian, 293:5
Claim, no c. upon your liberty,
103:1
  no easy victories, 285:9
Clanking of galling chains, 100:1
Clapping, one note everybody c.,
261:6
Clare, the trouble with C., 182:7
Clarity, everything but c., 398:4
Clash between freedom and
exploitation, 297:6
Class, America's black middle c.,
482:7
  capitalist c. use women to reduce
wages, 129:4
  emancipated c. under former
master c., 118:3
  more important than race, 366:1
  oppression, 379:6
  Race First and c. after, 165:6
  separate race from c. from sex
oppression, 573:14
  Solidarity, 165:6
Classroom looked at me like I was a
nut, 499:5
Clay, feet part of iron and c.,
23:23
  had she paints or c., 337:4
  like c. in a season of drought,
284:2

Clean glass of water, 196:3
new broom sweep c., 575:16
Cleanse me from secret faults, 16:7
Clear as the sun, 21:11
he might make c. for them, 54:7
is that c., 198:6
out poverty plant new life, 227:1
Clerks, whippersnapper c. call our
name, 206:3
Cliché, love is the most empty c.,
340:4
Clichés of adolescent narcissism,
446:4
Click, locks c. on the doors of cars,
530:1
Clifford, my name is C. Pepperidge,
298:4
Cliffs shelve surely to foam, 332:5
Climate change does not respect
borders, 383:8
Climb, aint trying to c., 555:5
lifting as we c. onward upward,
140:5
Lifting As We C., 571:10
more hills to c., 267:5
Climbing higher ground, 230:7
up the Rough Side of the
Mountain, 201:4
Cling to guns or religion, 525:4
Cloak of righteousness, 231:5
Close, through dance c. to God as we
get, 433:3
Closed, case is c., 53:3
father's lips c. in silence and grief,
65:8
Closer and closer in touch with
nature, 142:3
Just a C. Walk with Thee, 579:9
Clot, created man of a blood c., 57:6
Clotel on the auction block, 97:1
Cloth, gray c. brings dark wood to
life, 487:4
Clothed and in right mind, 32:12
naked and you c. me, 30:11
Clothes, dressed in old raggedy c.,
485:5
matchbox hold my c., 195:6
style of c. one wears, 142:5
with my c. on, 301:3
wrapped in swaddling c., 33:3
Clothing, in sheep's c. are ravening
wolves, 27:11
strength and honor are her c.,
19:10

Clothing (continued)
wolf in sheep's c., 45:8
Cloud, black-gray mountains of c.,
258:1
by day in a pillar of a c., 9:15
dark and dismal is the c., 89:3
of witnesses unseen, 348:3
smoking gun a mushroom c., 498:4
Clouds, as fleeting as the c., 55:9
gray skies are just c. passing, 202:1
return after rain, 20:11
she's walking through c., 420:7
when the c. clear, 386:2
Cloven tongues like fire, 37:7
Cloven-footed, parteth the hoof is c.,
10:13
Clown, tears of a c., 405:2
thick lips white teeth, 280:3
Clubs, billy c. couldn't beat it out,
274:4
hoses guns jails, 249:5
in Spanish Harlem, 262:1
jazz c. houses of worship, 312:4
Clues, used abused without c., 518:2
Clutching, on elevator and woman c.
her purse, 530:1
Coal, black as c., 519:1
Coalition, the real rainbow c., 410:4
Coast, on the c. a slave ship, 69:2
Coat, in my boxcar c., 379:5
stripped Joseph of his c. of many
colors, 8:14
Coat of Arms, more than National
C. make a nation, 237:6
Coats, dark solemn c., 322:4
Cobra, strike like a c., 395:7
Cock, before the c. crow, 31:7
Cocoa pods and alligator pears,
175:5
shades of delight c. hue, 299:8
Coconut, Peas an' Rice an' C. Oil,
575:3
Code, live by justice c., 300:2
Coffee, integrated cup of c., 295:6
like caffeine in your c., 303:3
that's too black too strong, 294:6
won't know you ever had c., 294:6
Coffles, chained you in c., 205:4
Coiled in their own hearts and
houses, 79:5
Coin, eagle on the back of a c., 356:7
flinging c. to beggar, 320:1
two sides of same c. of existence,
468:3

Coincidences that became miracles,
562:6
Coins, tossing c. in praise, 174:8
Coke, in Georgetown snorting c.,
389:7
want some c. have some weed,
423:5
Cold, clothes on in the blueback c.,
243:3
hand of death, 63:5
hot and c. with same breath, 46:12
suddenly she was oddly c., 182:3
Collect all de common-sense ina
worl, 269:3
Collective, our fate as Americans is
c., 446:5
Collector, I shall become a c. of me,
360:7
College, from cotton fields to c.,
153:5
Colonial, dares to question c.
authority, 207:1
Colonialism, all of Africa against c.,
293:5
and its puppets, 294:1
whiplash of c., 310:3
Colonialist, underdevelopment a
product of c. exploitation, 427:4
Colonies, dark ghettos are economic
c., 246:2
greatest crime in the c., 207:1
Colonization, between c. and
civilization, 241:7
of Africa, 439:1
Colonize, failed to c. it with family,
397:8
Colonized, Britain c. you, 234:3
in their native land, 280:2
wretchedness of being c., 465:1
Colonizes, no one c. innocently,
242:2
Color, accomplishments have no c.,
305:6
all men regardless of c., 67:8
and complexion be what it will,
67:2
aside from c., 193:1
despair my c. shrouds me in, 218:7
difference of c. difference of
species, 569:9
discriminated for their c., 272:5
discrimination based on c. is
barbarous, 222:3
does c. impair my bravery, 68:2

Color *(continued)*

does c. impair my honor, 68:2

dressed in c., 224:6

easier to outgrow crime than c., 115:7

escape nemesis of my c., 183:3

every nameless woman of c., 543:3

extreme difference based upon c., 229:3

fate of our unfortunate c., 65:1

her c. variation a curse, 216:5

identifying one's own c., 246:7

in one place he had no c., 415:3

indicating one's c. preference, 246:7

irrespective of c. and race, 117:6

is a political reality, 284:6

is of no more significance, 183:6

knew how I'd change the c., 238:1

know the c. of the sky, 386:2

known by c. under British flag, 569:12

light c. status symbol, 263:1

line, 139:7

line problem of twentieth century, 143:1

lines within the c. line, 184:6

met by the c. line, 106:8

music is not a c. to me, 534:4

never destroyed self-respect, 153:5

no escape from badge of c., 395:4

not a c. question, 142:1

not exchange my c. for wealth, 153:5

not judged c. of skin, 318:2

of our skin is the most fundamental, 427:3

of skin, 90:2

oppression based on c. of skin, 140:7

permit no man no matter c., 132:9

prejudice against c. is the question, 79:5

prejudice creates attitudes, 184:6

proud of my c. or ashamed, 263:1

purple, 444:5

stop charging failures to c., 160:3

that is life, 224:6

their c. a diabolic die, 71:4

there is no c. called blood, 388:4

until c. no significance is a war, 449:9

use of c. in my paintings, 184:3

was a false distinction, 227:5

Color *(continued)*

Water doesn't have a c., 509:3

why does our c. make a difference, 237:9

worth not related to c., 276:1

written about this c. thing, 408:2

Colorblind casting, 452:7

criminal justice system is not c., 523:4

Color-blind society eludes us, 253:2

Colorblindness, in the era of c., 545:9

Colored, American citizen and c., 179:3

and married to white woman, 290:1

because I am a c. girl, 125:6

destiny of c. American, 106:2

disillusioned c. pioneers, 375:2

drop of black blood makes a c. man, 214:2

every c. woman dying, 337:5

girl an evil woman, 466:5

gonna love it bein c. all yr life c., 467:3

ground c. man occupies disputed, 105:5

I am c., 178:7

I don't eat c. people, 343:1

in company of c. people, 90:3

kill a c. sonofabitch, 298:3

love one another hate skins c., 105:4

man look to white folks, 451:3

man must be philosopher, 164:2

mechanic an elevator of his race, 104:6

men getting rights but not c. women, 83:5

men have one handicap race, 141:2

nobody called c. motherfucker, 290:3

not trust white or c., 96:4

overnight c. people become blacks, 290:3

people don't want me either, 289:8

people free and slaves, 88:6

people most degraded since world began, 77:4

people scared of whitefolks, 444:8

people understand white people, 147:4

persons more white than black, 134:2

Colored *(continued)*

problem confronting c. peoples, 193:4

question before c. people, 115:2

regular c. girl, 466:3

rob c. people of their money, 233:1

secondarily as c. people, 207:5

Soldiers of the Revolution have no historian, 103:2

tragically c., 179:1

traitors even among c. people, 96:4

turn up noses near c. person, 99:4

whether or not c. man can rise, 80:2

why repugnant to marry c. persons, 93:1

woman has two handicaps sex and race, 141:2

women can't afford self-pity, 227:3

wreck and ruin of c. youth, 140:6

you are C. Americans, 79:4

Colorful, most things are c. things, 164:8

Color-Line barbarous, 222:3

Colorphobia is a contagious disease, 99:4

Colors, arbitrary c. of scientists, 241:5

beautiful different c., 334:5

of the Negro race, 272:5

Red Black Green, 272:5

stripped Joseph of his coat of many c., 8:14

they were of all c., 295:8

Colours in salt teeth of foam, 345:6

Colts on the plains, 276:2

vagabond kids run like c., 276:2

Columbus of my ships, 325:2

Comb, scraped life with fine-toothed c., 258:9

to scratch your head, 277:4

tyranny and torture of the c., 193:2

Combine, let us c., 259:2

Come, all things must c. to pass, 30:3

back to you one of these days, 171:6

behold I c. quickly, 45:6

by here my Lord, 579:10

crossed the waters to c. here, 65:6

evil days c. not, 20:11

far from where I started from, 579:8

from some weh fus, 268:6

he shall c. unto us as the rain, 24:4

Compose, can't talk so I c. music,
247:1

Composition for White Critics,
484:7

Comprehend the roaring of the tiger,
241:1

Compromise, on these we do not c.,
538:6

Compromising, don't believe in c.,
383:9

Conceal, do not c. truth knowingly,
53:8

words made to c. thought, 98:2

Conceals, who c. disease cannot be
cured, 565:2

Concede your flesh and blood, 301:6

Conceits, wise in your c., 38:19

Conceive, in sin did my mother c.
me, 17:4

it believe it achieve it, 410:2

Concept, race a biological c., 330:4

Conception of justice, 485:2

Concern, expressed c. abroad
premature, 191:2

plead cause in things which c. us,
80:1

soul is the c. of my Lord, 54:13

Concerning, question thee c. the
soul, 54:13

Concerns, hear all but attend only
which c. you, 172:9

the many tight and small c., 259:7

Conch-shell, voiceless c., 356:3

Conch-shell's invocation, 332:4

Condemn, neither do I c. thee, 36:4

Condemnest, thou c. thyself, 38:4

Condition, acquiesces in that c. of
things, 128:2

blacks have a c., 289:2

common c. rather than common
consciousness, 168:1

happy contented love this c., 101:2

lowest c. of society to highest, 96:2

made our c. more hopeless, 126:4

of his class slavery, 103:7

position of people c. of females,
94:2

the term black denotes c., 452:6

their c. was slavery, 397:4

towards bettering our c., 123:1

Conditioned to their existence,
231:3

Condom, crown with a c. on it,
347:10

Conduct, duty to render account of
my c., 68:1

on our c. their salvation depends,
79:3

Conductors, I say what most c. can't
say, 111:4

Confer with the ignorant man, 1:4

Confess, deny me c. me, 49:3

you who c. me deny me, 49:3

Confession, art is a kind of c., 283:4

full of curiosities, 340:7

Confetti of flesh, 368:8

Confidence in destiny of my people,
125:2

Muhammad's c. in Allah, 348:4

no nation can obtain c., 123:5

Conflict, resolve c. before the
military stage, 382:4

worsted in the c., 127:3

Confused, resistance c. power, 319:6

Confusion about good neighbor
policy, 519:5

all over the land, 448:5

ball of c. that's the world today,
436:3

Congo, born in the c., 431:2

dances of Place C., 389:2

independence of the C., 293:6

no white can understand music of
C., 290:9

Congo's green, 306:1

Congregation said Amen, 256:3

Connection to its slaveholding past,
275:2

Connections as a human being,
471:1

Conquer, conquering and to c., 44:6

dishonorable to c. to be slaves, 73:3

opportunity to achieve, 286:2

Conquering and to conquer, 44:6

Conquest, forced upon African by
military c., 197:5

Conscience beats feebly, 189:2

behold his c., 81:7

freedom of c., 239:3

salves its c., 231:5

seared with a hot iron, 42:5

void of offense, 37:19

without compunction of c., 140:3

Consciousness, basic tenet of black
c., 454:6

common condition rather than
common c., 168:1

humanity called to shift c., 401:6

Consciousness *(continued)*
of Everlasting Arms, 125:5

of survival, 422:2

of the problems, 208:2

precedes unity, 417:12

Conscription for war, 239:3

Consequence of idle imagination,
337:4

of the single story, 562:9

racism was the c. of slavery, 237:5

Consequences, bear all the c., 275:2

they lead to evil c., 60:2

Consider loneliness, 381:3

me Black to the bone, 518:6

Consideration, ask c. and fairness,
125:1

Considered, you're c. black, 277:5

Constitutional, protect enjoyment of
c. rights, 125:3

Conspiracy, society in c. to oppress,
107:2

to destroy Black boys, 493:8

Conspirators, passive group of c.,
493:8

Constantly, white people c. talk of
black people, 107:6

Constituency unwilling to assert the
tragic optimism, 446:5

Constitution did not survive the
Civil War, 230:2

rights given us in C., 125:1

slavery question embedded in C.,
524:3

tragic optimism intrinsic to the C.,
446:5

Constitutions do not act to right
wrong, 228:6

Consume rather than preserve, 362:6

they raise produce we c. it, 93:5

Consumed, days c. like smoke, 18:2

the bush was not c., 8:22

Consumers, white men are
producers we are c., 93:5

Consumption, blues like c., 193:6

Contact with Egyptian Antiquity,
279:6

Contemporary Negro life, 167:6

Contempt, familiarity breeds c.,
45:14

of God, 53:6

of self, 53:6

Content, a race c. in midst of
wrongs, 127:5

deeper c. never spoken, 164:7

Content *(continued)*
  with your lot, 46:7
Contented, happy c. love this
    condition, 101:2
  is the caged lion c., 101:3
  to make a c. slave, 104:4
  with life dinner and wife, 85:2
Continence, give me chastity and c.,
    52:6
Continent, Africa a free c. to be,
    312:5
  carved up by great powers, 197:5
  half free half enslaved, 245:4
  why described the Dark C., 413:5
Continual sorrow in my heart,
    72:3
Continue, things will not always c.
    the same, 569:11
Continues, the struggle c., 567:13
Continuous play of history, 344:1
Contract, we've got to start with a c.,
    349:4
Contracted, enlarge the c. mind,
    72:1
Contracts, prisoners cannot enter
    into c., 266:7
  sign c. without reading, 277:8
Contradiction, African American is a
    c., 573:15
  deal in c. of terms, 131:1
  that divides the world, 443:2
Contrary effects of liberty and
    slavery, 74:3
Contribute, life that does not c. to
    history, 227:2
Contributions, withholding our own
    c., 264:7
Contributors, black major c. art of
    country, 335:2
Control, bullet c., 544:5
Controllable, if you are free you are
    not c., 373:1
Controlled, always be those c. by the
    past, 349:7
Controversies, victory in c. of all
    kinds, 159:1
Controversy, where man stands
    times of c., 318:6
Convenient, when I have a c. season,
    37:20
Conventional, challenge stale and c.,
    373:3
Conventions, holding c. for years,
    111:6

Conversation, Ibo art of c., 322:8
  in the c. itself, 522:3
Converted rock of oppression into
    steppingstone, 460:3
Conveyed as dry goods to a free
    state, 100:1
Convict attackers on the spot, 298:5
  not every black person is a c.,
    508:9
Conviction, full and unshaken c.,
    77:4
Convulsed, world c. for freedom,
    64:3
Cook, ugly and can't c. but I'm here,
    444:7
Cool, don't blow your c., 299:9
  down papa, 269:6
  make government c. again, 523:5
  to rule my world, 514:5
  too c. for words, 379:5
  used to be hot becomes c., 294:6
  way the wind blows is c. with me,
    502:4
  we real c., 259:8
Cooled, whose lives were c. felt the
    heat, 475:5
Cooperate, demand the right to c.,
    145:6
  stay and c., 182:1
  with white Americans, 145:6
Cooperative, ujamaa c. economics,
    410:8
Cop, and hey Mr. C., 449:6
Copacetic, everything is c., 160:1
Cope, shoot'n' dope just to c., 548:6
Copious perspirations, 69:3
Copper's brackish hue, 306:1
Coral, branches of c., 345:8
Cord, sever that c., 361:9
  umbilical c. was severed, 362:8
Core, rotten to the c., 131:2
Corn, cut-worm's in de c., 569:5
  planted your c., 292:3
Corner, ole broom know c. best,
    575:16
  shine a light in a dark c., 406:9
  this was not done in a c., 38:3
Corners, four angels on four c.,
    44:8
  of American society, 317:6
Cornets, harps timbrels and c.,
    13:19
Cornrowed, little girl boy with c.
    style, 392:7

Corporate, liberation from c. society,
    393:6
Corpse, every c. is mine, 458:7
  have a good-looking c., 233:3
  love c. on show in museum, 535:4
  rather a c. than a coward, 98:1
  your body like a c., 381:4
Corridor to the gas chamber, 285:1
Corrupt, evil communications c.
    good manners, 40:6
  word is like a c. tree, 54:8
Corruptible must put on
    incorruption, 40:7
Corruptions, shadows of c., 288:1
Cosmic loneliness of unmated, 180:4
Cost, counted c. to make the
    sacrifice, 99:1
  of ignorance, 346:7
  of liberty, 144:8
  maintain position at any c., 383:6
  slaves to the c. of living, 242:5
Costs, achieve freedom at all c., 264:5
Cotton, bloomy c. whitened in vale,
    128:7
  boll-weevil's in de c., 569:5
  brought them here, 206:2
  Candy on a rainy day, 431:9
  claim to love the c. gin, 444:8
  from c. fields to college, 153:5
  old c. fields at home, 174:4
  painting is harder than pickin' c.,
    169:2
  pick a bale o' c., 569:6
  picked your c., 292:3
  woman from the c. fields, 142:7
Cotton Club chorus girl, 385:3
Couch, old c. stuffed with fleas,
    332:2
Could you be loved and be loved,
    449:14
Coumbite of farmers, 227:1
Counsel of thine own heart, 25:14
Counsels, hated me in your c., 50:3
Count 'em two make 'em three,
    158:4
  chickens before hatched, 45:10
Counted as the small dust, 22:16
  for my full value, 130:7
  nothing could be c. on, 339:1
  willing to be c. as nothing, 63:1
Countenance, black my c., 91:2
  lift up his c., 11:5
  like lightning, 32:3
Counter, eat at any c., 245:6

Counteract his mercies, 66:2

Counteroffensive, reply to enemy's c., 265:1

Counter-violence, violence can breed c., 266:3

Countries, decide what happens in other c., 559:3

hinders relations with c. known, 58:2

Country, acquainted them and all c., 62:2

affords pleasure, 107:4

America is the Black Man's c., 199:2

America more our c. than is whites, 78:3

apologies you are no c., 554:3

black men are a c., 573:7

can't run a c. and be soft, 269:5

didn't love us back, 178:4

doing undoing in this c., 257:3

forbidden from serving c., 528:1

gives vigor to spirits, 107:4

guilty of such atrocities, 272:5

had I lived in a c., 141:3

has never been for me or for mine, 413:1

have let my c. down, 561:4

I like c. music, 433:6

in America black is a c., 354:5

in the interest of my c., 351:9

invested in future of c., 270:2

is changing demographically, 381:1

man without a c., 289:8

may be cramped or vast, 390:1

mother c. has enslaved you, 234:3

my c. right or wrong, 179:3

one's c. is your mama, 214:5

open to hunters of men, 101:4

our c. is being depopulated, 57:10

serving my c. with zeal and fidelity, 68:2

slice-and-dice our c., 522:6

stepped 'n fetched a c., 306:5

this c. where I intend to live expect to die, 126:1

this is my c., 423:1

this is our home our c., 569:11

we have no C., 61:2

we love our c. she don't love us, 94:3

we loved our c., 178:4

we Negroes love our c., 107:3

Country (continued)

we're this c., 227:1

wealth of c. founded, 308:7

when I look at my c., 276:2

your c. how came it yours, 144:4

Countrymen, salvation of my c., 72:3

shame of my own c., 73:2

Counts, under it and that c. too, 501:4

Courage comes in believing in oneself, 478:6

displaces fear, 519:3

found the c. to keep it alive, 525:7

is admirable, 258:5

is hidden until after it's done, 346:9

must be the fuel, 166:2

quality of c. unsung, 304:1

to face life, 334:6

to stand up and fight, 198:5

truth is a letter from c., 180:17

Courageous, we're all c., 305:3

Course, in the c. of study, 52:5

swiftness of thy c., 71:8

throw the river out of c., 203:3

Courteous, less c. than Negroes, 193:3

Courts, justice in the c., 298:5

Cousin, my c. from the South, 315:4

Cousins, brothers sisters c., 334:5

Covenant, ark of the c., 12:7

Covenant, problem of the broken c., 482:7

the words of the c., 10:12

Covenanted with him for silver, 31:1

Cover, judge a book by its c., 397:2

not the c. of the book, 74:1

Covet, thou shalt not c., 10:8

Coward, rather a corpse than a c., 98:1

Cowardice, take patience too far and it's c., 409:9

Cowardly, we're all c., 305:3

Cowards, nation of c., 483:4

one hero worth million c., 113:2

Cowboy in the boat of Ra, 389:1

Co-workers with God, 317:2

Cowries, other money except c., 273:8

Crack, a world in a c., 402:5

rock gets into the country, 549:1

Cracker, goddamn best c., 522:1

Cradle, another had power to tear from c., 112:1

from c. to the grave, 109:6, 272:3

Cradle (continued)

of jazz, 178:2

woman rocks the c., 195:7

Cramp, not c. him but free him, 133:3

Cramps, I wish them c., 367:7

Crave, all c. all lost, 575:9

Craving to be mentally alive, 296:9

Crawled, soul c. out from hiding place, 180:7

Crawling, black snake c. in my room, 195:4

Crazy, I May Be C. but I Ain't No Fool, 155:8

let's go c. let's get nuts, 514:2

master was a little c., 562:4

on an ordinary day, 464:5

they wonder why we c., 556:4

to call somebody c., 558:3

Cream, integrate with c., 294:6

milking a bear to get c., 181:3

Create, fight to c. the new man, 351:6

sense of the hunger, 231:6

world he wanted to c. was doomed, 477:6

Created, Adam c. from whole earth, 59:5

Black man you are c. Black, 196:6

by him all things c., 41:14

by him for him, 41:14

for thy pleasure, 44:4

God c. man immortal, 25:5

he who c. you without you, 53:4

in the image of God, 341:8

male and female c. he, 6:4

man of a blood clot, 57:6

of a blood clot, 55:5

of a lump of flesh, 55:5

of a sperm drop, 55:5

of dust, 55:5

once and he was nothing, 55:3

one God c. us, 24:16

thou hast c. all things, 44:4

Creation fires my tongue, 81:1

lost in wonder of C., 62:3

of heavens and earth, 56:3

reaction rather than c., 393:6

variety throughout His c., 121:5

Creative art means you create yourself, 157:6

edge, 455:2

handed on the c. spark, 443:5

out of our own c. genius, 172:10

Creative *(continued)*
 people respect c. genius, 142:1
 politics for c. intellectual, 255:9
 process not a switch, 333:1
Creativity, kuumba c., 410:8
 SAT tests do not measure c., 366:3
Creator has a master plan, 405:4
 remember now thy C., 20:11
 uncreated, 4:4
Creature, every c. of God is good,
   42:6
 man is a wonderful c., 72:4
 peculiar alien c., 86:3
 preach gospel to every c., 32:16
 shallow vain shadowy c.
   advertised, 162:8
Creatures, all c. must die and vanish,
   61:1
Credentials of status and beauty,
   507:4
Credit to my race, 191:7
Creeds, denominations and c., 181:7
Crematorium, flames at the c., 271:4
Crescent, terror did not come with
   star and c., 470:2
 walked to the fertile c., 431:2
Cried, boy c. wolf, 45:15
 for T.J. and the land, 435:6
Cries, all my help was c. and tears,
   73:1
 no one c. when a street dies, 480:2
 one who c. out and listen, 51:4
Crime, black-on-black c., 553:6
 complexion construed into c.,
   92:3
 easier to outgrow dishonor of c.,
   115:7
 greatest c. in the colonies, 207:1
 greatest virtue becomes greatest c.,
   207:1
 innocence constitutes the c.,
   284:1
 long after the c. has ended, 412:5
 shackles and binds, 553:6
 sympathize with Negro c., 145:5
 tried to make black love a c.,
   495:7
Crimes by Negroes discredit the race,
   128:1
Criminal, black c. prey on his own,
   145:5
 called c. for advocating, 299:1
 hope always a c., 299:1
 is past reformation, 139:8

Criminal *(continued)*
 justice system is not colorblind,
   523:4
 made by law a c., 266:4
 no doubt she was the c., 217:1
 until segregation made c., 234:4
Criminals, black race not a race of c.,
   128:1
 defend Negro c., 145:5
 legal to discriminate against c.,
   545:9
Crises, humanitarian rights c., 383:2
 in midst of our own c., 252:6
Crisis, biggest goddamn c. in history,
   504:6
 in national economy, 239:5
 of living, 377:2
 of Negro intellectual, 255:9
Criterion of rights, 92:3
Critic, question for black c. today,
   342:6
 toughest c. is myself, 301:1
Criticism, accept c. and do self-c.,
   351:6
Critics, Composition for White C.,
   484:7
 film c. don't write about it, 508:9
Crocodile, don't insult the c., 565:4
 log will never be a c., 564:16
Crocodiles, routinely fed to c., 506:4
Crooked shall be made straight,
   22:14
Crops failed sold my children, 513:3
 want c. without plowing, 105:9
Cross, bear no c. wear no crown,
   571:11
 by way of the Bible, 285:5
 go on c. that sea, 484:6
 one more river to c., 577:6
 suffered the C., 299:4
 under the weight of its c., 240:7
 willing to c. waters to return, 65:6
Crossed line so long been dreaming,
   111:3
 the waters to come here, 65:6
Crow, before the cock c., 31:7
Crowd, in the motley c., 301:7
 is gone, 277:6
 keep the c. cold bored, 539:2
 know ourselves as c., 310:4
 never end up a face in the c., 485:6
Crown, all God's chillun got a c.,
   577:13
 bear no cross wear no c., 571:11

Crown *(continued)*
 been bought and paid for, 285:7
 no victory to c. her banners, 113:5
 of glory fadeth not, 43:9
 of life, 43:21
 put the c. on what he say, 451:3
 shall receive c. of life, 43:1
 with a condom on it, 347:10
 you can't eat a c., 303:9
 your nakedness, 280:4
Crowned, Faith c. with grace, 190:5
 Freedom's army c. with laurels,
   102:5
Crownest the year with goodness,
   17:6
Crucible, race relationships in c.,
   177:3
Crucified, let him be c., 31:15
 was she not c., 445:2
Cruel, compassionate and c., 50:1
 don't be c. to heart that's true,
   333:4
 heart can be c., 478:4
 jealousy is c. as the grave, 21:14
 master treats with unkindness,
   62:1
 remain in this c. uncertainty, 67:3
 tender mercies of the wicked are
   c., 18:16
 wrongs and injuries, 89:3
Cruelest, being a mother is the c.,
   183:1
Cruelties, compare your language
   with your c., 78:5
Cruelty and barbarism of men, 66:1
 example of fraud rapine and c.,
   70:1
 subtleties of refined c., 154:3
Crumb falls from tables of joy,
   213:4
Crumbs, dogs eat c. from masters'
   table, 29:4
 folk want bread cake pie c., 292:2
 tobacco c. vases fringes, 259:6
Crusade, call of one's c., 312:1
Crush apartheid, 266:6
 people then penalize them, 296:6
Crushed, a reptile to be c., 207:1
Crust eaten in peace, 46:1
Cry, a great c. in Egypt, 9:13
 best time to c. is at night, 378:8
 don't make me c., 277:4
 it's still okay to c., 536:4
 No Woman No C., 449:7

Cry *(continued)*
only because of beautiful things, 465:5
over their condition, 296:2
stones c. out, 34:17
when doves c., 514:4
Cryin', can't keep from c., 244:1
Crying, don't let sun catch you c., 228:3
gotta dance to keep from c., 466:2
Crystal, clear as c., 519:1
life ain't been no c. stair, 211:3
Crystals, magic c. pure and white, 521:1
Cud, cheweth the c. among the beasts, 10:13
Cultivated, cut off society its c. minds, 99:3
Cultivation of our own natures, 125:4
Cultivators, original c. of the earth, 422:1
Cultural, denial of c. activities, 278:5
half-castes, 225:4
identity is a matter of becoming, 344:1
integration leading to c. negation, 255:6
mulatto, 533:1
nationalism, 255:8
tool of the C. Imperialists, 452:7
zero, 168:2
Culture, accommodate dominant c., 252:8
American c. is mulatto, 257:1
black American c. is a New World creation, 534:8
Black Shadow of American c., 347:8
black women's c. unknown, 456:6
blues ain't c., 359:6
come when you buck up, 314:1
drum of African c., 381:2
excluded by American c., 231:4
expresses its own c., 295:10
is effective weapon, 278:5
Negroes inside outside our c., 231:7
politics of c., 255:9
symptomatic of a dying c., 379:1
to speak to assume a c., 290:7
transmitted through genes, 248:13

Culture *(continued)*
Western c. in love with own image, 518:9
without concessions, 301:6
Cultured hell that tests my youth, 175:6
Cultures, learn about another's c., 389:4
smothered c., 412:5
Cumbered about much serving, 34:4
Cunning, Segu is a garden where c. grows, 375:5
Cup, bitterness in somebody else's c., 466:5
drinking c. of bitterness, 317:8
integrated c. of coffee, 295:6
is new testament in my blood, 39:15
let this c. pass from me, 31:8
my c. runneth over, 16:10
took the c. gave thanks, 31:6
Cure, beside nettle grows c. for its sting, 90:5
no medicine to c. hatred, 565:19
those the doctor has failed, 566:12
Cured, who conceals disease cannot be c., 565:2
Curiosity, anything to engage c., 337:4
Negro regarded a c., 86:3
research is formalized c., 181:1
Curls, humpteen baby c., 258:6
swarthy neck black shiny c., 174:8
Curse, add mother to sound like c., 485:3
black is not a c., 290:9
bless them that c. you, 27:1
God and die, 15:1
her color variation a c., 216:5
in its own soul, 114:2
my pride, 50:2
no portion of globe exempt from c., 108:6
slavery a c. to whites blacks, 95:3
slavery far reaching c., 103:6
tried to make black history a c., 495:7
unemployment is like a c., 369:5
upon motherhood, 161:3
why do you c. and honor me, 51:2
Cursed be Canaan, 7:15
slavery, 118:4
thou art c. above all, 6:17

Curtains, chance for the c. to part, 423:7
comely as the c. of Solomon, 21:3
Curve, sliding c. of world, 325:5
Custom is despot of mankind, 85:3
to whom c. due, 38:23
Customs, ancient c. disrupted, 197:5
gods not born again, 330:7
habits of slavery oppression, 123:5
repudiation of one's c., 202:3
Cut deep bloody grooves, 336:2
eye don't kill, 575:12
it off, 26:14
my teeth as the black raccoon, 218:5
off society its cultivated minds, 99:3
Scriptures c. from men's hearts, 59:1
the thread of life, 63:5
window through on Europe, 86:7
Cutteth like a sword, 59:1
Cutting off man's legs and telling him to walk, 68:3
out man's tongue and telling him to talk, 68:3
Cycle, civil rights c. of Sixties, 255:10
Cycles in the circle, 386:1
Cymbals harps and psalteries, 13:19
Cypress, tall as a c. strong, 279:7
Czar, long live C. Dimitri Ivanovich, 86:2

D

Daddy is really gone, 475:2
rolling stone, 333:2
Daddy's, my dark d. knuckles, 516:1
Daffodils, once-bold d., 281:1
Dahomey, great-grandmammy a D. queen, 300:4
took me out of D., 403:2
Daily, give us our d. bread, 27:2
quota of Negro arrests, 332:6
Damage, how great the d., 57:10
one ignorant Negro can do, 395:9
Damages, racist system d. human beings, 246:1
Dame Poverty gave me my name, 218:6
Dammit, she can say D., 377:5
Damn, nobody really gives a d., 353:9
the lights watch the cars, 186:3

Damned, my constituency is the d., 410:3

Damning my native land, 231:5
those it cannot understand, 231:5

Dams, men may build d., 203:3

Dance came from the people, 332:7
can't talk so I d. it, 247:1
close to God through d., 433:3
do the ragtime d., 146:2
exists in memory, 490:3
gotta d. to keep from cryin, 466:2
is bigger than the physical body, 433:2
it, 353:4
naked under palm trees, 223:3
science in d. and art in science, 504:4
she knew how to d. better than any, 223:4
teach a barren world to d., 443:2
they stay to see that d., 169:8
time to d., 19:17
whirl whirl, 210:8
with Bovanne, 394:4
you d. because you have to, 232:5

Danced, David d. before the Lord, 13:20

Dancer, be a d., 353:4
tap d. as my occupation, 455:6

Dances, not talk any more about d., 497:1
of 19th-century New Orleans, 389:2

Dancing, all that music all that d., 214:6
girl whose eyes are bold, 210:7
in the street, 396:3
not shuffling, 558:1
one note everybody d., 261:6
spirit, 433:2

Danger, bodies between you and d., 388:1
caused by deceitful fables, 59:1
difficulty and d. old acquaintances, 251:1
from hatred in my heart, 282:9
great d. America faces, 371:2
my real life in d., 282:9
prefer self-government with d., 233:4
same ol d. brand new pleasure, 430:2
to hold both old and new, 166:5
your body between them and d., 388:1

Dangerous and blue, 571:5
as sleepwalkers, 248:1
departure is d., 251:1
generalizations are d., 112:3
marked D. If Not Treated, 412:7
obedient to our keepers d. to each other, 437:4
she became d., 337:4
two black men a d. mob, 544:4

Dangers, all God's d. ain't a white man, 168:4
delivered out of many D., 61:4

Daniel, didn't my lord deliver D., 578:13

Dare death than endure chains, 100:1
dispute with God, 63:6
now d. everything, 284:7
they d. not fire, 64:4
when I d. to be powerful, 358:4
your head and heart to d., 137:9

Dared, if we d. lift a finger, 112:1
to be free, 73:3

Dares to question colonial authority, 207:1

Daring every day to dream, 455:2

Dark, being d. I cannot bear, 218:7
body rosy black, 223:4
can't tell difference after d., 191:4
daughter of the d., 441:5
denied because d., 184:7
finding one's way through the d., 498:1
foreign presence, 324:2
like the women of Egypt, 153:9
Madison Avenue afraid of the d., 269:7
night of the Past, 123:3
robbed of my d. complexion, 99:2
shadow in light, 223:5
white black casts d. shadows, 185:3
why described the D. Continent, 413:5
World submit to its treatment, 145:4

Darken his moral mental vision, 104:4

Darkened, sun moon or stars be not d., 20:11
windows be d., 20:11

Darker, I am the d. brother, 211:2
where the lighter is the d., 214:6

Darkest pages of life, 108:3

Darkey, sing out d. nigger, 99:4

Dark-eyed Harlem, 176:2

Darkly, see through glass d., 39:17

Darkness and light are alike, 18:6
deny our d., 322:6
earth in d. as if in death, 4:7
hovers earth is silent, 5:1
how in d. did you know, 147:8
hurl words into this d., 231:6
lest d. overtake us, 87:2
light can drive out d., 318:7
not of night nor d., 41:21
of division, 458:8
of injustice and ignorance, 56:6
only light in this d., 282:3
symbol evil inferior, 322:6
upon face of the deep, 5:4

Darky's, old d. heart longed to go, 130:1

Darling you have not died in vain, 275:6

Dart, eagle stricken with d., 47:*n*1
fish in the river d. before you, 5:2
the bright eye, 71:6

Dash thy foot against stone, 33:9

Dashed in pieces the enemy, 10:2

Daughter, as is the mother so the d., 23:17
I am mother and d., 49:1
last words to a d., 487:3
Left-lonesome d., 148:5
of a rabbi married a black man, 509:2
of dining-car worker, 287:8
of ocean waters, 441:1
of the dark, 441:5

Daughters born to pamper lusts, 100:6
O d. of Jerusalem, 21:10
of Africa awake, 88:7
of Africa, 89:1
of all those dusty things, 486:4
of Ethiopia were honoured, 59:2
of Jerusalem, 21:3
of music brought low, 20:11
of Zion were rejected, 59:2

David, and D. his ten thousands, 13:11
chose five smooth stones, 13:9
danced before the Lord, 13:20
died full of days, 14:12
in the city of D., 33:4
played before the Lord, 13:19
prevailed over Philistine, 13:10

Dawn, at the end of d., 240:6
new d. of American leadership, 526:3
new d. on African horizon, 424:3
of Liberty, 190:5
saw the blush and called it D., 150:1
Day black man takes step, 296:1
born this d. a Savior, 33:4
Bring Judgment D., 174:*n*2
by d. in a pillar of a cloud, 9:15
children of the d., 41:21
crazy on an ordinary d., 464:5
evening and morning were the first d., 6:1
every d. a test and trial, 339:1
every d. a wilderness, 487:4
every d. gives praise to him, 4:5
Every D. I Have the Blues, 254:5
faint in the d. of adversity, 19:3
folds up like money, 554:2
frivolous all d., 2:1
from this d. forward, 349:3
give peace in our d., 70:2
great and dreadful d. of the Lord, 24:18
has just begun, 340:2
he shall come out into the d., 2:7
heat of the d., 29:16
let me wear the d. well, 360:2
makes d. seep into night, 56:7
makes night seep into d., 56:7
many have died for this d., 532:1
O D.-O, 575:1
of death better than d. of birth, 20:2
of the great reckoning, 2:6
of the Lord cometh, 41:20
on the seventh d. God ended his work, 6:6
part of the night before d. break, 108:7
possession over judgment d., 236:7
pulse of this new d., 308:4
remember the sabbath d., 10:7
serious all d., 2:1
seventh d. thou shalt not work, 10:7
star arise in your hearts, 43:11
there breaks this d., 190:5
third d. he will raise us up, 24:3
thou knowest not what a d. may bring, 19:5
till the quick d. is done, 210:8
to make a better d., 512:7

Day *(continued)*
we shall overcome some d., 578:15
welcome d. with song, 88:1
would not break into life, 388:3
wrestled a man until the breaking d., 8:11
Daydream, tinker and d., 372:7
Daylight come me wan' go home, 575:1
kill in broad d., 298:3
Days, all the d. of my life, 16:10
all the d. of thy life, 6:17
all the d. of Methuselah, 7:8
are past, 15:11
as thy d. so thy strength, 12:5
born in the d. of Herod, 25:18
consumed like smoke, 18:2
David died full of d., 14:12
evil d. come not, 20:11
fasted forty d. and forty nights, 26:10
forty d. and forty nights, 10:12
freedom until end of my d., 266:2
in the d. of Herod, 25:18
may be long upon the land, 10:8
on earth are a shadow, 14:11
our best d. are coming, 390:6
rain was forty d. and forty nights, 7:11
seven d. shall ye eat unleavened bread, 9:12
teach us to number our d., 17:19
turn midnights into d., 128:6
two d. will he revive us, 24:3
Dead, all the gods are d., 362:4
and alive again, 34:11
black boy on trial for own murder, 560:1
blessed are the d., 44:19
Christ risen from the d., 40:4
eye of earth, 241:4
faith without works is d., 43:3
forgotten as a d. man, 16:14
Freddie's d., 423:3
from the week's bombing, 382:1
Hip Hop Is D., 559:7
let the d. bury their d., 27:14
my affections were not d., 72:2
neither the living nor the d., 349:5
not a house where there was not one d., 9:13
opera of d. on arrival, 462:3
people d. haven't been buried, 164:4

Dead *(continued)*
presidents, 540:4
rather be d. than echo of someone, 472:5
resurrection of the d., 40:4
riddles that only the d. can answer, 515:5
seek the living among the d., 35:1
shall be raised, 40:7
slavery is d. spirit still lives, 115:6
societies without change are d., 496:3
the d. are not d., 458:7
the d. he slew at his death, 12:17
upon d. man's brow, 158:3
we have seen their d. bodies, 86:2
when I die won't stay d., 292:5
when you're d. you're done, 228:5
with all the music, 247:5
with the d. and we were them, 463:2
Deadness, moan my d., 386:1
Deafness afflicting the black race, 296:9
thrown against the clamor, 241:4
Deal in contradiction of terms, 131:1
not holding up their end in d., 376:7
Dealers, can drug d. be role models, 533:4
Dear Friend I, 465:7
Mr. President despite bombings, 245:5
Death am universal, 94:6
behold a pale horse his name was D., 44:7
better than day of birth, 20:2
black gates of d., 232:8
blacker world on d. row, 495:8
by inches minutes hours days, 415:4
by man came d., 40:4
cold hand of d., 63:5
courage to face d., 334:6
dare d. than endure chains, 100:1
deliver me from body of d., 38:12
did not stop the war, 507:3
died a good d., 323:4
earth in darkness as if in d., 4:7
faithful unto d., 43:21
fight to the d. preferably not her own, 444:1
got some style, 451:5
hath no dominion over him, 38:8

Death (continued)
heroin was slow d., 370:2
if not liberty would have d., 111:2
impression only d. can erase, 187:3
in d. they were not divided, 13:15
is a slave's freedom, 430:3
is fearful indeed, 90:6
is slow sure drifting in, 146:6
is what Slave Trade was about, 475:1
knocking at my front door, 557:2
last enemy destroyed is d., 40:5
living on edge of d., 306:5
love is strong as d., 21:14
mourn your d., 386:1
nigger is a slow d., 520:2
no d. do us part in slavery, 445:8
only thing not chaotic is d., 369:6
or pain or any kind of passion, 491:2
pictured my own d., 456:2
poverty smells of d., 180:9
pronounced its own d. sentence, 156:7
row will find this writer, 495:8
spirits live beyond d. before birth, 458:7
stops the body's work, 545:3
swallow up d. in victory, 22:10
swallowed in victory, 40:8
talking about d. part of life, 451:6
that drips to to to, 566:11
the dead he slew at his d., 12:17
they call Life you called D., 50:3
through envy of devil came d., 25:5
two places all go after d., 64:2
valley of the shadow of d., 16:10
wages of sin is d., 38:10
was deliberate, 337:1
where is thy sting, 40:8
will kick your ass, 451:5
within shadow of her d., 321:9
Debasement of the Negro woman, 130:6
Debasing, slavery in America was d., 130:6
Deborah arose, 12:13
awake D. utter a song, 12:14
Debt of forty acres and two mules, 426:2
small was the d. I thought, 150:7
Debtors, as we forgive our d., 27:2
Debts, forgive us our d., 27:2

Decadent civilization, 241:6
Decay of society leaves few options, 310:2
Deceit, civilization that uses d., 241:6
Deceitful fables and imaginings, 59:1
heart is d., 23:14
Deceitfulness of riches, 28:14
Deceived, be not d., 41:8
too long has the public been d., 80:1
Deceiveth, Satan d. the world, 44:15
Deceiving, appearances are d., 45:9
Decently and in order, 40:2
Decide what happens in other countries, 559:3
Deciding, living dying d., 557:7
Deciphering with a wild surmise, 199:4
Decision, reaffirmed steadfast d., 286:2
Decision makers, you have black d., 461:4
Decisions made quickly can be good, 534:1
political d. made with the bullet, 446:2
Declaration, see your D. Americans, 78:5
Declare, fishes shall d. unto thee, 15:8
Declaring war on the enemy within, 351:8
Decolonize our minds, 301:5
Deed, let soul look for d. it performed, 57:3
Deeds, man witness unto his d., 57:5
not just with words with d., 525:3
perform the d., 253:2
where black d. are done, 175:2
Deep in my heart I believe, 578:15
when thou art on mighty d., 109:7
Defeat deserve d. if spirit of indifference, 127:4
enemies in our country, 286:4
man reveals himself in d., 365:3
our most common foe, 490:7
poverty and racism, 286:4
Defects, point out my d., 125:6
Defend, right to d. themselves, 299:1
Defender says come, 142:8
Defense, fuck the world my d. came, 550:7
race needs no d., 124:5

Defense (continued)
sacrificed everything to your d., 73:4
snakelike our d. has turned on us, 457:4
Deferred, dream d., 213:5, 213:6
Deficiency, from d. of law distress damage result, 184:1
Define what it means to be American, 494:6
Defines, no one d. your life only you, 500:1
Degradation, economic d. begets environmental d., 543:4
environmental d. begets social d., 543:4
Degrade, do not d. magnates, 2:4
soul by making me hate, 132:9
Degree, exalted them of low d., 32:21
pursue a d. from University of Mississippi, 351:9
the difference is d., 302:2
Dehumanized, blessed are the d., 385:4
Dehumanizes blacks and whites alike, 246:1
Dehumanizing society, 548:6
Delegation, give me back my d., 356:1
Deliberate, death was d., 337:1
Delicate, love too d. to have thrown on my face, 466:6
Delicious, Hungering to be called D., 506:3
Delighted, what they d. in telling, 60:2
Delighteth, king d. to honor, 14:14
Deliver, didn't my lord d. Daniel, 578:13
I will d. him unto you, 31:1
me from body of death, 38:12
messages instructed to me, 116:4
us from evil, 27:2
words that might d. them, 493:1
Deliverance from a foreign yoke, 76:4
from chains, 104:1
from point of view of d., 207:5
in our power, 252:6
little hope of d., 375:2
prayer for d., 104:1
Delivered out of many Dangers, 61:4
Deliverer, Lord is my d., 13:23

Demand of the world a free Africa, 171:1

power concedes nothing without d., 106:1

right to live and labor, 101:6

rights given us in Constitution, 125:1

the right to cooperate, 145:6

your sympathy and aid, 116:3

Demanded any moment, 94:7

Demanding, we are d. $500,000,000, 310:1

Demands, justify black d., 277:7

Democracy can be noisy messy complicated, 528:4

cannot be coaxed supporting the D., 124:1

equally applicable to all, 186:8

for all or none, 173:3

free trade as d. in the marketplace, 407:1

fruit of American d., 292:2

is an act of faith, 252:7

majority rule not reliable instrument of d., 477:2

means everybody but me, 213:1

never destroyed, 184:7

obstacles to d., 383:6

people do not buy d. at the market, 493:3

prostituted to dignify enslavement, 220:3

strip the cloak of false d., 197:3

Democratic, evrybady claim dem d., 489:5

Party is a means to an end, 384:7

practice a work in progress, 498:6

state is not proven, 372:2

Democratization, battle between imperialism and d., 495:5

Democrats, Blue States for D., 522:6

Den of thieves, 29:19

Denial of cultural activities, 278:5

of man's continuous evolution, 427:6

Denied because dark, 184:7

by the Laws of the Land, 64:3

one morsel of wealth, 64:3

Denominations and creeds, 181:7

Deny me confess me, 49:3

part of ourselves and we did, 488:3

thou shalt d. me thrice, 31:7

you who confess me d. me, 49:3

Depart, thy servant d. in peace, 33:6

when ye d. that house, 28:3

Departed into their own country another way, 26:1

sleep d. from our eyes, 75:3

Department store architecture, 552:7

Departure is dangerous, 251:1

Depend, learn not to d. on anything, 263:2

on others never obtain rights, 155:4

Dependence, scorn unmanly d., 101:6

Dependent one upon the other, 66:4

Depopulated, our country is being d., 57:10

Depression, whites unemployed it's called a d., 409:10

Deprive them half their virtue, 70:1

us of that which belonged to us, 170:7

Deprived of bliss through toil and pain, 81:2

Depth, tests d. of river with both feet, 565:17

Deputy, did not shoot the d., 449:3

Derrière, blessed with intelligent d., 223:2

Descend to earth place thy throne, 72:1

Descendant, Negro d. of one family stock, 170:6

Descendants of a suffering people, 170:7

Descending, angels ascending and d., 35:12

behold angels ascending and d., 8:8

spirit d. like a dove, 26:8

Describe what I saw on that slab, 275:8

Desegregation is not an easy task, 229:8

Desert, burden of the d. of the sea, 22:5

Deserve a chance to pursue, 526:5

defeat if spirit of indifference, 127:4

to be enslaved, 280:2

Deserves, not everybody d. love, 561:5

Designation of division, 51:5

Desire, all you d. is Freedom, 100:3

art is expression of belief and d., 235:2

follow d., 1:6

follow your d., 1:6

Desire *(continued)*

hast given him his heart's d., 16:8

his d. is toward me, 21:13

I have one burning d., 419:9

lessen the time of following d., 1:6

more as a favor than d. to revisit past, 509:2

of information springs up, 109:3

of returning home, 72:2

of those in power, 383:6

politics d. to satisfy basic needs, 425:3

satisfiest d. of every living thing, 18:8

to be has become d. to belong, 189:3

to make good, 167:3

Desired, equally d. equally attained, 166:2

I d. mercy, 24:5

knowledge of God, 24:5

more d. than fine gold, 16:6

to hear and have not heard, 33:15

to see and have not seen, 33:15

what they d. to speak, 60:2

Desires, blossoms of our d. will burst, 140:5

he may still our d., 1:1

Despair a poor chisel, 320:5

as final response, 319:4

burden'd heart breaking in d., 112:4

perplexed but not in d., 40:10

they will reduce us to d., 59:6

Desperate foolishness, 513:3

my constituency is the d., 410:3

Desperation is energy, 328:4

Despise my fear, 50:2

Despised, my constituency is the d., 410:3

when things go wrong, 324:2

Despot, custom is d. of mankind, 85:3

Destiny, bound single garment of d., 320:6

calling, 523:2

confidence in d. of my people, 125:2

Haitians have a d. to suffer, 226:6

in the hands of God, 171:6

in the land of our birth, 111:9

is in our hands, 106:7

lifted to a higher d., 113:6

no d. separate from nation, 91:5

Die *(continued)*
  would we d. as some have done, 210:4
  ye shall d. like men, 17:13
  you does kind of d. inside, 321:8
  you gotta d. someday, 221:4
Died a good death, 323:4
  father d. after my misfortune, 62:2
  have d. the Present teaches, 150:8
  he d. for her also, 76:6
  heart of the city has not yet d., 440:2
  many have d. for this day, 532:1
  Missus d. she'd set me free, 568:10
  my people d. to build this country, 568:10
  people I did not know d., 471:5
  she d. and I lived, 321:9
  someone d. continuing to live, 550:5
  wid a hammer in his han', 568:1
Dies, great wrong never d., 322:1
  man ain't happy unless man d., 514:6
  no one cries when a street d., 480:2
  the man d. in all who keep silent, 361:5
  when a griot d., 274:2
Dieth, how d. the wise man, 19:16
  man d. and wasteth away, 15:9
Difference based upon race or color, 229:3
  between dream and vision, 94:4
  between exploitation and slavery, 379:6
  between God and luck, 516:3
  between integration and separation, 196:2
  can't tell d. after dark, 191:4
  diversity is accepted d., 310:5
  doesn't make any d., 396:1
  is difficult, 313:3
  little d. Antebellum South New South, 138:5
  matters, 536:1
  no d. between African Negro, 170:6
  no d. between killer and killed, 185:2
  now what's the d., 244:6
  of color a d. of species, 569:9
  produced by unequal opportunities, 132:3
  reduce all signs of d. to zero, 202:3

Difference *(continued)*
  sameness is d., 310:5
  the d. is degree, 302:2
  trivial d. make no d., 286:5
  why does our color make a d., 237:9
Differences into one undifferentiated mass, 400:1
  still believe our d. define us, 401:2
Different, adults a d. species, 494:1
  conceive life being d., 299:3
  it was never any d., 253:3
  just because you're black, 532:7
  no d. from other colored women, 227:3
  strokes for d. folks, 570:11
Differently, it's packaged slightly d., 548:8
Difficult, advance is d., 251:1
  giving all to a d. task, 527:2
  love is d. always, 340:3
  nothing easy becomes d., 48:2
  nothing so d. may be found out, 47:9
Difficulties, mask no d., 285:9
Difficulty and danger old acquaintances, 251:1
  hope in the face of d., 522:7
Digestion, getting angry hurt your d., 197:1
Digged the hole and the whole held him, 535:3
Dignity at any price, 267:4
  children robbed of d., 317:9
  enough humanity to treat with d., 493:4
  in tilling field, 131:6
  is first, 239:4
  national d. beaten down, 197:5
  raise slave to d. of man, 75:1
  rob me of my d., 267:4
  silence at least has d., 258:4
Dilemma, problem of prejudice moral d., 316:5
Dimensions, black man has two d., 290:6
  the dead are alive in new d., 458:7
Dimitri Ivanovich, long live Czar D., 86:2
Dinah has blowed de horn, 146:3
Diner, call myself a d., 295:2
Dining, frightens them from d. table, 99:4

Dinner, contented with life d. and wife, 85:2
Dinners, finds comfort in good d., 180:11
Diploma, tombstone will be d., 304:6
Diplomat, garbageman dignified as d., 260:5
Dips one's tongue in the ocean, 345:8
Direct us in the right path, 53:7
Direction, failure way to show us moving in wrong d., 500:2
Dirges, lamenting songs and d., 85:5
  no organ-piped d., 480:2
  singing d. and ditties, 255:1
Dirt, eat a peck of d. before you die, 570:6
  off your shoulder, 550:8
Dirty glass of water, 196:3
  laughing kids, 276:2
  wata scarce and d. tuff, 268:5
  water can put out fire, 574:8
Disabilities imposed in South, 118:1
  of color, 115:7
Disadvantage, forgets I am at a greater d., 91:3
Disappear by the river, 519:2
Disappointment follows in its wake, 67:4
Disaster, stumble one d. to next, 288:2
  to have no ideal to capture, 187:2
Discharge, no d. in that war, 20:7
Disciple not above master, 28:5
  street's d., 559:6
Disciples, Jesus gave bread to the d., 31:6
Discipline, freedom without d., 261:1
  is the tenet of education, 383:11
Disciplined, one who is free is d., 261:1
Discord in songs of freedom, 76:4
Discount her memory, 519:2
Discouraged, lest they be d., 41:17
Discouragement, in the face of d., 132:4
Discourse of the elders, 25:11
Discover Promised Land, 224:6
  who I am I'll be free, 248:7
Discovered something to die for, 317:5
  world d. it was white, 145:3
Discrepancy too great to be ignored, 246:7

Dreams (*continued*)
who profits by our d., 189:11
zippers broken but d. alive, 485:5
Dress, how they can't d., 558:9
lifts a d. of silken gold, 210:7
new d. same old broad, 227:6
same rating as basic black d., 256:7
Dressed in old raggedy clothes, 485:5
well d. does not prevent being
poor, 565:9
Dresses, shapeless house d., 322:4
Drifting, yes d. d., 146:6
Drink, a bitter bitter d., 149:5
eat d. and be merry, 20:8
in remembrance of me, 39:15
it new with you, 31:6
let us eat and d., 22:7
neither eat bread nor d. water,
10:12
strong d. is raging, 18:22
thirsty and ye gave me d., 30:11
this fruit of the vine, 31:6
this is my blood, 31:6
Drinking cup of bitterness, 317:8
gourd, 569:8, 576:9
Son of man came eating and d.,
28:7
the life of my soul, 232:8
Dripping, indigo dye d. from cloth,
566:11
Drips, Shango is the death that d.,
566:11
Drive off the beast of fear, 180:16
Driven by political demagogues,
132:5
Driver's, for once in the d. seat, 239:1
Drives off the powers of Seth, 3:1
Driving a Caddy you're fixin' a Ford,
539:2
Drones, society becomes drumming
of d., 166:3
Drop, boiled down to a d., 180:5
of a bucket, 22:16
one d. of black blood, 136:4
Dropping revolution like a pick-up
line, 467:6
Drought of Afro-American
resources, 332:6
Drove, so he d. out man, 7:2
Drown, neither can floods d. it,
21:15
Drowned, inner tube d. at sea, 356:3
Pharaoh's army got d., 578:5
Drowning in past, 284:2

Drowns, silent water d. a man,
565:16
Drug, can d. dealers be role models,
533:4
of the damned, 370:2
violence a potent d. for oppressed,
359:3
Drugs, cradled by d. by jazz, 243:6
Drum, beat d. lak in de Affica soil,
124:6
foot-drop find d., 489:3
if the d. is a woman, 369:2
is sacred instrument, 305:1
of traditional culture, 381:2
skin whip lash, 324:3
slaves not allowed to use d.,
262:1
Drumming of drones, 166:3
Drums, blow your shells roll your d.,
108:7
electric bongo d., 214:6
Drunk and disorderly, 364:5
Drunkard, palm-wine d., 273:8
Drunken officer of British rule,
330:5
Dry bones hear the Lord, 23:21
conveyed as d. goods, 100:1
don't miss water till well runs d.,
571:6
never miss water till well runs d.,
151:7
Duchamp never even considered me,
494:5
Duchess, return to my family a d.,
531:3
Due, beginning of reparations d.,
310:1
custom to whom custom d.,
38:23
fear to whom fear d., 38:23
honor to whom honor d., 38:23
it's past d., 198:1
receive wages d. him, 166:1
tribute to whom tribute is d.,
38:23
Duel, fight aerial d., 195:8
Dues, render their d., 38:23
Duke, fly away d., 398:2
Dumb as a robe and halo, 502:3
let who fear be d., 91:6
more than d. we invisible, 481:1
opposed to a d. war, 522:4
Dumbness afflicting the black race,
296:9

Dunk, won't make you d. like me,
533:5
Duppy know who to frighten,
574:10
Dusk, skin like d. on the horizon,
188:5
Dusky dream Harlem, 215:3
Dust, and d. shalt thou eat, 6:17
arise from this d., 100:6
awake and sing ye that dwell in d.,
22:11
counted as the small d., 22:16
created of d., 55:5
enemies shall lick the d., 17:10
God formed man of the d. of the
ground, 6:7
like d. I'll rise, 307:4
man lost in d. of own raising,
93:2
shake off the d., 28:3
shaking the d. of ages, 85:8
slaves to d. and ashes, 78:1
thou art unto d. shalt thou return,
7:1
walk in the d., 181:10, 537:3
Dusty, daughters of all those d.
things, 486:4
Dutch nigger and English in me,
331:6
Duty, answer the call of d., 155:3
artist's d. is to reflect the times,
352:8
as slaves to obey masters, 63:6
do our d. to our new masters, 78:6
I did my d., 157:4
indispensable d. to do so, 67:2
of interest in Africa, 108:5
of man, 21:1
of self-respect, 108:5
of slave husband to endure, 98:4
of younger Negro artist, 211:5
stood firm at my post of d.,
124:1
to cast off grave-clothes, 108:4
to claim this heritage, 279:6
to render account of my conduct,
68:1
to use every means, 100:3
Dwell, awake and sing ye that d. in
dust, 22:11
God is pleased for her to d., 59:2
he shall d. in the tents of Shem,
7:17
in house of the Lord, 16:10

Dwelleth not in temples made with hands, 37:13

Dwelling shaped like a bird, 445:1
thou hast been our d. place, 17:17
with windows but no doors, 412:4

Dye, indigo d. dripping from cloth, 566:11

Dying befo' yo' time is out, 179:6
but fighting back, 175:4
give out'n de notion a d. at all, 569:10
groans of the d., 69:3
hand of racism, 380:2
into that new life, 291:3
is a d. civilization, 241:6
like a stump, 337:5
living and d. for freedom, 428:7
mourn death of a people d., 291:3
not all d. is the physical self, 394:7
supposed to be d. equal, 415:2
to hell with d., 442:6
white people better or above d., 539:6

Dysfunction of Vietnam veterans, 390:8

E

Each one teach one, 570:15

Eager to shift blame on others, 217:1

Eagerness of slaves to become masters, 80:3

Eagle, fourth beast like a flying e., 44:3
imprisoned on back of coin, 356:7
judge my soul e. nor mole, 199:3
let my spirit soar like an e., 453:6
my soul is an e., 252:2
protects his nest, 406:2
riches fly as an e., 19:1
stricken with dart, 47:n1
will never fly, 356:7

Eagle's, like an e. lightning flash, 224:6
own plumes, 47:1

Eagles ride low, 345:4
swifter than e., 13:15

Ear, envious heart makes a treacherous e., 180:1
of jealousy heareth all things, 25:3
reach nation's e. we need earthquake, 105:2

Earn, e. baby e., 230:5

Earrings, bamboo e. at least two pair, 548:4

Ears, have e. and hear not, 23:8
he that hath e. let him hear, 28:6
of saturday night specials, 368:8
they have e. but hear not, 18:5

Earth, Adam created from whole e., 59:5
and a new e. will rise, 360:5
brightens in lightland, 5:1
cast forth upon e., 51:4
creation of heavens and e., 56:3
darkness hovers e. is silent, 5:1
days on e. are a shadow, 14:11
descend to e. place thy throne, 72:1
four winds of the e., 44:8
giants in the e. in those days, 7:9
go with at her pace, 323:2
God created heaven and e., 5:4
God is light of heavens and e., 55:7
God take the black e., 281:3
he shall walk on e. among the living, 2:7
heaven and e. shall pass away, 30:5
heaven and e. to witness, 11:11
hurt not the e. sea nor trees, 44:9
I adore the e., 356:8
in darkness as if in death, 4:7
in e. as it is in heaven, 27:2
independent mortal on e., 66:4
language of all the e., 8:1
let a new e. rise, 255:2
live long upon e., 2:4
marriages consummated on e., 153:8
meek shall inherit the e., 17:1
Mother E., 491:10
new birth of freedom on E., 523:2
new heaven and new e., 45:3
our work here on E., 527:6
peace on e., 33:5
pregnant e. to our hearts, 388:3
remembered who we were, 488:2
replenish the e. and subdue it, 6:5
salt of the e., 26:13
shall teach thee, 15:8
they shall inherit the e., 26:12
this e. is yours, 350:1
tyrant wars made e. a grave, 129:1
walk not on e. exultantly, 54:12
way of all the e., 12:11
wealth moves the e., 123:6
where Sky touches E. is End, 564:4

Earth (continued)
who knows this book on e., 2:7
without form and void, 5:4
you made the e. as you wished, 5:3

Earthly love by love of self, 53:6

Earthquake, reach nation's ear we need e., 105:2

Earths, spinning of a thousand e., 434:6

Ease on down the road, 442:2

Easier for camel to go, 29:14
into enemy's toils than out, 46:18

East, face neither e. nor west, 234:1
movin' on up to the E. Side, 447:2
of the garden of Eden cherubims, 7:2
olive tree neither E. nor West, 55:7
shake it to the e., 571:1
star in the e., 25:18
wise men from the e., 25:18

Easy, ABC e. as 123, 434:2
ain't no e. thing to do, 150:3
burden, 346:8
life of TV and gasoline, 491:3
like Sunday morning, 473:1
mothafucking e. to kill, 298:3
my yoke is e., 28:8
nothing e. becomes difficult, 48:2
once you learn how to fly, 476:2
to hit a son, 282:1
to win applause and approval, 166:4
universal quest e. answers, 318:4

Easy Rider's, wonder where my E. gone, 151:5

Eat, and say sit here e., 331:1
at any counter, 245:6
at the welcome table, 579:4
black man sitting down to e., 99:4
dogs e. crumbs from masters' table, 29:4
drink and be merry, 20:8
his pleasant fruits, 21:9
I don't e. colored people, 343:1
I e. of its brightness, 4:1
in kitchen when company comes, 211:2
it in haste, 9:10
kill him e. him to survive, 289:6
let us e. and drink, 22:7
neither e. bread nor drink water, 10:12
of the tree I did not e., 6:16
of the tree of life, 43:20

Eat (*continued*)
  serpent beguiled me and I did e.,
    6:17
  shall ye not e., 11:1
  Take e. this is my body, 31:6
  take e. this is my body, 39:14
  they shall e. the flesh in that night,
    9:9
  what's on that plate, 295:2
  with bitter herbs they shall e., 9:9
  ye shall e. the fat of the land, 8:17
Eaten, crust e. in peace, 46:1
Eating, men e. on the moon, 366:4
  Son of man came e. and drinking,
    28:7
  which I liked to do, 197:1
Eats, dem what e. can say grace,
    570:16
Eavesdropping, you know you are e.,
    415:1
Ebony phoenix in her own time,
    479:3
Ecce homo, 37:n1
Echo, rather be dead than e. of
    someone, 472:5
  wait for an e., 231:6
Echoes, love-cry e. of your soul,
    391:1
Economic access depends on
    literacy, 365:2
  Forced upon African by e.
    domination, 197:5
  dark ghettos are e. colonies, 246:2
  degradation begets environmental
    degradation, 543:4
  ladder, 239:6
Economically, Negro women neither
    e. free, 168:3
Economics, traditional e. disrupted,
    197:5
Economy, build a green e. strong,
    548:1
  success of e., 526:6
  unresolved crisis in national e.,
    239:5
Eden, after E. was surprise, 331:4
  Lord God planted a garden in E.,
    6:8
Edge, don't push 'cause close to e.,
    520:6
  living on the creative e., 455:2
Edges and kitchen, 450:6
  nappy e., 467:2
Edification, for our own e., 279:5

Edifieth, charity e., 39:10
Education and work uplift people,
    143:3
  comes in to practice daily, 163:5
  democracy's life insurance, 160:6
  discipline is the tenet of e., 383:11
  for Our People, 426:3
  homemade e., 296:9
  ignorance more costly than e.,
    132:6
  industrial e. for the Negro, 133:3
  is the medium, 172:5
  is the teaching of citizenship, 229:4
  it's time we try e., 347:9
  let e. cease enslave the mass, 99:3
  most viable means of
    empowerment, 368:5
  nor e. finished until we die, 109:6
  of a nation is rich powerful, 109:4
  opportunities for e., 103:7
  problem of e. among Negroes,
    143:2
  progress through e. and industry,
    572:2
  real e. means to inspire, 154:5
  robbed of my e., 91:4
  role of e. in modern society, 239:6
  the real solution is e., 368:6
  university e. one of privileges,
    178:1
  which bravest men followed, 109:5
  will not whitewash them, 474:4
Effects, contrary e. of liberty and
    slavery, 74:3
  of racism, 320:11
Effort, aim to make e. not measure
    it, 189:6
  and grace, 466:1
  incentive to e. snatched away,
    140:6
Eggs, golden e. empty of albumen,
    345:5
Ego in heart of cosmos, 290:9
  non flocci pendere, 48:n2
Egos, check your e. at the door, 351:3
Egypt, a great cry in E., 9:13
  I will pass through the land of E.,
    9:10
  image great in E., 50:3
  one more plague upon E., 9:8
  out of E. I called my son, 26:2
  princes shall come out of E., 17:9
  there arose a new king over E.,
    8:20

Egypt (*continued*)
  this day in which you came out
    from E., 9:14
  way down in E. land, 576:10
Egyptian, contact with E. Antiquity,
    279:6
Egyptians, Christians in style of the
    E., 58:1
Eighteen inches between a pat and a
    kick, 192:1
Either I'm nobody or a nation, 331:6
Either-or, question of e., 242:4
Élan, their ingenuity their é. vital,
    243:9
Elasticity in their spirits, 115:5
Elation all from God, 300:7
Elbow, some e. room up here, 434:1
Elders, children listening to e., 283:5
  discourse of the e., 25:11
  respect for e., 60:2
Electric bongo drums, 214:6
  hog in the e. chair, 350:7
Electricity, Soul is like e., 326:8
Elegance all from God, 300:7
Elements, the e. God's deliberate eye,
    545:2
  weak and beggarly e., 41:4
Elephants, when e. fight grass suffers,
    564:6
Elevated, become e. cultivate and
    practice, 102:4
Elevation, accomplishes e.
    admiration increased, 96:2
  herself capable of e., 116:2
  measure of our e. in society, 79:3
  our e. result of self-efforts, 93:6
Elevator, colored mechanic an e. of
    race, 104:6
  escalator e. choices say who we are,
    552:7
  on e. and woman clutching her
    purse, 530:1
Eleven o'clock Sunday morning,
    321:1
  people murdered, 415:5
Eli lama sabachthani, 32:2
Eligible to all employment, 67:8
Elijah, mantle of E., 14:6
  the prophet, 24:18
  went up by whirlwind, 14:4
Elite, responsible e. in the Negro
    community, 186:1
  where the e. always meet, 177:2
Elizabeth is an imposter, 289:3

Emancipate yourselves from mental slavery, 450:1

Emancipated class under former master class, 118:3

Negro race must be e., 171:4

who e. the modern Negro, 216:3

Emancipation, achieved political e., 266:9

came and vested interests lost, 139:4

Negro signs his own e., 320:3

soon after E., 138:1

Emancipation Proclamation, the word Negro not outlawed in E., 141:4

Emancipator, I am the e., 344:3

Embark on open-ended war, 456:1

Embarrassment, for my mother e. I was black, 216:1

Embrace, me without fear, 241:2

time to e., 19:17

Embraced, We have e. Islam, 56:11

Embraces, tear your wives from your e., 100:6

Embracing blackness, 355:3

time to refrain from e., 19:17

Emerge from prison undiminished, 267:3

Emigrate, Mom and Pop chose to e., 380:3

Eminence engenders enemies, 207:8

Emmanuel, call his name E., 25:17

Emotion, I Second That E., 403:10

love the most powerful e., 340:4

thought and magic sound, 85:7

Emotions, tangled e. vague and dim, 158:5

Emperors, under E. Kings and Princes, 72:5

Employed, means e. against me, 68:2

Employees, Black perspective and Black e., 461:4

Employment, eligible to all e., 67:8

Empower victims of evil, 372:7

Empowerment, change based on e., 288:2

education most viable means of e., 368:5

Empty, dream am e. thing, 94:4

the rich he sent e. away, 32:22

wagon rattles, 570:14

Encounters, if I count my sexual e., 367:2

Encouragement, Negro has no e., 103:7

Encouragements, what e. none absolutely none, 103:7

End, after the e. of the world, 250:8

all things come to their e., 385:6

born to draw to our e., 25:6

colonial domination, 286:2

everything has an e., 564:5

freedom until e. of my days, 266:2

hope to the e., 43:6

I am the beginning and e., 45:7

I'm gonna find the e., 188:3

is a greater America, 384:7

is in the beginning, 248:2

is not yet, 30:3

is this my beginning or e., 429:8

nothing in the e. is lost, 393:3

of peace there shall be no e., 22:3

of the world, 32:5

right here everything e., 332:5

rope got two e., 574:6

start with one e. with another, 486:5

to humiliating slavery, 293:6

when I go will be the e. of it, 137:7

where Sky touches Earth is E., 564:4

you are the end the beginning, 393:4

Endangered, black men are not e. species, 483:2

Ended, summer is e., 23:11

Endings, lie has seven e., 564:9

Endless, carry into e. bondage, 93:7

love, 473:5

Endowment, improvisation heroic e., 257:6

Ends, needle that pricks at both e., 567:2

of strings somebody else pulls, 203:5

Endure, all who e. shall be saved, 70:3

his name shall e. for ever, 17:11

weeping may e. for a night, 16:13

what storms may come, 527:3

what we e. is what America is, 231:2

Endured in spite of our wounds, 360:5

Endureth, blessed the man that e. temptation, 43:1

charity e. all things, 39:16

Enemies, eminence engenders e., 207:8

give e. means of our destruction, 47:1

in the presence of mine e., 16:10

love your e., 27:1

makes e. by great service, 68:6

saved from our e., 33:2

shall lick the dust, 17:10

sworn e. of liberty, 68:5

within without the race, 127:3

Enemy, ancient e. employs his woe, 377:1

and avenger, 15:22

close friend can become close e., 566:3

cold remains of the e., 440:3

dashed in pieces the e., 10:2

ignorance ferocious e., 285:3

last e. destroyed is death, 40:5

love transforming e. to friend, 319:1

not under dining table but outside, 512:8

of black survival, 495:1

war on the e. within, 351:8

Enemy's, easier into e. toils than out, 46:18

Energy at the start, 535:6

can move things, 328:4

living dying deciding, 557:7

their almost frightening e., 243:8

we neither feel nor see, 557:7

Engage in struggle, 265:1

Engaged in nation building, 171:3

Engagement can lift suspicion and fear, 529:1

Engineer, lawyer is a social e. or parasite, 191:1

Engineering, social e. no more difficult than space e., 246:6

England Is a Bitch, 489:4

lose my E. and now liberty, 513:2

English, distorting everything not E., 271:2

Dutch nigger and E. in me, 331:6

from the Jews to the E. nation, 72:5

into hands of the E., 75:2

proper wages like E. servants, 79:1

English *(continued)*
 upbringing was something I was
  not E., 472:3
Englishman, de misery o' de E.,
  313:2
 virtual E. treated as African cargo,
  513:2
Enjoy fruits of our toil, 101:6, 198:8
 goodness fruit of democracy,
  292:2
 grudge what they cannot e., 46:5
 the fruits of our labors, 76:5
 you will e. it, 360:2
Enjoying the same privileges, 74:3
Enlarge the close contracted mind,
  72:1
Enough, being beautiful is not e.,
  379:2
 being was e., 393:1
 Can't Get E. of Your Love Babe,
  445:6
 Don't Stop 'Til You Get E., 511:3
 it isn't e., 270:6
 not e. for others, 76:3
Enrich not Africans, 234:2
Enslave, let education cease e. the
  mass, 99:3
 man will e. own blood, 105:7
 me on film in celluloid, 510:3
 what better way to e. a man, 427:7
 white man's power to e., 104:2
Enslaved at same rate being set free,
  432:5
 deserve to be e., 280:2
 half free half e., 245:4
 mind e. body never free, 320:3
 mother country has e. you, 234:3
 people of an alien race, 121:6
 white womanhood too e., 302:2
Enslavement, democracy prostituted
  to dignify e., 220:3
 Negroes in Africa prior to e.,
  155:6
 of African people, 439:1
Enslaving behavior caused by
  prejudices, 189:15
Ensnarings of others worst kind of
  robbery, 72:6
Enter into joy of thy lord, 30:8
 kingdom of God, 29:14
 not into temptation, 31:9
 when and where I e., 135:5
Enterprise, no race has monopoly on
  e., 365:7

Enters, whole Negro race e. with me,
  135:5
Entertain, be not forgetful to e.
  strangers, 42:19
Entertained angels unawares, 42:19
 idea of being free, 88:6
Entertainer, ain't no e., 300:9
Entertainment and Relaxation to
  avoid Reflection, 519:5
 gold-rush culture of popular e.,
  446:4
 providing whites e. while
  embarrassing blacks, 389:5
Entitled, rights to which we are e.,
  171:4
 to enjoy equally with others,
  131:4
Entitlement for many years of
  wrongs, 412:6
Entrance into Heaven, 122:5
 to Texaco, 493:7
Entrapped, love of you has e. me,
  3:3
Entrenched cannot tremble, 321:5
Envious heart makes a treacherous
  ear, 180:1
Environment for academic
  achievement, 383:11
 mismanaged undermines quality
  of life, 401:5
 not strange not friendly, 182:6
Environmental degradation begets
  social degradation, 543:4
Envisioned, rise and attain the e. self,
  454:3
Envy, natives e. the tourist, 471:8
 of the devil, 25:5
 the glory of others, 68:6
 them their public love, 339:6
 you e. of the world, 337:3
Epidermalized, men had e. Being,
  465:1
Epigram-surprise, with an e., 85:1
Epitaph, the line will probably be
  my e., 375:*n1*
Epithet, nigger e. generates epithets,
  497:5
Epithets, first e. immigrants learned,
  249:2
 nuclear bomb of racial e., 549:5
 same contemptuous e., 166:4
Epitome a public enemy, 518:2
Epitomes, Black women e. of Black
  womanhood, 437:5

Equal, all are e. all are free, 526:5
 black men accorded e. treatment,
  272:5
 chance in battle of life, 124:5
 chance to obtain ideals, 152:4
 citizenship under the law, 524:3
 knock and ask for e. chance,
  140:5
 of their murderers, 284:8
 Pan-Africanism wants e.
  opportunity, 215:6
 parity and opportunity, 292:3
 privilege which nothing else can e.,
  65:7
 share e. privileges, 76:5
 supposed to be dying e., 415:2
 to Him is not anyone, 57:8
 to ourselves, 284:8
Equality among all men, 220:2
 complete e., 296:4
 give me my e., 352:5
 in the vineyards of e., 230:6
 language lead into e. of power,
  372:6
 make e. for himself, 97:4
 nobody can give you e., 296:3
 some will always reject e., 362:6
 speculated moralized e., 93:4
 talk of e. ring true, 286:4
Equally, bondage e. intolerable,
  70:5
 desired e. attained, 166:2
 entitled to enjoy e. with others,
  131:4
 liberty e. precious to Black as to
  white, 70:5
Equals, make wives e. not
  subordinates, 129:6
Equation, craving other half of e.,
  337:4
 one part of e., 250:5
Equity of law, 184:1
Era of colorblindness, 545:9
 of little tyrants, 282:1
Erase the past from the present of a
  slave, 476:7
Erotic in development of our power,
  358:1
Error, response to e. that counts,
  431:3
Errors, acknowledge our e., 494:4
Eruption, centuries burst into
  volcanic e., 207:9
 volcano in full e., 260:7

Escalator elevator choices say who we are, 552:7

Escape, affinity with slaveholders worked for my e., 99:2

he cannot e. it completely, 348:2

nemesis of my color, 183:3

no e. from badge of color, 395:4

opportunity how make my e., 61:3

resolved to venture on my e., 82:4

the blow impending over him, 98:7

the imputation of vanity, 68:7

the mark of racial inferiority, 185:8

Escaped alone to tell thee, 14:18

with skin of my teeth, 15:12

Escapes, not much e. the Lord, 54:5

Eschewed evil, 14:15

Essence of a thing returning to origin of thing, 521:6

of the fight, 351:6

Establish the work of our hands, 17:20

Eternal, gift of God is e. life, 38:10

God is thy refuge, 12:6

lay hold on e. life, 42:10

or eternalist, 540:6

oughtness, 319:4

the struggle is e., 217:7

Verities, 162:8

Eternity, above kingly banners until all e., 4:2

bear fruit throughout e., 115:3

found for all e., 3:4

image of his own e., 25:5

let E. be our measurement, 172:11

nothing between myself and e., 472:8

sole one who traverses e., 4:4

Ethics and aesthetics are one, 379:1

do well in e. not politics, 93:4

Ethiopia, King of E. is exalted, 59:3

people of E. were chosen, 59:2

shall stretch out her hands, 17:9

Ethiopia's queens will reign again, 194:2

Ethiopian, can E. change his skin, 23:13

gone was the E. nose, 193:2

Ethnic, American e. minorities, 330:2

group aspirations, 255:7

Europe, cut window through on E., 86:7

technique and style of E., 290:5

European, duplicity of E. imperialism, 207:2

Eve, Adam called his wife's name E., 7:1

Even, never get angry get e., 363:5

Even-handed justice for the Negro, 103:5

Evening and morning were the first day, 6:1

in e. it withereth, 17:17

of our history, 288:1

rest at pale e., 210:8

will be fair weather, 29:5

Event, one e. happeneth to all, 19:15

Events, little person to stir up great e., 472:6

Ever no kindness e. wasted, 45:12

Everlasting arms, 12:6

consciousness of E. Arms, 125:5

from e. to e., 17:17

God the E. Refuge, 57:8

his name shall be e. Father, 22:3

life, 35:18

utmost bound of the e. hills, 8:19

Every beast is mine, 17:3

creature of God is good, 42:6

Day I Have the Blues, 254:5

goodbye ain't gone, 572:6

living thing of all flesh, 7:10

man did right, 12:19

man is free, 212:8

man's sword against his brother, 23:22

mountain shall be made low, 22:14

one his own way, 48:13

time I feel the spirit, 578:2

to e. thing there is a season, 19:17

valley shall be exalted, 22:14

Everybody can be great, 320:10

can be wrong, 271:5

Democracy means e. but me, 213:1

deserves love no, 561:5

fightin' about a spoonful, 251:6

got something with everything, 509:4

I know live without, 452:5

knows about Mississippi, 352:4

knows I'm here, 251:4

likes my Rocket '88, 341:4

wants to be right in world, 480:4

Everybody's got a little light under the sun, 407:5

Everyday living seen through a veil, 180:14

people, 435:1

Everyone has a plan until punched in mouth, 545:7

we all e. of us, 427:2

Everything, attainable to e., 51:5

can change all at once, 533:7

cannot be first in e., 46:7

comes out of tap dancing, 455:6

else is fruits, 252:1

everybody got something with e., 509:4

goes and turns around, 393:3

has an end, 564:5

I Do Gonna Be Funky, 391:6

is copacetic, 160:1

is e., 560:7

papers are e., 550:3

rock 'n' roll good for e., 303:3

sacrificed e. to your defense, 73:4

say they could do e., 265:6

tries e. before arms, 48:9

was changing pushing me out, 439:3

what else to say but e., 260:1

will be alright, 556:5

yet nothing, 48:5

you need you got, 302:3

You're the First the Last My E., 445:7

Everywhere, hated and loved e., 50:3

prejudice like atmosphere e., 84:3

there is e. here, 460:7

we feel the chain, 84:3

Evidence, faith is e. of things not seen, 42:18

got to leave e. to hold up, 470:4

to convince most prejudiced, 110:2

Evil, atom's weight of e., 57:7

blow the trumpet against e., 75:1

colored girl an e. woman, 466:5

communications corrupt, 40:6

days come not, 20:11

deliver us from e., 27:2

enters like needle spreads like oak, 566:2

eschewed e., 14:15

fear no e., 16:10

for e., 38:19

hearted women, 236:8

I would not I do, 38:11

Evil *(continued)*
  integrate with e. be destroyed with e., 196:2
  leave untouched an e. institution, 95:7
  money is root of e., 156:5
  money root of all e., 42:9
  of fulfillment, 336:8
  overcome e. with good, 38:22
  say e. against you falsely, 26:12
  societies kill consciences, 273:2
  sons of men snared in e. time, 20:9
  stubborn heart shall fare e., 25:7
  they lead to e. consequences, 60:2
  tree of knowledge of good and e., 6:9
  with indifference notes e. and good, 86:1
  without e. without a witness, 2:6
  ye shall know good and e., 6:14
Evils, Africa resolved to end such e., 197:4
  among e. slavery more deadly, 108:6
  comfort victims of e., 372:7
Evolution, America is the denial of man's e., 427:6
Exalt, whosoever shall e. shall be abased, 30:2
Exaltation all from God, 300:7
Exalted, every valley shall be e., 22:14
  he shall humble himself shall be e., 30:2
  King of Ethiopia is e., 59:3
  them of low degree, 32:21
Exalteth, wisdom e. her children, 25:8
Examined, strange men e. me, 78:6
Example, best e. of motherhood, 255:3
  from others take e., 48:14
  he will set a good e., 1:3
  of fraud rapine and cruelty, 70:1
  woman your e. is powerful, 89:6
Examples have ye set the rising generation, 88:7
Excel the boasted ruling race, 133:8
Excellent is always beautiful, 502:8
  things more e., 38:6
Exceptional, makes e. also make lonely, 328:1
Excess, my heart was sweet to e., 3:5

Exchange, would not e. color for wealth, 153:5
Excitements of colts, 276:2
Exclude, right to e., 231:4
Excluded by American culture, 231:4
  on account of complexion, 120:3
Excluding those who look different, 231:5
Excuse, any e. will serve a tyrant, 46:9
  double e. no time to rest, 121:1
  for lawlessness or anarchy, 229:7
  me while I kiss the sky, 420:3
  only e. capital punishment attempts, 139:8
  talent not e. for bad manners, 289:7
Excused, writer cannot be e., 323:3
Exemplar of purest grace, 86:6
Exempt, no portion e. from curse, 108:6
  nor necessary to be morally e., 457:3
Exercise kindness and love, 58:5
  of political rights, 132:5
Exhale, ever be able to e., 483:7
Exhaust the little moment, 259:1
Exhausted, words of God not be e., 56:5
Exhibited to all kinds of people, 210:5
Exile in own land, 317:6
  place where there is no e., 345:1
  rise in the lands of e., 119:4
  who longs for homeland, 59:4
Exist, cannot e. slaves on this territory, 67:8
  pointless to pretend it doesn't e., 328:3
  pretending it did not e., 260:7
  there shall e. no distinction, 67:8
  whys do not e., 562:3
Existed, as if thing believed actually e., 553:2
Existence, black women's e. invisible, 456:6
  conditioned to their e., 231:3
  hate demands e., 291:1
  surrender is to surrender my e., 108:2
  two sides of the same coin of e., 468:3
Exists, nigger e. only in his mind, 343:11

Exodus from land of bondage, 100:4
  going to our Father's land e., 449:11
Exotic, people want from black artists the e., 548:8
Expansion, painful process of e., 515:2
Expatriate driven from one's fatherland, 206:5
Expect chaos in innocent moments, 477:5
  in life e. trouble, 478:5
  of the world a free Africa, 171:1
Expected to please other people, 494:3
Expedient, all things lawful not e., 39:13
Expeditions, out of all colonial e., 241:7
Expensive to be poor, 283:6
Experience, authentic Negro e., 491:7
  Black e. an American e., 226:4
  black women's e. invisible, 456:6
  having no e. of liberty, 111:1
  learn by bitter e., 119:1
  music is your own e., 273:5
  very few African Americans who haven't had the e., 530:1
Experienced, have you ever been e., 419:8
Experiences inform how community interprets one night in Florida, 530:1
  mirror of e. in America, 231:2
  of each generation, 444:2
Explain, don't e., 253:8
  hush now don't e., 253:8
  in great detail, 275:8
Explanation, unless verbal e., 326:10
Explanations for things we don't have an explanation for, 534:2
Exploit their helplessness, 329:5
Exploitation, all forms e. identical, 291:2
  clash between freedom and e., 297:6
  cultural self-defense against e., 373:3
  excesses of e., 379:6
  of Africa, 439:1
  prerequisite of e., 278:5
  will not bow down to e., 427:1

Exploited, half rich half e., 245:4
keep separated and you will be e., 172:2
Exploits, white America still e. black, 310:1
Explore, travel and e., 253:4
Expose lies whenever told, 285:9
their predatory aims, 197:3
their stony bones, 276:2
Exposed as hypocrites, 286:4
Express, dissatisfaction felt but could not e., 116:2
Expression, Lyric E. Due to Self-Limiting Concerns, 484:7
Extend opportunity to every heart, 526:6
Extensions in her hair, 548:4
Extensive, iniquity is general and e., 62:1
Exterminated, in danger of being e., 155:5
Extermination, justify e. of men, 290:8
External view about the Negro, 167:5
Extraordinary, every child has potential to become e., 538:5
Extreme difference based upon color, 229:3
law is e. justice, 48:1
Extremists, what kind of e. we will be, 317:3
Exultantly, walk not on earth e., 54:12
Eye, apple of the e., 16:4
as far as the e. could see, 148:2
blinking of an e., 225:2
bright E. of Horus comes, 3:1
cut e. don't kill, 575:12
dart the bright e., 71:6
devours seascape, 330:6
for e., 10:9
hesitancy of man with one e., 135:10
His e. is on the sparrow, 579:7
if thy right e. offend thee, 26:14
look them e. to e., 190:3
of a grownup, 494:1
of the beholder, 181:9
open on the sea, 345:3
see e. to e., 22:17
through e. of needle, 29:14
wind rain God's deliberate e., 545:2

Eyes, Africa of your e., 554:3
beauty in everything in her e., 453:7
black girl yearns blue e., 336:8
boys with blue e., 300:10
breath e. and memory, 550:1
bright and shining light for e., 58:3
dancing girl whose e. are bold, 210:7
dark e. know mine, 336:3
dry shuttered e., 325:4
full of e. within, 44:3
has not a Negro e. as a white man, 569:10
have e. and see not, 23:8
have they but they see not, 18:5
his e. are on the town, 566:8
kindling smiles in ladies' e., 85:1
look into the e. of five-year-olds, 485:5
mask that shades our e., 150:2
my ox bled e., 368:8
new hope in their e., 276:2
nothing hidden from e. of world, 86:5
of that House of Hunger, 490:4
on the prize, 572:11
right in his own e., 12:19
sharp as the e. of hate, 489:2
she walks with downcast e., 116:1
sleep departed from our e., 75:3
to the blind, 15:19
Watcher turns his e. away, 179:9
white tiger's blue e., 199:4
wipe your weeping e., 571:1
your e. shall be opened, 6:14

F

Fables, deceitful f. and imaginings, 59:1
Fabulating, and in our f. way, 537:2
Fac animo haec praesenti dicas, 48:n3
Face, beyond the f. of fear, 367:6
brown bamboo colored blk berry f., 359:5
cannons on the battlefield, 194:3
darkness upon f. of the deep, 5:4
falsely-smiling f., 174:8
flat ruined f., 325:4
God moved upon f. of the waters, 5:4
Jezebel painted her f., 14:8
lifts f. unashamed, 260:4

Face *(continued)*
Linda's f. pale as a pecan, 486:6
make his f. shine upon thee, 11:5
Moses hid his f., 9:1
my black f. fades, 461:6
my f. and rump were famous, 232:2
my f. is black not my fault, 138:2
neither east nor west, 234:1
never end up a f. in the crowd, 485:6
of America red yellow brown black white, 410:4
of the moon, 223:5
pallid f. and flaxen head, 107:5
power in f. of more power, 297:5
put on f. of cheerfulness, 109:1
seen many times, 283:2
third beast had f. as a man, 44:3
thou canst not see my f., 10:11
to f., 39:17
up to shortcomings, 494:4
warrior's black f., 225:8
why hidest thou thy f., 17:16
woman counts on her f. is a fool, 561:8
your f. has the beauty, 226:1
your own damn f., 394:2
Faced if only one is forced to face it, 475:1
nothing changed until f., 283:10
Faces, ain't no smiling f., 399:5
at the bottom, 324:1
I am what I see in your f., 291:3
I remember the f., 379:4
peeling with freudian dreams, 359:4
wall of my cell 47 black f., 336:3
Fact, never get away from the f., 277:5
Factor, race f. in diverse student body, 498:5
Factories standing idle, 332:6
Facts, violence of which f. are formed, 552:8
Fadeth, crown of glory f. not, 43:9
Fading, mountains are f. too, 276:2
Faggot deleted from our vocabulary, 425:5
Fail, they succeed who refuse to f., 131:4
Failed, accept first of all we have f., 469:5
Failing to serve the cause, 274:6

Far *(continued)*
no matter how f. person can go, 180:6
peace to him f. and near, 23:4
We've Come This F. by Faith, 579:5
Fare, tell me f. from you, 214:6
Farewell, bid f. to rule of slavery, 293:5
grandmother bid me f., 102:3
Farmer, primary idea was to help f., 142:2
Farmers, coumbite of f., 227:1
they are f. I am thief, 336:3
Fascist-minded, no f. people will drive me from it, 198:6
Fashion, black urban f., 510:6
of the shaft, 47:*n1*
passeth away, 39:9
Fast black energy space, 355:1
car, 536:8
hold f. that which is good, 42:3
live f. die young, 233:3
Fastballs and bigotry, 353:4
Fasted forty days and forty nights, 26:10
Fasten as a nail in a sure place, 22:8
Fastened woman, 506:5
Faster, run f. than man in front, 186:5
Fasting, devoting time to f. and prayer, 87:4
Fat, is as f. is as f. is, 480:7
no sex if you're f., 430:8
on its own flesh, 532:4
trousers full of f., 281:7
ye shall eat the f. of the land, 8:17
Fate, at odds with its f., 240:7
dice of f., 308:6
I know longer doubted my f., 69:2
is being kind to me, 201:7
is sealed and ought to be sealed, 128:2
merit the f. of ungrateful people, 73:4
of our unfortunate color, 65:1
of the people of Black Metropolis, 235:5
our f. as Americans is collective, 446:5
practical man your f. is here, 214:1
turns up the bitter cup, 149:5
unfortunate f. engulfing me, 92:1

Father, Abraham f. of many nations, 8:4
against son, 448:5
died after my misfortune, 62:2
do not go, 110:1
forgive them, 34:22
have we not all one f., 24:16
help your children, 473:3
his name shall be everlasting F., 22:3
honor thy f. and mother, 10:8
I am mother of my f., 49:1
in the name of the F., 32:4
into thy hands, 34:25
is shrouded in mystery, 105:6
it is my f., 335:7
my f. was a slave, 198:6
my resembling my f., 102:1
of many little slaves, 95:2
our F. which art in heaven, 27:2
richest man in town, 273:8
shall a man leave his f. and mother, 6:13
took to his grave, 475:2
worked for Mr. Pullman, 173:6
Father's, from his f. property, 2:4
going to our F. land exodus, 449:11
having her f. baby, 336:6
in F. house are many mansions, 36:13
lips closed in silence and grief, 65:8
Fatherland, driven from one's f., 206:5
Fatherless, judge the f., 21:17
Fathers, between f. and sons, 416:1
blood of your f., 100:6
dark tones of f. dying, 434:6
given your f. the least provocation, 78:5
iniquity of the f., 10:6
provoke not your children, 41:17
sins inflicted upon their f., 173:1
sins of its f. not visited today, 275:2
slavery does away with f., 105:6
speak from graves, 100:6
white f. told us, 358:6
your f. have lived died, 104:7
Fatted, bring f. calf, 34:10
Faucet, love is like a f., 253:6
Fault is the blood of an outcast race, 113:3
me I say na your f., 387:1

Fault *(continued)*
my face is black not my f., 138:2
Faults, cleanse me from secret f., 16:7
share these f. of character, 231:5
Fauna, cut off from f. and flora, 240:7
Favor, found f. in thy sight, 8:5
freedom yet deprecate agitation, 105:9
in f. with God and man, 33:7
to men of skill, 20:9
Favored, hail thou art highly f., 32:17
Favorite, regard myself a f. of heaven, 69:1
Favors, ask no special f., 101:6
fortune f. the brave, 48:*n4*
I don't want f., 238:1
no special f. but plead for justice, 101:6
seeking no f. because of color, 140:5
Fear, accorded through motives of f., 130:8
and trembling, 15:3
be not afraid of sudden f., 18:12
beyond the face of f., 367:6
choosing hope over f., 523:7
dehumanized look of f., 369:1
denies change, 419:2
despise my f., 50:2
drive off the beast of f., 180:16
embrace me without f., 241:2
engagement can lift suspicion and f., 529:1
Fearless didn't f. anything, 491:2
freedom from f., 245:5
God, 43:7
hate and f. cause time to snag, 491:6
is a noose that strangles, 189:10
is an illusion, 534:5
let who f. be dumb, 91:6
masks we f. cannot live without, 284:4
move in packs ingesting f., 555:1
new f. known to me, 402:1
no evil, 16:10
no f. in love, 43:15
no law divine, 81:7
no need to f. others, 284:8
not, 33:4
nothing to f., 127:3
of hunger hell and the Devil, 402:1
of the Lord is beginning of wisdom, 18:3

Fear *(continued)*
  passion of f. hath slain thousands,
    67:1
  remain in the world without f.,
    566:12
  slough off our f., 523:2
  strength and f., 49:3
  thrill of f., 490:5
  to live without f., 198:8
  to whom f. due, 38:23
  vanity is f., 346:5
  walk behind you who f. me, 371:6
  wept with f. and guilt, 388:2
  whom shall I f., 16:11
  younger artists express without f.,
    211:6
Feared, go through life f. by anyone,
    130:8
  God and eschewed evil, 14:15
  potential of what is f., 361:8
  the sky should fall, 47:n9
Fearful, why are ye f., 27:15
Fearfully and wonderfully made,
    18:7
Fearing, I'm not f. any man, 321:4
Fearless didn't fear anything, 491:2
Fears, no longer merged in f., 116:6
  of years, 336:2
  she who exists in f., 50:2
  throw away f. and prejudices, 78:4
Feast, a f. to the Lord, 9:11
  of moon and men, 188:8
  throughout your generations, 9:11
Feathered, harmonious lays the f.
    race, 71:6
  with eagle's plumes, 47:1
Feathers, fine f. make fine birds, 46:3
  in my mouth like f., 325:5
  parsley green, 487:1
  with our own f., 47:n1
Fed, I f. the wind, 240:6
Fed up, I know you're f. ladies, 556:3
Federating, ain't F. no more, 364:3
Federation, they didn't want F.,
    364:3
Feeblest, society trample on f., 114:2
Feed his flock like a shepherd, 22:15
  the worm shall f. on him, 15:15
Feeds me bread of bitterness, 175:6
Feel, I f. good, 347:3
  I f. therefore I can be free, 358:6
  instantly American, 249:2
  You Make Me F. Mighty Real,
    464:4

Feeling, greatest f. in my life, 301:3
  hot hot hot, 470:1
  sense of f. is exceedingly fine, 77:2
  when I get that f., 396:8
Feelings, my f. are too intense, 233:2
  upon parting with last relative,
    102:3
Feet, Big Bessie's f. hurt, 260:5
  cast in the iron of soul, 200:4
  come on f. do your thing, 346:2
  fell at his f., 43:19
  giver of speed to the f., 58:3
  guide my f. while I run this race,
    578:1
  I would place at your f., 396:4
  like unto fine brass, 43:18
  part of iron and clay, 23:23
  put off thy shoes from thy f., 8:23
  tests depth of river with both f.,
    565:17
  to the lame, 15:19
Feets is tired but soul is rested, 204:3
Fell among thieves, 34:1
  at his feet, 43:19
  down and worshipped him, 26:1
  into the burning fiery furnace,
    23:24
  not where you f. but where you
    slipped, 567:11
  one f. swoop, 123:8
  seeds f. by the way side, 28:12
Fellow, sword against his f., 13:6
Fellowship, right hands of f., 41:3
Female, as a black f. writer, 339:5
  male and f. created he, 6:4
  more obstacles than being black,
    287:2
Femaleness, devalue f., 488:3
Females, position of people
    condition of f., 94:2
  stereotyping of f. begins, 287:2
Femininity, he spoke to her f.,
    508:1
Feminist Warrior Poet Mother,
    359:1
  womanist is to f., 443:4
Fences, black iron-grille f., 321:7
  build f. to keep others out, 186:4
Festivity, Two Lands are in f., 5:1
Fettered, free and f., 383:2
Fetters, clanking of their f., 76:4
  lend aid in bursting f., 100:1
  of brass, 12:16
  strike off his f., 80:2

Fetus, love affair with the f., 348:1
Fever all through the night, 333:3
  burning in Harlem, 176:2
  when you kiss me, 333:3
Few, freedom not reserved for the f.,
    528:7
  many called f. chosen, 29:21
Fib, Mary had little lamb a f., 547:3
Fiction is preserver of customs,
    136:2
  is record of growth development,
    136:2
Fictions generated by imagination,
    323:5
Fiddle, second f. to no one, 201:8
Fidelity, serving my county with f.,
    68:2
Field, cursed above all of the f., 6:17
  dignity in tilling f., 131:6
  lilies of the f., 27:4
  potter's f., 31:13
  reap thy f., 11:3
  to bury strangers in, 31:13
Fields, from cotton f. to college,
    153:5
  glean in f. they have not sown,
    210:3
  old cotton f. at home, 174:4
  promoted from f. to washtub,
    142:7
  red blood in the f., 461:1
  rice f. in swamp did reap, 128:7
Fifteen dollars for every black
    brother, 310:1
Fifth, smote under f. rib, 13:18
Fig, land of vines and f. trees, 11:15
Fight aerial duel to avenge race,
    195:8
  against the Serpent, 87:6
  American people did not choose
    this f., 528:3
  born to f., 536:9
  can't keep swinging f. over, 224:3
  can't win what you don't f. for,
    380:1
  children need people to f. for
    them, 485:5
  come I will show you how to f.,
    84:7
  courage to stand up and f., 198:5
  don't give up the f., 449:2
  don't have to be man to f., 296:5
  don't want to die so I can f., 137:6
  enemies in our country, 286:4

Fight *(continued)*
essence of the f., 351:6
for freedom or slavery, 198:3
for freedom yourself, 240:1
for Liberty Freedom Life, 172:7
for what they deserve, 299:1
for your life, 285:1
fought a good f., 42:13
if we don't f. don't resist, 369:1
it did not have to f., 393:1
justice without a f., 437:1
not f. your battles on my body,
537:5
of faith, 42:10
off their asses and f., 299:1
resolved to f. and live or die, 162:8
the good f., 42:10
the powers that be, 518:4
they get boys to f. wars, 378:5
to create the new man, 351:6
to f. be intelligent, 296:5
to get in the kitchen, 554:1
to the death preferably not her
own, 444:1
whatever the obstacles, 131:4
why f. what's known, 85:3
willing to f. for it and so are you,
505:1
Fighter, being a f. to stay out there,
405:3
never been another f. like me,
417:6
Fightin like dogs, 247:3
Fighting, better die f. than die like rat
in a trap, 140:4
dying but f. back, 175:4
for human rights, 295:7
for ideas, 285:8
for survival, 450:3
freedom until end of days, 266:2
solidarity is forces f. for the same
end, 351:5
the power is good, 471:3
words are braver than all f., 2:3
Fights, roof f. rain sheltered ignores
it, 566:7
Fig-leaf, guilt pins a f., 164:6
Figure out the patterns, 553:4
Fill it with thy fire, 72:1
their minds they will adore you,
441:3
Filled the hungry with good things,
32:22
they shall be f., 26:12

Filled *(continued)*
with the Holy Ghost, 37:7
Film critics don't write about it,
508:9
enslave me on f., 510:3
Filthy, let him be f. still, 45:6
Final word in reality, 319:5
Finance, poverty complicated as
high f., 272:2
Find, can't f. what you can't see,
384:3
ourselves beyond ourselves, 557:6
out who he is, 451:3
seek and ye shall f., 27:7
sin will f. you out, 11:10
Sister Caroline, 148:6
they will f. me there, 52:1
through jungle to f. me, 335:7
whosoever lose life shall f. it, 29:10
your passion, 500:3
Finding one's way through the dark,
498:1
Fine, feathers make f. birds, 46:3
feet like unto f. brass, 43:18
Fine-toothed, scraped life with f.
comb, 258:9
Finger, black f. pointing upwards,
161:5
git you' f. bit stick it at a 'possum,
568:6
if we dared lift a f., 112:1
the f. of God, 9:7
Fingers, many heavens as pointing f.,
447:3
separate as f. one as hand, 132:1
thick f. of vines, 462:1
time leaves marks of rough f., 65:2
Fingertips, this poem has his f., 388:6
Finish it off with a laugh, 181:11
Finished, it is f., 37:3
Fir wood harps and psalteries, 13:19
Fire, ain't no f. here, 278:3
always a new lie on the f., 205:2
and gunpowder do not sleep
together, 565:14
better to save brother's house on
f., 66:3
burning in the souls, 274:4
by night in a pillar of f., 9:15
catch a f. so you can get burn, 449:5
chariot of f., 14:4
cloven tongues like f., 37:7
dutty water can put out f., 574:8
fill it with thy f., 72:1

Fire *(continued)*
hide de f. but what do wid smoke,
570:19
horses of f., 14:4
hoses and nightsticks, 401:1
if hiding don't light a f., 565:15
light the f. at bottom of the pile,
166:2
lips to touch the sacred f., 147:8
maketh ministers a flame of f.,
42:16
no more water f. next time, 284:7
not light is needed but f., 105:2
of life and youth in his veins, 130:3
over f. watch fever grow, 469:6
purifying ourselves in their f.,
351:6
revealed by f., 39:4
roast with f. and unleavened
bread, 9:9
set hearts on f. with zeal, 166:2
set this world on F., 174:1
should not approach the f., 281:7
stand next to your f., 419:9
the bush burned with f., 8:22
they do not f., 64:4
those being burned know f., 194:5
to burn the world, 441:5
went through f. and water, 17:8
without warmth, 377:1
ya'll think it's a f. in here, 278:3
Fired, last hired first f., 570:7
Fires, made banked f. blaze, 243:3
of April were not weather, 475:5
of faith kept burning, 177:3
passed through f. of tribulation,
125:5
Firm, who believe stand f. by His
Word, 54:8
Firm-footed, stand f. unchanging,
86:7
First and great commandment, 30:1
as citizens of the world, 207:5
beast like a lion, 44:3
cannot be f. in everything, 46:7
class citizenship for the Negro,
270:4
evening and morning were the f.
day, 6:1
fruits, 40:4
He is the f. and last, 57:2
I am f. and last, 49:1
I am the f. and last, 45:7
last shall be f., 29:15

First *(continued)*
    man to sit on top of the world, 169:1
    my f. and only one, 247:6
    name ourselves f., 418:1
    never as good as the f. time, 516:7
    shall be last, 29:15
    should be last, 87:6
    show piety at home, 42:7
    sprinkle of unrest, 280:4
    the last should be f., 87:6
    time in my life proud of my country, 538:1
    try f. thyself, 46:*n*2
    waiting for other to make f. move, 194:7
    You're the F. the Last My Everything, 445:7
Firstborn, brought forth her f. son, 33:3
    smite all the f. in Egypt, 9:10
First-class citizen, 208:3
    citizens, 183:6
    made Negro f. citizen, 216:3
    second-class don't pay f. taxes, 343:4
Fish, after f. spoil 'e spoil, 575:8
    dart among their bones, 545:2
    dominion over the f. of the sea, 6:5
    every f. eena sea no shark, 576:1
    in the belly of the f., 24:10
    in the river dart before you, 5:2
Fishers of men, 26:11
Fishes, five loaves two f., 28:20
    shall declare unto thee, 15:8
    taken in evil net, 20:9
Fist, if you raise your f. and yell, 368:6
    more to it than just your f., 436:10
    violent act from f. stick knife to gun, 485:4
Fit, if it doesn't f. you must acquit, 375:3
    isn't f. to live, 317:5
    the rest must simply f. in, 494:6
Five loaves two fishes, 28:20
    smooth stones, 13:9
    were wise f. were foolish, 30:7
Fix gaze on guiding star, 261:4
    me no breakfus', 179:8
Flag, American f. a dirty rag to Negro, 122:4
    black girl waving american f., 442:7

Flag *(continued)*
    more than National F. to make a nation, 237:6
    salute the f., 271:1
    used to love grand old f., 122:4
    wave my freak f., 420:2
Flagons, stay me with f., 21:6
Flamboyant hooker on the street, 385:3
Flame falls in the hay, 3:2
    graceful as the tongues of f., 223:4
    maketh ministers a f. of fire, 42:16
    reflected light of this inner f., 167:1
    slower to see f. of truth, 166:5
    tomorrow bright like a f., 211:1
Flames at the crematorium, 271:4
    long after f. city still smoldering, 475:5
    of April came out of season, 475:5
Flanks, touch sisters on the f., 382:2
Flares, meteoric f. and flights, 207:9
Flatters, wolf hates when it f., 53:2
Flaw, in everything we find a f., 152:1
Flaws of character into virtues, 471:2
Flaxen, pallid face and f. head, 107:5
Fleas in the pores of your desert skin, 439:6
    lie down with dogs get up with f., 570:5
    old couch stuffed with f., 332:2
Fleeting as the clouds, 55:9
    pleasures, 52:1
Flesh and blood talking to you, 469:3
    and bone rebel, 199:1
    bone of my bones f. of my f., 6:12
    confetti of f., 368:8
    every living thing of all f., 7:10
    fat on its own f., 532:4
    hair of my f., 15:4
    is weak, 31:9
    man is left only f. and passions, 363:7
    needs feed upon f., 302:2
    no tears I'm stone I'm f., 461:6
    of their f., 11:1
    outa f., 372:5
    profiteth nothing, 35:24
    that weeps laughs, 338:9
    they shall be one f., 6:13
    they shall eat the f. in that night, 9:9
    thorn in the f., 41:1
    Word was made f., 35:8
Flew, they f. like blackbirds, 370:6

Flies, popping off like f., 332:6
Flight, we had done it achieved f., 488:2
Float like a butterfly, 417:4
    through life, 261:4
Flock, feed his f. like a shepherd, 22:15
    valiant shepherd who drives his f., 4:5
Flogging, more rigorous system of f., 102:2
    one hundred lashes, 102:2
Flood, accustomed to f. famine fear, 506:4
    carried away as with a f., 17:17
Floods, neither can f. drown it, 21:15
Floor, down on the killin' f., 234:8
    Floorboards under my feet, 378:7
Floors, roam all over coliseum f., 539:4
Florida, how community interprets what happened one night in F., 530:1
Flourisheth, in the morning it f., 17:17
Flower, more than National F. to make a nation, 237:6
    of their age, 13:1
    plant your f. grow a pearl, 414:5
    time cracks into furious f., 260:4
    with petals of blood, 388:4
Flowers droop and sigh, 192:7
    of many sorts many colors, 193:5
    unseen f. under your feet, 377:8
Flowing, a land f. with milk and honey, 9:2
Flunkeys of order, 240:6
Fly away and be at rest, 17:5
    away duke, 398:2
    easy anyone can f., 330:1
    easy once you learn how to f., 476:2
    riches f. as an eagle, 19:1
    rode upon a cherub and did f., 16:5
    shoo f. don't bother me, 569:2
    sparks f. upward, 15:6
    straighten up f. right, 269:6
    the eagle will never f., 356:7
    they say the people could f., 370:6
    upon the wings of wind, 16:5
    wanna f., 337:7
Fly's, doomed f. wings, 491:6
Flying among stars, 330:1
    and floating that shit in, 549:1

Flying *(continued)*
  bird alone f. low, 329:3
  fourth beast like a f. eagle, 44:3
  I see a f. saucer comin, 357:2
Foe, defeat our most common f., 490:7
Fog a-fall an de sun a-fail, 313:2
Foil voice of drum, 469:6
Fold, in the f. of old wounds, 486:4
  sheep I have are not of this f., 36:9
Folk, all music is f. music, 204:5
  Companions and the pious f., 60:2
  games black f. play on one another, 546:4
  if black f. allowed to participate, 231:1
  listen to the f., 362:7
  nibble the cakes of other f., 182:7
  one mind for white f. to see, 570:3
  scholarly and righteous f., 60:3
  want bread cake pie crumbs, 292:2
Folklore of white supremacy, 257:2
Folks, come north all f. good and bad, 142:8
  different strokes for different f., 570:11
  hearin bout old f., 271:6
  might understand you by and by, 423:2
  Us are the F., 323:9
  ways of white f., 212:3
  white f. still ahead, 204:7
Folk-song rhythmic cry of slave, 144:3
Folksy, However Too Trite and Too F., 484:7
Follow desire, 1:6
  goodness and mercy shall f., 16:10
  me, 26:11
  the drinking gourd, 569:8, 576:9
  the North Star, 569:7
  things which make peace, 39:1
  you to moon in the sky, 484:4
Followed, being f. in a department store, 530:1
  Hell f. with him, 44:7
Follows, disappointment f. in its wake, 67:4
Folly, answer a fool according to his f., 19:4
  laughing at our f., 89:1
  to revise God's mind, 181:6

Food affirms our humanity, 553:9
  if you do not have f., 289:6
  is life, 384:1
  money to buy f. on earth, 366:4
  Necessity like f. water, 326:9
  prepared by Negro mothers, 229:3
  soul f. is more than chitlins, 384:2
Fool, always been f. who believes, 328:4
  and water go the way they are diverted, 566:6
  answer a f. according to his folly, 19:4
  any f. living in the world, 444:6
  griefs that f., 260:6
  hath said there is no God, 16:2
  I can't f. myself, 484:3
  I May Be Crazy but I Ain't No F., 155:8
  me once shame on you, 572:8
  of no consequence, 280:3
  played the f., 13:14
  time f. has learned game players dispersed, 565:13
  wisdom higher than f. can reach, 71:3
  with a dick can make a baby, 548:9
  woman counts on her face is a f., 561:8
  you a f. it's my hair, 501:2
Fool's, a f. mouth is his destruction, 18:20
  silence is a f. program, 127:5
Fooleries of beings, 360:9
Foolish, five were wise five were f., 30:7
  hear now this f. people, 23:8
  things to confound the wise, 39:3
  to trust in things, 363:1
Foolishness, desperate f., 513:3
Fools Fall in Love, 401:3
  grapes too green only for f., 45:n3
  heart of f., 20:3
  suffer f. gladly, 40:15
  take people for f., 373:6
  you are f. and old women, 84:7
Foot, dash thy f. against stone, 33:9
  for f., 10:9
  society's f. on throat, 329:4
  soldiers on the march, 303:6
Football, black kids want to play f., 457:10

Footin', as long as I'm f. the bills, 293:3
Footstool of the other races, 172:1
For what for a piano, 451:10
  whites only, 317:9
Forbearance of the poor, 208:1
  spirit of f. we can exert, 97:7
  tested in our f., 133:2
Forbid, God f., 8:16
Forbidden from serving country, 528:1
  in vain f. to write, 82:3
Force is able to exterminate wicked, 60:1
Forced to tell whole story, 283:4
Forces ruining the Negro, 136:3
Forcible, how f. are right words, 15:7
Forebears, stolen labor of our f., 412:6
Forefathers, bloodshed of their f., 376:10
  made being here possible, 250:9
Foreign, dark f. presence, 324:2
  no rights as f. workers, 329:5
Foreigner in the country of his birth, 454:6
Foreigners, treated as well as F., 76:5
Forests of columns, 279:6
Forever and ever and ever there it is, 369:1
  his name shall not perish f., 2:7
  servitude f. abolished, 67:8
  sometimes f. yet so brief, 373:2
Forget, 518:8
  how long wilt thou f. me, 16:1
  I'm Black, 441:4
  no right to f. history, 311:6
  the womb shall f. him, 15:15
  they f. who got them where they are, 439:2
  they tell us to f., 199:1
  things don't want to remember, 179:10
  we can forgive never f., 267:7
Forgetful, be not f. to entertain strangers, 42:19
Forgetfulness, dreamer roused from f., 465:4
Forgets, worth what one f., 311:3
Forgetting while stealin, 466:7
Forgive, as we f. our debtors, 27:2
  Father f. them, 34:22

Free *(continued)*
  my soul feels f. to travel, 73:5
  not cramp him but f. him, 133:3
  nothing is f., 365:4
  now f. I weave together, 85:7
  older and white and somewhat f.,
    213:7
  on paper, 510:3
  one who is f. is disciplined, 261:1
  only f. men negotiate, 266:7
  ourselves can f. our minds, 450:1
  prejudice in f. society, 120:4
  see ya when I f. ya, 556:2
  shaking f. from traditions of past,
    119:4
  the dream to be f., 198:8
  the privileged white, 246:3
  to eat and sleep, 264:7
  to tell a man he is f., 131:1
  trade for some protection for
    others, 407:1
  truth shall make you f., 36:5
  walk until we are f., 245:6
  was I same person now I was f.,
    111:3
  you mind and your ass will follow,
    407:3
Freed, cannot rise until f., 118:3
  the white race f. me, 215:1
Freedom, a great sum obtained this
    f., 37:15
  achieve f. at all costs, 264:5
  advance guard for f., 176:6
  African is conditioned to a f.,
    181:12
  aid in the fight for F., 172:7
  all you desire is F., 100:3
  among all men, 220:2
  armed with f. defense and guns,
    424:8
  a-waitin' to carry you to f., 576:9
  begging for f., 286:2
  being jeopardized, 296:1
  believe in f. of Africa, 272:5
  better than slavery, 113:4
  birthright of humanity, 135:9
  born into a kind of f., 478:3
  can't separate peace from f., 297:3
  carry precious light of f., 529:4
  clash between f. and exploitation,
    297:6
  comes with responsibilities, 528:5
  complete f., 296:4
  complete, 488:4

Freedom *(continued)*
  death is a slave's f., 430:3
  determined to gain my f., 102:2
  discord in songs of f., 76:4
  elect to fight for f. or slavery, 198:3
  everybody wants f., 252:5
  favor f. yet deprecate agitation,
    105:9
  fight for f. yourself, 240:1
  fighting f. until end of days, 266:2
  for all human Race, 64:3
  for f. of soul and body, 121:2
  for one deny to others, 304:5
  for one group, 304:5
  for whole world or no world,
    185:4
  from war springs f., 113:6
  full f. will satisfy us, 240:4
  genesis of their f., 254:4
  gift of f., 527:3
  give us f. from fear, 245:5
  having lover who has no control,
    95:4
  held him back from f., 113:5
  in full sense of the word, 126:4
  in hearts not on paper, 184:7
  in this village, 507:2
  is a privilege, 65:7
  is limited by necessities, 207:7
  is oxygen of the studio, 200:1
  is the sense of option, 203:4
  issue is whether f. can be
    permanent, 103:4
  jazz musicians symbolize f., 446:4
  learning to read the pathway to f.,
    104:2
  let f. reign, 267:1
  let us use our f., 264:7
  living and dying for f., 428:7
  long road to f., 267:5
  marchin' up to f. land, 579:2
  more unbearable than f., 283:3
  must be demanded, 316:8
  my mind set on f., 577:11
  never granted it is won, 176:4
  never handed on silver platter,
    233:5
  never voluntarily given, 316:8
  new birth of f., 523:2
  no f. by appealing to moral sense,
    463:5
  no f. for patriarchal men, 488:4
  no word in 1776 to us about F.,
    432:7

Freedom *(continued)*
  nobody can give you f., 296:3
  not reserved for the few, 528:7
  Now, 573:5
  objective necessity to objective f.,
    207:3
  of conscience, 239:3
  of every slave on every plantation,
    92:5
  of speech watch what you say,
    511:1
  of the forest and plain, 101:3
  oh f. over me, 577:7
  on the march to f., 303:6
  oppression and f. umbilically tied,
    428:8
  our f. and we want it now, 400:5
  people will never fight for your f.,
    240:1
  preservation of f., 64:3
  psychological f., 320:3
  ring, 318:3
  slaves in the midst of f., 76:4,
    93:7
  soon got used to f., 115:1
  story ends with f., 95:5
  strange f. to be adrift in the world,
    202:5
  the cause of f., 274:6
  to fight for f., 296:5
  train running toward f., 292:1
  tried to make black f. a pipe
    dream, 495:7
  until the f. gates are open, 237:7
  want to taste f., 111:5
  we have waited too long for f.,
    266:8
  We Want F., 426:1
  we who believe in f. cannot rest,
    217:4
  when f. is taken away, 267:2
  without discipline, 261:1
  women Black Panthers as f.
    fighters, 446:3
  words devoted to quelling f.,
    506:6
  worth paying for, 316:1
Freedom's army crowned with
    laurels, 102:5
  sing in light of f. morn, 129:1
  sweet f. way, 212:8
  walk f. road, 300:2
Freelands reek from peak to peak,
    161:2

Future *(continued)*
of endless possibility, 523:2
of my people, 115:5
optimistic about the f., 284:10
past on one side f. on the other, 496:7
past useful to present and f., 104:7
preserve for f. reference, 125:5
reality of a f. punishment, 71:2
slavery remembered as past, 114:1
tell the f. we did not exist, 535:2
the f. perfect, 561:6
upon ourselves depend our f., 171:5
was sunset, 339:1
we know who holds the f., 573:10
will be a now then, 472:10
without hope can be no f., 495:1

G
G, nuthin' but a G thang, 556:8
Gain, to live is Christ to die is g., 41:12
whole world lose own soul, 29:10
Gained, when riches are g., 1:6
Gaining, something might be g. on you, 224:2
Gal, brown skin g., 575:4
got a g. up on the hill, 221:3
long time g., 575:5
young g. good for start, 300:4
Galaxy, imagine a great web across g., 418:2
Gall, bitter as the g. of birds, 3:4
our haughty neighbor, 86:7
Gallery, freedom is the oxygen of the g., 200:1
to be a star not a g. mascot, 517:6
Galling, clanking of g. chains, 100:1
feel the chain g. us, 84:3
forever wear g. chain, 117:4
of the chains, 69:3
Gambling your way out of sad, 559:8
Game, beat him at his own g., 358:3
business was the white man's g., 363:2
called on account of hugs, 515:4
don't hate player hate the g., 574:2
enough to take punishment, 303:8
got on my pimp g., 550:7
messing with my g., 378:7
name of the g. ain't baseball, 359:7
of getting, 179:2
of keeping what one has, 179:2

Game *(continued)*
old observation g., 506:4
only g. you know is do or die, 423:6
running down a beautiful g., 379:5
the beautiful g., 402:4
time fool has learned g. players dispersed, 565:13
Games black folk play on one another, 546:4
invent your own g., 430:7
memory g. in casino of the past, 458:4
Gang, workin' on the chain g., 334:1
Gangrene of empty hours, 369:5
Gangsta rap ghetto life ignored by Americans, 510:4
Gangsters say My word is my bond, 394:1
Gao, traveler to G., 59:4
Gap in the side of mountain, 46:8
Garbage, burn them up like g., 415:5
snow fell obscuring the g., 238:6
Garbageman dignified as diplomat, 260:5
Garden, come into g. and eat his fruits, 21:9
in my hat in a foreign g., 397:7
in search of mother's g. I found my own, 443:6
Lord God planted a g. in Eden, 6:8
must never satisfy, 472:9
sail g. round, 325:2
voice of the Lord God in the g., 6:15
where cunning grows, 375:5
Gardenia thing she was into, 379:4
Gardenias in your hair, 254:2
Gardens of their servitude, 243:5
Garment, best the g. be loose, 285:4
bound single g. of destiny, 320:6
Garments, put on her g. of gladness, 25:2
Gash, be it g. or gold, 259:1
Gasoline, easy life of TV and g., 491:3
volatile as alcohol g., 306:3
Gasoline Point Alabama, 257:7
Gasp, at the last g., 25:16
Gate, sign on front g., 298:4
strait is the g., 27:10
this is the g. of heaven, 8:10
wide is the g., 27:10

Gatekeeper, bribe for the g., 365:5
Gates, black g. of death, 232:8
of hell shall not prevail, 29:8
until the freedom g. are open, 237:7
Gather, glean and g., 12:21
the gleanings, 11:3
the lambs with his arm, 22:15
time to g. stones, 19:17
up the fragments, 35:22
Gathered, all the saints g., 59:3
before him all nations, 30:10
one scattered and g., 50:3
them into Armageddon, 44:20
two or three g. together, 29:11
Gave birth to a puzzle, 361:7
his only begotten Son, 35:18
Lord g. and hath taken, 14:19
up the ghost, 34:26
Gay, because I was a g. man, 502:5
black man living in a world, 502:5
Black men proudly g., 496:4
our troops and yes some are g., 528:1
spot a g. man, 502:1
Gayness a rupture in the order of things, 509:5
Gays, The New Niggers Are G., 240:2
unnatural because not straight, 509:5
Gaza, brought him to G., 12:16
Gender, supposed purity of g. race, 485:2
General, iniquity is g. and extensive, 62:1
Generalizations are dangerous, 112:3
Generation, breed new g. of aristocrats, 257:8
examples set before rising g., 88:7
experiences of each g., 444:2
New G. Blacks, 410:2
stubborn and rebellious g., 17:12
third and fourth g. that hate me, 10:6
younger meaner g., 503:1
Generations, delivered safely to future g., 527:3
feast throughout your g., 9:11
live for g. and g. and g. and g., 327:8
of black men, 416:1
pay for the bloodshed, 376:10
quality of life and future g., 401:5

Generations (continued)
shall call us blessed, 171:2
yet unborn, 88:7
Generous, Lord is most g., 57:6
Genes and chromosomes, 518:6
Genesis of their freedom, 254:4
Genetic mulatto, 533:1
racism and sexism are not g., 368:4
Genitals public other parts private, 531:4
Genius + Soul = Jazz, 326:7
born of his spiritual g., 120:1
does not grow on trees, 399:4
man has demonstrated little spiritual g., 220:4
no race has monopoly on inventive g., 365:7
out of our own creative g., 172:10
proof accessible to the g., 185:1
talent hide its luster, 90:2
Genocide begins with killing one man, 383:3
evidence of our g., 483:3
Gentle, treat it g., 194:9
Gentleness, hear me in g., 51:4
Gently lead those with young, 22:15
Geographical lines, 173:3
Geography, my original g., 241:5
you got a g. of your own, 367:4
Geometry of my shed blood, 241:5
George Bush doesn't care about black people, 563:4
Georgetown, in G. snorting coke, 389:7
Georgia, higher'n a G. pine, 221:6
red hills of G., 318:1
German, gurgles in G., 200:5
Gesture, friendly g. or not, 362:8
Get, going to g. it what's mine, 464:6
it if you really want, 464:8
Let's G. It On, 396:7
off your asses and do something, 504:6
oh you'll g. used to it, 396:2
on board little children, 577:8
out of my way, 452:3
over it I'm best for Washington, 366:6
over the water, 555:4
ready cause here I come, 403:9
Rich or Die Tryin', 560:4
thee behind me Satan, 29:9
time to g., 19:17
up stand up, 449:2

Get (continued)
used to me, 417:8
what you can take, 176:8
whatever you g. that's you, 219:5
Getting, game of g., 179:2
great g. up morning, 578:4
Jiggy wit It, 549:4
with all thy g. get understanding, 18:13
Ghetto, barriers of the g., 246:3
bastard, 551:5
dopefiends in the g., 370:2
gangsta rap g. life ignored by Americans, 510:4
Harlem capital of every g., 446:1
in which whites live imprisoned, 246:3
past the g. on to Mardi Gras, 508:3
smaller g. to larger one, 317:9
stage is the g., 547:3
stay the fuck outta the g., 551:6
the g. talkin' bout the g., 448:4
wonder if heaven got a g., 556:6
Ghetto's invisible walls, 246:2
smash something g. need, 282:10
Ghettoes, teen-ager in these g., 297:2
Ghettos, God's will is not that we be confined to g., 469:4
Ghost, gave up the g., 34:26
man giveth up the g., 15:9
Ghosted you up a swell story, 212:2
Ghosts, big g. in a cloud, 307:1
clothes hang like g., 175:8
falling in love again with g., 483:6
of the past, 304:2
we once were, 385:5
Giants, they were g. in the earth, 7:9
gift, free g. to mankind, 163:3
her g. for metaphor, 337:4
music as much a g., 475:3
of freedom, 527:3
of God is eternal life, 38:10
of the Negro people, 144:3
unspeakable g. of Almighty God, 80:4
word better than a g., 25:12
Gifted, to be young g. and black, 328:2
usta be young usta be g. still black, 455:1
with double vision, 231:7
young g. and black, 433:1
Gifts, presented unto him g., 26:1
we start with g., 189:5

Giggle, ha'd to g. w'en nuffin' in the pot, 150:6
Gild dark horrors of the grave, 81:5
Gilead, balm in G., 23:12
balm in G., 579:3
is there no Balm in G., 377:1
Gin, we thin g., 259:8
Ginger-root, bananas ripe and g., 175:5
Girded, let your loins be g., 34:6
with your loins g., 9:10
Girl, average g. from video, 561:1
because I am a colored g., 125:6
black g. yearns blue eyes, 336:8
brown g. in the ring, 574:12
can take g. out the projects, 497:8
exotic as a chorus g., 385:3
gets sick of a rose, 258:10
growing up Southern Black g., 305:7
if a g. was colored, 238:2
look at a fine fine g., 574:15
next door, 502:7
no place in America for a black g., 428:8
slave g. black as ebony fair as mistress, 95:1
talkin' 'bout my g., 404:1
they shoot white g. first, 340:2
wasn't the only black g., 217:1
when doctor says it's a g., 287:2
with extensions in her hair, 548:4
Girls, brown g. rouged, 176:1
four black g. blown up, 384:3
gonna make you g., 251:4
I'll show them g., 258:6
machine makes little blonde g., 362:1
Give, ask bread will g. him a stone, 27:9
can't g. nothing away if you poor, 436:9
enemies means of our destruction, 47:1
freely g., 28:2
gold the goose could g., 46:13
his angels charge over thee, 33:9
I will g. you rest, 28:8
it up you got to g. it up, 237:4
me back my delegation, 356:1
me chastity and continence, 52:6
me John Baptist's head, 28:19
me my equality, 352:5

Give *(continued)*

me neither poverty nor riches, 19:9

more blessed to g. than receive, 37:14

now g. me money, 315:2

peace I g. unto you, 36:17

peace in our day, 70:2

salvation g. with tender Love, 63:2

such as I have g. I thee, 37:8

the young man knowledge and discretion, 18:11

thee crown of life, 43:21

thee keys of the kingdom, 29:8

up the shit, 337:7

us this day our daily bread, 27:2

what we g. makes a life, 428:3

what will ye g. me, 31:1

what you command, 52:9

world giveth g. I unto you, 36:17

Give-and-take between two black people, 415:7

Given, ask and it shall be g., 27:7

hast g. him his heart's desire, 16:8

it was g. to me this way, 327:6

much is g. much required, 34:7

of knowledge but little, 54:13

this world I didn't make it, 556:5

to hospitality, 38:18

to Moses and Jesus and the Prophets, 53:9

unto every one that hath g., 30:9

want nothing unless freely g., 130:8

Giver, every gift has personality of its g., 447:6

of needs undefined, 381:3

Gives, if white man g. you anything, 262:5

more fame than gold and silver, 58:3

you nothing, 277:2

Giveth, spirit g. life, 40:9

to all life and breath, 37:13

unto the poor, 19:7

up the ghost, 15:9

world g. give I unto you, 36:17

Giving liberates the soul, 308:5

tired of g. in, 245:1

Glad, after dey free us we so g., 124:6

ain't-cha g. we get along, 192:4

Gladly, suffer fools g., 40:15

Gladness, put on her garments of g., 25:2

Glam-glow twinkle and gold, 557:6

Glamour, 'bout time I got some g., 258:6

Glance, satisfied with a g., 280:3

Glass, blue g. in the house sing, 516:1

broke g. cold blades, 489:2

clawed in g. and brick, 250:1

encased in g. as glistening star, 55:7

see through g. darkly, 39:17

tower filled with headaches, 224:7

Glean and gather, 12:21

thy vineyard, 11:3

Gleanings, gather the g., 11:3

Glimmer of resurrection morn, 190:5

Gloom, in g. and sadness I may rise, 82:2

Glorify, tales of the hunt g. the hunter, 567:12

Glorious, become g. in power, 10:2

city of God, 53:5

Eye of Horus, 3:1

Gloriously, he had triumphed g., 9:17

Glory, crown of g. fadeth not, 43:9

envy the g. of others, 68:6

give God the g., 577:4

life and bliss unknown, 71:5

of the Lord is risen upon thee, 23:5

of the Lord shone round, 33:4

rise to zenith of g., 119:3

taste of g. like sweet wine, 239:1

thine is the power and the g., 27:2

to God in the highest, 33:5

Gluttonous, behold a man g., 28:7

Gnaws, life that g. in us all, 231:6

Go, a long long way to g., 316:3

and do likewise, 34:3

and sin no more, 36:4

away I said, 240:6

down Death bring her to me, 148:6

down Moses, 576:10

for what you know, 518:4

from strength to strength, 17:15

gotta g. for all we know, 392:6

hell no we won't g., 292:2

into the world, 32:16

let g. because you can, 337:10

let her g. God bless her, 572:4

let my people g., 9:4

light on vices, 224:2

Lord be with thee, 13:8

Go *(continued)*

round the rocks, 567:7

shorty it's your birthday, 560:3

tell it on the mountain, 576:8

thou goest I will g., 12:20

where they still must g., 251:2

zombie no g. tell am to g., 386:5

Goal, Africa has single g. independence, 197:6

my g. as an artist, 302:4

tragedy lies in having no g., 187:2

upward I look I seek my g., 82:2

Goals, we believe in g. and timetables, 292:3

Goat, traveled aimless g. paths, 337:6

Goats, as a shepherd divideth sheep from g., 30:10

God accepted the peoples cast away, 59:2

ain't that how G. planned it, 518:6

all from G., 300:7

am a jealous G., 10:6

and G. saw that it was good, 6:2

angels of G. ascending and descending, 8:8

arm's too short to box with G., 148:4

be still and know that I am G., 17:2

behold the Lamb of G., 35:10

believe in G. believe in me, 36:13

black g. made me, 312:5

bless Africa, 152:*n*1

bless Africa, 267:1

bless child that's got his own, 253:7

bless you make haste, 82:4

blessed be Lord G. of Israel, 33:1

blessed be the Lord G. of Shem, 7:16

blessedness comes from G., 201:10

bones G. gave us our own, 112:1

breathed the breath of life, 6:7

bringest G. and angels as a surety, 54:14

built you noble, 179:5

cannot see the kingdom of G., 35:15

cannot serve G. and mammon, 27:3

changes not people until they change, 54:6

children of G., 26:12

Christ from G. and a woman, 83:1

Christ Son of the living G., 29:7

645

God *(continued)*

contempt of G., 53:6
co-workers with G., 317:2
created heaven and earth, 5:4
created in image of G., 341:8
created man immortal, 25:5
curse G. and die, 15:1
damn white people anyway, 238:1
dare dispute with G., 63:6
desired knowledge of G., 24:5
destiny in the hands of G., 171:6
didn't G. know we'd have trouble
    if black, 237:9
didn't place only roses on earth,
    193:5
difference between G. and luck,
    516:3
enter kingdom of G., 29:14
every creature of G. is good, 42:6
every race believe they look like G.,
    122:3
fear G. and keep commandments,
    21:1
fear G., 43:7
feared G. and eschewed evil,
    14:15
filled my soul with melody, 147:1
fool hath said there is no G., 16:2
for G. nothing shall be impossible,
    32:18
forbid, 8:16
formed man of the dust of the
    ground, 6:7
gave Noah rainbow sign, 284:7
gift of G. is eternal life, 38:10
give G. the glory, 577:4
glorious city of G., 53:5
glory to G. in the highest, 33:5
gracious and merciful, 300:6
guideth to His light, 55:7
guideth whom He will, 56:1
has called you, 357:4
has stirred the nation, 113:5
hath joined together, 29:13
he that loveth not knoweth not G.,
    43:14
hear the voices of G., 136:1
heirs of G., 38:13
help him to help himself, 46:*n*2
help us G. make Humanity divine,
    144:10
his name shall be the mighty G.,
    22:3
i found g. in myself, 467:1

God *(continued)*

if G. for us who can be against us,
    38:14
if G. will, 55:1
in favor with G. and man, 33:7
in my pocket, 544:9
in the house, 434:6
in the image of G. made he man,
    7:13
in the name of G., 53:7
is black, 395:1
is G. dead, 82:5
is light, 43:12
is light of heavens and earth, 55:7
is love, 43:14
is no respecter of persons, 37:12
is not mocked, 41:8
is pleased for her to dwell, 59:2
is smiling but frowning too, 520:7
is swift at the reckoning, 55:8
is the color of water, 509:3
is the sequel of all things, 56:4
is their only friend, 62:1
is thy refuge, 12:6
it's the way G. wants it, 504:7
Kingdom of G. appeared, 304:4
kingdom of G. within you, 34:15
knows what you'll go through,
    520:7
learned the first man to read, 80:4
lends aid to the worker, 46:*n*2
let G. be our limit, 172:11
let her go G. bless her, 572:4
looked around said I'm lonely,
    148:1
Lord our G. is one Lord, 11:12
love G. in words hate brother in
    works, 92:4
love is G., 340:3
love of G. burned within me, 77:1
love of G., 53:6
made all of the same blood, 79:4
made us what we are, 172:10
make a joyful noise unto G., 17:7
make straight a highway for our
    G., 22:13
man more just than G., 15:5
man sent from G. was John, 35:6
may send hand of death, 63:5
most merciful G., 53:7
mother's house there is G., 327:4
moved upon face of the waters, 5:4
neither g. nor angels nor men,
    100:3

God *(continued)*

no man hath seen G., 35:9
not even G. wise enough, 564:15
O G. give me words, 190:4
of ancient times modern days,
    90:1
of great kindness, 14:13
of such is kingdom of G., 32:14
of the living, 34:18
of truth, 12:4
of war, 362:4
offense toward G. toward men,
    37:19
on the seventh day G. ended his
    work, 6:6
one G. created us, 24:16
one G. one Aim one Destiny, 170:5
our G. is a walking G., 389:6
people call hurricanes acts of G.,
    514:9
pisses G. off, 444:5
please forgive those people, 496:5
Praise be to G., 53:7
prayed to G. to learn me to read,
    80:4
prayer to G. for deliverance, 104:1
prayers to unknown g., 255:1
preserve us from such things, 60:2
Put a Rainbow in the Sky, 236:1
put on armor of G., 41:11
rainbow people of G., 342:2
rejected Israel, 59:2
respond to call of G., 186:6
reveal future to man, 88:3
said Let there be light, 5:4
said Let us make man in our
    image, 6:3
said so Family, 334:5
said unto Moses I AM THAT I
    AM, 9:3
saints of G. are gathered home,
    128:4
save the king, 13:4
sees when He looks down, 477:8
separate us from love of G., 38:16
setteth forth parables, 55:7
shall smite thee, 37:16
shall wipe away all tears, 45:4
shapes laws of man to laws of G.,
    230:7
sin against Grace G. can not save
    you, 164:5
so loved the world, 35:18
Sole G. beside whom is none, 5:3

Golden eggs empty of albumen, 345:5
lived by g. rule, 299:9
oh dem g. slippers, 130:2
seven g. candlesticks, 43:17
Gold-tipped, dog with black g. hair, 232:7
Goliath, nobody roots for G., 367:1
Gone, every goodbye ain't g., 572:6
Joe Turner's come and g., 568:5
many thousand g., 578:3
'til November, 551:2
Good, a g. character is remembered, 2:5
Americans g. guys, 286:4
and faithful servant, 30:8
and God saw that it was g., 6:2
any g. come out of Nazareth, 35:11
atom's weight of g., 57:7
be of g. cheer, 28:23
be of g. cheer, 36:21
black don't crack, 573:11
born for g. luck, 251:5
died a g. death, 323:4
do g. to them that hate you, 27:1
every creature of God is g., 42:6
evil communications corrupt g. manners, 40:6
example to the children, 1:3
feel so strange but sure is g., 385:2
fight the g. fight, 42:10
filled the hungry with g. things, 32:22
for your everything, 303:3
fought a g. fight, 42:13
hold fast that which is g., 42:3
I bring you g. tidings, 33:4
I feel g., 347:3
I would I do not, 38:11
I'm as g. as anyone, 178:5
if he had not been born, 31:5
in a g. old age, 8:3
it is not g. that man be alone, 6:10
jealous of g. not themselves accomplished, 68:6
law is g., 42:4
make use of the great g. in us, 220:2
man and just, 34:27
mornin' blues, 174:5
neighbor policy, 519:5
never as g. as the first time, 516:7
night Willie Lee see you in the morning, 443:8

Good (continued)
no matter what not g. enough, 332:8
once g. like the Virgin Mary, 173:6
overcome evil with g., 38:22
peace from men's g. will, 293:7
proofs of my g. citizenship, 67:3
rich in g. works, 42:11
seemed like a g. idea at the time, 376:3
shepherd, 36:8
so g. of you being so g., 259:4
times roll, 228:5
tree of knowledge of g. and evil, 6:9
we all g. woman, 486:4
when your g. woman is gone, 187:7
white folks working for me, 500:4
who will speak for the common g., 371:2
will never have g. time, 2:1
will toward men, 33:5
with indifference notes evil and g., 86:1
word is like a g. tree, 54:8
works better in sight of thy Lord, 55:2
ye shall know g. and evil, 6:14
you are as g. as they are, 79:4
zealously affected in a g. thing, 41:5
Good morning daddy, 213:5
Goodbye, every g. ain't gone, 572:6
is a stone on my tongue, 545:1
long and short g., 520:3
Good-bye mr wigin, 351:1
Good-looking, have a g. corpse, 233:3
Goodness and mercy shall follow, 16:10
crownest the year with g., 17:6
essential g. of my fellow man, 220:1
gracious, 333:6
sold itself, 564:10
Goodnight Irene, 174:2
Goods, conveyed as dry g., 100:1
kills thief and owner of stolen g., 567:1
not take g. with him, 1:2
Good-will, conquered in an evening's g., 282:11

Goose, gold the g. could give, 46:13
killed to find nothing, 46:13
voice of the wild g., 3:3
Gorilla, if you say G. My Love, 394:1
Gospel, not believed the g., 52:11
preach g. to every creature, 32:16
train's a-coming, 577:9
Gossiping about you, 567:6
Got, if you g. to ask you ain't g. it, 221:7
they g. things and we ain't, 230:9
Gourd, follow the drinking g., 569:8
follow the drinking g., 576:9
let this g. let this g. break, 360:8
Government can no longer tolerate, 229:3
failure of G. to enforce, 191:2
if g. had right to free us, 138:1
incomprehensible that g. is powerless, 208:8
make g. cool again, 523:5
of America has failed you, 196:1
that gave us liberty, 125:3
unable to protect Negro citizen, 139:5
violence can breed counter-violence, 266:3
what g. does in our name, 503:3
Governments, alien g. forced upon African people, 197:5
follow progress, 129:3
prodded by g. into needless war, 220:5
Grace, being an athlete a kind of g., 533:2
carried to the throne of g., 72:3
dem what eats can say g., 570:16
effort and g., 466:1
Faith crowned with g., 190:5
fallen from g., 41:6
full of g. and truth, 35:8
heart full of g., 320:10
Madonna exemplar of g., 86:6
sin against God G. can save you, 164:5
sways in wicked g., 260:4
yes and I take it quiet quiet, 493:6
Graceful as the tongues of flame, 223:4
Gracious, God g. and merciful, 14:13
unto thee, 11:5
Graduating every day, 229:2
Grandeur, girdled with g., 113:1

Grandfather not an Indian chief, 178:7

Grandfather's grave with American flag, 234:9

Grandma, high yellow g., 531:2

Grandma's hands clapped in church, 392:4

Grandmother appears to speak to me, 397:7
  bid me farewell, 102:3

Grandmother's, nights behind g. porch, 486:6

Grandmothers handed on the creative spark, 443:5

Granite, hiding inside the black g., 461:6
  Negro remains like g., 106:6

Grape, if loneliness were a g., 431:9
  of thy vineyard, 11:3

Grapes are not ripe, 45:n3
  are sour, 45:11
  our vines have tender g., 21:7

Grapeshot, canisters packed with g., 412:7

Grapevine, heard it through the g., 436:1

Grapple with slavery not at arm's length, 79:5

Grasped, speech that cannot be g., 51:5

Grasping at the shadow, 46:10

Grass, in the morning like g. groweth, 17:17
  snakes in that g., 392:4
  when elephants fight g. suffers, 564:6

Grass roots, change will come from g., 522:2

Grateful for the trust, 526:4
  for what I've got, 483:6

Gratified, often sorry if wishes g., 46:16

Grave, birthday boy headed for g., 478:2
  from cradle to the g., 109:6
  from cradle to the g., 272:3
  gild dark horrors of the g., 81:5
  Grandfather's g. with American flag, 234:9
  I'll be buried in my g., 577:7
  immortalize names beyond the g., 88:7
  jealousy is cruel as the g., 21:14

Grave *(continued)*
  lay down in my g., 306:4
  make me a g. but not where men are slaves, 114:8
  resurrection from g. of slavery, 100:2
  trouble to follow me to my g., 191:5
  tyrant wars made earth a g., 129:1
  where is thy victory, 40:8
  within step of the g., 63:5

Graven, among idols and g. images, 59:2
  images of gods, 22:6
  not make unto thee any g. image, 10:5

Graves, fathers speak from g., 100:6
  free from sinking in inglorious g., 91:1

Graveyard, tractor getting closer to that g., 350:5
  trouble take you to g., 353:4

Gravity, defy g. to feel tugged back, 557:5

Gray jail looming, 292:7
  like some magistrate grown g., 86:1
  skies are just clouds passing, 202:1

Great balls of fire, 333:6
  black men once g. shall be g. again, 172:2
  everybody can be g., 320:10
  gettin' up morning, 578:4
  gods ride little horses, 574:7
  good that is in us, 220:2
  is Truth, 24:19
  little person to stir up g. events, 472:6
  Many g. men are under me, 57:9
  men not always wise, 15:20
  ones of the countries bow down, 4:1
  she whose wedding is g., 49:1
  think I'm g. if play like idiot, 457:8
  to be g. yet small, 133:2

Greater love hath no man, 36:18
  only thing g. than yourself, 274:3
  than civil rights is human rights, 295:7
  the handicap g. the triumph, 266:1

Greatest, I am the g., 417:3
  of these is charity, 39:17
  virtue becomes g. crime, 207:1

Great-grandmammy a Dahomey queen, 300:4

Greatness, measure our g. by the least, 537:6
  respect to the great paves own g., 567:10

Greed no longer saps the soul, 212:8

Greedy, we're all a little g., 305:3

Greeks, I am the wisdom of G., 50:3
  judgment of G. and barbarians, 50:3

Green, build a g. economy strong, 548:1
  grapes too g. only for fools, 45:n3
  lie down in g. pastures, 16:10
  Red Black G. colors, 272:5
  wave to lift all boats, 548:1

Greet yourself arriving, 331:1

Grenade fallen like jackfruit, 462:6

Grenades, brandishing hand g., 297:9

Grew up like a neglected weed, 111:1

Grey bone and white surf, 332:4
  make a g. turn to face it, 345:6

Grief and wailing o'er silent dead, 82:1
  cooperate with g., 394:6
  father's lips closed in silence and g., 65:8
  history of g., 92:1
  in much wisdom is much g., 19:14

Griefs, beware the easy g., 260:6

Grievances overshadow opportunities, 131:6

Grievously, I have been g. afflicted, 61:4

Grime, snow fell obscuring the g., 238:6

Grin, silly rabbit g., 537:2

Grind in the prison house, 12:16

Grinders cease, 20:11

Grinding, sound of the g. is low, 20:11

Griot, when a g. dies, 274:2

Groans of the dying, 69:3

Groove, One Nation Under G., 407:6

Grooves, bloody g. across backs, 336:2

Ground, at least get off the g., 180:15
  broken unto the g., 22:6
  brother's blood crieth from the g., 7:5
  Cain was a tiller of the g., 7:3
  climbing higher g., 230:7

Ground (*continued*)
colored man occupies disputed, 105:5
God formed man of the dust of the g., 6:7
opens up and envelops me, 354:1
whereon thou standest is holy g., 8:23
Group, imitation of the dominant g., 202:3
Groups, collection of interest g., 371:2
in g. less guilt to swallow, 555:1
multitudinous g. of people, 229:1
Groveling, he goeth g., 57:4
Grow, did not g. up in any inner city, 503:7
full the river still wants to g., 565:6
know how to g. hair as g. cotton, 142:7
men g. strong in action, 114:4
Growing is relentless as life, 189:7
love is g. up, 283:7
Grown, I'm a g. man now, 158:3
scion of youth is g., 81:4
up slaves always, 64:1
Grownup, eye of a g., 494:1
Grudge what they cannot enjoy, 46:5
Guarantee future of children, 285:8
Guard, advance g. of revolution, 176:6
be on your g., 50:2
Guardian animal I must hide, 225:3
Guardians of the liberty you cherish, 73:4
Guards, prison g. cannot hold down an idea, 425:4
Gudgeons, swallow g. ere they're catched, 45:*n*2
Guess I wait and see, 357:2
why this is so is anybody's g., 437:7
Guest, well-mannered g. at party, 305:4
Guest-workers from third world, 329:5
Guidance, those who yield to g., 56:1
Guide my feet while I run this race, 578:1
Guideposts, democracy and human rights are our g., 538:6
Guideth, God g. to His light, 55:7
God g. whom He will, 56:1
Guiding, gaze on g. star, 261:4

Guilt, bear pain of g. and shame, 92:2
in groups less g. to swallow, 555:1
of lifetime floated away, 456:2
pins a fig-leaf, 164:6
so deep so long unfelt, 81:7
wept with fear and g., 388:2
without sin without g., 2:6
Guilty, absolutely 100 percent not g., 464:2
of act detested in others, 66:2
of such atrocities, 272:5
we too are g. of murder, 186:8
Guinea, sang the g. hen, 61:1
Guinea's, choruses above the g. squawk, 188:6
Guise, under the g. of liberation, 220:3
Guitar, grip g. as somebody's throat, 497:2
play g. like ringing a bell, 299:7
Gulf, between us a g., 34:14
invisible signs form a g. between us, 401:2
Gumbo, jazz is a musical g., 178:3
Gun basic tool of liberation, 425:1
boys with g. and uniform, 413:2
Joe where you going with g., 420:1
smoking g. a mushroom cloud, 498:4
violent act from fist stick knife to g., 485:4
Gunfire and rocks, 245:5
from the mountains, 512:8
Gunpowder, fire and g. do not sleep together, 565:14
Guns, armed with freedom defense and g., 424:8
cling to g. or religion, 525:4
clubs hoses g. jails, 249:5
I have all the g. and money, 428:6
lack the body of human truths, 448:1
leave your house take your g., 108:7
pursued with g. and bloodhounds, 99:1
trusty g. in my belt, 130:3
two men holding g., 351:2
votes must go with g., 288:3
we don't like to use 'em, 534:9
we have no g. only stones, 373:5
Gush, makest a spring to g. forth, 54:14

Guy, can't be torn apart from my g., 403:7
Gypsy to get my fortune told, 187:6
woman hypnotized me, 422:4

H

H.I.V./AIDS, let us give publicity to H., 267:8
Habit is Heaven's own redress, 85:6
of surviving, 263:2
takes the place of happiness, 85:6
Habitation, there is her h., 59:2
Habits, bad h. lead to bumps on head, 397:7
censuah othah folks about dey h., 149:1
customs h. of slavery oppression, 123:5
fixed for higher attainments, 109:2
vile h. acquired in servitude, 74:3
Hail, blues falling down like h., 237:2
Master, 31:11
thou art highly favored, 32:17
Hair, adore my kinky h., 242:7
appreciate my hair, 444:10
bad h. day, 561:3
blonde girls with stringy h., 362:1
braid my h., 371:7
complexion of skin texture of h., 139:7
curly crinkly woolly h., 182:2
dog with black gold-tipped h., 232:7
extensions in her h., 548:4
gardenias in your h., 254:2
gone was the nappy h., 193:2
good h. that's the expression, 489:1
I Am Not My H., 561:2
intended to be nappy, 461:3
like a h. across your cheek, 194:8
like white folks' h., 489:1
long luxurious blond h., 501:2
my h. is wooly, 352:6
of my flesh, 15:4
texture of my h. had changed, 346:4
write it's like braiding h., 550:2
yellow h. brown h. black h., 182:2
Hairdo, I am remembered as a h., 437:6
Hairdressers, years of enduring h., 444:10

Haiti is parish of the poor, 493:1
Haitians have a destiny to suffer, 226:6
Half because I was game, 303:8
  craving other h. of equation, 337:4
  deprive them h. their virtue, 70:1
  free h. enslaved, 245:4
  he was h. black h. white, 74:2
  liked my h. did you like yours, 74:2
  made to feel h. a man, 436:11
  rich h. exploited, 245:4
  women hold up other h. of sky, 473:8
Half-and-half, since dem h. dem choice, 269:1
Half-baked solutions, 318:4
Half-castes, we are all cultural h., 225:4
Half-told, truth has never been h., 79:2
Hallelujah I Love Her So, 326:5
Hallowed be thy name, 27:2
Hallways, in wine-stained h., 284:5
Halo, dumb as a robe and h., 502:3
Ham, I want my h., 452:2
  in the meat house, 256:7
Hambone where you been, 571:4
Hammer, died wid a h. in his han', 568:1
  loaded h. swung like a ton, 205:7
  of armed struggle, 266:6
  swing dat h., 205:3
Hand, behold the hour is at h., 31:10
  capitalistic h. around throat, 548:6
  cold h. of death, 63:5
  dying h. of racism, 380:2
  every man's h. against me, 114:3
  for h., 10:9
  he may carry away in h., 20:1
  if thy right h. offend thee, 26:14
  is pure as sorrow, 360:8
  keep h. wide open, 329:1
  kingdom of heaven is at h., 26:5
  lead me by the h., 251:4
  lend helping h., 66:3
  mek me hold yuh h., 575:5
  nuthin but sweat inside my h., 540:4
  of all that hate us, 33:2
  raise a h. to shade eyes, 233:6
  raised right h. stood for power, 442:4

Hand (continued)
  reach out touch somebody's h., 406:3
  right h. not to know what left h. doing, 110:5
  right h. hath dashed the enemy, 10:2
  right h. is become glorious, 10:2
  separate as fingers one as h., 132:1
  someone puts h. on you, 294:5
  take my h. precious Lord, 200:9
  take our children by the h., 75:1
  the stopper's in my h., 191:6
  thou openest thine h., 18:8
  upon trembling slave, 113:5
  what one h. removes, 281:6
Handicap, colored men have one h. race, 141:2
  colored woman has double h. of race and sex, 141:1
  for oppressed to depend on a leader, 217:6
  greater the h. greater the triumph, 266:1
  have not let color h. me, 153:5
  white woman one h. sex, 141:2
Handicapped on account of race, 141:3
Handicaps among so-called Negroes, 196:5
  associated with race, 379:6
  one of my two h., 287:2
Handkerchief, mother had h. and song, 440:3
Handle, way to h. it is destroying it, 264:4
Handled, strange men h. me, 78:6
Hands, abomunists join nothing but their h., 292:4
  destiny in the h. of God, 171:6
  destiny is in our h., 106:7
  destiny we hold in our h., 198:8
  done shook h. and gone, 188:4
  Ethiopia shall stretch out her h., 17:9
  Father into thy h., 34:25
  future in the h. of the young, 400:7
  Grandma's h. clapped, 392:4
  her h. like precious stones, 440:3
  I am pure of mouth of h., 2:6
  into h. of the English, 75:2
  into the h. of sinners, 31:10

Hands (continued)
  Lady Lady I saw your h., 165:1
  looked at h. to see if I was same, 111:3
  must be very important, 432:3
  my h. against every man, 114:3
  not by others' h., 47:n1
  on the h. of your two sisters, 3:1
  power in your h., 181:10
  prey in h. of white race, 196:4
  right h. of fellowship, 41:3
  the work of our h., 17:20
  throw up both my h., 396:5
  took water and washed his h., 31:16
  train your head and h. to do, 137:9
  two men h. hands, 351:2
  we can't hold, 324:4
  work of our own h., 93:6
  wounds in thine h., 24:15
Hanging by thread of life, 63:5
Hangs, the man h. twenty feet above, 384:6
Hannah, go down ol' H., 174:1
Happen, could never h. to someone like me, 515:3
  some things that h., 562:3
Happeneth, one event h. to all, 19:15
  time and chance h. to all, 20:9
Happening because this is how it happens, 421:2
Happens to me at least before I was a senator, 530:1
Happily, let us live h., 567:8
Happiness, achieve our own h., 286:2
  full measure of h., 526:5
  habit takes the place of h., 85:6
  induce sadness to attain h., 465:6
  is a perfume, 170:2
  is living seen through a veil, 180:14
  love and h., 455:3
  of liberty, 75:2
  or unhappiness, 259:5
  peace and h. for every man, 405:4
Happy birthday boy headed for grave, 478:2
  contented love this condition, 101:2
  I sing because I'm h., 579:7
  man ain't h. unless man dies, 514:6
  man h. as a baby boy, 221:5
  man says slaves are h., 78:7

Have-Nots, World divided into Haves and H., 215:5

Haves, World divided into H. and Have-Nots, 215:5

Having nothing yet possessing all, 40:13

Hawks and crows, 388:5

Hay, flame falls in the h., 3:2

Hazards of the high seas alone, 233:6

He believeth in me shall live, 36:10
  can run he can't hide, 249:4
  cannot escape it completely, 348:2
  is before all things, 41:14
  is risen, 32:15
  is the first and last, 57:2
  is the Rock, 12:4
  is wise tries everything before arms, 48:9
  knoweth all things, 57:2
  not with me is against me, 28:9
  saved others, 32:1
  shall come out into the day, 2:7
  shall humble himself shall be exalted, 30:2
  shall inherit the wind, 18:15
  shall walk on earth among the living, 2:7
  that trusteth his riches shall fall, 18:14

Wasn't Last Night, 548:5

without sin among you, 36:3

Head, anointest my h. with oil, 16:10
  give me John Baptist's h., 28:19
  go h. held high, 300:2
  in the lion's mouth, 248:6
  keep your h. up, 556:3
  makes your big h. so hard, 228:2
  never lose your h., 186:2
  pallid face and flaxen h., 107:5
  the whole h. is sick, 21:16
  train your h. and hands to do, 137:9
  your h. and heart to dare, 137:9

Headaches, glass tower filled with h., 224:7

Heads, black skins and wooly h., 107:5
  proudly gay with h. held high, 496:4

Headway, can't make h. in this country, 163:6

Heal and re-create ourselves, 444:3
  helped h. wounds, 279:1

Heal *(continued)*
  how can love h. the mouth shut, 462:2
  not believe doctors h., 337:1
  physician h. thyself, 33:10
  the world, 512:5
  time to h., 19:17

Healing begins where the wound was made, 445:3
  for all men's h. let me sing, 218:10
  if apology is a prerequisite for h., 508:4
  of the wounds, 266:9
  sexual h., 396:8

Health, better care of horses than own h., 121:1
  is a human right, 286:7
  spirit of success and h., 163:3

Healthy boy ain't wrong when he kills, 490:8

Heaps up gold and silver, 58:4

Hear, have ears and h. not, 23:8
  he that hath ears let him h., 28:6
  me in gentleness, 51:4
  Miss Jane jus h. from 'Merica, 268:7
  now this foolish people, 23:8
  O Israel, 11:12
  of wars and rumors of wars, 30:3
  the other side, 52:10
  the voices of God, 136:1
  they have ears but h. not, 18:5
  those things ye h., 33:15
  you may h. what I h., 357:5

Heard it through the grapevine, 436:1
  Jezebel h. of it, 14:8
  none but Jesus h., 82:6
  the sighs of wonder, 210:5
  they h. the voice of the Lord God, 6:15
  voice saying God bless you make haste, 82:4
  will not retreat and will be h., 110:4

Hearest, thou h. the sound thereof, 35:16

Heareth, ear of jealousy h. all things, 25:3

Hearin bout old folks, 271:6

Hearing, blind have the sense of h., 77:2
  locks click on the doors of cars, 530:1

Heart, a hope arose in my h., 74:4
  a lot of h. and soul, 384:2
  abundance of the h., 28:11
  according to the size of his h., 390:1
  an instrument we never understand, 478:4
  and you'll see into my h., 158:4
  beauty strikes my h., 224:6
  begging us to keep a good h., 78:6
  big as a whale, 226:5
  black labs of the h., 354:4
  blues ain't nothin' but a h. disease, 193:6
  burden'd h. breaking in despair, 112:4
  can be cruel, 478:4
  cheer men cheer in the h., 108:7
  come from the h., 153:6
  committed adultery in his h., 26:14
  continual sorrow in my h., 72:3
  counsel of thine own h., 25:14
  cruel to h. that's true, 333:4
  did not our h. burn within us, 35:3
  ego in h. of cosmos, 290:9
  engage h. of each others lives, 373:2
  envious h. makes a treacherous ear, 180:1
  fool hath said in his h., 16:2
  free hand free, 157:8
  full of grace, 320:10
  hatred in my h., 282:9
  he hardened Pharaoh's h., 9:6
  he thinketh in his h., 19:2
  human h. can bear misfortune, 103:3
  I tell my h. to go ahead, 173:8
  if your h. ain't rock, 195:5
  in my h. I do not yield, 128:3
  intents of the h., 42:17
  is deceitful and wicked, 23:14
  knows down in my h., 156:1
  Lady Lady I saw your h., 165:1
  lak a rock cast in the sea, 151:4
  let not h. be troubled, 36:17
  let not your h. be troubled, 36:13
  living chords of my h., 113:1
  lock your h., 165:2
  long my buried h. is lain, 85:5
  Lord looketh on the h., 13:7
  love the Lord with all thy h., 30:1
  love your h. the prize, 338:9

Heart (*continued*)

man after own h., 13:5
my h. left long ago, 413:1
my h. turns this way and that, 4:3
my h. was sweet to excess, 3:5
mystery of the universe, 134:5
of a woman, 169:3
of fools in house of mirth, 20:3
of Muhammad, 56:13
of the human world, 189:2
of the moment, 311:4
of true integration, 454:3
of wise in house of mourning,
    20:3
old darky's h. longed to go, 130:1
one love one h., 449:12
powerful h. can endure the pulse,
    513:5
proud h. survive, 322:9
racial h. of the American Negro,
    166:1
records of a h. in pain, 84:8
seal upon thine h., 21:14
she had a loving trusting h., 116:1
slave trade at war with h. of man,
    69:4
songs of the slave sorrows of h.,
    104:1
source of joy for the h., 58:3
spirit moving in my h., 578:2
stubborn h. shall fare evil, 25:7
tell hungry belly take h., 575:14
the whole h. faint, 21:16
thoughts of the h., 42:17
today blues of mind and h.,
    268:4
way of world makes h. cold,
    414:5
when belly full h. glad, 575:13
whole h. and soul, 23:15
wise and understanding h., 13:24
with bleeding h. we smile, 150:2
without a h. it cannot sing, 61:1
without love woman's h. hardens,
    376:1
your head and h. to dare, 137:9
Heart's, hast given him his h. desire,
    16:8
Heartease, eye know how far h. is,
    460:5
Heart-miles, hundred h. could scarce
    measure it, 153:9
Hearts, a country in their h., 573:7
    apply our h. unto wisdom, 17:19

Hearts (*continued*)

cheerfulness when h. are torn,
    109:1
day star arise in your h., 43:11
do not forgive, 322:1
freedom in h. not on paper, 184:7
hope in their h., 115:5
imagination of h., 32:21
in h. know it is right, 194:7
inevitably complicated tragic,
    510:7
know and respect quality of their
    h., 510:7
of men do not change themselves,
    229:5
peace from men's h., 293:7
pregnant earth to our h., 388:3
rustle secrets, 325:1
Scriptures cut from men's h., 59:2
set h. on fire with zeal, 166:2
set their h. upon you, 48:10
shrieks of breaking h., 97:2
study their h., 65:5
that dream held in our h., 198:8
the serpent coiled in their own h.,
    79:5
unharnessed h. can survive, 340:5
what your h. have amassed, 53:11
Heat and hunger of the streets,
    490:1
neither sun light nor h., 44:12
of the climate, 69:3
of the day, 29:16, 148:6
wave burnin' in my heart, 408:5
whose lives were cooled felt the h.,
    475:5
your body loses its h., 381:4
Heaven and earth shall pass away,
    30:5
and earth to witness, 11:11
and Hell, 64:2
as it is in h., 27:2
beams of h. as I go, 128:6
calls you to arise, 100:6
de 'lectric light o' Heaven, 149:6
entrance into H., 122:5
every purpose under h., 19:17
four winds of the h., 24:12
God created h. and earth, 5:4
handed down to man from h.,
    70:4
Harlem was Seventh H., 296:7
helps not men who will not act,
    46:*n*2

Heaven (*continued*)

in h. and in earth, 41:14
key to h. is language, 497:3
keys of the kingdom of h., 29:8
kingdom of h. is at hand, 26:5
life is h., 145:10
like a net cast into the sea, 28:16
like to mustard seed, 28:15
likened unto ten virgins, 30:7
Lord of h. and earth, 37:13
new h. and new earth, 45:3
New York was h., 296:7
no telephone to h., 454:7
one h. earth queen, 289:3
our Father which art in h., 27:2
people go to hell not to h., 267:8
poor man to get in h., 365:5
regard myself a favorite of h., 69:1
sends down the love of her, 3:2
shoot where stars will fall, 345:3
suddenly a sound from h., 37:6
theirs is the kingdom of h., 26:12
there is a h. there is a hell, 150:5
this is the gate of h., 8:10
war in h., 44:14
wonder if h. got a ghetto, 556:6
ye shall see h. open, 35:12
Heaven's, habit is H. own redress,
    85:6
splendid you rise in h. lightland,
    4:6
your splendor is like h. splendor,
    4:4
Heavenly love by love of God, 53:6
Heavens, as many h. as there are
    beings, 447:3
as many h. as there are pointing
    fingers, 447:3
boiled down to a drop, 180:5
creation of h. and earth, 56:3
God is light of h. and earth, 55:7
lifted baby to the h., 274:3
loud noise in the h., 87:6
she was the world and h., 180:5
towards h. lost to him, 240:6
Heavy, all ye that are h. laden, 28:8
Heel, he knows who holds the h.,
    93:7
Heels, take to their h. and run, 79:5
took to my h., 48:11
Heights of Itoko, 361:7
Heir, every American h., 317:7
Heirs of God, 38:13
    we are h. of a past, 135:4

Hell, cultured h. that tests my youth, 175:6

followed with him, 44:7

gates of h. shall not prevail, 29:8

Heaven and H., 64:2

militaristic stairway into h., 319:5

no we won't go, 292:2

people go to h. not to heaven, 267:8

Satan to own there is a h., 71:2

slavery form of h., 308:6

there is a heaven there is a h., 150:5

who the h. told Black woman, 335:3

whole body not be cast into h., 26:14

without satisfaction life is h., 145:10

Hello Massa bottom rail on top dis time, 570:4

Helmet for the head, 58:3

the hope of salvation, 42:1

Help, all my h. was cries and tears, 73:1

God h. him to h. himself, 46:*n*2

gods h. them that h. themselves, 46:15

hurt something to h. something, 350:6

I can't h. myself, 408:10

the gods h. those who h. themselves, 139:1

used to h. you out, 374:1

who need a woman's h., 90:4

Helped, really h. heal wounds, 279:1

Helpfulness must be the fuel, 166:2

Helping, far from h. me, 16:9

lend h. hand, 66:3

Helplessness, exploit their h., 329:5

Helps, fortune h. the brave, 48:12

not men who will not act, 46:*n*2

He-male, put h. an' she-male asunder, 570:2

Hemingses, in the case of the H., 510:7

Hence these tears, 47:3

Henry, remember H. Aaron, 353:3

roll with me H., 385:1

Her, call h. she replies with wisdom, 566:12

he died for h. also, 76:6

Herbs, beasts browse on their h., 5:2

of every joyous kind, 55:5

with bitter h. they shall eat, 9:9

Here, ain't got long to stay h., 578:6

am I, 13:2

any place but h., 298:4

come by h. my Lord, 579:10

come the judge, 221:6

crossed the waters to come h., 65:6

I shouldn't be h., 298:4

I'm pore I'm black I'm h., 444:7

if neither there nor h. then what, 349:5

in America, 559:3

right h. everything end, 332:5

taken me a lifetime to get h., 441:6

there is everywhere h., 460:7

we can't stay h. no more, 451:2

we're h. aren't we, 456:5

Heritage, I have a h., 16:3

recapture lost artistic h., 168:2

repudiation of one's h., 202:3

Hero, not a h. because I got HIV, 515:3

worth more than a million cowards, 113:2

Herod, born in the days of H., 25:18

should not return to H., 26:1

Heroes, children of battle are your h., 430:7

kings and h. die and vanish, 61:1

my h. on no stamps, 518:5

where are your h. little Black ones, 430:6

wrong kinds of h., 297:2

Heroin was slow death, 370:2

Heroism is sober and undramatic, 428:1

Herself, invisible and precious and only h., 546:*n*2

Hesitate, tell me now why do you h., 151:6

Heterogeneity, Black h., 557:1

Hewers of wood, 12:10

Hey Joe, 420:1

say h., 336:4

Hi, de h. de h., 226:5

Hidden castle of your skin, 304:7

he is manifest and h., 57:2

more h. than malachite, 1:4

nothing h. from eyes of world, 86:5

you have h. and appear, 51:1

Hide behind national sovereignty, 383:1

de fire but what do wid smoke, 570:19

genius talent h. its luster, 90:2

he can run he can't h., 249:4

nowhere to h., 409:2

the Ancestor, 225:3

thyself for a little moment, 22:12

whenever you appear I will h., 51:1

you in the night, 381:4

Hidest, why h. thou thy face, 17:16

Hidin, not be h. and lyin, 271:5

Hiding, if h. don't light a fire, 565:15

soul crawled out from h. place, 180:7

truth like trying to bury water, 493:2

High, master your h., 555:4

High school, h. was best, 300:10

Higher, move on up a little h., 195:2

wisdom h. than fool can reach, 71:3

Highest, Glory to God in the h., 33:5

High-tech lynching for uppity blacks, 468:4

Highway, intellectual h., 447:1

key to the h., 184:4

make straight a h. for our God, 22:13

memory is a h., 458:6

Hijacked airplane as a missile, 498:3

Hillbilly music is like the Stock Exchange, 433:6

Hills and valleys he come through, 327:7

cattle upon a thousand h., 17:3

more h. to climb, 267:5

red h. of Georgia, 318:1

utmost bound of the everlasting h., 8:19

Him, by h. all things consist, 41:14

equal to H. is not anyone, 57:8

to H. we surrender, 53:9

who knows this book on earth, 2:7

Himself, by h. in the perfect quiet, 370:5

he cannot save, 32:1

Hinc illae lacrimae, 47:*n*3

Hinders relations with countries known, 58:2

Hip hop the hibbie hibbie, 374:5

Hip Hop Is Dead, 559:7

Hip-hop, ballet h. and kung fu, 557:4
  is cool, 557:4
  is real description of suffering
    people, 510:1
  is something you live, 542:2
  like pieces of puzzles complicated,
    541:3
Hips, these h. have never been
    enslaved, 367:3
Hired, last h. first fired, 570:7
His eye is on the sparrow, 579:7
  firm Word, 54:8
  mercy endureth for ever, 14:10
  name shall endure for ever, 17:11
  name shall not perish, 2:7
Historian, Colored Soldiers of the
    Revolution have no h., 103:2
Historians know practically nothing,
    155:6
History, absolved of h. did not
    commit, 331:8
  accept one's h., 284:2
  Africa will write own h., 294:1
  ambiguities of h., 319:4
  America frightened of h., 231:5
  answer the call of h., 529:4
  black h. is American h., 377:3
  Black H. Month, 377:3
  cannot believe h. sacred or
    profane, 77:5
  children are the seeds of h., 395:6
  continuous play of h., 344:1
  curiosities in the h. books, 542:3
  depends on the beholder, 341:6
  don't want a Black H. Month,
    377:3
  Education that Teaches Our True
    H., 426:3
  evening of our h., 288:1
  from point of view of deliverance,
    207:5
  full of great events, 472:6
  great men make h., 207:7
  hope to be remembered by h.,
    279:1
  if we search h., 72:5
  in parade of God's h., 197:7
  let's look to h., 302:2
  life that does not contribute to h.,
    227:2
  make h. or remain the victims,
    492:1
  matrix in which h. happens, 418:2
  memory without h., 226:1

History *(continued)*
  much h. under them skin, 313:4
  must restore what slavery took
    away, 152:3
  need not be lived again, 308:3
  no right to forget h., 311:6
  not exclusively h. of problems,
    330:2
  of America written in bloody
    terms, 232:4
  of glory and dignity, 294:1
  of liberty born of struggle, 105:9
  of Negro in America, 232:4
  one day have its say, 294:1
  pages of h. blistered with tears,
    127:2
  people without a positive h., 454:4
  poverty and dysfunction traced to
    difficult h., 530:1
  pride in its own h., 295:10
  spiral of h., 248:3
  tells people where what, 251:2
  three centuries human h., 301:7
  trapped in h., 282:6
  tried to make black h. a curse, 495:7
  unboastful unbiased h., 162:4
  understanding of h., 251:2
  will remember your judgment,
    183:4
  will repeat itself, 171:6
  write me down in h., 307:4
Hit the road Jack, 273:4
Hitchhike when I walked in my
    sleep, 216:2
Hitter, the h. can never be the judge,
    477:7
H.I.V./AIDS, let us give publicity to
    H., 267:8
HIV because I had unprotected sex,
    515:3
Ho, de h. de h., 226:5
Hoard, people who h., 377:4
Hog in the electric chair, 350:7
  want you like a h. wants slop, 438:5
Hogs, die not like h., 175:3
Hold, danger to h. both old and new,
    166:5
  fast that which is good, 42:3
  fast to dreams, 210:6
  her squeeze her, 412:1
  keep what you can h., 176:8
  lay h. on eternal life, 42:10
  me like a River Jordan, 512:6
  on, 572:11

Hold *(continued)*
  on honey sanctify yourself, 514:11
  something's got a h. on me, 385:2
  the door open for me, 196:7
  their peace, 34:17
  You've Really Got a H. on Me,
    403:6
Holding black people back, 277:3
  more comfortable h. guns than h.
    hands, 351:2
Holds, we know who h. the future,
    573:10
Hole at one end will sink us all, 383:8
  boring the same h. like a worm,
    200:6
  digged the h. and the whole held
    him, 535:3
  making h. bigger to stay in, 200:6
Holidays, Black only on weekends
    and h., 500:6
Holier, I am h. than thou, 23:7
Holler, makes me wanna h., 396:5
Hollywood, elevated the Negro to H.
    star, 216:3
  is the manipulator, 248:14
  province of H. is illusion, 248:14
  roles for African-Americans, 508:9
Holy, I am whore and h. one, 49:1
  let him be h. still, 45:6
  temple of God is h., 39:5
  the bones of our ancestors, 391:2
  whereon thou standest is h.
    ground, 8:23
Holy Ghost, filled with the H., 37:7
  in name of Father Son and H., 32:4
Home a place riddled with
    questions, 513:6
  allow children to come back h.,
    376:2
  at h. somewhere at h. everywhere,
    203:1
  Bring It on H. to Me, 334:3
  carry me h., 577:1
  change things there, 322:3
  charity begins at h., 47:5
  daylight come me wan' go h., 575:1
  desire of returning h., 72:2
  first show piety at h., 42:7
  for Russia sigh, 85:5
  God tries to steal h., 479:2
  goin' h. like a shootin' star, 84:1
  going back h., 257:4
  going h. to biceps triceps thighs,
    514:11

Home *(continued)*
hauling ass back h., 298:4
hoped for more came h. to less, 390:8
I will bring you h., 517:4
is where the hatred is, 474:3
Jane and Louisa will soon come h., 574:13
lead me h., 200:9
line that takes me halfway h., 378:7
long ways from h., 576:7
mammy went h. with nothing, 78:6
must come h. again, 427:2
my native land my h., 174:7
no house I call my h., 254:3
not able to stay h. brother, 474:1
oldest place in world, 257:4
place where I am most at h., 345:1
poor Nigger hain't got no h., 569:5
returning h. embittered life to us, 75:3
saints of God are gathered h., 128:4
she's only just gone h., 148:5
sit at h. and see it all, 306:1
stay h. mind baby, 575:4
steal away h., 578:6
take h. with me wherever I go, 476:8
tell 'em I'm not at h., 234:6
there's no going h., 545:5
they say we are dogs without any h., 97:6
think of h. think of a place, 442:3
this is our h. our country, 569:11
welcome in palace and humblest h., 126:2
what at h. is the greatest virtue, 207:1
when I think of h., 442:3
where is nigger's h., 324:5
wherever his hat was his h., 436:7
woman not safe in her h., 536:7
woman rules the h., 195:7
you almost h. boy, 484:6
Homecoming, sole witness to my h., 346:1
Homeland, dragged you from h., 205:4
exile who longs for h., 59:4
Homemade education, 296:9
Homes, ruin of nation begins in h. of its people, 565:18

Homesick for Negroes, 182:4
Hometown, brown-skinned h. boy, 257:5
Homey's, South Central h. newly risen, 458:5
Homo sum, 47:*n6*
Homogenized chocolate milk, 358:8
Homosexuality, end silence and stigma around h., 505:4
Homosexuals, accept black h. and love them, 540:2
are not enemies of the people, 425:5
Honest men and pickpockets skilled, 151:8
nation secure only while h., 107:1
whatsoever things are h., 41:13
Honesty in both directions, 132:7
Honey, a land flowing with milk and h., 9:2
Harlem of h. and chocolate, 215:3
land of oil olive and h., 11:15
like h. from the bee, 176:9
locusts and wild h., 26:7
love the way he talks, 315:4
sugar pie h. bunch, 408:10
sweeter than h. and honeycomb, 16:6
Honeycomb, sweeter than honey and h., 16:6
Honeysuckle Rose, you're much sweeter H., 192:7
Honey-talk on streets, 176:2
Honor all men, 43:7
and advantage arise from equity of law, 184:1
before h. is humility, 18:18
does color impair my h., 68:2
ideals by upholding them, 527:4
king delighteth to h., 14:14
prophet not without h., 28:18
strength and h. are her clothing, 19:10
the birth of a son, 487:2
the king, 43:7
thy father and mother, 10:8
to whom h. due, 38:23
why do you curse and h. me, 51:2
Honored, daughters of Ethiopia were h., 59:2
one and scorned one, 49:1
Hoochie Coochie Man, 251:4
low-down h. coocher, 226:5

Hood, what's going on in the 'h., 549:2
Hoo-de hoo de oh, 364:4
Hoof, parteth the h. is cloven-footed, 10:13
Hooked baby nobody else's fault, 521:1
Hooked on Phonics, won't spend $200 on H., 376:7
Hooker, flamboyant h., 385:3
Hooks, spears into pruning h., 22:1
Hoop, to the h. magic Johnson, 398:3
Hope, absence of h., 527:5
always a criminal, 299:1
arose in my heart, 74:4
audacity of h., 522:7
audacity to h., 416:4
audacity to h., 416:5
choosing h. over fear, 523:7
desperate for a reason to h., 505:1
ends despair, 519:3
faintest h. of resurrection, 114:1
finally making a comeback, 538:1
helmet the h. of salvation, 42:1
humans create, 353:5
ideal I h. to live for, 266:5
in his mercy, 64:1
inclined to h. without work, 189:9
is a song in a weary throat, 235:1
keep h. alive, 410:6
kept safe, 369:4
man saved h. maintained, 226:2
new h. in their eyes, 276:2
no h. for the youth, 556:4
now abideth h., 39:17
of all the world, 527:6
of the slave, 307:5
prisoners of h., 24:13
the white h., 159:4
then burn and blaze forever, 81:3
to the end, 43:6
tried to make black h. a joke, 495:7
we wanted to give h., 265:6
where there's life there's h., 48:3
who against h. believed in h., 38:7
wisdom two words wait h., 88:3
without h. can be no future, 495:1
Hoped, faith is substance of things h. for, 42:18
Hopeful for tomorrow, 139:6
Hopeless, made our condition more h., 126:4

Hopes, closer than our closest h., 393:5

Hopeth, charity h. all things, 39:16

Hordes, whip-scarred h., 391:3

Horizon, keep eyes on h., 261:4
- new dawn on African h., 424:3
- no nouns no h., 331:2
- of your face, 225:8
- sail forever on h., 179:9
- shine like Re in the h., 3:1
- skin like dusk on the h., 188:5
- so much more beyond h., 233:6
- way beyond you, 180:6

Horn, able to blow my h., 204:4
- Dinah has blowed de h., 146:3
- it won't come out of your h., 273:5
- outdo white on my h., 300:10
- play my h., 300:9

Horror at the heart, 336:8
- how came this h. be, 302:2
- scene of h. inconceivable, 69:3

Horrors of American Slavery, 98:5
- of police brutality, 317:9

Horse and his rider thrown into sea, 9:17
- behold a pale h., 44:7
- cares more than for a lame h., 79:1
- dollar fer a ole blin' h., 568:7
- keep your h. in hand, 165:4
- mustn't ride you, 390:2
- never heard no h. sing song, 204:5
- saddled the h. for the first time, 82:4

Horsemen, chariot of Israel and h., 14:5

Horses, better care of h. than own health, 121:1
- great gods ride little h., 574:7
- of fire, 14:4

Horus, bright Eye of H. comes, 3:1

Hoses, can't put out with h., 278:3
- clubs h. guns jails, 249:5
- fire h. and nightsticks, 401:1
- water h. couldn't wash it out, 274:4

Hospitality, given to h., 38:18

Hostages, not informed become h. to prejudice, 421:3

Hostility to colored people, 88:6

Hosts, O Lord of h., 17:14
- of prejudice, 104:6

Hot and cold with same breath, 46:12
- Buttered Soul, 419:6

Hot (continued)
- conscience seared with a h. iron, 42:5
- de co'n pone's h., 149:6
- used to be h. becomes cool, 294:6

Hotel, going to dinner table at h., 106:4

Hotels of the cities, 317:9

Hottentot, au naturel end for thuh Miss H., 535:4
- I am called Venus H., 531:3

Hound of deviltry, 161:2

Hounds, moon men and barking h., 188:8

Hour, behold the h. is at hand, 31:10
- don't let minute spoil h., 312:7
- mine h. is not yet come, 35:13
- segregated h. of America, 321:1
- to weep in, 149:2
- wait 'til the midnight h., 411:2
- watch with me one h., 31:9

Hours, how the h. would turn, 165:3
- truth within twenty-four h., 356:2

House, better to save brother's h. on fire, 66:3
- built by black men, 104:6
- built h. upon sand, 27:13
- built with stones I hauled myself, 440:4
- divided against itself, 32:9
- dwell in h. of the Lord, 16:10
- especially from White H., 270:6
- every h. a tower, 104:6
- God in the h., 434:6
- if h. is burning, 327:1
- in Father's h. are many mansions, 36:13
- in south of France, 283:1
- in the h. of generations, 357:4
- inherited great world h., 320:8
- integrated into a burning h., 284:3
- is lonesome, 195:5
- keepers of the h. shall tremble, 20:11
- leave your h. take your guns, 108:7
- Master's Tools Will Never Dismantle the Master's H., 358:2
- mother's h. there is God, 327:4
- my h. shall be called, 29:19
- no h. I call my home, 254:3
- not a h. where there was not one dead, 9:13

House (continued)
- of Hunger, 490:4
- of Israel played before Lord, 13:19
- of mirth, 20:3
- of mourning, 20:3
- of prayer, 29:19
- out of the h. of bondage, 9:14
- peace be to this h., 33:13
- set thine h. in order, 14:9
- shalt not covet neighbor's h., 10:8
- this is the h. of God, 8:10
- to be set in order, 253:1
- to h. take every man, 108:7
- touch this h. at your peril, 388:5
- when ye depart that h., 28:3
- whose h. is this, 340:1
- wounded in h. of my friends, 24:15

Houses, the serpent coiled in their h., 79:5
- they build h. we rent them, 93:5

Housewives, group of ordinary h., 322:4

How a man was made slave, 104:3
- a slave was made man, 104:3
- amiable are thy tabernacles, 17:14
- are the mighty fallen, 13:16, 13:17
- can these things be, 35:17
- choose Africa and English tongue, 330:5
- does one scream in thunder, 360:4
- forcible are right words, 15:7
- I got over Lord, 577:14
- I should make my escape, 61:3
- in the hell could God, 281:3
- keep from going under, 520:6
- long not long, 319:7
- Long the Train's Been Gone, 568:4
- long wilt thou forget me, 16:1
- soon it runs its morning race, 81:4
- Sweet It Is to Be Loved by You, 408:8
- take refuge in h., 336:7
- to survive prison intact, 267:3

Howdy, tell him h., 205:6

Huddled you spoon-fashion, 205:4

Hues, variety of tongues and h., 56:3

Hugs, first game called on account of h., 515:4

Hully Gully, 389:2

Human, at the service of h. needs, 176:7
- being first, 296:11
- being is a researcher, 362:8
- beings are of infinite value, 341:8

Idea *(continued)*
  seemed like a good i. at the time, 376:3
  that really sounds good, 378:4
  this central i. to be African, 198:2
  today the triumph of an i., 342:5
Ideal a disaster to have no i., 187:2
  for which I am prepared to die, 266:5
  of democratic free society, 266:5
Idealist shall move the earth, 323:2
Idealists see things better, 327:5
Ideals, enduring power of our i., 526:3
  honor i. by upholding them, 527:4
  worth living for, 198:2
Ideas, art about i., 309:3
  not fighting for i., 285:8
  scattered i. like seeds, 438:8
Identical, unity does not require we be i., 358:8
Identification, race relevant label of i., 488:3
Identify covers nakedness of self, 285:4
Identifying one's own color, 246:7
Identities I never wanted to claim, 509:6
Identity always being negotiated, 481:4
  authentic i. for the African is the tribe, 562:5
  Black i., 557:1
  measured by struggle, 291:3
  Racial/Cultural I. in Poetry, 484:7
  respectability without losing i., 121:6
  sense of racial i., 239:4
  womanhood as aspect of i., 488:3
Ideological, judges not to have i. views, 468:5
Ideologies of racism and sexism are not genetic, 368:4
Ideology, divesting ourselves of the i., 351:6
  judges not to have i., 468:5
  of Black Panther Party, 420:9
Idiot, proof accessible to the i., 185:1
  think I'm an i. even if I'm great, 457:8
Idle, if we are lazy and i., 74:5
  words seemed i. tales, 35:2

Idols, among i. and graven images, 59:2
  city unsullied by worship of i., 60:3
If a man calls me nigger, 343:11
  alive what ails you, 65:4
  God for us who can be against us, 38:14
  I Did It, 464:3
  my life has any meaning, 287:8
  sky were to fall, 47:10
  That's Your Boy Friend, 548:5
  they do I'm still looking for it, 353:5
  they take you in the morning, 285:1
  this world were mine, 396:4
  we know and do nothing, 285:1
  we must die not like hogs, 175:3
  when they do i. they do, 385:6
  you come softly, 357:5
  you don't know me by now, 429:2
  you love me too, 333:11
  you're not white, 277:5
Igbo, I was I. before the white man came, 562:5
Ignorance allied with power, 285:3
  and prejudice belong to slavery, 75:4
  darkness of injustice and i., 56:6
  knowledge and i., 49:3
  more costly than education, 132:6
  the cost of i., 346:7
  veil of i., 572:2
  where i. prevails, 107:2
Ignorant, confer with the i. man, 1:4
  do not be i. of me, 49:1
  know me i. of me, 49:3
Ignores, roof fights rain sheltered i. it, 566:7
Ill, speak i. of another in absence, 56:10
Illegal business controls America, 541:7
  nothing is i. if businessmen do it, 346:6
Illness, symptoms of the i. in its music, 507:1
  which he'd been smitten, 85:4
Illusion, fear is an i., 534:5
  remain but a fleeting i., 183:6
Ill-will, separateness breeds i., 186:4
Image, conventional exotic i., 311:2
  corrupted by white people, 263:1
  created in i. of God, 341:8

Image *(continued)*
  great in Egypt, 50:3
  in love with own white i., 518:9
  in the i. of God made he man, 7:13
  let us make man in our i., 6:3
  my mirrored i. reflected a future, 346:4
  no i. among barbarians, 50:3
  not make unto thee any graven i., 10:5
  of his own eternity, 25:5
  proclaim her beautiful i., 328:7
Images, among idols and graven i., 59:2
  anti-Negro i. of films, 248:14
  dish water gives back no i., 223:3
  graven i. of gods, 22:6
  negative i. of black people, 508:9
  positive Black i., 265:6
  surrounded by white i., 322:6
Imagination a magic carpet, 250:3
  consequence of idle i., 337:4
  fictions generated by i., 323:5
  is the bridge, 558:6
  just my i., 436:4
  mixing i. with the product, 190:2
  no nation but i., 331:7
  of hearts, 32:21
  set the i. to work, 215:4
  sing thy force, 71:8
Imaginations, african i., 354:6
Imaginings, deceitful fables and i., 59:1
Imani faith, 410:8
Imitate, never failed to i., 283:5
  verses I would become a poet, 82:3
Imitation of the dominant group, 202:3
  of the nature of another, 125:4
Immigrants, first epithets i. learned, 249:2
Immortal, God created man i., 25:5
  happy saint on i. throne, 71:5
Immortality, children are our i., 395:6
  mortal must put on i., 40:7
Immortalize names beyond the grave, 88:7
Immune, attribute i. deficiency to a virus, 424:2
Impact of sexism on social status, 488:3

Impair, does color i. my bravery, 68:2

does color i. my honor, 68:2

Impatient Ancestors, 224:7

idealist move the earth, 323:2

of airs of superiority, 90:3

Impediment, slavery the i., 106:5

Imperfect, we're all i., 305:3

Imperfection, what i. in our minds, 569:9

Imperfections, struggle against i., 305:3

Imperialism, all of Africa against i., 293:5

battle between i. and democratization, 495:5

divided into Haves and Have-Nots, 215:5

is the arsonist, 473:11

racial i., 488:4

real motives i. in Africa, 207:2

whiplash of i., 310:3

Imperialism's, each time i. tentacles cut off, 463:7

Imperialisms, prey of rival i., 181:12

Imperialist, poisoned by i. education, 207:2

strip i. vultures and expose, 197:3

underdevelopment a product of i. exploitation, 427:4

Imperialists, tool of the Cultural I., 452:7

Impervious indestructible, 279:7

Implosion, self-destroying i., 306:3

Importance other than being white, 301:4

Important, enough heartbeats and time do what is i., 457:5

talk is i., 270:6

thing to do in the meantime, 464:9

values most real and i., 189:1

Importunities, weary them with i., 89:2

Impossible, for God nothing shall be i., 32:18

now is not i., 275:1

We Specialize in the Wholly I., 160:4

with faith nothing is i., 153:4

Imposter, Elizabeth is an i., 289:3

Impoverishment, Africa's i., 234:2

Impress, may not i. the neighbors, 181:4

Impressive, love myself looking i., 179:7

Improve, strive to i. spiritually, 349:3

Improvement, thought i. was white, 216:4

Improvident avarice of their purchasers, 69:3

Improvisation heroic endowment, 257:6

Imputation, escape the i. of vanity, 68:7

In other words I am three, 277:8

Inaction, our i. can make inevitable, 156:7

In-between, there's never no i., 559:5

Inborn, hate is not i., 291:1

Incarnation, I am black the i., 290:9

Incentive to effort, 140:6

Inch, one piece one i., 275:8

Inches between pat on back and a kick, 192:1

Incidental or accidental, 261:4

Incidents create revolutions, 232:6

we retain are those of strength, 418:4

Included, finally i. in We the People, 371:1

Includes, that i. me, 530:1

Inclusion is a passion, 384:7

Incomplete, mek yu weep feel i., 489:6

Incomprehensible that government is powerless, 208:8

Inconsistencies, detect no i. in slavery, 104:4

Inconvenient, being a colored man i. in America, 156:4

Incorruption, corruptible must put on i., 40:7

Increaseth, he that i. knowledge i. sorrow, 19:14

Incurable activist, 288:5

Inde irae et lacrimae, 47:n3

Indeed, Lord is risen i., 35:4

Independence, Africa has goal of its own i., 197:6

bled to purchase i., 76:5

have i. or cease to live, 75:5

is we nature, 269:2

nothing short of absolute i., 75:5

possess spirit of i., 89:2

right of countries to i., 473:9

Independence *(continued)*

Self-reliance Is the Fine Road to I., 111:8

was at the door, 364:3

Independent, not an i. mortal on earth, 66:4

Indian, grandfather not an I. chief, 178:7

high chiefs frolicking, 301:7

Indians are Red Americans, 79:4

did in ambush lay, 65:9

root for I. against the cavalry, 343:8

Indifference, justice sleeps by our silence and i., 127:5

notes with i. good and evil, 86:1

spirit of i., 127:4

through i. perpetuate it, 493:8

Indignation, until the i. be overpast, 22:12

Indignity, drama of i., 208:7

of being the skunk, 267:1

Indispensable duty to do so, 67:2

Individual, beyond i. an answer given, 202:5

ceased to exist as an i., 373:4

equally enjoy the blessings, 66:1

in disadvantaged group, 330:3

is a minority, 248:9

pernicious dismissal of i. will, 498:2

worth is valued, 384:7

worth of an i., 276:1

Individualism as philosophic value, 330:3

Indivisible, I am i., 359:1

justice i., 320:9

Industrial, emancipated from i. bondage, 171:4

Industry, progress through education and i., 572:2

Infamous, I am i., 124:1

Infancy, back to the days of i., 87:3

Inferior because not white, 509:5

make a man feel i., 154:6

one race superior another i., 183:6

races are all fictions, 323:5

Inferiority, black bourgeoisie has i. complex, 185:7

in segregated a feeling of i., 186:4

mark of racial i., 185:8

Infinite, human beings of i. value, 341:8

I am one with the i., 181:7

Jamaica, deal with honorable J., 287:9
  dragged to J. in chains, 380:3
James Brown, Bach and J., 476:4
  music of J. without lyrics, 389:2
Jane and Louisa will soon come home, 574:13
Janie looked down on him, 180:7
Japheth, God shall enlarge J., 7:17
Jaw, black enduring j., 325:4
Jaybird don't rob his own nes', 570:18
Jazz a swinging dialogue, 521:3
  American musical art form, 269:4
  as roots of today's rap, 453:2
  basic thing about j., 261:6
  beat from Sanctified Church, 236:4
  clubs houses of worship, 312:4
  cradled by drugs by j., 243:6
  Genius + Soul = J., 326:7
  giving birth is like j., 531:6
  is a musical gumbo, 178:3
  is my adventure, 264:1
  is my religion, 312:4
  is the nobility of race, 521:2
  it's always j., 227:6
  known over the world, 269:4
  music our black anthem, 312:6
  musicians symbolize freedom, 446:4
  no America no j., 269:4
  radio on midnight kick, 293:1
  the cradle of j., 178:2
  unfree created freest forms blues and j., 495:6
  was like the trunk of a tree, 219:2
  we j. June, 259:8
Jazzers, six long-headed j. play, 210:7
Jealous, am a j. God, 10:6
  of good not accomplished themselves, 68:6
Jealousies, same j. as love, 375:6
Jealousy, ear of j. heareth all things, 25:3
  is cruel as the grave, 21:14
Jean and Dinah Rosita Clementina, 364:2
Jellyroll, Ain't Gonna Give Nobody None o' This J., 185:6
Jeopardized, own freedom being j., 296:1
Jericho, Joshua fit the battle of J., 576:6

Jerusalem as bride adorned, 45:3
  came wise men to J., 25:18
  certain man from J., 34:1
  daughters of J., 21:3
  new J., 45:3
  O daughters of J., 21:10
  temple of J., 54:10
Jesus, Blessed J. Heavenly Dove, 63:2
  call my J. up, 333:8
  came to J. and kissed him, 31:11
  gave bread to the disciples, 31:6
  given to Moses and J., 53:9
  if J. came this morning we failed, 469:5
  increased in wisdom and stature, 33:7
  nobody knows but J., 576:5
  none but J. heard, 82:6
  said this is my body, 31:6
  said Woman thou art loosed, 508:1
  stained-glass windows of J., 256:3
  steal away to J., 578:6
  stink of our own breathing J., 368:1
  the King of the Jews, 31:18
  they would beat J. if he was black, 204:4
  took bread and blessed it, 31:6
  typical life of J., 299:4
  walking on the sea, 28:22
  was born in Bethlehem, 25:18
  wept, 36:11
  worshipping a white J., 281:3
Jesus Christ is born, 576:8
  testimony of J., 43:16
  the same for ever, 42:20
Jew, when Negro hates the J., 282:2
Jewel, Liberty is a J., 70:4
  of the Antilles, 291:4
Jewels of elegant pain, 280:4
  scramble vowels j., 326:1
Jewish daughter married a black man, 509:2
  demanding from J. synagogues, 310:1
I'm Puerto Rican J. colored, 290:1
  intellectuals a social force, 255:8
  people of J. ancestry run entertainment industry, 509:1
Jews, from the J. to the English nation, 72:5
Jesus the King of the J., 31:18
King of the J., 25:18

Jezebel heard of it, 14:8
Jiggy, Getting' J. wit It, 549:4
  stay real j., 550:6
Jim crowing us impartially, 166:4
Jim Crowed me during the war, 215:1
Job, all I want is a j., 238:1
  get a j. doin' nothin', 216:2
  like a j. I report to every day, 272:4
  the patience of J., 43:5
  to sit by the door, 327:3
Jobs, advance guard for j., 176:6
Jockey, to be great j. have stopwatch in head, 165:4
Joe Turner's come and gone, 568:5
  where you going with gun, 420:1
John, man sent from God was J., 35:6
  saw new Jerusalem, 45:3
John Baptist's, give me J. head, 28:19
John Henry hain't ever comin' back, 568:1
  what we need now J., 205:7
John Laws, anything to do with J., 298:4
Johncrow, out of j. sky, 325:5
Johnnie thereafter forever, 461:2
Join nothing but hands legs or other same, 292:4
Joined, God hath j. together, 29:13
  with future generations, 190:1
Joining in this shit, 298:3
Joint is jumpin', 192:9
Joint-heirs with Christ, 38:13
Joke to be laughed at, 280:3
  tried to make black hope a j., 495:7
Joker, some j. got lucky, 236:5
Jonah was in the belly of the fish, 24:10
Jonathan loved him, 13:12
Jordan, hold me like a River J., 512:6
  in the midst of J., 12:7
  looked over J., 577:1
Joseph, stripped J. of his coat of many colors, 8:14
Joshua fit the battle of Jericho, 576:6
Journal, in this journey you're the j., 540:6
Journalist, you're the journal I'm the j., 540:6
Journey, Amistad was an American j., 505:1
  in this j. you're the journal, 540:6

Journey *(continued)*
long j. to this moment, 305:2
never tires of j., 335:7
our j. is not complete, 529:2
tell the glories of our j., 253:4
towards a preordained time, 56:7
Journeyman, the soul's a j., 545:3
Joy and pain sunshine and rain, 454:1
cometh in the morning, 16:13
crumb falls from tables of j., 213:4
enter into j. of thy lord, 30:8
food affirms j. of being alive, 553:9
for the heart, 58:3
heart can give j., 478:4
is finding a pregnant roach, 431:1
of a new beginning, 274:5
of being a mother, 438:3
of being loved tenderly, 67:4
of colts, 276:2
pint of j. to peck of trouble, 149:2
roll it let 'em jump for j., 221:5
share our j. in the satisfying, 358:1
simple j. could shake you, 338:5
sorrow treads on nation's j., 114:1
source of j. for the heart, 58:3
take your sorrows give you j., 163:3
that your j. may be full, 36:20
you're my j. and pain, 253:8
Joyful, make a j. noise unto God, 17:7
Joys, count our j. not by what we have, 151:1
my childish j. are past, 110:1
Juba skin dat Yaller Cat, 568:8
Jubilee, year of J., 577:4
jubilees, singing blues and j., 255:1
Judge, here come the j., 221:6
listening like a j. supreme, 85:1
my soul eagle nor mole, 199:3
no one will j. me, 51:6
not according to appearance, 36:1
not that ye be not judged, 27:5
the fatherless, 21:17
the hitter can never be the j., 477:7
Judged by content of character, 318:2
every race nation should be j., 147:5
judge not be not j., 27:5
Judges not to have agendas, 468:5
Judgest, thou j. another, 38:4

Judging people on content of character, 530:2
Judgment and all exactitude, 1:3
bring every work into j., 21:1
Bring J. Day, 174:n2
God will remember your j., 183:4
he sits in silence to pass j., 566:8
his ways are j., 12:4
knowledge without j., 64:5
of Greeks and barbarians, 50:3
possession over j. day, 236:7
seek j., 21:17
sworn it was j. day, 513:8
upon what God has seen fit to do, 121:5
Judgments of the Lord are true, 16:6
Judicial tyranny, 419:4
Jug, got the world in a j., 191:6
Jugular, nearer than his j. vein, 56:12
Juices, keep j. flowing, 224:2
Jukebox, poet is not a j., 250:2
Jump, allowed to j. into liberty, 97:4
at de sun, 180:15
down turn around pick a bale a day, 569:6
made a parachute j., 181:5
notion to j. into ocean, 204:2
off that bandwagon, 438:6
over ocean in smooth j., 315:3
June, we jazz J., 259:8
Juneteenth Negro telegraph reached last slave, 456:3
Jungle, it's like a j. sometimes, 520:6
through j. to find me, 335:7
Junk, smack j. snow poison, 370:2
Junkie walking through twilight, 474:3
Jury, showed up for j. duty, 554:4
Just a Closer Walk with Thee, 579:9
compensation, 412:6
contemplates alike j. and unjust, 86:1
enough for the city, 481:11
give me my equality, 352:5
he was a good man and j., 34:27
man more j. than God, 15:5
not a j. man that sinneth not, 20:5
nothing to do with that j. man, 31:14
whatsoever things are j., 41:13
Justice and law are distant cousins, 513:1
appearance of j., 375:4
arc may bend toward j. but not on its own, 531:1

Justice *(continued)*
arouse j. from its slumbers, 127:5
bends toward j., 319:7, 319:n1
blood cry for j., 299:4
complete j., 296:4
conception of j., 485:2
criminal j. system is not colorblind, 523:4
democracy's life insurance, 160:6
do j., 2:4
every man's birthright, 103:5
everybody wants j., 252:5
extreme law is extreme j., 48:1
for all, 267:1
for all overthrows injustice, 519:3
for the Negro, 103:5
for us is to be set apart, 196:2
in the courts, 298:5
in the eye of beholder, 181:9
indivisible, 320:9
injustice is threat to j., 316:6
knock at the bar of j., 140:5
live by j. code, 300:2
Mais l'extrême j. est une extrême injure, 48:n1
makes change inevitable, 419:2
never given it is exacted, 176:4
no j. no peace, 366:8, 573:12
no special favors but plead for j., 101:6
nobody can give you j., 296:3
peace means j., 499:3
rolls down like waters, 317:9
social peace through social j., 535:1
superhighway of j., 319:3
tomorrow's j., 320:5
transform power into j., 522:3
watching j. die, 312:2
we ask, 127:1
what j. to take this life, 350:7
where j. is denied, 107:2
without a fight, 437:1
won't get quiet until we get j., 499:3
Justifiable, protect one's rights j., 272:5
Justified, nation will never stand j., 222:4
wisdom j. of children, 28:7
Justifies, no reason or cause j. war, 183:5
Justify black demands, 277:7
extermination of men, 290:8
he will not j. you without you, 53:4
Justly, do j., 24:11

K

Kaffir, called me K. boy, 518:10
Kedar, comely as tents of K., 21:3
Keep a knockin', 344:2
  all who k. silent, 361:5
  America free and make it freer, 208:4
  cotton will k. them here, 206:2
  fear God and k. commandments, 21:1
  from going under, 520:6
  going, 111:5
  got to k. movin', 237:2
  hands on the plow, 261:4
  hope alive, 410:6
  juices flowing, 224:2
  Lord bless thee and k. thee, 11:5
  me from winning, 275:4
  my commandments, 10:6
  not what I meant to k., 281:1
  on a-walkin', 579:2
  on calling, 234:6
  on living, 163:7
  on pushin', 422:5
  on truckin', 226:7
  pushin', 422:7
  swinging at them, 353:4
  the faith baby, 230:3
  the way of the tree of life, 7:2
  time to k., 19:17
  time to k. silence, 19:17
  what you can hold, 176:8
  your eyes on the prize, 572:11
  your head up, 556:3
Keeper, Abel was a k. of sheep, 7:3
  am I my brother's k., 7:4
Keepers of the house shall tremble, 20:11
Keepin' still and mindin' things, 67:6
Keeping, game of k. what one has, 179:2
Kerchiefs, tomato-red k., 506:6
Kettle, pot calling the k. black, 238:8, 570:10
Kettles, beneath iron pots and k., 89:1
Key is to reign over yourself, 553:8
  no purer k. than Liberty, 117:5
  secrets we preserve provide a k., 447:7
  to heaven is language, 497:3
  to the highway, 184:4
  who was a k., 260:2

Key *(continued)*
  why does lock fit my k., 340:1
  with lover's k. trust is a temptation, 460:2
Keys, black k. as beautiful as white k., 320:7
  gri-gri k. of birmingham, 398:2
  of the kingdom of heaven, 29:8
  permits another the k. to his destiny, 202:4
Kick, don't care where they k., 514:7
  eighteen inches between a pat and a k., 192:1
Kid remember to be adult, 314:6
Kidnapped by some of my own complexion, 73:2
Kidnappers ensnarers and slave holders, 72:6
Kids, clean dirty-faced k., 314:5
  dirty laughing k., 276:2
  vagabond k. run like colts, 276:2
  we raise our k. to do the same, 529:5
Kill, cut eye don't k., 575:12
  do not k., 2:4
  evil societies k. consciences, 273:2
  him eat him to survive, 289:6
  if they k. us we shall die, 89:4
  if you will not k. me I will live with you, 84:5
  in broad daylight, 298:3
  mothafucking easy to k., 298:3
  our prophets, 450:2
  slower ways to k. ourselves, 559:8
  some people she'd like to k., 552:5
  terrible thing to k. a man, 130:4
  the fatted calf, 34:10
  thou shalt not k., 10:8
  time to k., 19:17
  truth be told though it k., 131:3
  well k. us, 387:*n*2
  why not k. a white person, 539:6
  without fear punishment, 298:3
Killed for a single beautiful word, 487:2
  ma pa but will vote for him, 468:1
  never closes till somebody k., 151:8
  no difference between killer and k., 185:2
  or captured and taken to South, 99:1
  the goose to find nothing, 46:13

Killer, no difference between k. and killed, 185:2
  world's biggest k. is extreme poverty, 424:*n*2
Killeth, letter k. life, 40:9
Killing destroying everything, 277:8
  one man for who he is, 383:3
  people to save to free them, 243:7
  they're k. us faster now, 415:2
  until the k. of black men as important, 217:4
Kills, Africa k. her sons, 413:5
  healthy boy ain't wrong when he k., 490:8
  owner of slave and slave runs away, 567:1
  thief and owner of stolen goods, 567:1
Kin, human touch makes whole world k., 137:1
  web of k., 480:6
Kind, fate is being k. to me, 201:7
  hearted woman, 236:8
  of fire we have, 278:3
Kindheartedness, the moment k. walks in, 463:1
Kindness, exercise k. and love, 58:5
  gains by k. and attachment, 95:4
  God of great k., 14:13
  no k. ever wasted, 45:12
  show k. to parents, 54:11
Kindreds, all nations and k., 44:10
King delighteth to honor, 14:14
  dependent from k. to the beggar, 66:4
  God save the k., 13:4
  honor the k., 43:7
  Jesus the K. of the Jews, 31:18
  no k. in Israel, 12:19
  of Ethiopia is exalted, 59:3
  of kings, 45:1
  of the Jews, 25:18
  stood at parting of the way, 23:18
  there arose a new k. over Egypt, 8:20
  yesterday I was k., 403:1
  your love is k., 516:5
Kingdom and the power and glory, 27:2
  bring k. to ruin, 276:3
  cannot see the k. of God, 35:15
  enter k. of God, 29:14
  keys of the k. of heaven, 29:8

Kingdom *(continued)*
    of God appeared, 304:4
    of God within you, 34:15
    of heaven is at hand, 26:5
    of heaven like a net, 28:16
    of heaven like to mustard seed,
        28:15
    of such is k. of God, 32:14
    outside k. of the Lord, 183:4
    rich man to enter k., 29:14
    right at our feet, 160:7
    theirs is the k. of heaven, 26:12
    thy k. come, 27:2
Kingdoms, devil showed him k., 33:8
    of world are k. of Lord, 44:13
Kingly, falcon rises above k. banners,
    4:2
Kings and heroes die and vanish,
    61:1
    King of k., 45:1
    prophets and k., 33:15
    under Emperors K. and Princes,
        72:5
    want in Africa to live like K., 59:6
    we either niggas or k., 559:5
Kinsmen, my brethren my k., 72:3
Kiss, 'scuse me while I k. the sky,
    420:3
    I kissed a k. in youth, 158:3
    want extra time and your k.,
        514:5
Kissed, angel k. the sleeping Night,
    150:1
    came to Jesus and k. him, 31:11
    sun k. me, 502:2
Kisses, love k. were the best kind,
    467:5
Kissing, brown lips sweet k., 176:1
Kitch come to bed, 277:4
Kitchen, come on in my k., 236:5
    eat in k. when company comes,
        211:2
    fight to get in the k., 554:1
    in Sorrow's k., 181:8
Kleptomaniac workin hard, 466:7
Kneel-in, we will k., 245:6
Knees, return to our k., 287:9
Knew, each k. all the other said,
    164:7
    taught Man that he k. not, 57:6
Knife on things held together,
    323:1
    sharpening oyster k., 179:1
    some paper and a pen k., 552:5

Knife *(continued)*
    violent act from fist stick k. to gun,
        485:4
Knight in shining armor, 473:4
Knives, live among k. and forks,
    478:7
Knob, left holding the k., 309:5
Knock 'em out I pick the round,
    417:5
    and it shall be opened, 27:7
    go up there and k. on that, 452:1
    I stand at the door and k., 44:2
    the table of privilege over, 492:4
Knocking, keep a k., 344:2
Knocks, school of the hard k., 550:6
Know, 'nother for what I k. is me,
    570:3
    about the events of September 11,
        503:2
    as I am known, 39:17
    be still and k. that I am God, 17:2
    change gonna come, 334:2
    did you k. I was waiting, 312:8
    didn't read books so didn't k.,
        180:5
    disposition of women, 48:10
    don't k. what to do about it, 252:3
    don't k. which way I'm travelin',
        205:1
    don't you k. that yet, 250:8
    get to k. you this Christmas, 448:6
    gotta go for what you k., 518:4
    how in darkness did you k., 147:8
    how much to k., 227:4
    I do k. that I love you, 333:11
    if we k. and do nothing, 285:1
    if you gotta ask you'll never k.,
        204:8
    if you had known what I k., 213:3
    mad but never let them k. it, 270:1
    me ignorant of me, 49:3
    men k. so little of men, 144:2
    not known me k. me, 49:3
    not who may grasp throat, 93:7
    one thing I k., 36:6
    people I did not k. died, 471:5
    pretend-to-be-cats don't k., 555:3
    sinner or no I k. not, 36:6
    skin skin ya na k. me, 574:11
    terrible thing to k., 321:8
    that I bend, 480:5
    that I smile, 480:5
    the color of the sky, 386:2
    their native culture, 248:10

Know *(continued)*
    they can never k. you, 304:7
    they did not k. how to die, 163:7
    they k. not what they do, 34:22
    those being burned k. fire, 194:5
    we k. as part as crowd, 310:4
    we k. less about Africa, 155:6
    we k. not how soon, 63:5
    we k. who holds the future,
        573:10
    we no k. ourselves, 386:4
    what did I k. what did I k., 243:4
    what is right for me, 453:1
    what to k. to stay alive, 337:6
    won't k. you ever had coffee,
        294:6
    world thinks we k. nothing, 89:1
    you don't k. me, 545:6
    you they will kill you, 304:7
    you will never k. me, 429:2
Knowest, thou k. not what a day may
    bring, 19:5
Knoweth, He k. all things, 57:2
    he that loveth not k. not God,
        43:14
    man k. not his time, 20:9
Knowledge, access to k. superb,
    338:1
    and ignorance, 49:3
    aware of his k., 2:3
    concealed attempt to destroy, 304:7
    desired k. of God, 24:5
    given of k. but little, 54:13
    he that increaseth k. increaseth
        sorrow, 19:14
    I am the k., 51:4
    is better than riches, 565:23
    is the prime need, 153:2
    key of k., 113:6
    little progress in k., 75:4
    of barbarians, 50:3
    oppressive language limits k.,
        339:8
    profess not k. thou hast not, 25:7
    puffeth up, 39:10
    slaveholder to keep k. to himself,
        120:4
    to young man k. and discretion,
        18:11
    traveled the wombs with the k.,
        478:3
    tree of k. of good and evil, 6:9
    wealth well earned, 554:6
    without judgment, 64:5

Known by colour under British flag, 569:12
  by the way you parked car sideways, 513:7
  hinders relations with countries k., 58:2
  I'd live this long I'd taken better care, 165:5
  if you had k. what I know, 213:3
  know as I am k., 39:17
  not k. me know me, 49:3
  once k. myself to be, 471:4
  rivers ancient as the world, 211:7
  terrified of being k., 304:7
  throughout villages beyond, 322:7
  tree k. by his fruit, 28:10
  why fight what's k., 85:3
Knows, everybody k. about Mississippi, 352:4
  God k. what you'll go through, 520:7
  who holds the heel, 93:7
  you when you're down and out, 163:1
Knuckles, my dark daddy's k., 516:1
Komitas, art leaves her lover as a K., 199:4
Kow-tow to an old order, 468:4
Ku Klux Klan, terror called the K., 470:2
Kujichagulia self-determination, 410:8
Kumbaya, 579:n1
Kung fu is kill the opponent, 557:4
Kunta, carrying K. in his arms, 274:3
Kuumba creativity, 410:8

L

Label, race relevant l. of identification, 488:3
Labor, all ye that l., 28:8
  man must be free of l., 257:8
  Negro l. inseparable from white l., 239:5
  of love, 41:19
  proud of l. in building America, 201:5
  six days shalt thou l., 10:7
  solace of my l. pains, 49:1
  stolen l. of our forebears, 412:6
  take nothing of his l., 20:1
  unpaid l. a stepping-stone, 83:7
  we ask to enjoy the fruits of our l., 76:5
  with all our might, 87:2

Labors, affluence from our l., 65:1
  in vain, 230:6
Labours, may dead rest from their l., 44:19
Labs, black l. of the heart, 354:4
Lace, he spoke to the l. in her, 508:1
Lack, shalt not l. any thing, 11:15
Ladder, he dreamed a l. set up on earth, 8:8
  highest rung of human l., 172:1
  lower rungs of economic l., 239:6
  of our vices, 52:13
  rise to top of the l., 136:3
Ladder's 'bout to fall, 481:8
Laden, all ye that are heavy l., 28:8
Ladies, hate the l. that make the babies, 556:3
  twenty thousand different l., 367:2
Ladies', kindling smiles in l. eyes, 85:1
Lady, Act Like a L. Think Like a Man, 504:2
  Black L. in Mourning, 291:3
  hurry to see your l., 3:2
  I saw your hands, 165:1
  I'm your knight in shining armor, 473:4
  if you got to ask, 221:7
  once twice three times a l., 473:2
  two l. birds, 292:7
  was not alone, 301:6
Laid him in a manger, 33:3
  out in my green velour, 379:5
Lake lay down for you, 334:4
Lakes crossed in painted boats, 340:1
  rivers of tears l. of blood, 118:4
Lamb, a l. for a burnt offering, 8:7
  began to follow the wolf, 45:8
  behold the L. of God, 35:10
  blood of the l., 44:11
  Mary had little l. a fib, 547:3
  same as a butcher would a calf a l., 78:6
  to the slaughter, 23:2
Lambs, gather the l. with his arm, 22:15
Lame, cares more than for a l. horse, 79:1
  feet to the l., 15:19
Lamenting songs and dirges, 85:5
Lamp, God's light like a l., 55:7
  light the clear-oil l., 224:8

Land, a l. flowing with milk and honey, 9:2
  a stranger in a strange l., 8:21
  adjudged the leastwise of the l., 259:3
  already in the promised l., 375:2
  back to this l. of mine, 241:2
  black of that black l., 175:2
  damning my native l., 231:5
  days may be long upon the l., 10:8
  denied by the Laws of the L., 64:3
  entire l. sets out to work, 5:2
  Exodus from l. of bondage, 100:4
  first sight of Free L., 113:1
  I am the l., 479:1
  I want l. I out to get, 314:2
  I will pass through the l. of Egypt, 9:10
  I've seen the promised l., 321:4
  in search of a promised l., 495:2
  in the l. of Canaan, 8:2
  love the l. that gave me birth, 126:1
  marchin' up to freedom l., 579:2
  my native l. my home, 174:7
  of Dreams, 177:2
  of my mothers, 312:5
  of the living, 15:17
  poor shall never cease out of l., 12:2
  revolution always based on l., 295:6
  that knew my love my pain, 85:5
  that never gave a damn, 517:8
  this is the l. where I suffered, 440:4
  where every man is free, 212:5
  whose stones are iron, 11:15
  ye shall eat the fat of the l., 8:17
Landless people dependent on landed people, 114:7
Landmarks and place names, 257:4
  are not exactly what they were, 532:5
Language alone protects us, 339:10
  artists express universal l., 335:2
  compare your l. with your cruelties, 78:5
  key to heaven is l., 497:3
  lead into equality of power, 372:6
  make our l. conform to truth, 372:6
  Merica people no talk Mendi l., 118:2
  no l. is neutral, 332:3
  not based on l. of body, 375:6

Life (continued)

believe not what l. told you to, 442:1

best things in l. are free, 315:2

better for people living in the dark, 406:9

black l. treated with short worth, 559:5

bloom of l., 256:3

book of l., 44:1, 45:2

but one great school, 109:6

can't spend your l. talking like a victim, 448:2

conceive l. being different, 299:3

contented with l. dinner and wife, 85:2

courage to face L., 334:6

crown of l., 43:21

cut the thread of l., 63:5

doesn't frighten me, 307:1

dying into that new l., 291:3

easy l. of TV and gasoline, 491:3

equal chance in battle of l., 124:5

everlasting l., 35:18

fight for your l., 285:1

fire of l. and youth in his veins, 130:3

float through l., 261:4

food is l., 384:1

for African not l., 264:6

framed by his absence, 475:2

gift of God is eternal l., 38:10

give love live l., 329:1

giveth to all l. and breath, 37:13

glory l. and bliss unknown, 71:5

God breathed the breath of l., 6:7

goes in a circle, 238:7

gray cloth brings dark wood to l., 487:4

growing is relentless as l., 189:7

hanging by thread of l., 63:5

he that loveth her loveth l., 25:8

I am the bread of l., 35:23

I am the resurrection the l., 36:10

I am the way the truth the l., 36:15

if ever I touched a l., 431:7

in it l. resides and manifests itself, 167:2

in l. expect trouble, 478:5

in midst of l. problems, 252:6

in the great race of l., 186:5

insist upon your l., 329:4

is a broken-winged bird, 210:6

Life (continued)

is a lie, 428:5

is complicated, 485:2

is just a short walk, 272:3

is like boxing, 470:3

is short make it sweet, 173:9

is tension, 370:1

is the miracle, 457:6

is the real Olympics, 244:5

keep the way of the tree of l., 7:2

Last Abode is L., 56:2

lay down his l. for friends, 36:18

lay hold on eternal l., 42:10

left a l. never found, 330:7

letter killeth l., 40:9

lives grown out of his l., 243:1

Lord is the strength of my l., 16:11

make l. adventurous dream, 254:7

miniature replica of l., 167:4

more like rain, 334:4

more than he slew in his l., 12:17

my l. in danger, 282:9

my l. is my music, 204:4

my l. is painting, 221:1

narrow meaning to l., 363:7

neatly fitted into pegs, 282:8

no one defines your l. only you, 500:1

not without laughter, 212:1

of the bayou, 153:9

of the moment, 311:4

painting is kind of talking about l., 235:3

participate fully in American l., 208:3

piece of l. for herself, 238:4

place in your own special l., 452:4

plant a new l., 227:1

proper mask to wear in l., 394:2

quality of l. and future generations, 401:5

requires preparation, 141:8

responsibility l. imposes, 349:1

returning home embittered l. to us, 75:3

righteous man regardeth l. of beast, 18:16

sacrificed for something, 275:6

scraped l. with fine-toothed comb, 258:9

seems full of clouds and rain, 156:2

shall receive crown of l., 43:1

shepherd giveth his l., 36:8

Life (continued)

spirit giveth l., 40:9

struggle against imperfections, 305:3

struggle is my l., 266:2

succeed in the race of l., 106:7

suckle l. not bombs and rhetoric, 360:3

Sunshine of My L., 481:7

that does not contribute, 227:2

that gnaws in us all, 231:6

that is the l. of men, 179:9

the soft and hard parts of l., 521:5

the trick in l., 475:4

the way l. used to be, 409:7

the way which leadeth unto l., 27:10

they call L. you called Death, 50:3

this is L., 162:1

too short to hold bitterness, 160:2

tree of l., 43:20

true riches of l., 268:3

typical l. of Jesus, 299:4

uncertainty of l., 63:5

We give l. to everything, 55:4

what justice to take this l., 350:7

what we play is l., 204:6

where there's l. there's hope, 48:3

whole l. of man, 259:5

whosoever lose l. shall find it, 29:10

whosoever save l. shall lose it, 29:10

will flow into not by you, 200:4

woman herself not the tree of l., 445:2

you had before buried, 353:4

your l. belongs to you, 562:8

Life's, meet l. terms, 189:8

piano melodies brotherhood, 320:7

time to accomplish l. work, 297:1

walking down l. road, 329:4

Lifelong sadness, 561:9

Lifetime wife and mother, 484:2

Lift ev'ry voice and sing, 147:2

Lifted the veil of ignorance, 572:2

Lifting as we climb onward upward, 140:5

As We Climb, 571:10

Light, arise shine for thy l. is come, 23:5

be not darkened, 20:11

Lips, a boy's l. are soft as baby's skin, 486:6
  brown l. sweet kissing, 176:1
  father's l. closed in silence and grief, 65:8
  slack anciently everted l., 325:4
  to touch the sacred fire, 147:8
  we can't kiss, 324:4
Liquor stores and weed, 558:2
Listen in Berlin either, 298:4
  one who cries out and I l., 51:4
  really l. this time, 480:3
  to the folk, 362:7
  to the people talking, 567:6
  wearily I sit and l., 149:5
  you a wonder, 367:4
Listened to groans chains prayers, 127:2
Listener, patient l. lives in larger world, 521:5
Listeners always have more friends, 521:5
Listening forces you to recognize others, 521:5
  if someone is l., 416:2
  like a judge supreme, 85:1
  somewhere l. for my name, 475:7
  to elders, 283:5
Literacy, economic access depends on l., 365:2
Literature is a big sea full of fish, 212:7
  is an old couch, 332:2
  measure of greatness is l., 147:9
  outstrips earthly limitations, 138:3
  Race L. not by race or creed, 138:3
  rises out of the Common People, 166:3
  speaking teaches natural l., 481:3
  the Negro in American l., 206:1
Little bird must you scold me, 3:5
  boy in you, 274:1
  did so much when we had so l., 363:6
  foxes that spoil the vines, 21:7
  given of knowledge but l., 54:13
  light of mine, 578:16
  O thou of l. faith, 29:1
  O ye of l. faith, 27:15
  one shall become a thousand, 23:6
  person to stir up great events, 472:6
  suffer the l. children, 32:14
  world a world within himself, 72:4

Live and die and do your work, 104:7
  as long as you l., 1:6
  beginning of learning to l., 227:4
  better and in peace, 285:8
  born l. and die free and French, 67:8
  born Queen must l. like Queen, 59:6
  can these bones l., 23:20
  Can't L. Without My Radio, 548:3
  couldn't l. where I wanted, 244:6
  die before you can l., 278:2
  die freemen than l. to be slaves, 100:5
  don't have to l. next to me, 352:5
  fast die young, 233:3
  for one another, 370:4
  have independence or cease to l., 75:5
  he that believeth in me shall l., 36:10
  if I'd known I'd l. this long, 165:5
  if man die shall he l. again, 15:10
  if they save us we shall l., 89:4
  if you will not kill me I will l. with you, 84:5
  in a state of war, 70:1
  in bondage forever, 264:5
  in peace with the other, 272:5
  let us l. happily, 567:8
  lives without living in the wounds, 486:4
  long l. Czar Dimitri Ivanovich, 86:2
  long upon earth, 2:4
  make my dream-children l., 190:4
  man never learned to l. with himself, 220:4
  never again l. apart l. in peace, 320:8
  none like us may l. again until time no more, 77:4
  older you get more l. in the past, 491:5
  peaceably with men, 38:20
  resolved to fight and l. or die, 162:8
  right attain the highest standards, 159:5
  see me one thing l. with me another, 576:2
  someone died continuing to l., 550:5
  something to l. for, 254:7

Live (continued)
  sure did l. in this world, 337:5
  they will l. and not die again, 52:1
  this is the urgency l., 260:3
  to do in the meantime is l., 464:9
  to l. is Christ, 41:12
  trying to l. without friends, 181:3
  want in Africa to l. like Kings, 59:6
  we l. here they l. there, 230:9
  we shall l. in his sight, 24:3
  with head in lion's mouth, 248:6
  with one's own pain, 284:9
  without fear, 198:8
Lived, linked with all who ever l., 190:1
  never l. among your own, 200:2
  shadow of her death, 321:9
Lives, Bird L., 312:3
  by the l. they lead, 285:2
  fleshing his dream, 243:1
  how long one l. but how well, 186:7
  look into l. as into mirror, 48:14
  miracle our l. be saved, 130:5
  our l. so diversified, 181:2
  swinging their l. as bats, 398:6
  without living in the wounds, 486:4
Living and dying for freedom, 428:7
  crisis of l., 377:2
  dying deciding, 557:7
  God of the l., 34:18
  just enough for the city, 481:11
  just like l. in jail, 230:9
  keep on l., 163:7
  land of the l., 15:17
  make life better for people l. in the dark, 406:9
  neither the l. nor the dead, 349:5
  no interest in l., 133:6
  on the creative edge, 455:2
  satisfiest desire of every l. thing, 18:8
  seek the l. among the dead, 35:1
  seen through a veil, 180:14
  service is the rent we pay for l., 395:3
  signs for all l. beings, 56:3
  slaves to the cost of l., 242:5
  sons of the l. God, 24:1
  tell-tale sign of l., 467:2
  their l. was not in vain, 348:3
  virtues of right l., 163:5
  we who are the l., 273:2

Living (continued)
what's necessary to keep on l., 475:4
Lizard cannot pretend to be a boa, 567:3
Load, sags like a heavy l., 213:6
Loaded spoons into belly of Jesus, 368:1
Loan, poor was the l. at best, 150:7
Loathsome smells, 69:3
Loaves, five l. two fishes, 28:20
Lock, jails couldn't l. it out, 274:4
up our minds, 281:8
up something invisible, 281:8
why does l. fit my key, 340:1
Locked, who l. you up, 355:4
Locked-down, hearts survive a l. life, 340:5
Locks, hearing l. click on the doors of cars, 530:1
Locusts and wild honey, 26:7
Lodge, thou lodgest I will l., 12:20
Lodgest, thou l. I will lodge, 12:20
Log will never be a crocodile, 564:16
Logy, makes you l., 277:2
Loins, let your l. be girded, 34:6
who had come from her l., 255:3
with your l. girded, 9:10
Loneliness as a weaver of want, 381:3
did marriage end l., 180:4
that can be rocked, 339:3
that roams, 339:3
were a grape, 431:9
Lonely, God said I'm l., 148:1
lusty because it is l., 231:5
Mag Smith, 116:1
makes exceptional also make l., 328:1
these arms of mine are l., 411:6
Lonesome, house is l., 195:5
so regular, 272:4
Long, ain't no rush l. ways to go, 205:3
days may be l. upon the land, 10:8
how l. but how well, 186:7
how l. not l., 319:7
How L. the Train's Been Gone, 568:4
how l. wilt thou forget me, 16:1
it's been a l. time coming, 526:1
live Czar Dimitri Ivanovich, 86:2
Lord how l., 22:2
Oh Lord how l. how l., 118:4
old road, 188:3

Long (continued)
road to freedom, 267:5
tall Sally, 344:6
time gal me never see yuh, 575:5
too l. have others spoken for us, 80:1
ways from home, 576:7
we have a l. l. way to go, 316:3
Longevity has its place, 321:4
Look at a fine fine girl, 574:15
at yourselves, 422:1
don't l. back, 224:2
for me all around you, 172:7
for the woman, 88:5
into lives as into mirror, 48:14
let soul l. for deed it performed, 57:3
man all I am, 300:9
must not speak up nor l. amiss, 79:1
on me and be renewed, 279:7
one can l. out but never leave, 412:4
stand aside and l., 450:2
they might l. just like me, 357:2
up to white folks, 193:3
Up You Mighty Race, 173:2
when I l. at my country, 276:2
Looketh, Lord l. on the heart, 13:7
on outward appearance, 13:7
to lust after her, 26:14
Looking at one's self through others, 143:6
back at you, 371:4
for God and He's in my pocket, 544:9
I'm still l. for it, 353:5
sees you even when not l., 566:8
trouble always l. for you, 298:4
Looks, sour l. and rude words, 90:3
Lord, a feast to the L., 9:11
and the L. set a mark upon Cain, 7:7
and the L. went before them, 9:15
angel of the L. came upon them, 33:4
army of the L., 256:3
be with thee, 13:8
being dark I cannot bear, 218:7
bless thee and keep thee, 11:5
blessed be L. God of Israel, 33:1
blessed be name of the L., 14:19
blessed be the L. God of Shem, 7:16

Lord (continued)
called Samuel, 13:2
come by here my L., 579:10
confound the language of all the earth, 8:1
David danced before the L., 13:20
day of the L. cometh, 41:20
didn't my l. deliver Daniel, 578:13
dry bones hear the L., 23:21
dwell in house of the L., 16:10
enter into joy of thy l., 30:8
fear of the L. is beginning of wisdom, 18:3
gave and hath taken, 14:19
glory of the L. is risen upon thee, 23:5
glory of the L. shone round, 33:4
God caused a deep sleep, 6:11
God formed man of the dust, 6:7
God made he a woman, 6:11
God planted a garden in Eden, 6:8
God said unto the serpent, 6:17
God will wipe away tears, 22:10
got the L. but need another mortal, 469:3
great and dreadful day of the L., 24:18
hath chosen thee, 11:13
have mercy on them both, 54:11
how long, 22:2
I am the L. thy God, 10:4
I have waited for salvation O L., 8:18
I want to be in that number, 577:12
I will sing unto the L., 9:17
If We Ever Needed the L. Before, 201:3
in memory of all saints, 274:5
is a man of war, 10:1
is it I, 31:4
is most generous, 57:6
is my light, 16:11
is my rock, 13:23
is my salvation, 16:11
is my shepherd, 16:10
is my strength and shield, 16:12
is my strength and song, 9:17
is the strength of my life, 16:11
is with thee, 32:17
judgments of the L. are true, 16:6

Love *(continued)*

heaven sends down the l. of her, 3:2

heavenly l. by l. of God, 53:6

his banner over me was l., 21:6

how can l. grow from pain, 397:1

how can l. heal the mouth shut, 462:2

I did not just fall in l., 181:5

I do know I l. you, 333:11

I envy their public l., 339:6

I Just Called to Say I L. You, 482:4

I l. a lot of things, 315:4

i too old to learn of l., 360:1

I used to l. her, 445:9

in l. for the first time, 502:2

in l. with loving, 52:4

instill the l. of you, 2:5

is a many-splendored thing, 508:2

is an addiction, 552:1

is blind, 86:4

is God, 340:3

is like a baby, 565:7

is like a faucet, 253:6

is like rain, 549:8

is like singing, 181:4

is so powerful, 377:8

is strong as death, 21:14

is stronger than pride, 517:2

is supreme and unconditional, 201:9

is the oestrum of the poet, 66:*n*1

is the only true adventure, 432:6

is war, 283:7

kisses were the best kind, 467:5

labor of l., 41:19

land that knew my l. my pain, 85:5

leaves us numb to l., 373:2

let brotherly l. continue, 42:19

like a hydrant turns on off, 571:8

Love's in Need of L. Today, 482:2

lovers' quarrels are renewal of l., 47:4

making l. your moans like blues, 462:4

many waters cannot quench l., 21:15

me like a mother, 512:6

mercy, 24:11

more l. for your brother, 448:5

my l. fantasy, 484:3

my man better than myself, 170:4

my man, 253:5

Love *(continued)*

myself laughing, 179:7

nice to see folks you l. together, 429:9

no l. for self is root cause of hate, 196:5

no l. or l. and no sex, 430:8

nobody better'n yo'self, 179:6

nor l. for his or her own kind, 196:5

not everybody deserves l., 561:5

not those who remind them of their sins, 105:8

of God burned within me, 77:1

of mankind, 377:7

of money root of all evil, 42:9

of money, 429:6

of you has entrapped me, 3:3

oh careless l., 571:9

oh loveless l., 151:10

one another hate skins colored, 105:4

one another, 36:12, 38:23

one l. one heart, 449:12

our country but she don't l. us, 94:3

passed the muse appeared, 85:7

peace and l. on this planet, 518:6

please send me someone to l., 273:3

profess to believe men l. one another, 105:4

renewing of l., 47:*n*4

root revival of l., 450:7

salvation give with tender L., 63:2

savin' my l. for you, 192:5

self-crushing l., 180:7

sending out our major l., 511:7

separate us from l. of God, 38:16

smitten with l. of wisdom, 58:3

spirit of brotherly l., 170:6

standing in shadows of l., 409:5

stop in the name of l., 409:3

such method is l., 319:2

Supreme, 300:6

takes off the masks, 284:4

taught me who was the boss, 406:5

the answer was l., 428:7

the brotherhood, 43:7

the Lord with all thy heart, 30:1

the way he talks, 315:4

their native culture, 248:10

throbbing with l., 176:1

Love *(continued)*

thy neighbor as thyself, 11:4, 30:1

time to l., 19:17

to be of service, 90:4

to my brothers in the pen, 556:2

too delicate to have thrown on my face, 466:6

train, 429:3

transcends hate, 519:3

transform sentiment into l., 522:3

transforming enemy to friend, 319:1

tried to make black l. a crime, 495:7

unconditional l. final word, 319:5

unlocked the interlacings of l., 200:7

victory in l., 159:1

want to die while you l. me, 169:4

was like an unread book, 219:1

was not a false distinction, 227:5

was the tragedy, 394:8

we build and work and l., 529:5

weapon of choice, 340:6

what I wanted was your l., 371:7

what nation will trust your l., 196:5

what we are, 383:5

when is time l. somebody, 327:7

when too old for l., 180:11

where are our union and l., 88:7

Where Did Our L. Go, 408:9

who shall separate us from l. of Christ, 38:15

who were the first to l., 422:1

Why Do Fools Fall in L., 401:3

why hate those who l. me, 49:3

you 'cause you're mine, 486:3

you for your brownness, 209:3

you save may be your own, 434:3

your enemies, 27:1

your heart the prize, 338:9

your l. is king, 516:5

Love's austere and lonely offices, 243:4

in Need of Love Today, 482:2

Love-cry echoes of your soul, 391:1

Loved as his own soul, 13:12

black women want to be wanted and l., 510:5

could you be l. and be l., 449:14

even though I no longer l. her, 471:6

God so l. the world, 35:18

Loved (*continued*)

hated and l. everywhere, 50:3

her l. her fiercely, 467:1

I found you l. you, 151:2

joy of being l. tenderly, 67:4

sacrificing what he l., 158:5

she l. to dance around, 223:4

so amazing to be l., 484:4

too late I l. you, 52:8

we l. our country, 178:4

Lovely, isn't she l., 481:12

whatsoever things are l., 41:13

Lover, art leaves her l. as a Komitas, 199:4

freedom having l. who has no control, 95:4

I found my l. on his bed, 3:5

lookin' for a l., 397:2

with a l. I could really laugh, 474:5

Lover's, with l. key trust is a temptation, 460:2

Lovers, anger of l. renews love, 47:*n*4

anger of l. renews strength of love, 47:*n*4

falling out of l., 47:*n*4

Lovers' quarrels are renewal of love, 47:4

Loves both Africa and America, 377:5

caldron of dissolute l., 52:3

dove l. when it quarrels, 53:2

says he l. no one but me, 170:3

two cities formed by two l., 53:6

Loveth, he that l. her l. life, 25:8

he that l. him chasteneth him, 18:17

he that l. not knoweth not God, 43:14

Loving, Baby I Need Your L., 408:7

been l. you too long, 411:7

in love with l., 52:4

price of hating is l. less, 362:3

wasn't l. her was stabbing her, 520:5

wonder who is l. you, 403:5

Low, daughters of music brought l., 20:11

sound of the grinding is l., 20:11

the down l. is everything and nothing, 540:3

Low-down hoochie coocher, 226:5

Lowdown dirty deal, 179:1

Lower, man little l. than angels, 15:22

not asking to l. qualifications, 292:3

the wing of submission, 54:11

Lowly, I am meek and l., 28:8

Loyal blood demanding loyalty, 225:3

men and of being l., 118:1

Loyalty, loyal blood demanding l., 225:3

Lucifer, anyone could be L., 377:9

Luck, bad l. soul, 187:6

born for good l., 251:5

hard l. started when I was born, 155:7

same hard l. been my bes' fren', 155:7

Such is your l., 87:5

survival is l. or unlucky, 424:4

the wounds of bad l., 369:5

trick is to swallow your good l., 487:3

when it leaves does not go far, 516:3

Lucky, folds like money if you're l., 554:2

freedom not reserved for the l., 528:7

legend that he was l., 209:6

some joker got l., 236:5

Luke the beloved physician, 41:18

Lump of flesh, 55:5

Lumumba is my given name, 256:5

Lunatic hurricanes, 369:7

Lure of you eye and lip, 162:3

Lurking, always l. under the surface, 361:6

Lust, looketh to l. after her, 26:14

Luster, genius talent hide its l., 90:2

Lusts, daughters born to pamper l., 100:6

victim of its l. and pride, 101:2

Luta, a l. continua, 567:13

Lute, the l. but a piece of wood, 61:1

Luxuries, no such l. in contemporary world, 427:3

Luxury, money power l. like that, 354:3

of having multiple careers, 484:2

Lynch law last relic of barbarism, 139:1

Lynched, by a committee of U.S. Senate, 468:4

the white race l. me, 215:1

Lynchers, law must bear upon l., 138:6

Lynching a barbarous practice, 272:5

etches impression on mind and soul, 187:3

high-tech l. for uppity blacks, 468:4

is an unwritten law, 140:1

meet l. with l., 298:5

still murdering and l. him, 138:5

substituted discrimination for l., 291:1

us impartially, 166:4

Lynchings, victim of a thousand l., 231:3

Lyre, power and beauty of minstrel's l., 147:8

M

M. C. Higgins, he was M. higher than everything, 370:5

Ma'am, say Yes m. for working's sake, 306:2

Machete will do for me, 137:6

Machine makes little blonde girls, 362:1

Machinery creaks, 157:1

Machines, God-breathing m. no more, 94:8

more important than people, 319:9

Mad but never let them know it, 270:1

I am not m., 38:2

much learning doth make thee m., 38:1

raise humble dogs or m. dogs, 227:3

Made, anything can be m., 532:2

fearfully and wonderfully m., 18:7

for special use of devils, 100:6

God m. all of the same blood, 79:4

I never had it m., 271:1

in the image of God m. he man, 7:13

light of it, 29:20

me feel rich, 329:6

no man m. them, 331:3

of one blood all nations, 37:13

the crooked shall be m. straight, 22:14

Made *(continued)*
   white in blood of the lamb, 44:11
Madison Avenue afraid of the dark,
   269:7
Madness of clashing winds, 369:7
   of their forefathers, 376:10
   war, 489:2
Madonna exemplar of purest grace,
   86:6
Mag Smith, lonely M., 116:1
Magi, holy the M. for sending him to
   us, 391:2
Magic, believe the m. inside your
   heart, 442:1
   blk m. you lookin at, 467:3
   hips, 367:3
   imagination a m. carpet, 250:3
   lingering after people, 443:7
   stitched m. into chitlin circuit air,
      398:6
   where is woman is m., 467:4
Magic Kingdom remains closed,
   400:3
Magician, no colored m. gonna
   make you white, 467:3
Magicians, and unfair we are black
   m., 354:4
Magicien de la terre, 548:8
Magics, no m. or elves, 259:2
Magistrate, hate struck down Chief
   M., 296:8
   like some m. grown gray, 86:1
Magistrates, to the children of the
   m., 1:3
Magnates, a wise man is a school for
   m., 2:3
   do not degrade m., 2:4
Magnificent, make your history m.,
   173:1
Magnify, my soul doth m. the Lord,
   32:20
Mahogany, taupe m. bronze, 182:2
Maid, as with m. with mistress,
   22:9
   rather play a m. than be a m.,
      192:*n*2
   why complain $7,000 a week
      playing a m., 192:2
Mainstream, liberation from m.
   culture, 393:6
   polluted m. of Americanism,
      342:6
Maintain their position at any cost,
   383:6

Mais l'extrême justice est une
   extrême injure, 148:*n*1
Majority, minorities will be the m.,
   381:1
   present-day white m., 275:2
   rule not reliable instrument of
      democracy, 477:2
   tyranny of The M., 477:3
Make a way out of no way, 571:12
   aim to m. effort not measure it,
      189:6
   follow things which m. peace, 39:1
   I want to m. myself, 337:2
   it happen inside of us, 374:4
   let us m. man in our image, 6:4
   my dream-children live, 190:4
   no division, 53:9
   ourselves what we want to be,
      172:10
   some elbow room, 434:1
   the wounded whole, 579:3
   to m. contented slave m.
      thoughtless, 104:4
   truth shall m. you free, 36:5
   use of the great good in us, 220:2
   you do wrong m. you do right,
      455:3
   you mo' pretty still, 179:5
Make-believe, what I do ain't m.,
   547:4
Maker, as their m. rests in lightland,
   5:1
Makes day seep into night, 56:7
   enemies by great service, 68:6
   night seep into day, 56:7
   you logy half alive, 277:2
Maketh angels spirits, 42:16
   ministers a flame of fire, 42:16
Making of truth is violence too, 552:8
Malachite, more hidden than m., 1:4
Malcolm is worthy of death, 348:4
   was our manhood, 261:2
Male and female created he, 6:4
   being Black and m. in America,
      505:4
   black m. patriarchs, 488:3
Mama, Afouyéké oh my sweet m.,
   574:14
   ask your m., 214:4
   Don't Want No Peas an' Rice an'
      Coconut Oil, 575:3
   I'll always love my m., 429:5
   one's country is your m., 214:5
   said I'm priceless, 551:5

Mama *(continued)*
   that's all right now m., 221:8
   the tell me of the m. is the answer,
      214:6
   told me, 404:2
Mammon, cannot serve God and m.,
   27:3
Mammy, Adam never had no M.,
   156:1
   says de blessin', 149:6
   went home with nothing, 78:6
Mammy's little baby loves short'nin'
   bread, 569:3
Man, a good m. and just, 34:27
   a wise m. is a school, 2:3
   Act Like a Lady Think Like a M.,
      504:2
   after own heart, 13:5
   ain't nothing but a m., 338:4
   all God's dangers ain't a white m.,
      168:4
   all m. hath will he give for his life,
      108:*n*1
   ancestors three-fifths of a m., 498:6
   and every m. is free, 212:8
   and his wife were not ashamed,
      6:13
   at war with heart of m., 69:4
   be a Negro than a poor white m.,
      569:4
   be born again, 35:15
   be both m. and woman, 358:5
   became a living soul, 6:7
   black m. I'm a black m. I'm black,
      384:4
   black m. in white world, 271:1
   black m. you cain't shine, 568:9
   born dies and does not come
      again, 564:3
   born unto trouble, 15:6
   bring him up a m., 282:5
   by m. came death, 40:4
   by m. came resurrection, 40:4
   ceases to be a m., 104:4
   certain m. from Jerusalem, 34:1
   confer with the ignorant m., 1:4
   created m. of a blood clot, 57:6
   dieth and wasteth away, 15:9
   distribution unto every m., 37:9
   do not oust a m., 2:4
   dog-faced m., 389:1
   don't have to be a m. to fight,
      296:5
   doth not live by bread only, 11:14

Massacre, when Indians won it was a m., 343:8

Masses make the nation and the race, 172:4

new spirit awake in the m., 167:6

uniting the Negro m., 166:2

Master adopts rigorous system, 102:2

before spoken first syllable of m., 477:6

disciple not above m., 28:5

emancipated class under former m. class, 118:3

Hail M., 31:11

hello M. bottom rail on top, 570:4

most merciful M., 53:7

thinkin' of a m. plan, 540:4

to tell him he has no m., 131:1

tried to m. the things I knew I could do, 434:7

was a little crazy, 562:4

your high, 555:4

Master's in How to Take Care of Everybody, 484:2

sun's cutting heat, 324:3

Tools Will Never Dismantle the M. House, 358:2

Masters, colored men m. over the women, 83:5

do our duty to our new m., 78:6

duty to obey our m., 63:6

if the m. let you marry, 445:8

mind our m., 63:6

no man can serve two m., 27:3

no more in sight of their m., 94:8

old m. seizing their slaves, 75:3

reproaches from my m., 68:4

slaves become m., 80:3

waiting for m. to come lay claim, 93:7

when m. abandon their slaves, 62:1

Masters', crumbs from their m. table, 29:4

Master-slave relationship, 488:4

Masturbation, in regard to m., 347:9

Matchbox hold my clothes, 195:6

Matches boxes of m. and petrol, 373:5

Materialism, giant triplets of m., 319:9

Math and science literacy, 365:2

Mathematicians, musicians are m., 264:3

subconsciously m., 264:3

Mathematics medicine science, 279:6

Matrix in which history happens, 418:2

into the m. of the Republic, 199:2

Matter, certain things don't m., 178:6

of death, 334:6

root of the m., 15:14

Maud went to college, 258:9

May not get there with you, 321:4

the tide that is entering now, 367:6

Maybellene why can't you be true, 299:5

Mayflower, long before the M., 308:7

trace family tree back to M., 501:4

Mayor who cared about people, 279:1

who stood the watch, 279:1

Maze, groping through this dreary m., 81:3

Me, 'nother for what I know is m., 570:3

a witness against m., 2:6

believe in God believe in m., 36:13

do in remembrance of m., 34:19

he not with m. against m., 28:9

I am m. they are thee, 336:3

Lord remember m. when thou comest, 34:23

Lord remember m., 579:6

my mother was like m., 550:1

myself and I, 547:4

myself I, 474:7

rescue m. protect m., 2:6

that includes m., 530:1

thou art with m., 16:10

We, 417:n1

Wheee, 417:9

white folks working for m., 500:4

Mean, don't m. black at all, 277:3

love myself looking m., 179:7

world is m., 355:2

you gotta m. it, 194:9

Meaning, full m. of liberation, 424:1

know the m. of our numbers, 176:6

without m. can be no struggle, 495:1

Meanings, did dreams have m., 223:6

heavy with weight of all m., 494:2

values and m. most real, 189:1

Means as pure as the ends, 317:4

by any m. necessary, 296:4

by any methods and m., 264:5

duty to use every m., 100:3

employed against me, 68:2

of our destruction, 47:1

use any m. necessary, 296:1

we use pure as ends we seek, 317:4

Meantime, to do in the m. is live, 464:9

Measure, aim to make effort not m. it, 189:6

him right, 327:7

our greatness by the least, 537:6

progress in how far we have to go, 270:4

ultimate m. of man, 318:6

Measured by a different yardstick, 496:6

by shiny illusion of cars clothes guns, 429:1

rumble, 381:2

Measurement, let Eternity be our m., 172:11

Meat, hungered and ye gave me m., 30:11

on my soul, 360:7

was locusts and wild honey, 26:7

you will even eat m. every day, 562:4

Mecca, sacred temple of M., 54:10

Media chief arm of white propaganda, 389:5

made a leader and may undo him, 217:6

Medicine, faithful friend is m., 25:10

give zombies a taste of their m., 458:5

no m. to cure hatred, 565:19

Medium, Education is the m., 172:5

Meek, I am m. and lowly, 28:8

shall inherit the earth, 17:1

Meet, if no more on earth do m., 109:7

life's terms, 189:8

me at ten thousand feet, 195:8

Meeting place of caravans and boats, 60:3

Melodies, silence distills in yellow m., 345:8

silences are m. heard, 345:7

Melody, God filled my soul with m., 147:1

Melting, great m. pot, 230:1

pot Harlem, 215:3

Mercy *(continued)*
  wing of submission through m., 54:11
  wrought by angels, 101:4
Meridian's, in M. chest a breaking, 444:1
Merit comes from what we make of them, 189:5
  talent rewarded on basis of m., 215:6
Mermaids, quadroon m. sang, 242:8
Merry, eat drink and be m., 20:8
Meshach fell into the fiery furnace, 23:24
Mess, don't you m. with me, 251:5
  whole m. of sorrow, 181:11
Message, came to believe m. was him, 500:8
  can't sing a song that doesn't have a m., 236:3
Messages, deliver m. instructed to me, 116:4
Messenger, an angel as m., 54:14
  has God sent mortal as m., 54:14
  I will send my m., 24:17
  with language of his folk, 54:7
Messing with my game, 378:7
  with no broke niggas, 563:3
Messy, democracy can be m., 528:4
Metaphor for the outsider, 249:2
  Negro is America's m., 232:4
Meteoric flares are meaningless chaos, 207:9
Method, man must evolve a m., 319:2
  my m. of working, 552:5
  revealed moment I am inspired, 141:7
  the big cities used, 238:5
Methods, by any m. and means, 264:5
Methuselah, all the days of M., 7:8
Metropolis, people of Black M., 235:5
Michael and angels fought dragon, 44:14
  row the boat ashore, 577:3
Michelangelo, like M. painted pictures, 315:6
  sweep streets like M., 315:6
Microscope, bugs under a m., 553:4

Middle, America's black m. class, 482:7
  in the m. of war, 378:6
  passage blacks in a net, 384:3
  start in m. and hold on tight, 239:6
  we buck in the m., 206:3
Middle Passage, routes of the M., 251:3
  voyage through death, 243:2
Midnight, burn the m. oil, 305:5
  celestial wishbone snap at m., 462:5
  hour, 411:2
  no white man coming after m., 343:2
  round about M., 293:1
Midnights, turn m. into days, 128:6
Midst, I am in the m. of them, 29:11
Midwife, I am the m., 49:1
Midwives of Africa's Renaissance, 424:3
Might, strengthened with m., 41:9
Mightier, there cometh one m. than I, 32:6
Mighty above all things, 24:19
  bring back our m. dream, 212:5
  fallen in midst of battle, 13:16
  hips, 367:3
  his name shall be the m. God, 22:3
  Look Up You M. Race, 173:2
  men of old of renown, 7:9
  put down the m., 32:21
  rushing m. wind, 37:6
  weak things to confound the m., 39:3
Migrants kept coming, 263:6
Migration, season of m., 476:8
Mikuyu, chattering wagtails of M. Prison, 439:6
Miles, broad plains m. and m., 130:3
Militarism, giant triplets of m., 319:9
Military, forced upon African by m. conquest, 197:5
  resolve conflict before the m. stage, 382:4
Milk, a land flowing with m. and honey, 9:2
  homogenized chocolate m., 358:8
Milking a bear to get cream, 181:3
Millions of voices are calling, 100:6
  of voices calling for change, 523:8
  with m. under his care, 4:4
Millstone, soul is a m., 260:8

Millstones, women slaves at the m., 1:4
Mimic, if they m. you return compliment, 172:8
Mimics, role of m. is to deny competence, 452:7
Mind, a man's m. strongest thing going for him, 483:5
  almost lost my m., 326:4
  anything you want if make up your m., 222:2
  blackness is a state of m., 573:9
  circus m. that's running wild, 420:7
  clothed and in right m., 32:12
  don't reckon I'll m. suh, 210:2
  enlarge the contracted m., 72:1
  enslaved body never free, 320:3
  free your m. and your ass will follow, 407:3
  her m. traveled crooked streets, 337:6
  his m. is the nigger, 343:11
  How to Pretend You Don't M. but I do m., 484:2
  is a terrible thing to waste, 573:6
  love the Lord with all thy m., 30:1
  lynching etches impression on m., 187:3
  makes everything work, 458:2
  my m. feels cycles old, 127:2
  my m. is like a rowboat, 187:5
  my m. set on freedom, 577:11
  not supposed to m., 377:6
  one m. for white folk to see, 570:3
  our masters, 63:6
  persuaded in his own m., 38:24
  placid slumbers sooth each m., 71:7
  powers of our own m., 125:4
  prepare bread and m., 51:4
  presence of m., 48:8
  restless youthful m., 84:6
  speak your m. or lose it, 552:4
  sweat your m., 169:2
  today blues of m. and heart, 268:4
  unshackle my m., 91:4
  weapon of oppressor is m. of oppressed, 454:5
  with a present m., 47:*n3*
Mindful of the sacrifices, 526:4
Mindin', keepin' still and m. things, 67:6

Minds, barriers of their m., 246:3
  black power must mean trained
    m., 187:4
  cut off society its cultivated m.,
    99:3
  decolonize our m., 301:5
  fill their m. with stories they adore
    you, 441:3
  leave their m. free to roam they
    will hatch plans, 441:3
  lives of people fill our m., 119:2
  lock up our m., 281:8
  nothing to occupy their m., 370:3
  ourselves can free our m., 450:1
  teach children their m. are pearls,
    410:2
  what imperfection in our m.,
    569:9
Mine hour is not yet come, 35:13
  if this world were m., 396:4
  this is m. ain't yr stuff, 466:7
Mingle, can't m. with people, 252:4
Miniature replica of life, 167:4
Minister, feel like an ordained m.,
    433:3
Minister's wife, 173:6
Ministering wants of their nature,
    99:3
Ministers, maketh m. a flame of fire,
    42:16
Ministry, call to m., 72:3
Minnie the Moocher, 226:5
Minorities, concern for m. abroad,
    191:2
  discussions of ethnic m. drift,
    330:2
  will be the majority, 381:1
Minority, American blacks crucial
    m., 255:10
  authority to kill a m., 542:4
  individual is a m., 248:9
  member of embattled m., 271:3
  no longer silence voice of m.,
    129:3
  white m. racist rule, 266:6
Minstrel's, power beauty of m. lyre,
    147:8
Minstrel-smile, hidden by a m.,
    209:2
Minute, don't let m. spoil hour,
    312:7
  less than one m. old, 481:12
  to smile, 149:2
Minutes that know no life, 386:1

Miracle, Next in Line for a M.,
    383:10
  our lives be saved, 130:5
  you are the m., 457:6
Miracles happen all the time we're
    here, 456:5
  we are the m. God made, 515:6
Mirage, works of unbelievers a m.,
    55:8
Mirror, at own door own m., 331:1
  black folk are a m., 231:2
  look into lives as into m., 48:14
  of original nakedness, 360:9
  past is a m., 108:2
  reflects my life, 108:2
  standin' up into m., 314:1
  tell me m. what is wrong, 547:4
Mirrors, no m. in Nana's house,
    453:7
  you are my m., 291:3
Mirth, house of, 20:3
Misanthrope, wonder colored
    person is not a m., 122:7
Misbehavin', ain't m., 192:5
Miseducation, the beginning of my
    m., 366:7
Misery always leaves its
    thumbprints, 550:4
  don't call ahead, 341:1
  endure extreme m., 383:7
  o' de Englishman, 313:2
Misfortune, father died after my m.,
    62:2
  human heart can bear m., 103:3
  in the cracks of everyday life, 369:5
Misrepresentations in things which
    concern us, 80:1
Missed, how much I m. them, 271:4
Missile, hijacked airplane as a m.,
    498:3
Missiles called peace keepers, 536:7
Missing out on what's passing by,
    555:4
Mission, fail our m. as a democratic
    nation, 446:5
  make world free, 286:4
Missionaries, Talented Tenth m. of
    culture, 143:4
Missionary, I am a lawyer not a m.,
    229:6
Mississippi, born in hard time M.,
    481:10
  Goddam, 352:4
  Negro in M. cannot vote, 317:9

Mississippi *(continued)*
  next to go Alleluia, 364:6
  pursue a degree from University of
    M., 351:9
  the middle of the iceberg, 364:6
Mistake, I'll make a fatal m., 137:7
  making m. when Negro, 491:8
Mistaken, slaves to a m. public
    opinion, 124:3
Mistakes are a fact of life, 431:3
  cannot repeat past m., 456:1
  mask no m., 285:9
Mister it's my business, 275:3
  say m. to spindling boys, 206:3
Mistletoe, hang all the m., 448:6
Mistress, as with maid with m., 22:9
  music is my m., 201:8
  slave girl black as ebony fair as m.,
    95:1
Misunderstanding between the
    races, 525:1
Mix strains of blood, 469:6
Mixing, avoided m. in society, 87:4
Mixture of arrogance insecurity,
    306:3
Moaning, hear her m. night and
    morn, 151:5
Moans come double, 149:2
Mob, hungry mouth is an angry m.,
    449:8
  in flickering light the m. swayed,
    185:1
  law is abnormal public opinion,
    131:2
  reign over the m., 145:2
  two black men a dangerous m.,
    544:4
Mobilization, watchword must be
    m., 265:1
Mobilized grass roots, 522:2
  into action, 265:1
Mobs, North's lynch m., 238:5
Mocked, God is not m., 41:8
Mocker, wine is a m., 18:22
Mockery, banner in m. waves,
    112:5
Model, aid-dependency m., 551:4
  did not set out to become role m.,
    353:1
  more than a role m., 502:6
Models, can drug dealers be role m.,
    533:4
Moderate in exercise of political
    rights, 132:5

Moron, proof accessible to the m., 185:1

Morsel, denied one m. of wealth, 64:3

devours m. of a sail, 330:6

Mortal, got the Lord but need another m., 469:3

independent m. on earth, 66:4

must put on immortality, 40:7

Mortals, if we m. love or sing, 151:1

Moses, given to M. and Jesus, 53:9

go down M., 576:10

God said unto M. I AM THAT I AM, 9:3

hid his face, 9:1

smote the rock twice, 11:6

Motels of the highways, 317:9

Mother, add m. to sound like curse, 485:3

against daughter, 448:5

as is the m. so the daughter, 23:17

begging us to do duty to our masters, 78:6

being a m. is the cruelest, 183:1

beneficent m. of gods and men, 4:5

Black m. within each of us, 358:6

came toward me, 471:6

condition of m. determines child, 94:2

country has enslaved you, 234:3

Earth, 491:10

embarrassment for m. I was black, 216:1

had handkerchief and song, 440:3

honor thy father and m., 10:8

I am m. and daughter, 49:1

I am m. of my father, 49:1

I imagine my m. dreaming, 416:3

I'm a black m., 247:3

in sin did my m. conceive me, 17:4

joy of being a m., 438:3

Lesbian Feminist Warrior M., 359:1

lifetime wife and m., 484:2

love me like a m., 512:6

may I go downtown, 249:5

members of my m., 49:1

mer was both m. and sea, 332:4

my m. is now me, 460:6

my m. religious-negro, 450:5

Nile Valley, 279:6

quintessential m., 491:10

said I'd be alone, 325:2

Mother (continued)

said pick the very best one, 506:4

shall a man leave his father and m., 6:13

told me I was blessed, 201:10

too many of you crying, 396:9

was like me, 550:1

weep not, 92:1

Mother Earth, you go back to M., 254:6

Mother's, grandfather on the m. side, 178:7

house there is God, 327:4

praying was theater, 490:2

search of my m. garden I found my own, 443:6

Motherfucker, nobody called colored m., 290:3

Motherhood, best example of m., 255:3

curse upon m., 161:3

is the off-and-on light, 447:8

pride of m., 438:2

Motherless, I feel like a m. child, 576:7

Motherlove, is unfailing l., 457:7

Mothers, food prepared by Negro m., 229:3

handed on the creative spark, 443:5

land of my m., 312:5

of those children, 229:3

weeping for children, 97:2

Motives move imperialism in Africa, 207:2

to undertake insurrection, 87:3

Motley, in the m. crowd, 301:7

of ugliness and beauty, 182:2

Motto, let your m. be Resistance, 101:1

that is our m., 88:2

Mountain, ain't no m. high enough, 405:5

brought forth a mouse, 46:n1

bury me on a m. top, 453:6

Climbing up the Rough Side of the M., 201:4

every m. shall be made low, 22:14

gap in the side of m., 46:8

go tell it on the m., 576:8

go up to the m., 321:4

stand on top of the m., 211:6

stood on m. with harp and sword, 181:8

Mountain (continued)

to die for the people heavier than m., 425:6

weights of sorrow lay, 112:6

wrapped in rainbows, 181:8

Mountains and valleys he roams, 389:6

as fleeting as the clouds, 55:9

beyond m. there are m., 276:n1

gunfire from the m., 512:8

My command stands firm like the m., 4:2

valleys and m. upon my body, 358:5

Mountaintop, a King who took us to the m., 524:1

last few steps to the m., 542:3

Mourn death of a people dying, 291:3

I will weep wail m., 291:3

time to m., 19:17

your death, 386:1

Mourning, Black Lady in M., 291:3

house of m., 20:3

Mouse laughs at cat hole is nearby, 565:3

mountain brought forth a m., 46:n1

tiny m. came forth, 46:8

Mouth, a fool's m. is his destruction, 18:20

beat me on the m. if I marched, 204:4

filled with a bitter taste, 471:6

find music in my m., 454:8

head in the lion's m., 248:6

his m. is most sweet, 21:10

I am pure of m. and hands, 2:6

in her m. was an olive leaf pluckt off, 7:12

like feathers, 325:5

open its m. and examine its teeth, 377:6

open my m. and sing, 288:6

out of abundance m. speaketh, 28:11

out of the m. of babes, 15:22

shut m. catch fly, 574:5

spake by m. of his holy prophets, 33:2

the words, 253:2

toothless without a tongue, 447:5

your m. and madness, 162:3

Mouth-in-the-dust and lash, 440:4

Mouths, they have m. but speak not, 18:5
Move around the room as they please, 506:6
  beyond old racial wounds, 525:2
  couldn't m. without man's assistance, 129:5
  don't m. out until you can stay out, 165:4
  jangling gently as you m., 224:2
  let's m., 538:3
  on up a little higher, 195:2
  social conscience, 319:7
  together we can m. it, 281:5
  waiting for other to make first m., 194:7
Moved, authority of Church m. me, 52:11
  God m. upon face of the waters, 5:4
  we shall not be m., 577:10
Movement, at the peak no m., 269:8
  Black Arts M., 379:1
  humans create, 353:5
  lost and in constant m., 440:5
Movie, in my m. draftees fleeing, 554:5
  walked into middle of m., 378:9
Movin', got to keep m., 237:2
Moving from silence into speech, 488:5
  on up, 422:7, 447:2
Mozart, life lived without knowing M., 452:7
Mr. Black Man watch your step, 194:2
Mr. Wigin, good by m. tell them im strong, 351:1
Much, did so m. when we had so little, 363:6
  faithful in least faithful in m., 34:13
  unjust in least unjust in m., 34:13
Muck, the story of M., 552:6
Mud, blood's thicker than the m., 435:4
  pray for rain deal with m., 575:6
Muddled, textbooks deliberately m., 279:5
Muddy, Frye Street is like m. water, 200:5
Mug, with your m. of a copper, 240:6
  your m. of a pig, 240:6
Muhammad, heart of M., 56:13

Muhammad's confidence in Allah, 348:4
Mulatto, American culture is m., 257:1
  cultural m., 533:1
  genetic m., 533:1
Mule could tell folks how it's treated, 444:9
  forty acres and a m., 499:2
  forty acres and my m., 300:3
  nigger woman m. uh de world, 180:2
  we didn't get the m., 499:2
Mules, forty acres and two m., 426:2
Multiplicity, lurid dream of m., 465:4
Multiply, be fruitful and m., 6:5
Multitude, I we all of us are one and the m., 425:7
Murder, can't m. liberation, 464:10
  dead black boy on trial for m., 560:1
  no need to m. others, 284:8
  price of truth has become m., 446:2
  she conceived the Chinaman's m., 441:2
  we too are guilty of m., 186:8
  you can m. a liberator, 464:10
Murdered, eleven people m., 415:5
Murderer, not every black person is a m., 508:9
  shoot m. in chest, 323:4
Murderers don't turn into patriots, 137:5
  equal of their m., 284:8
  we know men are m. sinful, 252:3
  worse than m. hired, 285:1
Murders, avalanche of m., 290:5
  doing something about the m., 402:1
Murmur my name, 59:4
Muse, love passed the m. appeared, 85:7
  were mine to tempt, 149:4
Museum, love corpse in m. please visit, 535:4
  in m. signs that said white and colored, 401:2
Mushroom cloud, 498:4
Music, all American m. derives from blues, 148:7
  all m. is folk m., 204:5
  all that m. all that dancing, 214:6

Music (continued)
  as much a gift, 475:3
  basic thing about jazz m., 261:6
  best in m. class, 300:10
  born into m. die into m., 411:1
  boundary line to m., 273:5
  brings stability, 537:1
  comes out the radio, 454:8
  daughters of m. brought low, 20:11
  I've changed m., 301:4
  if you can it ain't m., 254:1
  is a world within itself, 482:1
  is my mistress, 201:8
  is not a color to me, 534:4
  is your own experience, 273:5
  it's not my m., 398:1
  jazz m. our black anthem, 312:6
  my life is my m., 204:4
  name doesn't make m., 269:4
  no more m. of thy tongue, 71:5
  of James Brown without lyrics, 389:2
  of the Congo, 290:9
  pages perfumed with m., 226:1
  playing m. away from trouble, 298:4
  poured through our veins, 406:8
  rock-wise tumble-doun m., 489:3
  symptoms of the illness in its m., 507:1
  that's what m. is to me, 300:5
  there is m. in me, 173:4
  when it hits you, 449:1
  why our m. is sweet, 515:6
  you feel it or not, 326:10
Music's, poetry is m. twin, 381:2
Musical, American m. art form, 269:4
  found m. heritage roots, 262:1
  jazz is a m. gumbo, 178:3
Musician, I am one thing a m., 300:9
  keeps records of his time, 288:4
  you just ain't a m., 264:2
Musicians are mathematicians, 264:3
  jazz m. symbolize freedom, 446:4
Must be my used to be, 169:7
Mustang Sally, 352:1
Mustard, heaven like to m. seed, 28:15
Mutual obligation to one another, 537:6
  regards cancel enmity, 519:3
Muzzled, I refuse to be m., 499:7

Nation *(continued)*

question for n. to solve, 106:3

secure only while honest, 107:1

shall not lift up sword, 22:1

small one a strong n., 23:6

spiritual heritage of n., 144:3

transformed society of love, 304:3

true strength of our n., 526:3

we remain a young n., 526:5

what it is today, 249:1

what n. will trust your love, 196:5

white Christian n., 161:3

whole n. to bear witness, 275:8

will never stand justified, 222:4

Nation's dividends must be ours, 83:7

reach n. ear we need earthquake, 105:2

sorrow treads on n. joy, 114:1

National crime is lynching, 140:1

crisis in n. economy, 239:5

dignity beaten down, 197:5

liberation of a people, 286:1

more than n. boundaries make a nation, 237:6

security crises, 383:2

sing the n. anthem, 271:1

National Basketball Association, like saying N. mostly African Americans, 509:1

Nationalism, activists of n., 255:9

is obstacle to peace, 221:1

Nationhood beaten down, 197:5

Nations, Abraham father of many n., 8:4

agitated for freedom, 64:3

all n. and kindreds, 44:10

are as a drop in the bucket, 22:16

astonishment among all n., 12:3

become free then rich and learned, 135:1

before him all n., 30:10

by-word among the n., 89:1

dem call us Underdeveloped N., 387:3

footstool of the other n., 172:1

obtain respect of other n., 123:5

rush like the rushing of waters, 22:4

teach all n., 32:4

term themselves civilized, 95:6

Nation-state, limited frontiers of the n., 215:6

Native, damning my n. land, 231:5

my n. land my home, 174:7

naturalized and all colors, 162:9

son dancing, 385:7

Natives envy the tourist, 471:8

of this country, 76:5

Natural la that the Refugees bring, 560:5

literature, 481:3

Nature abhors a vacuum, 441:3

beauty of N., 167:2

describe their n., 1:1

God speaks to us through n., 142:4

his very n. will demand one, 154:6

imitation of the n. of another, 125:4

in his genius man has harnessed n., 220:4

in touch with n. and its teachings, 142:3

isness of man's n., 319:4

made us what we are, 172:10

make human n. thy study, 65:5

preserved rights of n., 66:1

thy anthems raise, 81:1

true n. inspires the man, 81:6

unity of N., 167:2

violence was foreign to his n., 187:1

were condescending to art, 503:6

Natures, cultivation of our own n., 125:4

Navigate easily in the white world, 533:1

Nazarene, he shall be called a N., 26:4

Nazareth, any good come out of N., 35:11

Near, better is a neighbor n., 19:6

peace to him far and n., 23:4

whenever you're n., 408:11

Nearer than his jugular vein, 56:12

Neatly fitted into pegs, 282:8

Necessary, builder of the n., 422:3

by any means n., 296:4

peculiarly n. to comfort and safety, 88:6

use any mean n., 296:1

what's n. to keep on living, 475:4

Necessities, freedom is limited by n., 207:7

Necessity for me like food water, 326:9

has no law, 52:12

no n. can warrant them to rob, 72:6

Necessity *(continued)*

objective n. to objective freedom, 207:3

virtue was not a n., 130:6

Neck, chain fastened about own n., 106:9

is as a tower of ivory, 21:12

Necklaces, boxes of matches and n., 373:5

Necktie, ladies' bowtie gentleman's n., 569:1

Need, Baby I N. Your Loving, 408:7

baby love I n. you, 408:6

everything you n. you got, 302:3

oppressed oppressor n. each other, 341:8

smash something ghetto's n., 282:10

storm whirlwind and earthquake, 105:2

what we n. now John Henry, 205:7

what you n. is within you, 252:6

what you n. you know I got it, 411:8

you don't n. anything else, 295:9

Needle, evil enters like n., 566:2

that pricks at both ends, 567:2

through eye of n., 29:14

Needless, prodded into n. war, 220:5

Needs, giver of n. undefined, 381:3

politics desire to satisfy basic n., 425:3

satisfy n. with all senses, 268:3

Negated, bourgeois n. being black, 491:7

Negation, integration leading to cultural n., 255:6

Negations of man, 290:5

Negative attitude that runs the show, 547:3

Black images, 265:6

images of black people, 508:9

Negativism is like cancer, 417:2

Negotiate, only free men can n., 266:7

Negress symbol of selflessness, 519:5

Negritude is not a stone, 241:4

neither tower nor cathedral, 241:4

Negro, about the N. rather than of him, 167:5

advise N. in exercise of political rights, 132:5

American flag a dirty rag to N., 122:4

Negro *(continued)*

American N. is just plain
American, 193:1
and beautiful, 211:5
and the African, 282:11
authentic N. experience, 491:7
awareness I was N., 185:1
be a N. than a poor white man,
569:4
blessing aid white more than N.,
124:2
blood flowing in his veins, 108:5
blood is powerful just one drop,
214:2
can attain progress, 239:2
children suffer, 228:7
citizenship is a fiction, 154:4
colors of the N. race, 272:5
compliments their tans, 298:1
condition of N. labor, 239:5
contemporary N. life, 167:6
crisis of N. intellectual, 255:9
damage one ignorant N. can do,
395:9
debasement of the N. woman,
130:6
descendant of one family stock,
170:6
destiny of N. lies in the future,
166:1
doesn't qualify you to understand
race, 343:9
effect of acculturation on the N.,
252:8
elevated the N. to Hollywood star,
216:3
feels his twoness an American a
N., 143:6
first class citizenship for the N.,
270:4
folk-song, 144:3
food prepared by N. mothers,
229:3
for the N. intellectual, 255:8
given N. bad check, 317:7
government unable to protect N.
citizen, 139:5
hair more educated, 242:7
has no encouragement, 103:7
has undeniable right to liberty,
70:5
history of N. in America, 232:4
I am a N. black as night, 211:4
I'm an American N., 298:4

Negro *(continued)*

if a N. got legs, 338:2
in American literature, 206:1
in corners of society, 317:6
in Mississippi cannot vote, 317:9
in the south, 298:5
industrial education for the N.,
133:3
insulted in places average N. could
never go, 289:9
is America's metaphor, 232:4
is an American citizen, 128:2
is bone of your country, 124:4
justice for the N., 103:5
literature is external view, 167:5
made N. first-class citizen, 216:3
making mistake when N., 491:8
may occupy highest rung, 172:1
must strive to help himself, 143:8
never eliminated as political
factor, 128:2
new N. a sober sensible creature,
162:8
new person in the N., 239:1
no difference between African N.,
170:6
no limits to the N. in arts in letters,
133:3
nobody called N. bastard, 290:3
only N. in the United States, 178:7
people of the world, 272:5
price for oppression of the N.,
316:5
problem rather than N. known,
167:5
Problem, 256:4
race in America stolen ravished,
222:4
race must be emancipated, 171:4
reduced N. to cultural zero, 168:2
regarded a curiosity, 86:3
remains like iron or granite, 106:6
represents a paradox, 231:4
responsible elite in N. community,
186:1
risk martyrdom, 319:6
role of N. created by Western man,
357:3
saved by Talented Tenth, 143:2
signs his own emancipation, 320:3
slave markets and N. pens, 97:2
sold to a N. trader, 102:1
stereotype N. character, 206:1
story of the N., 252:8

Negro *(continued)*

telegraph reached last slave, 456:3
the leap the N. made when freed,
132:2
thinks he's white man, 453:4
to recognize he is a hybrid, 282:11
travelers, 571:13
until every N. in America can vote,
245:6
wants what all Americans want,
152:4
was in vogue, 212:6
what does the N. want, 208:3
when N. hates the Jew, 282:2
whenever he sees a N., 348:2
whole N. race enters with me,
135:5
women, 168:3
word N. not outlawed in
Emancipation, 141:4
world looks up to American N.,
197:3
you cannot do without N., 124:4
you want to shut up every N.,
198:5
Negro's capacity to adjust
accommodate, 252:8
essential self, 271:3
great stumbling block, 317:1
qualities as an individual, 271:3
survival in America, 252:8
vested interests in the N. body,
139:4
Negroes a race more in name than in
fact, 168:1
are outsiders, 231:7
assumption that law-abiding N.,
145:5
black as Cain join angelic train,
71:4
bleaching theirself trying to be
white, 216:4
crimes by N. discredit the race,
128:1
got blindyitis, 453:4
handicaps among so-called N.,
196:5
hated N. for not standing up,
402:1
have had white allies, 209:1
homesick for N., 182:4
in Africa prior to enslavement,
155:6
inside outside our culture, 231:7

Negroes *(continued)*
  integration of n. with black
    people, 421:7
  lighter skinned N., 154:3
  New N., 210:5
  observe everything, 257:3
  overnight N. become blacks, 290:3
  prejudice kept white from N.,
    120:4
  quarter of the N., 214:6
  to keep N. in their place, 238:5
  unthinkable N. will go to war,
    270:*n*1
  we N. love our country, 107:3
  why single out N., 229:1
Negrohood, sobbing school of N.,
  179:1
Neighbor, better is a n. near, 19:6
  gall our haughty n., 86:7
  good n. policy, 519:5
  love thy n. as thyself, 11:4, 30:1
  love thy n., 11:4
  mole don't see what n. doing,
    570:17
  not bear false witness against n.,
    10:8
Neighbor's, shalt not covet n. house,
  10:8
  shalt not covet n. wife, 10:8
Neighborhood after midnight,
  343:2
  girl next door whose n., 502:7
Neighbors, forsake friends n. or die a
  slave, 99:1
  may not impress the n., 181:4
Neither do I condemn thee, 36:4
  the living nor the dead, 349:5
  there nor here then what, 349:5
Nemesis, escape n. of my color,
  183:3
  restlessness is my n., 559:4
Neo-colonialism, British n.
  strangling your countries,
    234:3
  paradox highlights n., 234:2
Neoconservatives are formidable
  adversaries, 246:5
Neo-HooDoo is a Lost American
  Church, 389:2
Neon, screams of your n. name,
  398:3
Nerves, takes n. to stay out there,
  405:3
  you shake my n., 333:6

Nervous, not n. not paying
  attention, 300:8
Nest, jaybird don't rob his own n.,
  570:18
Nests, birds fly from their n., 5:2
Net, kingdom of heaven like a n.,
  28:16
Nettle, beside n. grows cure for its
  sting, 90:5
Neurotics keep from being sane,
  354:3
Neutral is to side with the powerful,
  341:5
  no language is n., 332:3
  race n. means are preferable,
    498:5
  time is n., 316:4
Never accept life's terms, 189:8
  Again, 499:1
  as good as the first time, 516:7
  be white again, 282:7
  buy puss in a bag, 574:9
  could n. happen to someone like
    me, 515:3
  end up a face in the crowd, 485:6
  failed to imitate, 283:5
  forget that I'm Black, 441:4
  get angry get even, 363:5
  get away from the fact, 277:5
  gonna quit, 445:5
  heard a slave say so, 78:7
  I n. had it made, 271:1
  if left to time time will n. come,
    123:8
  lose a thing belongs to you,
    329:1
  lose your head, 186:2
  lost a passenger, 111:4
  made it into the pot, 230:1
  man spake like this man, 36:2
  no more war n. again, 341:3
  paid reparations, 335:1
  received reproaches from masters,
    68:4
  run my train off track, 111:4
  there's n. no in-between, 559:5
  they can n. know you, 304:7
  Wait always meant N., 316:7
New, and a n. earth will rise, 360:5
  Beauty ancient and n., 52:8
  blood of the n. testament, 31:6
  broom sweep clean, 575:16
  cup is n. testament in my blood,
    39:15

New *(continued)*
  danger to hold both old and n.,
    166:5
  Day is always beginning, 432:8
  dress same old broad, 227:6
  dying into that n. life, 291:3
  era of peace, 527:1
  era of responsibility, 527:2
  fight to create the n. man, 351:6
  form old monster will assume,
    106:5
  from root of old a n. one sprung,
    480:8
  Generation Blacks, 410:2
  heaven and n. earth, 45:3
  Jerusalem, 45:3
  Negroes, 210:5
  no n. thing under the sun, 19:12
  nothin' n. white folks still ahead,
    204:7
  person in the Negro, 239:1
  skin old snake will come forth,
    106:5
  society we must create, 242:4
  struggle for n. world, 320:2
  The N. Niggers Are Gays, 240:2
  there arose a n. king over Egypt,
    8:20
  woman has made her bow, 129:5
New Negro, at a loss to account for
  N., 167:6
New Orleans, can't have N. no other
  way, 504:7
  dances of 19th-century N., 389:2
  in N. you're born into music, 411:1
  is the cradle of jazz, 178:2
  Land of Dreams, 177:2
New South, little difference
  Antebellum South N., 138:5
New World, black American culture
  is a N. creation, 534:8
New York, I am n. city, 368:8
  in the streets of N., 75:3
  never did to me in N., 298:4
  not from Africa I'm from N., 501:4
  warn the innocent people of N.,
    503:2
  was heaven, 296:7
New Yorker, you are a N., 553:1
News, Bible says it still is n., 253:7
  I've got n. for them too, 522:6
  tell Tchaikovsky the n., 299:6
Newspaper people smart but I'm
  smarter, 98:2

Next, don't have to live n. to me,
352:5
you're flying among stars, 330:1
Nia purpose, 410:8
Niagara, seen rainbow-crowned N.,
113:1
Niagaras of the little people, 199:2
Nibble the cakes of other folk, 182:7
Nice is such a rip-off, 466:4
starving it's what being n. gets,
551:5
we always do it n. and rough,
399:1
Nickel, can't borrow a n., 326:4
Nickname was Scooter, 257:7
Nigeria, white man created N., 562:5
Nigger, all-American trump card,
549:5
comes to 15 dollars per n., 310:1
Don't Call Me N. Whitey, 435:2
Dutch n. and English in me, 331:6
epithet generates epithets, 497:5
five years CIA n., 327:3
his mind is the n., 343:11
I was a n. for twenty-three years,
402:6
I'm that n. in the alley, 423:5
if a man calls me n., 343:11
immigrants learned n., 249:2
is a slow death, 520:2
is described, 277:3
is destined to remain, 497:6
is word in the English lexicon,
542:5
no amount of political correctness
will remove it, 542:5
nuclear bomb of racial epithets,
549:5
play role of Negro, 357:3
poked out tongue and called me
N., 218:4
poor N. hain't got no home, 569:5
run N. run it's almos' day, 568:11
sing out darkey n., 99:4
the word n., 277:3
they have never called us n., 374:2
treated as a n. in America, 495:4
where I learned I was a n., 428:8
woman mule uh de world, 180:2
Nigger's, where is n. home, 324:5
Niggerization N. doesn't just apply
to black people, 256:1
of black people, 495:7
result of oppression, 256:1

Niggers, black n. my beauty, 359:4
do you see any n., 403:4
happy hewers of wood, 281:3
hear of solitary n., 337:3
holding black back, 277:3
love black people hate n., 544:3
messing with no broke n., 563:3
The New N. Are Gays, 240:2
there's black people and there's n.,
544:3
we either n. or kings, 559:5
white n., 277:3
yaller n. bear the prejudice, 154:3
Night, best time to cry is at n.,
378:8
black as the n. is black, 211:4
by n. in a pillar of fire, 9:15
carried His servant by n., 54:10
coming for us that n., 285:1
coming tenderly, 210:8
covered by a friendly n., 314:5
dark n. of the Past, 123:3
die sweetly in the n., 485:1
has come land is dark, 386:3
hide you in the n., 381:4
is buried under our skins, 440:5
leading me to morning, 283:1
lives in primordial n., 226:3
long n. physical slavery, 320:3
makes day seep into n., 56:7
makes n. seep into day, 56:7
not of n. nor darkness, 41:21
part of the n. before day break,
108:7
rich as n. Afro Blue, 299:8
rock me all n. long, 293:2
the n. is thick, 369:4
there shall be no n., 45:5
they shall eat the flesh in that n.,
9:9
thief in the n., 41:20
this n. thou shalt deny me, 31:7
victims of the n. eternal, 232:8
watch in the n., 17:17
we own the n., 354:4
weeping may endure for a n.,
16:13
Your Boy Friend He Wasn't Last
N., 548:5
Nightgown, floated like a nylon n.,
456:2
Nightmare, I see American n.,
295:3
wake up it's a n., 563:6

Nightmares of shipwrecked bones,
398:5
our n. are tight compacted, 379:3
Nights behind grandmother's porch,
486:6
fasted forty days and forty n.,
26:10
five n. of bleeding, 489:2
forty days and forty n., 10:12
rain was forty days and forty n.,
7:11
southern n., 392:1
Nightsticks, fire hoses and n., 401:1
Nighttime, so black they call me n.,
247:4
Nil tam difficile est quin quaerendo
investigari possiet, 47:n8
Nile, lotus flow'r drinking at the N.,
209:2
mother N. Valley, 279:6
Ninety-Nine and a Half Won't Do,
411:3
Nipples, marquee of false n., 368:8
Nkosi sikelel' iAfrika, 152:2
No America n. jazz, 269:4
better thing under the sun, 20:8
black people we n. know, 386:4
boundary line to art, 273:5
choose none, 576:3
discharge in that war, 20:7
go and sin n. more, 36:4
hell n. we won't go, 292:2
how does one say N. in thunder,
345:5
justice n. peace, 573:12
man hath seen God, 35:9
man might buy or sell, 44:16
more auction block, 578:3
more water fire next time, 284:7
new thing under the sun, 19:12
one goes away and comes back, 1:2
one makes war on anyone, 58:1
one steps outside his territory,
58:1
one who can return from there, 1:1
one will judge me, 51:6
one will speak for us, 564:1
person is left out, 384:7
profit without wisdom, 58:4
ring, 484:1
room in the inn, 33:3
Stoppin' Us Now, 469:2
telephone to heaven, 454:7
there is n. God but He, 54:2

695

Number, I put the n. 39 on my back, 479:2

Lord, I want to be in that n., 577:12

runner is like Santa Claus, 281:2

teach us to n. our days, 17:19

telleth the n. of the stars, 18:10

Numbers, know the meaning of our n., 176:6

Numerous sins, 52:1

Nurtured, race n. in oppression, 113:3

Nuthin' but a G thang, 556:8

N-word, the n. without feeling its sting, 542:5

O

O Beauty ancient and new, 52:8

O.J., please think of the real O., 464:1

Oak, enters like needle spreads like o., 566:2

when you talk to an o. tree, 350:2

Oaths, vain words in your o., 53:11

Obedience, do not hate my o., 50:2

Obedient to thy will, 92:2

Obey cheerfully and freely, 63:6

laws were created to o. men, 424:6

the word, 63:4

while slaves duty to o. masters, 63:6

Object, exploitation against same o. man, 291:2

Objective necessity to o. freedom, 207:3

Objects of satisfaction, 358:1

Obligation, mutual o. to one another, 537:6

Obligations, how far do our o. reach, 522:3

Obliged to leave many friends, 75:2

Obnoxious to white inhabitants, 88:6

Obscure, shadows upon a sea o., 55:8

Observation, function of art is o., 263:4

old o. game, 506:4

Observe has meant remember it, 519:4

Negroes o. everything, 257:3

the opportunity, 25:9

Observer sees them as projections, 207:9

Obstacle, nationalism is o. to peace, 221:1

Obstacles, fight whatever the o., 131:4

more o. than being black, 287:2

no more o. in his path, 193:2

success measured by o. overcome, 132:8

to democracy, 383:6

Obvious, what is o. we turn from with disgust, 68:7

Obviously I'm not white, 289:8

Occupation, tap dancer as my o., 455:6

Ocean falls at your feet, 357:1

I have crossed an o., 480:8

notion to jump into o., 204:2

singing its wild chorus, 113:1

want o. without waters, 105:9

Odds, all the o. against a cruel fate, 163:7

Oestrum, love is the o. of the poet, 66:n1

Off to a bad start, 253:3

Offend, if thy right eye o. thee, 26:14

if thy right hand o. thee, 26:14

Offense, my name an o., 240:5

toward God toward men, 37:19

Offering, a lamb for a burnt o., 8:7

myself to suffer the lash, 98:4

Offerings, burnt o., 24:5

Officer, cursed drunken o., 330:5

Offspring of queens, 441:5

ruler of my o., 49:1

Oh freedom, 577:7

Mary don't you weep, 578:5

no not again, 270:5

Oil, anointest my head with o., 16:10

Ointment, good name better than precious o., 20:2

Okonkwo was well known, 322:7

Old broom know corner best, 575:16

children and o. folks tell the truth, 178:6

danger to hold both o. and new, 166:5

folks always somebody else, 271:6

for I was twenty and very o., 165:3

i too o. to learn of love, 360:1

in a good o. age, 8:3

man a-waitin' to carry you, 576:9

men shall dream dreams, 24:7

my mind feels cycles o., 127:2

never give in to o. age, 399:2

not being o., 433:5

now the world is o. I am young, 165:3

Old (continued)

Virginny, 130:1

when too o. for love, 180:11

when you get real o., 178:6

Older and white and somewhat free, 213:7

de moon brighter it shine, 575:15

people say, 276:2

you get more live in the past, 491:5

Olive, in her mouth was an o. leaf pluckt off, 7:12

land of oil o. and honey, 11:15

tree neither East nor West, 55:7

Oliver walked in and began to talk, 462:6

Olympics, life is the real O., 244:5

Omega, I am Alpha and O., 45:7

Omelet, wrote a good o. after loving you, 432:4

Omnipotence, choral hymn of O., 113:1

Omoro completed the naming ritual, 274:3

On your guard, 50:2

Once, created o. and he was nothing, 55:3

fool me o. shame on you, 572:8

twice three times a lady, 473:2

Once-bold daffodils, 281:1

Once-upon-a-time slaves, 478:3

One, all for o. o. for all, 88:2

among a thousand, 15:21

body part at a time, 275:8

by o. or in fell swoop, 123:8

cease to be o. nation, 371:2

don't care o. straw, 48:7

God created us, 24:16

God o. Aim o. Destiny, 170:5

have we not all o. father, 24:16

heaven o. earth o. queen, 289:3

I can only do o. thing, 300:9

I we all of us are o. and the multitude, 425:7

little o. shall become a thousand, 23:6

Lord our God is o. Lord, 11:12

man among a thousand found, 20:6

more river to cross, 577:6

my first and only o., 247:6

Nation Under Groove, 407:6

old people ask if he's the O., 350:3

people pledging allegiance, 522:6

taken the other left, 30:6

Passing *(continued)*
the love of women, 13:17
Passion, death or pain or any kind of
p., 491:2
divine p. without affection, 64:5
find your p., 500:3
for categorization, 282:8
inclusion is a p., 384:7
of fear hath slain thousands, 67:1
Passions, disgraceful p., 52:1
grabbed my soul, 494:1
man is left only flesh and p., 363:7
Passive group of conspirators, 493:8
Passover, Christ our P. is sacrificed,
39:8
it is the Lord's p., 9:10
Past, accept one's p., 284:2
America is false to the p., 105:1
doll-baby woman thing of the p.,
194:3
drowning in p., 284:2
erase the p. from the present of a
slave, 476:7
future is just more of the p., 518:7
future slavery remembered as p.,
114:1
ghosts of the p., 304:2
harvest is p., 23:11
I live the p. as if it is the present,
356:4
invented p., 284:2
is a mirror, 108:2
is best forgotten, 267:7
is now then, 472:10
it's p. due, 198:1
just came up and kicked me, 535:7
let us shut door on p., 342:3
made to touch my p. at an early
age, 470:5
more a favor than desire to revisit
her p., 509:2
my childish joys are p., 110:1
my days are p., 15:11
necessary to man as roots to tree,
162:5
Negro must remake his p., 152:3
no perfect p. to go back to, 407:8
older you get more live in the p.,
491:5
on one side future on the other,
496:7
one must begin with p., 253:1
present was an egg laid by the p.,
180:13

Past *(continued)*
promotes reconciliation peace,
267:7
recovery of the p., 344:1
shadows of the p., 304:2
so we rely on the p., 516:7
something to leave behind, 339:1
the p. is tense the future perfect,
561:6
the P. was forgotten, 123:3
too many scars from the p., 486:4
useful to present and future, 104:7
we are heirs of a p., 135:4
we possess the p., 273:2
what has been said in the p., 1:3
Pastime, rape is a national p., 457:2
studying for survival the only p.,
490:9
Pastures, lie down in green p., 16:10
Pat, eighteen inches between a p. and
a kick, 192:1
Path, another case about the wrong
p., 543:1
departure from accepted p., 251:1
direct us in the right p., 53:7
followed p. of their ancestors, 60:2
great rock across our p., 281:5
lead them in p. of virtue, 75:1
no more obstacles in his p., 193:2
of a more perfect union, 525:2
to a more perfect union, 525:3
to more knowledge, 255:8
Pathology, fakelore of black p., 257:2
Paths, aimless goat p., 337:6
make his p. straight, 26:6
no p. in water no signposts,
513:4
of righteousness, 16:10
Pathway, learning to read the p. to
freedom, 104:2
of human bones, 251:3
Pathways, god of p., 325:1
Patience and forbearance of the
poor, 208:1
blest with a p. not yet known,
171:2
for today, 139:6
has its limits, 409:9
is a dirty word, 400:5
is a visit from another age, 397:5
nothing to lose but p., 385:4
of Job, 43:5
sadistic p., 412:5
tested in our p., 133:2

Patient, Black people to be p., 437:2
most p. of all people, 270:5
we cannot be p., 400:5
we will not and cannot be p., 400:6
you are a p. people, 100:6
Patmos, isle called P., 43:16
Patois, in Antillean p., 332:4
of furious rains, 369:7
Patriarchal, no freedom for p. men,
488:4
Patriarchs, absolute power for p.,
488:4
black male p., 488:3
Patriarchy, sexual politics under p.
pervasive, 573:14
Patriotism, blind with p., 297:4
confidence in p. of people, 126:1
response to p., 125:3
Patriots, murderers don't turn into
p., 137:5
Pattern after pine tree, 179:5
of foam like a broken zip, 532:3
Patterns, figure out the p., 553:4
historical p. isolation, 335:2
Paul said But I was free born, 37:15
son of a Pharisee, 37:18
thou art beside thyself, 38:1
Pauper, free p. than rich slave, 316:1
Paws, white tiger's pink p., 199:4
Pay, if you can't p. you can't have,
129:2
me my money down, 572:9
people p. for what they do, 285:2
us all they owe us, 198:1
Paycheck, we bring more than a p.,
453:5
Paying, ain't p. that price, 298:3
the cost to be the boss, 293:3
Peace, all men should live in p., 272:5
and blessings manifest, 554:6
and happiness for every man,
405:4
and love on this planet, 518:6
be to this house, 33:13
bias for p., 220:1
body and soul together in p., 369:3
can't separate p. from freedom,
297:3
crust eaten in p., 46:1
dominates war, 519:3
dream of everlasting p, 183:6
exhaust every recourse to save p.,
221:2
follow things which make p., 39:1

Peace *(continued)*
  for all, 267:1
  from men's hearts, 293:7
  give p. in our day, 70:2
  goddamned p., 420:10
  has no parade, 383:4
  his name shall be Prince of P., 22:3
  hold their p., 34:17
  I give unto you, 36:17
  I leave with you, 36:17
  in Africa our contribution to p.,
    197:4
  in our time a world at p., 220:2
  in the valley, 201:2
  in time of p. and war, 172:9
  it's wonderful, 163:2
  live better and in p., 285:8
  live with each other in p., 320:8
  means justice, 499:3
  missiles called p. keepers, 536:7
  nationalism is obstacle to p., 221:1
  new era of p., 527:2
  no justice no p., 366:8, 573:12
  no p. because no justice, 341:7
  of p. there shall be no end, 22:3
  on earth, 33:5
  past which promotes p., 267:7
  people speak words of p., 322:1
  progress and liberty, 423:7
  quest for p., 473:9
  social p. through social justice,
    535:1
  there is no p., 22:17
  threat to international p., 245:4
  thy servant depart in p., 33:6
  time of p., 19:17
  to him far and near, 23:4
  ushering in new era of p., 527:1
  want p. got to fight for it, 420:10
  what hast thou to do with p.,
    14:7
  when there is no peace, 23:9
  when we say P. on earth, 374:4
Peaceably, live p. with men, 38:20
Peaceful, afford a safe and p. retreat,
    70:2
Peak, at the p. no movement, 269:8
  want to go out in my p., 563:9
Peaked, but have I p. yet, 563:9
Pearl, plant your flower grow a p.,
    414:5
Pearls, cast p. before swine, 27:6
  teach children their minds are p.,
    410:2

Pears, cocoa pods and alligator p.,
    175:5
Peas an' Rice an' Coconut Oil, 575:3
Peasant that reads is prince in
    waiting, 491:4
Peasants accept will of the gods as
    theirs, 291:4
Pebble, I am a Rock you are a p.,
    555:2
Pecola having father's baby, 336:6
Peculiar, ain't that p., 397:1
  feel p. living as they do, 371:5
  slavery the p. institution, 106:5
Peculiarly necessary to comfort and
    safety, 88:6
Peek, want a p. at the back, 258:10
Pegs, life neatly fitted into p., 282:8
Pen and ink of selfhood, 320:3
  books p. ink paper not allowed,
    98:6
  brothers in the p., 556:2
  no p. can express horrors of
    Slavery, 98:5
Pendulum, time is a p., 210:1
Pennsylvania, small towns in P.,
    525:4
Peonage, emancipated from p., 171:4
People, advancement of free colored
    p., 96:1
  advancing when respect
    education, 109:2
  afraid of certain p., 252:4
  all p. and tongues, 44:10
  All Power to the P., 573:4
  are surprised, 242:1
  are ultimate source of power,
    573:1
  arose as one man, 12:18
  bear all they can, 302:1
  between white and colored p.,
    106:3
  black p. are an African p., 414:1
  black p. around white p., 520:1
  black p. catch it, 353:6
  black p. magical faces, 324:1
  black p. we no know, 386:4
  bugs p. especially white, 301:2
  can't mingle with p., 252:4
  cared enough to help me, 303:8
  chosen to be special p., 11:13
  colored p. don't want me either,
    289:8
  colored p. understand white p.,
    147:4

People *(continued)*
  coloured p. most degraded since
    world began, 77:4
  confidence in destiny of my p.,
    125:2
  dance delivered back to the p.,
    332:7
  dead haven't been buried, 164:4
  descendants of a suffering p., 170:7
  do not buy liberty at the market,
    493:3
  do not choose rebellion, 289:1
  don't trust reactions, 326:10
  dwell among mine own p., 123:4
  dying into that new life, 291:3
  finally included in We the P.,
    371:1
  future of my p., 115:5
  get ready, 422:6
  God changes not p. until they
    change, 54:6
  god damn white p. anyway, 238:1
  gods behave like p., 180:8
  grudge what they cannot enjoy,
    46:5
  hear now this foolish p., 23:8
  I am everyday p., 435:1
  I am the candidate of the p., 287:5
  I got it from the p., 398:1
  I see all types of p., 403:4
  I think what the p. will say, 4:3
  in those skins, 271:2
  informed p. will do the right thing,
    421:3
  judging p. on content of character,
    530:2
  landless p. dependent on landed
    p., 114:7
  leader and commander to the p.,
    23:3
  less advanced in refinement, 95:6
  let my p. go, 9:4, 576:10
  like being p., 394:5
  like p. like priest, 24:2
  listen to the p. talking, 567:6
  love black p. hate niggers, 544:3
  magic lingering after p., 443:7
  merit the fate of ungrateful p.,
    73:4
  monsters we make of p., 553:3
  most patient of all p., 270:5
  music of a peasant p., 173:4
  my p. my p., 181:2
  negative images of black p., 508:9

People *(continued)*

newspaper p. smart but I'm smarter, 98:2

not fighting for ideas, 285:8

nothing could destroy a p., 255:3

of Black Metropolis, 235:5

of Ethiopia were chosen, 59:2

of Israel were rejected, 59:2

oppressed p. in South Africa, 264:5

out of Common P. rise sources of art, 166:3

paper pen knife and some p. to kill, 552:5

passing ending of p. dying, 291:3

pay for what they do, 285:2

picture of the p. in glory, 521:2

power of the p., 351:7

racism does to young p., 332:8

rainbow p. of God, 342:2

refuse to see me, 247:7

rob colored p. of their money, 233:1

secondarily as colored p., 207:5

see you so call you lazy, 321:8

shouted great shout, 12:9

signs for god-fearing p., 54:3

Socialist Tribunes of all the p., 482:6

song of the p., 444:2

soul is to feel oneness with black p., 368:3

start running four ways, 290:1

suffer and are without soul, 444:2

that oppresses another p., 293:5

there's black p. and there's niggers, 544:3

they are p. not commas, 208:7

they say the p. could fly, 370:6

they will come out as Black p., 474:4

thy p. shall be my p., 12:20

traitors even among colored p., 96:4

trapped in history, 282:6

used to white p. by 1948, 490:5

visited and redeemed his p., 33:1

waging war in the streets, 490:1

want from black artists the exotic, 548:8

what p. want is simple, 371:3

what p. would reap fruits of our labors, 73:3

what shall we do with the white p., 107:6

People *(continued)*

where no vision p. perish, 19:8

white p. are White Americans, 79:4

white p. talk of black p., 107:6

who have to die, 289:5

who remained unnoticed, 86:3

will never fight for your freedom, 240:1

will try to be what other p. are, 505:2

with african imaginations, 354:6

witness to the p., 23:3

world needs p. who have come alive, 203:6

you are a patient p., 100:6

People's art is the genesis, 254:4

other p. money, 112:2

votes p. guns inseparable twins, 288:3

Peoples, all p. in the same boat, 185:5

God accepted the p. cast away, 59:2

problem confronting colored p., 193:4

Pepper, salt and p. what it should be, 222:6

Perambulator every morning, 387:2

Perfect, absolute idea of p. harmony, 116:5

being is complete p., 302:3

her vision of the p. slave, 394:8

his vision of the p. woman, 394:8

his work is p., 12:4

kept from the p. thing, 151:1

love casteth out fear, 43:15

no p. past to go back to, 407:8

strength p. in weakness, 41:2

Perform, do not p. more than ordered, 1:6

the deeds, 253:2

Performers taking our hearts, 520:3

Perfume, happiness is a p., 170:2

Perfumed, pages p. with music, 226:1

Periculum ex aliis facito tibi quod ex usu siet, 47:*n7*

Perish, black folk p. America will p., 231:2

his name shall not p., 2:7

money p. with thee, 37:10

one of thy members should p., 26:14

take the sword p. the sword, 31:12

where no vision people p., 19:8

Perish *(continued)*

whosoever believeth should not p., 35:18

Perished, weapons of war p., 13:17

who ever p. innocent, 15:2

Permanent, issue is whether freedom can be p., 103:4

Permit no man to degrade soul, 132:9

Permits another the keys to his destiny, 202:4

Permitted, see what we're p. to see, 459:4

Perpetual childlike state, 551:4

Perplexed but not in despair, 40:10

Persecute, despitefully use and p. you, 27:1

when men revile and p. you, 26:12

Persecuted but not forsaken, 40:10

for righteousness's sake, 26:12

Persecution by secular authority, 299:4

more hateful in United States capital, 140:7

Perseverance, SAT tests do not measure p., 366:3

tested in our p., 133:2

Person can run for years, 322:3

is shiftless lazy, 277:3

little p. to stir up great events, 472:6

no p. is left out, 384:7

over-loving gentle p., 277:8

turn up noses near colored p., 99:4

was I same p. now I was free, 111:3

who seizes two things, 564:8

Personal, success is merely p., 443:7

Personality, distortion of p., 228:7

every gift has p. of its giver, 447:6

regaining historical p., 286:1

Person-oriented society, 319:9

Persons, God is no respecter of p., 37:12

neither p. nor property safe, 107:2

Perspective, tell our story from our p., 461:4

Perspirations, copious p., 69:3

Persuaded in his own mind, 38:24

Perversities, tales told of strange p., 212:1

Petals, flower with p. of blood, 388:4

pressed of forget, 281:1

Peter, thou art P., 29:8

Plant a tree that bears fruit, 532:6
clear out poverty p. new life, 227:1
the seed and pick the fruit, 410:1
time to p., 19:17
women to p. roots of progress, 114:5
Plantation, freedom of every slave on every p., 92:5
marketable as pigs on the p., 95:2
slave and p. describe state of mind, 480:9
still working on a p., 254:2
Plantations, going in chains to p., 308:7
slaves poured from p., 260:7
Planted, I have plowed and p., 82:6
myself inside you, 451:7
your corn, 292:3
Planting, who is going to do the p., 417:1
Plate, with nothing on my p., 295:2
Plateau, barren p. of truth, 258:4
Platter, never handed over on a silver p., 233:5
Play, don't p. what public wants, 263:7
games black folk p. on one another, 546:4
like you p., 219:5
my horn, 300:9
something for me Berniece, 451:10
something sweet, 391:7
teach us old ones how to p., 430:7
what we p. is life, 204:6
your own way, 263:7
Played the fool, 13:14
Players in this drama, 208:7
time fool has learned game p. dispersed, 565:13
Playing, bop is like p. Scrabble, 201:6
Plead, ask no favors but p. for justice, 101:6
case before whites, 89:4
for the widow, 21:17
our own cause, 80:1
Pleasant, in a p. place, 50:2
many are the p. forms which exist, 52:1
Please, always trying to p. us back, 444:6
baby baby baby p., 508:5
expected to p. other people, 494:3
not to p. ourselves, 39:2
send me someone to love, 273:3

Pleased, God is p. for her to dwell, 59:2
Pleasing God is all God care about, 444:6
Pleasure, created for thy p., 44:4
dissipate in p. and riot, 109:1
I have no p. in them, 20:11
indulge every p., 257:8
of my company, 179:4
same ol danger brand new p., 430:2
turn their boredom into p. for yourself, 471:8
Pleasures, fleeting p., 52:1
tales told of dangerous p., 212:1
Pledge from this day forward, 349:3
to Americans black and white, 160:7
Pledging allegiance to stars and stripes, 522:6
Plot, tending the family p., 234:9
Plow, keep hands on the p., 261:4
one thing for something else to grow, 350:6
Plowed, I have p. and planted, 82:6
Plowing, want crops without p., 105:9
Plowshares, beat swords into p., 22:1
Pluck it out and cast from thee, 26:14
the man and boy apart, 158:4
time to p. up, 19:17
Pluckt, in her mouth was an olive leaf p. off, 7:12
Plug in turn on cop out, 474:1
Plume, shake the painted p., 71:6
Plumes, borrowed p., 46:2
eagle's own p., 47:1
Plush safe he think, 517:5
Plymouth Rock, we didn't land on P., 295:1
Pocket, dig into my p., 540:4
God in my p., 544:9
Poem, dignity in writing p., 131:6
do not resist this p., 388:6
I woodah write a p., 489:6
only p. you will hear, 385:7
Poems I do in the dark, 372:1
Poet and Giant wander on, 391:2
Feminist Warrior P. Mother, 359:1
imitate verses I would become a p., 82:3
is not a jukebox, 250:2

Poet (continued)
love is the oestrum of the p., 66:n1
religion could not produce a p., 66:n1
should stand at center of drum, 381:2
we did and I the p. still do, 353:8
whispers in our dreams, 358:6
Poetic irony of race relations, 246:3
Poetry, among the blacks is not p., 66:n1
blues as much social reference as p., 354:2
if worth its salt, 331:5
is music's twin, 381:2
is one of the realities that persist, 158:2
men pass hand to mouth, 331:5
only way to get from here to there, 531:8
rap is rhythm and p., 541:2
say something that is p., 481:3
That Is Ultimately Perhaps Beautiful, 484:7
we cry our cry of p., 310:4
what you find in the dirt, 531:8
what you overhear on the bus, 531:8
Poet's head full with double-entendres, 398:4
Poets, grew up among p., 322:4
Who Think African-American P., 484:7
Point out my defects, 125:6
Tipping P., 533:7
Pointed the way to the Promised Land, 524:1
Poison is the wind that blows, 396:6
potent p. of your hate, 175:9
smack junk snow p., 370:2
Poisoned, America's soul p., 319:8
blood of both, 330:5
by British education, 207:2
Maria Godunov and son p. themselves, 86:2
Polar bears and poor kids too, 548:1
Polaroid, shake it like a P. picture, 560:2
Pole, like the p. vaulter begins his run, 269:8
Police, all children should feel protected by p., 559:1
always come late if at all, 536:6

Police *(continued)*
  brutality, 317:9
  inna Inglan gat liesense fi kill,
    489:7
Policemen denied daily quota, 332:6
Policy, good neighbor p., 519:5
Polished piano with her tears, 451:10
  she cleaned p. and prayed over it,
    451:10
Political, challenge for p. prisoner,
    267:3
  color is a p. reality, 284:6
  decisions made with the bullet,
    446:2
  driven by p. demagogues, 132:5
  every Black man woman prisoner
    a p. prisoner, 461:5
  exercise of p. rights, 132:5
  history otherwise, 249:1
  Negro never eliminated as p.
    factor, 128:2
  not candidate of p. bosses, 287:5
  position of stars, 493:5
  win every p. office, 262:5
Politically disinherited face, 202:2
Politician, I am not a p., 289:4
Politics desire to satisfy basic needs,
    425:3
  do well in ethics not p., 93:4
  for creative individual, 255:9
  not engaged in domestic p., 171:3
  of culture, 255:9
  sexual p. pervasive, 573:14
  sexual p., 491:9
Polls, kept from the p. by ruffians,
    128:2
Polluted mainstream of
    Americanism, 342:6
Pomegranate, sweet p. wine, 3:4
Pomegranates, land of p., 11:15
Pone's, de co'n p. hot, 149:6
Poor, Ah sees rich men n p. men,
    230:8
  and black and shut out, 238:4
  be a Negro than a p. white man,
    569:4
  best for the p. is not to be one,
    365:6
  can't give nothing away if you p.,
    436:9
  don't rest nor permitted
    relaxation, 242:6
  expensive to be p., 283:6
  fill p. man's dinner pail, 142:2

Poor *(continued)*
  giveth unto the p., 19:7
  gon be p. all yuh life, 321:8
  I am the p. the hungry, 479:1
  is a state of mind, 343:6
  leave for the p. and stranger, 11:3
  man I ain't p., 436:9
  man to get in heaven, 365:5
  man's wife is starvin', 188:2
  money for wars but can't feed p.,
    556:4
  parish of the p., 493:1
  patience and forbearance of the p.,
    208:1
  race in a land of dollars, 143:7
  rich and p., 64:2
  rich rob p. and p. rob one another,
    84:2
  rich today p. tomorrow, 66:4
  rob not the p., 18:24
  save polar bears and p. kids too,
    548:1
  shall never cease out of land, 12:2
  sold the p. for a pair of shoes, 24:8
  well dressed does not prevent
    being p., 565:9
  when p. you are despised, 565:20
  ye have the p. always, 30:13
Popcorn, 389:2
Position for women in SNCC is
    prone, 413:6
  maintain p. at any cost, 383:6
  of people condition of females,
    94:2
  political p. of stars, 493:5
Positive Black images, 265:6
Possess spirit of independence, 89:2
Possessing, having nothing yet p. all,
    40:13
Possession, deliverance in our p.,
    252:6
  found in p. of women slaves, 1:4
  is hanging up the nation, 364:1
  it is Seth who would take p., 3:1
  of rights as men and citizens, 79:3
  over judgment day, 236:7
Possessions, having no p. I possessed
    all, 425:8
Possessiveness, same p. as love, 375:6
Possibility, sweet p. never quite
    maturing, 431:9
Possible, being a star made it p. to
    get insulted, 289:9
  show a faith in what's p., 505:1

Possible *(continued)*
  without faith nothing is p., 153:4
Post Traumatic Slave Syndrome,
    506:1
Post-black was the new black, 541:4
Postman, wait a minute Mr. P.,
    408:4
Post-racial society, 530:2
Pot calling the kettle black, 238:8,
    570:10
  great melting p., 230:1
  ha'd to giggle when nuffin' in the
    p., 150:6
  Negro never made it into p., 230:1
Potential, harnessing black p., 255:10
  of what is feared, 361:8
Pots, licked out all the p., 181:8
Pottage, bread and p. of lentils,
    147:n1
Potter's field, 31:13
Pound, top dog everybody want you
    in the p., 533:6
Pour too much cream in it, 294:6
Poverty and dysfunction traced to
    difficult history, 530:1
  complicated as high finance, 272:2
  easy burden to eliminate p., 346:8
  gave me my name, 218:6
  give me p. nor riches, 19:9
  in liberty, 278:4
  rather die in p., 316:1
  simply lack of funds, 272:2
  smells of death, 180:9
  take your p. give you prosperity,
    163:3
  where p. is enforced, 107:2
  world's biggest killer is extreme p.,
    424:n2
Poverty-stricken, spiritually p. as the
    world, 167:1
Powder, white p. looked innocent,
    370:2
Power, afraid of my p., 50:2
  all in my p. while life and strength
    last, 123:1
  become glorious in p., 10:2
  becoming the p. is better, 471:3
  black access to p., 366:1
  black p. is the brain p., 230:5
  can lead to freedom can be
    destructive, 153:3
  concedes nothing without
    demand, 106:1
  desire of those in p., 383:6

Power *(continued)*

enduring p. of our ideals, 526:3

faith in each other that is our p., 529:5

humans create, 353:5

ignorance allied with p., 285:3

in communities, 549:6

in face of more power, 297:5

in your hands, 181:10

is ours, 567:14

it does not matter who is in p., 155:4

little that lies in my p., 123:1

measured by shiny illusion of cars, 429:1

money p. luxury like that, 354:3

never takes a back step, 297:5

no p. over benefit, 54:1

of deliverance, 252:6

of millions of voices for change, 523:8

of oppressor rests on submission of the people, 424:7

of redemptive suffering, 299:4

our p. is p. of the people, 351:7

people are ultimate source of p., 573:1

productive p. of modern times, 242:4

protection against Injustice is P., 172:3

race oppressed by p., 113:3

relationship between athletes and owners, 480:9

resistance paralyzed p., 319:6

seek black p., 230:4

sent forth from p., 48:15

spit truth to p., 510:2

structure of the art world, 204:1

tested in our p. to endure, 133:2

thine is the p. and the glory, 27:2

to build black institutions, 230:4

to control our own lives, 369:1

to make things right, 186:8

to tear from cradle and sell, 112:1

to the People, 573:3

transform p. into justice, 522:3

we have the p., 186:8

we have to build our p., 262:5

We Want P. to Determine the Destiny, 426:1

white man's p. to enslave, 104:2

whites seeking p. and authority, 78:2

Power *(continued)*

world respects p., 153:3

zig-zag lightning of p., 181:10

Powerful and powerless, 383:2

black is p., 214:2

capitulation to the p., 202:3

language of the p., 372:6

love the most p. emotion, 340:4

nobody's as p. as we make them, 443:1

when I dare to be p., 358:4

Powerless, incomprehensible that government is p., 208:8

powerful and p., 383:2

Powers, fight the p. that be, 518:4

of our own mind, 125:4

Practical man your fate is here, 214:1

Practice, democratic principle and p., 498:6

in daily life the virtues, 163:5

Practices which violate principles, 280:2

Praesentia animi, 48:*n*3

Praise be to God, 53:7

if there be any p., 41:13

leader on whom blame or p. falls, 84:4

let us p. famous men, 25:15

me point out my defects, 125:6

song walking forward, 532:2

tossing coins in p., 174:8

Praised, the Lord's name is to be p., 18:4

weaknesses overlooked, 132:7

Pray, and he did not p., 388:2

don't p. when it rains, 224:5

for only one thing, 273:7

for rain deal with mud, 575:6

for them which despitefully use you, 27:1

for them which persecute you, 27:1

I will p., 578:2

pass not away I p. thee, 8:5

to gods when times hard, 291:4

watch and p., 31:9

we can p. about it, 374:4

without ceasing, 42:2

Prayed, as any blessing ever p. for, 475:3

to God to learn me to read, 80:4

Prayer, devoting time to fasting and p., 87:4

for deliverance, 104:1

Prayer *(continued)*

for mothers 'neath the shadows, 115:9

house of p., 29:19

in the arms of p. and faith, 72:3

of chicken hawk does not get chicken, 564:13

Prayers, no whispered p., 480:2

praying their p., 255:1

Praying, mother's p. was theater, 490:2

their prayers, 255:1

what's the use of p., 115:4

Preach about being single, 514:11

can't p. if don't know what folk saying, 362:7

gospel to every creature, 32:16

if man may p. why not woman, 76:6

we can p. about it, 374:4

Preacher, devil is an old p., 71:1

now black is the p. shouted, 248:4

quoting Negro slave p., 316:3

Precinct, whose p. We have blessed, 54:10

Precious as gold and unused chances, 463:1

can't stop now P., 481:2

in God's sight, 410:4

invisible and p. and only herself, 546:*n*1

liberty equally p. to Black as to white, 70:5

take my hand p. Lord, 200:9

Predictable, if free you are not p., 373:1

Preferable, time before is preferable and good, 540:1

Preference indicating one's color p., 246:7

Preferred, many p. before me, 97:7

Pregnant, if men could get p., 256:2

Prejudice, act as if p. did not exist, 159:6

against color is the question, 79:5

allied hosts of p., 104:6

avoiding race p., 159:6

bigotry and p. are winning, 498:2

blinded by p., 133:8

cast down thorn of p., 190:5

color p. creates attitudes, 184:6

hostages to p., 421:3

if p. could reason, 162:7

Prejudice (*continued*)
  ignorance and p. belong to slavery, 75:4
  in free society during slavery, 120:4
  in hopes p. was not in this land, 569:12
  inoculate victims against own p., 497:4
  is like the atmosphere, 84:3
  is to blame, 498:2
  leak caused by color p., 185:5
  live down the p. crush it out, 133:8
  pride of race antidote for p., 152:3
  problem of p. moral dilemma, 316:5
  race proscribed by p., 113:3
  responsible for color p., 166:4
  the floating wreckage of slavery, 146:7
Prejudiced against colored man, 110:2
  assassin, 186:8
Prejudices, free men from our p., 189:15
  give time to get over p., 123:8
  throw away fears and p., 78:4
Preordained, journey towards a p. time, 56:7
Preparation, life requires p., 141:8
Prepare bread and mind, 51:4
  himself to battle, 40:1
  I go to p. a place, 36:13
  the way of the Lord, 26:6
  thrifty to p. today, 46:6
  ye the way of the Lord, 22:13
Prepared, food p. by Negro mothers, 229:3
  ideal for which I am p. to die, 266:5
  to die before you can live, 278:2
  to fight for freedom, 240:1
Preparest a table before me, 16:10
Prerequisite of exploitation, 278:5
Prescribed the remedy Racial Solidarity, 165:6
Prescription, can't write a p., 252:3
  their p. Class Solidarity, 165:6
Presence, dark foreign p., 324:2
  in the p. of mine enemies, 16:10
  of mind, 48:8
Present, absent in body p. in spirit, 39:7
  America is false to the p., 105:1

Present (*continued*)
  erase the past from the p. of a slave, 476:7
  I live the past as if it is the p., 356:4
  one cannot begin with p., 253:1
  past useful to p. and future, 104:7
  the p. had the future inside, 180:13
  was an egg laid by the past, 180:13
  will be a now then, 472:10
  with a p. mind, 47:n3
Present-day white majority, 275:2
Presented unto him gifts, 26:1
Preservation of books, 109:3
  of freedom, 64:3
Preserve, consume rather than p., 362:6
  for future reference, 125:5
  republican institutions, 125:3
  us from such things, 60:2
Preserved rights of nature, 66:1
Preserving and promoting these interests, 168:5
President, being p. reveals who you are, 538:4
  Dear Mr. P. despite bombings, 245:5
  who the fake p., 355:4
Presidents, get some dead p., 540:4
Press forward at all times, 230:7
Pressed petals of forget, 281:1
  to the wall, 175:4
Pressure, dignity under any p., 267:4
Pretend, Let's P. and we did, 353:8
  lizard cannot p. to be a boa, 567:3
  Ph.D. in How to P. You Don't Mind but I do mind, 484:2
  someone died p. hasn't happened, 550:5
  to read God's mind, 181:6
Pretend-to-be-cats don't seem to know, 555:3
Pretty as a picture, 519:1
  sex object if p., 430:8
Prevail, gates of hell shall not p., 29:8
Prevent, powerless to p. abuse, 208:8
Prevented men from believing, 54:14
Prey in hands of white race, 196:4
  lion that roars catches no p., 565:12
Price and promise of citizenship, 527:2
  dignity at any p., 267:4
  for oppression of the Negro, 316:5
  for ticket to become white, 285:6

Price (*continued*)
  of hating is loving less, 362:3
  of its own destruction, 316:5
  of liberty paid in full, 572:1
  of repression, 144:8
  of truth has become murder, 446:2
  of wisdom above rubies, 15:18
  paying p. for belonging, 298:3
  that must be paid, 252:5
  we've got to pay, 408:3
  weighed for my p., 24:14
Priceless, Mama said I'm p., 551:5
Pricks, needle that p. at both ends, 567:2
Pride, curse my p., 50:2
  failure not prick its p., 322:9
  goeth before destruction, 18:19
  in its own history, 295:10
  love is stronger than p., 517:2
  naked p. against myself, 225:3
  of motherhood, 438:2
  of race, 144:7
  of race antidote for prejudice, 152:3
  sacrifice his p. for his people's, 353:6
  victim of its lusts and p., 101:2
  wounded p. in asking for money, 153:7
Priest, every artist a p., 389:3
  he is the Pillar-of-his-Mother p., 3:1
  like people like p., 24:2
  revilest God's high p., 37:17
Priests stood firm on dry ground, 12:7
Prince, black shining P., 261:2
  Blessed P., 355:3
  of Peace, 22:3
  peasant that reads is p. in waiting, 491:4
Princes, fall like one of the p., 17:13
  put not your trust in p., 18:9
  shall come out of Egypt, 17:9
  under Emperors Kings and P., 72:5
Principal, wisdom is the p. thing, 18:13
Principle, democratic p. and practice, 498:6
  in soul makes man woman, 90:2
Principles emerge badly cracked, 157:1
  practices which violate p., 280:2

Printed, my words p. in a book, 15:13

Prison bars to our souls, 186:4
born black skin born in p., 294:3
cannot be victorious, 425:4
chattering wagtails of Mikuyu P., 439:6
emerge from p. undiminished, 267:3
grind in the p. house, 12:16
how to survive p. intact, 267:3
I was in p. and ye came, 30:11
in p. studying for survival, 490:9
is death by inches minutes hours days, 415:4
men were glad to go to p., 370:3
prepared for p., 409:8
the air in p. is different, 539:8
time a metaphorical death, 415:4
what for Americans keep us in p., 118:2

Prisoner, challenge for every p., 267:3
every Black man woman p. a political p., 461:5
love can set p. free, 81:5

Prisoner's life enclosed within parenthesis, 415:4

Prisoners cannot enter into contracts, 266:7
of hope, 24:13
seemed happy, 370:3
take no p., 383:9

Prisons designed to break human beings, 437:4
sea-shell p., 379:3

Private, genitals public other parts p., 531:4
satisfy their p. interests, 371:2

Privilege, black access to p., 366:1
freedom is a p., 65:7
no greater higher p., 90:4
table of p., 492:4
this privacy p. breached, 416:1
to be purchased, 286:7
to stand here has been won, 410:5
which nothing else can equal, 65:7

Privileged and humiliated, 383:2
cannot tremble, 321:5
free the p. white, 246:3
inhabitants, 383:7

Privileges, depend on others never obtain p., 155:4
enjoying the same, 74:3

Privileges (continued)
of citizenship enjoyed, 228:6
share equal p., 76:5
sue for rights and p., 89:2
university education one of p., 178:1

Prize, but one receiveth the p., 39:12
highest p. at parish fairs, 175:5
keep your eyes on the p., 572:11
love your heart the p., 338:9

Prizes to boys with blue eyes, 300:10

Problem, Caucasian p. is real and universal, 193:4
disinherited face is survival possible, 202:2
in common rather than life in common, 168:1
Negro P., 256:4
Negro p. rather than Negro known, 167:5
no p. of human relations is insoluble, 220:1
of prejudice moral dilemma, 316:5
of the broken covenant, 482:7
part of solution or of p., 362:5
wasn't a p. until Iowa, 549:1
whites have the p., 289:2
you were solution p., 339:1

Problematic, an dat is p., 489:5

Problems, consciousness of the p., 208:2
in midst of life p., 252:6
inherit the p., 231:7
know what human p. are, 252:3
law of life that p. arise, 240:3
Mo Money Mo P., 557:3
solutions to our p. come from us, 401:4
solving p. it creates, 241:6

Process of people finding themselves, 207:6

Proclamation to make war against us, 108:7

Prodded into needless war, 220:5

Prodigal, before your presence a p., 345:2
son wasted his substance, 34:9
you feel p., 200:2

Produce, they raise p. we consume it, 93:5

Producers, white are p. we are consumers, 93:5

Product of slaves, 441:5

Profane, cannot believe history sacred or p., 77:5
heights of Itoko, 361:7

Profess not knowledge thou hast not, 25:7
to believe men love one another, 105:4

Profiling, racial p. program, 559:1

Profit, does it p. a man to vote, 427:7
it will not p. you, 2:4
no p. without wisdom, 58:4
riches will not p., 1:6
seldom loses, 287:4

Profited, for what is a man p., 29:10

Profiteth, flesh p. nothing, 35:24

Profits, who p. by our dreams, 189:11

Progress, achieve our own p., 286:2
community p. result from individuals, 157:2
democratic principle a work in p., 498:6
does require us to act in our time, 529:3
governments follow p., 129:3
in changing attitudes to race, 530:2
international p. results by nations, 157:2
is painful, 130:7
little p. in knowledge, 75:4
little p. toward human brotherhood, 220:4
measure p. in how far we have to go, 270:4
Negro can attain p., 239:2
never rolls on wheels, 317:2
no struggle no p., 105:9, 495:*n1*
peace p. and liberty, 423:7
quiet force of p., 527:2
real p. is growth, 135:3
revolutions create p., 232:6
story of human p., 527:6
through education and industry, 572:2
tolerance is a work in p., 459:5
voice of protesting minority moves p., 129:3
we have made little p., 111:6
what we designate as p., 324:2
women to plant roots of p., 114:5
work for the p. of humanity, 157:2

Projections of the sub-soil, 207:9

Racial *(continued)*

insults, 497:5

mark of r. inferiority, 185:8

move beyond old r. wounds, 525:2

neither geographical nor r. lines, 173:3

nuclear bomb of r. epithets, 549:5

oppression of black people, 379:6

profiling program, 559:1

redesigned r. caste, 545:9

signposts, 497:7

snake pit of r. hatred, 458:8

Solidarity, 165:6

terror is an acknowledgment, 361:8

until r. discrimination made criminal, 234:4

Racism and sexism are not genetic, 368:4

beneficiaries of reverse r., 297:9

creates our condition, 289:2

dying hand of r., 380:2

easy burden to eliminate r., 346:8

form of psychosis, 353:6

hurts and inconveniences, 428:2

is a bitch, 403:3

is a disease, 246:4

is entirely made by people, 428:2

is invisible, 287:3

let r. be someone else's burden, 380:2

liberation from the system of r., 393:6

never excuse for not doing your best, 428:4

regret the discomfort your r. is causing me, 465:7

roots of r. deep, 320:11

tears down insides, 332:8

through silence allow r. to continue, 493:8

triplets of r., 319:9

truth about r. in South Africa, 265:2

victims of white r., 297:9

wait for r. to be obliterated, 457:1

whiplash of r., 310:3

will not bow down to r., 427:1

Racist, at the hands of a r. society, 424:5

don't want to see because are r., 492:2

never believe white people aren't r., 457:3

Racist *(continued)*

system destroys human beings, 246:1

white minority r. rule, 266:6

world no longer r. or sexist, 488:4

Racists, are there black r., 389:5

Radiation hits the children before conceived, 453:5

Radio, Can't Live Without My R., 548:3

jazz r. on midnight kick, 293:1

Rag, American flag a dirty r. to Negro, 122:4

Rage and tears, 47:*n3*

die from r. or someone else's, 503:1

Raging, strong drink is r., 18:22

Ragtime, all night r. and blues, 176:2

do the r. dance, 146:2

Raiment white as snow, 32:3

Rain, a-fall an de snow a-r., 313:2

a-fall river dah-flood, 268:5

beats leopard's skin but not wash out spots, 565:10

clouds return after r., 20:11

comes to you, 334:4

he shall come unto us as the r., 24:4

help understand these r., 326:1

joy and pain sunshine and r., 454:1

laughing in the purple r., 514:3

life more like r., 334:4

looking at the r., 302:5

love is like r., 549:8

pray for r. deal with mud, 575:6

roof fights r. sheltered ignores it, 566:7

thunder not yet r., 564:12

to wash off the stink, 369:3

umbrella in 40 years of r., 274:4

want r. without thunder, 105:9

was forty days and forty nights, 7:11

Rainbow, God gave Noah r. sign, 284:7

God Put a R. in the Sky, 236:1

is full of harmonies, 345:6

people of God, 342:2

symbol of hope promise, 302:4

the real r. coalition, 410:4

Rainbows, mountain wrapped in r., 181:8

Raindrop, paramountacy is like a r., 439:5

water in a r., 325:5

Rains, don't pray when it r., 224:5

patois of furious r., 369:7

Raise humble dogs or mad dogs, 227:3

no shade for sun, 165:2

takes a village to r. a child, 574:3

they goddamn self, 563:8

they r. produce we consume it, 93:5

third day he will r. us up, 24:3

Raised, dead shall be r., 40:7

Raisin in the sun, 213:6

Raising, man lost in dust of his own r., 93:2

Ramble, social r. ain't restful, 224:2

Random, subject to r. violence, 495:4

Ranks, close r. before group can enter society, 414:3

Ransom, love can r. every slave, 81:5

Rap, believe r. is art, 542:1

gangsta r. ghetto life ignored by Americans, 510:4

is black America's TV station, 518:3

is rhythm and poetry, 541:2

is something you do, 542:2

jazz and blues roots of today's r., 453:2

Rape is national pastime, 457:2

nobody believes Negro men r. white women, 139:3

to whom will she cry r., 328:7

was an insurrectionary act, 362:2

Rapine, example of fraud r. and cruelty, 70:1

Rapist, I became a r., 362:2

not every black person is a r., 508:9

Rare, I wanted to be r., 385:3

kind of r. beast, 86:3

Rarely, what is uncommon is r. believed, 68:7

Rash, opposed to a r. war, 522:4

Rasta, Dreadlock R., 450:3

Rat, better die fighting than die like r. in trap, 140:4

ravaged by r. woodworm, 325:4

Rats don't dance in cat's doorway, 565:5

stop biting in the North, 273:1

Rattle, Shake R. and Roll, 208:5

Rise *(continued)*
    up from one end to the other, 227:1
    up in righteousness, 492:4
    whether or not colored man can r., 80:2
Risen, Christ r. from the dead, 40:4
    glory of the Lord is r. upon thee, 23:5
    he is r., 32:15
    Lord is r., 35:4
Rises like a bitterness in the throat, 348:2
Rising of the sun unto going down, 18:4
    time to get up, 355:1
Risk, I r. my all, 91:1
    willing to r. prison even death, 502:9
Rite of passage, 491:1
Ritual, completed the naming r., 274:3
Rituals of blood on the burning, 489:2
River, at last r. will get to the sea, 203:3
    born by the r., 334:2
    disappear by the r., 519:2
    full the r. still wants to grow, 565:6
    goin' to the r. there's reason why, 151:9
    hold me like a R. Jordan, 512:6
    lay down for you, 334:4
    of black struggle, 353:5
    of time, 382:2
    one more r. to cross, 577:6
    take me to the r., 455:4
    tests depth of r. with both feet, 565:17
    throw the r. out of course, 203:3
    time is not a r., 210:1
    walking out over the r., 322:5
Rivers, all r. run into the sea, 19:11
    are drowned in the sea, 390:3
    many r. to cross, 464:7
    not craziness when you talk to r., 350:2
    soul grown deep like the r., 211:7
Riverside, down by the r., 578:11
Roach, squashing a pregnant r., 431:1
Road, all kind of r. to take in life, 486:4
    clear the r. we go forward, 106:7
    don't let fall by side of the r., 473:3

Road *(continued)*
    ease on down the r., 442:2
    from Montgomery to Oslo, 319:3
    hit the r. Jack, 273:4
    is smooth and easy, 328:6
    it's a long old r., 188:3
    long r. to freedom, 267:5
    reach a fork in the r., 329:4
    Self-reliance Is the Fine R. to Independence, 111:8
    there's a r., 536:2
    walk freedom's r., 300:2
    walking down life's r., 329:4
Roads lie open when you rise, 5:2
Roam all over coliseum floors, 539:4
    sea's expanse unpent, 85:5
Roams, loneliness that r., 339:3
Roar, lion may cease to r. but is still lion, 101:3
Roaring, words of my r., 16:9
Roast, left in sun to r. like pigs, 506:4
    with fire and unleavened bread, 9:9
Rob colored people of their money, 233:1
    jaybird don't r. his own nes', 570:18
    me of my dignity, 267:4
    no necessity can warrant them to r., 72:6
    not the poor, 18:24
    rich r. poor and poor r. one another, 84:2
    society in conspiracy to r., 107:2
Robbed me of labor and liberty, 99:2
    of humanity, 267:2
    of my dark complexion, 99:2
    of my dearest right, 108:1
    of my education, 91:4
    of the fruits of his labor, 138:5
    restoring rights r. me, 100:1
Robbers of men, 72:6
Robbery, end the R. of our Black Community, 426:2
    rebelled against r., 108:1
    worst kind of r., 72:6
Robbing your way out of sad, 559:8
Robe, dumb as a r. and halo, 502:3
Rock a rhyme that's right on time, 539:3
    converted r. of oppression into steppingstone, 460:3
    crack r. gets into the country, 549:1

Rock *(continued)*
    founded upon a r., 27:12
    great r. across our path, 281:5
    he is the R., 12:4
    I am a R. you are a pebble, 555:2
    it up, 344:5
    Lord is my r., 13:23
    me all night long, 293:2
    me baby, 293:2
    steady baby, 418:6
    to the planet r., 501:1
    upon this r. build my church, 29:8
    wanna r. with you, 511:2
    was landed on us, 295:1
Rock and roll, architect of R., 344:3
    beat from Sanctified Church, 236:4
    good for the soul, 303:3
    take a dose of r., 303:3
Rock-a my soul, 578:9
Rocked, loneliness that can be r., 339:3
Rocket ship explodes everybody wants to fly, 514:6
Rocket '88, everybody likes my R., 341:4
Rockin, don't stop the r., 374:5
Rocks, go round the r., 567:7
    gunfire and r., 245:5
    on the Isle de Vaches, 258:1
Rod, Aaron's r. swallowed up their rods, 9:6
    he that spareth his r., 18:17
    take thy r., 9:5
    thy r. and staff comfort me, 16:10
Rode, he r. upon a cherub, 16:5
Role, can drug dealers be r. models, 533:4
    did not set out to become r. model, 353:1
    more than a r. model, 502:6
    of Negro created by Western man, 357:3
    play r. of Negro has been the Nigger, 357:3
Roles, Hollywood r. for African-Americans, 508:9
Roll it let 'em jump for joy, 221:5
    let the good times r., 228:5
    over Beethoven, 299:6
    Shake Rattle and R., 208:5
    who shall r. the stone away, 112:6
    with me Henry, 385:1
    your drums, 108:7

Rolling, Papa was a r. stone, 436:7

Rolls, justice r. down like waters, 317:9

Roma locuta est, 53:*n*1

Romans, I do as the R. do, 130:8

Romanticism, infinite caprice and r., 207:9

of a Brahms, 248:10

Rome has spoken, 53:3

here or in Heaven, 324:5

Roof fights rain sheltered ignores it, 566:7

no r. over head but he has a car, 490:6

Roofs, left in the sun on the r., 506:4

Room, black snake in my r., 195:4

for many a more, 577:8

in their rented back r., 259:6

made me go to my r., 501:2

no r. in the inn, 33:3

scarcely r. to turn, 69:3

Roost, coming home to r., 296:8

Root, because no r. they withered, 28:13

for Indians against the cavalry, 343:8

from r. of old a new one sprung, 480:8

money is r. of evil, 156:5

of all evil, 42:9

of the matter, 15:14

revival of love, 450:7

Roots, blues are the r., 252:1

from our r. draw sustenance, 401:7

of racism deep, 320:11

strength of their r., 311:2

without understanding its r., 525:1

women to plant r. of progress, 114:5

Rope got two end, 574:6

I will skip without your r., 440:1

time longer dan a r., 575:7

Rose, girl gets sick of a r., 258:10

of Sharon, 21:5

to respectability without losing identity, 121:6

Rot, absence of hope can r. a society, 527:5

which imprisoned everything, 393:1

Rotten to the core, 131:2

Rough, let it come r. or smooth, 87:5

places made plain, 22:14

Rough (*continued*)

time leaves marks of r. fingers, 65:2

we always do it nice and r., 399:1

Roughness, learn of me in r., 51:4

Roulette, slave trade was r. wheel, 308:6

Round about Midnight, 293:1

go r. the rocks, 567:7

the world and back again, 571:4

Routes, African bones marking the r., 251:3

Row the boat ashore Alleluia, 364:6

Rowboat, like a r. on the stormy sea, 187:5

Royalty inherited from another, 201:10

Rub, if my blackness would r. off, 214:4

Rubies, price of wisdom above r., 15:18

Rude in speech, 40:14

Ruffians, terrorized by r., 128:2

Ruin, bring kingdom to r., 276:3

enemies plotting our r., 127:3

of nation begins in homes of its people, 565:18

Ruins, buries all sentiments in r., 69:4

Rule, lived by golden r., 299:9

of international morality, 183:6

people think we cannot r. ourselves, 562:2

white minority racist r., 266:6

Ruled, women r. by their bodies, 546:2

Ruler of my offspring, 49:1

who the r., 355:4

Rules are fixed, 396:1

woman r. the home, 195:7

Rulest, thou who r. wind and water, 128:5

Ruling, excel the r. race, 133:8

over Church and State, 110:4

Rum, Harlem of caramel and r., 215:3

Rumble, boogie-woogie r., 213:5

labored out in measured r., 381:2

Rumbling, Harlem r. into a tunnel, 215:3

Rumors, hear of wars and r. of wars, 30:3

Rump, my face and r. were famous, 232:2

Run, all rivers r. into the sea, 19:11

faster than man in front, 186:5

he can r. he can't hide, 249:4

I will just r. and r. and r., 413:4

never r. my train off track, 111:4

Nigger r. it's almos' day, 568:11

nowhere to r. to, 409:2

race r. all but one prize, 39:12

this race in vain, 578:1

to when already in promised land, 375:2

Runaway from birth, 137:2

stopped being r. when slavery ended, 137:4

Runneth, my cup r. over, 16:10

Running, ain't done r. around, 187:8

avoid r. at all times, 224:2

kept r. into myself, 351:4

learned r. away to perfection, 98:6

no more r., 338:3

people start r. four ways, 290:1

Runs, when slave r. away, 102:2

Rush, ain't no r. long ways to go, 205:3

Rushing mighty wind, 37:6

nations rush like the r. of waters, 22:4

Russia, there at home for R. sigh, 85:5

Russia's chondria for short, 85:4

Rust on the razor, 305:7

Ruthless, men are unkind r. cruel, 252:3

S

Sabachthani, Eli lama s., 32:2

Sabbath made for man, 32:8

proper time to keep S., 79:1

remember the s. day, 10:7

without soul, 377:1

Sable, view s. race with scornful eye, 71:4

Sacrament, abortion a s., 256:2

Sacred, cannot believe history s. or profane, 77:5

drum is s. instrument, 305:1

new yam reapings, 480:6

no right so s. as choice, 117:2

obligation, 317:7

right to freedom, 286:2

temple of his being, 277:8

temple of Mecca, 54:10

Saturday and Sunday's fun to sport around, 214:3

   mornings listened to Red Lantern, 353:8

Saucer, I see a flying s. comin, 357:2

Saul hath slain thousands, 13:11

Savage to be satiated, 280:3

Savagery, relics of unreasoning human s., 222:3

Savages, admiration from hearts of s., 139:5

Savanna, desolate s. where cacti grow, 376:1

Save anybody but themselves, 393:2

   himself he cannot s., 32:1

   if each will not s. himself, 393:2

   if they s. us we shall live, 89:4

   killing people to s. to free them, 243:7

   love you s. may be your own, 434:3

   polar bears and poor kids too, 548:1

   thy people, 70:2

   United Nations s. what it can, 264:6

   us from our lesser selves, 144:10

   whosoever s. life shall lose it, 29:10

Saved, all who endure shall be s., 70:3

   from our enemies, 33:2

   he s. others, 32:1

   miracle our lives be s., 130:5

   we are not s., 23:11

Saves, a man is what he s. from rot, 199:3

Saving my love for you, 192:5

Savior, Black woman god damn s., 335:3

   born this day a S., 33:4

   which is Christ the Lord, 33:4

Saviors, never be any s., 393:2

Saviour, is he not a whole S., 76:6

Savor, if salt have lost s., 26:13

Savoy, stompin' with you at the S., 192:8

Say, and s. sit here eat, 331:1

   'em loud s. 'em clear, 275:5

   hey, 336:4

   I s. what I think, 301:2

   I s. what most conductors can't s., 111:4

   it loud, 347:4

   it plain, 532:1

   nothing to s. except why, 336:7

Say (continued)

   something worth breath, 462:2

   tell me what'd I s., 326:6

   Thankyuh sah, 206:3

   they could do everything, 265:6

   watch what you s., 511:1

   what else to s. but everything, 260:1

   what we hear others s., 459:4

   what you do want to s., 470:6

   Yes ma'am, 306:2

Scandal, burst the dam of s., 225:3

Scapegoat in the wilderness, 11:2

Scarcely room to turn, 69:3

Scarceness, eat bread without s., 11:15

Scared, being s. all the time, 378:9

   if s. keep going, 111:5

   spirit struggles loose, 90:6

   tired of being s. for our boys, 558:9

   white race talking s. of me, 215:1

Scarf, black s. stood for black pride, 442:4

Scariness of things with no names, 339:10

Scarlet, sins be as s., 21:17

Scars of war, 512:8

   we wear our s. like armor, 486:4

Scattered, one s. and gathered, 50:3

   pathway of bones, 251:3

   the proud, 32:21

Scene of horror inconceivable, 69:3

Scented salams from an exile, 59:4

Schemes, schemeless s., 151:10

Schizophrenia, sexual s., 435:8

Scholarly and righteous folk, 60:3

Scholars, gather my s. about me, 123:4

School age you cannot control, 229:2

   for the magnates, 2:3

   funds unequally divided, 272:5

   learned hate and shame at s., 343:7

   life but one great s., 109:6

   of the hard knocks, 550:6

   subject of slavery in s. books lost, 92:4

   take our children to any s., 245:6

   we left s., 259:8

   white children to s. with Negroes, 229:3

Schools, inferior separate s., 272:5

   segregation in public s., 228:7

   white and colored s., 272:5

Science as the end-all of life, 167:1

   in dance and art in s., 504:4

   math and s. literacy, 365:2

   of living together, 185:5

   religion not rivals, 318:5

   what is man and all his s., 167:1

Scientific genius has transformed world, 220:4

Scientists do the same to Bushmen, 377:6

Scion of youth is grown, 81:4

Scooter, nickname was S., 257:7

Scorn and shouts malign, 92:2

   let not men laugh to s., 56:10

Scorned, honored one and s. one, 49:1

   I've been 'buked and s., 578:7

Scorpions whose sting sings like brain, 439:6

Scourge and terror of race, 82:1

   spleen that s. of Britain, 85:4

Scrabble, playing S. with the vowels missing, 201:6

Scramble together vowels jewels, 326:1

Scream, how does one s. in thunder, 360:4

   why do we s. at each other, 514:4

Scriptures cut from men's hearts, 59:1

   search the s., 35:20

Sea, all rivers run into the s., 19:11

   and a slave ship, 69:2

   burden of the desert of the s., 22:5

   dominion over the fish of the s., 6:5

   go on cross that s., 484:6

   horse and his rider thrown into s., 9:17

   hurt not the earth s. nor trees, 44:9

   into the midst of the s., 9:16

   Jesus walking on the s., 28:22

   life awaits man as s. awaits river, 390:3

   like a net cast into the s., 28:16

   literature is big s. full of fish, 212:7

   love can still the raging s., 81:5

   mer was both mother and s., 332:4

   propellers undress the s., 532:3

   rays in the midst of the s., 5:2

   red s. humming, 325:5

   shadows upon a s. obscure, 55:8

   sparkling in the sun, 291:4

Sea *(continued)*
the river will get to the s., 203:3
the s. is not full, 19:11
things that drive men to s. is women, 465:3
Sea-fever globules of anguish, 345:5
Seal upon thine arm, 21:14
upon thine heart, 21:14
Sealed, fate is s. and ought to be s., 128:2
letter they could not read, 443:5
with seven seals, 44:5
Seals, seven s., 44:5
Search for something to lean upon, 259:5
the scriptures, 35:20
Searched, I s. for you, 52:8
Seared, conscience s. with a hot iron, 42:5
Sea's, roam s. expanse unpent, 85:5
Seas, seven s. of ink, 56:5
Seascape, starved eye devours s., 330:6
Sea-shell prisons, 379:3
Season of migration, 476:8
Tamarind S., 460:4
to every thing there is a s., 19:17
when I have a convenient s., 37:20
Seasons, he makes the s. with the months, 4:5
mix de bag-o' tricks, 313:2
Seat, in the driver's s., 239:1
Seats, come all this way for no two s., 262:3
put down mighty from their s., 32:21
there are no reserved s., 176:8
Second beast like a calf, 44:3
fiddle to no one, 201:8
Secondarily as colored people, 207:5
Second-class citizen don't pay first-class taxes, 343:4
citizens, 183:6
citizens in United States of America, 198:4
Secret, cleanse me from s. faults, 16:7
my s. is my eternal burden, 360:9
nothing is s., 33:12
of my going on, 426:6
of our lack of union, 96:1
staging s. woodland ceremonies, 460:7
tell you a s. I'm better, 178:5
Secretary, artist is like a s., 288:4

Secrets define us, 447:7
linking us and setting us apart, 415:7
love contained the s. of tomorrow, 422:1
Secure, nation s. only while honest, 107:1
world never fully s., 383:7
Secured Liberty without resistance, 101:1
Security, national s. crises, 383:2
threat to international s., 245:4
See, cannot s. the kingdom of God, 35:15
cant s. white can't s. black, 230:8
do not the unbelievers s., 55:4
eye to eye, 22:17
eyes have they but they s. not, 18:5
have eyes and s. not, 23:8
I was blind now I s., 36:6
lets go and youll s. for yrself, 535:6
me one thing live with me another, 576:2
mole don't s. what his naber doing, 570:17
O can't you s. it, 188:5
only the monsters we make, 553:3
people refuse to s. me, 247:7
s. rider s. what you done, 571:7
they shall s. God, 26:12
those things ye s., 33:15
through glass darkly, 39:17
what sorrow sees, 357:5
what we're told that we s., 459:4
when will I s. you again, 429:8
ya when I free ya, 556:2
ye shall s. heaven open, 35:12
you are unable to s., 492:2
young men shall s. visions, 24:7
your Declaration Americans, 78:5
Seed, children of long-sown s., 412:7
heaven like to mustard s., 28:15
I planted a s., 451:7
of our destruction, 510:5
plant the s. and pick the fruit, 410:1
repay s. for sins inflicted, 173:1
repay your s., 173:1
Seeds, children are the s. of history, 395:6
did not sprout, 336:6
fell by the way side, 28:12
scattered ideas like s., 438:8

Seek and ye shall find, 27:7
black power, 230:4
continuing city we s. to come, 42:21
judgment, 21:17
the living among the dead, 35:1
the southern surges, 85:5
those who s. me, 48:15
to suppress truth, 361:4
where else can you s. survival, 234:3
Seeking, liberty worth s. for, 64:1
may be found out by s., 47:9
no favors because of color, 140:5
Seemed like a good idea at the time, 376:3
Seen, blessed they have not s. yet believed, 37:5
how one is s. as black, 492:2
no man hath s. God, 35:9
not being s., 492:2
they had to see what I had s., 275:8
Sees, what one s. in a white world, 492:2
whenever he s. a Negro, 348:2
you even when not looking, 566:8
Seeth, Lord s. not as man s., 13:7
Segregate somebody in front, 343:3
Segregated a feeling of inferiority, 186:4
discrimination scars soul of s., 186:4
hour of America, 321:1
kill to preserve s. way of life, 402:2
schools in Topeka, 228:7
to nonsegregated society, 275:2
Segregation, bitter swill of s., 527:1
enables to ignore, 257:2
in public schools, 228:7
rid of s., 387:n2
that would remake rules, 446:5
until s. made criminal, 234:4
Segregator, discrimination scars soul of s., 186:4
Segu is a garden where cunning grows, 375:5
Seize, merchants daily s. our subjects, 57:10
our time, 374:3
Seized and sold for a slave, 62:2
my property and papers, 68:3
one pursued and s., 50:3
Self, contempt of s., 53:6
earthly love by love of s., 53:6

723

Self *(continued)*
 identify covers nakedness of s., 285:4
 looking at one's s. through others, 143:6
 my private s. doesn't exist, 373:4
 rise and attain the envisioned s., 454:3
 why pose a s. other than you, 376:9
Self-ambush, accomplice in s., 394:6
Self-conceit to self-destruction, 46:4
Self-control, do not love my s., 50:2
Self-defense, cultural s. against exploitation, 373:3
 revolution always s., 289:1
Self-destruction, self-conceit to s., 46:4
Self-determination, kujichagulia s., 410:8
 right of nations to s., 473:9
Self-division result of subjugation, 290:6
Self-efforts, our elevation result of s., 93:6
Self-esteem powerful weapon, 320:3
Self-government handed over on silver platter, 233:5
 prefer s. with danger, 233:4
Selfhood, affirms its own s., 295:10
 children stripped of s., 317:9
 pen and ink of s., 320:3
Selfish, let us not be s., 250:9
 men are mean s., 252:3
 prudence between duty and human life, 120:5
Self-pity, colored women can't afford s., 227:3
Self-possession, last barrier to the kind of s., 457:4
Self-realization, lack of s., 230:10
Self-reliance Is the Fine Road to Independence, 111:8
Self-respect and remain patient, 270:5
 color never destroyed s., 153:5
 kindred duty of s., 108:5
 oppression robs s., 108:4
Sell, I s. the shadow, 83:3
 in shambles like a brute, 112:1
 no man might buy or s., 44:16
Sellers, if no buyers there would be no s., 73:2
Selling, the company's s. it, 541:8
Sell-outs, see us as s., 542:3

Senator, at least before I was a s., 530:1
Send angels with sound of trumpet, 30:4
 please s. me someone to love, 273:3
 skyscrapers toppling, 230:11
Senility, don't worry about s., 376:5
Sense, blind have s. of hearing acute, 77:2
 make s. all this pain, 326:1
Senseless, I am s. and wise, 50:2
Senses, satisfy needs with all s., 268:3
Sensibility, tear of s., 75:1
Sensitivity to that afflicting race, 296:9
Sent an angel as messenger, 54:14
 for my baby and she don't come, 236:9
 for you yesterday here you come today, 219:4
 forth from power, 48:15
 man s. from God was John, 35:6
 me to France, 68:3
Sentiments, buries all s. in ruins, 69:4
 proofs of my republican s., 67:3
Separate as fingers one as hand, 132:1
 can't s. peace from freedom, 297:3
 from the first ones, 51:2
 neither life nor death s. us from love of God, 38:16
 who shall s. us from Christ, 38:15
 why give Negroes s. treatment, 229:1
Separated, keep s. and you will be exploited, 172:2
Separateness breeds ill-will and hatred, 186:4
 lurid dream of s., 465:4
Separation, difference between integration and s., 196:2
Separatism, demands for s., 277:7
Separatists, real s. moved to suburbs, 277:7
September 11 erased over there and over here, 503:3
Sequel, God is the s. of all things, 56:4
Serfdom, emancipated from s., 171:4
Serious, no one's s. makes me furious, 423:4
 one who is s. all day, 2:1
Serpent, a s. is a s., 94:1
 beguiled me and I did eat, 6:17

Serpent *(continued)*
 called the Devil and Satan, 44:15
 coiled in their own hearts, 79:5
 it shall become a s., 9:5
 Spirit said S. loosened, 87:6
Serpents, all the s. bite, 5:1
Servant, a s. of servants shall he be, 7:15
 borrower is s. to the lender, 18:23
 Canaan shall be his s., 7:16, 7:17
 carried His s. by night, 54:10
 good and faithful s., 30:8
 high and yet the s. of all, 133:2
 not above his lord, 28:5
 speak Lord for thy s. heareth, 13:3
 thy s. depart in peace, 33:6
Servants, proper wages like English s., 79:1
 white men's s., 438:1
 whose s. and soldiers are we, 96:3
Serve and hate will die unborn, 211:8
 any excuse will s. a tyrant, 46:9
 cannot s. God and mammon, 27:3
 cannot s. people by giving orders, 155:2
 everybody can s., 320:10
 no man can s. two masters, 27:3
 others at whatever cost, 428:1
 we don't s. colored people here, 343:1
Served, food s. by Negro mothers, 229:3
Service, African spirit is spirit of s., 120:1
 is the rent we pay for living, 395:3
 love to be of s., 90:4
 makes enemies by great s., 68:6
 measures success, 142:5
 of human needs not profits, 176:7
 spirit of s. in black man, 120:1
Serving, forbidden from s. country, 528:1
 Martha cumbered about s., 34:4
 my country with zeal and fidelity, 68:2
Servitude, better in a state of s., 74:5
 forever abolished, 67:8
 in tranquility, 233:4
 lush ice gardens of their s., 243:5
 vile habits acquired in s., 74:3
Set, bitch s. me up, 366:5
 did not s. my traps today, 3:3
 thine house in order, 14:9

Seth, it is S. who would take possession, 3:1

Setteth, God s. forth parables, 55:7

Seven days shall ye eat unleavened bread, 9:12
    golden candlesticks, 43:17
    lie has s. endings, 564:9
    seals, 44:5
    seas of ink, 56:5
    until seventy times s., 29:12

Seventeen hundred and forty-six, 65:9

Seventh day God ended his work, 6:6
    day thou shalt not work, 10:7
    Harlem was S. Heaven, 296:7

Seventies, civil rights cycle of S., 255:10

Seventy times seven, 29:12

Sever that cord, 361:9

Sew, I must sit and s., 154:2
    time to s., 19:17

Sewed stars and roads into quilts, 536:2

Sex, double handicap race and s., 141:1
    exploit s. and at same time repress it, 435:8
    got HIV because I had unprotected s., 515:3
    it's a s. object if pretty, 430:8
    learn about s. in the streets, 389:4
    like a s. machine, 347:6
    machine to all the chicks, 419:7
    money like s., 283:9
    no s. if you're fat, 430:8

Sexism, before we begin to address s., 457:1
    impact of s. on social status, 488:3
    never excuse for not doing your best, 428:4
    racism and s. are not genetic, 368:4

Sexist, world no longer racist or s., 488:4

Sexual healing, 396:8
    if I count my s. encounters, 367:2
    oppression, 379:6
    politics, 491:9
    politics pervasive, 573:14
    schizophrenia, 435:8

Sexually stereotyped, 564:1

Shackles, crime s. and binds, 553:6

Shade, raise a hand to s. eyes, 233:6

Shades, different s. of blues, 326:2
    different s. of singer, 326:2
    of delight cocoa hue, 299:8

Shadow, Black S. of American culture, 347:8
    body make s., 314:1
    dark s. in light, 223:5
    days on earth are a s., 14:11
    grasping at the s., 46:10
    I grew up in your s., 224:6
    I sell the s., 83:3
    maneuvering her s. to the floor, 487:5
    not the s. but the act, 248:14
    of American army, 113:6
    of the dollar, 214:6
    of thy wings, 16:4
    of time s. of blood, 242:8
    time is a s., 25:4
    today is s. of tomorrow, 250:4
    under which we live, 140:6
    valley of the s. of death, 16:10
    within s. of her death, 321:9

Shadows all about me, 232:8
    casting s. on the sun, 382:1
    flung into space, 232:8
    mothers who dwell 'neath s., 115:9
    of corruptions, 288:1
    of the past, 304:2
    on s. of men, 232:8
    on the wall, 307:1
    standing in s. of love, 409:5
    trees' s. like men's spirits, 137:3
    upon a sea obscure, 55:8
    victims of the s., 232:8
    wait in the s., 280:4
    where your eye-lids rest, 209:3
    white black casts dark s., 185:3

Shadrach fell into the fiery furnace, 23:24

Shaft, 419:7
    fashion of the s., 47:n1
    with own feathers, 47:n1

Shake it like a Polaroid picture, 560:2
    it to the one you love best, 571:1
    it up, 344:5
    off the dust, 28:3
    Rattle and Roll, 208:5
    the painted plume, 71:6
    Your Moneymaker, 265:4

Shakespeare, life lived without knowing S., 452:7
    like S. wrote poetry, 315:6

Shaking the dust of ages, 85:8

Shalimar, what S. knew, 337:9

Sham, your celebration is a s., 105:3

Shambles, sell in s. like a brute, 112:1

Shame, ain't that a s., 309:6
    and boldness, 49:3
    bear pain of guilt and s., 92:2
    crying s. how they do us, 415:2
    driving me out, 147:6
    fool me twice s. on me, 572:8
    I wear like a tattoo, 517:3
    learned s. at school, 343:7
    lynching s. to civilization, 272:5
    of my own countrymen, 73:2
    should know no s., 81:7
    speak of proud country's s., 112:5
    with a great amount of s., 561:4
    younger artists express without s., 211:6

Shameless, I am s., 49:3
    you have been s. to me, 50:3

Shango is death that drips to to to, 566:11

Shanty Town, 407:7

Shape, fiends who bear the s. of men, 95:1

Shapen, I was s. in iniquity, 17:4

Shapes the laws of man, 230:7

Share equal privileges, 76:5
    His martyrdom, 299:4
    of the pie, 394:3
    our joy in the satisfying, 358:1
    the bounties of the earth, 212:8
    these faults of character, 231:5
    with Angels s., 63:2

Sharecroppers, strong as a dozen s., 462:1

Shark, every fish eena sea no s., 576:1

Sharon, rose of S., 21:5

Sharpening my oyster knife, 179:1

Sharper, word of God s. than sword, 42:17

She a gold digger, 562:3
    came s. loved s. went away, 162:2
    died and I lived, 321:9
    is for everyone soup before dinner, 537:4
    passin' fe wite, 268:7
    replies with wisdom, 566:12
    was a woman now, 434:5
    what s. could and would have been, 508:1
    who cries out, 51:4
    who does not bear, 49:1

She (*continued*)
  who exists in fears, 50:2
  who is weak, 50:2
  whose wedding is great, 49:1
Sheaves, reapers among s., 12:21
Sheba, queen of S. heard of
    Solomon, 14:3
Sheep, Abel was a keeper of s., 7:3
  all s. have gone astray, 23:1
  as a shepherd divideth s., 30:10
  black men s. among wolves, 196:1
  but some a wolf an some a s.,
    489:5
  found s. which was lost, 34:8
  I have are not of this fold, 36:9
Sheep's clothing, 27:11
  wolf in s. clothing, 45:8
Shell, future inside its s., 180:13
Shells, blow your s. roll your drums,
    108:7
Shem, blessed be the Lord God of S.,
    7:16
  dwell in the tents of S., 7:17
She-male, put he-male an' s.
    asunder, 570:2
Shepherd divideth sheep from goats,
    30:10
  feed his flock like a s., 22:15
  I am the good s., 36:8
  Lord is my s., 16:10
  valiant s. who drives his flock, 4:5
Shepherds keeping watch over flock,
    33:4
Sheriff, I shot the s., 449:3
Shield for the breast, 58:3
  lay down my sword and s.,
    578:11
  Lord is my strength and s., 16:12
Shielded by her unshakable
    humanity, 546:3
Shine, arise s. for thy light is come,
    23:5
  black man you cain't s., 568:9
  brilliant wit will s., 90:2
  I'm gonna let it s., 578:16
  like Re in the horizon, 3:1
  older de moon brighter it s.,
    575:15
  swam on, 571:14
Shines, pray when the sun s., 224:5
Shining, burning s. light, 35:19
  star, 414:4
  you are a s. star, 473:6
  you are my s. star, 484:3

Ship, big s. need da wata, 575:11
  freshly launched, 233:6
  like a s. upon the sea, 128:5
  only safe s. in a storm is
    leadership, 435:9
  slave s. riding at anchor, 69:2
  who owned the slave s., 355:4
Ships at a distance, 179:9
  fare north fare south, 5:2
  first s. arrived from Africa, 253:3
Shipwrecked bones, 398:5
Shirt, nuh-uh fool that's a s., 501:2
Shit, flying and floating that s. in,
    549:1
  life ain't s., 451:5
  weighs you down, 337:7
  white man's s., 359:6
  you all believe that s., 281:3
Shiver, we s. together, 506:6
Shock, looked up with s. on his face,
    378:3
Shoe, lifted out a s., 250:1
  my baby wore, 250:1
  one thing common s.
    uncomfortable, 573:16
  this is my new s., 533:5
Shoes, being black in America like
    ill-fitting s., 573:16
  come walk in my s., 401:1
  I am not worthy to unloose, 32:6
  in the s. of those attacked by police
    dogs, 401:1
  it'll only make you have s. like me,
    533:5
  on your feet, 9:10
  put off thy s. from thy feet, 8:23
  sold the poor for a pair of s., 24:8
Shone, glory of the Lord s. round,
    33:4
Shoo fly don't bother me, 569:2
Shook, I'm in love all s. up, 333:5
Shoot slugs from my brain, 559:6
  the white girl first, 340:2
Shooting your way out of sad,
    559:8
Shop, shattered Sunday s., 325:4
  you better s. around, 404:2
Short, life is s. make it sweet, 173:9
Shortcomings, charging our s. to
    white people, 166:4
  face up to our s., 494:4
Short-term visitors, 373:2
Shorty, go s. it's your birthday,
    560:3

Shoulder, dirt off your s., 550:8
  put our s. to the wheels, 108:7
  put s. to the wheel, 46:14
  weep on world's s., 227:3
Shoulders, lay burdens on men's s.,
    101:5
Shout, shouted great s., 12:9
  you make me wanna s., 378:1
Shouters, spectators tune s. out, 482:8
Shouts, racial discussions two levels
    s. or whispers, 482:8
Shove, when they s. me in, 556:2
Show, don't s. the anger, 273:6
  him of Our tokens, 54:10
  kindness to parents, 54:11
  yo bum rush the s., 518:4
  your own kind of S. Way, 536:2
Shower, not the gentle s. but
    thunder, 105:2
Showing, all you're doing is s. off,
    499:4
Shown off to all kinds of people,
    210:5
Shriek rose wildly on the air, 112:4
Shrieks of breaking hearts, 97:2
  of the women, 69:3
Shrine, no s. to worship, 363:7
Shrink, time and distance cannot s.
    it, 180:10
Shrouds, battling billows while s.
    rattling, 85:5
  despair my color s. me in, 218:7
Shuffling, dancing not s., 558:1
Shut, doors s. in the streets, 20:11
  mouth catch fly, 574:5
  poor and black and s. out, 238:4
  you want to s. up every Negro,
    198:5
Shutting myself in a box, 100:1
Shy about being capitalists, 472:1
  you're playing s., 277:4
Sick and tired of being s. and tired,
    262:4
  and ye visited me, 30:11
  for I am s. of love, 21:6
  kills his black brother who is s.,
    490:8
  the whole head is s., 21:16
Sickness among the slaves, 69:3
  of laughing giggling, 298:3
  take your s. give you health, 163:3
Side, decide which s. you want to live
    on, 496:7
  hear the other s., 52:10

Side *(continued)*

neutral is to s. with the powerful, 341:5

reads one page without other s., 94:5

we are on God's s., 249:3

Sides, Pharaohs on both s. of waters, 100:4

the artist must take s., 198:3

thorns in your s., 12:12

Sideshow of open beaks, 368:8

Sigh, there at home for Russia s., 85:5

Sighing for what one adores, 67:5

Sighs of wonder of the New Negroes, 210:5

Sight, first s. of Free Land, 113:1

in absence out of your s., 550:5

no more in s. of their masters, 94:8

swingin' low then out of s., 329:3

walk by faith not s., 40:11

we shall live in his s., 24:3

Sign, God gave Noah rainbow s., 284:7

Men Only s. off White House door, 459:1

of barbarity and immorality, 87:1

of the letter, 51:5

on front gate, 298:4

Signals carrying s. & planets, 325:5

Signed our last wills and testaments, 387:4

Sealed Delivered I'm Yours, 482:5

Signifying, monkey kept on s., 571:15

Signposts, no paths in water no s., 513:4

racial s., 497:7

Signs for all living beings, 56:3

for god-fearing people, 54:3

for whites only, 317:9

invisible s. form a gulf between us, 401:2

of the times, 29:6, 103:7

Silence, achieve personal s., 305:8

at least has dignity, 258:4

bear our sorrows in s., 109:1

bless them in s., 515:6

change lay in our s., 332:5

distills in yellow melodies, 345:8

end s. around homosexuality, 505:4

father's lips closed in s. and grief, 65:8

Silence *(continued)*

he sits in s. to pass judgment, 566:8

I am still as s., 441:5

I am the s., 49:2

I greet you in s., 225:1

into speech, 488:5

is a fool's program, 127:5

is killing us, 505:3

listening for a s. deep enough, 399:3

no longer s. voice of minority, 129:3

of the oppressed, 488:3

pigeon s., 477:4

quiet means suffer in s., 499:3

through s. allow racism to continue, 493:8

time to keep s., 19:17

when in s. thou doest walk, 109:7

will not protect you, 358:7

Silences are melodies heard, 345:7

Silent, by and large s., 488:3

gesture to speak volumes, 442:5

I could not keep s., 504:3

in the face of tyranny, 361:5

shall be s. among s., 50:3

until the enemy, 554:5

water drowns a man, 565:16

Silhouette am I, 223:5

Silk thread of sunlight, 345:4

Silver, ambush the S. Screen, 391:1

and gold have I none, 37:8

covenanted with him for s., 31:1

heaps up gold and s., 58:4

more fame than gold and s., 58:3

never handed on s. platter, 233:5

sold the righteous for s., 24:8

speak s., 564:11

teethed on a s. spoon, 218:5

thirty pieces of s., 24:14, 31:1

tossed into the icy s. bowl, 506:3

treasures of gold and s., 58:3

Similar yet differentially not, 250:5

Simmer, rape a people s. for centuries, 469:6

Simón Bolivar, I also saw S., 301:7

Simple, give subtilty to the s., 18:11

joy could shake you, 338:5

what people want is s., 371:3

Sin against Grace God cannot save you, 164:5

go and s. no more, 36:4

he without s. among you, 36:3

in s. did my mother conceive me, 17:4

not failure but low aim is s., 187:2

one s. slavery committed, 91:4

taketh away the s. of the world, 35:10

wages of s. is death, 38:10

we sing s., 259:8

will find you out, 11:10

without s. without guilt, 2:6

Sinew in your wing to help you soar, 218:1

Sinful as bolshevism, 233:1

Sing a song full of faith, 147:3

about the Stars and Stripes, 122:4

and dream sweet things, 515:6

awake and s., 22:11

can't s. a song that doesn't have a message, 236:3

don't know how to s. Black, 534:4

for all men's healing let me s., 218:10

I just open my mouth and s., 288:6

I s. because I'm free, 579:7

I too s. America, 211:2

imagination s. thy force, 71:8

in light of freedom's morn, 129:1

never heard no horse s. song, 204:5

out darkey nigger, 99:4

shout dream about, 324:3

song wanta s. but s., 353:4

the names of the dead, 532:1

the national anthem, 271:1

the same song, 254:1

unto the Lord a new song, 18:1

want us to s. God Bless America, 416:6

we can s. about it, 374:4

when we stand to s., 321:1

why I s. the blues, 293:4

without a heart it cannot s., 61:1

Singer, be a s., 353:4

cage the s. not the song, 303:4

different shades of s., 326:2

Singing, better than s. is more s., 261:5

hit comes to real right s., 150:3

in the night, 329:3

love is like s, 181:4

slave songs, 255:1

Slave *(continued)*

barracks was my house, 440:4
before I'd be a s., 577:7
believing s. better than an idolater,
    53:10
born a s. in captive society, 409:8
bought and sold like ox, 98:7
chains do not make the s., 129:1
discarding my s. name, 355:3
domestic traffic in s. state, 101:4
driver table is turn, 449:5
duty of s. husband to endure, 98:4
folk-song rhythmic cry of s.,
    144:3
forsake wife child or die a s., 99:1
four centuries s. trade, 251:3
Fourth of July to American s.,
    105:3
free pauper than rich s., 316:1
freedom of every s. on every
    plantation, 92:5
girl black as ebony fair as mistress,
    95:1
hand upon trembling s., 113:5
her vision of the perfect s., 394:8
how man was made a s., 104:3
how s. was made a man, 104:3
I am s. of who prepared me, 49:1
I have been a s. myself, 78:7
is a human being, 98:7
kills owner of s. and s. runs away,
    567:1
love can ransom every s., 81:5
markets and Negro pens, 9:2
more secure than we, 93:7
my father was a s., 198:6
Negro telegraph reached last s.,
    456:3
never heard a s. say so, 78:7
Post Traumatic S. Syndrome,
    506:1
raise s. to dignity of man, 75:1
remember you're not a s., 541:1
seized and sold for a s., 62:2
ship riding at anchor, 69:2
singing s. songs, 255:1
skin of s. bind American Liberty,
    77:3
songs of the s. sorrows of heart,
    104:1
to be a s. was to be human, 397:4
to make contented s., 104:4
trade at war with heart of man,
    69:4

Slave *(continued)*

Trade was all about death, 475:1
trade was roulette wheel, 308:6
unlike other men is denied, 98:7
when s. runs away, 102:2
who owned the s. ship, 355:4
Slaved, the white race s. me, 215:1
three hundred years we s., 199:1
Slaveholder did break ten
    commandments, 79:2
judgment and conscience of the s.,
    79:3
to keep knowledge to himself,
    120:4
Slaveholders, affinity with s. worked
    for my escape, 99:2
false logic about good s., 120:2
Slaveholding, connection to its s.
    past, 275:2
spirit must die, 83:4
Slavekeeping, practice of s. is illicit,
    70:5
Slave-owners, sons of former s.,
    318:1
Slavery a curse to whites and blacks,
    95:3
attempts to make man brute,
    101:2
bid farewell to rule of s., 293:5
branded from the time of s.,
    350:4
broken the bands of s., 98:6
calamities of war and s., 70:2
condition of his class s., 103:7
contrary effects of liberty and s.,
    74:3
cursed s., 118:4
customs habits of s., 123:5
deeds of brave opposers of S.,
    110:4
different kind of s. today, 329:5
does away with fathers families,
    105:6
elect to fight for freedom or s.,
    198:3
end to humiliating s., 293:6
far reaching curse, 103:6
find a nation in s., 72:5
form of hell, 308:6
future s. remembered as past,
    114:1
grapple with s. not at arm's length,
    79:5

Slavery *(continued)*

has hulled empty a whole race,
    412:5
history must restore what s. took
    away, 152:3
I was born in s., 67:7
if s. is right then its horrors are
    right, 120:2
ignorance and prejudice belong to
    s., 75:4
in America was debasing, 130:6
is dead spirit still lives, 115:6
is not a just cause, 72:5
is the worst kind of robbery, 72:6
long night physical s., 320:3
lynch law last relic of s., 139:1
made us tough, 115:1
mental illness is a kind of s., 475:6
mental s., 450:1
monster of s., 111:9
nations fall into s. too great
    wealth, 135:1
no death do us part in s., 445:8
one sin s. committed, 91:4
or banishment, 113:4
partakes of the excesses of
    exploitation, 379:6
pathway from s. to freedom,
    104:2
question embedded within
    Constitution, 524:3
racism was the consequence of s.,
    237:5
reduced Negro to cultural zero,
    168:2
resurrection from grave of s.,
    100:2
riches in s., 278:4
seeking information of S., 110:4
sweat of s., 302:2
taking away liberty by s., 72:6
testimony against s., 104:1
the horrors of American S., 98:5
the impediment, 106:5
the peculiar institution, 106:5
the social system, 106:5
their condition was s., 397:4
this is s., 79:1
to argue to discredit effects of s.,
    132:3
transition from s., 275:2
treats him as beast, 101:2
vestige of s., 452:6
was not born of racism, 237:5

Snow fell obscuring the ugliness, 238:6
  queens, 518:9
  raiment white as s., 32:3
  sins as white as s., 21:17
  smack junk s. poison, 370:2
Snows, Atlas Mountain s., 225:2
Snuff, not quite up to s., 332:8
Sober, be s. be vigilant, 43:10
Soberness, words of truth and s., 38:2
Social engineering no more difficult, 246:6
  environmental degradation begets s. degradation, 543:4
  force to be reckoned with, 255:8
  in Africa all art is s., 225:6
  in all things s. separate, 132:1
  lawyer is a s. engineer or parasite, 191:1
  new s. planning, 176:7
  our s. system a disgrace, 126:1
  peace through s. justice, 535:1
  ramble ain't restful, 224:2
  slavery the s. system, 106:5
Socialist Tribunes of all the people, 482:6
Socially constructed barriers, 455:2
  disinherited face, 202:2
  Negro women neither s. free, 168:3
Societies, evil s. kill consciences, 273:2
  without change are dead, 496:3
Society, a new s. we must create, 242:4
  absence of hope can rot a s., 527:5
  advancing when respect education, 109:2
  at the hands of a racist s., 424:5
  avoided mixing in s., 87:4
  becomes drumming of drones, 166:3
  Blue Vein S., 134:2
  close ranks before group can enter s., 414:3
  color-blind s. eludes us, 253:2
  cut off s. its cultivated minds, 99:3
  decolonize s., 301:5
  dehumanizing s., 548:6
  did not ask s. to take me up, 97:3
  from segregated s., 275:2

Society (continued)
  harmonious s. shapes the laws, 230:7
  in conspiracy to oppress, 107:2
  is rotten to the core, 131:2
  leaves few options, 310:2
  likes whites better, 245:7
  lowest condition of s. to highest, 96:2
  measure of our elevation in s., 79:3
  needs of white s., 324:2
  Negro in corners of s., 317:6
  nonracial s., 265:2
  of love of justice, 304:3
  of peace and brotherhood, 304:3
  outlaw of s., 266:4
  person-oriented s., 319:9
  prejudice in free s., 120:4
  purged from s., 311:5
  role of education in modern s., 239:6
  tells me I am black, 503:7
  that will crush people, 296:6
  that works requires simply, 279:4
  thing-oriented s., 319:9
  trample on weakest, 114:2
  united democratic s., 265:2
  what kind of s. will we be, 365:1
  which racial boundaries disappeared, 497:7
Society's bottom of s. well, 324:1
  foot on throat, 329:4
Socks, flashing white silk s., 490:5
Sodom, pitched his tent toward S., 8:2
Soft, can't run a country and be s., 269:5
Softly as wind within the trees, 357:5
Soil, black s. this rhythm was born, 500:8
  his blood is in their s., 282:11
  is no longer rich, 276:2
  was hard and rocky, 451:7
Solace of my labor pains, 49:1
Solarium a rage of light, 487:4
Sold, bought and s., 122:6
  cause them to be s., 57:10
  seized and s. for a slave, 62:2
  the poor for a pair of shoes, 24:8
  the righteous for silver, 24:8
  to a Negro trader, 102:1
  you to give gentlemen ease, 205:4
Soldier, fearless black s., 256:3
  fellow s. is wounded, 289:6
  I am a professional s., 289:4

Soldiers, all s. angel warriors, 378:5
  Colored S. of the Revolution have no historian, 103:2
  gallant colored s., 149:4
  giggling murdering, 298:3
  we are foot s., 303:6
  whose servants and s. are we, 96:3
Sole God beside whom is none, 5:3
Solidarity, their prescription Class S., 165:6
  is mutual aid between forces, 351:5
  Racial S., 165:6
Solitude, in s. thoughts ripened, 114:4
  out of the s., 345:4
Solomon, comely as the curtains of S., 21:3
  fame of S., 14:3
  wisdom of S., 14:2
Solomon's, song of songs is S., 21:2
Solution, no s. to race question, 234:4
  part of s. or of problem, 362:5
  the real s. is education, 368:6
  war is the s., 362:6
  you were s. problem, 339:1
Solutions, half-baked s., 318:4
  must come from us, 401:4
  no s. to anything in life, 258:4
Solve, question for nation to s., 106:3
Solved, until we've s. it, 408:1
Solving problems it creates, 241:6
Somalia is an open sore, 447:5
Somebody, always wanted to be s., 303:8
  be a fake s., 545:8
  else carries on, 217:7
  I am s., 410:7
  somethin' from s. sometime, 156:3
  they were s., 239:1
  to lean on, 392:5
Someday We'll Be Together, 375:1
Someone, could never happen to s. like me, 515:3
  has to care, 556:1
  will be killed, 387:4
Somersets, make our figgers turn s., 206:3
Something die for, 317:5
  every line means s., 517:7
  everybody got s. with everything, 509:4

Something *(continued)*
  I am s. you'll never understand,
    514:1
  just happened, 275:4
  might be gaining on you, 224:2
  struck me honey, 302:5
  to live for, 254:7
  wanna be startin' s., 511:6
  wonder if other guys have s., 353:5
Something's got a hold on me, 385:2
Sometime, you are my s., 426:5
Sometimes it comes and it goes,
    516:7
Somewhat free, 213:7
Somewhere, all you need s. to go,
    330:1
  listening for my name, 475:7
Son, Absalom my s., 13:22
  am I not Afric's s., 175:2
  behold thy s., 37:2
  brought forth her firstborn s., 33:3
  Christ S. of the living God, 29:7
  easy to hit a s., 282:1
  gave his only begotten S., 35:18
  grief-stricken s., 148:5
  honor the birth of a s., 487:2
  in the name of Father S. and Holy
    Ghost, 32:4
  is not this the carpenter's s., 28:17
  my first and only s., 247:6
  native s. dancing, 385:7
  now that's somebody, 338:4
  of man came eating and drinking,
    28:7
  of man is betrayed, 31:10
  out of Egypt I called my s., 26:2
  Paul s. of a Pharisee, 37:18
  prodigal s. wasted his substance,
    34:9
  succour man's afflicted s., 72:1
  the kid is not my s., 511:5
  this is my beloved S., 26:9
  thou art the S. of God, 29:2
  today it was my s., 544:2
Song awake Deborah utter a s.,
    12:14
  cage the singer not the s., 303:4
  doesn't have strength can't lift
    you, 236:3
  he spoke to the s. in her, 508:1
  hope is a s. in a weary throat, 235:1
  in search of itself, 451:9
  Lord is my strength and s., 9:17
  never heard no horse sing s., 204:5

Song *(continued)*
  of songs is Solomon's, 21:2
  of the people, 444:2
  praise s. walking forward, 532:2
  same old s., 409:1
  shall swell a s. of hope, 190:5
  sing a s. full of faith, 147:3
  sing the same s., 254:1
  sing unto the Lord a new s., 18:1
  siren s. sung in bass, 270:2
  spread universal s. of praise, 81:1
  wailing for the s., 379:4
  welcome day with s., 88:1
Song-lit race of slaves, 188:7
Songs a thousand and five, 14:1
  are celebration, 303:5
  discord in s. of freedom, 76:4
  folk s. from soul sounds, 188:8
  for the people, 115:8
  in spite of our sorrow s., 360:5
  lamenting s. and dirges, 85:5
  of deliverance mingle with war,
    113:6
  of the slave sorrows of heart, 104:1
  singing slave s., 255:1
  song of s. is Solomon's, 21:2
  to stir like a battle-cry, 115:8
Sons, Africa kills her s., 413:5
  barren one and many s., 49:1
  fallen s. of Africa, 89:3
  gathering stalk and root, 210:3
  of Africa apply for redress, 62:1
  of former slave-owners, 318:1
  of former slaves, 318:1
  of men snared in evil time, 20:9
  of the living God, 24:1
Soon I will be done, 578:14
  we die s., 259:8
  we know not how s., 63:5
Sooner marriage of harmony, 129:6
  men learn wives equals, 129:6
Soothe my troubled soul, 82:2
Soprano, under a s. sky, 360:6
Sorcery a gift given to a few, 465:2
Sorrow, blue-to-black s., 516:1
  continual s. in my heart, 72:3
  dammed up in my soul, 179:1
  hand is pure as s., 360:8
  he that increaseth knowledge
    increaseth s., 19:14
  in spite of our s. songs, 360:5
  is a wave without end, 390:2
  mountain weights of s. lay, 112:6
  pray no more s. I'll see, 201:2

Sorrow *(continued)*
  see what s. sees, 357:5
  the only faithful one, 247:2
  treads on nation's joy, 114:1
  whole mess of s., 181:11
Sorrowful, exceeding s., 31:4
Sorrow's kitchen, 181:8
Sorrows, bear our s. in silence, 109:1
  songs of the slave s. of heart, 104:1
  take your s. give you joy, 163:3
Sorry, ain't s. for nothing, 453:1
  change can't come until we feel s.,
    349:2
  don't feel s. for me, 464:1
  don't have time to feel s., 277:1
  often s. if wishes gratified, 46:16
Sort, two of every s. bring into the
    ark, 7:10
Soul, a bad marriage kills the s.,
    416:7
  a lot of heart and s., 384:2
  agonies of centuries crowd my s.,
    127:2
  American blacks call that s., 233:2
  America's s. poisoned, 319:8
  bad luck s., 187:6
  charge not s. save to its ability,
    55:6
  crawled out from hiding place,
    180:7
  curse in its own s., 114:2
  cuts the fibers of the s., 89:5
  drinking the life of my s., 232:8
  equal nobleness of s., 155:3
  feels free to travel, 73:5
  feet cast in the iron of s., 200:4
  feets is tired but s. is rested, 204:3
  filled my s. with melody, 147:1
  folk songs from s. sounds, 188:8
  food is more than chitlins, 384:2
  fragment of the Great S., 179:3
  freedom of my s., 184:2
  gain the world and lose your s.,
    449:10
  gain whole world lose own s.,
    29:10
  Genius + S. = Jazz, 326:7
  giving liberates the s., 308:5
  got s. and I'm superbad, 347:7
  grown deep like the rivers, 211:7
  Hot Buttered S., 419:6
  in this ark, 357:4
  is a millstone, 260:8
  is like electricity, 326:8

Soul *(continued)*
  is the concern of my Lord, 54:13
  is to feel oneness with black
    people, 368:3
  judge my s. eagle nor mole, 199:3
  let s. look for deed performed, 57:3
  light of my s., 91:2
  little sweetness down in my s.,
    352:3
  looked back and wondered, 577:14
  love the Lord with all thy s., 30:1
  loved as his own s., 13:12
  lynching etches impression on s.,
    187:3
  man, 411:4
  man became a living s., 6:7
  meat on my s., 360:7
  men alike in s., 144:6
  my s. beyond their reach, 122:6
  my s. doth magnify the Lord,
    32:20
  my s. is an eagle, 252:2
  no s. shall be wronged, 56:8
  not too late to catch thy s., 188:7
  of a freeman, 67:7
  of my sad people's s., 209:2
  passions grabbed my s., 494:1
  peculiar wrenching of the s., 144:1
  people suffer and are without s.,
    444:2
  permit no man to degrade s., 132:9
  principle in s. makes man woman,
    90:2
  question thee concerning the s.,
    54:13
  restoreth my s., 16:10
  rhythm is s. of life, 305:1
  rock 'n' roll good for s., 303:3
  rock-a my s., 578:9
  sabbath without s., 377:1
  soothe my troubled s., 82:2
  sorrow dammed up in my s., 179:1
  straight and narrow or s. gets cast,
    543:1
  thinking about your s., 282:4
  whispereth within him, 56:12
  whole heart and s., 23:15
  why castest thou off my s., 17:16
  wiggles in the dark of her s., 354:3
Soul's a journeyman, 545:3
  your s. on ice, 548:7
Souls, all s. are steeped in, 301:6
  are open skies, 379:3
  calluses on our s., 343:10

Souls *(continued)*
  fire burning in the s., 274:4
  in every race and hue, 144:10
  lighten world's weight, 331:9
  of Black America, 274:4
  prison bars to our s., 186:4
  rest unto your s., 28:8
  silent like their s., 153:9
  weakness of limbs innocent not s.,
    52:2
Sound, name of s. and s. of name,
    51:5
  name of the s., 51:5
  of my own background music,
    399:3
  of the genuine in yourself, 203:5
  of the grinding is low, 20:11
  of the men workin' on chain,
    334:1
  of the name, 51:5
  of trumpet, 12:9
  quiet has a hidden s., 158:7
  send angels with s. of trumpet,
    30:4
  stood still in the riot of s., 305:8
  suddenly a s. from heaven, 37:6
  thou hearest the s. thereof, 35:16
  trumpet give uncertain s., 40:1
  voice as s. of many waters, 43:18
Sounds, folk songs from soul s.,
    188:8
  lay down the s., 264:2
Sour, grapes are s., 45:11
Source of joy for the heart, 58:3
South, captured and taken to
    extreme S., 99:1
  colored people at s. free and slaves,
    88:6
  did not grow up in the rural s.,
    503:7
  disabilities imposed in S., 118:1
  dogs stop biting in the S., 273:1
  even go back S., 298:4
  freeze to death in S. a slave, 142:8
  goin' back down s. child, 244:1
  muffled strain in Silent S., 135:2
  of the ghosts, 385:5
  ships fare north fare s., 5:2
  whether I live North or S., 130:7
  whirlwinds in the s., 22:5
South Africa, oppressed people in S.,
    264:5
  truth about racism in S., 265:2
  we have a vision of S., 265:2

South Africa *(continued)*
  white man of S., 518:10
South Central homey's newly risen,
    458:5
Southern, growing up S. Black girl,
    305:7
  Harlem S. Harlem, 215:3
  nights, 392:1
  seek the s. surges, 85:5
  white man owned Negro body
    soul, 139:4
Southern Africa, there is no peace in
    S., 341:7
Sovereignty, hide behind national s.,
    383:1
  implies responsibility, 382:5
Soweth, whatsoever a man s., 41:8
Sown, glean in fields they have not s.,
    210:3
  they have s. the wind, 24:6
Soza, this s. is wonderful thing, 413:2
Sozaboy, call myself S., 413:4
Space belongs to all of us, 504:4
  choc-full of traffic, 557:7
  fast black energy s., 355:1
  shadows flung into s., 232:8
Spaces, influenced by the nature of
    s., 543:2
Spaceship comin, 357:2
Spake as a child, 39:17
  never man s. like this man, 36:2
  three thousand proverbs, 14:1
Spanish Harlem, little clubs in S.,
    262:1
Spareth, he that s. his rod, 18:17
Spark, divine s. runs through all
    human creation, 401:2
  handed on the creative s., 443:5
Sparkle, today's sharp s., 532:2
Sparks fly upward, 15:6
Sparrow, His eye is on the s., 579:7
  take over now, 364:2
Spasms, progress never made by s.,
    135:3
Speak after manner of men, 38:9
  all men s. well of you, 33:11
  burn him if he s., 161:2
  can't s. for any million people, 270:2
  do not s. of Segu in Segu, 375:5
  fathers s. from graves, 100:6
  for freedom of every slave, 92:5
  for us but ourselves, 564:1
  free to write to s., 264:7
  I s. for you, 248:8

Spoons, better to be packed like s., 478:7

into belly of Jesus, 368:1

Sport, boxing is only s. get your brain shook, 438:7

life a diversion and s., 56:2

Spot, one s. to call my own Harlem, 215:1

Spots, leopard change his s., 23:13

Spray, white boil of s., 258:1

Spread, I have s. you abroad, 24:12

way he s. his wings, 195:1

Sprigs, tiny green s. men wore in their capes, 487:2

Sprout, seeds did not s., 336:6

Spyglass, chinaberry tree my s. tree, 257:7

Squeeze her never leave her, 412:1

St. James Infirmary, 572:4

St. Louis, got de S. Blues, 151:4

Missouri back in 1944, 301:3

Stabbing, wasn't loving her was s. her, 520:5

Stability in an uncivilized time, 537:1

Stackolee was a bad man, 568:3

Staff in your hand, 9:10

thy rod and s. comfort me, 16:10

Stage is the g-h-e-t-t-o, 547:3

wide world is my s., 194:4

Stagnation, forces of social s., 317:2

Stagolee was a man they killed, 568:2

Stain, foul and indelible thy s., 89:3

Stained-glass windows of Jesus, 256:3

Stair, feet won't climb the s., 307:2

life ain't been no crystal s., 211:3

Stairway, militaristic s. into hell, 319:5

Stake out a piece of life for herself, 238:4

Stale, challenge s. and conventional, 373:3

Stalk, gathering s. and root, 210:3

Stallion, like a s. on the track, 3:2

Stammerer spoke freely, 77:1

Stamps, my heroes on no s., 518:5

Stand, 435:3

alert, 280:4

aside and look, 450:2

aside hear voices of God, 136:1

by me, 128:5, 386:3

by you, 406:2

chance to s. on own legs, 106:4

don't s. on the track, 292:1

Stand *(continued)*

firm-footed unchanging, 86:7

gotta s. up once in this life, 435:7

I'm gon' s., 427:1

in opposition to oppression, 457:3

on top of the mountain, 211:6

tall and in proud shoes, 234:9

up be wrong right out, 271:5

up for your rights, 449:2

when we s. to sing, 321:1

Standards, beauty s. are our own invention, 489:1

live right attain the highest s., 159:5

Standing against the sky, 276:3

between myself and eternity, 472:8

in shadows of love, 409:5

like tree s. by water, 577:10

on the blood of our ancestors, 349:1

Stands forever in the middle, 277:8

in the wild weed, 260:5

Star, being a s. made it possible to get insulted, 289:9

day s. arise in your hearts, 43:11

encased in glass as glistening s., 55:7

every man is within his s., 186:6

gaze on guiding s., 261:4

give him the morning s., 43:22

giving divine light, 431:2

goin' home like a shootin' s., 84:1

in the east, 25:18

question every stripe every s., 349:6

terror did not come with s. and crescent, 470:2

to be s. not a gallery mascot, 517:6

you are a shining s., 473:6

you are my shining s., 484:3

Stars and skyscraper buildings, 329:6

be not darkened, 20:11

disgrace to have no s. to reach, 187:2

dreamed of the s., 169:3

everyone looks for s., 247:4

flying among s., 330:1

out under the moon s., 274:3

political position of s., 493:5

strung for a rattle, 218:5

telleth the number of the s., 18:10

when s. begin to fall, 577:5

Stars and Stripes, love the S., 126:1

pledging allegiance to s., 522:6

Stars *(continued)*

should never be polluted, 127:1

Star-spangled banner millions of slaves, 112:5

Start in middle and hold on tight, 239:6

learning what life is about, 436:8

off to a bad s., 253:3

saying now Black Power, 414:*n*1

talking about our plan, 539:9

when to s. when the beats commence, 539:1

with one end with another, 486:5

Started, far from where I s. from, 579:8

Starting, wanna be s. somethin', 511:6

Starvation wages, 321:2

Starve, men can s., 230:10

who cares million s., 331:9

Starved eye devours seascape, 330:6

the white race s. me, 215:1

Starving it's what being nice gets, 551:5

State, better in a s. of servitude, 74:5

democratic s. is not proven, 372:2

domestic traffic in slave s., 101:4

live in a s. of war, 70:1

Stature, Jesus increased in wisdom and s., 33:7

Status, credentials of s. and beauty, 507:4

impact of sexism on social s., 488:3

light color s. symbol, 263:1

not accept a lesser s., 208:6

Status quo, change in the s., 321:5

Stay, ain't got long to s. here, 578:6

and cooperate, 182:1

black and die, 573:8

cain't s. here, 205:1

here and have a part of it, 198:6

me with flagons, 21:6

real jiggy, 550:6

the fuck outta the ghetto, 551:6

we can s. where we want to s., 401:2

we can't s. here no more, 451:2

Steady, slow and s. wins race, 45:13

Steal away home, 578:6

away to Jesus, 578:6

God tries to s. home, 479:2

thou shalt not s., 10:8

Stealing, forgettin while s., 466:7

Step on dog's tail he will bite you, 565:22

within s. of the grave, 63:5

Steppingstone, converted rock of oppression into s., 460:3

Stepping-stone, unpaid labor a s., 83:7

Stereotype, basic truth beneath the s., 235:4

    Negro character, 206:1

Stereotyped, sexually s., 564:1

Stereotypes are incomplete, 562:9

Stereotyping of females begins, 287:2

Stew, w'en de s. is smokin' hot, 150:6

Stewards of the planet, 362:6

Stick, violent act from fist s. knife to gun, 485:4

Stigma around homosexuality, 505:4

Still and quiet with a smile, 200:4

    be s. and know that I am God, 17:2

    beside s. waters, 16:10

    keepin' s. and mindin' things, 67:6

    stood s. in the riot of sound, 305:8

    we are slaves, 84:3

Sting, beside nettle grows cure for its s., 90:5

    death where is thy s., 40:8

    like a bee, 417:4

    of truth, 482:8

Stink of our own breathing Jesus, 368:1

    rain to wash off the s., 369:3

Stir social conscience, 319:7

Stitch, dreams torn hard to s., 547:3

Stock Exchange, hillbilly music is like the S., 433:6

Stole from a silvered world, 164:8

Stolen, kills thief and owner of s. goods, 567:1

Stomach, laugh until s. ache, 306:2

    pacify s. with cool thoughts, 224:2

Stomp on mothafuckas' like herd of Bi-son, 395:7

Stompin' with you at the Savoy, 192:8

Stone, ask bread will give him a s., 27:9

    bones gone home to s., 398:5

    cast the first s., 36:3

    Christ was hit by a s., 493:7

    daddy rolling s., 333:2

    dash thy foot against s., 33:9

    each hurt swallowed is a s., 487:6

    faces of s., 224:7

    fall that morning, 325:5

    heart must be marble s., 195:5

    my age the s. age, 240:5

Stone *(continued)*

    no tears I'm s. I'm flesh, 461:6

    on my tongue, 545:1

    sling and s., 13:10

    the builders rejected, 364:6

    uniform red-brown s., 321:7

    who shall roll the s. away, 112:6

Stones cry out, 34:17

    five smooth s., 13:9

    house built with s. I hauled myself, 440:4

    left to be unearthed, 438:8

    throw s. at the bandwagon, 438:6

    time to cast away s., 19:17

    time to gather s., 19:17

    voices hitting walls like s., 305:8

    we have no guns only s., 373:5

Stop, being black does not s. you, 222:2

    can't s. me now, 436:2

    can't s. now Precious, 481:2

    doggin' me around, 512:3

    dogs s. biting in the South, 273:1

    Don't S. 'Til You Get Enough, 511:3

    in the name of love, 409:3

    one monkey don't s. no show, 572:5

    trying to be white, 196:6

    we will not s., 273:1

Stop-and-frisk, 559:1

Stopper's in my hand, 191:6

Stopping, Ain't No S. Us Now, 469:2

Store, build a s. of your own, 89:1

Stories, a space our s. tell, 416:2

    are letters, 415:1

    available to as many people's s., 500:9

    Brooklyn-born don't have no sob s., 539:7

    our s. are singular, 526:3

    sung by minstrels of old, 153:9

    the s. must be told, 416:1

    thousand different s. collide, 552:8

Storm, bleached by s., 276:2

    need s. whirlwind and earthquake, 105:2

    proud of having waded through a s., 450:5

    wrapped in s. shall I be battling, 85:5

Storms, endure what s. may come, 527:3

    of life are raging, 128:5

Stormy skin, 225:3

    we laugh at s. weather, 192:4

Story 'bout Minnie the Moocher, 226:5

    called Bible but it's dead now, 212:2

    each in her own time had a s., 479:3

    ends with freedom, 95:5

    fat ancestors that tell their s., 532:6

    forced to tell whole s., 283:4

    ghosted you up a swell s., 212:2

    great long s. to tell, 237:1

    hurting black s., 489:3

    I can set down this s., 515:2

    not a s. to pass on, 339:4

    of human progress, 527:6

    of Muck, 552:6

    of the Negro, 252:8

    one s. the only s., 562:9

    part of the larger American s., 523:1

    tell the s. how we've overcome, 128:4

    too horrible to hear, 79:2

    whatever you get that's your s., 219:5

    when you tell a s., 471:1

Story-making animal, 323:7

Storytelling problem, 534:2

Straight ahead can lead nowhere, 328:6

    and narrow or soul gets cast, 543:1

    gays unnatural because not s., 509:5

    make his paths s., 26:6

    make s. a highway for our God, 22:13

    talked s. two and two are four, 354:3

    the crooked shall be made s., 22:14

    we strike s., 259:8

Straighten up fly right, 269:6

Straights as well as white queers, 518:9

Strait is the gate, 27:10

Strand, two women on lone wet s., 157:7

Strange, a stranger in a s. land, 8:21

    environment not s. not friendly, 182:6

    feel so s. but sure is good, 385:2

    freedom to be adrift in the world, 202:5

    in that s. place, 174:8

Sun (continued)
  sometime s. shines in my life, 426:5
  subordinated s. and moon, 56:7
  sure as the s. will shine, 464:6
  when the s. goes down, 188:5
Sunday morning when we sing, 321:1
  today is S., 224:7
Sundays my father got up early, 243:3
Sunlight, child flying toward s., 314:7
  luminous with heat, 158:7
  ray of s. under earth, 290:9
  silk thread of s., 345:4
Sunny, Afric's s. sky, 85:5
Sunshine, ain't no s. when she's gone, 392:3
  joy and pain s. and rain, 454:1
  of My Life, 481:7
  on a cloudy day, 404:1
Suo quoque mos, 48:n5
Superbad, got soul and I'm s., 347:7
Superficial, disregard the s. for the real, 133:2
Superfly make your fortune, 423:6
Superhighway of justice, 319:3
Superior advantage of being white, 97:7
  one race s. another inferior, 183:6
  races are all fictions, 323:5
  what is this s. thing, 302:2
Superiority, impatient of airs of s., 90:3
  myth of white s., 193:4
  skin white proof of s., 185:1
Superstar, 'bout to burn out s., 563:7
Superstitious writing's on the wall, 481:8
Superstructure, economic infrastructure a s., 290:4
Superwoman, 491:10
Suppress his instincts, 353:6
Supremacists, white s. said, 302:2
Supremacy, Africa resolved to end white s., 197:4
  folklore of white s., 257:2
  legacy of white s., 495:3
  protest white man's s., 239:1
Supreme destiny in hands of God, 171:6
  listening like a judge s., 85:1
  love is s. and unconditional, 201:9

Supreme (continued)
  Love S., 300:6
Supreme Court, your appointment to S., 311:6
Surely God Is Able, 195:3
  the Lord is in this place, 8:9
Surf, white s. as it crashes, 332:4
Surface, always lurking under the s., 361:6
Surgery, it's not brain s., 499:4
Surges, seek the southern s., 85:5
Surmise, deciphering with a wild s., 199:4
Surname is depending who you speak to, 356:5
Surprise, after Eden was s., 331:4
Surprised, aggression that s. no one, 493:7
  to see a white man, 490:5
Surrender, is to s. my existence, 108:2
  to Him we s., 53:9
Surrenders, whosoever s. to God, 56:4
Surrounded, soon s. by strange men, 78:6
Survival, black s., 495:1
  consciousness of s., 422:2
  fighting for s., 450:3
  in prison studying for s., 490:9
  is luck or unlucky, 424:4
  Negro's s. in America, 252:8
  of the fittest attitude, 422:2
  on how swiftly leak is caulked, 185:5
  there is no s. here, 412:3
  what terms is s. possible, 202:2
  where else can you seek s., 234:3
Survive, hearts s. a locked-down life, 340:5
  how to s. prison intact, 267:3
  in warfare to s., 289:6
  kill him eat him to s., 289:6
  never meant to s., 357:7
  only the strong s., 430:1
  resisters need only s., 358:9
Surviving, habit of s., 263:2
Survivors, bitterness in s., 316:2
Sushi and fried catfish, 476:4
Suspicion crossed my mind, 494:1
  engagement can lift s. and fear, 529:1
  segregation fosters s., 157:5

Swaddling, wrapped in s. clothes, 33:3
Swagger, tough-guy s. looks dumb, 502:3
Swallow gudgeons ere they're catched, 45:n2
  up death in victory, 22:10
Swallowed, death s. in victory, 40:8
Swam, and Shine s. on, 571:14
Swamp of hatred, 380:2
  rice fields in s. did reap, 128:7
Sweat and blood done drenched this earth, 350:1
  blood and s. of the innocent, 410:5
  first bead of s., 331:4
  nuthin but s. inside my hand, 540:4
  of slavery, 302:2
  will get you change, 409:13
  your mind, 169:2
Swede, strike terror in S., 86:7
Sweep of sky, 258:1
Sweet, 287:n1
  Afouyéké oh my s. ma-ma, 574:14
  black angel, 195:1
  freedom's way, 212:8
  his mouth is most s., 21:10
  How S. It Is to Be Loved by You, 408:8
  life is short make it s., 173:9
  my heart was s. to excess, 3:5
  never find a s. man like me, 572:4
  play something s., 391:7
  pomegranate wine, 3:4
  sing and dream s. things, 515:6
  so cold so s. so fair, 572:4
  why our music is s., 515:6
Sweeter, blacker the berry s. the juice, 571:2
  no s. note than Liberty, 117:5
  than honey and honeycomb, 16:6
  you're s. goodness knows, 192:7
Sweetest taboo, 517:1
Sweetness, little s. down in my soul, 352:3
Swift, God is s. at the reckoning, 55:8
  race not to the s., 20:9
Swifter than eagles, 13:15
Swiftness of thy course, 71:8
Swill, bitter s. of civil war, 527:1
Swim, learn how to s., 334:4
  like me, 571:14
Swine, cast pearls before s., 27:6
  is unclean to you, 11:1

Swing dat hammer, 205:3
  Don't Mean a Thing If It Ain't Got That S., 219:3
  low sweet chariot, 577:2
Swinging, can't keep s. when fight's over, 224:3
  keep s. at them, 353:4
  low then out of sight, 329:3
Swoop, one by one or in fell s., 123:8
Sword against his fellow, 13:6
  cutteth like a s., 59:1
  every man's s. against his brother, 23:22
  fallen by the s., 25:13
  flaming s. which turned every way, 7:2
  lay down my s., 578:11
  my word is my s., 544:1
  nation shall not lift up s., 22:1
  take the s. perish the s., 31:12
  with harp and s., 181:8
  word of God sharper than s., 42:17
Swords, beat s. into plowshares, 22:1
Symbol, darkness made into s., 322:6
  is useful to the spirit, 189:4
  light color status s., 263:1
  of limits, 249:2
  rainbow s. of hope, 302:4
Symbols, trees are s. of peace and hope, 401:7
Sympathy, beg and plead for your s., 397:3
  demand your s. and aid, 116:3
  I came not here for s., 123:2
  I don't beg for s., 273:3
  tears will get you s., 409:13
Symphony, I hear a s., 408:11
Symptoms of the illness in its music, 507:1
Synagogues, abetted by white churches and s., 310:1
Syncopation, vine of s., 500:8
Syndrome, Post Traumatic Slave S., 506:1
Synthetic myths, 393:6
System, born under a s., 299:3
  criminal justice s. is not colorblind, 523:4
  that s. meant for us, 287:9
  where a white man can destroy, 343:10
Systematic oppression, 359:2
Systems, immoral social s., 519:3

T

Tabernacles, how amiable are thy t., 17:14
  thy t. O Israel, 11:9
Table, crumbs from their masters' t., 29:4
  crumbs that fall from t., 292:2
  eat at the welcome t., 579:4
  enemy not under dining t. but outside, 512:8
  going to dinner t. at hotel, 106:4
  lay it all on the t., 178:6
  not going to sit at your t., 295:2
  of brotherhood, 318:1
  of dark breasts, 225:8
  of privilege, 492:4
  preparest a t. before me, 16:10
  sit at whatever t. they want, 506:6
  slave driver t. is turn, 449:5
  stretched out on long white t., 572:4
Tables, crumb falls from t. of joy, 213:4
  of the moneychangers, 29:18
Tablet, personal mythic t., 381:3
Taboo, give me the sweetest t., 517:1
Taboos, old t. of the land, 437:7
Tag, I know my t. Slam, 378:7
Tailor-mades and hand-me-downs, 151:8
Tainted with the hateful virus, 271:2
Take a dose of rock 'n' roll, 303:3
  back your God damn rib, 292:8
  cannot go forward unless you t. us, 218:1
  care say with presence of mind, 48:8
  eat this is my body, 31:6, 39:14
  for ourselves, 262:5
  get what you can t., 176:8
  heart, 575:14
  I'll t. you there, 399:5
  it, 296:3
  it or leave it as it was, 283:8
  me as I am, 241:3
  me to the river, 455:4
  my yoke, 28:8
  no prisoners, 383:9
  nothing of his labor, 20:1
  refuge in how, 336:7
  smash reach in t. what I want, 458:5
  thank you I can t. that too, 406:6

Take *(continued)*
  the A train, 254:8
  the sword perish the sword, 31:12
  thy rod, 9:5
  up read, 52:7
  up thy bed, 32:7
  what rightfully belongs, 492:4
  what she wants from both, 377:5
  when it comes you won't t. it, 115:4
  white man will t. it back, 262:5
  you to task, 53:11
  your guns, 108:7
Taken away that which he hath, 30:9
  liberty can be t. away, 203:4
  Lord gave and hath t., 14:19
  one t. the other left, 30:6
  shall not be t. away from her, 34:5
  when freedom is t. away, 267:2
Takers, nation of t., 528:7
Takes a village to raise a child, 574:3
Taketh away the sin of the world, 35:10
Tale, alive to tell the t., 130:5
  spend our years as a t. is told, 17:18
  to tell, 282:3
Talent, genius t. hide its luster, 90:2
  not excuse for bad manners, 289:7
  rewarded on basis of merit, 215:6
  uses its own t., 295:10
  wins games, 534:7
Talented Tenth missionaries of culture, 143:4
  Negro race saved by T., 143:2
Tales of the hunt glorify the hunter, 567:12
  words seemed idle t., 35:2
Talk any more about dances, 497:1
  cannot all t. at once we can take turns, 477:3
  do more t. less, 111:6
  for the rest of my life, 275:8
  is important, 270:6
  make our t. ring true, 286:4
  theology, 299:2
  to black guy down the street, 533:3
  when you t. to an oak tree, 350:2
  will be no art t., 385:7
  with each other about race, 483:4
Talked about sure's you born, 578:7
  down to working cheap, 277:8

Talked *(continued)*
   straight about the world, 354:3
Talking about a revolution, 536:5
   about death part of life, 451:6
   back, 488:5
   blues is life's way of t., 451:4
   'bout my girl, 404:1
   'bout the ghetto, 448:4
   'bout you and me, 309:7
   keep on a-walkin' keep on a-t.,
      579:2
   like a victim, 448:2
   listen to the people t., 567:6
   of Companions and pious folk,
      60:2
   painting is kind of t. about life,
      235:3
   start t. about our plan, 539:9
Talks, love the way he t., 315:4
   to me in my dreams, 546:1
Tall as a cypress strong, 279:7
   as fairy tale beanstalk, 257:7
Tamarind Season, 460:4
Tambourine, Grandma's hands
   played the t., 392:4
Tampon, and the last t., 367:7
Tangent, some t. about Islamic
   terrorism, 470:2
Tangerines and mangoes, 175:5
Tans, white people on t., 298:1
Taped wall 47 black faces, 336:3
Tar Beach, sleeping on T. was
   magical, 329:6
Tar-heat, sticky t. roofs, 506:4
Task, giving all to a difficult t., 527:2
   righteousness of one's t., 312:1
   sew a useless t. it seems, 154:2
   take you to t., 53:11
Taste him in the dusty air, 462:6
   of glory like sweet wine, 239:1
   truth leaves bad t. in mouth, 134:4
   want to t. freedom, 111:5
Taste-making of mass media, 446:4
Tastes, leisure to cultivate t., 257:8
Tattoo, shame I wear like a t., 517:3
Taught Man that he knew not, 57:6
   to look up to white folks, 193:3
Taupe mahogany bronze, 182:2
Tax, nobody insults colored man in
   T. Office, 110:3
Taxes, second-class citizen don't pay
   first-class t., 343:4
Taxing, being Black is emotionally t.,
   500:6

Tchaikovsky, tell T. the news, 299:6
Tea, waters them with t., 460:6
Teach a barren world to dance, 443:2
   all nations, 32:4
   beasts shall t. thee, 15:8
   each one t. one, 570:15
   earth shall t. thee, 15:8
   education must t. work t. Life,
      143:3
   him what has been said, 1:3
   me who I might be without race,
      415:8
   me who you might be without
      race, 415:8
   our children, 410:2
   us not to give a fuck, 556:1
   us old ones how to play, 430:7
   us to number our days, 17:19
Teachers, bunch of substitute t.,
   544:8
Teaches, he who learns t., 566:1
   religion t. us to respect, 294:5
Teaching, asked on a t. application,
   368:7
   important the work incessant,
      111:7
   of the three R's, 229:4
   slaves to read and write, 209:1
Teamwork and intelligence win
   championships, 534:7
Tear, gonna t. this building down,
   451:2
   of sensibility, 75:1
   right to their own t., 536:4
Tearing everything down, 451:2
Tears, all my help was cries and t.,
   73:1
   and blood sacrificed, 83:7
   are very close to my eyes, 465:5
   enriched America with blood and
      t., 78:3
   fell into hand, 325:2
   fire blood, 293:6
   God shall wipe away all t., 45:4
   hence these t., 47:3
   Lord God will wipe away t.,
      22:10
   no one will wipe my t., 291:3
   no t. I'm stone I'm flesh, 461:6
   of a clown, 405:2
   pages of history blistered with t.,
      127:2
   polished piano with her t.,
      451:10

Tears *(continued)*
   rage and t., 47:*n3*
   rivers of t. lakes of blood, 118:4
   the t. we save, 432:1
   tracks of my t., 404:4
   wasted water's all that is, 392:6
   will get you sympathy, 409:13
Teenage, antifamily everything but
   t., 485:3
Teen-ager in these ghettoes, 297:2
Teeth, cut my t. as the black raccoon,
   218:5
   open its mouth and examine its t.,
      377:6
   skin of my t., 15:12
Teethed on a silver spoon, 218:5
Telegraph, Negro t. reached last
   slave, 456:3
Telephone, no t. to heaven, 454:7
   somebody's calling over my t.,
      234:6
Televised, revolution will not be t.,
   474:2
Tell alive to t. the tale, 130:5
   don't care who you t., 548:2
   'em I'm not at home, 234:6
   fowls shall t. thee, 15:8
   go t. it on the mountain, 576:8
   him howdy, 205:6
   him what you want, 333:8
   Me How Long the Train's Been
      Gone, 568:4
   me what'd I say, 326:6
   no lies, 285:9
   the glories of our journey, 253:4
   the truth, 561:9
   them about the dream, 236:2
   them im strong, 351:1
   truth about me lie about me, 49:3
Telleth the number of the stars,
   18:10
Telling, cutting off man's legs and t.
   him to walk, 68:3
   tired of t. young men they can't,
      558:9
   what they delighted in t., 60:2
Tell-tale sign of living, 467:2
Temperate in exercise of political
   rights, 132:5
Temple, Chinaberry Tree became a
   T., 164:1
   library t. of learning, 297:8
   of God is holy, 39:5
   of Jerusalem, 54:10

Thing, a mind is a terrible t. to waste, 573:6
   always try to do the right t., 508:7
   beautiful needful t., 243:1
   Don't Mean a T. If It Ain't Got That Swing, 219:3
   essence of t. returning to origin of t., 521:6
   every little t. gonna be all right, 449:13
   it's a black t., 574:4
   it's your t., 378:2
   never lose t. belongs to you, 329:1
   no new t. under the sun, 19:12
   that makes you exceptional, 328:1
   to every t. there is a season, 19:17
   upsets a t. know how to rearrange it, 565:21
   written about this color t., 408:1
Thing-oriented society, 319:9
Things, affection on t. above, 41:15
   ain't what they used to be, 396:6
   all t. come to pass, 385:6
   all t. must come to pass, 30:3
   best t. in life are free, 315:2
   buying t. for kids, 376:7
   by him all t. consist, 41:14
   certain t. don't matter anymore, 178:6
   created by him all t., 41:14
   filled the hungry with good t., 32:22
   foolish to trust in t., 363:1
   he is before all t., 41:14
   He knoweth all t., 57:2
   how can these t. be, 35:17
   I am made all t. to men, 39:11
   keepin' still and mindin' t., 67:6
   moderation in all t., 47:2
   more excellent, 38:6
   no bright bickle no nuff, 268:5
   plead cause in t. which concern us, 80:1
   prove all t., 42:3
   remembrance of t. to come, 19:13
   seizes two t. one always slips, 564:8
   that drive men to sea is women, 465:3
   they got t. and we ain't, 230:9
   unto the pure all t. pure, 42:15
   vicissitudes in all t., 48:6
   visible and invisible all t., 41:14
   we find ourselves in, 252:6

Things (continued)
   will not always continue the same, 569:11
   with no names, 339:10
Think, Act Like a Lady T. Like a Man, 504:2
   black, 421:6
   kindly too of others, 181:10
   let your mind go, 419:1
   on these things, 41:13
   pains people having to t., 318:4
   play like you t., 219:5
   say nothing but t. a great deal, 76:2
   what man shall t. what he will do, 154:6
   what we're told we t., 459:4
Thinketh, he t. in his heart, 19:2
Thinking, confined to ghetto t., 469:4
   no more backward t., 486:1
   time for t. ahead, 486:1
   virtues of right t., 163:5
Third and fourth generation that hate me, 10:6
   beast had face as a man, 44:3
   day he will raise us up, 24:3
Third world, dem go call us T., 387:3
   guest-workers from t., 329:5
Thirst, he that believeth on me shall never t., 35:23
   hunger and t. after righteousness, 26:12
   neither t. any more, 44:12
Thirsty and ye gave me drink, 30:11
Thirty pieces of silver, 24:14
This little light of mine, 578:16
   was not done in a corner, 38:3
Thorn, cast down t. of prejudice, 190:5
   in the flesh, 41:1
Thorns in your sides, 12:12
Thou art ever with me, 34:12
   art the man, 13:21
   art the Son of God, 29:2
   art with me, 16:10
Thought as a child, 39:17
   wake t. in a man, 180:12
   words made to conceal t., 98:2
Thoughtless, contented slave make a t. one, 104:4
Thoughts, contribute our good t., 190:2
   effluvia of endless t., 240:6
   God lies under the t. of man, 434:6

Thoughts (continued)
   hurt like real pain, 272:1
   in solitude t. ripened, 114:4
   of the heart, 42:17
   pacify with cool t., 224:2
Thousand, cattle upon a t. hills, 17:3
   little one shall become a t., 23:6
   many t. gone, 578:3
   one among a t., 15:21
   one man among a t. found, 20:6
   songs a t. and five, 14:1
   three t. proverbs, 14:1
   twenty t. different ladies, 367:2
   years are as yesterday when past, 17:17
Thousands, and David ten t., 13:11
   of pilgrims, 295:8
   passion of fear hath slain t., 67:1
   Saul hath slain t., 13:11
Thread, cut the t. of life, 63:5
Threads, diamond tooth n' flashy t., 500:8
   of life, 63:5
Threat to international peace, 245:4
Three, I am t., 277:8
   times a lady, 473:2
Three-fifths, ancestors t. of a man, 498:6
Three-year-old, revelations of a t., 337:6
Thrice, thou shalt deny me t., 31:7
Thrifty to prepare today, 46:6
Thrill, but what a t., 333:6
   of fear, 490:5
Thrills, that t. me to death, 403:2
Throat, capitalistic hand around t., 548:6
   grip guitar as somebody's t., 497:2
   hope is a song in a weary t., 235:1
   know not who may grasp t., 93:7
   like bitterness in the t., 348:2
   razor threatens the t., 305:7
   sinks tiger's tooth into t., 175:6
   society's foot on t., 329:4
   when I clear my t., 547:1
Throne, carried to the t. of grace, 72:3
   descend to earth place thy t., 72:1
   happy saint on immortal t., 71:5
   Madonna thou shalt t., 86:6
Through envy of devil came death, 25:5
   fire and water, 17:8

Throw away fears and prejudices,
  78:4
  it away t. it away, 329:1
  too much invested to t. it away,
    270:2
  up both my hands, 396:5
Thumbprints, misery always leaves
  t., 550:4
Thunder, ain't afeared of t. and
  lightning, 210:2
  catch the t., 280:4
  grumbling t. in your wake, 181:10
  how does one say No in t., 345:5
  how does one scream in t., 360:4
  is not yet rain, 564:12
  none but him dat makes de t.,
    570:2
  not the gentle shower but t., 105:2
  skin streaks with t., 225:3
  want rain without t., 105:9
Thy kingdom come, 27:2
Thyself, physician heal t., 33:10
Ticket, price for t. to become white,
  285:6
  to anywhere, 536:8
Tickets, strip t. still illusion, 214:6
Ticks in cracks of cement floors,
  439:6
Tide that is entering even now, 367:6
Tidings, bringer of good t., 54:1
  I bring you good t., 33:4
Ties, creates t. to torture us, 260:8
Tiger, roaring of the t., 241:1
Tiger's, sinks t. tooth into throat,
  175:6
Tiller, Cain was a t. of the ground,
  7:3
Timbrels harps cornets and cymbals,
  13:19
Time and chance happeneth to all,
  20:9
  and distance cannot shrink it,
    180:10
  as much t. in library as on
    basketball, 458:3
  becomes ally of stagnation, 317:2
  before birth, 226:1
  before is preferable and consoling,
    540:1
  bitter fruits of t., 515:6
  black artist has wasted t., 280:2
  cracks into furious flower, 260:4
  crumble before the breath of t.,
    158:2

Time *(continued)*
  do not lessen the t., 1:6
  don't have t. to feel sorry, 277:1
  dreams mocked by T., 179:9
  falleth suddenly upon them, 20:9
  for healing of the wounds, 266:9
  for martyrs now, 297:7
  give t. to get over prejudices, 123:8
  go with T. and leave him there,
    158:1
  has come the question to be met,
    79:5
  in t. of peace and war, 172:9
  is a pendulum, 210:1
  is a shadow, 25:4
  is at hand, 31:2
  is neutral, 316:4
  journey towards a preordained t.,
    56:7
  leaves marks upon all things, 65:2
  left to t. t. will never come, 123:8
  longer dan a rope, 575:7
  love and hate cause t. to drag
    down, 491:6
  man knoweth not his t., 20:9
  moves on, 536:3
  moves slowly but passes quickly,
    444:4
  never stops does it end, 557:6
  no man ahead of his t., 186:6
  nothing destroys but t., 56:9
  now is the accepted t., 40:12
  of peace, 19:17
  of times and a half t., 122:5
  of war, 19:17
  on side of oppressed, 295:9
  passage of t. to quietly erode, 521:6
  removes distress, 47:8
  shadow of t., 242:8
  shall close the door, 158:1
  short in transitory world, 87:2
  snared in an evil t., 20:9
  the wasting of t., 1:6
  thinking about soul, 282:4
  to accomplish life's work, 297:1
  to be born, 19:17
  to break down, 19:17
  to build is upon us, 266:9
  to build up, 19:17
  to cast away stones, 19:17
  to dance, 19:17
  to die, 19:17
  to embrace, 19:17
  to every purpose, 19:17

Time *(continued)*
  to gather stones, 19:17
  to get, 19:17
  to get together, 355:1
  to hate, 19:17
  to heal, 19:17
  to keep, 19:17
  to keep silence, 19:17
  to kill, 19:17
  to laugh, 19:17
  to lose, 19:17
  to love, 19:17
  to mourn, 19:17
  to plant, 19:17
  to pluck up, 19:17
  to refrain from embracing, 19:17
  to rend, 19:17
  to sew, 19:17
  to speak, 19:17
  to weep, 19:17
  touches with destroying hand,
    134:3
  upholds or overturns, 259:7
  want extra t. and your kiss, 514:5
  will always be, 386:1
  will bring about civil rights, 123:8
Time's wheel still rolls, 545:4
Times, let the good t. roll, 228:5
  of challenge and controversy,
    318:6
  signs of the t., 29:6, 103:7
  these are tryin' t., 448:5
  until seventy t. seven, 29:12
Timetable for another man's
  freedom, 317:1
  name on L&N t., 257:7
Timetables, we believe in goals and
  t., 292:3
Timing, mastering the art of t., 479:4
Tinker and daydream, 372:7
Tinted thoughts to paint you true,
  175:7
Tipitina tra la la la, 268:1
Tipping Point, 533:7
Tips, father worked for white
  people's t., 173:6
Tire, if he no t. dem go t. am, 387:2
Tired and jest resting, 451:1
  building somebody else's
    civilization, 173:7
  don't feel no ways t., 579:8
  feets is t. but soul is rested, 204:3
  if t. keep going, 111:5
  of giving in, 245:1

Truths, guns lack body of human t., 448:1

its own breed of t., 485:2

one falsehood spoils thousand t., 565:11

Try first thyself, 46:*n*2

no matter how hard you t., 436:2

you must t. and t., 464:8

Trying, afraid of not t., 551:1

Get Rich or Die T., 560:4

I can't accept not t., 534:6

times, 448:5

to live without friends, 181:3

you does stop t. after time, 321:8

Tub, every t. on its own bottom, 570:13

Tumbling, walls come t. down, 576:6

Tune, trying to t. out the whipping, 459:2

Tunnel, Harlem rumbling into a t., 215:3

Turn, approach slowly and quickly t. away, 67:4

do not cast nor t. away, 51:2

it up, 518:1

thee behind me, 14:7

Turtledove, voice of the t. speaks out, 3:5

TV, easy life of T. and gasoline, 491:3

rap is black America's T. station, 518:3

Tweedledee, choose between T. and Tweedledum, 427:7

Twelve baskets full, 28:21

Twenty-four, truth in t. hours, 356:2

Twice, fool me t. shame on me, 572:8

Twilight, child out of t., 314:7

glowed with t., 225:8

Twin, poetry is music's t., 381:2

Twins, votes and guns inseparable t., 288:3

Twist, let's do the t., 303:2

Twisted like crumpled roots, 165:1

Two black men a dangerous mob, 544:4

can t. walk together, 24:9

cities formed by t. loves, 53:6

days will he revive us, 24:3

five loaves t. fishes, 28:20

just straight t. and t. are four, 354:3

Lands are in festivity, 5:1

no man can serve t. masters, 27:3

Two *(continued)*
of every sort bring into the ark, 7:10

on these t. commandments hang law and prophets, 30:1

or three gathered together, 29:11

places all go after death, 64:2

wisdom t. words wait hope, 88:3

Twoness, feels his t. an American a Negro, 143:6

Tyranny, inoculate victims against own t., 497:4

judicial t., 419:4

of The Majority, 477:3

silent in the face of t., 361:5

within that t., 304:1

Tyrant, any excuse will serve a t., 46:9

timeless and elastic, 381:3

wars made earth a grave, 129:1

Tyrants, era of little t., 282:1

make the t. tremble, 75:1

not free men, 304:2

pronounce it cursing the day, 73:4

U

Ugliness, motley of u. and beauty, 182:2

snow fell obscuring the u., 238:6

you learn how to use, 290:2

Ugly, an u. thing a tourist, 471:7

and can't cook but I'm here, 444:7

black is u., 276:1

I know I'm dreadfully u., 290:2

to the bone, 571:3

white is u., 276:1

Uh that's the sound of men workin', 334:1

Ujamaa cooperative economics, 410:8

Ujima responsibility, 410:8

Ultimate source of power, 573:1

Umbilical cord stretches across oceans, 361:9

cord was severed, 362:8

Umbilically, oppression and freedom u. tied, 428:8

Umbrella in 40 years of rain, 274:4

Umoja unity, 410:8

Unafraid, less important whether I am u., 358:4

Un-American as bolshevism, 233:1

Un-Americans, you are the u., 198:7

Unarmed people are slaves, 424:8

truth final word, 319:5

Unawares, entertained angels u., 42:19

Unbearable as freedom, 283:3

shame u. shame, 147:6

Unbelievers, do not the u. see, 55:4

in pursuit of happiness, 465:6

works of u. a mirage, 55:8

Unborn, foundation laid for generations u., 88:7

Unbought and Unbossed, 286:3

Unbroken chain of ancestors, 190:1

thorny brush, 537:3

Uncertainty of life, 63:5

remain in this cruel u., 67:3

Unchanging, stand firm-footed u., 86:7

Uncle Sam, colored soldiers fought for U., 149:4

Unclean, she became an u. thing, 136:4

swine is u. to you, 11:1

Uncommon, what is u. is rarely believed, 68:7

Unconditional love final word, 319:5

love is supreme and u., 201:9

Under, keep from going u., 520:6

Many great men are u. me, 57:9

no better thing u. the sun, 20:8

we were u. it and that counts too, 501:4

Underclass, black u., 366:2

Underdeveloped countries are exploited, 427:4

Nations, 387:3

Underdog, anti-intellectual u., 542:3

Underground Railroad, transact the business of U., 110:5

Understand argument without punishment, 60:1

colored people u. white people, 147:4

I am something you'll never u., 514:1

it better by and by, 128:4

my hatred, 209:4

where you are, 261:4

you by and by, 423:2

Understanding, candle of u., 25:1

draw u. to yourself, 200:4

of history, 251:2

where is place of u., 15:16

with all thy getting get u., 18:13

Understood as a child, 39:17
  I am u. but partially so, 91:3
Undertaker, name in the u. book, 438:7
Undo, do not u. me I bear you sacrifice, 566:10
Undoing, doing u. in this country, 257:3
Unemployed, blacks u. called lazy, 409:10
  whites u. called depression, 409:10
Unemployment is like a curse, 369:5
  victims of u., 176:7
Unequal, difference produced by u. opportunities, 132:3
Unfailing, motherlove is u., 457:7
Unfair, and u. we are black magicians, 354:4
  we are u., 354:4
Unfamiliar moving from familiar to u., 248:10
Unfortunate, fate of our u. color, 65:1
Unfree people created freest forms blues and jazz, 495:6
Unhappiness, happiness or u., 259:5
Unharnessed hearts can survive, 340:5
Unheard, riot the language of u., 320:4
Uniform, boys with gun and u., 413:2
Union gives strength, 46:17
  path of a more perfect u., 525:2
  path to a more perfect u., 525:3
  secret of our lack of u., 96:1
  where are our u. and love, 88:7
Unions, forbidden to form u., 329:5
Unique as the white tiger's blue eyes, 199:4
Unite, call for black people to u., 414:2
  the intellectuals, 166:2
United mass action, 266:6
United Nations get name for us, 387:3
  not history taught in U., 294:1
  save what it can, 264:6
United States, not dragged to the U., 380:3
  only Negro in U., 178:7
Uniting the Negro masses, 166:2

Unity, apparent u. among Caucasians, 348:5
consciousness precedes u., 417:12
does not require we be identical, 358:8
never achieve u. under white supremacy, 348:5
never between white non-white, 295:8
over division, 523:7
umoja u., 410:8
U.N.I.T.Y. that's a u., 553:7
want of u. in action, 96:1
way to u. is through hearts, 166:2
Universal, artists express u. language, 335:2
Caucasian problem is u., 193:4
death am u., 94:6
in order to create u., 328:5
song of Creator's praise, 81:1
suffering is u., 202:7
Universe, arc of moral u., 319:7, 319:n1, 531:1
driven by intricate twists of story line, 514:8
revolves in rhythm, 305:1
the city is the U., 250:7
this is a big beautiful u., 300:5
University education one of privileges, 178:1
Unjust, contemplates alike just and u., 86:1
in least u. in much, 34:13
let him be u. still, 45:6
to ask black community, 275:2
Unknown that does not terrify, 310:4
Unlearned, I am u., 51:1
Unleavened, roast with fire and u. bread, 9:9
seven days shall ye eat u. bread, 9:12
Unliberated, territory remains u., 233:7
Unlock the races, 189:15
Unlocked the interlacings of love, 200:7
Unloose, shoes I am not worthy to u., 32:6
Unlucky, survival is luck or u., 424:4
Unnatural, gays u. because not straight, 509:5
Unnecessary to march on Washington, 400:4

Unnoticed, envied people who remained u., 86:3
Unpaid labor a stepping-stone, 83:7
Unprotected, unsafe u. random violence hated, 495:4
Unrecognizable, everything was u., 439:3
Unrest, catch first sprinkle of u., 280:4
Unsafe unprotected violence hated, 495:4
Unseen, cloud of witnesses u., 348:3
Unselfishness must be the fuel, 166:2
Unshackle my mind, 91:4
Unshakable humanity, 546:3
Unspeakable horrors, 317:9
Unsullied, city u. by worship of idols, 60:3
Untarnished, make your history u., 173:1
Untied the monsters, 240:6
Until the indignation be overpast, 22:12
Unwhole, so used to being u., 394:6
Upbringing was something I was not English, 472:3
Upright, forgot what it was to walk u., 394:6
  he walketh u., 57:4
Upset, don't know what causes the u., 509:1
Upsetter, I am the u., 373:6
Upsweep, gimme an u. Minnie, 258:6
Upward I look I seek my goal, 82:2
Urban, America's u. blacks, 208:2
  black u. fashion, 510:6
  survival in the u. areas, 422:2
Urgency, this is the u. live, 260:3
Ursa Corregidora, I am U. have tears for eyes, 470:5
Us are the Folks, 323:9
  remember u. we the people, 539:9
  they are u., 555:1
Use any means necessary, 296:1
  your brains, 436:10
Used, must be my u. to be, 169:7
  to love her, 445:9
  you will get u. to it, 396:2
Useful as a tool to the hand, 189:4
Useless, love the most u. word, 340:4
Utmost bound of the everlasting hills, 8:19
Utterance of my name, 49:2

V

Vacuum, nature abhors a v., 441:3
Vagabond kids run like colts, 276:2
Vain, he did not die in v., 187:1
  labors in v., 230:6
  not take name of Lord thy God in
    v., 10:6
  the Present teaches but in v., 150:8
  their living was not in v., 348:3
  too v. to play anything bad, 301:1
  was the war in v., 126:4
  when all your love's in v., 237:3
  words in your oaths, 53:11
  you have not died in v., 275:6
Valiant men to slay, 65:9
  shepherd who drives his flock, 4:5
Valley, every v. shall be exalted, 22:14
  full of bones, 23:19
  mother Nile V., 279:6
  of the shadow of death, 16:10
  peace in the v., 201:2
Valleys and mountains upon my
    body, 358:5
  hills and v. he come through,
    327:7
  lily of the v., 21:5
  mountains and v. he roams, 389:6
Valor, men of v., 12:8
Valuable, more visible but not more
    v., 457:9
Value, accepted white v. systems,
    463:4
  cannot be counted for my full v.,
    130:7
  fiction of v. to any people, 136:2
  human beings of infinite v., 341:8
  not come a single human v., 241:7
  of winning access, 239:6
  systems that reduce human
    dignity, 454:6
  teach v. of useful books, 116:2
Values and meanings most real,
    189:1
  created predominantly
    materialistic, 220:4
  good and bad, 395:6
  integration involves change in v.,
    309:2
  right wing family v. man, 389:7
  spiritual v. have lagged behind,
    220:4
Vampires of thought, 232:8
Vandalism, repeated acts of v., 279:5
Vanilla suburbs, 407:4

Vanish, all creatures must die and v.,
    61:1
  I shall be buried and v., 61:1
Vanity is fear, 346:5
Variations, no matter what the v.,
    247:2
  on theme by morning, 292:7
Variety of tongues and hues, 56:3
  throughout His creation, 121:5
Vases beads receipts dolls, 259:6
Vaulted, through v. skies, 71:6
Veil, do not v. the truth, 53:8
  living seen through a v., 180:14
  mysterious v. he entered the
    world, 209:6
  of Color, 144:1
  of ignorance, 572:2
Vein, dark v. of intolerance, 381:1
  divided to the v., 330:5
  nearer than his jugular v., 56:12
  vibrant v. bent crooked, 382:2
Veins, Blue V., 134:2
  fire of life and youth in his v.,
    130:3
  Negro blood flowing in his v.,
    108:5
Velour, laid out in my green v., 379:5
Veneer isn't worth anything, 141:8
Venetian, African river no
    resemblance to V. canal, 513:5
Vengeance is mine, 38:21
  shall be taken on him, 7:7
Venus Hottentot, 531:3
Verb, my name should be a v., 547:1
Vernacular, speak street v. and job
    interview, 558:5
Versailles, palms greater than V.,
    331:3
Verses, copied the best v., 82:3
Vessel, chosen v., 37:11
  I am like a broken v., 16:14
  lone v. confidently sets sail, 233:6
Vestige of slavery, 452:6
Veterans, return of Vietnam v.,
    390:8
Vibrations, was bout v., 394:4
Vice, no monopoly on v., 276:1
Vices, go light on v., 224:2
  ladder of our v., 52:13
  of white man copied by Negro,
    140:2
Vicious cycle of black community,
    457:10
Vicissitudes in all things, 48:6

Victim, can't spend life acting like a
    v., 448:2
  of a thousand lynchings, 231:3
  of its lusts and pride, 101:2
Victimhood, enshrinement of v.,
    542:3
Victimization, victims the cause of
    their own v., 246:5
Victimized, tempo of triumph by v.,
    361:8
Victims ad infinitum, 412:5
  before they were its v., 242:1
  black folk not v., 327:2
  comfort v. of evil, 372:7
  make history or remain the v.,
    492:1
  of the night eternal, 232:8
  of the shadows, 232:8
  of white racism, 297:9
  rob it of its v., 391:1
  to the improvident avarice, 69:3
Victories, claim no easy v., 285:9
Victory, death swallowed in v., 40:8
  eve of complete v., 222:5
  for Black people, 463:7
  grave where is thy v., 40:8
  in the ring, 159:1
  lasts, 225:2
  march till v. won, 147:3
  no v. to crown her banners, 113:5
  peace has no pantheon of v., 383:4
  swallow up death in v., 22:10
  this v. truly belongs to you, 526:2
  when cavalry won it was a v., 343:8
Video, average girl from v., 561:1
Viet Cong, no quarrel with them V.,
    417:7
Vietnam, autopsy read V., 319:8
  good guys in V., 286:4
  return of V. veterans, 390:8
View, accepted white man's v. of
    ourselves, 463:4
Vigilance, future security rights
    depend on v., 503:3
Vigilant, be sober be v., 43:10
Vile habits acquired in servitude,
    74:3
Village, freedom in this v., 507:2
  take a v. to raise a chile, 563:8
  takes a v. to raise a child, 574:3
  to the edge of the v., 274:3
Villages, nine v. and beyond, 322:7
Vine, fruit of the v., 31:6
  of syncopation, 500:8

Vines, land of v. and fig trees, 11:15
  little foxes that spoil the v., 21:7
  our v. have tender grapes, 21:7
Vineyard, glean thy v., 11:3
  grape of thy v., 11:3
  labored long in my v., 148:6
Vineyards of equality, 230:6
Violating law in interest of a people,
    437:3
Violence a potent drug for
    oppressed, 359:3
  and injury grow, 184:1
  black-on-black v., 503:1
  can breed counter-violence, 266:3
  detaining by fraud and v., 66:2
  has always been around, 485:4
  in poor black neighborhoods
    borne of violent past, 530:1
  is as American as cherry pie, 427:5
  is immoral, 316:2
  is v., 189:13
  making of truth is v. too, 552:8
  meet v. with v., 298:5
  oppressive language is v., 339:8
  our fight is against v., 145:2
  overcome non-violence, 387:4
  subject to random v., 495:4
  was foreign to his nature, 187:1
  wrong abroad, 294:4
  wrong in America, 294:4
Violent act from fist stick knife to
    gun, 485:4
Violets and soul's forgotten dream,
    154:1
Violin tongues whispering, 292:7
Viper, serpent none the less a v., 94:1
Virgin, behold a v. with child, 25:17
  I am wife and v., 49:1
Virgin Mary, once good like the V.,
    173:6
Virginny, carry me back to old V.,
    130:1
Virgins, heaven likened unto ten v.,
    30:7
Virtue, breaking the barriers of v.,
    69:4
  deprive them half their v., 70:1
  greatest v. becomes greatest crime,
    207:1
  if there be any v., 41:13
  knows no color line, 139:7
  lead them in path of v., 75:1
  no monopoly on v., 276:1
  was not an ornament, 130:6

Virtues, carelessness of civic v., 135:1
  flaws of character into v., 471:2
  of white man copied by Negro,
    140:2
  one drop neutralized her v., 136:4
  practice in daily life the v., 163:5
Virus, attribute immune deficiency
    to a v., 424:2
  tainted with the hateful v., 271:2
Visible and invisible all things, 41:14
  more v. but not more valuable,
    457:9
Vision are a reality, 94:4
  difference between dream and v.,
    94:4
  gifted with double v., 231:7
  her v. of the perfect slave, 394:8
  his v. of the perfect woman, 394:8
  I had a v., 87:5
  of South Africa, 265:2
  pursuit of highest v., 261:4
  virus attacked their v., 271:2
  where no v. people perish, 19:8
Visions, seeing secret v., 393:5
  young men shall see v., 24:7
Visit, if you ain't been to v. you,
    552:3
  the birds again in sleep, 477:4
Visited and redeemed his people,
    33:1
  sick and ye v. me, 30:11
Visitors, short-term v., 373:2
Visual markers that reveal you to
    world, 492:2
Vocabulary of the civilized, 95:6
Vocal, I use my v. cords, 544:1
Vocation no measure of inner
    feelings, 159:5
  which is God-inspired, 239:3
Vogue, Negro was in v., 212:6
Voice as sound of many waters,
    43:18
  breaking sadness in your v.,
    209:3
  cast my vote raise my v., 124:1
  feeble v. were strong, 149:4
  foil v. of drum, 469:6
  have to be a v. for them, 502:6
  I am the v., 49:2, 329:2
  in the wilderness, 22:13, 26:6
  let no v. but own speak to you,
    172:9
  liberated v., 488:5
  lift ev'ry v. and sing, 147:2

Voice *(continued)*
  lift v. in chamber of the nation,
    117:6
  of many waters, 44:17
  of protesting minority, 129:3
  of the Lord God in the garden,
    6:15
  of the turtledove speaks out, 3:5
  of the wild goose, 3:3
  of their wrongs, 76:4
  of vision in his own time, 361:3
  reproduce V. of Black Woman,
    135:2
  rise at the v. of the bird, 20:11
  said do you see any niggers, 403:4
  saying God bless you make haste,
    82:4
  the only v. is your own, 480:3
  the wind heard your v., 356:8
  will float on every note, 547:1
Voiceless conch-shell, 356:3
Voices hitting walls like stones,
    305:8
  in the joining of v., 522:3
  of everybody here, 372:6
  power of millions of v. for change,
    523:8
  secret v. of our purpose, 393:5
Void, conscience v. of offense,
    37:19
Volatile as alcohol gasoline, 306:3
Volcano in full eruption, 260:7
Vomit the anguish up, 283:4
Voodoo, I'm a v. chile, 420:8
  king v. queen witch doctor, 548:8
Vote, a Negro who does not v., 274:6
  any person does not v., 274:6
  cast my v. raise my voice, 124:1
  does it profit a man to v., 427:7
  every v. counts, 384:7
  killed ma pa but will v. for him,
    468:1
  right to v., 558:8
  until every Negro in America can
    v., 245:6
Votes and guns inseparable twins,
    288:3
  must go with guns, 288:3
Vowels, playing Scrabble with the v.
    missing, 201:6
  scramble v. jewels, 326:1
Voyage through death, 243:2
Vultures, strip imperialist v. and
    expose, 197:3

751

W

Wade in the water children, 578:10

Wagadu, four times W. rose W. fell, 61:1

Wages, capitalist class use women to reduce w., 129:4

  of sin is death, 38:10

  proper w. like English servants, 79:1

  receive w. due him, 166:1

  starvation w., 321:2

Wagon, an empty w. rattles, 570:14

Wagtails of Mikuyu Prison, 439:6

Waifs, wailing out its liquid w., 381:3

Wail, I will weep w. mourn, 291:3

Wait a minute Mr. Postman, 408:4

  always meant Never, 316:7

  being a woman you can w., 200:4

  for an echo, 231:6

  guess I w. and see, 357:2

  how long will I have to w., 151:6

  in the shadows, 280:4

  is the reason, 460:4

  it is that moment I w. for, 269:8

  'til the midnight hour, 411:2

  we can no longer w., 266:8

  wisdom two words w. hope, 88:3

Waited for salvation O Lord, 8:18

  we have w. too long for freedom, 266:8

Waiting, all in line w. for you, 511:7

  for me to stumble in, 416:3

  for the other to make first move, 194:7

  for you, 312:8

  raise on up your band's w., 398:2

  to carry you to freedom, 576:9

  we are the ones we have been w. for, 372:3

  we are the ones we've been w. for, 524:2

Waits, in another place he watches and w., 415:3

Wake a pang in thee, 92:1

  closing in its w., 532:3

  disappointment follows in its w., 67:4

  git it when you w. up, 179:8

  more heav'nly more refin'd, 71:7

  thought in a man, 180:12

  thunder in your w., 181:10

  up, 508:6

  up America, 400:6

  up and demand their share, 394:3

Wake *(continued)*

  up everybody, 486:1

  up like that anymore, 563:6

  you up puts to sleep, 294:6

Walk ahead through the thorny brush, 537:3

  arise and w., 32:7

  by faith not sight, 40:11

  come w. in my shoes, 401:1

  cutting off man's legs and telling him to w., 68:3

  he shall w. on earth among the living, 2:7

  humbly with God, 24:11

  I'll never w. that slowly, 431:5

  in humble places, 181:10

  in the dust, 181:10, 537:3

  it slow, 355:2

  Just a Closer W. with Thee, 579:9

  life is just a short w., 272:3

  lightly w. behind you who fear me, 371:6

  not on the earth exultantly, 54:12

  on faith each day, 333:9

  quickly w. through the doors, 237:10

  the good American earth, 198:8

  together children, 578:12

  until we are free, 245:6

  up on the air, 370:6

  when I w. along, 247:4

Walked into middle of movie, 378:9

  long road to freedom, 267:5

  off wid alla my stuff, 466:7

Walketh, he w. upright, 57:4

Walking, I see men as trees w., 32:13

  I'm w. yes indeed, 309:7

  is too slow, 184:4

  Jesus w. on the sea, 28:22

  keep on a-w. keep on a-talkin', 579:2

  out over the river, 322:5

  through twilight, 474:3

Walks, I like the way he w., 315:4

Wall, no brothers up on the w., 508:8

  pressed to the w., 175:4

  waters were a w. unto them, 9:16

Wall Street hardly any black people, 549:1

Walls come tumbling down, 576:6

  four w. that ain't so pretty, 481:10

  ghetto's invisible w., 246:2

  prison w. cannot hold down an idea, 425:4

Walls *(continued)*

  we must tear down, 525:6

Wander, wonder and wonder until you w., 200:3

Wanna be startin' somethin', 511:6

  fly, 337:7

Want a little sugar in my bowl, 352:3

  can get it if you really w., 464:8

  I shall not w., 16:10

  if you w. to get what you w., 349:4

  lan' I w. lan' I out to get, 314:2

  make ourselves what we w. to be, 172:10

  my God what do we w., 286:5

  Negro wants what all Americans w., 152:4

  nothing in w., 48:5

  nothing unless freely given, 130:8

  our freedom and w. it now, 400:5

  tell him what you w., 333:8

  weaver of w., 381:3

  what does any human w., 286:5

  what does the Negro w., 208:3

  what people w. is simple, 371:3

  what we w. is what America is, 231:2

  why should I w. to be white, 211:5

  you can have anything you w., 221:2

  you like a hog wants slop, 438:5

  you play what you w., 263:7

  you to get out of my way, 452:3

  your extra time and your kiss, 514:5

Wanted, black women want to be w. and loved, 510:5

  to be rare noticed glamorous, 385:3

  what I w. was your love, 371:7

Wants, ministering the w. of their nature, 99:3

  of tomorrow, 46:6

  take what she w. from both, 377:5

War, ain't gonna study w., 578:11

  and peace, 49:3

  aversion to suffering overcome in w., 126:3

  begets further w., 221:2

  bias against w., 220:1

  calamities of w., 70:2

  calamities of w. and slavery, 70:2

  cause of w. is preparation for w., 145:1

  conscription for w., 239:3

  death did not stop the w., 507:3

War *(continued)*
 declaring w. on enemy within,
  351:8
 easy burden to eliminate w.,
  346:8
 every winter was a w., 516:6
 from w. springs freedom, 113:6
 gaining liberty but seen camps and
  w., 75:4
 god of w., 362:4
 in heaven, 44:14
 in the heat of the streets, 490:1
 infringe upon rights w. inevitable,
  272:5
 is a w., 449:9
 is at us my black skins, 108:7
 is Old not wise, 445:4
 is the solution, 362:6
 Jim Crowed me during the w.,
  215:1
 live in a state of w., 70:1
 Lord is a man of w., 10:1
 love is w., 283:7
 no discharge in that w., 20:7
 no more w. never again, 341:3
 no one makes w., 58:1
 no reason or cause justifies w.,
  183:5
 open-ended w., 456:1
 opposed to a dumb w., 522:4
 propaganda itself an instrument of
  w., 220:3
 scars of w., 512:8
 slave trade at w. with heart of man,
  69:4
 the panoply of w., 154:2
 time of w., 19:17
 waged in living rooms, 512:8
 was deeply within us, 378:6
 was the w. in vain, 126:4
 we at w. with ourselves, 563:2
 weapons of w. perished, 13:17
 what is it good for, 436:5
 which may at worst destroy them,
  220:5
Warehouse of language, 398:4
Warfare, in w. to survive, 289:6
Warmth, fire without w., 377:1
Warned in a dream, 26:1
Warner, I am only a w., 54:1
Warning property belongs to a
  wizard, 388:5
Warrior Poet Mother, 359:1
Warrior's black face, 225:8

Warriors, angel w., 378:5
 transformed w. who dared not cry,
  406:7
Wars, all the w. in history, 297:8
 hear of w. and rumors of w., 30:3
 money for w. but can't feed poor,
  556:4
 not all w. have casualties, 394:7
 they get boys to fight w., 378:5
 tyrant w. made earth a grave,
  129:1
Wash, hoses couldn't w. it out, 274:4
Washed robes in blood, 44:11
 took water and w. his hands, 31:16
Washington, I'm best for W., 366:6
 not history taught in W., 294:1
 unnecessary to march on W.,
  400:4
Waste, it's such a w., 277:2
 mind is a terrible thing to w., 573:6
Wasted, no kindness ever w., 45:12
 prodigal son w. his substance, 34:9
Wasteth, man dieth and w. away,
  15:9
Wasting time is an abomination to
  the spirit, 1:6
 time wishing and hoping, 483:6
Watch, a Mayor who stood the w.,
  279:1
 and pray, 31:9
 damn the lights w. the cars, 186:3
 in the night, 17:17
 Mr. Black Man w. your step,
  194:2
 shepherds keeping w. over flock,
  33:4
 what you say, 511:1
 with me one hour, 31:9
 you eat, 295:2
Watcher turns his eyes away, 179:9
Watches, I know He w. me, 579:7
Watchword must be mobilization,
  265:1
Water, afraid of w., 506:4
 big ship need da w., 575:11
 bigger than the world, 451:8
 clean glass of w., 196:3
 cold w. better than wine, 66:3
 dirty glass of w., 196:3
 dish w. gives back no images,
  223:3
 don't miss w. till well runs dry,
  571:6
 drawers of w., 12:10

Water *(continued)*
 dutty w. can put out fire, 574:8
 everybody deserves clean w., 561:5
 fool and w. go way they are
  diverted, 566:6
 Frye Street is like muddy w., 200:5
 get over the w., 555:4
 get your ass in the w., 571:14
 God is the color of w., 509:3
 God's a-gonna trouble the w.,
  578:10
 hoses couldn't wash it out, 274:4
 in a raindrop, 325:5
 in the summer of 2005, 506:4
 in the world for us, 444:3
 in w. she became herself, 466:3
 like trying to bury w., 493:2
 necessity like food w., 326:9
 need more w., 327:1
 neither eat bread nor drink w.,
  10:12
 never miss w. till well runs dry,
  151:7
 no more w. fire next time, 284:7
 no paths in w. no signposts, 513:4
 silent w. drowns a man, 565:16
 under w. in Charleston harbor,
  384:3
 until you cross the w., 565:4
 upon earth quivers and swells,
  55:5
 wade in the w. children, 578:10
 was made wine, 35:14
 went through fire and w., 17:8
Watered-silk dresses and money to
  grow food, 531:3
Waterline, gull-glittering w., 331:9
Water's ceaseless drip, 149:5
 tears wasted w. all that is, 392:6
Waters, beside still w., 16:10
 birth w. sang like rivers, 460:6
 both sides of blood-red w., 100:4
 cast thy bread upon the w., 20:10
 crossed the w. to come here, 65:6
 God moved upon face of the w.,
  5:4
 justice rolls down like w., 317:9
 many w. cannot quench love,
  21:15
 nations rush like the rushing of w.,
  22:4
 of hate rushing in, 185:5
 of mercy, 225:7
 voice as sound of many w., 43:18

Waters *(continued)*
   voice of many w., 44:17
   want ocean without w., 105:9
   were a wall unto them, 9:16
   willing to cross w. to return, 65:6
Wave, green w. to lift all boats, 548:1
   my freak flag, 420:2
Waves crashed thunderous fury, 258:1
   wage war on rocks sand, 157:7
Way, a w. outa no w., 372:5
   broad is the w., 27:10
   every one his own w., 48:13
   find another w., 287:9
   he spread his wings, 195:1
   I am the w. the truth the life, 36:15
   keep the w. of tree of life, 7:2
   king stood at parting of the w., 23:18
   make a w. out of no w., 571:12
   narrow is the w., 27:10
   of the world makes heart so cold, 414:5
   prepare the w. of the Lord, 26:6
   that leadeth to destruction, 27:10
   that's the w. it is, 538:7
   we have come a long long w., 316:3
   we have come this w. before, 532:5
   you do the things you do, 405:1
   your own kind of Show W., 536:2
Ways, amend your w., 23:10
   his w. are judgment, 12:4
   of white folks, 212:3
We ain't what w. was, 316:3
   all everyone of us, 427:2
   are Africans, 414:1
   are and shall be, 360:5
   are free at last, 318:3
   are moving forward, 390:6
   are not for sale, 287:9
   are not saved, 23:11
   are the change that w. seek, 524:2
   are the ones w. have been waiting for, 372:3
   are the ones we've been waiting for, 524:2
   are the world, 512:7
   are therefore I am, 336:5
   ask are you men, 100:6
   believe in God, 53:9
   can forgive never forget, 267:7
   can never be satisfied, 317:9

We *(continued)*
   carry on, 529:5
   complain, 272:5
   either bitches or queens, 559:5
   either niggas or kings, 559:5
   face forward, 234:1
   finally included in W. the People, 371:1
   have come a long long way, 316:3
   have come this way before, 532:5
   have fallen apart, 323:1
   have no Children, 61:2
   have no City, 61:2
   have no Country, 61:2
   have no guns only stones, 373:5
   have no Property, 61:2
   have no Wives, 61:2
   have the power, 186:8
   live here they live there, 230:9
   Negroes love our country, 107:3
   own the night, 354:4
   possess the past, 273:2
   real cool, 259:8
   remain in the beginning, 324:2
   remember us w. the people, 539:9
   rise and fall, 324:2
   shall have independence or cease to live, 75:5
   shall know color of the sky, 386:2
   shall not be moved, 577:10
   shall overcome, 578:15
   shall rise to the occasion, 401:4
   shiver together, 506:6
   Specialize in the Wholly Impossible, 160:4
   still w. are slaves, 84:3
   who are the living, 273:2
   will be your friends, 78:4
   will find another way, 287:9
   will get to the promised land, 321:4
   will not stop, 273:1
Weak and beggarly elements, 41:4
   bear infirmities of the w., 39:2
   flesh is w., 31:9
   more w. she became the easier, 182:5
   she who is w., 50:2
   things to confound the mighty, 39:3
   used to be strong becomes w., 294:6
   welfare of the w., 372:2

Weakest enjoy the highest rights, 176:5
   society trample on w., 114:2
Weakness of children's limbs is innocent, 52:2
   strength perfect in w., 41:2
Weaknesses, praised w. overlooked, 132:7
Wealth and children are adornment of life, 55:2
   Black love is Black w., 430:5
   denied one morsel of w., 64:3
   flowing current of w., 377:4
   knowledge w. well earned, 554:6
   made from African, 335:1
   maketh many friends, 18:21
   moves the earth, 123:6
Weapon, culture is effective w., 278:5
   of choice love, 340:6
   of oppressor is mind of oppressed, 454:5
   paint is the only w., 268:2
Weapons of war perished, 13:17
   Saddam Hussein has biological w., 380:5
Wear, all we have to do is w. it, 285:7
   it like a banner, 213:2
   let me w. the day well, 360:2
   the exaggerated look of captivity, 369:1
Weariness, much study is w., 21:1
Weary, don't you get w., 578:12
   the more w. the more weak, 182:5
Weather, fair w. for the sky is red, 29:5
   we laugh at stormy w., 192:4
Weave, now free I w. together, 85:7
Weaver of want, 381:3
Web of kin, 480:6
   snag like a spider's w., 491:6
Wedding, didn't print w. announcements, 265:5
   she whose w. is great, 49:1
Weed, anger is a w., 53:1
   grew up like a neglected w., 111:1
   liquor stores and w., 558:2
   she stands in the wild w., 260:5
   through our own screaming w., 259:2
   want some coke have some w., 423:5
   where hungry w. grows, 258:10
Weeds, bitter stalks of w., 281:1
   of death, 306:4

Whosoever believeth should not perish, 35:18

liveth and believeth in me shall never die, 36:10

shall exalt shall be abased, 30:2

surrenders to God, 56:4

Why are ye fearful, 27:15

Democracy means everybody but me, 213:1

Do Fools Fall in Love, 401:3

do you all push us around, 245:2

do you curse and honor me, 51:2

does our color make such a difference, 237:9

don't ask me I don't know w., 538:7

fight what's known, 85:3

hast thou forsaken me, 16:9, 32:2

hate those who love me, 49:3

have you hated me, 50:3

I sing the blues, 293:4

is an unanswerable word, 258:4

is difficult to handle, 336:7

kill my brothers and sisters, 415:5

should I want to be white, 211:5

Should White Guys Have All the Fun, 421:5

single out Negroes, 229:1

sit here and die, 89:4

you hate me love me, 49:3

you so black, 384:5

Whys do not exist perhaps not necessary, 562:3

Wicked, force is able to exterminate w., 60:1

heart can be w., 478:4

heart is deceitful and w., 23:14

no peace unto the w., 22:17

tender mercies of the w. are cruel, 18:16

wickedness from the w., 13:13

Wickedness from the wicked, 13:13

Wide is the gate, 27:10

Wide-awake to our own interest, 127:4

Widow, do not oppress the w., 2:4

how is she become as a w., 23:16

plead for the w., 21:17

Wife, contented with life dinner and w., 85:2

forsake w. child or die a slave, 99:1

I am w. and virgin, 49:1

lifetime w. and mother, 484:2

Lot's w. looked back, 8:6

Wife (continued)

man and his w. were not ashamed, 6:13

once good like the Minister's w., 173:6

poor man's w. is starvin', 188:2

remember Lot's w., 34:16

shalt not covet neighbor's w., 10:8

want to die before my w., 376:6

Wife's, your w. living like a queen, 188:2

Wiggles in the dark of her soul, 354:3

Wild about Harry, 176:9

at the w. w. west, 534:9

locusts and w. honey, 26:7

voice of the w. goose, 3:3

women don't have the blues, 194:1

Wilderness, black people in America's w., 495:2

every day a w., 487:4

go out into the w., 253:4

scapegoat into the w., 11:2

voice in the w., 22:13, 26:6

Will among Afro-Americans to hold, 304:1

command what you w., 52:9

good w. toward men, 33:5

if God w., 55:1

it and say Be and it is, 54:9

must be stronger than the skill, 417:10

my w. I had complete dominion, 471:4

not as I w. but as thou wilt, 31:8

not my w. but thine, 34:20

pernicious dismissal of individual w., 498:2

thy w. be done, 27:2

when you w. they won't, 48:10

you be there, 512:6

you broke my w., 333:6

Willie Gee, Sandy Star and W., 158:4

Willie Lee, good night W., 443:8

Willing, spirit is w., 31:9

to cross waters to return, 65:6

Win, can't w. what you don't fight for, 380:1

every political office, 262:5

some but just lost one, 560:6

we fought to w. it, 293:6

we shall w. without a doubt, 310:3

Win (continued)

won't w. until learn how to lose, 458:1

Wind, awake O north w., 21:9

bleached by w., 276:2

bloweth where it listeth, 35:16

cries Mary, 420:4

echoes and sings like you, 356:8

fly upon the wings of w., 16:5

I am the w. the voice calling, 479:1

I fed the w., 240:6

inherit the w., 18:15

is in the cane, 188:6

no w. in sweep of sky, 258:1

of doctrine, 41:10

rain God's deliberate eye, 545:2

rushing mighty w., 37:6

the in-dark answered with w., 418:3

the w. you hear, 385:7

they have sown the w., 24:6

way the w. blows is cool with me, 502:4

Window, cut w. through on Europe, 86:7

I stand at the w., 283:1

Jezebel looked out w., 14:8

Windows be darkened, 20:11

dwelling with w. but no doors, 412:4

stained-glass w. of Jesus, 256:3

Winds, ancient as the w., 382:2

four w. of the earth, 44:8

four w. of the heaven, 24:12

Windstorm, slouching in a W., 377:1

Wine, better is thy love than w., 21:8

cold water better than w., 66:3

is a mocker, 18:22

Noah awoke from his w., 7:14

sweet pomegranate w., 3:4

water was made w., 35:14

Winebibber, behold a w., 28:7

Wing, lower the w. of submission, 54:11

Wings, doomed fly's w., 491:6

fly upon the w. of wind, 16:5

four beasts had each six w., 44:3

like a dove, 17:5

pressing close to my side, 169:5

riches make themselves w., 19:1

shadow of thy w., 16:4

way he spread his w., 195:1

Wink to remember him by, 487:3

Winner, day has come we're a w.,
422:7

Wins, slow and steady w. race, 45:13

Winter, cooled by the same w. as a
white man, 569:10
every w. was a war, 516:6
God the w. summer, 434:6
my mother named me W., 539:7

Winters, full of w. when we want
sun, 354:6

Wipe, Lord God will w. away tears,
22:10

Wisdom, apply our hearts unto w.,
17:19
better than treasures of gold, 58:3
exalteth her children, 25:8
fear of the Lord is beginning of w.,
18:3
higher than fool can reach, 71:3
in much w. is much grief, 19:14
is finest beauty of a person, 567:5
is justified, 28:7
is not bought, 564:14
is the principal thing, 18:13
Jesus increased in w. and stature,
33:7
no man can snatch w., 58:4
no profit without w., 58:4
of Solomon, 14:2
opportunities lost of gaining w.,
84:6
philosophy without w., 64:5
price of w. above rubies, 15:18
she replies with w., 566:12
smitten with love of w., 58:3
two words wait hope, 88:3
where shall w. be found, 15:16
worth more than silver gold,
449:10

Wise, a w. man is a school, 2:3
and understanding heart, 13:24
bread to the w., 20:9
five were w. five were foolish,
30:7
foolish things to confound the w.,
39:3
great men not always w., 15:20
he is w. tries everything, 48:9
heart of w., 20:3
how dieth the w. man, 19:16
I am senseless and w., 50:2
in your conceits, 38:19
men from the east, 25:18
not even God w. enough, 564:15

Wise (continued)
oppression makes w. man mad,
108:4
proof accessible to w. man, 185:1
there is none born w., 1:3
War is Old not w., 445:4

Wish, call me anything you w., 164:3
every man's w. on board, 179:9
I could break all the chains, 275:5
I could say all the things, 275:5
I do not w. to be free, 64:1
I knew how it would feel, 275:5
I was back again, 177:1
no w. to die for fame alone, 61:1
them a strange town, 367:7

Wishbone, celestial w. snap at
midnight, 462:5

Wished, you made the earth as you
w., 5:3

Wishes, often sorry if w. gratified,
46:16
yes 3 w. is all you get, 467:3

Wit, brilliant w. will shine, 90:2
without discretion, 64:5

Withered, because no root they w.,
28:13

Withereth, in the evening it w., 17:17

Within, thumping from w., 135:7
what you need is w. you, 252:6
you w. me and I out of myself,
52:8

Without a witness against me, 2:6
beckoning from w., 135:7
don't want to live my life w., 452:5
he w. sin among you, 36:3

Witness, heaven and earth to w.,
11:11
I was sole w. to my homecoming,
346:1
man is w. unto his deeds, 57:5
thou shalt not bear false w., 10:8
to the people, 23:3
whole nation to bear w., 275:8
without evil without a w., 2:6

Witnesses, cloud of w. unseen,
348:3
share what they have seen, 552:8

Wives, make w. equals not
subordinates, 129:6
tear your w. from your embraces,
100:6
we have no W., 61:2

Wives' fingers sparkling with rings,
89:1

Wizard a track, 259:2
of the crow, 388:5

Woe unto you, 33:11

Woke this morning mind on
freedom, 577:11

Wolf, boy cried w., 45:15
every w. taking a bite at you, 196:1
hates when it flatters, 53:2
in sheep's clothing, 45:8
lamb began to follow the w., 45:8
spotted w. of sameness, 361:1

Wolves, black men sheep among w.,
196:1
in sheep's clothing are ravening
w., 27:11

Woman ain't done running around,
187:8
although I am a w., 287:5
always a w. has swayed me, 159:3
among those have I not found,
20:6
aren't I a w., 82:6
awakening of Afro-American w.,
138:4
be both man and w., 358:5
behold thy son, 37:2
being a w. you can wait, 200:4
black w. mythology, 491:10
black w. wells of strength, 255:4
Christ from God and a w., 83:1
doll-baby type of w., 194:3
every colored w. dying, 337:5
every nameless w. of color, 543:3
friend of your mind, 339:2
gypsy w. hypnotized me, 422:4
happening because I'm a w., 421:2
heart of a w., 169:3
herself not the tree of life, 445:2
his vision of the perfect w.,
394:8
I am a black w., 279:7, 287:8
I am a blk w., 358:5
I am the Black w., 441:5
I am w. from the cotton fields,
142:7
I got a w., 326:3
if man may preach why not w.,
76:6
if the drum is a w., 369:2
I'm every w., 406:4
I'm not a w. not a man, 514:1
injury to one w. injury to all
women, 138:4
kind hearted w., 236:8

Woman (*continued*)

let us look for the w., 88:5

light the clear-oil lamp, 224:8

Lord God made he a w., 6:11

love a black w., 553:7

messed with too many times, 506:5

naked w. black w., 224:6

new w. has made her bow, 129:5

nigger w. mule uh de world, 180:2

nobody insults colored w. in Tax Office, 110:3

not safe in her home, 536:7

only the Black W. can say, 135:5

oughta be a w., 372:4

phenomenal w. that's me, 307:3

principle in soul makes man w., 90:2

reproduce Voice of Black W., 135:2

rocks the cradle, 195:7

rules the home, 195:7

she was a w. now, 434:5

sings lovely as chandeliers, 360:6

suffer as w. suffer for race, 183:2

the w. from America, 377:5

the w. gave me of the tree I did not eat, 6:16

the w. said The serpent beguiled me, 6:17

thou art loosed, 508:1

we all good w., 486:4

what have I to do, 35:13

what if I am a w., 90:1

what is a w., 416:2

when your good w. is gone, 187:7

where is w. is magic, 467:4

who counts on her face, 561:8

who told Black w. she savior, 335:3

who will revere Black w., 328:7

wide-awake w. forging ahead, 194:3

your example is powerful, 89:6

Womanhood as aspect of identity, 488:3

Black innocent w., 328:7

Black women epitomes of Black w., 437:5

undisputed dignity of w., 135:5

white w. enslaved too, 302:2

Womanist is to feminist, 443:4

Woman's heart hardens without love, 376:1

tryin' to quit me, 221:3

Woman's (*continued*)

who need a w. help, 90:4

Womb, anarchism carries liberty in w., 129:7

ancestors and w. one the same, 486:2

asleep in that w., 441:1

blessed is the fruit of thy w., 32:19

hatches in time's w., 385:7

loneliness as a w., 381:3

shall forget him, 15:15

Women, African-American w. do what we have to do, 237:8

Black Panthers as freedom fighters, 446:3

black w. carry the handicaps, 379:6

Black w. epitomes of Black womanhood, 437:5

black w. not homogenized chocolate milk, 358:8

black w. sexually stereotyped, 564:1

blessed art thou among w., 32:17

calling all w., 287:7

capitalist class use w. to reduce wages, 129:4

colored men getting rights but not w., 83:5

colored w. can't afford self-pity, 227:3

countless w. in my life, 159:3

disposition of w., 48:10

distrust between black men black w., 491:9

don't want to remember, 179:10

evil hearted w., 236:8

fairest among w., 21:4

friendship between w. can resemble love, 375:6

hold up other half of sky, 473:8

join hands with you as w., 245:6

laboring w. of my race, 121:1

men and w. liberate, 189:14

monument erected in worship of w., 447:8

must've been w., 170:1

Negro w. like w. in general, 168:3

Negro w. no less than white w., 168:5

of Brewster Place, 479:3

of Liberia of Africa of the world, 390:5

Women (*continued*)

passing the love of w., 13:17

preserve account of these w., 125:5

pretty w. wonder, 307:3

return to children as butterflies, 550:1

ruled by their bodies, 546:2

shrieks of the w., 69:3

slaves at the millstones, 1:4

subjugation of black w., 488:4

subjugation of w., 488:4

suffer doubly, 473:7

things that drive men to sea is w., 465:3

to plant roots of progress, 114:5

white w. liberationists, 488:3

wild w. don't have the blues, 194:1

turn world right side up, 83:2

you are fools and old w., 84:7

Women-as-mothers, offered w. their due worth, 447:8

Women's, black w. existence, 456:6

not candidate of w. movement, 287:5

sexual politics in Black w. lives, 573:14

Wonder, and w. until you wander, 200:3

if other guys have something, 353:5

lost in w. of Creation, 62:3

what is worryin' me, 169:7

Wonderful, his name shall be W., 22:3

isn't she w., 481:12

world this would be, 333:11

Won't know you ever had coffee, 294:6

when you will they w., 48:10

Wood, fir w. harps and psalteries, 13:19

God's bits of w., 281:4

gray cloth brings dark w. to life, 487:4

hewers of w., 12:10

if loneliness were a w., 431:9

lips speak so we see, 325:1

nature of w. to rot, 393:1

the lute but a piece of w., 61:1

took shape, 325:4

Woodwork image of anger, 325:4

Woooooooman, i am a blk w., 359:5

Word better than a gift, 25:12
corrupt w. is like a corrupt tree, 54:8
destroy with a single w., 343:10
doers of the w., 43:2
every w. slides out of mouth, 315:4
final w. in reality, 319:5
give thou the w., 92:2
good w. is like a good tree, 54:8
His firm W., 54:8
in beginning was the W., 35:5
killed for a single beautiful w., 487:2
my w. is my sword, 544:1
no w. to us about Freedom, 432:7
obey the w., 63:4
of God, 43:16
of God is quick and powerful, 42:17
of Lord cutteth like sword, 59:1
patience is a dirty w., 400:5
question every w. spoken, 349:6
was made flesh, 35:8
was with God and was God, 35:5
Words are braver than fighting, 2:3
books that hold the w., 493:1
bridge of w., 231:6
bullets or butterflies, 315:1
devoted to quelling freedom, 506:6
dreamers toss w. on their tongues, 494:2
falsify w. of my mouth, 566:10
far from the w. of my roaring, 16:9
grasping w. ruined a damn good thing, 520:4
how forcible are right w., 15:7
I am tired of w., 332:2
in constant flow of propaganda, 220:3
less w. need love, 326:1
like liberty make me cry, 213:3
lose all respect for w. per se, 372:6
love God in w. hate brother in works, 92:4
made to conceal thought, 98:2
mouth the w., 253:2
my w. printed in a book, 15:13
not just with w. with deeds, 525:3
of God not be exhausted, 56:5
of truth and soberness, 38:2
on a parchment not enough, 524:3
seemed idle tales, 35:2
some w. spoken split world in two, 504:5

Words (continued)
sour looks and rude w., 90:3
too cool for w., 379:5
tumbling w. spend themselves, 398:4
vain w. in your oaths, 53:11
wisdom two w. faith hope, 88:3
Work, black power must mean hard w., 187:4
bring every w. into judgment, 21:1
came here to w. and w. hard, 123:2
death stops the body's w., 545:3
democratic principle a w. in progress, 498:6
don't mind hard w., 79:1
finish w. that needs to be done, 523:2
for all, 267:1
for w. it was leaning was w., 259:5
hard w. and sacrifice pursue our dreams, 525:7
heartbreaking w., 311:6
his w. is perfect, 12:4
if stop w. I have not enough, 76:3
in 1891 before I'd w., 575:2
inclined to w. without hope, 189:9
let's go to w., 279:2
let's try to w. it out, 521:3
live and die and do your w., 104:7
man's w. made manifest, 39:4
no matter how hard you w., 321:8
nothing worth having except of hard w., 133:1
of his ancestors, 279:6
of insurrection will go on, 76:1
of our hands, 17:20
of our own hands, 93:6
on yourself, 552:3
our w. here on Earth, 527:6
ourselves out of business, 288:5
plenty of w. for hard working man, 142:8
seventh day thou shalt not w., 10:7
time to accomplish life's w., 297:1
we build and w. and love, 529:5
with Me Annie, 303:1
100 percent harder, 183:3
Worker, God lends aid to the w., 46:n2
Workers, fight for rights of w., 198:5
no rights as foreign w., 329:5
Workin', been w. and w., 300:1
Working for nothing, 277:8
on the chain gang, 334:1

Working (continued)
together to correct the past, 267:6
white folks w. for me, 500:4
Workman that needeth not to be ashamed, 42:12
Works, faith without w. is dead, 43:3
good w. better in sight of thy Lord, 55:2
love God in words hate brother in w., 92:4
of unbelievers a mirage, 55:8
reward according to his w., 42:14
rich in good w., 42:11
what w. remain for devils, 101:4
World, a w. in a crack, 402:5
Africans of the w., 563:5
after the end of the w., 250:8
alive in a living w., 203:2
all the w. to me a wonder, 157:8
all the w. was mine, 151:2
as big as you make it, 169:5
becomes unbearable, 558:6
below us and beyond, 330:7
black man in white w., 271:1
blacker w. on death row, 495:8
boiled down to a drop, 180:5
brought nothing into w., 42:8
bulb-lit w. below, 314:5
but the w. is growing up, 361:9
can't go wrong w. behind you, 222:5
care of this w., 28:14
convulsed for freedom, 64:3
cool to rule my w., 514:5
crises in one part of the w., 383:2
devil showed him all the w., 33:8
discovered it was white, 145:3
distance and elusive, 231:6
divided into Haves and Have-Nots, 215:5
done whipped him so, 327:7
done with troubles of the w., 578:14
end of the w., 32:5
expect of the w. a free Africa, 171:1
explored the w., 397:8
fellow citizen of the w., 525:5
first as citizens of the w., 207:5
first man to sit on top of the w., 169:1
freedom for whole w. or no w., 185:4

World (*continued*)

fuck the w. my defense came, 550:7

gain whole w. lose own soul, 29:10

giveth give I unto you, 36:17

go into the w., 32:16

God so loved the w., 35:18

got the w. in a jug, 191:6

half rich half exploited, 245:4

has had to limp along, 135:10

has run amok, 361:2

having passed through the w., 141:5

heal the w., 512:5

hope of all the w., 527:6

I didn't make this w., 327:6

I dream a w., 212:8

I was given this w., 556:5

if this w. were mine, 396:4

I'll make me a w., 148:1

instill the love into all the w., 2:5

integrated intellectual w., 255:7

interracial conflicts in parts of w., 496:1

into a w. of bad spirits, 69:2

is before you, 283:8

is full of riddles, 515:5

is mean, 355:2

is my stage, 194:4

is not their friend, 62:1

is one great battlefield, 128:3

is tossing me, 128:5

is white no longer, 282:7

It's a Man's Man's Man's W., 347:2

jazz known over the w., 269:4

kingdoms of w. are kingdoms of Lord, 44:13

let another w. be born, 255:2

let w. know our numbers, 176:6

let's stick up the w., 550:6

lose ourselves in the w., 145:7

make the w. a safer place, 390:7

make this w. a better place, 406:3

man is a little w. within himself, 72:4

mission make w. free, 286:4

music is a w. within itself, 482:1

my w. defined by my skin, 431:6

my w. got bigger, 339:5

navigate easily in white w., 533:1

needs people who have come alive, 203:6

Negro people of the w., 272:5

World (*continued*)

never fully secure, 383:7

nigger woman mule uh de w., 180:2

no longer racist or sexist, 488:4

nowhere in the w., 272:5

of negative Black images, 265:6

of street, 314:6

of tomorrow, 226:2

on the tip of tongue, 497:1

once the w. was young, 165:3

overcome the w., 36:21

promised for this w. just so long, 137:7

provin' to w. black was beautiful, 216:4

remain in the w. without fear, 566:12

remake our part of the w., 265:2

'round the w. and back again, 571:4

Satan deceiveth the w., 44:15

set this w. on Fire, 174:1

she was the w. and heavens, 180:5

sins of the w., 43:13

skunk of the w., 267:1

sliding curve of w., 325:5

so all the w. can see, 275:7

some words spoken split w. in two, 504:5

spectacle unto the w., 39:6

strange freedom to be adrift in the w., 202:5

stranger in w. and pilgrim here, 63:1

struggle for new w., 320:2

suffer for the w., 387:1

sure did live in this w., 337:5

taketh away the sin of the w., 35:10

talk to women of the w., 390:5

that had a problem with both, 502:5

they shared twisted perverted everything, 510:7

thinks we know nothing, 89:1

time short in transitory w., 87:2

to give him a name, 418:3

trouble all over this w., 578:8

true Light cometh into the w., 35:7

wanted to create was doomed, 477:6

was his oyster, 193:2

water in the w. for us, 444:3

World (*continued*)

way of w. makes heart cold, 414:5

we are the w., 512:7

we must remake the w., 153:1

weep at the w., 179:1

where there ain't no right or wrong, 480:4

whether you have what w. wants, 142:1

with slightest push can be tipped, 533:8

without end in suffering, 218:10

women turn w. right side up, 83:2

wonderful w. this would be, 333:11

you envy of w., 337:3

World's beauty becomes enough, 337:10

biggest killer is extreme poverty, 424:*n*2

Harlem is black w. community, 255:5

number one sufferer, 334:6

weep on w. shoulder, 227:3

white race w. archdeceivers, 196:4

Worlds and systems small and great, 117:3

passed in and out of their w., 502:1

underneath friendship one could find w., 472:7

within without Veil of Color, 144:1

Worm, boring the same hole like a w., 200:6

shall feed on him, 15:15

Worriation, what is sense of so much w., 215:2

Worried, not w. about anything, 321:4

Worry, don't w. 'bout a thing, 449:13

don't you w. 'bout a thing, 481:9

when you w. make it double, 478:5

wild women don't worry, 194:1

Worryin', wonder what is w. me, 169:7

Worrying as long as I have been black, 215:2

Worship, Americans w. money, 544:9

are come to w. him, 25:18

jazz clubs houses of w., 312:4

none save Him, 54:11

thee we w. and beg assistance, 53:7

Yes I'm almost done, 174:6
  that's correct, 367:2
  we can, 391:5, 522:5, 524:1, 524:*n*1
Yesterday I was king, 403:1
  sent for you y. here you come today, 219:4
  thousand years are as y. when past, 17:17
Yield and ask no questions, 182:5
  in my heart I do not y., 128:3
  those who y. to guidance, 56:1
Yields, what the orchard y., 210:3
Yo bum rush the show, 518:4
Yodeling or something not music, 254:1
Yoke, deliverance from a foreign y., 76:4
  my y. is easy, 28:8
  take my y., 28:8
Yoruba, distance between as great as Ibo and Y., 433:7
  girl dancing, 406:8
You a city of a woman, 367:4
  ain't a bitch or a ho, 553:7
  are a New Yorker, 553:1
  are all of these, 280:3
  are appreciated, 556:5
  are as good as they are, 79:4
  are colored Americans, 79:4
  are none of these, 280:3
  Are the Sunshine of My Life, 481:7
  are the un-Americans, 198:7
  are unable to see, 492:2
  Be Illin', 539:5
  better shop around, 404:2
  between y. and danger, 388:1
  bodies between y. and danger, 388:1
  can cage the singer, 303:4
  can get it if y. really want it, 464:8
  can't hurry love, 409:6
  created y. without y., 53:4
  don't know me, 545:6
  don't need anything else, 295:9
  give me fever, 333:3
  hate me love me, 49:3
  have to let yourself be, 562:7
  he without sin among y., 36:3
  if y. ain't been to visit y., 552:3
  in the end you'll still be y., 435:3
  justify y. without y., 53:4
  lie y. lie, 574:15

You *(continued)*
  lied about me tell truth about me, 49:3
  Make Me Feel Mighty Real, 464:4
  make me wanna shout, 378:1
  might win some, 560:6
  no one defines your life only y., 500:1
  reaching for y. whoever y. are, 372:1
  Send Me, 333:10
  take it, 296:3
  they are no better than y., 79:4
  this victory truly belong to y., 526:2
  were a solution problem, 339:1
  whatever you get that's y. your story, 219:5
  why pose a self other than y., 376:9
  within me and I out of myself, 52:8
  your life belongs to y., 562:8
Young, for the y. know nothing, 165:3
  future in the hands of the y., 400:7
  gently lead those with y., 22:15
  gifted and black, 433:1
  live fast die y., 233:3
  may look with hope, 96:2
  men shall see visions, 24:7
  once the world was y., 165:3
  racism does to y. people, 332:8
  to be y. gifted and black, 328:2
  to y. man knowledge and discretion, 18:11
  too famous too y., 201:7
  usta be y. usta be gifted still black, 455:1
  we remain a y. nation, 526:5
  who dare run against the storm, 426:6
  woman ain't done running around, 187:8
Youngblood fearless black soldier, 256:3
Your body between them and danger, 388:1
  life belongs to you, 562:8
  way out of sad, 559:8
You're a shining star, 414:4
  Africa to me, 306:1
  Next in Line for a Miracle, 383:10
  the First the Last My Everything, 445:7

Yours, this earth is y., 350:1
  tomorrow it might be y., 544:2
Yourself, draw understanding to y., 200:4
  reign over y., 553:8
  sound of the genuine in y., 203:5
  work on y., 552:3
  you have to let y. be, 562:7
Yourselves, look at y., 422:1
  no claim upon your liberty but y., 103:1
Youth, cultured hell that tests my y., 175:6
  determined from y. to gain freedom, 102:2
  drunk of the fountain of y., 134:3
  enlightened y. to undertake tasks, 155:3
  no hope for the y., 556:4
  scion of y. is grown, 81:4
  wreck and ruin of colored y., 140:6
You've Really Got a Hold on Me, 403:6

Z

Zeal, serving my country with z., 68:2
Zealously affected in a good thing, 41:5
Zebra is not supposed to mind, 377:6
Zebras Lions Buffalo and Bushmen, 377:6
Zephyr, the gentle z. plays, 71:6
Zero, cultural z., 168:2
  reduce all signs of difference to z., 202:3
Zig-zag lightning of power, 181:10
Zion, daughters of Z. were rejected, 59:2
  was taken away, 59:2
Zippers broken but dreams alive, 485:5
Zombie have long been with us, 483:3
  O z., 386:5
Zombies a taste of their medicine, 458:5
Zoo-man, they call me Z., 395:7
Zounds, 65:4